America's Most

Charming

Towns & Villages

A *"masterpiece of small-town boosterism ..."*
Los Angeles Times

*"A basic primer to the country's better small towns.
Most are worth seeing."*
Fort Worth Star Telegram

*"Virtually all the spots chosen are off the mainstream, from trout
fishing to wine tasting."*
Newsday

*"Profiles of 200 picturesque places travel agents don't know much
about."*
US News & World Report

Recommended by **Endless Vacation**, **Coast to Coast**, **Out West**,
and many other publications!

ABOUT THE AUTHOR

A native Midwesterner, Larry T. Brown was educated at the University of Kentucky, University of Edinburgh (Scotland), and Princeton University. He was a member of the psychology faculty at Oklahoma State University from 1961 to 1990. While at Oklahoma State University, he authored or co-authored numerous research publications, several teaching manuals, and a psychology textbook. After taking early retirement, Brown turned his attention to three areas of special love – travel, conservation, and American cultural history.

Dr. Brown now lives with his wife, Ausma, in Tulsa, Oklahoma.

BE A TRAVELER, NOT A TOURIST – WITH OPEN ROAD TRAVEL GUIDES!

Open Road Publishing has guide books to exciting, fun destinations on four continents. As veteran travelers, our goal is to bring you the best travel guides available anywhere!

No small task, but here's what we offer:

•All Open Road travel guides are written by authors with a distinct, opinionated point of view – not some sterile committee or team of writers. Our authors are experts in the areas covered and are polished writers.

•Our guides are geared to people who want to make their own travel choices. We'll show you how to discover the real destination – not just see some place from a tour bus window.

•We're strong on the basics, but we also provide terrific choices for those looking to get off the beaten path and experience the country or city – not just see it or pass through it.

•We give you the best, but we also tell you about the worst and what to avoid. Nobody should waste their time and money on their hard-earned vacation because of bad or inadequate travel advice.

•Our guides assume nothing. We tell you everything you need to know to have the trip of a lifetime – presented in a fun, literate, no-nonsense style.

•And, above all, we welcome your input, ideas, and suggestions to help us put out the best travel guides possible.

America's Most
Charming
Towns & Villages

Larry T. Brown

OPEN ROAD PUBLISHING

To all who believe that our small-town American heritage
must be preserved.

Acknowledgments

I remain forever grateful to the representatives of hundreds of chambers of commerce, regional and state tourism offices, historical societies, magazines, newspapers, state parks, museums, inns, and restaurants. As with the first two editions, these people not only willingly provided the information and advice I sought, they did so with a friendliness that frequently transformed toil into real enjoyment.

I remain grateful also to my publishers, Jonathan Stein and Avery Cardoza, for their sometimes sobering but always sound advice.

Special thanks continue to my wife, Ausma, for her patience and encouragement during our many miles of travel and my many hours before the monitor. I especially appreciate her objectivity, a trait that in travel writing can easily become victim to wishful fantasy. Finally, special thanks are due my friends and fellow travelers for sharing with me their many observations and suggestions.

Front cover photo courtesy of Virginia Division of Tourism (Colonial Williamsburg). Maps by Rob Perry.

The author has made every effort to be as accurate as possible, but neither the author nor the publisher assume responsibility for the services provided by any business listed in this guide; for any errors or omissions; or any loss, damage, or disruptions in your travels for any reason.

TABLE OF CONTENTS

OTHER CHARMING TOWNS!

*At the end of each chapter, you'll find a selection of **Other Charming Towns** in that state. Enjoy all the towns and villages in our guide!*

INTRODUCTION

If you're looking to get off the beaten path and experience small-town America's most enchanting, historical, and interesting destinations, this book is for you! If you enjoy historic inns and bed-and-breakfasts, arts and crafts festivals, antiquing, hiking, walking, cross-country skiing, or just strolling down a quaint Main Street in a new place, then you'll want to own this unique guide.

No one place in America has cornered the market on charm. In every region, we've got wonderful towns and villages that keep a window open to America's past. Americans love to explore new and special places – especially places with a sense of character and a sense of place – that seemingly live on from a bygone era, hidden over a hill or tucked away in a quiet valley.

In this guide, I'll show you where to find beautiful covered bridges and great places to fish. I'll take you to incredible seaside towns where waves crash against vintage historic lighthouses. I'll lead you to my favorite white-pillared antebellum Southern homes and through old riverboat port towns, and to unspoiled steamboat stops along the mighty Mississippi. I'll show you where you can pick apples and peaches, watch for bald eagles, and linger beside lovely, award-winning flower gardens.

I'll take you to terrific wine-tasting villages in California's unbeatable wine country, guide you to classic New England commons, and tell you where to witness picture-perfect fall foliage. And I'll show you places where spreading vistas are an everyday affair, and where friendly folks can't wait to help make your stay more enjoyable and help you learn more about their hometown.

Each destination is described briefly, so that its general character and principal points of interest can be seen in a quick scan. Lodging and restaurant suggestions are restricted to bed-and-breakfasts, historic inns and hotels, and locally-owned dining establishments.

With this book as your essential travel companion, you'll be ready to hit the open road in search of Charming America! We know you'll have a great trip.

OVERVIEW – CHARMING AMERICA!

Anyone observing the American scene at the turn of the 20th century would surely make note of the theme park, with its bizarre blend of thrills, fantasy, and nostalgia. An institution not unrelated to the theme park–something I have come to call the *charmtown*–might be overlooked, however. The reason for this would be that the charmtown evolved from something so very similar to it, i.e., the *charming town*, that in many cases the current specimen might be confused with its ancestor and, hence, go unnoticed.

No one with any kind of honesty should or would pretend that the charmtown is simply a spruced-up version of its ancestor. Homes that residents of charmtowns *restore* with historical accuracy in mind were in the past *modernized* with comfort and convenience the major incentives. What is now a quaint shop might once have been a tavern or pool hall in front of which older men, seated on wooden benches, gossiped and spat tobacco juice. The chickens and guinea fowl that once livened the yards of charming towns have been replaced by petunia beds and potted geraniums.

All of this is not to belittle the charmtown, however. In charmtowns, worthy buildings from the past are carefully restored and converted to museums, shops, and comfortable, sometimes even luxurious, bed and breakfasts. Cafes that once specialized in fat and frying reopen as attractive little restaurants with menus designed for the most discriminating and health-conscious. Galleries of every description allow artists and craftspeople an opportunity to create, maybe even to make a living.

Of even greater importance, charmtowns help keep past generations just a little bit alive, maybe enough to ensure that younger generations will know just a little bit about them. And of greatest importance, the charmtown and its visitors make it possible for many of our country's most treasured little towns to survive–period.

> *Ten percent of the author's proceeds from this book are donated to The American Farmland Trust, working to stop the loss of productive farmland and to promote farming practices that lead to a healthy environment.*

It is my privilege to be able to continue to explore and report on America's charming towns and villages and the process whereby they evolve with grace, beauty, and of course charm, into that highly adaptable new species, the charmtown.

PRICE CODES

Unless otherwise noted, the coded prices for **lodgings** refer to rates for a double room (double occupancy):
- **$**, *most rooms $50 or less*
- **$$**, *most rooms in $51 to $80 range*
- **$$$**, *most rooms $81 or more*

Rates for bed and breakfasts always include breakfast. Unless a listing states "full breakfasts" or "Cont. 'plus' breakfasts," assume that breakfasts are Continental, consisting of fruit and/or juice, pastry, and hot beverage. Continental "plus" breakfasts, also known as "deluxe" Continental breakfasts, consist of a wider variety of selections (pastries, cereals, etc.) than Continental breakfasts, but usually do not include egg, meat, and/or cheese dishes.

Rates for inns and historic hotels often do not include breakfast. For this reason, the nature of the breakfast, *including* Continental breakfasts, has been indicated for all inns and hotels whose rates include breakfast.

Full-service means that evening meals are served on the premises and that guest rooms have, at the very least, private baths, phones, and usually TVs. *Restaurant* or *dining room* indicates an eating establishment that is also open to non-guests.

Except for establishments serving lunch only, the **restaurant** code designates the prices of evening meals, excluding alcoholic beverages, tips, or taxes:
- **$**, *most meals $10 or less*
- **$$**, *most meals in $11 to $20 range*
- **$$$**, *most meals $21 or more*

It is usually safe to assume that lunch prices average about 60% to 70% of dinner prices.

The lodging and restaurant listings are given as an illustrative list, and are not meant to be an exhaustive or "best-of" compilation. Part of the joy of visiting these destinations is discovering your own favorites, so please consider branching out from those suggested here.

TRAVEL SUGGESTIONS

This guide is intended only as an introduction to a town or village's general character and principal points of interest. More detailed information, including admission fees and schedules and calendars of special events, is available from chambers of commerce, visitors bureaus, and (oftentimes) innkeepers.

The majority of the listed communities publish brochures for self-guided tours. This is sometimes noted, but not always.

Almost all national parks, national monuments, state parks, state historic sites, major museums, and large churches are open year-round. Many other sites and attractions, however, restrict visiting hours or close altogether during the winter months. *Always* inquire in advance when planning a visit after Labor Day and before Memorial Day.

Many of the communities can be very crowded during summer (and sometimes autumn) weekends. It may therefore be wise to schedule visits during weekdays or the off-season. This is especially true for Lenox/Stockbridge (MA), Cape May (NJ), Southampton (NY), Williamsburg (VA), and other popular towns near large metropolitan areas. Off-season travelers should bear in mind also that virtually every community but the tiniest sponsors some kind of "Victorian" Christmas celebration.

When planning itineraries and scheduling travel time, remember that most American towns of 10,000 or more population have developed lengthy commercial strips that can significantly slow travel. If a bypass is available, use it; if not, whenever possible try to remain on interstates or other limited-access highways, or on two-lane roads that pass only through very small towns.

SUGGESTED ITINERARIES

SIX SUGGESTIONS FOR WONDERFULLY CHARMING ROAD TRIPS!

I've designed these six driving tours to give you a few ideas for some scenic trips to America's charming travel treasures and gems. Most of the towns below are detailed in later chapters; check the Table of Contents or index for full listings. I welcome your input, so please let me know how these trips work for you. Happy trails!

1. THE BERKSHIRES & SOUTHERN VERMONT
• *Point of Departure and Return: Danbury, Connecticut*
• *Four Days, 535 Miles*

Hugging famous US 7, the first half of this tour passes through or near some of America's loveliest and most fabled towns and villages. The second half follows less known roads that wind through Vermont's **Green Mountains**, Massachusetts' **Berkshire Hills**, and rural Connecticut's rolling parkland. One of the tour's major gems – **Litchfield, Connecticut** – is reserved for the last day.

This is side-trip country, so take every opportunity to try the back roads, especially those leading off US 7. Side trips in Vermont to **Dorset** and to Robert Todd Lincoln's *Hildene* near Manchester are musts. Some other recommendations include lunch at the **Red Lion Inn** in Stockbridge, Massachusetts (reservations), a leisurely stroll about the campus of **Middlebury College** in Vermont, and a walking tour of Litchfield's Georgian homes.

Day 1 – *105 miles*

From intersection of I 84 with US 7 east of Danbury, drive north on US 7 to **Bull's Bridge** (covered bridge).

Continue north on US 7 to **Kent** (see listing).

Continue north on US 7 (visiting Kent Falls State Park en route) to **West Cornwall** (covered bridge).

Continue north on US 7 to intersection with CT 112. Drive west on CT 112 (via Lime Rock) to intersection with CT 41. Drive north on CT 41 to **Salisbury**.

Drive northeast on US 44 to intersection with US 7 (at Canaan). Drive north on US 7 to **Sheffield**, Massachusetts (covered bridge).

Continue north on US 7 to **Great Barrington**. Take side trip through **South Egremont** and other nearby Berkshire villages.

Continue north on US 7 to **Stockbridge** (see listing). Take side trip to **West Stockbridge**.

Continue north on US 7 and then 7A to **Lenox** (see listing).

Day 2 – *145 miles*

Continue north on US 7 (via Pittsfield) to **Williamstown** (Williams College, Sterling & Francine Clark Art Institute).

Continue north on US 7 to Bennington, Vermont, then north on US 7 or 7A to **Manchester Village/Manchester Center** (see listing). Visit nearby **Dorset** (see listing).

Continue north on US 7 (via Rutland) to **Middlebury** (see listing).

Day 3 – *130 miles*

Drive east on VT 125 (via Middlebury Gap) to intersection with VT 100 (at Hancock). Wind south on VT 100 to intersection with US 4. Drive east on US 4 to **Woodstock** (see listing).

Return via US 4 and VT 10A to intersection with VT 100. Travel south on Vt 100 to **Weston** (Guild of Old Time Crafts & Industries, Vermont Country Store).

Continue south on VT 100 to intersection with VT 11 (at Londonderry). Travel west on VT 11 to Manchester/Dorset (see above).

Day 4 – *155 miles*

Return south on US 7 or 7A (via Bennington) to Williamstown, Massachusetts. Drive east on MA 2 to intersection with MA 8. Wind south on MA/CT 8 through Berkshire Hills to Torrington, Connecticut. Drive southwest on US 202 to **Litchfield** (see listing).

Drive southwest on US 202 (via New Milford) to Danbury.

2. NORTHERN CALIFORNIA

• *Point of Departure and Return: San Francisco*
• *3 days, 420 miles*
• *optional Ferndale excursion: 5 days, 750 miles*

A Spanish-American plaza, a traditional American square, a piece of New England, a slice of Victoriana, all form a collage that pays tribute to

California's rich cultural diversity. Mediterranean vineyards, Pacific palisades, redwood groves, secluded beaches, these in turn pay tribute to the state's considerable scenic diversity.

The first part of this tour focuses on California's famed wine country, so take full advantage of the many winery tours, tasting rooms, and vineyard picnic sites. Then, your knowledge of California wines warmly extended, head westward along one of the country's most beautiful highways, CA 128, toward the beaches and cliffs of the blue Pacific beyond.

Tour additions might include the **Ferndale** excursion, described below, or **Half Moon Bay** south of San Francisco. If you've got two or three days more to spare, consider crossing the Central Valley for a night in **Grass Valley** or **Nevada City** in the foothills of the Sierra Nevadas. Or a tour of **Lake Tahoe** and little **Genoa**, Nevada, on the other side.

Day 1 – *100 miles*

Drive north from San Francisco on US 101 to intersection with CA 37. Drive east on CA 37 to intersection with CA 121. Drive north on CA 121 to intersection with CA 12. Continue north on CA 12 to **Sonoma** (see listing).

Return south on CA 12 to intersection with CA 121. Drive east on CA 12/121 to intersection with CA 29. Travel north on CA 29 through Napa Valley (vineyards, wineries) to **St. Helena** (wineries, Bale Grist Mill State Historic Park, Silverado Museum).

Continue north on CA 29 to **Calistoga** (springs, vineyards, Old Faithful Geyser of California, Petrified Forest, Sharpsteen Museum).

Day 2 – *140 miles*

Drive west on Calistoga Road to intersection with Mark West Springs Road. Turn right on Mark West Springs Road and continue to intersection with US 101 north of Santa Rosa. Drive north on US 101 to **Healdsburg** (plaza, winery tasting rooms).

Continue north on US 101 to intersection with CA 128 (at Cloverdale). Making sure you have a tank full of gas, drive northwest on beautiful CA 128 to intersection with CA 1 on Pacific Coast. Drive north on CA 1 along coast to **Mendocino** (see listing).

Continue north on CA 1 to **Fort Bragg** (see listing).

Day 3 – *180 miles*

Returning south on CA 1, drive along coast to **Gualala** (arts center, Point Arena Lighthouse).

Continue south on CA 1 along coast to intersection with US 101. Drive south on US 101 to San Francisco (starting point).

20

Optional Excursion to Ferndale – *two days, 330 miles*
- **Day 1** – From Healdsburg (see Day 2 above), drive north on US 101 (visiting redwood groves & *Avenue of the Giants* en route) to Fernbridge/ Ferndale exit south of Eureka. Travel west to Victorian **Ferndale** (see listing).
- **Day 2** – Inquire locally concerning loop road via Lost Coast and Petrolia back to US 101. Depending on weather, time of year, nature of vehicle, and hardiness of travelers, the better option may be to return directly to US 101. Drive south on US 101 to intersection with CA 1. Drive south on CA 1 to Fort Bragg (see Day 2 of above itinerary).

3. THE LOWER MISSISSIPPI RIVER
- *Non-looping tour along Mississippi River from Vicksburg, Mississippi to Baton Rouge, Louisiana.*
- *3 days, 255 miles*

The white-pillared mansions and the sleepy little towns of the romantic old South still exist in places. This tour explores one of the grandest and best preserved of these places, the stretch of cotton-rich land that winds along the **Mississippi River** south of Vicksburg, Mississippi.

The Deep South can be enjoyed any month of the year, but it is in late March and early April that the antebellum romance seems to reach full blossom. This is when many towns – **Natchez, St. Francisville**, and **Vicksburg** among them – open their doors during "pilgrimages." It's a busy time, and reservations should be made as early as possible. (October and Christmas can also be busy times down here.)

If this tour sharpens your desire to see more of the Old South, Alabama's **Black Belt**, another plantation area rich in pre-Civil War memories, is just two or three hours east of Jackson. Although little known, in and around **Demopolis, Forkland, Eutaw** (see listing), and farther east, **Lowndesboro**, lies another superb collection of antebellum mansions.

Day 1 – *45 miles, from Vicksburg*
From Jackson, Mississippi drive west (or from Shreveport, La., drive E) on I 20 to exit 4B in **Vicksburg**. Drive north into city (antebellum mansions, Old Court House Museum, Toys & Soldiers Museum, Vicksburg National Military Park).

Drive south on US 61 to **Port Gibson** (see listing). Take side trip to Grand Gulf State Park on the Mississippi River. Also, inquire locally for information on (and advisability of) side trip to ghost town of Rodney. Spend balance of day relaxing on verandah and grounds of plantation home B&B in Port Gibson or Lorman areas.

Day 2 – *130 miles*

Continue south on US 61, or alternatively, the Natchez Trace Pkwy., to **Natchez** (tours of antebellum homes and churches).

Continue south on US 61 to **Woodville** (see listing). Take side trip on Pinckneyville Rd. to Pond Store and Clark Creek Nature Area.

Continue south on US 61 to **St. Francisville** (see listing), Louisiana.

Day 3 – *80 miles*

Cross Mississippi River by ferry and drive south on LA 10 to **New Roads** in "French Louisiana." Return to St. Francisville.

Drive east on LA 10 to **Jackson** (see listing).

Continue east on LA 10 to **Clinton** (antebellum buildings).

Return west on LA 10 to intersection with LA 68 (just east of Jackson). Drive south on LA 68 to intersection with US 61. Continue south on US 61 to Baton Rouge.

4. SOUTHERN COLORADO & NORTHERN NEW MEXICO

• *Point of Departure and Return: Denver*

• *6 days, 1,150 miles*

Colorado and New Mexico are doubly blessed. Each can boast some of the country's most spectacular scenery, and each can lay claim to an especially colorful collection of charming little towns. The itinerary first leads through several of Colorado's best-preserved old mining towns, each miniaturized against a breathtaking mountain backdrop. Along the way are the **San Juan Mountains** of southwestern Colorado, possibly the most beautiful mountain range in the U.S.

The second part of the itinerary includes legendary **Santa Fe** and **Taos** as well as several tiny Spanish-American villages hidden on the back roads. Here in northern New Mexico lies the birthplace of the "Santa Fe look," that special cultural blend known around the world for its unique architecture, painting, furniture, jewelry, clothing, and cuisine. The scenery is also impressive, as the drive through the **Sangre de Cristo Mountains** east of Taos will soon make clear.

While in Colorado, take a Jeep tour for an exciting excursion into a back country dotted with old mining camps and ghost towns. And while in New Mexico, try both the red and the green chilis to decide which you prefer with your enchiladas (and have the chili served on the side).

Day 1 – *170 miles*

From Denver drive west on I 70 to **Georgetown** (see listing).

Continue west on US 70 to intersection with CO 91. Drive south on

CO 91 to **Leadville** (old mining town, Victorian buildings, Healy House, museums, train tour).

Drive south on US 24 via **Buena Vista** to intersection with US 285 (at Johnson Village). Drive south on US 285 to intersection with CO 291. Continue south on CO 291 to **Salida** (see listing).

Day 2 – *185 miles*

Drive west on US 50 to **Gunnison** (Pioneer Museum).

Continue west on US 50 along Blue Mesa Reservoir to Montrose. Drive south on US 550 to **Ouray** (see listing).

Continue south on US 550 (the *Million Dollar Hwy.*) to **Silverton** (see listing).

Day 3 – 150 miles

Drive south on US 50 via spectacular Molas Divide to intersection with US 160 at Durango. Drive west on US 160 to Mesa Verde National Park.

Return on US 160 to Durango.

Day 4 – *225 miles*

Drive east on US 160 to Pagosa Springs. Drive south on US 84 via **Abiquiu**, New Mexico to **Santa Fe** (Plaza, Palace of the Governors, Mission of San Miguel of Santa Fe, museums, Canyon Road for galleries and charm).

Day 5 – *100 miles*

Drive north on US 84 to intersection with NM 502. Drive west on NM 502 to **San Ildefonso Pueblo** (pottery).

Return east on NM 503 to intersection with US 84 and continue east (now NM 503) to intersection with NM 520. Drive north on NM 520 to **Chimayo** (El Santuario de Nuestro Senor de Esquipulas).

Drive east on NM 76 via Spanish-American villages of **Truchas** and **Las Trampas** (church) to intersection with NM 75. Drive west on NM 75 via **Dixon** to intersection with NM 68. Drive north on NM 68 to **Taos** (see listing).

Day 6 – 320 miles

Drive east on US 64 through Sangre de Cristo Mountains to **Cimarron** (old outlaw town).

Continue east on US 64, paralleling Santa Fe National Historic Trail, to intersection with I 25. Drive north on I 25 for return to Denver (starting point).

5. SOUTHERN INDIANA & KENTUCKY'S BLUEGRASS COUNTRY

• *Point of Departure and Return: Indianapolis*
• *6 days, 800 miles*

Indiana and Kentucky have long been associated with the nostalgia of the long ago and far away. Just listen to the words of their state songs: *On the Banks of the Wabash, Far Away* and *My Old Kentucky Home.* Along the byways of this nostalgic itinerary lie more than a dozen towns and villages in parts of these states that especially suggest the long ago and far away: the rolling woodland of southern Indiana and the incomparable Bluegrass Country of Kentucky.

Two of the towns were founded as Utopian communities, Indiana's delightful little **New Harmony**, which in fact sits right on the Banks of the Wabash, and Kentucky's pastoral **Pleasant Hill**, with its quaint Shaker simplicity. Two of the towns are widely respected for their art and crafts, **Berea**, Kentucky, and **Nashville**, Indiana. Several of the towns in Kentucky's Bluegrass have historic inns that could stand proudly alongside their Virginia cousins. Indiana's **Madison** is probably the loveliest town on the **Ohio River**. And just in case the present be forgotten, **Columbus**, Indiana, scatters buildings of superb late 20th-century design about a town with a late 19th-century Main Street.

You'll want to spend *at least* half of your last day, Day 6, in Madison. But should you still have several hours to spare, consider winding northeast by back roads from Madison up to the little canal town of **Metamora** (see listing) and then returning to Indianapolis by US 52.

Day 1 – *100 miles*

From Indianapolis drive south on I 65 to **Columbus** (contemporary buildings designed by world-famous architects).

Drive west on IN 46 to **Nashville** (see listing). Tour Brown County State Park, **Bean Blossom** (covered bridge), **Story**, and other Brown County sites (listed under Nashville).

Day 2 – *175 miles*

Continue west on IN 46 to **Bloomington** (Indiana U. campus).

Drive south on IN 37 to intersection with IN 60 (at Mitchell). Drive east on US 60 to Spring Mill State Park and **Spring Mill Village**.

Return via IN 60 to IN 37. Drive south on IN 37 to intersection with US 150 (at Paoli). Drive west on US 150 to intersection with IN 56. Drive south on IN 56 to **French Lick/West Baden Springs** (see listing).

Continue south on IN 56 to intersection with US 231. Drive south on US 231 to intersection with I 64. Drive west on I 64 to intersection with IN 68 (exit 12). Drive southwest on IN 68 to **New Harmony** (see listing).

Day 3 – *200 miles*

Drive east on IN 66 (via Evansville and along the Ohio River) to intersection with IN 462 (at Sulphur). Drive east on IN 462 to **Corydon** (see listing).

Drive north on IN 135 to I 64. Drive east on I 64 to intersection with I 65 (in Louisville, Kentucky). Drive south on I 65 to intersection with KY 245 (exit 112). Drive east on KY 245, stopping at the gardens of the Bernheim Forest, to **Bardstown** (see listing).

Day 4 – *110 miles*

Drive south on US 150 to intersection with US 68 (at Perryville). Drive north on US 68 to **Harrodsburg** (see listing).

Continue north on US 68 to **Pleasant Hill** (see listing).

Drive south on KY 33 to **Danville** (Constitution Square State Historic Site, McDowell House).

Drive east on KY 52 via **Lancaster** to intersection with KY 21. Drive south on KY 21 to **Berea** (see listing).

Day 5 – *165 miles*

Drive north on I 75 (stopping en route at White Hall State Historic Site, exit 95) to intersection with US 27/68 (in Lexington). Drive east on US 27/68, past horse farms, to **Paris**.

Drive west on US 460 via **Georgetown** to **Frankfort** (State Capitol, Frankfort Cemetery, Liberty Hall Historic Site, Old Governor's Mansion, Old State Capitol/Kentucky History Museum).

Drive north on US 421 (crossing Ohio River) to **Madison**, Indiana (see listing).

Day 6 – *50 miles*

Drive north on IN 7 to intersection with I 65 (at Columbus). Return north on I 65 to Indianapolis (starting point).

6. THE CAROLINAS & GEORGIA UPCOUNTRY

• *Point of Departure and Return: Asheville, North Carolina*
• *4 days, 395 miles*

This itinerary is not to be hurried. To hurry through the **Upcountry** would be to miss the very soul of the countryside and its people. For generations a place of summer retreat from Southern coastal climes, and more recently a four-season place of retirement from Eastern cities, the Upcountry is for leisurely strolling, forest hiking, river rafting, fishing, golfing. Even in the car, enjoyment of the winding roads, scenic overlooks, streams, and waterfalls demands time. Moreover, the people in this corner of the world are especially friendly, and their hospitality does not allow for haste – or worry.

The tour begins with the sophisticated resort towns of Upcountry North Carolina and then turns south toward historical little towns in Upcountry Georgia and South Carolina. Along the way lies the delightful little Bavarian village of **Helen**, Georgia. Not to be missed in the North Carolina towns are the performing arts. Check with the chambers of commerce in advance for schedules and information. Also, be on the lookout throughout the tour for local crafts – the people of the **Blue Ridge Mountains** have a long tradition of quality craftsmanship.

For a non-looping tour, wind westward across the mountains of northern Georgia from **Dahlonega** or **Helen** (Day 3) to the little mountain resort of **Mentone**, Alabama.

Day 1 – *45 miles*
From **Asheville** (Biltmore Estate, Biltmore Homespun Shops, Thomas Wolfe Memorial) drive south on I 26 to **Hendersonville** (exit 18; see listing).
Drive west on US 64 to **Brevard** (see listing).

Day 2 – *150 miles*
Drive west on US 64 via **Cashiers** (mountain resort) to **Highlands** (see listing).
Wind north on US 64 through mountains to Franklin. Drive west on US 64 to intersection with NC 175. Drive south on NC 175 (becoming GA 75) to **Hiawasee**, Georgia (mountain resort, Georgia's highest peak).
Drive west on US 76 to intersection with US 19 (at Blairsville). Turn south on US 19 to **Dahlonega** (see listing).

Day 3 – *100 miles*
Drive east on GA 52 to intersection with GA 115. Continue east on GA 115 to intersection with US 129 (at Cleveland). Drive north on US 129 about 1 mile to intersection with GA 75. Continue north on GA 75 to **Helen** (see listing).
Drive east on GA 17 to Toccoa. Continue east on US 123 to Westminster, SC. Turn north on SC 183 to old German town of **Walhalla**.
Drive south on SC 28 to US 123/76. Drive east on US 123/76 to **Clemson** (Clemson University, Fort Hill plantation house, Hanover House).
Drive south on SC 28B to **Pendleton** (see listing).

Day 4 – *100 miles*
Drive south on US 76 to I 85. Drive east on I 85 to US 25 (in

Greenville). Travel north on US 25 to I 26 (in North Carolina). Turn south on I 26 to **Saluda** (next exit, exit 28).

Return north on I 26 to Asheville (starting point).

GREAT VINTAGE TRAIN RIDES

- **Black River & Western Railroad** (between Flemington & Ringoes, NJ) – Flemington, NJ
- **California Western Railroad** *Skunk* **trains** (between Ft. Bragg & Willits, CA) – Fort Bragg, CA
- **Durango & Silverton Narrow Gauge Railroad Company** (between Durango & Silverton, CO) —Silverton, CO
- **Eureka Springs & North Arkansas Railway** (Ozark Mountains) — Eureka Springs, AR
- **French Lick, West Baden, & Southern Railroad** (Hoosier National Forest) — French Lick, IN
  Georgetown Loop (between Georgetown & Silver Plume, CO) – Georgetown, CO
- **Minnesota Zephyr** (St. Croix River Valley) — Stillwater, MN
- **New Hope & Ivyland Rail Road** (Pennsylvania countryside) – New Hope, PA
- **Scenic Ozark Railway** (Ozark Mountains) — Van Buren, AR
- **Valley Railroad Company** (between Essex & Chester, CT) — Essex/ Chester, CT
- **West Shore Railroad** (Pennsylvania countryside) — Lewisburg, PA

TOP 10 TOWNS OF THE OLD SOUTH

- Abbeville, SC
- Eufaula, AL
- Harrodsburg/Pleasant Hill, KY
- Holly Springs, MS
- Jefferson, TX
- Jonesborough, TN
- Madison, GA
- Oxford, MS
- St. Francisville, LA
- St. Marys, GA

TOP 10 TOWNS OF THE WILD WEST

- Abilene, KS
- Deadwood, SD
- Fort Benton, MT
- Fort Davis, TX
- Genoa, NV
- Medora, ND
- Saratoga, WY
- Silverton, CO
- Tombstone, AZ
- Wallace, ID

WONDERFUL COLONIAL VILLAGES
- Beaufort, NC
- Camden, SC
- Chestertown, MD
- Edgartown, MA
- Essex, CT
- Exeter, NH
- Odessa, DE
- Old Lyme, CT
- Rockport, MA
- St. Mary's City, MD
- Wickford, RI

INTERESTING OLD MILLS
- **Fly Creek Cider Mill** (1856), Cooperstown, NY
- **Ledford Mill** (1884), Lynchburg, TN
- **Meek Grist Mill** (1878), Bonaparte (Van Buren County), IA
- **The Old Mill** (1746), Nantucket Town, MA
- **Old Stone Mill** (1836), Clinton, NJ
- **Prallsville mills** (18th & 19th century), Delaware & Raritan Canal State Park, Stockton, NJ
- **Red Mill** (ca 1763), Clinton, NJ
- **Red Mill** (1855), near Rural, WI
- **Waterloo Village mills** (18th & 19th century), Waterloo Village, NJ
- **White's Mill**, Abingdon, VA
- **Zeitinger's Mill** (1859), Maeystown, IL

CLASSIC COVERED BRIDGES
Bean Blossom Bridge (1880), near Nashville, IN
Brown County State Park Bridge (1838, double-barreled), near Nashville, IN
Bull's Bridge, near Kent, CT
Emily's Bridge, near Stowe, VT
Goddard Covered Bridge (1820), near Maysville/Washington, KY
Green Sergeants Bridge, near Stockton, NJ
Pulp Mill Bridge (1806, double-barreled), near Middlebury, VT
Red Mill Bridge (1970, from original plans), near Rural, WI
Sheffield Bridge (1837, rebuilt 1995), near Great Barrington, MA
Sunday River Bridge (1870), near Bethel, ME
White Caps Bridge, near Stowe, VT

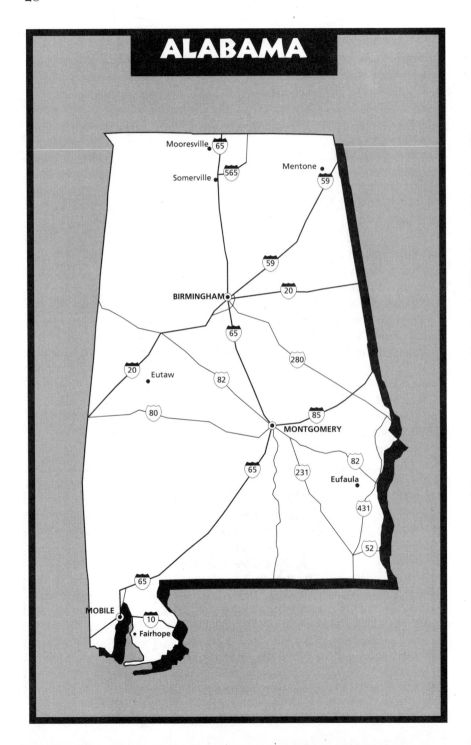

ALABAMA

Eufaula

Population 13, 320

With antebellum houses azaleas, dogwoods, and a history of wealth centering on cotton, **Eufaula** (you FALL uh) is unmistakably the Deep South. Located on the **Chattahoochee River**, the town was once an ideal riverboat port for planters from across a broad swath of Alabama, Georgia, and Florida. And as was so often true in the South during the 1840s and 1850s, the planters and merchants converted their wealth into magnificent homes, churches, and other buildings.

Spared by the Yankees (the Confederacy had surrendered by the time Union troops reached the town), many of the antebellum structures still stand. In the post-war years many other beautiful structures went up, and these too have been preserved. The result is that Eufaula, with over 700 historic buildings, boasts Alabama's finest 19th-century small-town commercial district as well as its grandest collection of domestic Italianate architecture. Many of the historic houses are in the Seth Lore-Irwinton Historic District and many of the historic commercial buildings are on Broad Street.

The oldest commercial structure in town - and also the oldest frame structure – is **The Tavern**, originally an 1830s inn, later a Confederate hospital, and now a private residence listed on the National Register of Historic Places.

The best-known home is the **Shorter Mansion** (open to the public). Built in 1884 and enlarged and rebuilt in 1906, it is one of Alabama's finest Neoclassical mansions. Another find mansion, **Fendall Hall** (1860), is topped by a square cupola so characteristic of the Italianate style. Waterford chandeliers, hand-stenciled walls, and murals grace the interior (open Mon., Thurs., & Sat.).

The **Holleman-Foy Home** (1907) and its columned rotunda entrance provide a magnificent example of turn-of-the-century Neoclassical Eclectic architecture. The house has been in the same family since 1909. Other important Eufaula houses include the Greek Revival **Hart-Milton House** (1843) and **Kendall Manor**, a stately Italianate mansion (listed below as a bed and breakfast).

Brochures for walking and driving tours of the many homes in the historic district are available at the Visitors Bureau (CoC). Most of the homes are private, but during Eufaula's Pilgrimage in April many of the owners open the doors and allow visitors to explore the rooms and family heirlooms within. The pilgrimage also features open-air art exhibits, tea gardens, concerts, and a major antique show.

Special Features

Bordered by 640 miles of shoreline, **Lake Eufaula** is sometimes called *The Bass Capital of the World*. The 25-year-old reservoir is surrounded by many weedy sloughs and stump rows and is dotted with 48 fish attractors. Two full-service marinas and many public-use areas serve fishermen as well as other water sportsmen.

> • *The twice-weekly local newspaper carries the phrase, "Symbol of the Old South, Cradle of the New."*

Where to Stay

KENDALL MANOR INN, *534 W. Broad St., (334) 687-8847.* 1872 Italianate home on National Register, full-service inn, columned veranda & distinctive cupola, antiques, 16-ft ceilings, fireplaces, full breakfasts, afternoon refreshments, dinner by reservation, gardens, croquet, bicycles. $$$

ST. MARY'S B&B, *206 Rivers Ave., (334) 687-7195.* Circa 1850 Italianate home, antiques, pumpkin pine floors, Oriental rugs, private baths, porch swing. $$

Where to Eat

THE CREEK RESTAURANT, *431 South St., (334) 687-0083.* Seafood, poultry, steaks; "located a stone's throw from Cheneyhatchee Creek." $

OLD MEXICO, *114 N. Eufaula Ave., (334) 687-7770.* Authentic Mexican cuisine served in historic Bluff City Inn. $ to $$

Further Information

Eufaula/Barbour County Chamber of Commerce, Visitors Bureau, *P.O. Box 697, Eufaula, AL 36072 (800) 524-7529.*

Directions

From Montgomery, US 82 southeast through Union Springs to Eufaula.

Eutaw

Population 2281

Eutaw is the seat of Greene County, a county known for its meandering rivers and white-pillared plantation houses. Located on the black, fertile soil of west Alabama, Greene County was (and to some extent still is) cotton country. Greene County fully participated in the romantic "Golden Era" of the plantation south, the period between 1840 and 1860.

In large part because of the defense provided by the bridgeless rivers surrounding the town, Union troops showed little interest in harming Eutaw, and much of the old town therefore survives. In the center of town is a charming public square, and on the square sits a lovely little Greek Revival **courthouse** (1839\68). Rural, and distant from anything that isn't, the place smacks of another era. The town even boasts a country store with a high ceiling that still delivers groceries and cuts off pieces of cheese from a large round (called "hoop" cheese).

A few of Eutaw's buildings are open to the public. In cases of doubt, simply ask – you'll find that Eutaw is an especially friendly town.

The meticulously restored **Kirkwood Mansion** (1860) is one of the most striking of Eutaw's more than 40 antebellum structures. The four-story mansion is lined on two sides with massive columns and has wrought-iron railings, four tall chimneys, and a reconstructed cupola. The **Captain Edwin Reese House** (1858), with four two-story fluted Ionic columns, and the Greek Revival **Coleman-Banks House** (ca 1847) are two other lovely houses. On the grounds of the latter are the original smokehouse and kitchen/wash-house.

One of the most interesting of the non-residential structures is the 1851 Greek Revival **First Presbyterian Church**. The church's slave gallery is still in place, as are the original whale-oil pulpit lamps.

Special Features

Ionic-columned **Thornhill** (1833) and what is possibly Alabama's most beautiful mansion, **Rosemount** (1832-39), are located in the tiny community of Forkland, 13 miles south of Eutaw on US 43.

The Greek Revival **Ebenezer Presbyterian Church** (1859) in Clinton, 6 miles north on AL 14, has been recently restored.

> • *Eutaw only came into being because, in 1838, Greene County needed a new government seat.*
> • *As with many Southern counties, the timber industry is today more important to Greene County than cotton.*

Where to Stay

KIRKWOOD B&B, *111 Kirkwood Rd., (205) 372-9009.* 1860 Greek Revival home with Ionic columns & wrap-around veranda, National Register, original furnishings, some private baths, full breakfasts, wooded gardens, tour of home, restoration award. $$

Where to Eat

COTTON PATCH, *Union Rd., P.O. Box 270, (205) 372-4235.* Old-fashioned fried chicken the dinner specialty. $

MAIN STREET EATERY & DELI, *208 Main St., (205) 372-0209.* Make-your-own-sandwiches, Shrimp Po Boy, Chick Tender Basket, Chick Fryz, Philly Cheese Steak. $

Further Information

Greene County Historical Society, *310 Main St., P.O. Box 746, Eutaw, AL 35462.*

Directions

From Birmingham, I 20 southwest to exit 40, AL 14 south to Eutaw.

Fairhope
Population 9, 816

Part bayside resort, part exclusive suburb, part artists' colony, part subtropical paradise, **Fairhope** is a beautiful place. The "Village of Fairhope," situated on the eastern shore of Mobile Bay, has beaches, boats, and broad sea views. The waterfront gives way very quickly, however, to gorgeous homes, moss-draped oaks, lush gardens of azaleas, roses, camellias, magnolias, and every other flower or plant that the gardener or artist might dream of. And not far away, still within the garden setting, is a delightful downtown area with canopied galleries, boutiques, and tempting specialty shops. There seems to be a feeling–one given substance by Fairhope's calendar–that an arts and crafts show isn't far off, in time or place.

Fairhope was founded in 1894 by a group of Iowans who were followers of American social reformer Henry George. It was George who proposed the idea of a single tax, one drawn exclusively from increases in the value of land; putting George's ideas into practice, Fairhope's settlers held the land in common ownership and enjoyed it individually through long-term leases. (For reasons that aren't completely clear, towns founded by 19th-century utopian societies seem to find their way into this book. Fairhope is no exception.)

One of the best places to begin a visit here is the **Fairhope Municipal Pier**, which houses a restaurant as well as fishing and marina facilities. Strolling the pier in the evening or early morning can be a truly memorable experience. At the foot of the pier is a stately **fountain**, and adjacent to the fountain an exceptionally lush waterside **park**. There is also a public **beach**. The area is best toured with the kind of timetable that allows for plenty of strolling, sea viewing, and just plain relaxing.

The **Eastern Shore Art Center**, a few blocks away, features monthly exhibitions of oils, watercolors, weavings, pottery, and other media. Concerts, films, and lectures are also offered.

Fairhope hosts a busy schedule of annual events ranging from Mardi Gras and Christmas parades to environmental activities to 4th-of-July fireworks on the pier. Between events visitors can enjoy sport fishing, jet skiing, and boating. Golfers will find the finest public course on Mobile Bay's Eastern Shore. And, of course, lovers of seafood will find flounder, crab, and shrimp fresh from the bay.

Special Features

Fairhope is within short-excursion distance of a number of attractions: historic **Fort Gaines** and **Fort Morgan** at the entrance to Mobile Bay, the beaches of **Gulf Shores**, the inimitable **Bellingrath Gardens** across the bay, **Historic Blakeley State Park** (site of the last major battle of the Civil War), and the many sights of **Mobile** and **Pensacola**.

> *• The Greek Orthodox Malbis Memorial Church (1965) in nearby Malbis is a copy of a Byzantine church in Athens (guided tours).*

Where to Stay

BAY BREEZE GUEST HOUSE, *742 S. Mobile St., P.O. Box 526, (334) 928-8976.* Early 1930s stucco home on Mobile Bay, family heirlooms & antiques, private baths, cottage suite, decks, private pier with covered areas, camellia & azalea garden. $$$

CHURCH STREET INN, *51 S. Church St., P.O. Box 526, (334) 928-8976.* 1921 home on National Register, family antiques & heirlooms, private baths, front porch with high-back rockers, garden courtyard. $$$

THE GUEST HOUSE, *63 S. Church St., (334) 928-6226.* 1900 home on National Register, private baths, full breakfasts, near downtown & pier. $$$

MARRIOTT'S GRAND HOTEL, *One Grand Blvd., Point Clear (36564), (334) 928-9201.* 1847/1939 full-service bay-front resort hotel on 550 acres, 4 restaurants & lounges, private beach, marina, fishing pier, pool, water sports, 36 holes of golf, tennis, lawn sports, stables, health club, shops. $$$

THE PORCHES, *19190 County Rd. 13, (334) 928-4754/(888) 227-8291.* Two-story country home with screened wrap-around porches, swing bed, private baths, full "country" breakfasts, outdoor kennel available. $$$

Where to Eat

CLAYTON'S, *19270 Scenic Hwy. 98, (334) 928-0031.* Soups, salads, & sandwiches incl. Uncle Joe's Seafood Gumbo, Seafood PoorBoy; chicken, pasta, steak, & seafood entrees. $ to $$

GAMBINO'S, *18 Laurel St., (334) 928-5444.* Pomadora del Sol, Lasagna, fried seafood dinners, Shrimp Tortellini, Chicken Parmigiana, Prime Rib of Beef; wine list. $ to $$

GRAND DINING ROOM, *(see Marriott's Grand Hotel above).* Sauteed Grouper New Orleans–fresh grouper with lobster sauce, garnished with crawfish tails & asparagus spears; reservations. $$ to $$$

THE ROYAL OAK, *14 N. Church St., (334) 928-1714.* "A traditional British restaurant and pub" serving Roast Chicken, Steak & Mushroom Pie, Fish & Chips, Cottage Pie, Poached Fresh Salmon, Maid Marion's Filet of Beef. $ to $$

Further Information

Eastern Shore Chamber of Commerce, *327 Fairhope Ave., Fairhope, AL 36532 (334) 928-6387/fax (334) 928-6389.*

Directions

From Mobile, I 10 east across Mobile Bay to US 98, south to ALT 98 (US Scenic 98), south to Fairhope.

Mentone

Population 474

Wilderness, rippling streams, and spectacular mountain views may not be among the images conjured up by the mention of Alabama, yet these are the very kinds of things that describe the mountain-top village of **Mentone** in lovely northeastern Alabama. They are also the kinds of things that make Mentone so many places in one: in the warmer months, an artist colony, a golf resort, a dude ranch, a nature lover's paradise; in the winter, the Southeast's southernmost ski resort. During all times of the year, shops along the town square and elsewhere offer a variety of unique mountain arts and crafts. A good example are *Gourdies* – dolls made from gourds.

The cooler temperatures and clear mountain air attracted visitors here throughout the 19th century, but it wasn't until the construction of the **Mentone Springs Hotel** in the 1880s that the village began to enjoy widespread popularity as a vacation retreat. The hotel was an active resort from the late 19th century to the early 1930s. Recently renovated and opened as a bed and breakfast (see below) the *Grand Ol' Lady* stands as a living reminder of another era.

St. Joseph's-on-the-Mountain Episcopal Church began as a log cabin in 1870 and with the help of donated furnishings and decorations ended up a lovely church. The stained-glass windows, more than a century old, were hand-painted and fired in France.

Special Features

One of the best ways to take in the area's scenery is to drive south seven miles to **DeSoto State Park**. The top sites here are **Little River Canyon**, which is one of the deepest gorges east of the Mississippi River, and the majestic 110-foot **DeSoto Falls**.

> • *Mentone averages about 10 degrees (F) cooler than the surrounding valley.*
> • *Fort Payne, 13 miles south, is both the "Sock Capital of the World" and the home of Alabama, "The Country Group of the Last Decade."*

Where to Stay

MADAPERCA, *H. C. 68 (Box 20), (205) 634-4792*. Riverside retreat atop Lookout Mountain, TV & phones, private baths, suite available, in bird sanctuary. $$

MENTONE INN B&B, *P.O. Box 284, (205) 634-4836*. Redecorated 1927 mountain retreat, private baths, restaurant, housekeeping cottage, flowered grounds, outdoor hot tub. $$ to $$$

MENTONE SPRINGS HOTEL B&B, *6114 AL Hwy. 117, (205) 634-4040*. Renovated 3-story 1884 Queen Anne hotel, original ballroom, TV/library room, antiques, some fireplaces, some private baths, afternoon tea, some pets, original restaurant (Caldwell's–see below), veranda, croquet. $$

MOUNTAIN LAUREL INN, *P.O. Box 176, (205) 634-4673*. On Little River Canyon in wooded setting, private baths & entrances, porch with rockers, hiking. $$

RAVEN HAVEN, *651 County Rd. 644, (205) 634-4310*. On 10 acres of nature atop Lookout Mountain, private baths, full breakfasts. $$

VALHALLA, *672 CR 626, (205) 634-4006*. 1930s farmhouse & guest cottage on 20 acres adjoining DeSoto State Park, private baths, hiking trails to park. $$

THE WINSTON PLACE, *P.O. Box 165 (Valley Head 35989), (205) 635-6381*. Circa 1831 mansion on National Register, original furniture, TV, private baths, private access to veranda, fresh flowers/fruit. $$$

Where to Eat

CALDWELL'S, *(see Mentone Springs Hotel above)*. Filet Mignon, Beef Tips, Ham Steak, Shrimp Scampi, Vegetarian Lasagna; in original 1884 dining room with lots of windows & lace curtains. $

CRAGSMERE MANNA, *Lookout Mountain, (205) 634-4677*. Shrimp Provencale, Grilled Lemon Chicken, Aged Ribeye Steak; in one of oldest houses on mountain. $ to $$

LOG CABIN DELI, *Rt. 1 (Box 300), (205) 634-4560*. In building originally housing an Indian fur-trading post. $

Further Information

DeKalb County Tourist Association, *P.O. Box 1165, Fort Payne, AL 35967 (205) 845-3957. (ZIP for Mentone is 35984.)*

Directions

From Chattanooga (40 miles), I 59 south to exit 231, south on AL 117 to Mentone.

Mooresville

Population about 60

Mooresville was incorporated in 1818, making it the oldest incorporated community in Alabama. Both Andrew Johnson and James A. Garfield spent time here years before their presidential days. Small then and small now, the village doesn't go much farther than three or four blocks in any direction. Almost all of its buildings are on the National

Register, and all but one or two are lived or worked in. Though out of the past, picturesque little Mooresville is a living village.

Bypassed by the interstate, the village is kind of tucked away, unknown even to people in nearby towns. On most maps of the state it looks as though the village has disappeared into some kind of urban sprawl connecting Decatur and Huntsville. In actual fact, the community is surrounded by cotton fields. Large towns are not far away, and many of the townspeople commute to them, but Mooresville still retains its rural charm—and setting. It is peaceful here.

Spanning as they do more than 150 years, Mooresville's buildings vary in style, size, and construction. Some are brick, some are white or pastel frame. All are shaded by beautiful old oaks, magnolias, and other trees. The town's most famous building is probably the **Mooresville Post Office**, which has been in continuous use since 1844. The wooden cubby holes receiving mail today are the same that received mail in Civil War times.

Two churches are of special historic interest. One, the circa 1820 red brick **community church**, still has one of the original chandeliers and the slave balcony (though boarded up after the Civil War). The pulpit of the second, the 1854 white-frame **Church of Christ**, was where Garfield, then a teacher, read from the Bible.

Among the other buildings of special note is the old stagecoach stop/tavern, currently undergoing restoration, and a house dating from around 1825 that owes its survival to the Union general, Garfield, who ordered that it not be vandalized.

Special Features

The **Old State Bank** in neighboring Decatur is the oldest bank in the state (1833). Recently restored, the bank was one of only four buildings in Decatur still standing at the end of the Civil War. Decatur is also home to two well-preserved Victorian residential areas.

Mooresville borders the **Wheeler National Wildlife Refuge**, the largest wildlife refuge in Alabama. The refuge includes a wildlife interpretive center and an observation platform from which migratory waterfowl may be viewed.

• *Only ancient cedars lining the front walk remain of the Female Institute (1830). The institute, which had 55 "lady pupils, " was destroyed by Union soldiers.*

Where to Stay

DANCY-POLK HOUSE, *901 Railroad St. (Decatur, 35601), (205) 353-3579.* Restored 1829 Palladian home on National Register, antiques, Union headquarters during Civil War. $$

Where to Eat

MR. PRIME'S FAMILY STEAK HOUSE, *5700 Mooresville Rd. (corner of I 565 & Mooresville Rd.), (205) 340-0999.* Variety of steak, chicken & rotisserie selections; fresh seafood. $ to $$

OL' HEIDELBERG, *6125 University Dr. (Huntsville), (205) 922-0556.* German & American dishes, locally popular. $ to $$

SHELLEY'S IRONGATE RESTAURANT, *402 Johnston St. SD (Decatur), (205) 350-6795.* Homemade specialties, different menu each day; in restored Victorian home, popular. $ to $$

SIMP McGEE, *725 Bank St. (Decatur), (205) 353-6284.* Cajun cooking, seafood, steaks, red beans & smoked sausage, gumbo, etouffees. $ to $$

Further Information

Alabama Mountain Lakes Association, *P.O. Box 1075, Mooresville, AL 35649 (800) 648-5381.*

Directions

From Huntsville, I 565 west to Mooresville exit (just before intersection with I 65).

Somerville

Population 208

Known as *Morgan County's Grand Old Gal*, **Somerville** is one of those rare little towns where the flavor of the Old South—the real Old South—still lingers. Of course, some of the new has invaded the town. The **Town Hall** is new, for example, and there are telephones (at least in some of the buildings) and electricity. But as an old-fashioned stroll around the square should make clear, very little has happened here since the 19th century.

Settled around 1818, Somerville was a 19th-century cotton town. It served as the county seat until 1891, when despite an uproar and even threats of violence, county government was moved to Decatur. Then total quiet took over. In recent years the town has become a home for people working in Decatur and Huntsville, and this, combined with the beginnings of tourism, has stirred up some activity. But not much.

Somerville's most imposing building, and one straight out of the Old South, is the partially renovated **Old Morgan County Courthouse** (1837). The two-story Federal-style brick structure, listed on the National Register, is Alabama's oldest courthouse. The bell in the belfry is still rung to welcome in each new year. (An appointment is advised for visitors wishing to tour the interior—check at the Town Hall.)

Sprinkled about town are a number of old homes, all private residences. Architecturally the most interesting is the **Rice House** (ca 1835), a Federal-style Tidewater-type cottage. On the National Register, the one-and-a-half-story house has original woodwork and mantels. The house is unique in that the brick was laid in Flemish bond around the entire building rather than just in front.

Other interesting houses include the restored **Gilchrist-Williams House** (probably mid 19th-century), the late 19th-century **Lyle House**, and the antebellum **Mikell House**, with original Federal woodwork. The 1880 **Binford-Peck House** was home to the town's telephone switchboard during the 1930s. A visit to the lovely old **Somerville Cemetery** can provide a good introduction to local history.

Note: I wish to thank historian David W. Whitehorn, author of *Historic Somerville* for providing some of the information for this selection. A copy of *Historic Somerville* may be obtained by writing the Somerville Public Library, P. O. Box 178, Somerville, AL 35670.

Special Features

Huntsville is home to the **US Space and Rocket Center** (hands-on exhibits, Spacedome Theater, bus tours of NASA's Marshall Space Flight Center). Among the city's many other attractions is the **Twickenham Historic District**, containing one of Alabama's largest and finest collections of antebellum homes.

> • *To avoid what could have been an unpleasant confrontation over moving the county seat (in 1891), people from Decatur quietly removed the county records from Somerville by night.*

Where to Stay & Eat

See previous selection, "Mooresville, Alabama."

Further Information

Town Hall, *Somerville, AL 35670 (205) 778-8282.*

Directions

From Birmingham, I 65 north to exit 328, Al 36 east to AL 67, AL 67 north to Somerville.

Other Charming Alabama Towns

Demopolis
Lowndesboro
Marion

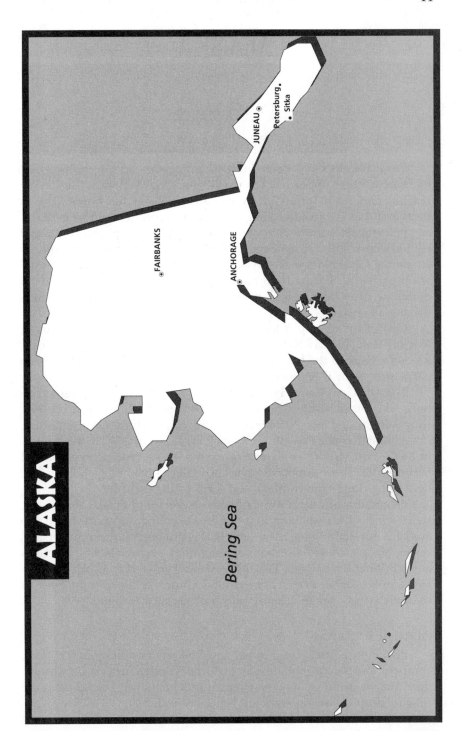

ALASKA

Petersburg
Population 3, 356

From the docks of **Petersburg's** harbor you can see snow-capped mountains, their upper reaches partly obscured by clouds, their lower reaches dark with forests. They rise steeply from the fjords. This is southeast Alaska's Inside Passage, not Norway, but it could be either.

Petersburg, or *Little Norway*, was settled by Norwegians (1897), and the heritage is still very important. The Chamber of Commerce sponsors an annual **Little Norway Festival** (see below), rosemaling decorates old Scandinavian-style frame buildings, and fishing and logging continue to dominate daily lives, just as in the Old Country (although tourism is making an entry).

One of the most picturesque of the older buildings is the **Sons of Norway Hall** (1912), a National Historic Site, constructed on pilings over a slough. Next to the hall is the *Valhalla*, a Viking ship built in 1976 to participate in the U.S. Bicentennial Parade of Ships in New York Harbor.

The **Clausen Memorial Museum** has a number of unusual attractions, like the giant lens from the Cape Decision Lighthouse, a 126.5-lb. King Salmon, and *Fisk* (Norwegian for "fish"), a lovely fountain sculpture.

Although small, Petersburg is a major fishing port—9th in the country in fact – and visitors enjoy exploring the docks of the three colorful harbors. The most popular catches are salmon (summer), halibut and herring (spring), crab (winter), and shrimp (all year).

Petersburg offers a variety of boat charters and rentals for fishing, sightseeing, whale watching, and wildlife observing. Air charters are also available for sightseeing. The area is a major migratory stopover and spring bird-watchers report fantastic sightings – especially of bald eagles at the **Stikine River Flats**. This is the Alaska Panhandle, Alaska's *banana belt*, and so the weather is much milder and far more supportive of outdoor activities than in more northerly parts of the state.

Special Features

People in Norwegian, Viking, and Valkyrie costumes dance, feast, compete, and have a good time at the **Little Norway Festival**, held on the third full weekend in May (Norwegian Independence Day). This is the time to sample from an authentic Smorgasbord.

Several Petersburg companies offer boat tours of beautiful **LeConte Glacier**, the world's southernmost active tidal glacier. The glacier can also be toured by air.

Spectacular scenery and navigational challenges make the ferry trip through the **Wrangell Narrows** especially interesting.

> • *A 2,000-year-old native fish trap archaeological site may be visited near Sandy Beach.*
> • *Alaskan King Crabs can have a "wingspan" of up to eight feet.*
> • *One of the best places to see bears is from the Fredrick Point Boardwalk, a nearby scenic hiking trail.*

Where to Stay

THE BROOM HUS B&B, *Box 427, (907) 772-3459.* 1920s home with kitchen, bath, etc., rented as unit; TV & phone, art, deck, scenic views, transportation available. $$$

MITKOF ISLAND B&B, *606 S. Nordic Dr., P.O. Box 864, (907) 772-3800.* Complete 2-bedroom apartment, TV & phone, waterfront location between ferry & downtown. $$$ (also weekly rates).

RAINSONG B&B HOME, *1107 Wrangell Ave., P.O. Box 968, (907) 772-3178.* Fully furnished 2-bedroom apartment, TV, baby grand piano, overlooking Wrangell Narrows. $$ (also weekly rates).

SCANDIA HOUSE, *P. O. Box 689, (800) 722-5006.* Downtown hotel with a "Norwegian flair," complimentary breakfasts, kitchenettes, car & boat rentals. $$$

WATER'S EDGE B&B, *P.O. Box 1201, (907) 772-3736.* Beachfront, private baths, living area/kitchenette, courtesy transportation, bikes & canoe. $$$

Where to Eat

HELSE, *Sing Lee Alley, (907) 772-3444.* Homemade soups, seafood, sandwiches, daily specials (incl. seafood chowder). $

HOMESTEAD CAFE, *N. Nordic Dr., (907) 772-3900.* Seafood, homemade pies; a favorite for breakfast, locally popular. $ to $$

JOAN MEI, *across from ferry terminal, (907) 772-4222.* American & Chinese dishes. $ to $$

Further Information

Petersburg Chamber of Commerce, *P.O. Box 649, Petersburg AK 99833, (907) 772-3646.*

Directions

Petersburg is on an island, so you'll have to make arrangements to get here by boat or plane. Alaska Airlines offers jet service to Petersburg from Seattle and Anchorage, and Wings of Alaska offers scheduled service between Petersburg and other Alaskan cities.

A spectacularly beautiful trip to Petersburg aboard a large ship (and ferry) is available through Alaska Marine Highway, Bellingham, Washington. Shallow waters prevent large cruise ships from putting to port here.

Sitka

Population 9, 000

Lucky–and wonderful–indeed is the town that can boast of spectacular scenery, a long and rich history, and a bountifulness of wildlife that would be the envy of any zoo or animal park. **Sitka** has all of these. From Russian and Indian dances to an onion-domed cathedral and stately totem poles, the town is full of reminders of the region's centuries-old Tlingit (KLINK et) and 19th-century Russian colonial cultures. In addition, Sitka is embraced by the Pacific Ocean on one side and gorgeous snowcapped mountains and forests of spruces and hemlocks on the others. And people travel thousands of miles to fish Sitka's waters for salmon and halibut and to view the area's many bald eagles, seabirds, and marine mammals, including humpback whales.

The Russians landed in the Sitka region in 1799 and, following a short period of courageous but ultimately futile opposition from the Tlingits, established Sitka as the capital of Russian Alaska. The town, called New Archangel by the Russians, became the base for the immensely profitable fur-trading Russian-American Company and, at least for a fortunate few, a place of relative luxury, the "Paris of the Pacific." Then, for several reasons, including the perceived likelihood that in time the colony would certainly fall to the British or Americans, the tsar decided to withdraw and in 1867 sold Alaska to the United States.

The domes of **St. Michael's Cathedral** (1844-48, rebuilt 1966) set a mood that is more Byzantine than Yankee or Western European. Within the National Historic Landmark are art treasures and memorabilia of the Russian Orthodox Church, among them a superb collection of icons (open to public). A second Russian building, the restored **Russian Bishop's House** (1842), is the largest Russian log structure in North America. Also a National Historic Landmark, the building contains original furnishings and other mementos of the Russian period (reservations advised).

Reminders of Russian Alaska continue with yet another National Historic Landmark, **Castle Hill** (Baranov Castle State Historic Site). Several buildings once existed here; surviving are the stone walls and cannons from the most famous, "Baranov's Castle" (1837), which burned in 1894. The castle was the site of the transfer of Alaska to the United States in 1867.

The 107-acre **Sitka National Historical Park** marks the site of a battle between the Tlingits and Russians in 1804. Within the visitors center is the **Southeast Alaska Indian Cultural Center**, where guests may watch and talk to native carvers and other native artists. A fine collection of totem poles lines the park's wooded pathways.

Two museums commemorate Sitka's and Alaska's colorful pasts. The many exhibits of the **Isabel Miller Museum** chronicle the histories of the Tlingits and Russian-Americans, as well as the region's logging, mining, and fishing industries. The excellent collections of the **Sheldon Jackson Museum** (building erected in 1895) focus on the cultural achievements of Alaska's many native peoples.

Sitka has two churches of special note in addition to St. Michael's Cathedral. The first, **Sitka Lutheran Church**, contains objects from the Finnish Lutheran Church (1843) that originally occupied the site. The second, **St. Peter's by the Sea Episcopal Church**, held its first service in 1899. Behind the church is the bishop's residence, or "**See House**" (1905).

Most of Sitka's in-town sights can be toured in the course of a short walk. Visitors wishing to take in the coastal and other scenery will find a nice selection of tours: narrated land tours, walking tours of forest trails, boat tours, air tours, and a variety of wildlife cruises. Sightseeing is just one of a number of activities available to the visitor. The fishing is fabulous, of course, and so are the hiking and biking. What is less well-known is that **Sitka Sound** offers some of the best kayaking in the world (rentals and instruction available). The incentives for another favorite activity, shopping, come in the form of stunning examples of Tlingit beadwork, basketry, and painting. As is true for the Indians of the Pacific Northwest in general, the woodcarving is magnificent.

Special Features

Whale Park, some 6 miles south of downtown, features a boardwalk from which to view wildlife, including whales. Whales are prominent in the early fall and winter, and again in March.

During the summer months birdwatchers can view a lifetime of puffins, petrels, and other seabirds on **St. Lazaria Island**, a federal wildlife refuge. The refuge is accessible by boat.

• Providing yet another example of the costs associated with the failure to conserve, a decline in the fur trade due to the over-hunting of sea otters and seals was one of the principal factors leading to Russia's decision to sell Alaska to the United States.

Where to Stay

ALASKA OCEAN VIEW B&B, *1101 Edgecumbe Dr., phone/fax (907) 747-8310.* All-cedar home with Alaskana library & business center, TV & phones, down comforters, private baths, private decks, full breakfasts, refreshments, some pets, spa, gardens, scenic views. $$$

CREEKS EDGE GUEST HOUSE, *P.O. Box 2941, 109 Cascade Creek Rd., (907) 747-6484.* English Country-style home with view of Mt. Edgecumbe, antiques, TV & phones, feather beds, some private baths, full breakfasts, 180-degree ocean view. $$

SEASIDE B&B, *2924 Halibut Point Rd., (907) 747-6066.* New Cape-Cod-style home with view of Sitka Sound, TV & phones, some private baths, full breakfasts, private entrance, covered porch, picnic tables. $$$

WILD STRAWBERRY INN, *724 Siginaka Way, P.O. Box 2300, (907) 747-8883/fax (907) 747-3646/(800) 770-2628.* Inn on water overlooking Mt. Edgecumbe, some private baths, full breakfasts, fishing/boating, courtesy van. $$

Where to Eat

ROOKIES SPORTS BAR & GRILL, *1615 Sawmill Creek Rd., (907) 747-7607.* 16 kinds of burgers, 9 chicken sandwiches, pasta, pizza, soups & salads; steak, chicken, & seafood specialties. $ to $$

Further Information

Sitka Convention & Visitors Bureau, *P.O. Box 1226, Sitka, AK 99835 (907) 747-5940/fax (907) 747-3739.*

Directions

Sitka cannot be reached by road and, as with nearby Petersburg (see selection), visitors must rely on boat or air transportation.

The Alaska Marine Highway offers ferry/passenger service from Prince Rupert, BC (18 hours) and Bellingham, WA (3 days). Cruise ships also put into Sitka. The protected waters of the Inside Passage make travel by private yacht yet another option.

tion service from Juneau. Car rentals and taxi service are
locally available.

Other Charming Alaska Towns

Skagway
Talkeetna
Valdez

ARIZONA

FLAGSTAFF

Sedona

Jerome

PHOENIX

Tombstone

ARIZONA

Jerome
Population 460

Founded in 1876 and incorporated in 1899, **Jerome** was by the 1920s a bustling copper-mining city of 15,000 people. In 1953 the mines closed, and by the late 1950s Jerome had become the world's largest ghost town–population maybe 50. Then in the 1960s and 1970s the town's winding hillside streets were rediscovered by artists and others of the rebellious generation in search of a simpler life. Today Jerome is a National Historic Landmark dotted with galleries, specialty shops, restaurants, bed and breakfasts, museums. The population is up to about 460.

Sundry buildings have been renovated to house Jerome's new businesses and handful of residents, but some structures remain abandoned. The place is in other words still part ghost town, and that inescapable perception can evoke a sense of nostalgia, a feeling even of downright unworldliness– especially when placed against the starkness of the desert-mountain setting. Striving to keep the visitor ever in the present, however, are working artists' studios, a fine collection of art galleries and artisans' shops, a selection of food establishments, and of course, a couple of genuine old-time saloons.

Two museums remind of a town that during its 70 years of active life yielded over a billion dollars worth of copper and other ores (and that still hides beneath its surface over 100 miles of tunnels and mine shafts). Central to **Jerome State Historic Park** is the **Douglas Mansion** (1916), originally the home of mining developer "Rawhide Jimmy " Douglas and now a museum focusing on the area's history. Among the exhibits of the second museum, the **Jerome Historical Society Mine Museum**, are local ores and examples of early mining equipment.

Special Features
Many of Jerome's homes and public buildings may be visited the second week in June during the **Annual Jerome Home Tour** (also called *Paseo de Casas*), the oldest such tour in Arizona.

Ruins of Indian pueblos occupied from the 12th to the 14th centuries may be toured at nearby **Tuzigoot National Monument**. Located at **Montezuma Castle National Monument**, a little farther away, is a well-preserved five-story cliff dwelling (circa 1050 to 1450).

The "Sliding Jail" slid 225 feet downhill and across the highway as a result of shock waves from dynamiting in the open-pit mines.

Where to Stay

THE COTTAGE INN, *East Ave., P.O. Box 823, (520) 634-0701.* 1914 home offering two suites, full breakfasts, private patio, pets, spectacular views. $$

GHOST CITY INN B&B, *541 Main St., (520) 634-4678.* 1898 home, antiques, TV, full "gourmet" breakfasts, afternoon teas, verandahs with views of red rocks, courtyard. $$$

HILLSIDE HOUSE B&B, *AZ 89A & Upper Gulch Rd., P. O. Box 305, (520) 634-5667.* 1904 home, private baths, Cont. "plus" breakfasts, wine, private patios, mountain views. $$

JEROME GRAND HOTEL, *200 Hill St., (520) 634-8200.* Full-service hotel renovated from 1927 hospital, National Historic Landmark, 1920s-style lounge & restaurant, at top of Jerome with panoramic views. $$ to $$$

THE SURGEON'S HOUSE, *101 Hill St., (800) 639-1452.* 1917 home on National Register, private baths, full breakfasts, wine & snacks, "panoramic elegance." $$$

Where to Eat

FLATIRON CAFE, *416 Main St., (520) 634-2733.* Popular tiny cafe serving artfully presented Grilled Panini & Lahvosh Roll sandwiches, salads, espresso. $

HOUSE OF JOY, *419 Hull Ave., (520) 634-5339.* Trout Amandine, Crab Imperial, Cornish Game Hen Kiev; in 12-ft-wide ca 1890 bldg. with history as bordello, dining by reservation only weekends. $$$

THE JEROME GRILLE, *309 Main St., P.O. Box 901, (800) 634-5094.* Smelter Nachos, Southwest Caesar Salad, Red Rock Enchilada, & Southwest Chicken Sandwich among lunch tempters; in 1899 bldg., lodging also available. $

Further Information

Jerome Chamber of Commerce, *P.O. Box K, Jerome, AZ 86331 (520) 634-2900.*

Directions

From Phoenix, I 17 north to AZ 260, northwest to AZ 89A (at Cottonwood), west to Jerome.

Sedona

Population 8, 875

It's hard to imagine that any town lying at the mouth of **Oak Creek Canyon** in central Arizona could avoid a listing in this book. The towering red rocks, fiery in the sun, dramatic in any season, make the area one of the most photographed in the country. Arizonans claim that "God created the Grand Canyon but He lives in Sedona." But even without the surroundings, **Sedona** has much to offer the visitor: first-class art galleries, boutiques, upscale restaurants, luxury resorts.

Sedona boasts over 40 galleries exhibiting creations by some of the most talented artists and craftspeople in the country. The picturesque Mexican-style **Tlaquepaque**, an arts and crafts village, is especially recommended for lovers of charm. Even people who hate to shop will enjoy a stroll through the village's quaint courtyards.

For an especially beautiful view of the red-rock formations, drive up to the **Chapel of the Holy Cross** (1956). The chapel is built on a nearly 250-ft-high spur that juts from a 1,000-ft-high rock wall.

Dramatic country like this is hardly of recent discovery: Native American settlers were attracted to the area hundreds of years ago. The remains of prehistoric cultures—cliff dwellings, villages, petroglyphs and pictographs – abound in the Sedona region.

The touring options form an appetizing menu: In addition to the usual driving and hiking tours, there are airplane, helicopter, even hot-air balloon tours for seeing the scenery. The back country, and the ancient Indian ruins in particular, can be explored by guided jeep or horseback tours. Jeeps can also be rented for self-guided touring.

Special Features

Some of the most photographed scenery in the world can be seen at **Red Rock Crossing/Crescent Moon Ranch**, a few miles west of town.

Eight miles southwest of town is **Red Rock State Park**, an environmental park where hikers, bikers, and others can experience first-hand the contrast between the coolness of tree-lined **Oak Creek** and the barrenness of the red cliffs and spires.

To the north, **Oak Creek Canyon**, a gorge with streams and waterfalls between sheer rock walls, provides one of the most scenic drives in the country.

A natural water slide at **Slide Rock State Park** tempts everyone, adult as well as kid, to jump in and go with the current. There are also natural swimming pools and opportunities for trout fishing.

> • *With over three million visitors, Sedona rivals the Grand Canyon in popularity.*
> • *A veritable back lot for Hollywood, many celebrities have worked and/or lived in Sedona. Among them – John Wayne, Elvis Presley, Lucille Ball, Orson Welles, Walt Disney.*

Where to Stay

CANYON VILLA B&B INN, *125 Canyon Circle Dr., (800) 453-1166.* Elegantly decorated rooms, stained-glass windows, fireplaces, private baths, whirlpools, full "gourmet" breakfasts, pool, red rock views, one of finest. $$$

CASA SEDONA B&B INN, *55 Hozoni Dr., (800) 525-3756.* Terraced guest rooms, fireplaces, private baths, spa tubs, "Southwestern" breakfasts, library, red rock setting. $$$

THE GRAHAM B&B INN & ADOBE VILLAGE, *150 Canyon Circle Dr., (602) 284-1425/(800) 228-1425.* Contemporary Southwest inn & casitas, arts & antiques, fireplaces, TV & phones, private baths & balconies, full breakfasts, refreshments, video libraries, fresh flowers, pool & spa, bicycles, wonderful views, highly rated. $$$

LANTERN LIGHT INN, *3085 W. Hwy 89A, (520) 282-3419.* Country French antique decor, private entries, TV, private baths, full breakfasts, tree-lined grounds. $$$

SADDLE ROCK RANCH, *P.O. Box 10095, (520) 282-7640.* Three-acre historic country estate on National Register, rock fireplaces & massive beamed ceilings, art & antiques, private baths, full breakfasts, afternoon snacks, pool & spa, incredible views. $$$

Where to Eat

ENCHANTMENT'S YAVAPAI ROOM, *525 Boynton Canyon Rd., (520) 282-2900.* Classic Southwest cuisine & decor; glass walls for views of canyon walls & cliff-dweller ruins. $$$

THE HEARTLINE CAFE, *1610 W. Hwy 89A, (520) 282-0785.* Inventive menu of European-Mediterranean-Asian ancestry. $$

THE HIDEAWAY, *P.O. Box 1757, (520) 282-4204.* "Italy on the banks of Oak Creek" serving pasta, pizza, sandwiches, salads, soups; spectacular setting. $

PIETRO'S CLASSIC ITALIAN RESTAURANT & CAFE, *2445 W. Hwy 89A, (520) 282-2525.* Farfalle Filippo, Linguine ai Fruitti di Mare, Pollo Formaggiano; intimate, Robert Shields's paintings, wonderful views. $$

Further Information

Sedona-Oak Creek Canyon Chamber of Commerce, *P.O. Box 478, Sedona, AZ 86339 (520) 282-7722/(800) 288-7336.*

Directions

From Flagstaff (28 miles), Hwy. 89A south to Sedona; from Phoenix (120 miles), I 17 north to Exit 298, AZ 179 north to Sedona.

Tombstone
Population 1, 220

It's not easy putting into words the kind of spell that Tombstone casts. For a short time in history the Old West took center stage here. It was quite a show. And then it was all over. The place didn't grow much, but "The Town Too Tough To Die" didn't rot away, either. Tourism eventually came and things were freshened up a bit, but not much more than was needed to preserve and restore what was. Some have likened Tombstone to a museum. To me it's rather more like an old attic, but an attic whose dusty inhabitants still sparkle with a little of their old color.

It all began in 1879 with the discovery of silver. A year later Tombstone was the fastest growing city between St. Louis and San Francisco. The quick wealth, brassy saloons, and countless gunfights–including the legendary shoot-out at the O.K. Corral–helped give substance to a chapter in American history that more often than not is fashioned by the novelist and screenwriter. The cast of characters included Wyatt Earp, Doc Holliday, and Bat Masterson. By the end of the 1880s, however, uncontrollable underground water and falling silver prices brought it all to an end.

The **Bird Cage Theatre**, in operation 24 hours a day from 1881 to 1889, provides the ideal starting place for a tour. After service as one of the wickedest spots in the country, the theater was boarded up and left that way until 1934, when it was opened as a historic landmark. It is preserved in its original state as a National Monument, more of an "attic" than a museum, with even the chairs in the poker room standing exactly where they were when the place was sealed.

The theater was named for the 14 crib compartments, suspended from the ceiling (and still in place), where prostitutes provided their services. The theater's massive grand piano and coin-operated juke box, as well as the original Boothill hearse trimmed in 24K gold and sterling silver, are among the exhibits.

Not far from the theater are the restored **Crystal Palace** (1879), the fabled saloon; the offices of *The Tombstone Epitaph* (founded 1880), with original equipment and presses; and the **O.K. Corral**, site of the infamous gun battle between the Earps and Clantons. The **Tombstone Historama**, adjacent to the corral, offers a unique audio-visual presentation of Tombstone's roaring history, narrated by Vincent Price.

Several buildings merit a special visit or walk-by. One of these is the **Tombstone Courthouse State Historic Park** (1882), whose exhibits provide a good glimpse of the area's early history. Others include the town's original **firehouse** (1880s), **city hall** (1882), and **St. Pauls Episcopal Church** (1882), now the oldest Protestant church building in Arizona.

And then there is of course **Boothill Graveyard** (used from 1879 to 1884), where authenticated grave sites mark the final resting places of a number of Tombstone's early residents, including many gunslingers. A visit here is almost obligatory, part of a pilgrimage to the Old West.

Tombstone's several streets are home to a variety of restaurants and saloons. There are also galleries and shops, including several specializing in Western wear and Indian jewelry. Theatrical groups present re-enactments of Western-style shoot-outs–inquire at the tourism office (see below) for details.

Tombstone is just the right size to be explored on foot. For added color, and maybe comfort, there are also horse-drawn tours and stage-coach rides.

> *The refrain, "She's only a bird in a gilded cage," was inspired by the crib compartments at the Bird Cage Theatre.*

Where to Stay

BUFORD HOUSE B&B, *113 E. Safford St., P.O. Box 98, (800) 263-6762/(520) 457-3969*. 1880 adobe home on National Register, antiques & White House memorabilia, some private baths, full breakfasts, wrap-around porch. $$

PRISCILLA'S B&B, *101 N. 3rd St., P.O. Box 700, (520) 457-3844*. 1904 clapboard home on National Register, full breakfasts, small pets, large grounds with flowers, original picket fence. $$

TOMBSTONE BOARDING HOUSE, *108 N. 4th St., (520) 457-3716*. Two 1880s adobe homes surrounded by picket fence, antique decor, private entrances & baths, full breakfasts, pets. $$

VICTORIA'S B&B, *P.O. Box 37, (800) 952-8216/(520) 457-3677*. 1880 adobe adjacent to historic district, TV, private baths, full breakfasts, artwork, wedding chapel. $$

Where to Eat

DON TEODORO'S MEXICAN RESTAURANT, *15 N. Fourth St., (520) 457-3647*. Burritos & chimichangas, platillos mexicanos, Barbacoa (beef in "Don Teodoro's secret sauce"), Pollo Asado, Enchilada Sonoran Style the chef's special. $

NELLIE CASHMAN'S RESTAURANT, Toughnut & 5th sts., (520) 457-2212. "Home Cooking with an International Flair"; sandwiches, "gourmet" burgers; in 1879 bldg. $

Further Information

Tombstone Office of Tourism, *P.O. Box 917, Tombstone, AZ 85638 (800) 457-3423*.

Directions

From Tucson, I 10 east to Exit 313 (Benson), AZ 80 south to Tombstone.

Other Charming Arizona Towns

Ajo
Carefree
Pine/Strawberry
Tubac
Wickenburg

ARKANSAS

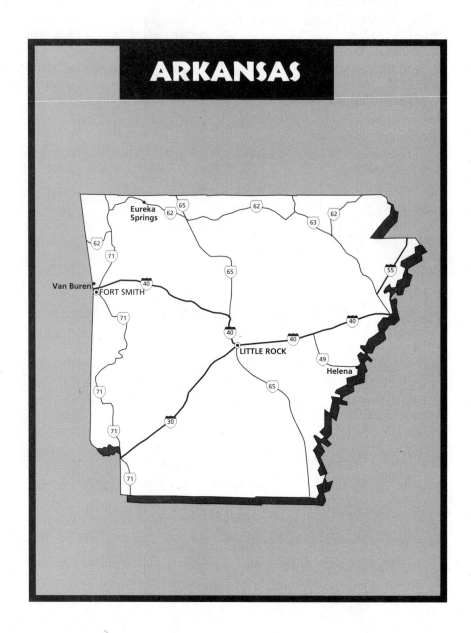

ARKANSAS

Eureka Springs
Population 1900

Eureka Springs is a beautifully unique blend of the Victorian and the Ozarks. The colorful array of Victorian buildings earned the entire downtown shopping district and residential area a listing on the National Register of Historic Places. But there are also narrow, winding mountain streets and lovely limestone walls built from native stone. Streets are sometimes hundreds of feet higher, or lower, than adjacent streets. And when streets cross, they never do so at right angles. You're in the **Ozarks**.

Belief in the healing powers of its spring waters was Eureka Springs's forebear. The town grew as thousands of health seekers journeyed, first by stagecoach and later by train, to the bathhouses of the growing resort. Today the town's native limestone buildings, gingerbread houses, shaded trails, springs, and gazebos preserve the Victorian atmosphere.

Eureka Springs is to be explored by some combination of trolley and foot, probably in that order. There are no fewer than six trolley routes, each designated by a color displayed on a sign in the front window, and they serve most of the town's places of lodging. Information on the trolley routes and a copy of the Scenic Walking Tours booklet can be obtained at the Chamber of Commerce.

Three Victorian homes are open to the public: the **Queen Anne Mansion** (1891), with exceptional interior oak and cherry woodwork; the lovely **Rosalie** (1880s), with period furnishings and accessories; and the **Gables**, known for its superb collection of Victoriana.

Just west of town (on US 62W) are two especially inspiring attractions, the exquisitely beautiful **Thorncrown Chapel**, an architectural masterpiece, and the **Eureka Springs Botanical Gardens**. The gardens span 33 acres of informal grounds and display a variety of hardwood trees and native plants.

Special Features

The Eureka Springs and North Arkansas Railway offers a lunch train, dinner train, and excursion train (departing hourly). A more leisurely tour of the mountains is available by cruise boat on scenic **Beaver Lake**.

> • *Eureka Springs is home to the regionally famous Great Passion Play, a spectacular outdoor drama depicting the life, death, and resurrection of Christ.*
> • *Known as an artists' colony as early as the 1930s and 1940s, Eureka Springs is now one of the most respected fine arts centers of the mid-South.*

Where to Stay

5 OJO INN, *5 Ojo St., (501) 253-6734*. Recipient of 1992 restoration award, fireplaces, private baths, whirlpools, "gourmet" breakfasts. $$$

BROWNSTONE INN, *75 Hillside, (501) 253-7505*. 1895 limestone building converted to elegant Victorian B&B, private entrances, private baths, full breakfasts. $$$

CRESCENT HOTEL, *75 Prospect St., (800) 342-9766*. Historic "Queen of the Ozarks," National Landmark, full service, Victorian guest rooms, restaurant, carriage rides. $$ to $$$

HEARTSTONE INN B&B/COTTAGES, *35 Kingshighway, (501) 253-8916*. Circa 1882 home, antiques, private entrances, TV, private baths, full "gourmet" breakfasts, tree-shaded decks, golf privileges, regional & national citations. $$ to $$$

PALACE HOTEL & BATH HOUSE, *135 Spring St., (501) 253-7474*. Restored Victorian hotel in historic district, antiques, private baths, bathhouse, small but elegant. $$$

PEABODY HOUSE, *7 Armstrong St., (501) 253-5376*. 1883 home overlooking historic downtown, antiques, TV, private baths, whirlpools, full breakfasts, restoration awards. $$$

ROGUE'S MANOR, *124 Spring St., (800) 250-5827/(501) 253-4911*. Themed suites with private entrances, TV, whirlpools, restaurant (with seafood flown in from Pacific Northwest), lounge. $$$

Where to Eat

AUTUMN BREEZE, *AR 23S, (501) 253-7734*. Clams Hoboken, Mahi-Mahi St. Thomas, Chicken Cordon Bleu, New York Strip (with choice of sauces); views, acclaimed. $$

CAFE ROYALE, *2A Spring St., (501) 253-8029*. Greek & American cooking: Mousaka, Chicken Breast Lemonato, Stuffed Grape Leaves, Prime Rib, Royale Baklava. $ to $$

CENTER STREET SOUTH, *10 Center St., (501) 253-8102*. Authentic Mexican & Latin American specialties: Red Snapper, Caribbean Chicken, Chalupas Compuestas, fajitas, fresh tamales, vegetarian dishes. $ to $$

DeVITO'S, *5 Center St., (501) 253-6807.* Chargrilled Trout, Chicken Bolognese, Fettuccine DeVito, Spaghetti; one of best in Arkansas. $$

GASKINS' CABIN, *AR 23N, (501) 253-5466.* Pan-fried Trout Amandine, Breaded Sauteed Chicken Gismondo, Prime Rib the house specialty; everything from scratch in historic bear trappers' cabin, reservations recommended. $$

Further Information

Eureka Springs Chamber of Commerce, *P.O. Box 551, Eureka Springs, AR 72632 (501) 253-8737.*

Directions

From Springfield (MO), US 65 south to US 62, west to Eureka Springs; from Little Rock, I 40 north to US 65 (at Conway), north to US 62, west to Eureka Springs.

Helena

Population 7, 491

Situated on a rise overlooking the Mississippi, **Helena** was described by Mark Twain as occupying "one of the prettiest situations on the river." Although much of Arkansas belongs geographically and culturally to the mid-South, Helena is unmistakably part of the Deep South. The second oldest city in Arkansas (founded in 1820), its history is that of steamboats, cotton, and the Mississippi Delta. Helena was the home of seven Confederate generals. It is today home to one of the Delta's major cultural events, the **Annual King Biscuit Blues Festival** (second weekend of October, Thursday - Sunday).

The **Cherry Street Historic District** is a well-preserved business district of the late 19th and early 20th centuries. The district's appearance and ambiance are those of a traditional river town. A top site is the new **Delta Cultural Center**, an important regional museum (costing $8.5 million) that chronicles the history of the Delta and its people. The center is housed in the 1903 **Helena Train Depot**.

Helena has a handsome collection of antebellum, Victorian, and Edwardian homes. Many are listed on the National Register of Historic Places (some offer tours by appointment – check with *Main Street Helena*, 338-9144). Three important antebellum homes are **Estevan Hall**, a magnificent home preserved by the descendants of the original owners; the 1860 red brick **Moore-Hornor Home**, with 18-foot ceilings and parlor doors that still bear shell marks from the Battle of Helena (see below); and the spacious 1858 Greek Revival **Tappan-Pillow Mansion**, with the original two-room brick kitchen out back.

Among the most elegant of the postbellum houses are the Italianate **Hornor-Gladin House** (1880), with original fireplaces and mantels; the grand Georgian-Revival **West-Webb House** (1900), with parquet floors and quarter-sawn oak woodwork; and the **Pillow-Thompson House** (1896), considered one of the finest examples of Queen Anne architecture in the south.

The restored **Old Almer Store**, constructed in 1872 of cypress, was once a market for dairy products and, later, a neighborhood grocery. Entered on the National Register, the store now serves as an area-wide arts and crafts cooperative.

High on Crowley's Ridge, the **Confederate Cemetery** offers a panoramic view of the Mississippi River. Another view of the water may be enjoyed from the boardwalk of **Riverfront Park**.

Special Features

Both the **St. Francis National Forest** and the **White River National Wildlife Refuge** offer superb opportunities for fishing and wildlife observation.

> • *The Battle of Helena was fought in 1863 as a Confederate attempt to relieve pressure on Vicksburg downriver. The Confederate troops suffered heavy casualties.*
> • *The riverboats "Delta Queen" and "Mississippi Queen" often put into Helena so that their passengers may tour Cherry Street.*
> • *The bridge at Helena is the only Mississippi River bridge between West Memphis (to the north) and Lake Village (to the south).*

Where to Stay

EDWARDIAN INN, *317 Biscoe St., (870) 338-9155/(800) 598-4749.* Restored turn-of-century mansion, original fireplace mantels, TV & phones, private baths, Cont. "plus" breakfasts, one of South's finest. $$

FOXGLOVE B&B, *229 Beech St., (870) 338-9391/(800) 863-1926.* Ca 1900 Georgian Revival mansion on National Register, parquet floors & double-seated staircase, TV & phones, private baths with whirlpools, full breakfasts, beverages/snacks, period pictures & maps. $$$

MAGNOLIA HILL B&B, *608 Perry St., (870) 338-6874.* 1900 Queen Anne home with wrap-around verandah on National Register, antiques,

TV & phones, private baths, 3-course "Southern" breakfasts on china, port & other beverages, Japanese porcelains, fresh fruit. $$

Where to Eat

BELL'S, *115 Cherry St., (870) 338-6655*. Seafood, prime rib, steaks. $ to $$

PASQUALE'S TAMALES, *211 Missouri St., (870) 338-6722*. Famous tamales simmered for 6 hours & hand-wrapped in corn shucks. $

Further Information

Phillips County Chamber of Commerce, *P.O. Box 447, 111 Hickory Hill, Helena, AR 72342 (870) 338-8327/ fax(870) 338-6445*.

Directions

From Little Rock, I 40 east to exit 216 (Brinkley), US 49 southeast to Helena.

Van Buren

Population 14, 979

Largely bypassed by much larger Fort Smith across the Arkansas River, **Van Buren** retains much of the quaint ole river town atmosphere. Narrow **Main Street**, which looks pretty much like it did 100 years ago, has appeared in several films and in the TV mini-series *The Blue and the Gray*. The street has seen everything from wagon trains to Union and Confederate troops to stagecoaches headed west. And wagons hauling freight to and from the many steamboats on the Arkansas. More than 70 buildings in the Main Street area are on the National Register of Historic Places.

Crawford County Courthouse, built in 1841 and rebuilt in 1877, is the oldest active county courthouse west of the Mississippi. The Seth Thomas clock in the tower has been tolling the hour for nearly 120 years.

The elegant 1890s **King Opera House** is currently undergoing restoration. Jenny Lind and William Jennings Bryant appeared here.

Van Buren's shops, respected throughout western Arkansas and eastern Oklahoma, display dolls, stained glass, jewelry, cutlery, quilts, pottery, and other items handmade by local artists. The emphasis is on the handcrafted and the Victorian. The fine arts are also represented.

Special Features

On selected days, April through November, the **Ozark Scenic Railway** offers three-hour excursions to the mountain village of **Winslow**. Passengers relax in early 1900s cars with restored inlaid mahogany interiors as they travel over trestles and through a tunnel built in 1882. The train embarks from the **Old Frisco Depot**, now restored and home to the Chamber of Commerce as well as to a collection of Bob "Bazooka" Burns memorabilia.

The towering bluffs along the Arkansas River can be seen from the decks of the 138-passenger *Frontier Belle*. The main deck is enclosed for comfort in all weather.

Across the river, the **Fort Smith National Historic Site**, **Belle Grove Historic District**, and the **Old Fort Museum** are especially worth a visit.

> • *Fort Smith was established in 1817 to help keep peace among the region's Indians.*
> • *On the back of the river wall in the Mike Meyer Riverfront Park is a mural history of Van Buren painted by Van Buren High School art students.*

Where to Stay

OLD VAN BUREN INN, *633 Main St., (501) 474-4202*. Second floor of High Victorian bank building, full breakfasts, said to be haunted. $$$

SILENT NIGHT LOFT, *614 Main St., (501) 471-1150*. Second floor of historic Main St. bldg., kitchenette & 2 bedrooms. $$ to $$$

Where to Eat

BOUDREAUX'S NEW ORLEANS CAFE & GIFT SHOP, *600 Main St., (501) 471-9579*. New-Orleans-style cooking. $

COTTAGE CAFE, *810 Main St., (501) 474-9895*. Home-style menu, daily Blue Plate Special, homemade pies. $

POP'S ICE CREAM PARLOR, *416 Main St., (501) 474-1244*. Sandwiches, variety of ice cream & fountain treats, brownies. $

WHISTLE STOP SANDWICH SHOPPE, *620-A Main St., (501) 474-6441*. New York deli-style fare, sandwiches, soups, salads, bagels, blackberry cobbler. $

Further Information

The Van Buren Chamber of Commerce, *P.O. Box 652, Van Buren, AR 72956 (800) 332-5889.*

Directions
From Little Rock, I 40 west to exit 5 (Van Buren/Fort Smith exit).

Other Charming Arkansas Towns
Hardy
Mountain View
Scott
Washington

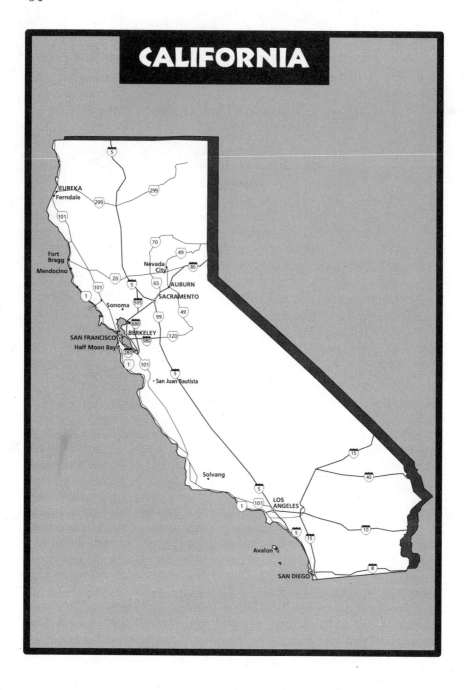

CALIFORNIA

CALIFORNIA

Avalon

Population 3200

Overlooking a gorgeous harbor, and ocean beyond, **Avalon** could be on the French or Italian Riviera. There are few communities in Southern California with its charm. There are even fewer with its beauty – the blue harbor, coastal hillsides, beaches, crystal-clear water, and clear skies (except when the wind's blowing from Los Angeles).

Situated on lovely **Catalina Island** some 20 to 30 miles off the California coast, Avalon has been a popular pleasure resort since the 1890s. The village is small, no more than about one square mile in area, and so its winding streets can be explored by foot. Although the foot may offer the best way to absorb the late 19th-century charm, there are others: tram tours, bus tours, golf cart and bicycle rentals.

The 1929 Art Deco **Casino Building**, located on one side of the harbor, includes the **Avalon Theatre** and **Casino Ballroom**. The Avalon Theatre, known for its excellent acoustics and murals by John Gabriel Beckman, has a full-scale pipe organ whose largest pipe measures 16 feet and shortest a mere 1/4 inch. The circular Casino Ballroom, the largest of its type in the world, was a symbol of the Big Band Era of the 1930s, 40s, and 50s (daily walking tours available).

Avalon's underwater scenery is spectacular: The octopus, barracuda, spiny lobsters, kelp forests, even wrecks make snorkeling and scuba diving very popular. There are glass-bottom boat tours, night as well as day, for underwater sightseers who wish to remain dry.

Special Features

The Seal Rocks down the coast can be visited by tour boat (migratory sea lions rather than seals sun on the rocks).

> • *Santa Catalina was once used as a base by Yankee, Russian, and other sailors and hunters in the sea-otter trade.*
> • *About 86% of the island is owned by the Santa Catalina Island Conservancy, a nonprofit group whose mission is to restore and preserve the land in a natural state.*
> • *Avalon is known for its fresh seafood, especially the swordfish.*

Where to Stay

CATALINA ISLAND SEACREST INN, *201 Clarissa, P.O. Box 128, (310) 510-0800.* Victorian-style home with country decor, fireplaces, TV, private baths, whirlpools, lace & wicker sun room, close to beach, romance & wedding packages. $$$

GULL HOUSE, *P.O. Box 1381, 344 Whittley Ave., (310) 510-2547.* Contemporary home, fireplaces, TV, private baths, suites, patio with pool & spa, quiet. $$$

INN ON MT. ADA, *398 Wrigley Rd., P.O. Box 2560, (310) 510-2030.* 1921 Georgian Colonial-style mansion overlooking bay, on National Register, antiques, fireplaces, private baths, full breakfasts, refreshments, restaurant, porch . $$$ (all meals & use of golf cart included)

THE OLD TURNER INN, *232 Catalina Ave., P.O. Box 97, (310) 510-2236.* Quiet setting in heart of Avalon, antiques, TV, fireplaces, private baths, Continental "plus" breakfasts, handmade linens, evening wine/appetizers, art. $$$

ZANE GREY PUEBLO HOTEL, *P.O. Box 216, (310) 510-0966.* 1926 Hopi-pueblo-style home of author Zane Grey, private baths, pool, decks & gardens, ocean & mountain views, courtesy taxi, packages. $$$

Where to Eat

ANTONIO'S PIZZERIA & CABARET, *230 Crescent Ave., (310) 510-0008.* Pizza, burgers, & more; waterfront dining, sawdust on floor, full bar & nightclub. $

ARMSTRONG'S FISH MARKET & SEAFOOD RESTAURANT, *306 Crescent Ave., (310) 510-0113.* Wide variety of fresh seafood, mesquite-charbroiled fish; on Avalon Bay, casual, a favorite. $$

THE BLUE PARROT, *205 Crescent Ave., (310) 510-2465.* Seafood, steak, chicken, pasta, & Cajun selections; live jazz in Coconut Bar, panoramic views. $$

DESCANSO BEACH CLUB, *around corner from Casino Bldg., (310) 510-7408.* Blue Pacific Fish & Chips, Local Fresh Fish Tacos, & Catalina Carne Asada the specialties; hot sandwiches, soups, "sensational" salads; bar on beach. $

PIRRONE'S, *417 Crescent Ave., (310) 510-0333.* Fresh local seafood, certified Angus prime rib & steaks, chicken & Italian specials; overlooking bay. $$

SALLY'S WAFFLE SHOP, *Crescent Ave., (310) 510-0355.* Omelets & waffles, on oceanfront. $

Further Information

Catalina Island Chamber of Commerce & Visitor's Bureau, *P.O. Box 217, Avalon, CA 90704 (310) 510-1520.*

Directions

Boats depart for Catalina Island from Long Beach, San Pedro, Huntington Harbour, and Newport Beach. Year-round helicopter service is available from Long Beach and San Pedro. Check with the Visitor Bureau for scheduling. Travel time to the island is one to two hours by sea and 15 minutes by helicopter.

Ferndale

Population 1, 331

The "**Victorian Village of Ferndale**" is tucked between the Eel River and northern California's "Lost Coast." Although geographically one of California's most western towns, Ferndale is architecturally one of the state's most eastern. **Main Street** (on the National Register) as well as the side streets are bordered by carefully restored, brightly painted Victorian buildings. Even the Victorian public restrooms are beautifully painted. The flower boxes and the nicely kept gardens add to the color, and the palm trees, camellias, roses, rhododendrons, and other lush plants impart a unique, almost enchanting beauty that sets the town apart from most other Victorian communities.

Situated in a rich dairying region, Ferndale became the agricultural center of northern California during the final decades of the 19th century. The area's wealth helped build ornate Victorian homes, nicknamed *Butterfat Palaces*. The town changed very little after the late 1800s. In the 1960s the picturesque buildings were discovered by artists and craftspeople and Ferndale's revitalization was underway. Today the thriving Main Street is lined with specialty shops, an old-fashioned mercantile, antique stores, and studios/galleries.

The principal architecture of the historic homes is Eastlake and Stick, although Gothic Revival and other Victorian styles are never far away. Some of the commercial structures are late Victorian, some early Modernistic (1920-1936). Much of the picturesque town can be taken in on a two-hour self-guided walking tour (especially with the assistance of the Chamber of Commerce's visitors' guide) or horse-drawn carriage tour. An excellent stop on the tour, if not in fact its starting point, is the **Ferndale Museum**. Among the museum's displays are Victorian room settings, a working forge, seismograph (earthquakes are not unknown here), and early agricultural equipment.

The **Ferndale Repertory Theatre** stages comedies, mysteries, the classics, and most popular of all, musicals. The performances, acclaimed and offered year-round, have played no small part in putting Ferndale back on the map.

Special Features

Ferndale consistently ranks in the top 20 of Audubon bird counts, with 355 varieties of birds spotted in the area. Good locations for bird watching, and nature watching in general, are the **Eel River State Wildlife Area**, the **Humboldt Bay National Wildlife Refuge**, and Ferndale's own **Russ Park**, a lovely 105-acre wilderness preserve. One of the best ways to see the giant redwoods is to drive along the **Avenue of the Giants**, a winding stretch of old US 101 southeast of Ferndale.

Ferndale is the gateway to California's "**Lost Coast**." Take the Wildcat Road to Petrolia and loop through the redwoods back to US 101 for a quick view of pristine shorelines (three-hour drive), or camp and hike in the **King Range** for a longer visit.

> *The verdant countryside of Northern California's Eel River Valley looked like home to the immigrating Danes of the last century.*

Where to Stay

GINGERBREAD MANSION INN, *400 Berding St., (707) 786-4000.* Opulent 1899 mansion with 4 parlors, private baths, full breakfasts, afternoon tea & cake, English garden, bicycles, one of loveliest in California. $$$

SHAW HOUSE INN B&B, *P.O. Box 1125, (707) 786-9958.* 1854 Gothic Revival home, fireplaces, "sumptuous" breakfasts, afternoon teas, fresh flowers, private balconies. $$ to $$$

VICTORIAN INN, *400 Ocean Ave., P.O. Box 1248, (800) 576-5949.* 1890 full-service inn named most beautiful bldg. in county, on National Register, antiques, down comforters, some fireplaces, private baths, full breakfasts, dining room, bar, pets. $$ to $$$

Where to Eat

DIANE'S, *553 Main St., (707) 786-4950.* A favorite place for lunch, everything freshly made from local produce. $

STAGEDOOR CAFE, *451 Main St., (707) 786-4675.* Fresh soups & salads, desserts, espresso drinks; in Ferndale Repertory Theatre bldg. $

VICTORIAN INN, *(see above).* Popular for meats & steaks, Crab Cioppino in season; fireside dining in stately 1891 hotel, bar. $ to $$

Further Information

Ferndale Chamber of Commerce, *P.O. Box 325, Ferndale, CA 95536 (707) 786-4477.*

Directions

From San Francisco, US 101 north to Fernbridge/Ferndale exit (south of Eureka), west to Ferndale.

Fort Bragg
Population 6, 078

Fort Bragg is an old coastal lumber mill town that is gradually turning into a tourist center. It is a town with many faces.

There is first of all Fort Bragg the American hometown. The facades of early 1900s buildings along downtown streets are painted in Victorian four-color schemes and decorated with canvas awnings. Bungalows of the Craftsman and other traditional California styles dot several adjacent neighborhoods.

Then there is Fort Bragg the coastal resort, with inns, fine restaurants, and other amenities for visitors wishing to enjoy the rugged Pacific scenery. Magnificent headlands, coves, natural arches, redwood forests, beaches, and tidepools are just minutes away.

Fort Bragg is also a fishing village. Down in **Noyo Harbor** is a commercial fishing fleet along with everything needed to service it. There are also facilities for recreational craft. Seafood restaurants, fishing charters, and boat excursions cater to the tourist, and add to the color.

An art center is beginning to look as though it may be Fort Bragg's newest identity. Several good galleries have grown up, including the **Northcoast Artist's Cooperative**. The **Fort Bragg Center for the Arts** sponsors exhibitions of photographs, weavings, collage art, sculpture, and other media.

Fort Bragg's logging history is recalled in two museums. The **Guest House Museum**, a handsome three-story 1892 home, displays photos and other artifacts of the lumber industry. The **Fort Bragg Depot**, a new marketplace museum, houses historic trains and logging artifacts under the same roof with a food court, art gallery, and very nice collection of little gift and craft shops.

Special Features

The famous California Western Railroad *Skunk* trains run 40 miles from Fort Bragg to the inland town of **Willits**. Once a logging railroad, the "Skunk" delivers mail and groceries to remote areas. The line's half-day and full-day round trips through the redwoods are one of Fort Bragg's top attractions. Sometimes the "trains" operate as motorcars on rails, at other times passenger cars are pulled by diesel or historic steam locomotives.

MacKerricher State Park north of town has miles of beautiful beaches.

• *Visitors to Glass Beach, once the town dump, can find interesting, often attractive ocean-cleansed glass and pottery shards.*

• *The 1906 Earthquake devastated Fort Bragg as well as San Francisco. However, San Francisco's demand for lumber to rebuild brought prosperity to Fort Bragg.*

Where to Stay

AVALON HOUSE B&B, *561 Stewart St., (707) 964-5555*. Restored turn-of-century Craftsman-style home, antiques, private baths, extra-thick towels. $$$

GLASS BEACH B&B INN, *726 N. Main St., (707) 964-6774*. 1920 Craftsman-style home, antiques, TV, fireplaces, private baths, full "country" breakfasts, hot tub. $$ to $$$

THE GREY WHALE INN, *615 N. Main St., (707) 964-0640/(800) 382-7244*. 1915 redwood bldg., phones, private baths, full breakfasts, tea/coffee, gardens, ocean view. $$$

THE LODGE AT NOYO RIVER, *500 Casa del Noyo Dr., (800) 629-1126*. 1868 redwood mansion perched on bluff, antiques & comforters, some fireplaces, some TVs, private baths, full breakfasts, suites, hot tubs, large deck, gardens, wildlife. $$$

THE PLATT HOUSE, *19100 Neptune Ave., (707) 961-9676*. 1990 "Victorian" mansion on bluff overlooking ocean, antiques, suites with sitting rooms & baths, high tea. $$ to $$$

Where to Stay

D'AURELIO'S, *438 S. Franklin St., (707) 964-4227*. Pizza, variety of pastas, Eggplant Parmesan, homemade minestrone, sandwiches, salads. $ to $$

NORTH COAST BREWING CO., *444 N. Main St., (707) 964-2739*. Linguine Fruitti di Mare, Shrimp Etouffee, North Coast Mixed Grill, Cajun-style dishes; home-brewed beers. $$

RENDEVOUS INN & RESTAURANT, *647 N. Main St., (707) 964-8142*. Spicy Crab Cakes, Pasta Santa Fe, Pepper Steak "Rendevous," house-made desserts; also, bed-&-breakfast accommodations. $$
THE RESTAURANT, *418 N. Main St., (707) 964-9800*. Bourride, Grilled Swordfish, New York Strip Steak, Vegetable Chili; original oils by Olaf Palm, live jazz. $$ to $$$
THE WHARF RESTAURANT, *780 N. Harbor Dr., (707) 964-4283*. Fresh Petrale Sole, Fresh Pacific Red Snapper, Prawn & Scallop Platter, steaks; overlooking river & ocean, locally popular, reservations suggested. $$

Further Information
Fort Bragg-Mendocino Coast Chamber of Commerce, *P.O. Box 1141, Fort Bragg, CA 95437 (707) 961-6300/(800) 726-2780.*

Directions
From San Francisco, US 101 north to CA 20 (at Willits), CA 20 west to Fort Bragg.

Half Moon Bay
Population 8, 886

Boasting miles of beautiful beaches and rugged bluffs, and separated from San Francisco by a half hour's drive and from the Silicon Valley by a coastal mountain range, it's only to be expected that **Half Moon Bay** should be a popular Bay Area retreat. The town is also the floriculture center of the **San Mateo Coast**: Fields of flowers can be seen from the road, and fresh cut flowers are a given in area homes, inns, and restaurants.

Many of the homes and commercial structures in Half Moon Bay's historic district, once known as Spanishtown, date to the 19th century. Restored storefronts provide an interesting backdrop for art and craft galleries, restaurants, and quaint gift shops. Group walking tours may be arranged through the Chamber of Commerce.

The **James Johnston House**, outside of town, is a saltbox structure (ca 1857) whose design was copied from the builder's Ohio home. Now on the National Register, plans call for the house and grounds to open after restoration is completed.

Located just north of town, **Pillar Point Harbor** is a bustling haven for pleasure craft and a commercial fishing fleet. The colorful harbor offers full marina services.

Widely known for its natural coastal beauty and abundant flora and fauna, Half Moon Bay provides a rich menu of recreational and sightseeing options. To list a few: whale-watching tours (January/April), air-taxi rides, horseback riding along the cliffs, salmon and rock fishing (charters available), sailing, beachcombing. Cyclists will fine a 12-mile coastal bicycle trail and golfers two courses that overlook the Pacific. Half Moon Bay also has an interesting variety of night clubs.

Special Features

A nature lover's paradise, the Half Moon Bay area offers the visitor a choice among a variety of field trips. Some suggestions:

For birdwatching – **Pescadero Marsh National Preserve**. (Twenty percent of all known North American species can be seen here.)

For hiking/biking among giant trees and wildflowers – **Purissima Creek Redwoods**.

For touring elephant-seal breeding grounds (December/March) – **Ano Nuevo State Reserve** (reservations).

For tide pooling – **Fitzgerald Marine Reserve**.

> *Visitors may pick their own berries, pumpkins, and kiwi at farms along the coastline.*

Where to Stay

MILL ROSE INN, *615 Mill St., (800) 900-7673*. English country inn with European antiques, TV & phones, private baths, full breakfasts, afternoon wine & cheese. $$$

OLD THYME INN, *779 Main St., (415) 726-1616*. 1899 Queen Anne home, fireplaces, private baths, whirlpools, "delicious" breakfasts, sherry, English herb gardens. $$ to $$$

THE PILLAR POINT INN, *P.O. Box 388 (El Granada 94018), (800) 400-8281*. Cape Cod harborside inn, fireplaces, TV & phones, European-style feather beds, private baths, full breakfasts, afternoon sherry. $$$

SAN BENITO HOUSE, *356 Main St., (415) 726-3425*. 1905 hotel with European feel, contemporary paintings, private baths with claw-foot tubs, full breakfasts, sauna, English-style garden, restaurant. $$ to $$$

ZABALLA HOUSE, *324 Main St., (415) 726-9123.* Circa 1859 home, antiques & oil paintings, fireplaces, private baths, whirlpools, full breakfasts, beverages, "well-behaved" pets. $$$

Where to Eat

MIRAMAR BEACH RESTAURANT, *131 Mirada Rd., (415) 726-9053.* Seafood & steaks, "unparalleled" view of Pacific, in Prohibition roadhouse dating to 1918. $$

MOSS BEACH DISTILLERY, *Beach Way & Ocean Blvd. (Moss Beach), (650) 728-5595.* Fresh seafood served in historic bldg., champagne brunches, spectacular views, patio, ghosts, murder mystery dinners. $$

PASTA MOON, *315 Main St., (415) 726-5125.* Pesce del Giorno, Linguine con Cape Sante, Involtini di Pollo, Lasagna di Polenta con Salmone; very good reviews. $$

SAN BENITO HOUSE, *(see above).* Mediterranean cuisine with European country inn ambiance, changing menu, very good reviews. $$

THE SHORE BIRD, *390 Capistrano Rd. (Princeton-by-the-Sea), (415) 728-5541.* Seafood, "Cape Cod on the California Coast." $$

Further Information

Half Moon Bay Coastside Chamber of Commerce, *520 Kelly Ave., Half Moon Bay, CA 94019 (415) 726-8380.*

Directions

From San Francisco, CA 1 south to Half Moon Bay.

Mendocino
Population 1008

When leaving CA 1 to enter **Mendocino**, take the northern approach (Lansing Street). Before you will appear a charming New England-like village looking down upon the blue Pacific. It's a beautiful sight. You'd have to travel nearly 3,000 miles - to the Maine Coast - to find anything like it.

Many of the loggers and mill workers attracted to Mendocino by the redwoods came from New England, hence the Cape Cod or Down East ambiance of the village they built. After the mill operations ceased in the 1930s, the town went into a sort of hibernation and remained there until artists and others rediscovered its charm. Today there is a commitment by the people to preserve that charm: The Mendocino Historical Review

Board, whose function it is to preserve Mendocino's traditional appearance, takes its job very seriously – just talk to anyone who has tried to build or remodel a house here.

Main Street is a wonderful juxtaposition of shops and businesses on one side and **headlands** (called palisades in Southern California) and ocean on the other. On the street is the **Mendocino Presbyterian Church** (1868), the oldest Presbyterian church in continuous operation in the state. The historic **Ford House** (1854), also on the street, is now a museum and visitor center for **Mendocino Headlands State Park** (see below).

The 1861 **Kelley House**, built of rough-sawn redwood boards, was erected by an early Mendocino entrepreneur. The house, gardens, and spring-fed duck pond are now a museum.

Along Main and the several inland streets are some first-class art galleries and an unusually broad variety of unique shops. The **Mendocino Art Center** is the arts headquarters, with galleries, an art shop, library, gardens, classes, and a theater.

Special Features

Mendocino is surrounded by **Mendocino Headlands State Park**. Get a map of the park at Ford House and take in the sights, sounds, and smell of the ocean from a walk on the headlands. Guided tours are sometimes available.

Aquatic opportunities include deep-sea fishing, snorkeling at Little River Beach, canoeing on Big River, and whale watching (out of nearby Noyo Harbor - winter months).

> • *Scenes for the "Maine" village of Cabot Cove in the TV series "Murder, She Wrote" were in fact filmed in Mendocino.*
> • *Mendocino's first known settler was the sole survivor of an 1850 shipwreck.*

Where to Stay

THE HEADLANDS INN, *Howard & Albion sts., (707) 937-4431.* Restored 1868 building, fireplaces, private baths, "creative" full breakfasts. $$$

JOSHUA GRINDLE INN, *P. O. Box 647, (707) 937-4143.* 1879 New England farmhouse on two landscaped acres, antiques, fireplaces, private baths, full breakfasts, ocean views. $$$

MENDOCINO HOTEL & GARDEN SUITES, *45080 Main St., (800) 548-0513.* Full-service hotel est. 1878, antiques, comforters, dining rooms, lounges, gardens. $$ to $$$

Where to Eat

955 UKIAH ST. RESTAURANT, *955 Ukiah St., (707) 937-1955.* California-French cuisine with emphasis on seafood, Apricot Tart & Strawberry-Rhubarb Sorbet among desserts; reservations recommended. $$

CAFE BEAUJOLAIS, *961 Ukiah St., (707) 937-5614.* Yucatecan-Thai Crab Cakes (served with spicy avocado salsa, achiote roasted tomato sauce, coconut rice, and black beans); regionally acclaimed. $$

LA SCALA, *at the Hill House, 10701 Palette Dr., (707) 937-2244.* Italian cuisine: Prawns Fra Diavalo, Chicken Parmigiana, Mixed Grill Contadino, Cheese Ravioli La Scala Style; largest selection of Italian wines on North Coast. $$

THE MOOSSE CAFE, *10390 Kasten St., (707) 937-4323.* Seafood, pasta, desserts, espresso. $$

MacCALLUM HOUSE RESTAURANT, *45020 Albion St., (707) 937-5763.* Broiled Local Rock Cod (with corn, roasted red bell pepper, black beans, and salsa verde); in 1882 mansion. $$

Further Information

The Mendocino Coast Chamber of Commerce, *P.O. Box 1141, Fort Bragg, CA 95437 (707) 961-6300. (Zip for Mendocino is 95460.)*

Directions

From San Francisco, CA 1 north to Mendocino.

Nevada City
Population 2855

Mix two parts Victoriana with one part Old West mining town. Make sure the Victoriana is colorfully painted and has plenty of balconies. Add winding streets, high-reaching trees, and natural-gas lights. Then place in the pine forests of the Sierra foothills. What you will have is an unusually pretty town with a truly distinctive charm.

Nevada City began in 1849 with a store selling miners' supplies. One year later the town had a government, post office, and population of some 10,000! Since that year the population has swung up and down, mostly down. Today, what began as a Gold Rush mining town is a kind of living museum with a kind of reputation that attracts artists, musicians, writers – and visitors. Strict building codes and underground wiring throughout are guaranteed to help preserve that reputation.

Nevada City's downtown, full of interesting shops, is listed on the National Register of Historic Places. Of special interest is the **National Hotel** (1854-57), California's oldest continuously-operating hotel. Herbert Hoover, Lola Montez, Jane Wyman, Martha Raye, and Tim Conway are among the many notables who have entered its doors. The square grand piano in the lobby once journeyed around Cape Horn, and the ornate back bar was originally the dining room buffet in the Spreckels mansion in San Francisco. Horse-drawn carriage tours can be taken from the hotel.

The Victorian bell tower and gingerbread trim of **Firehouse No. 1** were added after the building's construction in 1861. Its contemporary, **Firehouse No. 2** (1861), continues in use. The **Nevada Theatre** (1865) is the state's oldest building constructed as a theater. Musicians, actors, and others still perform here.

The many restored homes, some of them historic, merit a drive or walk through the neighborhoods surrounding the downtown. Evening strolls along the gas-lighted streets downtown are popular here.

Special Features

Grass Valley, similar to Nevada City in charm and history, is just four miles away, in the next valley.

> • *In the general election of 1856 only Sacramento and San Francisco cast more ballots than Nevada City.*
> • *During the 1960s and 70s hippies and back-to-the-landers began opening shops and other small businesses in the decaying downtown. Such efforts contributed much toward putting the town back on the map.*

Where to Stay

DEER CREEK INN, *116 Nevada St., (800) 655-0363*. 1870s Queen Anne home, private baths, full breakfasts, half-acre creekside setting, gardens. $$$

DOWNEY HOUSE, *517 W. Broad St., (800) 258-2815*. 1870s Eastland home, private baths, "generous" buffet breakfasts, fragrant gardens, sweeping views. $$ to $$$

GRANDMERE'S INN, *449 Broad St., (530) 265-4660*. 1856 Colonial Revival home on National Register, private baths, full breakfasts, lawns & gardens. $$$

KENDALL HOUSE, *534 Spring St., (530) 265-0405*. 1860s home on 2 secluded acres, art, fireplaces, private baths, full breakfasts, veranda, decks & heated pool, gardens & views, guest cottage with kitchen also available. $$$

RED CASTLE INN, *109 Prospect St., (530) 265-5135.* Four-story 1857 Gothic Revival landmark on Prospect Hill, private baths, "elaborate" buffet breakfasts, terraced gardens. $$$

Where to Eat

Note: Reservations are a must in Nevada city, especially on Saturdays.

CIRINO'S RESTAURANT, *309 Broad St., (530) 265-2246.* A favorite for Italian cuisine; bar, "fun - sometimes even noisy." $$

COUNTRY ROSE, *300 Commercial St., (530) 265-6248.* Country French menu, garden patio. $$

FRIAR TUCK'S RESTAURANT & WINE BAR, *111 N. Pine St., (530) 265-9093.* Fondue, seafood, steaks; bar, good wine list, entertainment. $$

KIRBY'S CREEKSIDE RESTAURANT & BAR, *101 Broad St., (530) 265-3445.* Seafood Ravioli (with chardonnay cream sauce), Fettuccine (with grilled sausage & roasted peppers), Vegetarian Sampler, Kirby's Steak Selection; multi-course dinners, broad & appetizing lunch menu. $$

POSH NOSH, *318 Broad St., (530) 265-6064.* Fresh seafood, "creative" soups, daily vegetarian specials, homemade breads; popular for lunch, garden patio. $$

Further Information

Nevada City Chamber of Commerce, *132 Main St., Nevada City, CA 95959 (530) 265-2692.*

Directions

From Sacramento, I 80 north to Auburn, CA 49 north to Nevada City.

San Juan Bautista

Population 1, 570

If you're looking for a little piece of Old California, you won't do much better than **San Juan Bautista**. Graced by a classic Spanish plaza, romantic old mission, and narrow streets flanked by quaint Mexican, Early Californian, and Victorian dwellings, San Juan Bautista is the kind of place that somehow managed to flirt with, but never really embrace, the 20th century. It's the kind of town where food is served in picturesque courtyards rather than fast-food drive-ups, and where shoppers browse in unique street-side shops rather than look-alike strip malls. Obviously impressed by San Juan Bautista's character and charm, Hollywood has chosen the town as a setting for a number of movies.

In 1797 Spanish Franciscan friars chose this as the site of their 15th California mission, and soon thereafter Mission San Juan Bautista (after St. John the Baptist) became the core of a thriving Mexican pueblo and early California city. At one time the population was served by no fewer than four newspapers, and four times that many saloons. Suffering the same fate as many towns in this book, however, San Juan Bautista was bypassed by the railroad, and this meant that to a large extent it was to be bypassed by the 20th century as well.

Mission San Juan Bautista (1797-1812), the largest and one of the best preserved of the 21 California missions (see also **Solvang** and **Sonoma**), comprises a colorful 40-foot-tall chapel along with a museum and gift shop. On the grounds are a garden and Indian/Early California cemetery. The mission continues as an active Roman Catholic church (open).

Adjacent to the mission on the plaza is **San Juan Bautista State Historical Park**, composed of four very brightly colored structures: the **Plaza Hotel**, an 1858 inn restored to its Victorian finest; the **Plaza Hall**, an 1860s building with a varied history, including unrealized service as a government hall; the 1860s **Plaza Stable**, now a museum featuring a remarkable collection of horse-drawn carriages and wagons; and the balconied 1830s **Castro-Breen Adobe**, a lovely old structure that functioned variously as a residence and as the headquarters of the Mexican government.

A strongly recommended way to tour San Juan Bautista's many other historic structures is by means of a walking-tour brochure distributed by the Chamber of Commerce. (Although guided horse-and-buggy tours offer a romantic alternative.) Making up the 41 historic sites are homes, mercantiles, cantinas, and other buildings from the mid and late 19th century. Most are of Spanish Colonial, Greek Revival, or Victorian ancestry. Some house private residences, others are open to the public as boutiques, art galleries, and restaurants. The range of craft and specialty items is remarkable for a town of this size.

Adding to San Juan Bautista's uniqueness are performances by the renowned **El Teatro Campesino**. The theater stages original productions year-round in its playhouse.

Special Features

Fremont Peak State Park, situated at the end of a winding 9-mile road south of San Juan Bautista, is the place to visit for spectacular sunsets and panoramic views of San Benito County, the Salinas Valley, and the Pacific

Ocean. The park is home to the Fremont Peak Observatory, which boasts a 30-inch reflecting telescope (open on selected dates).

Also south of town is **Pinnacles National Monument**, which contains remnants of an ancient volcano. Included among the attractions are miles of hiking trails, caves (bring your own flashlights!), and excellent rock-climbing opportunities. The monument is home to rare birds of prey as well as to displays of poppies, lupines, and other spring wildflowers.

Where to Stay

POSADA DE SAN JUAN HOTEL/INN, *310 Fourth St., P.O. Box 2130 (408) 623-4030*. Spanish Colonial-style inn, fireplaces, TV & phones, private baths with whirlpools, balconies. $$ to $$$

Where to Eat

CADEMARTORI'S, *600 First St., (408) 623-4511*. "Fine Italian cuisine," specializing in homemade pasta; beautiful views. $$

DONA ESTHER RESTAURANT, *25 Franklin St., (408) 623-4549*. "Authentic" Mexican food, lounge, patio dining, live entertainment weekends. $

THE DONKEY DELI & GERMAN RESTAURANT, *322 Third St., (408) 623-4521*. German specialties, self-service sandwich bar. $

LA CASA ROSA, *107 Third St., (408) 623-4563*. A favorite for Mexican cooking, patio dining. $

Further Information

San Juan Bautista Chamber of Commerce, *402A Third St., San Juan Bautista, CA 95045 (408) 623-2454/fax (408) 623-0674*.

Directions

From the Bay Area, US 101 south to CA 156, south and east 2 miles to San Juan Bautista.

Solvang
Population 4, 741

Separated from the Pacific by a coastal mountain range to the south, but open to climate-moderating ocean breezes from the west, lovely **Santa Ynez Valley** is sunny, temperate, and smog-free. The gently rolling valley is home to vineyards, horse ranches, apple orchards and, as unlikely as it may seem, the *Danish Capital of America*, **Solvang**.

Solvang (*sunny field* in Danish) was founded in 1911 by Danes from the Midwest seeking to establish a West-Coast Danish colony and folk school. Over the years the town began to look more and more Danish as the townspeople, perhaps encouraged by visits from Danish royalty, turned increasingly to Danish-style architecture.

Today the buildings sport exteriors of timber-framed white stucco, sloping green-copper or wood-shingle roofs, and lots of gables and dormers and towers. Up on top are hand-carved storks, down below are cobblestone sidewalks, outdoor cafes, and shops with leaded-glass windows. There are four windmills; one still turns. Visiting Danes say that the town looks more like Denmark than Denmark.

Specific Danish sites include the **Little Mermaid**, a half-scale copy of the original in Copenhagen harbor, and the **Bethania Lutheran Church**, a typical rural Danish church with hand-carved pulpit and a scale model of a Danish sailing ship hanging from the ceiling. The half-timbered **Elverhoj Museum**, once a residence, presents the story of Solvang with old photographs, crafts, period rooms, and other exhibits. The **Hans Christian Andersen Museum** honors the life and work of the father and master of the modern fairy tale.

Solvang's most historic site is not Danish. The adobe **Mission Santa Ines**, established in 1804 as the 19th of the 21 missions built in California by Spanish Franciscan priests, has been beautifully restored (visitors welcome). The chapel, in continuous use since 1817, is decorated with murals by Indian artists as well as by masterpieces of Moorish art and sculpture. The **Mission Museum** displays a number of treasures, among them 16th-century church vestments. On the grounds are the cemetery and semi-formal gardens.

Solvang boasts no fewer than 350 shops! Danish offerings include pastries (of course), music boxes, porcelain figurines, knitted sweaters, folk art, handmade lace, and Danish costumes. The shops are also noted for their selections of paintings and antiques. A delightful new downtown mall – complete with carousel! – maintains the tradition of upscale shops and Danish architecture.

Tours of Solvang may be taken on the Honen, a replica of a turn-of-the-century Copenhagen streetcar pulled by a pair of Belgian draft horses. Carriage tours are also offered. Gliders and bicycles offer two of the best ways to tour the valley: The air currents are ideal for the former, and the many delightful country roads are designed for the latter.

Critically acclaimed musicals, dramas, and comedies are staged in Solvang's outdoor **Festival Theater** from summer through early fall by the **Pacific Conservatory of the Performing Arts Theaterfest**. Four spectacular area courses offer a variety of golfing challenges.

Special Features

Over 20 **Santa Barbara County wineries** are open to visitors, most without appointment. Many provide picnic tables. A wine touring map may be picked up at the visitors center.

Lake Cachuma, 15 minutes southeast, is home to a host of wildlife, including 275 species of birds. Eagle boat cruises (winter), nature cruises (summer), and boat rentals are available.

The Pacific Ocean may be enjoyed at **Gaviota State Park** and **Refugio** and **El Capitan** state beaches.

> *All classic grape varieties can be grown in Santa Barbara County because of the many microclimates.*

Where to Stay

THE INN AT PETERSEN VILLAGE, *1576 Mission Dr., (800) 321-8985*. Replica of Danish village, TV, private baths, "European buffet" breakfasts, wine hour with grand piano music, dining room, garden. $$$

LOS OLIVOS GRAND HOTEL, *P.O. Box 526 (Los Olivos 93441), (800) 446-2455/(805) 688-7788*. Exquisite full-service little hotel, antiques, fireplaces, Cont. breakfasts, superb dining room, pool, bicycles. $$$

STORYBOOK INN B&B, *409 First St., (805) 688-1703*. Danish-style inn, antiques, fireplaces, TV, European beds, private baths, some whirlpools, full "gourmet" breakfasts weekends, scenic views. $$$

Where to Eat

BALLARD STORE, *2449 Baseline Ave. (Ballard), (805) 688-5319*. International menu offering Pacific Coast seafood, bouillabaisse, abalone; local wines, "gourmet" picnic boxes. $$ to $$$

CAFE ANGELICA, *490 First St., (805) 686-9970*. Bistro-style menu featuring fresh fish & "gourmet" specials, indoor & patio cafe dining. $ to $$

THE RIVER GRILL AT THE ALISAL, *150 Alisal Rd., (805) 688-7784*. Grilled Alaskan Halibut, Chicken Pot Pie, Roasted Pork Loin, Baked Eggplant; scenic views. $$

Further Information

Solvang Conference & Visitor's Bureau, *P.O. Box 70, Solvang, CA 93464 (800) 468-6765. (Zip for Solvang is 93463.)*

Directions

From Los Angeles, US 101 west to Buellton, CA 246 east to Solvang.

Sonoma

Population 8, 738

Old adobe buildings look on as children in **Sonoma's** enormous **plaza** play or point at ducks in the pond. Fountains splash and people enjoy their lunches or simply relax under the pines, palms, and redwoods. Flowers and sunshine are in every direction. There is Mexican blood in Sonoma's ancestry.

Mission San Francisco Solano de Sonoma was founded in 1823, when California was still a province of Mexico. The mission was the last and most northerly of California's 21 Franciscan missions. A few years after the mission was built, Mexican General Mariano Vallejo, headquartered here, laid out the 8-acre plaza (1834). The plaza was to become the center of Sonoma.

Still the center of Sonoma, the plaza today is bordered by historic buildings, quaint old hotels (see listing below), art galleries, and a host of inviting specialty shops. The best known of the buildings dating from Mexican times is the adobe **San Francisco Solano Mission church**, built by General Vallejo in 1840 to replace an earlier structure. The attached padres' quarters go back to about 1825 and are Sonoma's oldest structure. The 1836 **Sonoma Barracks** and 1850s **Toscano Hotel** (originally a general store and library) join the mission church in making up the **Sonoma State Historic Park**.

Among the historic houses on or near the plaza are the 1840s **Salvador Vallejo Home**, the 1836 adobe *Casa Grande*, and the 1847 **Nash-Patton Adobe**. A house of special interest away from the plaza is **Lachryma Montis**, the two-story Gothic Revival house built in 1851 by the now-American General Vallejo as his permanent home. The house, designated a state historical monument, was prefabricated and shipped around the Horn. Check with the Sonoma Valley Visitors Bureau on the plaza for touring information on these and many other historic buildings.

The visitors bureau also offers information on winery tours. Tours of the **Sebastiani Winery**, located just a few blocks off the plaza, are among the most popular. Sonoma's association with wine is nearly as old as the town itself. Cuttings of the Mission grape, used to make wines for the Mass, were brought to Sonoma as early as 1825 by Franciscan missionaries. The real birth of the wine industry, however, dates to 1857 when a

Hungarian nobleman introduced cuttings of old-world varietals to the area and established **Buena Vista Winery**. Lining the beautiful Tuscany-like **Sonoma Valley** are now 36 or so wineries and some 6,000 acres of vineyards. Most of the tasting rooms along the 17-mile-long valley are open year round, and tastings are free in about 99% of them.

The Sonoma Valley is the site of an all-too-common struggle between rural charm and urban sprawl. Although the sprawl seems to have an advantage in parts, the vineyards, a national treasure, continue to predominate.

Special Features

Jack London built his hillside ranch, which he called his *Beauty Ranch*, near Glen Ellen north of Sonoma. What is now **Jack London State Historic Park** comprises about 800 acres of trees and spectacular scenery. On the grounds are **The House of Happy Walls** built in 1919 by London's widow, Charmian, and the remaining walls of **Wolf House**, a stone mansion that mysteriously burned a few days before the Londons were due to move in. London memorabilia are on display in The House of Happy Walls.

The **Sonoma Valley** is made-to-order for picnics. Pick up some local cheese, French bread, and other items from the specialty food shops around the plaza and journey out to the vineyards to purchase a bottle of wine. Many of the wineries have set aside picturesque areas for picnics.

> *Sonoma Valley wines are by custom served only in distinctive blue-stemmed wine glasses.*

Where to Stay

El DORADO HOTEL, *405 First St. W., (707) 996-3030*. Full-service hotel with French windows & terraces, bed linens of goose down, restaurant, heated pool. $$$

GAIGE HOUSE INN, *13540 Arnold Dr. (Glen Ellen 95442), (707) 935-0237/(800) 935-0237/fax (707) 935-6411*. Turn-of-century home with pool & grounds, fireplaces, TV & phones, private baths, full breakfasts, wine & refreshments. $$$

SONOMA MISSION INN & SPA, *P.O. Box 1447, (707) 938-9000*. Lovely historic mission-style hotel, full-service, extensive grounds. $$$

SWISS HOTEL, *18 W. Spain St., (707) 938-2884*. 1830s home converted to hotel in late 1800s, full-service, 1934 bar with signed celebrity photos. $$$

TROJAN HORSE B&B, *19455 Sonoma Hwy., (707) 996-2430.* 1887 farmhouse with period decor, private baths, full breakfasts, social hour, outdoor whirlpool, gardens, bicycles. $$$

Where to Eat

DELLA SANTINA'S, *101 E. Napa St., (707) 935-0576.* Trattoria, rosticceria, pasticceria. $ to $$

THE DEPOT HOTEL RESTAURANT & GARDEN, *241 First St. W.,* *(707) 938-2980.* Innovative Northern Italian cuisine by chef-owner, fireside wine bar, in historic stone bldg. dating to 1870. $ to $$

GARDEN COURT CAFE & BAKERY, *13875 Sonoma Hwy. (Glen Ellen), (707) 935-1565.* Creative breakfast & lunch menu, interesting "healthy alternatives." $

THE GENERAL'S DAUGHTER, *400 W. Spain St., (707) 938-4004.* Mix of American classics & other ethnic/cultural choices, daily menu; in 1864 home built by Gen. Vallejo for daughter. $$

MURPHY'S IRISH PUB, *464 First St. E., (707) 935-0660.* Pub food, pasties, Irish stouts & international ales. $

Further Information

Sonoma Valley Visitors Bureau, *10 E. Spain St., Sonoma, CA 95476 (707) 996-1090.*

Directions

From San Francisco, US 101 north to CA 37, CA 37 northeast to CA 121, CA 121 north to CA 12, CA 12 north to Sonoma.

Other Charming California Towns

Calistoga
Cambria
Gualala
Healdsburg
Lone Pine
Quincy
St. Helena

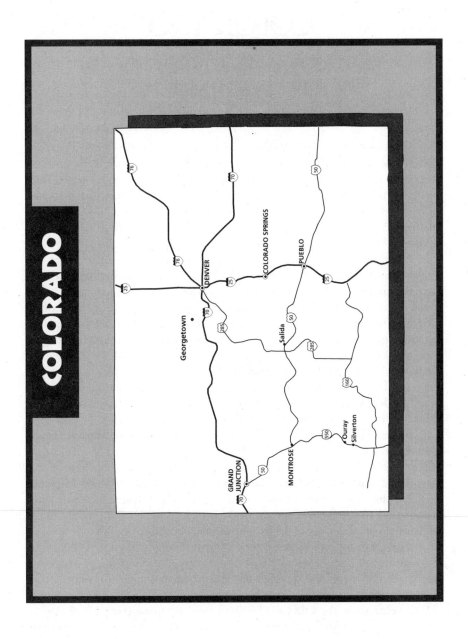

COLORADO

Georgetown
Population 950

With over 200 original Victorian buildings, narrow streets, a narrow-gauge railroad, and Rocky Mountain scenery, **Georgetown** is the quintessential Old West mining town. So much so in fact that it has served as a setting in films and television commercials. The town has a second, less obvious distinction as well: Its location just 45 miles west of Denver and within 45 minutes of some of the top sights and ski areas in Colorado makes it ideal as a base for getting to know this beautiful state.

Georgetown began in 1859 as a gold prospectors' camp, but it was silver that turned the town into a busy commercial and service center. Unlike many mining communities of the era, the town was never destroyed by fire (see, also, **Silverton**). Following the pattern common to so many well-preserved towns from the 19th century, prosperity reached a peak and then plunged, sending the town into decades of near oblivion–and safekeeping. The peak year was 1877, when the valley's population reached 5,000, and the year of bad fortune 1893, when the country went on a gold standard. True to pattern, the sleeping little town was rediscovered in the latter half of the 20th century, its valley declared a National Historic Landmark District, and restoration efforts begun.

Notable among Georgetown's historic buildings is the **Hamill House Museum**, a Gothic Revival home built in 1879 by the town's best-known silver baron. The house retains its original hand-painted wallpaper and imported marble fireplaces. Also of note is the **Hotel de Paris Museum** (1875), the restoration of an elegantly decorated hotel that was once renowned for its lavish accommodations and table. Among its many luxuries was steam heat, virtually unknown at the time.

The Georgetown Hydroelectric Station, constructed in 1900, is the second oldest hydroelectric plant in the state. Now an **Energy Museum**, much of the original equipment is still in use. Among the many other historic buildings are the **First Presbyterian** (1874) and **Grace Episcopal** (1869) **churches**, the **Old Jail** (1860s), and the **Alpine Hose No. 2** (1874).

The reconstructed **Georgetown Loop** offers a six-mile round trip between Georgetown and Silver Plume aboard a 1920 narrow-gauge steam train. Along the way is the spectacular 95-foot-high **Devil's Gate Viaduct**. A walking tour of the **Lebanon Silver Mine**, which can be reached only by the train, is optional. (Check with the Old Georgetown Station for schedules, reservations, etc.)

Georgetown can be toured by foot, but perhaps the most interesting (and informative) way to see the town is by means of a narrated tour by horse-drawn trolley. Private carriage tours are also available.

The area's eye-dazzling scenery can be enjoyed by driving from Georgetown to Grant over the **Guanella Pass Scenic Byway**, or less comfortably but more spectacularly by maneuvering a 4-wheel-drive over the very narrow and rocky **Saxon Mountain Road**. The **Notch Trail** offers hikers a 2.4-mile trail from Georgetown to Silver Plume. Then of course there are snowshoeing and cross-country skiing for seeing the landscape in the winter. Bikers should check locally for information on guided half-day downhill mountain-bike tours, complete with uphill transportation, bike, lunch, and more.

Special Features

Christmas Market, the first two weekends in December, is a time of crafts, special foods, and other holiday attractions. The evening reflections of the Christmas lights off the snow-packed streets adds to the special enchantment of the season.

Just 14 miles west of town is **Loveland**, Georgetown's own ski area, with slopes for all levels.

> *A herd of Rocky Mountain Bighorn Sheep (Colorado's state animal) can sometimes be seen from the Watchable Wildlife Viewing Station near Georgetown Lake (year-round viewing). The station is the only one of its kind in Colorado.*

Where to Stay

ALPINE HIDEAWAY B&B, *2045 Bluebird Dr., P.O. Box 788, (800) 490-9011/(303) 569-2800*. Modified A-frame nestled in pines by Georgetown Lake, fireplaces, private baths, whirlpool tubs, full "gourmet" breakfasts. $$$

CANDLEWOOD INN B&B, *201 Loop Dr., P.O. Box 372, (303) 569-2287/(888) 327-8460*. 1891 home with view of town & Rockies, TV, private baths, full breakfasts, outdoor spa. $$ to $$$

CREEKSIDE B&B INN, *610 7th St., P.O. Box 917, (303) 569-2664/ (800) 484-9493*. Turn-of-century home in Old Town Historic District, private baths, full breakfasts, gift shop. $$ to $$$

HARDY HOUSE B&B INN, *605 Brownell St., (800) 490-4802/(303) 569-3388*. Late 19th-century home with wood stove in parlor, TV, feather comforters, private baths, full candlelight breakfasts. $$ to $$$

HILLSIDE HOUSE, *1034 Main St., P.O. Box 266, (800) 490-9012/ (303) 569-0912*. Home on side of hill with panoramic valley view, stained glass windows, private baths, "famous" Belgian waffles, verandah. $$ to $$$

Where to Eat

THE RAVEN HILL MINING COMPANY, *612 6th St., (303) 569-2209*. Buffalo Prime Rib the specialty, "wonderful" pastas, daily vegetarian specials; Victorian mining atmosphere with lamplight & linen tablecloths/napkins. $ to $$

Further Information

Town of Georgetown Visitor Information, *P.O. Box 26, Georgetown, CO 80444 (303) 569-2888*.

Directions

From Denver, I 70 west to Georgetown (exit 228).

Ouray

Population 700

Travelers sometimes allot a couple of hours to **Ouray** before speeding on to their next destination. They often come back, but this time for a week, or more. True, Ouray (pronounced you RAY, but YOU ray will get the job done) is a quaint old Victorian mining town with no traffic lights, malls, freeways, or fast-food restaurants.

But Ouray is more than that, as visitors soon discover. Ouray is also a popular spa; the *Jeep Capital of the World*, with over 500 miles of off-road Jeep trails; a developing winter resort with excellent ice climbing and skating; and the proud owner of some of the most spectacular scenery on the planet. Lying 7,800 ft. up in the sky, and surrounded by mountains that soar yet another 5,000, the town's favorite descriptor is "heavenly."

All of Ouray is a National Historic District. The buildings, most of them restored, go back to the last two decades of the 19th century and the first decade of the 20th. Although quiet and charming today, Ouray was once wild and wide open: Not a few of the structures that now house respectable bed & breakfasts, restaurants, and residences were once saloons, brothels, and cribs.

The **Ouray County Museum** is the best place to start a tour of the town. The museum, once a miners' hospital (1887), contains 27 room-sized exhibits of everything from a cellblock out of the old **Ouray Jail** to a child's bedroom to an outstanding mineral collection.

Sweet, hot mineral water (105 degrees F) flowing from **Box Canyon** pours into the **Ouray Hot Springs Pool**. The pool is divided into several sections of differing temperatures. The hottest is a soaking section, the coolest a diving and lap lane section. The pool complex includes a fitness center and park and is very popular in the winter, especially with sore-muscled cross-country skiers and ice climbers. Waters from other mineral springs heat buildings and fill hotel hot tubs and vaporcaves.

The **Gary Davis My Country USA** is a family music variety show featuring classic country music, '50s music, gospel, an Elvis tribute, and a patriotic revue. Down the street, the **Silver Legacy Players** present Broadway-style comedy, drama, and musical theater at **Wright's Opera House** (1888; summer/fall).

Special Features

The surrounding country is laced with old mule trails, stagecoach trails, and mining roads that have found new life as 4-wheel-drive roads. Along these roads are old mines and boarding houses, ghost towns, alpine flowers, waterfalls, and other treasures. The best way to do these roads is by guided tour, at least on the first time out. If you think you'd be comfortable driving along the top of a 3,000-foot canyon, go for a rental.

A mine train carries visitors 3,500 horizontal feet into Gold Hill for a guided tour of the **Bachelor Mine** (silver was discovered here in 1884 by three bachelors). The silver and gold mine is about two miles from Ouray.

Canyon Creek plunges 285 feet through a rock to form spectacular **Box Canyon Falls**, on the outskirts of town. Trails, stairs, and bridges lead to views of both the top and bottom of the falls.

> • *Scenes from "True Grit" and "How the West Was Won" were filmed in the Ouray area.*
> • *Ouray Ice Park, the world's first ice-climbing park, offers climbers one-half mile of ice-covered canyon walls.*

Where to Stay

ABOVE TIMBERLINE B&B, *803 Main St., (970) 325-4125*. New Orleans-style bldg. with patio, TV, private baths & entrances, Cont. "plus" breakfasts, hot tub, balcony views. $$

CHINA CLIPPER B&B INN, *525 Second St., P.O. Box 801, (800) 315-0565*. Covered front porch, English-style furniture, fireplaces, TV, private baths, full breakfasts, refreshments, garden hot tub. $$$

THE DAMN YANKEE B&B INN, *100 6th Ave., (800) 845-7512.* Distinctive custom-built B&B inn, TV & phones, private baths, private entrances, "gourmet" breakfasts, refreshments, 3rd-story Observatory Lounge, hot tub, one of best in Colorado. $$ to $$$

HISTORIC WESTERN HOTEL B&B, *210 7th Ave., (970) 325-4645.* Restored Italianate hotel built in 1891 as a "miner's palace," antiques, period rooms, suites with private baths overlooking veranda, Western bar. $ to $$

MAINSTREET B&B, *322 Main St., (970) 325-4871.* Turn-of-century houses with decks, antiques, TV, private baths, full breakfasts, some kitchen suites, mountain views. $$ to $$$

THE MANOR B&B, *317 2nd St., (970) 325-4574.* 1890 Georgian Victorian hybrid on National Register, feather beds & down comforters, private baths, hot tub, full breakfasts, afternoon refreshments, whirlpool, flower gardens. $$

OURAY HOTEL, *303 6th Ave. & Main St., (970) 325-0500.* Restored 1893 hotel with original room decor, TV, private baths, suites. $$

ST. ELMO HOTEL, *426 Main St., P.O. Box 667, (970) 325-4951.* Restored 1898 hotel on National Register, fine antiques, stained glass, polished wood & brass trim, private baths, breakfast buffet, restaurant. $$ to $$$

Where to Eat

BON TON RESTAURANT, *(see St. Elmo Hotel).* Scampi Bon Ton, Chicken Chipeta, Beef Wellington, pasta entrees; award-winning wine list, reservations recommended. $ to $$

BUEN TIEMPO MEXICAN RESTAURANT & CANTINA, *206 7th Ave., (303) 325-4544.* "The best Mexican food and margaritas this side of Santa Fe," historical setting. $ to $$

CASCADE GROCERY & DELICATESSEN, *726 Main St., (303) 325-4089.* Homemade pizza, sandwiches, & soups served in little Victorian grocery store; picnic lunches. $

OUTLAW RESTAURANT, *610 Main St., (303) 325-4366/4458.* Popular steak house, rustic decor, full bar, home of Outlaw Mountain Cookout (reservations). $ to $$

THE PINON RESTAURANT & TAVERN, *737 Main St., (303) 325-4334/7307.* Loin of Venison, Pinon Pasta, Lobster Lasagna; Western artwork, sundeck with mountain views, reservations suggested. $$

Further Information

Ouray Chamber Resort Association, *P.O. Box 145, Ouray, CO 81427 (800) 228-1876.*

Directions

From Denver, I 70 west to exit 37 (before Grand Junction), CO 141 south to US 50, US 50 south to US 550 (at Montrose), US 550 south to Ouray.

Salida

Population 5, 500

Salida (sa LYE da) is easy to picture – simply conjure up an image of what a Colorado town ought to look like: Turn-of-the-century streets nestled in a valley surrounded by snow-capped mountains, crystal-clear streams, wildflower-covered slopes, and bright yellow aspens against Colorado blue skies. It is with good reason that Salida has been nick-named the *Heart of the Rockies.*

Established in 1880, Salida has an agricultural, mining, and railroad history – and the largest historic district in Colorado. The colorful and unusually healthy downtown doesn't look like it has changed much from the first half of the 20th century. Flanking the side streets is an interesting collection of turn-of-the-century brick apartment dwellings.

One of the most active of the historic sites is the **Salida Hot Springs Pool and Mixed Baths,** the largest indoor hot springs pool in Colorado. As popular today as 50 years ago, the odorless mineral waters are used for everything from swimming and water games to arthritis classes. There are three pools in addition to private hot baths.

Sometimes called the **Banana Belt** because of its surprisingly mild climate, Salida is a year-round sportsman's paradise. Rafting, kayaking, hiking, backpacking, golfing, horseback riding, and four-wheeling are all popular. The **Monarch Ski Area** is just minutes away. For mountain bikers there are leisurely rides, rides in the mid-ability range, and rides like the Monarch Crest Trail, considered one of the best in the world.

The **Arkansas River,** which flows through Salida, offers guided family float trips, high-adventure white-water trips, and everything in between, including fishing excursions. Trips vary from quarter-day to several-day and offer splendid opportunities to view wildlife and majestic scenery. Large brown, rainbow, cutthroat, and brook trout are plentiful in the Arkansas and in countless streams, lakes, and beaver ponds.

Special Features

The high country and several ghost towns can be visited by half-day to all-day car tours. A four-wheel drive isn't necessary. Check with the Chamber of Commerce for routings.

Buena Vista, another 19th-century Colorado town with a quaint downtown area, is 25 miles north of Salida.

> • *One of the most beautiful of the town's seasonal attractions occurs each year right after Thanksgiving when some 22, 000 colored lights are strung in the shape of an enormous Christmas tree on the side of Tenderfoot Mountain.*
> • *The Salida area is sometimes called the "14ers Region" because of the number of peaks over 14, 000 feet in the Sawatch Range to the west.*
> • *Over 40 percent of the trout used to stock Colorado's waters come from nearby Mt. Shavano Fish Hatchery.*

Where to Stay

THE CENTURY HOUSE B&B, *401 E. 1st St., (719) 539-7064*. 105-year-old French Victorian home, antiques, close to downtown. $ to $$

THE GAZEBO COUNTRY INN B&B, *507 E. Third St., (719) 539-7806*. 1901 home with white picket fence, full breakfasts, porch swing. $$

PINON & SAGE B&B, *803 F St., (719) 539-3227*. Turn-of-century home with "woods & textures of Southwest," extensive breakfast menu, library, outdoor hot tub. $$

RIVER RUN INN, *8495 County Rd. 160, (719) 539-3818*. Renovated 1892 brick farmhouse, some private baths, full breakfasts, refreshments, 104-year-old library lounge, stocked trout pond. $$

Where to Eat

FIRST STREET CAFE, *137 E. First St., (719) 539-4759*. Mexican platters, vegetarian dishes, daily specials; local favorite. $

IL VICINO, *136 E. Second St., (719) 539-5219*. "Neighborhood place" offering wood-fired pizza, pasta, salads, handcrafted ales, espresso & cappuccino. $

LAUGHING LADIES CAFE, *128 W. First St., (719) 539-6209*. Corn-meal-crusted Snapper, Jeff's Oowee Smoked Brisket, Grilled Polenta with Red Chile an appetizer; in turn-of-century bldg., paintings, outdoor seating, Colorado beers. $ to $$

MAMA D'S SANDWICH JOINT, *140 F St., (719) 539-2228*. Chicago-style sandwich joint popular with lunch crowd, framed caricatures on walls. $

Further Information

Heart of the Rockies Chamber of Commerce, *406 W. Rainbow Blvd., Salida, CO 81201 (719) 539-2068/fax (719) 539-7844.*

Directions

From Denver, I 25 south to exit 102 (Pueblo), US 50 west to Salida.

Silverton
Population 716

Nestled in a narrow valley in the county with the highest mean elevation of any county in the United States, **Silverton's** "low" altitude is a mere 9,318 feet. At this altitude you may need a blanket on a summer evening, but on a sunny day in winter you can sport in the snow with a tee-shirt instead of a jacket or sweater. The surrounding countryside is 100% scenery – there's not so much as one acre of agriculture in the entire county.

Victorian Silverton, now a National Historic Landmark, is one of the best-preserved but least-discovered of Colorado's romantic old mining camps. Having never experienced a major fire (unlike most mining towns), Silverton retains most of its original homes and commercial buildings. The **San Juan County Historical Society Museum** (1902), once the county jail, provides a good short introduction to the town and ideal starting point for a walking tour (maps available at Chamber of Commerce). The **San Juan County Courthouse** (1907), next to the museum, is one of the most beautiful in Colorado. Another impressive public building, the native stone **Town Hall** (1909), has been faithfully restored to its original self.

"Notorious" **Blair Street** once housed 40 saloons and brothels, integral parts of every proper mining and railroad town. The street has provided settings for several Western movies.

The **Old Hundred Gold Mine Tour** proves that there are experiences that can be both educational and exciting. The one-hour tour, set up by local miners, consists of a narrow-gauge train ride into an authentic gold mine deep in a mountain. An experienced miner serves as the guide.

Although tiny, Silverton is home to no fewer than 15 or so studios and galleries of local artists and craftspeople. A brochure for a gallery walking tour is distributed by the Chamber of Commerce.

There are several options for the evening. Enjoying the saloons, a time-honored recreation in any mining town, is one. Another is attending a production of *A Theatre Group* in the **Miners' Union Theatre**. The company stages the plays of George Bernard Shaw in the summer **Shaw Festival**. A variety of plays are staged the rest of the year.

Special Features

One of the best ways to enjoy the area's spectacular scenery is to board a coal-fired, steam-operated train of the **Durango & Silverton Narrow Gauge Railroad Company** for a trip to Durango. The train, serving Silverton since 1882, offers breathtaking views. During some months it is possible to take a railroad-operated bus to Durango and return to Silverton by train the same day. Another option is to make the Durango-Silverton-Durango loop and stop over for one or more nights in Silverton.

Daily tours are offered at the **Mayflower Gold Mill** two miles northeast of Silverton. The mill produced gold and silver from 1929 to 1991.

> • *Some of the nation's best 4-wheel-drive roads are in the Silverton area. Check with the Chamber of Commerce for a detailed Jeep map and for information on Jeep rentals and tours.*
> • *Some of the clearest and cleanest air in the U.S. is just south of Silverton on top of Molas Pass. Here you can hike or bike the Colorado Trail.*

Where to Stay

THE ALMA HOUSE HOTEL, *220 E. 10th St., (970) 387-5336*. Restored 1898 hotel, room service, pets. $$

EMPIRE STREET B&B, *P.O. Box 241, (970) 387-5857*. 1894 home, house of mayor during town's boom days, antiques, private bath available, full breakfasts. $ to $$

THE GRAND IMPERIAL HOTEL, *1219 Greene St., (970) 387-5527*. 1882 hotel with mountain views, private baths, two magnificent back bars, dining room. $$ to $$$

VILLA DALLAVALE, *1257 Blair St., (970) 387-5555/fax (970) 387-5965*. 1901 rooming house, antiques & art, TV & phones, private baths, buffet breakfasts, refreshments, some pets, magnificent views, gift shop/candy store. $$ to $$$

WINGATE HOUSE, *1045 Snowden St., P.O. Box 383, (970) 387-5520*. 1886 home, parlor with art, down pillows & comforters, mountain views. $$

Where to Eat

BENT ELBOW RESTAURANT & BAR, *P. O. Box 371, Blair St., (970)* *387-5775*. Rocky Mountain trout, steaks, Mexican buffet. $

THE FRENCH BAKERY, *1250 Greene St., (970) 387-5423*. Deli sandwiches, soups, gourmet pizzas, chili. $

GOLD KING DINING & HUB SALOON, *(see Grand Imperial Hotel)*. Traditional American fare, Baked French Onion Soup, pizza, dessert board; Victorian surroundings. $ to $$

HANDLEBARS RESTAURANT & SALOON, *117 E. 13th St., (970)* *387-5395*. American food served amongst hundreds of antiques, unique setting, bar. $ to $$

THE PICKLE BARREL, *1304 Greene St., (970) 387-5713*. Chili, hamburgers, sandwiches, hot specials, vegetarian options. $ to $$

Further Information

Silverton Area Chamber of Commerce, *P. O. Box 565, Silverton, CO* *81433 (970) 387-5654.*

Directions

From Denver, I 70 west to exit 37 (before Grand Junction), CO 141 south to US 50, south to US 550 (at Montrose), south to Silverton (about 8 hours); from Albuquerque (NM), I 25 north to NM 44 (at Bernalillo), north to NM 544 (at Bloomfield), north to US 550 (at Aztec), north to Silverton (about 5 1/2 hours).

Other Charming Colorado Towns

Crested Butte
Cripple Creek
Estes Park
Lake City
Leadville
Pagosa Springs
Redstone

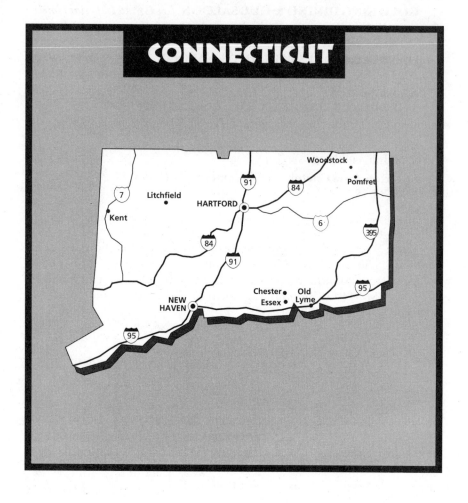

CONNECTICUT

Essex/Chester

Population 2, 500/1, 563

The villages of **Essex** and **Chester** are the kinds of places you go when you wish to experience that New England of Christmas cards, picture calendars, and romantic old movies. Here you can start the day by jogging or biking along a wooded country road past little clusters of white clapboard houses. You can then spend part of the day sightseeing along the beautiful **Connecticut River**, and the rest browsing in galleries, boutiques, and sophisticated shops. In the evening you can relax by the fire in a gorgeous old inn after seeing a good play and dining in a world-class restaurant. It doesn't come much better.

The **Connecticut River Museum** in Essex offers a thoroughly enjoyable introduction to the region. Housed in an 1878 dockhouse, the museum's permanent and seasonal exhibits recall the long and colorful history of the Connecticut River and its beautiful valley.

Quaint shops in both villages offer a wide selection of fine and decorative artwork. **The Artisans**, a craft gallery cooperative in Chester, displays paintings, furniture, pottery, clothing, and other works of its members. For arts and crafts from another time, there's the Colonial **Pratt House** (1732/1734) in Essex. Connecticut redware and American furnishings of the 17th, 18th, and 19th centuries are among the collections of this house museum.

The natural beauty of the **Connecticut River Valley** combines with the picturesque beauty of villages like Essex and Chester to make this region an especially attractive one. There are several good ways to take in the beauty. The **Valley Railroad Company** in Essex offers excursions in vintage 1920s' steam trains along the Connecticut River to Chester and back. The **North Cove Express**, Connecticut's only moving dinner train (also in Essex), offers a similar excursion aboard beautifully restored Pullman cars. For both trains, there's the option of getting off at **Deep River** for a riverboat cruise.

Chester Airport offers 25-minute scenic flights over the lower Connecticut River Valley. For more traditional (and shorter and cheaper) sightseeing, there's the trip across the river on the **Chester-Hadlyme Ferry**, one of the oldest continuously operating ferries in the nation.

The theater has long been important in Connecticut, and Essex and Chester maintain the tradition. Among the best-known productions are those of the **Ivoryton Playhouse** near Essex (summer repertory), the **National Theatre of the Deaf** in Chester (performances in sign language and spoken words), and the **Goodspeed-at-Chester/Norma Terris Theatre** (new musicals-in-progress).

> • *The last 38 miles on the Connecticut River have been designated one of the "Last Great Places" by The Nature Conservancy.*
> • *Although there is still some commerce and light industry in the region, Essex – like so many places in Connecticut – is better known today as an upscale residential community.*

Where to Stay

CAPTAIN DIBBELL HOUSE, *21 Commerce St. (Clinton 06413), (860) 669-1646/fax (860) 669-2300.* 1866 home close to shopping & harbor, art, private baths, full breakfasts, refreshments, gardens & gazebo, bicycles. $$ to $$$

THE INN AT CHESTER, *318 W. Main St. (Chester 06412), (860) 526-9541/(800) 949-7829.* Full-service inn "with 20th-century amenities & 18th-century ambiance," on 12 acres, dining room, tavern, exercise room, sauna, tennis. $$$

THE COPPER BEECH INN, *46 Main St. (Ivoryton 06442), (860) 767-0330.* Victorian home & gardens, antiques, private baths, famed restaurant, magnificent copper beech tree. $$$

GRISWOLD INN, *36 Main St. (Essex, 06426), (860) 767-1776.* Full-service country hotel, Cont. breakfasts, dining rooms, acclaimed barroom, library of historic firearms, collection of marine art. $$$

RIVERWIND INN B&B, *209 Main St. (Deep River 06417), (860) 526-2014.* 1790s home with informal country atmosphere, antiques & folk art, fireplaces, private baths, "Southern" buffet breakfasts, sherry, piano, porch. $$$

Where to Eat

THE COPPER BEECH INN, *(see above).* French country cuisine, award-winning, reservations. $$ to $$$

FIDDLERS SEAFOOD RESTAURANT, *4 Water St. (Chester), (860) 526-3210.* Baked Maine Crabcakes, Oysters Imperial, Grilled Scallops, Fillet of Sole Robert; appetizing seafood lover's luncheon menu. $$

GRISWOLD INN, *(see above).* Classic American dishes & traditional New England fare, famous meat pies, own sausages. $$

RESTAURANT DU VILLAGE, *59 Main St. (Chester), (860) 526-5301.* Regional French cuisine served in traditional country French setting complete with linen, silver, crystal, china, & country garden flowers; own baking, award-winning. $$$

STEVE'S CENTERBROOK CAFE, *Main St. (Centerbrook), (860) 767-1277.* Thai Shrimp, pastas; casual dining with bistro-style cuisine. $$

Further Information

Connecticut River Valley & Shoreline Visitors Council, *393 Main St., Middletown, CT 06457 (860) 347-0028/(800) 486-3346.*

Directions

From New Haven, I 95 east to exit 69, CT 9 north to Essex.

Kent

Population 2, 900

The three parallel lines on the map signify that **Kent** is nestled in some special countryside. One of the lines is scenic U.S. 7 winding its way through the **Litchfield Hills**. A second is the **Housatonic River**, flowing alongside the highway. The third, a little to the west, is the **Appalachian Trail**, synonymous with breathtaking scenery. In addition to its lovely countryside, Kent has many beautiful mementos of some three centuries of history. The village also offers some fabulous shopping.

The sites of Kent are neatly ordered along the three parallel lines. Approaching from the south, the visitor first passes **Bull's Bridge** (1842, with ancestry to 1760), one of the only two covered bridges in Connecticut open to automobiles. The bridge and the falls beneath it are very frequently viewed through camera lenses.

Kent Center, a little more up the road, is the place for antiques, museum-quality art galleries, and both traditional and contemporary American crafts. It is also the place for some of the finest and most unusual clothing shops around.

Two miles north of Kent Center is the **Sloane-Stanley Museum**, which features works of art by noted author and artist, Eric Sloane. There is also a re-creation of Sloane's studio, an extensive collection of Early American woodworking tools and implements, and the remains of the **Kent Iron Furnace**, in operation from 1826 to 1892.

Yet a little farther north is the **Flanders Historic District**, a cluster of houses that were once part of the center of Kent. Especially noteworthy here is the **Seven Hearths Museum**, the 1754 home of the great portrait painter, George Lawrence Nelson. The home, now a museum, displays an impressive collection of Nelson's artwork and lithographs.

Special Features

Kent Falls State Park, north on U.S. 7, is known for its dramatic 200-foot cascade, the largest in the state.

> *With its iron ore and many smelting furnaces, this part of Connecticut was able to supply the Continental Armies in the War for Independence with hundreds of cannon.*

Where to Stay

CHAUCER HOUSE, *88 N. Main St., (860) 927-4858*. 1948 Colonial home in convenient location offering "English hospitality," some private baths, full breakfasts, refreshments, lawns & maple trees. $$

CONSTITUTION OAK FARM, *Beardsley Rd., (860) 354-6495*. 1830s home on 200-acre farm, period furnishings, near Lake Waramaug. $$$

THE COUNTRY GOOSE B&B, *211 Kent Cornwall Rd., (860) 927-4746*. 1740 Colonial home, antiques, home baking, guest library, gazebo with scenic views. $$$

FIFE 'N DRUM, *P.O. Box 188, 59 N. Main St., (860) 927-3509*. Individually decorated guest rooms, antiques, TV, private baths, refreshments, restaurant, bar, gift shop. $$$

MAVIS' B&B, *230 Kent Cornwall Rd., (860) 927-4334*. 1860 Greek Revival home, private baths, den, also cottage apartment. $$$

Where to Eat

THE BISTRO CAFE, *31 Bank St. (New Milford), (860) 355-3266*. Steamed Mussels, Oven Roasted Long Island Duckling, Grilled New York Strip Steak; weekly menu. $$

BULLS BRIDGE INN, *333 Kent Rd., (860) 927-1617*. American menu: steaks, chicken, baked jumbo shrimp, grilled or pan-blackened fish, mixed grill; directly across from scenic Bull's Bridge. $$

FIFE 'N DRUM, *(see above)*. Mediterranean Fish Stew, Jumpin' Juniper Grilled Chicken Breast, Filet Mignon au Poivre, Caesar Salad for Two; pub for lighter fare, award-winning wine list. $$

RUDY'S, *122 Litchfield Rd. (New Milford), (860) 354-7727*. Lobster Newburg, Chicken Cordon Bleu, Wienerschnitzel, daily specials; Swiss decor. $$

VILLAGER RESTAURANT, *Main St., (860) 927-3945.* Home-style cooking in cozy & friendly atmosphere. $

Further Information

The Litchfield Hills Travel Council, *P. O. Box 968, Litchfield, CT 06759-0968 (860) 567-4506, Fax (860) 567-5214. (ZIP for Kent is 06757.)*

Directions

From New York City, I 684 north to I 84, east to exit 7, north on US 7 to Kent.

Litchfield
Population 1378

Litchfield is one of the finest examples of mid- and late-18th-century architecture in the U.S. It is also one of the most beautiful Colonial villages in New England. The village has been favorably compared with Williamsburg, Virginia.

The difference is that Williamsburg is a reconstruction and Litchfield is the real thing. The lovely **Litchfield Green** was laid out in the 1770s and hasn't changed much since. On the green are exactly what ought to be there: quaint shops, cozy restaurants, art galleries, and a **Congregational Church** (1829) that — of course — happens to be one of the most photographed in New England.

Grand maple-lined streets, gracious old homes, and "gentrification" in general carry the park-like Colonial charm beyond the green. Along CT 63 north and south of the green lie a living museum of gorgeous Colonial and Federal Georgian homes. To name just three: the house once owned by **Benjamin Tallmadge** (ca 1760), an aide to George Washington; **Sheldon's Tavern** (1760), where George Washington really did sleep; and the birthsite of **Harriett Beecher Stowe** (1775), author of *Uncle Tom's Cabin.*

Also on CT 63 (South) is the Neoclassical **Litchfield Historical Society Museum** with seven galleries featuring an especially fine selection of early Americana. The museum traces the history of Litchfield from Indian country to the village as it is today.

Just a little south of the museum is the **Tapping Reeve House and Law School**, the country's first law school (1774). Graduates included Vice Presidents Aaron Burr and John C. Calhoun, three Supreme Court justices, and well over a hundred cabinet members, governors, and members of Congress. The house, with finely furnished period rooms, and school are open to the public.

Special Features

Just west of Litchfield Center is Connecticut's largest natural lake, **Bantam Lake**. Bordering a major part of the shoreline is **White Memorial Foundation**, Connecticut's largest nature sanctuary (4,000 acres).

White Flower Farm, approximately two miles from the village, is a nationally recognized nursery. Five acres of display gardens may be explored—the tuberous begonias make a visit here in July and August imperative.

Situated atop a 1,230-ft knoll just east of the village, **Topsmead State Forest** offers several miles of excellent hiking and cross-country ski trails. An English-Tudor-style "cottage" (1924), the park's principal attraction, is open during the summer months.

> • *Litchfield's beautiful homes and tree-lined streets belie its early history as a manufacturing center.*
> • *Lourdes in Litchfield Shrine is modeled after Lourdes Grotto in France. The peaceful, non-commercial 35-acre shrine is a dedicated place of pilgrimage (open daily).*

Where to Stay

ABEL DARLING B&B, *102 West St., (860) 567-0384*. 1782 home with views of Litchfield Green, hand stenciling, exposed beams, antiques, period dining room. $$

COUNTRY B&B, *74 March Rd., (806) 567-4056*. Contemporary country home in woods, private bath, gardens, pool. $$$

THE LITCHFIELD INN, *Rte. 202, (203) 567-4503*. Full-service country inn, roaring fireplaces, hor d'oeuvres, restaurant. $$$

TOLL GATE HILL INN & RESTAURANT, *Rte. 202 & Tollgate Rd., (860) 567-4545*. Restored 1745 tavern on National Register, full-service inn, outdoor decks, restaurant. $$$

Where to Eat

TOLL GATE HILL INN & RESTAURANT, *(see above)*. Early American setting with contemporary American menu, award-winning. $$ to $$$

WEST STREET GRILL, *West St., On the Green, (860) 567-3885*. Grilled Atlantic Salmon, Housemade Opal Basil Pasta, Oven Roasted Chicken Breast; rated one of best in country. $$ to $$$

Further Information

Litchfield Hills Travel Council, *P. O. Box 968, Litchfield, CT 06759 (860) 567-4506/fax (860) 567-5214.*

Directions

From Hartford, I 84 to Farmington, CT 4 west to CT 118, CT 118 west to US 202, US 202 into Litchfield.

Old Lyme

Population less than 1, 000 in village

It sometimes happens that the best of an era becomes concentrated in one small spot on the map. When that happens, the beauty of the spot can become almost overwhelming. A common human reaction seems to be to grab a brush or a camera, as though caging the beauty were the only way to control it. And so it's been with **Old Lyme**.

Through the 18th century and well into the 19th, some of the most fortunate beneficiaries of the region's maritime commerce, including sea captains, built grand homes along **Lyme Street**. A few of the earliest houses were pre-Georgian; later ones displayed Georgian, Greek Revival, Italianate, and various mixtures of styles. The houses were, and are, separated by stone walls and vast, beautifully groomed grounds. Those on one side of the street back onto the **Lieutenant River**, and so views of water and salt marshes enter the scene.

It was only a matter of time before the landscape would begin attracting serious artists. And so it did, in 1899. From that year until 1937 Old Lyme was home to one of the country's first art colonies, and the center of American Impressionism. At the heart of the activity was Florence Griswold, daughter of a sea captain and heiress to one of Lyme Street's lovely mansions. Griswold didn't have the money to maintain the home, and so turned to innkeeping. The house-turned-inn became home to the art colony, and Florence Griswold became the colony's friend and advocate.

Sitting proudly on six landscaped acres, the 1817 Georgian mansion is now the **Florence Griswold Museum** and a National Historic Landmark. Painted on the doors and wooden dining-room panels of the house are various works of "Miss Florence's" boarders. Each has its story. The museum also presents four exhibitions each year of works from the Barbizon and American Impressionist schools of painting. A museum of history as well as art, the house features several period room settings. The site also includes the **Chadwick Studio**, an authentic turn-of-the-century artist's studio.

Art is also exhibited at other addresses on Lyme Street. Housed in a Federal-style home (1817, on National Register), the **Lyme Academy of Fine Arts** exhibits paintings, sculptures, and other works by students, faculty, and others. The gallery of the **Lyme Art Association** offers year-round shows of works by association members.

Even with its art aside, beautiful Old Lyme is worth some serious exploring. A National Historic District, the village is a living museum of gracious old mansions. It is also a center for fine antiques.

Special Feature

Down the coast in the southeastern corner of the state is another quintessential New England seaside village, **Stonington Borough**. The borough is home to the last commercial fishing fleet in Connecticut. Of special note here are the **Old Lighthouse Museum** and the many fine examples of 18th- and 19th-century architecture. The main street is flanked by boutiques, antique shops, and several fine restaurants.

> *Sound View Beach is a public beach with parking and other facilities. Local residents tend to avoid the place during the warmer months.*

Where to Stay

BEE & THISTLE INN, *100 Lyme St., (860) 434-1667*. 1756 Colonial home with riverside setting, carved staircase, antiques, private baths, full breakfasts (EP), sunlit porches, restaurant, cottage. $$ to $$$

OLD LYME INN, *85 Lyme St., (860) 434-2600*. 1850s mansion, Empire & Victorian furnishings, private baths, restaurant. $$$

Where to Eat

BEE & THISTLE INN, *(see above)*. American cuisine served in 4 small dining rooms, romantic setting with fireplaces, highly rated. $$ to $$$

HIDEAWAY, *Old Lyme Shopping Center, (860) 434-3335*. Broad menu with traditional, New England, California, Cajun, & Mexican roots; views of salt marshes & birds. $ to $$

OLD LYME INN, *(see above)*. Innovative menu, white table cloths with single roses set amongst royal blue furnishings, highly rated. $$$

Further Information

Southeastern Connecticut Tourism District, *P.O. Box 89, New London, CT 06320 (800) 863-6569*; or **Florence Griswold Museum,** *96 Lyme St., Old Lyme, CT 06371 (860) 434-5542.*

Directions

From New Haven, I 95 east to exit 70.

Pomfret/Woodstock
Populations 3, 220 & 6, 180

Pomfret and **Woodstock** are neighboring towns up in "Connecticut's Quiet Corner." This (the northeastern) corner of the state is called "quiet" because there are no major cities or geological formations or resorts to attract major crowds of visitors. There are countless things to see and do, however, and they're the kinds of things that can be selected and combined daily–or hourly–to please any whim of mood or weather. One day might be right for the antique and craft shops, a flea market or two, and maybe a little golf. Another day might include a country fair, a trip along scenic CT 169, an hour or so of apple picking. Some other options: fishing, shopping at roadside stands, reading by the fireside, exploring quaint country roads by foot, bike, or ski.

Pomfret and Woodstock are *towns* in the New England sense, which means they are geographical-political entities that include rural areas as well as clusters of villages. Both have similar histories–largely agricultural in the 1700s, a mix of agriculture and industry in the 1800s, summer colonies for New York City's wealthy in the late 1800s and early 1900s (earning the area the nickname "the other Newport"). In recent times the towns, especially Woodstock, have attracted several small businesses, but the overall character remains rural, albeit more residential-rural than agricultural-rural.

The oldest and one of the most charming of the towns' villages is **Woodstock Hill** (settled in 1686). The oldest stone in the village's cemetery is dated 1687; many of the houses go back to the late 1700s. The pointed arches and stained-glass windows of the village's most famous house, **Bowen House** ("Roseland Cottage," 1846), speak unmistakably of the Gothic Revival period. The house's furnishings date from the mid-19th century, as does the handsome boxwood parterre garden. Guests attending Independence Day parties here included four presidents and writer Oliver Wendell Holmes. (open to public)

The **Brayton Grist Mill** and **Marcy Blacksmith Museum** in Pomfret's **Mashamoquet Brook State Park** provide an interesting view of the towns' 19th-century industrial heritage. The three-generation Marcy Blacksmith Collection, housed on the fourth floor of the mill, includes tools used for horse-shoeing, wheelwrighting, and other aspects of iron manufacture and repair.

Pure New England towns like Pomfret and Woodstock can be counted on to have several interesting old churches, and maybe a private boarding school or two. Historic churches here include Woodstock's **Baptist Church** (1840) and Pomfret's **Congregational Church** (1832) and **Christ Church** (Episcopal, 1882); the latter has several windows of Tiffany design. Some of Pomfret's prettiest buildings belong to the private **Pomfret School** (founded 1894) and **Rectory School** (founded 1921).

Special Features

Woodstock's **Photomobile Model Museum** features solar-powered model cars, boats, planes, and trains. Demonstrations are held inside or outside year-round.

Nearby **Putnam** is known as the "Antique Capital of the Northeast."

> *The wolf den in Pomfret's Mashamoquet Brook State Park is said to be where Revolutionary War hero General Israel Putnam slayed the last she-wolf in northeastern Connecticut.*

Where To Stay

CHICKADEE COTTAGE B&B, *375 Wrights Crossing Rd., P.O. Box 110, Pomfret Center (06259), (860) 963-0587/fax (860) 963-0594.* 1910 Cape cottage on 10 acres, antiques, one private bath, Cont. "plus" breakfasts, across from Audubon Society Nature Preserve. $$ to $$$

KARINN B&B, *330 Pomfret St., Pomfret Center (06259), (860) 928-5492.* Late 19th-century home built as girls' school, library & music room, private baths, full breakfast menu, refreshments, bar, some pets, gardens. $$ to $$$

QUAIL RUN AT POMFRET, *1 Townhouse Dr., Pomfret Center (06259), (860) 928-6907.* Five-room apartment with two bedrooms, living room, fully-equipped kitchen, dining room, private bath, private entrance. $$$

TAYLOR'S CORNER, *880 Rt. 171, Woodstock (06281), (860) 974-0490/fax (860) 974-0498.* Ca 1795 home with central chimney, on National Register, antiques, fireplaces, some private baths, full breakfasts weekends, herb gardens. $$

THE INN AT WOODSTOCK HILL, *94 Plaine Hill Rd., P.O. Box 98, S. Woodstock (06267), (860) 928-0528/fax (860) 928-3236.* 1825 full-service inn on 14 acres, once private estate, fireplaces, floral chintz fabrics, Cont. "plus" breakfasts, award-winning dining room (see below). $$$

Where to Eat

THE INN AT WOODSTOCK HILL, *(see above).* Grilled Swordfish Steak, Broiled Sea Scallops & Shrimp, Chicken Piccata, New York Sirloin Steak; fine china & linen. $$ to $$$

THE VANILLA BEAN CAFE, *Corner of rtes. 44, 169, & 97, Pomfret (06258), (860) 928-1562.* Award-winning sandwiches & desserts, some dinner specials, singers & songwriters on weekend evenings. $

THE VINE BISTRO, *85 Main St. (Putnam 06260), (860) 928-1660.* 7 to 10 specials daily, salmon, rack of lamb, pastas. $$ to $$$

Further Information

Northeast Connecticut Visitors District, *P.O. Box 598, Putnam, CT 06260 (860) 928-1228/fax (860) 928-4720.*

Directions

From Hartford, I 84 east to exit 69, CT 74 east to US 44, east to Pomfret; also from Hartford, I 84 east to exit 73, CT 190 east to CT 197, east to North Woodstock; from Providence (RI), RI 101 or US 44 west to CT 169.

Other Charming Connecticut Towns

Madison
Salisbury
Stonington Borough
West Cornwall
Woodbury

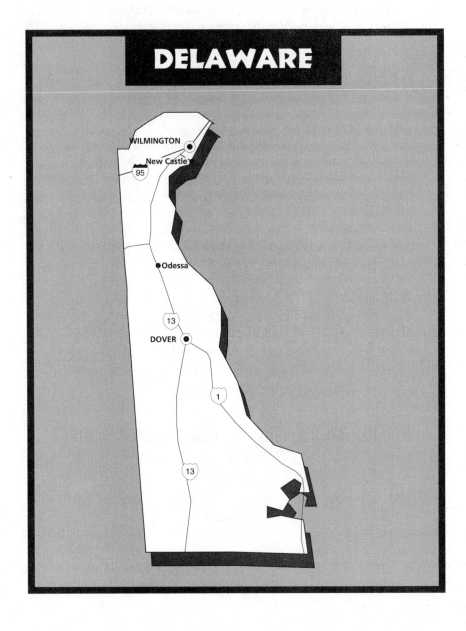

DELAWARE

New Castle
Population 4, 837

Located on the **Delaware River** just south of Wilmington, **New Castle** is one of our country's finest but least known Colonial treasures. In the historic part of town are not only buildings but whole streets, some even cobbled, that look very much like they did 200 years ago. Although a town today, New Castle was once a prosperous Colonial city. Which is what makes New Castle's historic district so very precious – it isn't a reconstructed village, it's a preserved 18th-century American city!

When an 18th-century American city enters the 21st century largely intact, something in history took a wrong turn. And so it did. During the 1600s New Castle shifted back and forth between Swedish, Dutch, and English control. In the 1700s the town became the capital of the colony and, later, state of Delaware. It also became the largest city in Delaware, and one known for its wealth and refinement.

Following the Revolution, the town prospered as a transportation and trade center. Then, it happened: Around 1840, long-distance rail lines were laid through Wilmington, not New Castle. The town/city remained virtually forgotten until rediscovery in the early 1920s.

New Castle's *Heritage Trail* comprises 26 historic sites, some of them entire streets or rows of houses. The buildings, usually brick, were built throughout the 18th and into the early 19th centuries. They show several architectural styles, including Dutch, Georgian, and Federal. Most of the houses are private residences.

The **Court House** was the Colonial capitol between 1732 (date of construction) and 1777, when Dover became Delaware's capital. Standing on the edge of the **Green** (1655), the building is now a Delaware State Museum Site. The prisoners' dock, witness stand, and judge's bench can be seen in the restored courtroom (group tours may be arranged).

Immanuel Episcopal Church (1703; tower, 1822) was the first parish of the Church of England in Delaware. The church was rebuilt, using the original walls, after a fire in 1980. Signers of the Declaration of Independence, governors, and other historic figures are buried in the cemetery.

There are three house museums, all with period furnishings. The first, the **Dutch House** (1700), is a rare and relatively undisturbed example of a house common in Colonial times. Standing in contrast, the elegant **Amstel House** (1738) was the home of Governor Van Dyke.

George Washington attended a wedding here in 1784. The third house is the Federal-style **George Read II House** (1801). With its 22 rooms and 14,000 square feet, it was once the largest house in the state. The formal garden, installed in 1847, is the oldest surviving garden in Delaware.

Special Features

Many historic homes and gardens are open to the public on *A Day in Old New Castle*, held the third Saturday in May.

Several lovely, historic mansions and gardens in or near Wilmington, several miles to the north, are open to the public. One of the most celebrated is **Winterthur**, where American decorative arts from 1640 to 1860 are displayed in two buildings on a nearly 1,000-acre estate. In one, a gallery, is an introductory exhibition; in the second, the mansion of Henry Francis du Pont, are 175 period room settings (guided tours). Complementing the house museum are 60 acres of carefully restored gardens. The garden landscape is noted for its color combinations, naturalistic planning, and finely orchestrated sequence of blooms. **Rockwood** (1851), another 19th-century estate, provides a superb example of Rural Gothic architecture and Gardenesque landscape design.

> • *Famous visitors to old New Castle included William Penn, George Washington, Thomas Jefferson, the Marquis de Lafayette, Harriet Tubman, Jenny Lind, and Enrico Caruso.*
> • *The interior and basement of the hexagonal Old Library Museum (1892) are illuminated in part by skylights and light-sinks.*

Where to Stay

THE ARMITAGE INN, *2 The Strand, (302) 328-6618*. 1732 home overlooking Battery Park & Delaware River, private baths, "gourmet" breakfasts. $$ to $$$

FOX LODGE AT LESLEY MANOR, *123 W. 7th St., (302) 328-0768*. 1855 Gothic Revival mansion, original pocket doors & chandeliers, private baths, pets. $$ to $$$

TERRY HOUSE B&B, *130 Delaware St., (302) 322-2505*. Circa 1860 brick town house, TV, private baths, porches, overlooking Battery Park & Delaware River. $$ to $$$

WILLIAM PENN GUEST HOUSE, *206 Delaware St., (302) 328-7736*. 1682 home, antiques, some private baths, Cont. "plus" breakfasts, lovely dining room, reputed lodging place of William Penn. $$

Where to Eat

THE ARSENAL ON THE GREEN RESTAURANT, *30 Market St., (302) 328-1290*. Chicken Chesapeake, Twin Filet Mignon, Pork Medallions Creole; in 1809 arsenal, tavern for lighter fare. $$

THE CELLAR GOURMET RESTAURANT, *208 Delaware St., (302) 323-0999*. Light fare, vegetarian selections, ice cream; family-oriented, quaint, patio. $

JESSOP'S TAVERN, *114 Delaware St., (302) 322-6111*. Tavern & Colonial restaurant in ca 1724 building serving "Dutch cheeses, English pub fare, Swedish sauces, & old American dishes." $ to $$

OPERA HOUSE VICTORIAN TEAROOM, *308 Delaware St., (302) 326-1211*. Full Victorian teas weekends, in 1879 Masonic Hall & turn-of-century opera house with 15-ft windows & Corinthian columns, antique mall. $

Further Information

New Castle Visitors Bureau, *P.O. Box 465, New Castle, DE 19720 (800) 758-1550*; or **George Read II House**, *42 The Strand, New Castle, DE 19720 (302) 322-8411*.

Directions

From Wilmington, DE 9 south to Historic Old New Castle.

Odessa

Population about 300

Rural **Odessa**, known until 1855 as **Cantwell's Bridge**, prospered during the 18th and 19th centuries from grain shipping and, later, the peach trade. The sources of prosperity didn't last, however, and the town's growth came to an end. Many handsome buildings from the 18th and 19th centuries survived, in large part because Odessa's commercial life had always proceeded in cooperation rather than competition with existing buildings. Today the buildings, some exquisitely restored, line the town's tree-shaded brick sidewalks.

Four of the town's most historic buildings are grouped as the **Historic Houses of Odessa**, owned and operated by the Winterthur Museum and Gardens (open to the public). Group tours are available by reservation (groups may enjoy boxed lunches – see below – or a formal coffee/tea).

The first of the Historic Houses of Odessa, the **Corbit-Sharp House** (1772/1774), is the finest example of mid-Georgian architecture in the state. Landscaped with sweeping lawns and formal gardens, the house is beautifully furnished in the style of the late 18th century.

The stately **Wilson-Warner House** (1769) typifies a simpler form of Georgian architecture commonly found in Delaware. Itemized lists of the house's contents from 1829 have aided the Winterthur Museum in selecting and arranging the furnishings. In the rear of the house are beehive ovens and a muskrat-skinning shack. One of Delaware's oldest houses, the early 18th-century **Collins-Sharp House** was formed by joining two small houses. The log-and-frame house is a center for the museum's hands-on educational programs for children.

The Federal-style "**Brick Hotel**" (1822), originally a hotel and later a residence, is now a gallery housing the country's largest collection of Belter furniture. (Belter was a mid-19th-century manufacturer known for his technologically innovative, highly carved creations. The furniture's style is described as Rococo Revival, but most people today would describe it simply as Victorian – and elegantly uncomfortable.)

Several lovely private homes in Odessa open their doors as part of the annual *Christmas in Odessa*, first weekend in December. One of them, the circa 1780 **January House**, commands a spectacular view of the **Appoquinimink Creek** and surrounding marshland. Another, the **Charles T. Polk House** (1852), is a mansion exemplifying the late Federal style.

Special Features

DE 9, which passes just to the east of town, is (deservedly) a designated scenic drive.

To the southeast of Odessa on DE 9 is the 15,122-acre **Bombay Hook National Wildlife Refuge**, a haven for waterfowl. Within the refuge are auto tour routes, walking paths, and observation trails and towers. The **Allee House**, a circa 1753 brick plantation house, is also part of the refuge (open to the public).

> *In 1855, the town optimistically renamed itself Odessa after the great Russian grain-shipping port.*

Where to Stay

CANTWELL HOUSE B&B, *P.O. Box 2, (302) 378-4179.* Circa 1840 house with Colonial antiques, private baths, homemade granola, also carriage house with living room/kitchen. $$ to $$$

Where to Eat

Historic Houses of Odessa will cater lunches for groups of 15 or more. The lunches (which include beverages, linens, and flatware) may be set up in any of several lovely locations. Menu options range from a fresh deli tray to a croissant box lunch to a lunch consisting of an entree with full accompaniments, including freshly baked pies and cakes.

Further Information

Historic Houses of Odessa, *P. O. Box 507, Odessa, DE 19730 (302) 378-4069.*

Directions

From Wilmington, US 13 south to Odessa.

Other Charming Delaware Towns

Arden
Bethel
Delaware City
Lewes

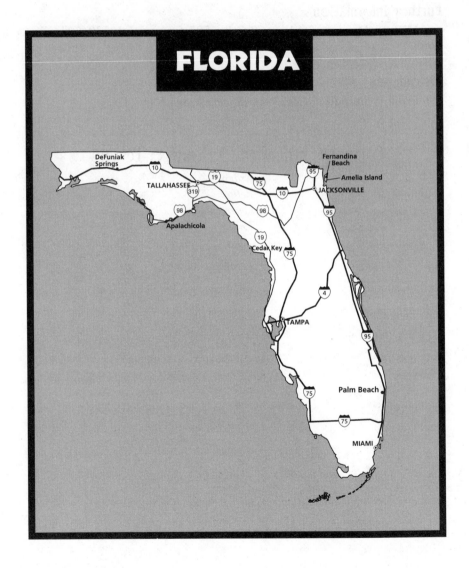

FLORIDA

Apalachicola

Population 2, 796

If the U.S. were to be divided according to its various brands of charm, the **Florida panhandle** would receive a separate listing. For it is here that the South begins to take on a hint of the tropics, and the mix can be lovely, even haunting. A very good example is **Apalachicola**, where antebellum homes and other buildings out of history share a water-surrounded town with fishing and shrimping vessels from the Gulf of Mexico.

Located at the mouth of the **Apalachicola River**, the port was one of the busiest on the Gulf in the 19th century. Before the Civil War, steamboats carried cotton, timber, and other products up and down the river between here and Georgia and elsewhere. In more recent times the economy has shifted to seafood; the surrounding waters now produce most of Florida's oysters and a major part of the shellfish.

Nestled as it is on Florida's *Forgotten Coast*, Apalachicola is a quiet town with one traffic light and no shopping mall within 50 miles. The moss-draped historic district and the fishing and shrimping boats have been joined by art galleries, an old-fashioned soda fountain, and families busy restoring the old houses. There are also three small but interesting museums. The **John Gorrie State Museum** features a replica of the world's first ice machine, invented by Gorrie. The **museum of the St. Vincent National Wildlife Refuge** has exhibits and information on coastal wildlife and is located in town because the refuge itself occupies a barrier island accessible only by private boat.

The third museum is the **Apalachicola Maritime Museum**, a nonprofit corporation committed to "informing the public about the maritime history of the American South, and especially that of the Apalachicola Bay area." The museum's prize possession is the *Governor Stone*, a fully restored 63-foot, two-masted schooner built in 1877. The oldest operational sailing vessel in the South, the *Governor Stone* has been declared a National Historic Landmark (daily two-hour and sunset cruises).

Apalachicola is obviously the place for those who love oysters, shrimp, scallops, crayfish, and/or fresh fish. The seafood industry is honored the first Saturday in November with the celebration of the **Florida Seafood Festival**. Among the festival's highlights are demonstrations of boat building and netmaking, an oyster-shucking contest, the blessing of the fleet, and arts and crafts exhibits.

Special Features

St. George Island State Park, located 10 miles east and south of Apalachicola, is considered one of Florida's most beautiful state parks. The island park has nine miles of undeveloped beaches and dunes. Along the island's beaches, salt marshes, and forests of slash pines and live oaks dwell osprey, raccoons, ghost crabs, diamondback terrapin, and many species of shorebirds.

> • *The structure for lovely Trinity Episcopal Church (1837) was prefabricated in New York of white pine and floated in sections by schooner down the Atlantic Coast and around the Florida Keys for assembly in Apalachicola. Trinity is the second oldest church in Florida with regularly scheduled services.*
>
> • *If you're thinking about building condominiums here, beware. Land for development is scarce and the ecological health of the Apalachicola River and surrounding waters is taken very seriously.*
>
> • *Private boaters headed for the St. Vincent National Wildlife Refuge should be prepared for the mosquitoes and other discomforts of this coastal wilderness.*

Where to Stay

COOMBS HOUSE INN, *80 Sixth St., (904) 653-9199*. 1905 mansion with ornate oak staircase & 9 fireplaces, antiques, TV, private baths. $$ to $$$

THE GIBSON INN, *at the bridge, (904) 653-2191*. Restored 1907 hotel, full-service, antiques, ambiance, restaurant & bar. $$

MAGNOLIA HALL GUEST HOUSE, *177 5th St., (904) 653-2431*. 1838 Greek Revival home on secluded grounds, on National Register, antiques & art, TV, private baths, full breakfasts, refreshments, veranda, pool, garden & views, airport pickup. $$$

WITHERSPOON, *94 5th St., (904) 653-9186*. 19th-century captain's home in historic district, on National Register, vaulted entrance hall, private baths, porches. $$

Where to Eat

APALACHICOLA GRILL SEAFOOD & STEAHOUSE, *100 Market St., (904) 653-9510*. Fried & chargrilled seafood, ribeye steak, "The Largest Fried Fish Sandwich in the World." $ to $$

BOSS OYSTER, *125 Water St., (904) 653-9364*. Oysters served chilled on half shell, steamed with melted butter, roasted in their shell, baked with choice of topping, etc.; also other fare. $ to $$

CAROLINE'S RIVERFRONT RESTAURANT, *123 Water St., (904) 653-8139*. Fresh local oysters, grouper, shrimp, scallops; house specialties; lounge, panoramic view of river. $$

CHEF EDDIE'S MAGNOLIA GRILL, *133 US 98 W., Ave. E, (904) 653-8000*. Renovated old home serving fresh seafood, generous portions, highly rated. $ to $$

THE GIBSON INN, *(see above)*. Grouper Papillote, Oysters Remick, Shrimp-Scallop-Crab Dijon. $$

OYSTER COVE SEAFOOD BAR & GRILL, *E. Pine at E. 2nd sts. (St. George Island), (904) 927-2600/(904) 927-2829*. Mama Shaw Southern Fried Deviled Crab, Apalachicola Bay Oysters, Shrimp Dijon, Louisiana Seafood Gumbo, Fresh Catch of the Day. $$

Further Information

Apalachicola Bay Chamber of Commerce, *84 Market Street, Apalachicola, FL 32320 (904) 653-9419*.

Directions

From Tallahassee, US 319/98 south to Apalachicola.

Cedar Key
Population 668

Three miles out in the **Gulf of Mexico** there is a little island community with just one main street, one grocery store, and no stoplights. The houses of tabby and wood, with porches and balconies, are home to families who have lived here for generations and who continue to maintain the island's traditions and memories. **Cedar Key's** atmosphere is something that has become very, very rare — something called Old Florida.

The island's 200-year history is highlighted in both the **Cedar Key State Museum** and the **Cedar Key Historical Society Museum**. Inquire at the Chamber of Commerce for information on a walking tour of the historic district. But take your time—hurrying doesn't agree with Cedar Key's culture, nor climate.

Very appropriately, this part of Florida's coast is called the *Nature Coast*. Cedar Key and the other tiny keys around it are a naturalist's paradise, with hundreds of species of birds and animals. Strolling along the shorelines and marshes is a favorite way to pass the time. Ospreys build their nests, Great Blue Herons and egrets wade the waters, pelicans dive and fish, dolphins play.

Cedar Key is understandably popular with seafood lovers. This is the place to sample, or gorge on if you like, smoked mullet, grouper, clams, shrimp, stone crab claws, blue crabs, soft shell crabs, oysters—all fresh from the Gulf.

Special Features

A pastime designed for lovers of charm is renting a **johnboat** and exploring the many uninhabited keys in the surrounding waters. Beyond the abundant wildlife, there's an 1850s lighthouse and artifacts, exposed by the shifting sands, from ancient Indian communities.

In addition to its first-magnitude spring, **Manatee Springs State Park** (near Chiefland) has canoe rentals and an elevated boardwalk that leads the visitor through cypress swampland on the Suwanee River.

> • *Naturalist John Muir walked 1000 miles in 1867 to reach his destination here. He wrote, "Today I reached the sea and many gems of tiny islets called keys."*
> • *There are probably more artists and writers per capita on Cedar Key than in any other Florida town.*

Where to Stay

CEDAR KEY B&B, *P.O. Box 700, (904) 543-9000.* Rambling 1880 home canopied by 500-yr.-old live oaks, on National Register, antiques, paddle fans, private baths, full breakfasts, afternoon tea, spa, rocking chairs on verandah, honeymoon cottage, extensive gardens, views. $$ to $$$

ISLAND HOTEL, *P.O. Box 460, (904) 543-5111.* 1859 inn on National Register, private baths, full breakfasts, long balcony with rockers, lounge bar & restaurant. $$$

Where to Eat

ANNIE'S CAFE, *6th St. & FL 24, (904) 543-6141.* Sandwiches, seafood, lots of local color. $ to $$

BLUE DESERT CAFE, *12518 FL 24, (904) 543-9111.* Eclectic menu featuring pastas, sandwiches, burritos, seafood & gourmet pizzas, calzones. $ to $$

CAPTAIN'S TABLE, *Dock St., (904) 543-5441.* Jambalaya, Stuffed Flounder, Crab Bisque, seafood platters; sunset views, bar. $ to $$

COOK'S CAFE, *2nd St., (904) 543-5548.* Daily specials, seafood platters, burgers; local ambiance, outside seating. $

THE HERON RESTAURANT, *2nd St., (904) 543-5666.* Crab au Gratin, Grouper ala Emeril, Scallops Limon, Baked Crab-stuffed Prawns, Pasta du Jour. $$

THE ISLAND HOTEL, *(see above).* Cedar Key menu with baked & sauteed local seafood, soft shell & stone crabs, clams, bouillabaisse, meat & vegetable dishes, homemade poppy-seed bread; fresh flowers, classical music, screened patio, lounge. $$

Further Information

Cedar Key Area Chamber of Commerce, *P.O. Box 610, Cedar Key, FL 32625 (904) 543-5600.*

Directions

From Tallahassee, US 27 east to US 19, US 19 east to FL 24 (at Otter Creek), west to Cedar Key. Note: From Clearwater/St. Petersburg consider using US 41 & 98 (via Brooksville) to bypass the excessive strip development on US 19 south of Spring Hill.

DeFuniak Springs
Population 5, 120

One natural event and one human event combined to produce what may be the most unique one-mile hike in the country. The natural event was the formation of a spring-fed lake, 60 feet deep and about one mile in circumference, that is almost perfectly round. It was inevitable that such a beautiful little lake would make **DeFuniak** (dee FEW nee ack) **Springs** a rather special kind of town.

The human event was the establishment of the winter capital of **Chautauqua** on the shores of the lake. Chautauqua was an institution formed in upstate New York in the latter part of the 19th century to provide summer cultural, educational, and religious programs (see Chautauqua, New York). From 1885 until the early 1920s the institution migrated to DeFuniak Springs for a winter session. Some of the people who migrated with it built handsome houses around the lake and, in some cases, became permanent residents.

The path about the lake therefore offers vistas of crystal-clear water on one side and a series of grand late 19th- and early 20th-century homes on the other. The Chamber of Commerce distributes a map and description of the buildings for a self-guided tour. Motorists may take the tour by following **Circle Drive**. The most prominent of the buildings is the **Chautauqua Auditorium** (1885, expanded in 1909), which once housed an auditorium with 4,000 inclined seats, as well as halls and classrooms. The building was reduced in size and altered in appearance by a 1975 hurricane.

One of the smallest buildings on the lake is the **Walton-DeFuniak Library**, which claims to be the "oldest structure in Florida built as a library and still serving that purpose." Inside is a substantial collection of swords and other weaponry.

Houses make up the majority of the buildings and illustrate a wide array of turn-of-the-century architectural styles. One of the most noteworthy is **Dream Cottage** (circa 1888), a Gothic Stick chalet-style house built by Wallace Bruce, American ambassador to Scotland. Four bells hanging from the gable produce a range of tones when stirred by the wind.

Two other imposing houses are **Magnolia House** (1887), which boasts 50 windows and 12 magnolia trees, and the **Elliot Home** (1907), decorated with massive Doric columns, five soaring chimneys, and an octagonal tent-roofed tower. The latter house was used to entertain celebrities during the Chautauqua sessions.

Special Features

An annual modern-day **Chautauqua Festival** is held around the lake in April.

The beaches of the **Gulf of Mexico** are only a half hour's drive to the south.

Vortex Springs at nearby Ponce de Leon offers the largest diving facility in Florida.

On the lake is a circa 1840 magnolia tree with a spreading crown of 72 feet and a trunk with a circumference of 12 1/2 feet.

Where to Stay

SUNBRIGHT MANOR B&B, *606 Live Oak Ave., (904) 892-0656.* Circa 1886 Queen Anne home on National Register, once home of Florida governor, private baths, full "Florida" breakfasts. $$

Where to Eat

EDIE'S, *301 N. 9th St., (904) 892-4847.* Unusual daily luncheon specials. $

McLAIN'S FAMILY STEAK HOUSE, *622 Hugh Adams Rd. (I 10 & US 331S), (904) 892-2402.* Steaks, Seafood Platter, Broiled Grouper, fried seafood, chicken; weekly catfish, rib, & seafood buffets. $ to $$

Further Information

Walton County Chamber of Commerce, *P.O. Box 29, 95 Circle Dr., DeFuniak Springs, FL 32435 (904) 892-3191.*

Directions

From Tallahassee, I 10 west to exit 14 (DeFuniak Springs exit).

Fernandina Beach
Population 8, 765

American Victoriana and an ocean beach make an unlikely couple, albeit an engaging one. When the setting is palmetto Florida, the coupling is even more unlikely, and engaging. Add to the scene draping Spanish moss and the scent of magnolias and you'll understand the lure of the old seaport of **Fernandina Beach** on **Amelia Island**.

There was a time back in the 19th century when it looked as though Fernandina Beach might become a major resort center. But then, in the parting years of the century, tycoon Henry M. Flagler's East Coast Railroad bypassed the village on its way south. The railroad – and more reliably warm winter temperatures – carried tourists farther south. Today Fernandina Beach, more Southern than Floridian, boasts some 450 structures built before 1927, and more than 50 blocks of the downtown area form a historic district listed on the National Register.

The **Palace Saloon** is Florida's oldest tavern (1878). The 40-foot hand-carved mahogany bar, the stuff of which great saloons are made, provides just one of several reasons why the visitor might want to step inside. General Ulysses S. Grant once stayed at the **Florida House Inn**, another gem in the historic district, now authentically restored and still very much in business (see listing below).

Centre Street, the hub of the district, has been returned to a turn-of-the-century shopping district with gas lanterns and cobblestone walks. A number of homes in the district are separately listed on the National Register; several are bed and breakfast inns (see below).

Special Features

Construction on the brick fort in nearby **Ft. Clinch State Park** began in 1847, and continued during the Union occupation in the latter part of the Civil War, but was never completed because of obsolescence. The soldiers' barracks, prison, guardhouse, and a wooden drawbridge are among the structures that can be visited. State park reenactors portray Union troops performing daily duties such as cooking and repairing rifles. Candlelight tours are conducted on some weekends. The park's unspoiled beaches afford a view of a Florida that has largely disappeared.

Amelia Island has 13 miles of dunes and white sand beaches. Beachside horseback riding and fresh and saltwater fishing are among the many activities that this beautiful island offers.

> • *Amelia Island is sometimes called the "Isle of Eight Flags" because it is the only land in the United States that has been under eight flags.*
> • *Fernandina Beach, which boasts a modern shrimp industry, is home to the world's largest producer of handmade shrimp nets.*

Where to Stay

AMELIA ISLAND WILLIAMS HOUSE, *103 S. 9th St., (904) 277-2328.* Antebellum home, antiques, museum collection of Oriental art & silks, TV & phones, fireplaces, private baths, whirlpools, "picture-book" breakfasts, porch, spa, garden, Jefferson Davis once a guest, acclaimed. $$$

BAILEY HOUSE, *P.O. Box 805, 28 S. 7th St., (904) 261-5390.* 1895 Queen Anne home on National Register, antiques, private baths, bicycles, beach towels. $$ to $$$

FAIRBANKS HOUSE, *227 S. 7th St., (800) 261-4838/(904) 277-0500.* Italianate home, private baths, some whirlpools, "gourmet" breakfasts, lovely pool setting. $$$

FLORIDA HOUSE INN, *P.O. Box 688, 22 S. 3rd St., (800) 258-3301.* Oldest continuously operated hotel in Florida (1857), on National Register, full-service, antiques, fireplaces, full breakfasts, restaurant, pub. $$ to $$$.

HOYT HOUSE, *804 Atlantic Ave., (800) 432-2085.* 1905 home, private baths, full breakfasts on china & silver. $$$

Where to Eat

BEECH STREET GRILL, *801 Beech St., (904) 277-3662.* Roasted Salmon Filet, Macadamia Crusted Local Grey Grouper, Grilled Prime Tenderloin of Beef; in 1889 house, solid wine list, one of Florida's best. $$

CAFE ATLANTIS, *22 S. 4th St., (904) 277-0042.* Southwestern Grilled Tuna with Tomato Chipotle Sauce, Roasted Pork Tenderloin Medallions with Truffled Demi-Glaze, Ginger-Soy Glazed Salmon with Sauteed Asian Greens; local artwork, covered patio. $$ to $$$

FLORIDA HOUSE INN, *(see above).* Country cooking served boarding-house style, oldest dining room in state. $

GOLDEN GROUPER, *5 S. 2nd St., (904) 261-0013.* Seafood the specialty – grilled, baked, broiled, sauteed, or fried; good selection of beers. $$

Further Information

Amelia Island Chamber of Commerce, *P.O. Box 472, Fernandina Beach, FL 32035 (800) 226-3542.*

Directions

From Jacksonville, I 95 north to exit 129, FL A1A east to Amelia Island.

Palm Beach

Population 9, 814 (x 2 or 3 during winter months)

The palms and the beaches are here, necessary but not sufficient. Part of the story. The other part has to do with what happens when enormous amounts of human wealth are used to turn the palms and the beaches and their 14-mile by 1/2-mile-or-so strip of land into a paradise. Not just any paradise, but a subtropical one with gorgeous flower beds and lush foliage and pastel-colored buildings that look part Spanish, part Moroccan, part Riviera. And fountains, sophisticated shops, and fashionable people. The result is **Palm Beach**, for generations an international symbol for the privileged at play.

Before Henry Morrison Flagler came along this strip of land may have looked good to shipwrecked sailors, but probably few others. Then in 1894 Flagler, one of the two or three tycoons who turned Florida into a resort state, built a large luxury hotel and connected it by means of a special spur to the main line of his Florida East Coast Railway. Other resort hotels followed and Palm Beach acquired a reputation as a playground of millionaires. Later, in the 1920s, an important part of the present town's character was molded when opulent Mediterranean palaces designed for winter escapees appeared.

The most important "sight" in Palm Beach is probably Palm Beach itself, for much of the town's beauty lies in its magnificently landscaped hotels (including the famed **Breakers**), apartment complexes, and mansions, and many of these can be enjoyed–at least from a distance–by foot, car, or bicycle (the trails are fabulous). Some of the grandest of the mansions face **Ocean Boulevard**. The resort's renowned shopping district–clad in charming Mediterranean style–lies along palm-lined **Worth Avenue**.

The single best-known site is the **Henry Morrison Flagler Museum** (1901), originally a home (*Whitehall*) built by Flagler for his wife Mary Lily, then a luxury hotel, and finally a museum restored to the house's original opulence. On view are the Flaglers' period rooms–the Louis XIV Music Room, for example–with many of their original furnishings. Exhibits include collections of family art and household treasures as well as artifacts of local and Florida history. On the grounds is the restored *Rambler*, Mr. Flagler's personal railroad car (1886).

Palm Beach has had a long love affair with the arts, maybe especially the performing arts, but certainly also the fine arts. **Society of the Four Arts** (Four Arts Plaza) includes an art museum, library, and lovely gardens, all open to the public. The **Hibel Museum of Art**, dedicated to the work of Edna Hibel, is located in the flowered and fountained Regency-style **Royal Poinciana Plaza** (1957).

Broadway and off-Broadway productions are hosted by the beautiful **Royal Poinciana Playhouse**, also in the plaza. A diversity of theatrical and musical performances, some 300 of them annually, are presented on the stages of the main concert hall, playhouse, and amphitheater of the world-class **Raymond F. Kravis Center for the Performing Arts** (1992).

Palm Beach may be a playground for the rich, but the not-so-rich may play here, too. There are public beaches, municipal tennis courts, and, as mentioned, great bicycle trails. And, of course, offshore sports fishing. As for golfing, Palm Beach County boasts some 145 courses!

Special Features

Other towns in **Palm Beach County**, just across the bridge, include **West Palm Beach**, **Lake Worth**, **Delray Beach**, and **Boca Raton**. Stop by the county's Convention & Visitors Bureau (see below) for information on the many, many attractions in these and other nearby towns.

The land occupied by Palm Beach is the closest in southern Florida to the climate-mellowing Gulf Stream.

The story goes that in 1878 the "Providencia" wrecked with a large cargo of coconuts and that the palms grown from the coconuts joined the beaches in prompting the choice of the young resort's name.

Where to Stay

PALM BEACH HISTORIC INN, *365 S. County Rd., (407) 832-4009.* Restored & renovated 1920s bldg. in heart of Palm Beach, TV & phones, private baths, Cont. "plus" breakfasts, one block to beach, highly rated. $$ to $$$

PLAZA INN-PALM BEACH B&B HOTEL, *215 Brazilian Ave., (800) 233-2632/(407) 832-8666.* Art deco hotel in tropical setting with pool, whirlpool, & waterfalls; TV & phones, private baths, full breakfasts, piano bar, pets, respected. $$$

Note: Palm Beach is virtually synonymous with posh resort hotels featuring tropical gardens, pools, tennis courts, fitness centers, formal and informal dining rooms, lounges, live entertainment, etc. Some are listed on the National Register of Historic Places. Daily rates for a double in the winter months can run into hundreds of dollars; during the warmer months, however, rates may fall to less than $150, sometimes less than $100. Among the grandest of the hotels are the **Brazilian Court**, **Breakers**, **Chesterfield Hotel**, **Four Seasons Resort Palm Beach**, **Palm Beach Hilton**, and **Palm Beach Hotel**.

Where to Eat

AMICI RISTORANTE & BAR, *288 S. County Rd., (407) 832-0201.* Large variety of risotti, paste Italiane, paste fatte in casa, carne, pesce, pizze; nightly menu, upscale, busy. $$ to $$$

Further Information

Palm Beach Chamber of Commerce, *45 Cocoanut Row, Palm Beach, FL 33480*; also, **Palm Beach County Convention & Visitors Bureau**, *1555 Palm Beach Lakes Blvd., Suite 204, West Palm Beach, FL 33401 (407) 471-3995/(800) 554-PALM.*

Directions

From Fort Lauderdale and Miami, north on I 95 or Florida's Turnpike to FL 704 (Okeechobee Blvd.), east to Palm Beach.

Other Charming Florida Towns

Cabbage Key/Useppa Island
Micanopy
Mt. Dora
Seaside
Starke
St. Augustine

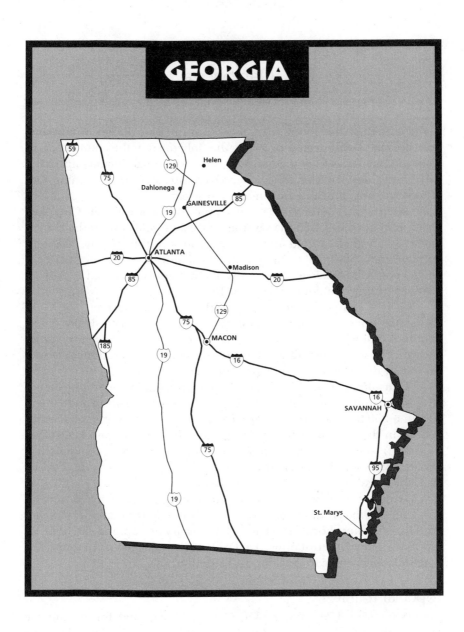

GEORGIA

Dahlonega
Population 3, 086

Nestled in the foothills of the beautiful **Blue Ridge Mountains**, picturesque **Dahlonega** is probably the only town in the country where you can pan for gold in the morning, shop for Appalachian crafts in the afternoon, dine on fried chicken served country-style in the evening, and canoe the next morning on a mountain stream.

Twenty years before gold was discovered in California, the Cherokee Nation in northern Georgia saw the first major gold rush in the United States. The smell of gold attracted thousands to the area in 1828, and prospectors continued coming for the next 20 years. Dahlonega (accent on second syllable) did well: Over $6 million in gold was coined by the U.S. Branch Mint in Dahlonega between 1838 and 1861.

Gold is still very much a part of the Dahlonega scene. The **Gold Museum**, once the **Lumpkin County Courthouse** (1836), is the oldest public building in north Georgia (it is also one of the state's most visited historic sites.) Here are displayed gold coins minted at Dahlonega as well as locally discovered gold nuggets, one over 5 ounces.

Consolidated Gold Mines, the largest gold mining operation east of the Mississippi (closed in the 1930s), offers tours which include a trip down a 250-foot hole (called *the Glory Hole*). Here and at several other places in the area visitors preferring the do-it-yourself (and keep-what-you-find) route are welcome to pan for gold. Prospecting equipment is available in shops in town and at the panning sites. Trying to "find color" is Dahlonega's most popular visitor pastime.

Around the square and on the surrounding streets are dozens of charming 19th-century houses and shops listed on the National Register of Historic Sites. Local crafts and gold jewelry are among the items of special regional interest offered in Dahlonega's many colorful shops. See the welcome center for walking and auto tours.

Special Features

What with 47% of Lumpkin County in national forest, and the **Appalachian Trail** and the **Desoto Falls Scenic Area** just a few miles away, hiking, camping, fishing, and canoeing opportunities abound.

> • *The Smith House (1884) is a 70-year-old restaurant, an old-fashioned mountain inn (see listings below), and beloved town landmark.*
> • *A prospecting party from nearby Auraria founded the first settlement at the present site of Denver, Colorado and named it after their hometown (Aurora is now a major Denver suburb).*

Where to Stay

CAVENDER CASTLE B&B, *Rt. 5 (Box 809)*, *(706) 864-4759*. 1989 Gothic-inspired castle, private baths, full candlelight breakfasts, dinner by appt., winery, mountain views. $$$

MOUNTAIN TOP LODGE, *447 Mountain Top Lodge Rd.*, *(800) 526-9754*. Cedar bldg. in secluded mountain location, large common area, antiques, some fireplaces, private baths, some whirlpools, full breakfasts, refreshments, guest kitchen, game loft, large decks, outdoor spa with view. $$$

ROYAL GUARD INN B&B, *203 S. Park St.*, *(706) 864-1713*. Close to square, private baths, "gourmet" breakfasts on china & silver, wine & cheese. $$

THE SMITH HOUSE, *202 S. Chestatee St.*, *(800) 852-9577*. 1884 home converted to inn in 1920s, full-service, Cont. breakfasts, wide verandahs, on vein of Dahlonega gold. $ to $$

WORLEY HOMESTEAD INN, *410 W. Main St.*, *(706) 864-7002*. Circa 1845/1872 home, antiques, "country" breakfasts. $$

Where to Eat

CARUSO'S/CURLY'S, *113 E. Main St.*, *(706) 864-4664*. Italian menu, Shrimp Scampi, pizza, nightly specials. $

RENEE'S CAFE & WINE BAR, *135 N. Chestatee St.*, *(706) 864-6829*. Greek Shrimp, Eggplant Parmesan, Spinach Mushroom Lasagna, Cajun Pasta, Crawfish Tails, Gourmet Individual Pizza; in 1870s home, fireplaces, wine bar. $$

THE SMITH HOUSE, *(see above)*. Fried chicken, sweet baked ham, beef stew, dumplings, angel biscuits, fried okra, candied yams; family-style service. $ to $$

Further Information

Dahlonega-Lumpkin County Chamber of Commerce, *13 South Park St., Dahlonega, GA 30533 (706) 864-3711.*

Directions

From Atlanta, US 19/GA 400N north to Dahlonega.

Helen

Population 300

The *Alpine Village of Helen* is a picture-book Bavarian village nestled among the mountains, forests, lakes, and waterfalls of northeast Georgia. Viewed from afar, the village is a cluster of old-world towers, rust-colored roofs, and gabled Bavarian facades.

Closer up, the place becomes a colorful mosaic of cobblestone alleys, balconies, outdoor cafes, and cascading flower baskets. Some of the townspeople dress in Bavarian attire. The little Georgia town obviously has a story to tell.

Helen's story has a much larger Cinderella component than do the stories of most towns. Originally a gold-mining town (part of Georgia's "Great Gold Rush"), then until the 1920s a sawmill town, Helen entered the post-war era without much of a future. In the late 1960s several local businessmen decided that the bleak little place could stand some improvement. They turned to John Kollock, a local artist, and within a week were presented with a set of water-color sketches of an Alpine Helen. Liking what they saw, a decision was made to proceed.

The transformation quickly became a community affair. Business people renovated their shops, the city put up quaint street lights and planters, and the townsfolk planted trees and flowers. New businesses put up new buildings. Power lines went underground. The work is still in progress.

More than 200 specialty and import shops now line Helen's streets and alleys. There is also a delightful collection of pubs and lodgings. The restaurant menus are about as loyal to their German and Austrian counterparts as menus on this side of the Atlantic are likely to get. For those not wishing to tour the town on foot, there are horse-drawn buggies and a village trolley.

Because the **Chattahoochee River** runs right through town, Helen is able to provide a morning of shopping to one part of the family while offering tubing, canoeing, gold mining, or trout fishing to another. Golfing is also an option. Hiking, backpacking, and horseback riding are just a few of the other activities pursued in the area. The **Appalachian Trail** passes north of town.

Special Features

Unicoi State Park, just north of Helen, provides a scenic setting for canoeing and fishing, and also has public beaches and a dining room.

Beginning just outside of town, the **Richard B. Russell Scenic Highway** (GA 348) winds through a particularly beautiful section of Georgia's **Blue Ridge Mountains**.

> • *Helen's 6-to-8-week Oktoberfest attracts as many as 150, 000 visitors.*
> • *Artist John Kollock's Alpine images were inspired by a stay in Bavaria with the army.*

Where to Stay

DUTCH COTTAGE B&B, *P.O. Box 757, Ridge Rd., (706) 878-3135*. "A Dutch setting with Southern hospitality," antiques, TV, private baths, "gourmet" breakfasts, front porch, overlooking waterfall, shuttle service to town. $$

EDELWEISS COUNTRY INN & RESTAURANT, *351 Duncan Bridge Rd. (Sautee 30571), (706) 865-7371*. Full-service German-style inn, breakfasts, great room with balcony, restaurant, volleyball court, nature trail, mountain views. $$

NACOOCHEE VALLEY GUEST HOUSE, *P.O. Box 249 (Sautee 30571), (706) 878-3830*. 1920s English cottage overlooking historic Nacoochee Valley, fireplaces, private baths, full breakfasts, dining room, large deck. $$

ROYAL WINDSOR COTTAGE, *4490 Hwy. 356 (Sautee 30571), (706) 878-1322*. English B&B on 20 acres of secluded woodland, private baths, private decks with mountain views, full English breakfasts. $$$

THE STOVALL HOUSE COUNTRY INN, *Rt. 1 (Box 1476) (Sautee 30571), (706) 878-3355*. Circa 1837 home on National Register, family antiques, private baths, restaurant. $$$

Where to Eat

ALT HEIDELBERG, *White Horse Sq., (706) 878-2986*. Georgia Mountain Trout, Chicken a la Mozart, Sauerbraten, Wiener Kalbs Schnitzel, Baurenwurst. $ to $$

HOFBRAUHAUS INN, *1 Main St., (706) 878-2248*. Extensive Bavarian-French-Italian-seafood menu, three dining rooms. $ to $$

NACOOCHEE VALLEY GUEST HOUSE, *(see above).* Shrimp Scampi, Chicken Picatta, Spaghetti Carbonara, Beef Wellington, napoleons & tarts; reservations a must. $ to $$

THE STOVALL HOUSE COUNTRY INN & RESTAURANT, *(see above).* Fresh Mountain Trout, Stuffed Chicken the house specialty, pastas, phyllo, daily specials. $ to $$

Further Information

Alpine Helen/White County Convention & Visitors Bureau, *P.O. Box 730, Helen, GA 30545 (706) 878-2181.*

Directions

From Atlanta, I 85 northeast to exit 45, I 985 / GA 365 north to GA 384, GA 384 to GA 75, GA 75 north to Helen.

Madison
Population 3483

Gone with the Wind was a work of fiction, but a Grand Old South did in fact exist in Georgia, at least for a fortunate few. General Sherman's march to the sea was not a work of fiction, but a few scenes from Georgia's Old South did survive the devastation. **Madison** was one of them. The town's National Historic District is an image from another era. Parts of it are virtually the same today as they were on the eve of the Civil War. Maybe they're even prettier.

The town lay smack in the middle of Sherman's path, and yet survived. It seems that as the Yankees advanced, a delegation of men led by Senator Joshua Hill pleaded with the general to spare the town. Sherman obliged – although the railroad station and some surrounding plantations were kindled – and the town was subsequently known as "the town Sherman refused to burn."

The welcome center, housed in the 1887 city hall and fire station, provides a brochure for a walking tour of the historic district. Among the over 40 structures on the tour are four whose doors are regularly open to the public: The oldest is the **Rogers House** (circa 1809-1810), which has been carefully restored to what it probably looked like in 1873. The house, a fine example of the Piedmont-Plain style of architecture, has mid-19th-century furnishings. The stately Greek Revival **Heritage Hall** (circa 1825) is currently the home of the **Morgan County Historical Society**. Built by a doctor who served with the Confederacy, the house is distinguished by its window etchings and ghost bedroom.

The **Madison-Morgan Cultural Center**, a restored 1895 Romanesque Revival school building, boasts a history museum, art galleries, original classroom, and antique auditorium. The **African-American Museum**, the fourth historic building open to the public, is housed in the recently restored **Horace Moore House** (circa 1895). The museum displays paintings, other works of art, and memorabilia honoring the area's Black heritage.

Many of the houses are shown during tours in April, May, October, and December. Private tours of some may also be arranged during other months. Whether or not their doors are open, the unusually well-restored and maintained homes in the historic district merit a walk- or drive-by.

Three antebellum churches also merit a visit: The **Advent Episcopal Church** (circa 1842) with its wrought-iron chandeliers and slave gallery, now used for the organ and choir; the **Madison Baptist Church** (1858), built by bricks hand-made by slaves on a local plantation; and the "Old English"-style **Presbyterian Church** (1842), noted for its Tiffany stained windows and a silver communion service, still in use, that was stolen during the Civil War and later returned by Federal orders. The churches are usually open daily.

Madison's preserved downtown is the kind designed to delight antique hunters, casual shoppers, and just plain lovers of charm. There are brick sidewalks, two old-fashioned soda fountains, and interesting shops. One of the largest antique stores is located in a restored 1880s hotel building.

> *• Madison was once described as the "wealthiest and most aristo-cratic town" on the stagecoach route between Charleston and New Orleans.*
>
> *• With 19, 000 acres, Lake Oconee, east of town, is the largest power-company lake in Georgia. The lake's shores and waters offer numerous golfing and fishing opportunities.*

Where to Stay

THE BRADY INN, *250 N. Second St., (706) 342-4400.* Victorian cottage with period antiques, private baths, full breakfasts, dinners available. $$$

BURNETT PLACE, *317 Old Post Rd., (706) 342-4034.* 1830 Federal-style home, period furnishings, private baths, full breakfasts. $$$

THE FARMHOUSE INN, *1051 Meadow Ln., (706) 342-7933.* Turn-of-century farmhouse overlooking 75 acres of pasture, antiques & quilts,

134 AMERICA'S MOST CHARMING TOWNS & VILLAGES

private baths, full breakfasts, hand-hewn log barn, river trail, fishing ponds. $$$

Where to Eat

AMICI ITALIAN CAFE, *113 W. Main St., (706) 342-0000*. A touch of Italy in historic downtown. $

MADISON CHOP HOUSE GRILLE, *202 S. Main St., (706) 342-0910*. Blackened Chicken Broccoli Alfredo, Fried Combo Platter, steaks, & Vegetable Platter among house specialties; salads, sandwiches, beers & wines. $

HUG'S, *2230 Eatonton Hwy. (US 441 S.), (706) 342-9730*. Italian-style cooking in Southern-home atmosphere. $

YE OLDE COLONIAL RESTAURANT, *108 E. Washington St., (706) 342-2211*. Southern cooking served cafeteria-style in old bank building. $

Further Information

Madison-Morgan Welcome Center, *P.O. Box 826, Madison, GA 30650 (706) 342-4454/fax (706) 342-4455*.

Directions

From Atlanta, I 20 east to exit 51, north on US 441.

St. Marys

Population 8, 187

With lovely antebellum buildings, gentle breezes off the sea, and wide avenues shaded by ancient live oaks, **St. Marys** is a town of many memories and moods. As the gateway to **Cumberland Island National Seashore** (see below) and neighbor to a naval base, St. Marys has a present and future as well as a past. But it is quiet here, and very beautiful.

Turbulent is perhaps the best term to describe St. Marys's past. Settled in 1787, the town has known smuggling, a slave trade, the scourge of yellow fever, periods of economic depression, and ravaging by the British in the War of 1812 and the Yankees in the Civil War. But there have also been times of peace and – thanks to shipping, timber, shrimping and, more recently, a paper mill and submarine base – periods of prosperity.

A 20-block area in the older section of town has been placed on the National Register of Historic Places. The streets in this district are the same as on the original 1788 town map and bear the names of the town's founders.

Orange Hall, St. Marys's venerable landmark, is a circa 1830 Greek Revival Mansion built by the town's first Presbyterian minister. The house is listed on the National Register and now serves as a welcome center for the tourism council (open daily).

Among the historic district's antebellum buildings are several churches with interesting credentials. The **First Presbyterian Church** (1808) is the oldest Presbyterian church in continuous use in Georgia. **St. Marys Methodist Church** (1858), organized in 1799, is the Mother Church of Methodism in Florida (which begins just across the St. Marys River). And the **Old Catholic Church** is housed in the oldest masonry bank building still standing in Georgia (1837).

The **Toonerville Trolley** is probably the district's most unique possession. A passenger rail car on the St. Marys Railroad from 1928 until 1938, the trolley was made famous in the nationally syndicated comic strip *Wash Tubbs and Easy* in 1935. It is still operated on special occasions.

Soldiers of every American war, yellow fever victims, Acadians, and others are buried in **Oak Grove Cemetery**. The oldest marked gravesites are dated 1801.

Surrounded by water, St. Marys is an ideal spot for photographers, hikers, bikers, birders, fishermen, and boaters. A good place to see the flora and fauna is on a nature trail at **Crooked River State Park**. Visitors are welcome on the greens of nearby **Osprey Cove Golf Course**.

Special Features

Boats depart daily from St. Marys for **Cumberland Island National Seashore**, located on the southernmost of Georgia's sea islands. Here there are 16 miles of undisturbed white-sand beach bordered by dunes that rise as high as 40 feet. Herds of horses graze openly on the island, and loggerhead turtles come ashore to lay their eggs. No vehicles are available, so walking and swimming (no lifeguards) are the only ways of moving about.

On some Sundays the boat to Cumberland Island puts in at **Plum Orchard Dock**. Plum Orchard is a magnificent thirty-room mansion constructed by Lucy Carnegie for her son and his wife in 1898. The building is currently undergoing restoration.

• *The Washington Pump, still around, was the only source of fresh water during the tidal wave of 1880.*
• *Many sites in the historic district are marked in Braille for sight-impaired visitors.*

Where to Stay

GOODBREAD HOUSE B&B, *209 Osborne St., (912) 882-7490.* 1870 home on National Register, antiques, TV & phones, fireplaces, private baths, full breakfasts, wine & cheese, verandah. $$

THE HISTORIC SPENCER HOUSE INN, *101 E. Bryant St., (912) 882-1872.* Renovated 1872 hotel, original moldings/floors, private baths, full breakfasts, three verandahs. $$ to $$$

RIVERVIEW HOTEL, *105 Osborne St., (912) 882-3242.* Full-service 1916 hotel on banks of river, dining room, verandah with rocking chairs. $ to $$

Where to Eat

SEAGLE'S RESTAURANT, *in Riverview Hotel (see above).* Fresh seafood, Rock Shrimp, steaks, acclaimed desserts; picnic lunches with basket & checkered tablecloth. $

Further Information

St. Marys Tourism Council, *P.O. Box 1291, St. Marys, GA 31558 (912) 882-4000.*

Directions

From Jacksonville (FL), I 95 north to exit 2, GA 40 east to St. Marys.

Other Charming Georgia Towns

Hiawasee
Newnan
Pine Mt./Warm Springs
St. Simons Island
Washington

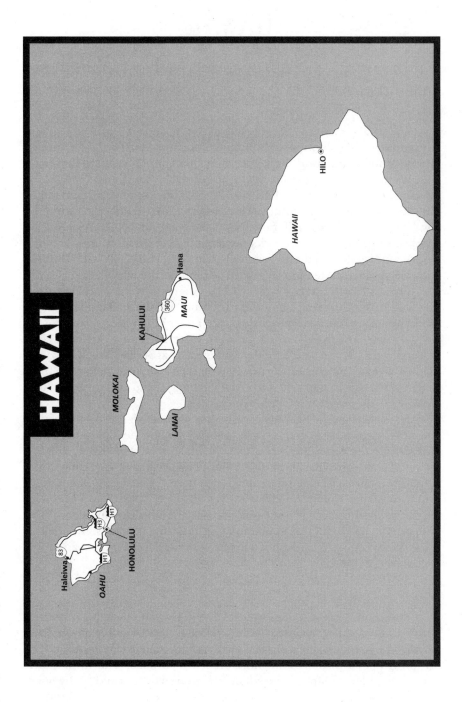

HAWAII

Haleiwa, Oahu

Population 2, 442

Haleiwa's brand of charm is one of the most delightfully unusual in the country. The old wooden buildings along the main road, or **Kam** (for **Kamehameha**) **Highway**, look very much like those you might find in an old Western town. Yet many of the shops sell clothing and supplies for distinctly non-Old-West surfers, snorkelers, and other ocean sports fans. In the restaurants, surf enthusiasts mingle with art enthusiasts attracted by Haleiwa's first-rate galleries. Down the road lies a picturesque little harbor offering charters for deep-sea fishing, snorkel excursions (summer), and whale-watch sails (winter). And then come miles of coastline boasting some of the most beautiful beaches in the world!

Oahu's **North Shore**, on which Haleiwa rests, is the world's surfing capital. Most of the year the waters are quiet, ideal for all kinds of water activities. But from November through January the waters become very active (and dangerous)—and a paradise for professional surfers. As an example, the average height of the winter waves at **Sunset Beach** is 15 feet. Monster waves measuring 35 and 40 feet are not unknown. Surfers from around the world come to meet the challenge, and surfing spectators follow for the excitement and beauty.

Haleiwa (hah lay EE vah) is of course also active during the winter months, in concert with the swells and those who ride and watch them. But during the rest of the year the town, like the water, is quiet. This is a part of Oahu that is still largely rural. The area is in fact called "the country." There are still pineapple fields here. Proud of its plantation/rural heritage, Haleiwa actively strives to preserve it. The facades of historic wood buildings are protected, and the historic appearance of Kamehameha Highway is maintained by imposing strict design codes on new construction. The result is a lovely little rural town on Hawaii's most urbanized island.

Special Features

Down the coast just a few miles is one of Hawaii's most beautiful and historic properties, **Waimea Valley**, home of 1,800-acre **Waimea Falls Park**. The park is home to native birds and animals and to thousands of tropical plants displayed in more than 30 gardens. The lush, exotic grounds and the 45-foot waterfall may be toured by foot and/or by open-air tram. Among the park's many attractions are cliff divers, demonstrations of traditional Hawaiian games, and performances by a resident hula troupe.

A garden featuring a variety of pineapple plants is open to the public at the **Dole Plantation** near **Wahiawa**.

> *Parks and Recreation personnel at the Surf Center at Haleiwa Alii Beach Park offer information on North Shore beaches, free use of ocean-sport gear, and free surfing and windsurfing lessons.*

Where to Stay

BACKPACKERS, *59-788 Kamehameha Hwy., (808) 638-7838/fax (808) 638-7515.* Hostel, Vacation Inn (studio apartments), & restored plantation cabins; cooking facilities, nightly meals, on beach, snorkeling gear & boogie boards, scuba diving, surfing, kayaking, hiking trips, airport pickups. $ to $$$

For information on bed and breakfast accommodations in Hawaii, contact: **Bed & Breakfast Honolulu** (statewide), *3242 Kaohinani Dr., Honolulu, HI 96817, (808) 595-7533/(800) 288-4666 from U.S. Mainland/ fax (808) 595-2030.*

Where to Eat

JAMESON'S BY THE SEA, *62-540 Kam. Hwy., (808) 637-4336.* Opakapaka (Hawaiian pink snapper), Ahi (yellow fin tuna), Mahi Mahi, Stir-fried Shrimp & Scallops with Fresh Vegetables, New York Steak; sunset dining upstairs, open-air pub lanai down. $$ to $$$

Further Information

North Shore News, *P. O. Box 1117, Haleiwa, Oahu, HI 96712 (808) 637-3138.*

Directions

From Honolulu, I H1 west to HI 99, HI 99 north to HI 83, HI 83 north to Haleiwa.

Hana, Maui

Population about 1, 200

Once a bustling sugar town, historic **Hana** is today a country-quiet village famed for its untouched natural beauty and relaxed lifestyle. Far from the intense development elsewhere on Maui, this is a peaceful tropical paradise, the enchanting Hawaii of picture postcard and movie. This is the Hawaii where swimmers may choose between a tropical pool or one of several ocean beaches – a black one, a red one, and a silver one.

Consistent with its gorgeous setting, Hana has little commercial development. And what little there is can be interesting. For example, the bank has a sign announcing that the doors are open from 3:00 to 4:30 p.m. daily, except on Fridays, when closing time is extended to 6:00. And **Hasegawa's General Store**, in business since 1910, stocks horseshoe nails, barbed wire, and bolo knives side by side with potato chips and pickled turnips.

One of the most interesting of Hana's historic structures is the **Wananalua Church** (circa 1840), built of lava rock. The area is rich with archaeological remnants from the early Hawaiian culture; most are unmarked, however, so inquire locally for information.

Driving to Hana is itself an eye-dazzling adventure. The narrow coastal road (HI 360) twists along cliffs, over streams and waterfalls, and through lush tropical foliage. People who have counted them report that the road has over 600 curves and 55 or so one-lane bridges. Allow about 3 hours each way.

Most visitors to Hana stay in towns like **Wailea** and **Kapalua** and take tour vans or rental cars out to Hana and back the same day. The area may also be reached by two commuter airlines, **Island Air** and **Air Molokai**.

Note: I wish to thank Carl Lindquist, long-time Hana resident and author of *On the Hana Coast*, for his contributions to this piece. (*On the Hana Coast* may be obtained by writing P. O. Box 507, Hana, Hawaii 96713.)

Special Features

Eleven miles down the coast from Hana is **Ohe'o Gulch**, renowned for its series of lovely stream-carved pools and tropical rain forest setting. Trails lead to several waterfalls. The gulch is a section of **Haleakala National Park**.

Cabins and camping are available at nearby **Waianapanapa State Park**. The park features a cave and scenic hiking trails along the shore.

> *One of the most popular tourist items in Hana is a tee shirt proclaiming that its wearer has "Survived the Road to Hana."*

Where to Stay

HOTEL HANA-MAUI, *Hana, Maui, (808) 248-8211/(800) 321-4262/ fax (808) 248-7202.* Small full-service hotel & cottages on old sugar plantation, Hawaiian art & antiques, fruit baskets, gardens & grounds, pool, wellness center, Jeep excursions, horseback riding, "Hawaii the way it used to be." $$$

Where to Eat

MAIN DINING ROOM, *Hotel Hana-Maui (see above).* Fresh Catch of the Evening from Hana Bay (choice of preparation), Braised Island Half Chicken in Pineapple Wine on White Beans a la Romana, Roast Prime Rib of Beef. $$$

Further Information

Maui Visitors Bureau, *1727 Wili Pa Loop, P.O. Box 580, Wailuku, HI 96793 (808) 244-3530. (ZIP for Hana is 96713.)*

Directions

From Kahului, HI 360 east to Hana.

Other Charming Hawaiian Towns

Hanalei, Kauai
Kailua Kona, Hawaii
Kilauea, Kauai
Lahaina, Maui

142

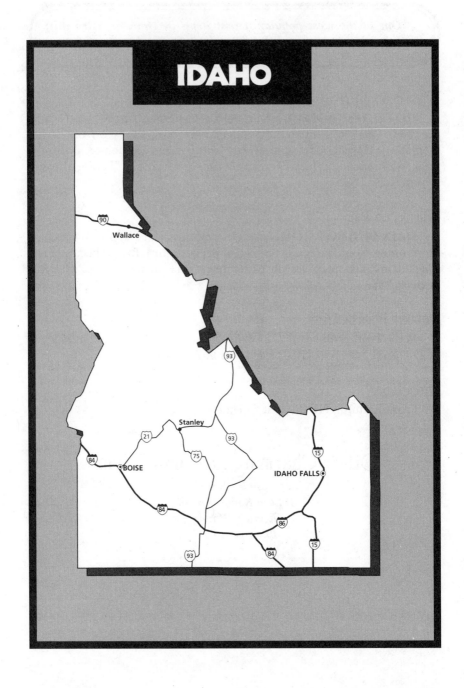

IDAHO

Stanley

Population 71

Only 71 souls and sundry aspens, pines, and firs live along **Stanley's** few streets. The streets are gravel, even the main street, and there are no sidewalks. Many of the homes are old cabins. Yet the town, elevation 6,260 feet, is surrounded by some of the most glorious scenery on the continent.

Situated on the Salmon River in the northern part of the spectacular **Sawtooth National Recreation Area**, Stanley is nestled among pristine mountain ranges, dense forests, and over 1,100 lakes. Three **National Forest Scenic Byways** – the **Sawtooth**, the **Ponderosa Pine**, and the **Salmon River** – converge on the town. Stanley was obviously designed for the nature lover, the outdoor sportsperson, the photographer, and the artist.

The **Stanley Museum** displays artifacts and photographs from the early days of the Sawtooth Valley and the Stanley Basin. The **Custer Museum**, 30 minutes north of town, features a ghost town and mining-history museum. Interesting old tombstones can be found in **Boot Hill Cemetery**, near the museum.

Virtually every land sport – and many of the water ones, too – known to the Western world can be pursued in these parts. Outfitters and guides abound. For snowmobilers there is the groomed *Highway to Heaven* trail from Boise or Lowman to Stanley. For hut skiers there are stationary circular tents with bunks, cooking equipment, and wood stoves. For wilderness floaters there is the **Middle Fork** of the beautiful **Salmon River** (three- to six-day trips by raft, oar boat, and paddle boat can be arranged in Stanley).

And for people in a hurry there are scenic air tours.

Special Feature

The **Sawtooth National Recreation** area is an eye-dazzling wilderness tamed only by the occasional guest ranch, resort, and horse trail. This is the kind of country that deserves to be seen from the back of a horse, and outfitters and guides are available to help you do just that.

Stanley really consists of two towns, incorporated upper Stanley and unincorporated lower Stanley. The two are about one mile apart and have different histories.

Where to Stay

IDAHO ROCKY MOUNTAIN RANCH, *HC 64 (Box 9934), (208) 774-3544*. 1930 handcrafted pine lodge & cabins, log furniture, rock fireplaces, private baths, dining room, natural hot water pool, horses, trails, spectacular views. $$$

SALMON RIVER LODGE, *Box 272, (208) 774-3422*. Rustic log lodge on river with panoramic view of Sawtooth Mts, private baths, quiet, fishing adjacent. $ to $$

SAWTOOTH HOTEL, *P.O. Box 52, Main St., (208) 774-9947*. Rustic 1931 log hotel, quilts, handmade lodgepole beds, restaurant, fishing guides. $$

Where to Eat

IDAHO ROCKY MOUNTAIN RANCH, *(see above)*. Idaho Ruby Rainbow Trout, steaks, pasta, creative chef specials, homemade breads & desserts, weekly Western Barbecue; reservations. $ to $$

SAWTOOTH HOTEL, *(see above)*. Homemade soup, bread, & cobbler; "world-famous" sourdough pancakes, popular for breakfast. $

STANLEY KASINO CLUB, *Main St., (208) 774-3516*. Roasted Prime Rib of Beef the house specialty, Clam Linguini, Kasino Chicken Bearnaise, Drunken Pork Chop, Salmon; cocktails, daily fresh sheet in summer. $$

Further Information

Stanley-Sawtooth Chamber of Commerce, *P.O. Box 8, Stanley, ID 83278 (208) 774-3411/(800) 878-7950*.

Directions

From Boise, ID 21 east and north to Stanley; from Twin Falls, ID 75 north to Stanley.

Wallace

Population 1010

Many of the descendants of late 19th-century mining towns are today among the West's most charming places. And so it is with **Wallace**, now listed on the National Historic Register and featuring turn-of-the-century buildings, unique shops, art galleries, museums, a new visitor center and park, even a melodrama.

Wallace's history is nicely wrapped up in its nickname, *The Silver Capital of the World*. At the turn of the century Wallace was the center of action in the **Silver Valley**, a scenic valley that happens (even to this day) to be one of the richest mining districts on the planet. As might be expected, most of Wallace's top attractions relate in one way or another to silver.

The displays and exhibits of the **Wallace District Mining Museum** portray without glamour life as it was in the old mines and mining camps. A 20-minute video presentation discusses the history and technology of mining. Included in the exhibits are old photographs, a collection of paintings by James R. Buckham (born and raised in Wallace), and the world's largest "silver" dollar, weighing in at 150 pounds.

The bricks used to build the **Northern Pacific Depot**, now a railroad museum, served as ballast in sailing ships coming over from China. The restored building houses photographs and artifacts from the mining district's early days.

The escorted tour of the **Sierra Silver Mine** proceeds through an underground tunnel that stretches for five blocks. Along the way is a 149-foot shaft now filled with water. A guide explains and demonstrates mining procedures, equipment, and safety precautions. A trolley carries visitors to and from the mine's entrance.

The **Oasis Bordello Museum** gives visitors a look at the bawdier side of old Wild West mining communities.

Some of Wallace's attractions are seasonal, but many are not. Skiers, snowmobilers, and other off-season visitors will discover that Wallace's charm can be enjoyed year-round.

Special Feature

The Wallace CoC distributes instructions for a scenic and historical loop that includes a "living ghost town," gold rush camps, ancient towering cedars, and the spot where Wyatt Earp owned and operated a saloon.

> • *Wallace was established in 1884 by prospector William R. Wallace, cousin to novelist, general, and statesman Lew Wallace.*
> • *Idahoans are proud to boast that the Silver Valley is the only place in the world that has produced a "billion" ounces of silver in less than a century.*

Where to Stay

21 BANK STREET, *21 Bank St., (888) 846-5051/(208) 752-1292.* 1916 home of former mayor, home-cooked breakfasts, afternoon snacks/wine, large front porch with wicker. $$

BEALE HOUSE B&B, *107 Cedar St., (208) 752-7151.* 1904 Colonial Revival home on National Register, original parquet floors, antiques, fireplaces, some private baths, full breakfasts, beverages, porch, spa, gardens, old photograph collection, scenic views. $$ to $$$

JAMESON B&B, *304 6th St., (208) 556-1554.* In restored turn-of-century hotel, period furnishings & decor, restaurant, seasonal. $$

THE McKINLEY INN, *210 McKinley Ave. (Kellogg 83837), (800) 443-3505.* Restored early 1900s hotel with "lively" history, each room with decor from different era, private baths. $$

Where to Eat

ALBI'S STEAKHOUSE, *6th St., (208) 556-1571.* Steak & seafood the specialties. $

BROOKS HOTEL & RESTAURANT, *500 Cedar St., (208) 556-1571.* Traditional cooking, "Best coffee in town!" $

JAMESON RESTAURANT & SALOON, *(see above).* American cooking served in restored 1900 dining room, saloon with mirrored back bar. $$

SILVER CORNER, *6th & Cedar, (208) 753-4261.* Tiny cafe offering daily lunch specials. $

SWEET'S CAFE & LOUNGE, *310 Sixth St., (208) 556-4661.* Traditional American menu, wide range of sandwiches, historic photo display. $

Further Information

West Wallace Visitor Center & Wallace Chamber of Commerce, *P.O. Box 1167, #10 River St., Wallace, ID 83873 (208) 753-7151.*

Directions

From Spokane (Washington), I 90 east to exits 61 and 62 (Wallace exits).

Other Charming Idaho Towns

Lava Hot Springs
McCall
Sandpoint

ILLINOIS

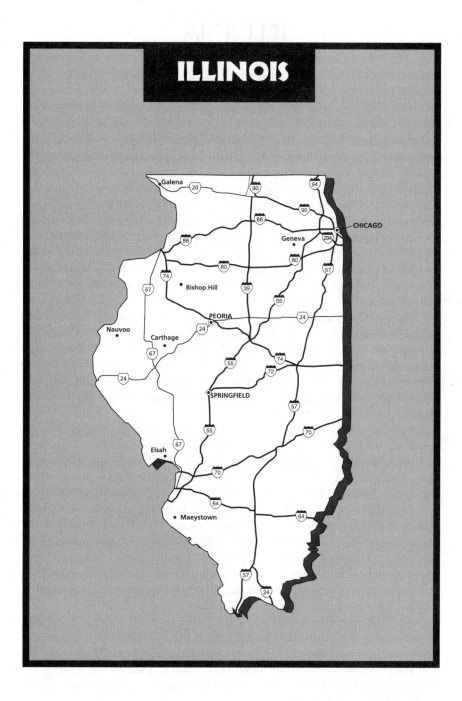

ILLINOIS

Bishop Hill

Population 135

Communal societies founded by groups of Europeans seeking religious freedom once dotted the fertile Midwestern countryside. The history of their settlement in America usually began with a year or so of hardship, continued with several years of prosperity, and then, for various reasons, ended in a period of abandonment and decay. In many cases the settlements' remnants were "discovered" a century later, a preservation society formed, and restoration begun. One of their legacies today is a group of unusually quaint towns and villages sprinkled across the rich American prairie. No fewer than five of them appear in this book: New Harmony, Ind.; the Amana Colonies in Iowa; Pleasant Hill, Ky.; Zoar Village, Ohio; and **Bishop Hill**, Ill.

Bishop Hill, called "Utopia on the Prairie," began in 1846 with a group of Swedish religious dissidents. After spending their first months hungry and living in dugouts, the colonists entered an era of amazing commercial and agricultural activity, and then, following the usual pattern, disbanded (in 1861)–in this case because of charges of financial mismanagement, internal dissension, and events associated with the Civil War.

Following a period of semiconsciousness, interest in preserving, restoring, and rebuilding the colony's buildings prompted the formation in 1962 of the Bishop Hill Heritage Association. Still undergoing restoration, Bishop Hill is today a quaint little town out on the Illinois prairie with status as a National Historic Landmark and State Historic Site.

The Illinois Historic Preservation Agency maintains three of the village buildings–the Colony Church, Colony Hotel, and Bishop Hill Museum–as well as the lovely village park (1853). The basement and first floor of the **Colony Church** (1848; open to public), the settlement's first permanent building, were used as living quarters. The sanctuary, on the second floor, is noteworthy for its simplicity and handmade black walnut pews. The women's and men's pews are separated by a divider.

The restored **Colony Hotel** (1852; open to public) sports a square cupola and a third-floor ballroom. Named the Bjorklund Hotel after its second proprietor, the establishment was once communally owned.

Paintings by folk artist and early resident Olof Krans are on display in the **Bishop Hill Museum**. These as well as other exhibits give a glimpse of the Bishop Hill Colony.

In addition to the Colony Church and Colony Hotel, 10 or so of the colony's original buildings still stand. Of special note is the **Steeple Building** (1854), which houses the exhibits of the **Bishop Hill Heritage Museum** (open to public).

Scattered about the village are a number of interesting shops stocked with antiques, collectibles, and gifts; as might be expected, many of the items are handcrafted and/or of Swedish import. The village also features craft demonstrations and an especially rich calendar of events (check with the heritage association–see below).

Special Features

The **Jenny Lind Chapel** is located in nearby **Andover**. The little Greek Revival chapel was endowed by the famous opera star.

A farm museum (tours available) is housed on the main floor of **Ryan's Round Barn** (1910), a beautifully preserved structure in **Johnson Sauk Trail State Park** a few miles east of Bishop Hill.

> *Many of the colony's first settlers walked the 160 miles from Chicago to Bishop Hill.*

Where to Stay

THE BISHOP HILL COLONY HOSPITAL B&B, *110 N. Olson St., P.O. Box 97, (309) 927-3506.* Ca 1855 Greek Revival colony building, period decorations, some private baths, full kitchen access, back porches for sunset views, mountain bikes. $ to $$

Where to Eat

P. L. JOHNSON'S DINING ROOM, *(309) 927-3885.* Lunches, Swedish meatballs, daily specials, sandwiches, soups, desserts; antique tables. $

THE RED OAK, *(309) 927-3539.* Lunches, Scandinavian open-faced sandwiches on home-baked rye bread, hot entrees (e.g., Swedish meatballs), soups, salads, homemade desserts; garden courtyard, authentic Swedish-style decoration. $

Further Information

Bishop Hill Heritage Association, *P.O. Box 92, 103 N. Bishop Hill St., Bishop Hill, IL 61419-0092 (309) 927-3345.*

Directions

From Peoria, I 74 north to US 34 (at Galesburg), north to CR 39 (west of Galva), north to Bishop Hill; from Chicago, I 55 south to I 80, west to exit 45 and (2 mi south) US 34, west & south on US 34 to CR 39, north to Bishop Hill.

Carthage

Population 2, 657

Settled in 1833, **Carthage** is a pretty little Midwestern town with an old courthouse on a square, a bustling downtown around the square, and tree-lined streets with homes representing over a century of architectural styles. The courthouse and 19th-century commercial buildings about the square have been designated an historic district. There are no discount stores or malls on Carthage's outskirts, so the downtown looks very much like the downtown of a traditional county seat.

The two-story limestone **Old Carthage Jail** is the site of the mob murder of Mormon prophet Joseph Smith and his brother Hyrum in 1844. Now a museum and visitor center, the jail has become a kind of Mormon shrine; thousands of people of the Mormon Church visit the site every year (although non-Mormons are by all means welcome).

The **Hancock County Court House** (1908), an unusually beautiful stone structure, is a favorite subject of photographers and painters. Inside is a large genealogical card index and collection of local artifacts.

Carthage is home to an interesting history and natural history museum, the **Alice Kibbe Museum**. The museum features collections of Native American, Mormon, Civil War, and late 19th century artifacts.

Special Features

Kids will enjoy the **World of Wonders Playground** (known locally as "WOW Park"), a 10,000-square-foot wooden playground with slides, mazes, even dragons and a pirate ship.

Several charming old two-story farmhouses can be spotted in the countryside around Carthage. Many of the old farmhouses here and elsewhere in the Midwest have weathered away or been destroyed, but fortunately, some farm families have invested considerable time and money to preserve these "gems of the prairie."

The **Great River Road** along the Mississippi is a few miles west of town.

> *You'll see fields of corn and soybeans around Carthage, but very few farm animals – farmers say they can no longer afford the feed and other supplies needed to keep livestock.*

Where to Eat

PLUM TREE SUPPER CLUB & LOUNGE, *69 S. Adams St., (217) 357-3518.* Chicken, steaks, seafood, ribs, Mexican dishes, specials. $ to $$

Further Information

Carthage Chamber of Commerce, *P.O. Box 247, Carthage, IL 62321 (217) 357-3024.*

Directions

From Peoria, US 24 southwest to US 136, US 136 west to Carthage.

Elsah

Population 851

Once a steamboat stop on the Mississippi, unspoiled little **Elsah** is the kind of village where you go to pick apples and peaches, watch for bald eagles, or linger beside old flower gardens. It's the kind of place where the local restaurant packs picnic lunches for passing bicycles. It's an enchanting spot.

The first village in the country to be listed in its entirety on the National Register of Historic Places, Elsah seems to be charmingly stuck in the last century. Indeed, most of the old and (thanks to stringent codes) new buildings are of an architecture belonging to the 1850-1900 period.

Guarded by bluffs, Elsah offers splendid views of the **Mississippi River Valley**. The riverside beauty can be enjoyed by renting a bike and cycling along the water on the newly paved **Vadalabene Bike Trail**. Horseback and boat rides are also popular. The **Great River Road** (IL 100) from Elsah to Alton offers sweeping views of the river on one side and beautiful limestone cliffs on the other.

Special Features

The lovely campus of nearby **Principia College** is worth a special visit. The college has been placed on the National Register of Historic Places.

Pere Marquette Park, about five miles west of Elsah, is the largest state park in Illinois (8,000 acres). The park overlooks the Illinois River and boasts an especially beautiful 1930s stone lodge.

Elsah's charm spills over onto **Grafton**, about 4 miles upriver, and **Alton**, about 10 miles downriver. Both of these towns are noted for their old homes and fabulous antiquing.

> • *Part of Elsah, now rebuilt, was damaged by the Great Flood of 1993.*
> • *Missouri can be easily reached by the ferry from Grafton to Calhoun Point.*

Where to Stay

THE CORNER NEST B&B, *P.O. Box 220, (618) 374-1892/(800) 884-3832.* 1883 home bound by limestone bluffs, on National Register, antiques, TV, some private baths, full breakfasts, snacks/sodas, overlooking river. $$ to $$$

GREEN TREE INN, *15 Mill St., P.O. Box 96, (618) 374-2821/(800) 701-8003.* 1850s-style country inn, private baths, home-cooked breakfasts, bicycles-built-for-two. $$

MAPLE LEAF COTTAGE INN, *P.O. Box 156, (618) 374-1684.* "Innchanting" cottages with antiques, private baths, full breakfasts, English herb garden. $$

TARA POINT INN, *P.O. Box 640 (Grafton 62037), (618) 786-3555.* New inn with wraparound deck & commanding river views, snacks, game room & bar, pool table. $$$

WILDFLOWER INN B&B, *Mason Hollow Rd. (Grafton 62037), (618) 465-3719.* Saltbox in valley with spring-fed creek, private baths, full breakfasts, gift baskets, hiking trails. $$

Where to Eat

ELSAH LANDING RESTAURANT, *18 LaSalle St., (618) 374-1607.* 4 homemade soups daily, 8 homemade breads, famed desserts; everything from scratch, highly rated. $

Further Information

Greater Alton/Twin Rivers Convention & Visitors Bureau, *200 Piasa, Alton, IL 62002 (800) 258-6645.* (ZIP for Elsah is 62028.)

Directions

From St. Louis (MO), US 67 north (across Mississippi River) to IL 100, IL 100 north to Elsah.

Galena

Population 3, 647

Surrounded by some of the most beautiful rolling countryside in Illinois, **Galena** is a little town of historic mansions, handsome brick commercial buildings, and churches with hand-carved altars and pulpits. The lure of this delightful place can be underscored by noting that Chicago CEOs have chosen to retire here and that several members of the renowned Chicago Symphony have selected this as their second home.

With economic roots in lead mining, smelting, and riverboating, Galena was once the largest Mississippi River port between St. Louis and St. Paul. But the railroad was to replace the riverboat, and this and other developments eventually plunged the town into a depression that lasted from the 1890s until the 1960s. The many grand old buildings were neither modernized nor torn down simply because no one had enough to money to do so. Artists from Chicago began restoring the town in the 1960s and, joined by other groups, changed Galena from a sleepy, decaying river town to one of the most charming and sophisticated spots in Illinois, the Midwest, and the United States.

Galena and **Jo Daviess County** claim 34 antique shops (making this a principal Midwestern antiquing center), 48 bed and breakfasts, 12 galleries, 20 private studios, and 150 specialty shops. Ranking as one of the most popular destinations in the Midwest, visitors may find accommodations scarce on weekends. Reservations are advised—only November and March can be relied on as truly "dead" months.

Eighty-five percent of Galena is listed on the National Register. Architectural styles include Federal, Italianate, Greek Revival, Queen Anne, Romanesque Revival, and Gothic Revival. The number of historic sites and other points of interest is greater than for many large cities. A good starting point for a tour of the town is the **Galena/Jo Daviess County History Museum**. Housed in an 1858 Italianate mansion, the museum features paintings, toys and dolls, household items, clothing, and a Civil War exhibit that includes Thomas Nast's original painting, *Peace in Union.*

One of Galena's most famous sites is the **Ulysses S. Grant Home State Historic Site**, the 1860 Italianate home that was presented to Grant in

1865 on his return from the Civil War. The restored home contains original furnishings and personal items of the Grant family.

The **Old Market House State Historic Site** is an 1845/1846 Greek Revival building that once served as the center of Galena's community life. Among its many functions today are a center for historical and architectural exhibits, an open-air farmer's market during the summer and fall, and a hospitality center during the Christmas season.

Among the historic homes open to the public are the **Dowling House** (1826) and the **Belvedere Mansion** (1857). The native limestone Dowling House, Galena's oldest house, contains primitive period furniture and a large collection of Galena pottery. The 22-room Italianate Belvedere Mansion has Victorian furnishings, items from Liberace's estate, and the famous green drapes from Tara in *Gone with the Wind*.

Also of interest are the limestone **Galena Post Office** (1857/1859), the second oldest continuously-operating post office in the United States; the Greek Revival **Galena Public Library** (1906), which has a reading room with a mosaic fireplace in the style of Frank Lloyd Wright; and the **Washburne House**, a Greek Revival home built in 1844 by a U.S. congressman. It was in the library of Washburne House that Grant received word of his election to the presidency (1868). The **Vinegar Hill Historic Lead Mine and Museum** offers a guided tour of an 1822 underground lead mine.

Recreational opportunities abound in the Galena area. A casino cruise ship plies the nearby **Mississippi River**. Mississippi riverboats also offer sightseeing excursions, including two-day round-trip cruises.

Summer sports include hiking, horseback riding, bicycling, and some of the best golfing in the country. With winter come skating, sledding, tobogganing, snow-shoeing, and some of the best downhill skiing in the Midwest. Horse-drawn sleigh rides are popular.

Cultural offerings range from chamber music to bluegrass to performances by a professional theatrical troupe.

Special Feature

Check with the Visitor Information Center for help on planning a scenic drive. **Jo Daviess County** is full of winding country roads.

Ulysses S. and Julia Dent Grant considered Galena their hometown even though the general actually lived in the town for no more than a total of about two years.

Where to Stay

ALDRICH GUEST HOUSE, *900 Third St., (815) 777-3323.* 1845 Greek Revival home, antique decor, full breakfasts, grand piano, library, screened porch. $$ to $$$

COLONIAL GUEST HOUSE, *1004 Park Ave., (815) 777-0336.* 1826 Greek Revival home, antiques, TV, private baths, Cont. "plus" breakfasts, private porch, scenic views, antique shop. $$

DeZOYA HOUSE B&B, *1203 Third St., (815) 777-1203.* 1830 limestone Federal house on two acres, antiques & art from Federal period, private baths, full breakfasts. $$$

HELLMAN GUEST HOUSE, *318 Hill St., (815) 777-3638.* 1895 Queen Anne home with stained glass, antique decor, private baths, overlooking downtown & countryside. $$$

THE PARK AVENUE GUEST HOUSE, *208 Park Ave., (800) 359-0743.* 1897 Queen Anne home with screened wrap-around porch, private baths, gardens, gazebo. $$ to $$$

QUEEN ANNE GUEST HOUSE, *200 Park Ave., (815) 777-3849.* 1891 Queen Anne home, antiques & art, private baths, whirlpools, Cont. "plus" breakfasts by candlelight, verandah, gardens, featured in TV commercial. $$ to $$$

Where to Eat

THE DeSOTO HOUSE HOTEL, *230 S. Main St., (815) 777-0090.* Leadminers Stew, Stuffed Pork Chops, hand-cut Midwestern steaks; in restored 1855 hotel on National Register. $ to $$

ELDORADO GRILL, *219 N. Main St., (815) 777-1224.* Fresh Roasted Local Trout Fillet, Grilled Beef Tenderloin with Oven Roasted Shallots, Wild Mushroom Quesadillas; rave reviews, reservations a must. $$

FRIED GREEN TOMATOES, *1301 N. Irish Hollow Rd., (815) 777-3938.* Pasta con Carne, Pasta di Mare, New York Strip, Bistecca al Jack Daniels, Pollo Vesuvio, Gamberetto Aglio; in transformed 1871 county poor farm, reservations suggested. $$

VINNY VANUCCHI'S, *201 S. Main St., (815) 777-8100.* Veal & Chicken Picatta, Seafood Italiano with Fresh Lobster Tail, Pasta ala Vinny, & Polo Compomare the house specialties; "great" sandwiches, hand-cut steaks, cappuccino, bar. $ to $$

Further Information

Galena/Jo Daviess County Convention & Visitors Bureau, *720 Park Ave., Galena, IL 61036 (800) 747-9377/fax (815) 777-3566.*

Directions

From Chicago, I 90 (Northwest Tollway) to US 20 at Rockford, US 20 west to Galena; also from Chicago, I 88 to I 39, I 39 north to US 20 at Rockford, US 20 west to Galena.

Geneva
Population 17, 500

Flowing just beyond the reach of Chicago's western suburbs is the beautiful **Fox River**. Each of the towns along the river has a waterside park, and the parks' bike trails have been connected to offer bicyclists, roller bladers, hikers, and joggers 25 miles of uninterrupted scenery.

Geneva is one of the prettiest and most historic of the towns along the river. The town's considerable charm is in part due to the convergence of its historic beauty, its 150-year-old reputation as a shopping center, and its lovely and unique location. Founded in the 1830s, Geneva has two historic districts and more than 200 homes, churches, and other buildings on the National Register of Historic Places. Most of the homes and churches were built in the middle of the 19th century, with the decades of the 1840s, 1850s, and 1860s predominating.

Encouraged by Geneva's beautiful setting – and the tastes of area residents – it was inevitable that during the decades of the 20th century the shops and the historic homes would begin to find each other. And so they did. Geneva boasts over 100 antique shops, galleries, specialty shops, restaurants, and cafes, many nestled within the walls of beautiful old homes. The union of upscale shopping with the town's architectural treasures and romantic riverside setting has earned Geneva a respected reputation in Chicagoland, and beyond.

The interior of the **Kane County Courthouse** is laced with wrought-iron balconies from the first to the fourth floors and displays eight large murals by Edward Holslag. The murals provide a good view of the surrounding countryside as it appeared in 1910. Among the local memorabilia showcased by the **Geneva Historical Society Museum**, in **Wheeler Park**, are furniture made by area cabinetmakers from local walnut and period costumes and hats from the shops of town merchants.

Special Features

Bikes and rollerblades can be rented riverside. The **Fox River bike trails** extend from Aurora to Elgin and beyond, and connect with a vast network of bike paths on Chicago's western outskirts. Also, Geneva's lovely Island Park is ideal for picnicking.

Where to Stay

THE HERRINGTON, *15 S. River Ln., (630) 208-7433*. Riverfront inn with Northern European/Scandinavian ambiance, fireplaces, private baths, whirlpools, dining room, fitness room, riverside gazebo. $$$

OSCAR SWAN COUNTRY INN, *1800 W. State St., (630) 232-0173*. 1902 Colonial Revival estate on 7 acres, antiques & art, TV & phones, private baths, full breakfasts weekends, pre-arranged meals, pets, pool, gardens. $$

Where to Eat

302 WEST, *302 W. State St., (630) 232-9302*. "Bold new American cuisine in an atmosphere of casual elegance." $$ to $$$

THE LITTLE TRAVELER, *404 S. Third St., (630) 232-6060*. 30-room mansion serving luncheon/snacks in Atrium Cafe, luncheon by reservation in Antique Courts; since 1922. $

MILL RACE INN, *4 E. State St., (630) 232-2030*. Grilled Raspberry Chicken Breast, Wild Game Medley, Swedish Meatballs; attractive setting, service for 60 years. $$

RISTORANTE CHIANTI, *207 S. Third St., (630) 232-0212*. Award-winning Italian cuisine, casual setting. $ to $$

RIVERWALK, *35 N. River Ln., (630) 232-1330*. Cioppino, Basil Brie Chicken, Jamaican Mixed Grill, Steak au Poivre; nice views. $$

Further Information

Geneva Chamber of Commerce, *P.O. Box 481, Geneva, IL 60134 (630) 232-6060*.

Directions

From Chicago, IL 38 west (approximately 35 miles).

Maeystown
Population 135

Cluster an old stone church, a little stone bridge, an inn, several stores, a few houses, and a handful of outbuildings on the rolling Illinois countryside, and you have the quaint little German village of **Maeystown**. The land was never graded to form level lots; instead, the buildings were set into the hillside. This means that to go upstairs you have the choice between climbing stairs or going outside and climbing a little hill to a door on the next floor. The effect is an integration of building and landscape; the overall result is a village straight out of a storybook.

The entire village of Maeystown, founded in 1852, is listed on the National Register. The village is so tiny that residents report two populations, the one given above and a larger one that includes the dogs and cats (and there are a lot of these around). Some of the more significant of the buildings include the original **stone church** (1865-67); the home (1860-65) of the town's founder, **Jacob Maeys**; and **Zeitinger's Mill** (1859), now the home of the preservation society. The picturesque old one-lane **stone bridge** (1881) is still in use.

Rent a bicycle and tour the village, or let a horse-drawn carriage do it for you. Everyone greets everyone else on the village's half dozen streets, and conversation comes easy. A very pleasant morning or afternoon can be spent by getting to know those lingering in the restaurant, inn, or old-fashioned general store.

Special Features

The original powder magazine and reconstructed north wall and guardhouse may be explored at **Fort de Chartres State Historic Site**, several miles south of town on the Mississippi. The original fort (1753) had 3-foot-thick stone walls and was built by the French to protect settlers in Prairie du Rocher.

> • *Services at the original stone church were sometimes held in German until 1943.*
> • *Many of the original barns, smokehouses, summer kitchens, sheds, and outhouses are still standing behind the village's homes.*

Where to Stay

CORNER GEORGE INN, *Main & Mill,* *(618) 458-6660.* Restored 1884 hotel – now country inn B&B, antiques, private baths, breakfast in ballroom. $$ to $$$

Where to Eat

HOEFFT'S VILLAGE INN, *Main & Mill sts., (618) 458-6425.* Country cooking, fried chicken, beef, daily specials, homemade pies; authentic old-time flavor. $

Further Information

The Innkeepers, *Corner George Inn, Maeystown, IL 62256 (618) 458-6660.*

Directions

From St. Louis, I 255 (across Mississippi River) to exit 6, IL 3 south to Waterloo (ask for directions to Maeystown Rd.).

Nauvoo

Population 1108

Located on a bluff overlooking the Mississippi, **Nauvoo** (nah VOO) is the idyllic early 19th-century American town with lovely shade trees and green parkland blended with stately old brick buildings. The atmosphere is small-town and peaceful. There is no commercialization, and in fact you're not likely to come across the town except by a lucky stumble. That is, unless you happen to know something about Mormon history.

Fleeing persecution elsewhere, the Mormons settled in Nauvoo in 1839. There, granted autonomy by the Illinois legislature, they prospered. During the 1840s, Nauvoo, which means *a beautiful place* in Hebrew, became the largest town in Illinois and the 10th largest in the country. Troubles continued to plague the church, however, and following the murder of Mormon leader Joseph Smith, the Mormons left Illinois. Nauvoo was abandoned.

In 1849 a group from France known as the Icarians chose Nauvoo for an experiment in communal living. The Icarian colony in Nauvoo survived until 1860. After its break-up, some of the members remaining in Nauvoo joined with their German and Swiss neighbors to begin the cultivation of grapes and the making of fine wines. Although Prohibition put an end to the wine industry, at least for a while, the wine cellars were found ideal for the aging of cheese and in 1936 a blue-cheese industry was born. The town celebrates its grape harvest with a festival every Labor Day weekend.

The best way to explore Nauvoo is by driving tour aided by a map and cassette obtained from the **Nauvoo Chamber of Commerce Uptown Tourist Center** (across from Hotel Nauvoo). The two best-known sites, or clusters of sites, help define the historic district, once inhabited by Mormons. Both are taken from the pages of Mormon history:

On the south side of the historic district is the **Joseph Smith Historic Center** (associated with the Reorganized Church of Jesus Christ of Latter Day Saints). The center comprises the log **Homestead** (1803), **Mansion House** (1842), and **Red Brick Store** (1842), all family properties of Joseph Smith. The Red Brick Store displays merchandise typical of the early 1840s. Near the store is the **Smith family cemetery**, burial place of Joseph Smith and his wife and brother, Emma and Hyrum.

The **LDS Visitors Center** (associated with the Church of Jesus Christ of Latter-day Saints), on the north side of the district, maintains the **Monument to Women Gardens**. The center provides a good introduction to the district and offers guided tours of its many beautifully restored homes and shops.

A goal of the **Icarian Living History Museum** is "to promote the preservation of French heritage in America." Among the items on display in the renovated 1846 house are artifacts of the Icarian period (1849-1860).

Special Features

Daily demonstrations of Nauvoo's old crafts are provided all over town, and because they are indoors, in all seasons. Woodworking, blacksmith, and cooper demonstrations are just a few that can be seen. All are performed by skilled artisans – the sheer intelligence and inventiveness of the craftsmanship are guaranteed to amaze.

> • *What with the bald eagles wintering in the area, the sleigh bells, and the traditional holiday decorations, many find December the best season to visit Nauvoo.*
>
> • *Held on the first week of August, the outdoor musical "City of Joseph" employs song, dance, costumes, fireworks, and a computerized sound and lighting system to tell the story of Nauvoo's Mormon period.*

Where to Stay

THE ANCIENT PINES, *2015 Parley St., (217) 453-2767*. Turn-of-century home with stained-glass windows & hand-carved woodwork, full breakfasts with homemade bread, piano, some pets, 142-year-old pines. $ to $$

HOTEL NAUVOO, *1290 Mulholland St., (217) 453-2211*. 1841 Italianate home converted to hotel in 1885, TV & phones, private baths, dining rooms, paintings by Lane K. Newberry. $ to $$

MISSISSIPPI MEMORIES B&B, *P.O. Box 291, (217) 453-2771*. On banks of Mississippi, flannel sheets, full breakfasts, seasonal fruit & flowers, library, piano, large decks, wooded setting. $$

ORTMAN'S B&B, *950 White St., (217) 453-2249*. 1865 brick structure near restored homes, antiques, full breakfasts, wine cellar, tours. $$

Where to Eat

GRANDPA JOHN'S CAFE, *1255 Mulholland St., (217) 453-2310.*
Popular for breakfast & lunch, homemade ice cream. $

HOTEL NAUVOO, *(see above)*. Buffet with numerous interesting
dishes, 7 distinctly decorated dining rooms. $ to $$

Further Information

Nauvoo Tourism, *P.O. Box 41, Nauvoo, IL 62354 (217) 453-6648.*

Directions

From Peoria, US 24 southwest to US 136, US 136 west to IL 96, IL 96
north (along Mississippi River) to Nauvoo.

Other Charming Illinois Towns

Golconda
Mt. Carroll
Petersburg (New Salem)
Woodstock

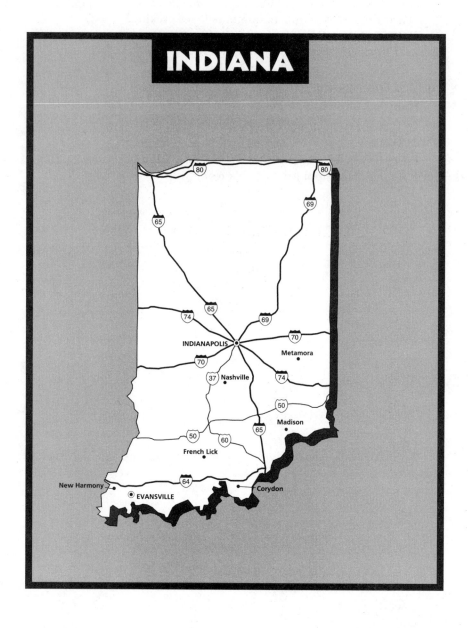

INDIANA

Corydon
Population 2, 661

Here and there among the hills and forests of southern Indiana are little towns whose streets look much as they did 50 years ago, or more. Too small to grow into cities, but too big to disappear, such towns somehow hang on, often with the help of tourist dollars attracted by a bit of Hoosier nostalgia. **Corydon** is a wonderful example of such a little town, and it has a lot of genuine Hoosier nostalgia to work with.

Corydon's downtown has an ambiance that beautifully complements the Hoosier heritage. Many of the businesses proudly display – and restore and preserve – ornamental iron store fronts from the 1890s. Included among the businesses are specialty shops, antique and art malls, restaurants, and a soda fountain. Corydon is especially known for its sculptured art glass objects.

On the square is the charming little **State Capitol Building**, Indiana's first state capitol (1816-1825). The 40-foot-square building, today a state historic site, is constructed of rough blue limestone and has first-floor walls that are 2 1/2 feet thick.

 Not far away is the 1817 Federal-style brick **Governor Hendricks's Headquarters**. This two-story building, open to the public, was the home and headquarters of William Hendricks while he was governor of Indiana (1822-1825). Also near the square is a one-story brick building (1817) that was rented to the state for offices, making it the first state office building (now a private residence).

Two other beautiful old buildings that are open to the public are the **Posey House**, a large brick house built in 1817 (operated as a museum by the D.A.R.), and the **Kintner House**, a delightful B&B inn (see below). Other historic buildings include the restored two-story log **Branham Tavern** (1800), the 1807 log **Westfall House**, and the Federal-style office of the weekly newspaper, the *Corydon Democrat*, originally built as a residence and drug store (1842).

Special Features

Scheduled trains operate 16-mile excursions on an 1883 scenic railroad. The excursions last about 1 1/2 hours.

In the rolling countryside not far from Corydon are some of the country's most beautiful caves. The best known, all open to the public, are

Wyandotte Cave, **Little Wyandotte Cave**, **Marengo Cave**, and **Squire Boone Caverns**. Many farmers have wild caves that they allow visitors to explore.

Along the **Ohio River Scenic Route** lie cypress swamps, river overlooks, rock outcroppings, caves, forested hills, and pieces of history and prehistory. Formed by IN 156, 56, 62, and 66, the route passes through Corydon.

> • *The Battle of Corydon Memorial Park south of town was the site of one of the few Civil War battles fought on Northern soil.*
> • *The Harrison County Fair is the oldest continuous fair in Indiana (dating from 1860). The fairgrounds are south of town.*

Where to Stay

KINTNER HOUSE INN B&B, *Capitol & Chestnut, (812) 738-2020.* Restored 1873 hotel featured on Christmas cards, on National Register, antiques, fireplaces, TV & phones, private baths, inviting large porch. $ to $$

Where to Eat

MAGDALENA'S RESTAURANT, *103 E. Chestnut (on the square), (812) 738-8075.* Lunch the main event - Oven-roasted Turkey, Country-fried Steak, Golden Fried Chicken; gourmet gift shop. $ to $$ (dinner)

OVERLOOK RESTAURANT, *P.O. Box 67 (Leavenworth), (812) 739-4264.* Creamed Chicken, Overlook's Chef Salad, & Beef Manhattan among the luncheon specialties; famous coconut cream pie; spectacular view of Ohio River. $ to $$ (dinner)

Further Information

Harrison County Chamber of Commerce, *310 N. Elm St., Corydon, IN 47112 (812) 738-2137.*

Directions

From Louisville (KY), I 64 west to exit 105, IN 135 south to Corydon.

French Lick/West Baden Springs

Population 2, 087

Nestled among the scenic knobs of southern Indiana, **French Lick** and **West Baden Springs** are, were, and have always been among the Midwest's great resorts. Belief in the medicinal and generally beneficial effects of the area's mineral waters turned French Lick and the neighboring village of **West Baden Springs** into a fashionable spa as early as the middle of the 19th century. The wealthy and the not-so-wealthy came here to take the waters, promenade, and enjoy the restaurants and black-tie casinos. Some of the wealthy even came in their own railroad cars. An opera house was built. As the resort seasoned, major-league baseball teams came here to train. The grandest of the spa's hotels, the **West Baden Spring's Hotel** and the neighboring **French Lick Springs Resort**, were built in 1902.

French Lick and West Baden Springs's popularity continued until the years of the Depression. Thereafter the resorts had their ups and downs, but never died. In 1991 the French Lick Springs Resort, by now listed as a National Historic Landmark, underwent extensive restoration. The result is a hotel whose reputation as the largest, most complete all-season resort in the Midwest continues unchallenged. The hotel features an Olympic-sized outdoor pool, a glass-domed indoor pool, two 18-hole golf courses, 18 tennis courts, 30 miles of trails for horseback riding, and a health and fitness spa.

The West Baden Springs's Hotel was famous for its 6-story free-span atrium dome, the largest in the world until the construction of Houston's astrodome in 1966. The hotel is currently undergoing restoration under the watchful eye of the Historic Landmarks Foundation of Indiana. Regularly scheduled tours are available (317-639-4646 for information).

French Lick and West Baden Springs can fill out a pleasant day even for those not staying at the resort. **Main Street** and a couple of adjacent streets in French Lick have an interesting assortment of gift and antique shops as well as the quaint appearance that people expect of southern Indiana. Several very pleasant hours can also be spent touring the West Baden Spring's Hotel and strolling the beautiful lobby, verandah, and vast landscaped grounds of the French Lick Springs Resort (on the grounds is the renowned **Pluto Spring** - see below).

Adjacent to the resort is the **Indiana Railway Museum**. A trip of less than two hours can be taken through 20 miles of the **Hoosier National Forest** on the **French Lick, West Baden and Southern Railroad**. Along the way is the 2,200-ft. **Burton Tunnel**, one of the longest railway tunnels in the state. The museum also displays several vintage locomotives and a number of old railroad cars.

> *The water from one of the artesian mineral springs, the Pluto Spring, was once bottled and widely distributed as "Pluto Water."*

Where to Stay

BEECHWOOD INN, *On the Boulevard, P.O. Box 96, (812) 936-9012.* 1915 21-room mansion, full-service inn, many original furnishings, full breakfasts, dining room; Irving Berlin, Joe Louis, & Al Capone once guests. $$$

FRENCH LICK SPRINGS RESORT, *French Lick, (800) 457-4042.* Historic full-service resort hotel, restaurants, golf, tennis, swimming pools, stables, health spa, bikes. $$$ (European & Modified American plans available)

Where to Eat

BEECHWOOD INN, *(see above).* Golden Halibut (the signature dish), Chicken Provolone, Tournedos of Beef, Pork Medallions, Chef's Pasta du Jour; elegant surroundings. $$ to $$$

FRENCH LICK SPRINGS RESORT (see above) features a variety of restaurants, menus, and price ranges. Among the more casual, moderately-priced are LeBistro and Pluto's Pavilion; at the more expensive, gourmet end are the Hoosier Dining Room (traditional ballroom) and Chez James.

Further Information

French Lick-West Baden Chamber of Commerce, *P.O. Box 347, French Lick, IN 47432 (812) 936-2405.*

Directions

From Indianapolis, IN 37 south to US 150 (at Paoli), west to Prospect, IN 56 south to French Lick / West Baden springs; from Louisville (KY), US 150 northwest to Prospect, as above.

Madison

Population 12, 006

Every visitor to Madison should reserve time for a stroll on the beautiful brick walk along the riverfront. On one side is the **Ohio River**, with the hazy hills of Kentucky beyond, and on the other are the wooded heights and limestone cliffs of Indiana overlooking and sheltering the finest concentration of early 19th-century architecture in the Midwest.

Madison's entire downtown, 133 blocks worth, is listed on the National Register of Historic Places. Most of the buildings on **Main Street** – one of the finest in the country – were in place at the time of the Civil War, yet the street is as alive as any main street ever was. Interwoven with the usual businesses, here and on adjacent streets, are some unusually fine antique, craft, and specialty shops. The charm of the district reaches a peak at N. Broadway and Main, where a Victorian fountain, called the **Broadway Fountain**, commands a little square. The fountain, originally cast in iron and recast in bronze in 1976, was presented in 1876 to the Philadelphia Centennial Exposition by France.

One of Madison's best-known citizens was financier James Lanier, who loaned financially troubled Indiana money during the Civil War so that the state could equip Union troops. Lanier built a Classic Revival mansion (1844) that has become Madison's most popular attraction. Now the **J. F. D. Lanier State Historic Site**, the splendid home has period furnishings and a south portico with a commanding view of the **Ohio River** that, by itself, would justify a trip to Madison. The lovely gardens, carefully restored, include fragrant 1850 peonies (thought to be original to the garden) and heirloom varieties of roses.

The Greek Revival **Shrewsbury House** (1849) is another lovely Madison landmark. Especially noteworthy inside are the plasterwork and three-story freestanding spiral staircase. The house and its period furnishings are open to public view.

The **Jeremiah Sullivan House** (1818), an outstanding example of Federal architecture, was probably Madison's first mansion (open). Also in the Federal style, the **Masonic Schofield House** (circa 1816) is believed to be the first two-story brick house/tavern in Madison (open).

The contents, including medical instruments, of **Dr. William D. Hutchings's Office** (1848) are exactly the same as they were at the time of Dr. Hutchings's death in 1903 (open).

Special Features

Several dramatic waterfalls, deep gorges, and bluffs overlooking the Ohio River can be found at nearby **Clifty Falls State Park**. Bowing a little to civilization, the park also offers an inn, Olympic-sized swimming pool, and more than 12 miles of moderate to rugged hiking trails.

Hanover College, founded in 1827, is seven miles west of town. The campus consists of thirty Georgian-style buildings located on a hilltop overlooking the Ohio River Valley.

IN 56E offers a picturesque tour of the countryside along the Ohio.

> • *The Fair Play Fire Company is Indiana's oldest existing volunteer fire department (1841).*
> • *Settlers often put into Madison for provisions on their way to their new homes in the Northwest Territory, now the eastern part of the Midwest.*

Where to Stay

AUTUMNWOOD, *165 Autumnwood Ln., (812) 265-5262.* 1840 Greek Revival home in wooded area, period furnishings, private baths, Cont. "plus" breakfasts served on Haviland china, patio with fountain, tours. $$$

CLIFF HOUSE, *122 Fairmount Dr., (812) 265-5272.* 1885 mansion high above historic district, antiques, private baths, Cont. "plus" breakfasts, tours. $$$

THE FEDERAL INN, *710 E. Main St., (812) 265-4501.* 1838 row house with antique appointments, TV & phones, private baths. $$

MAIN STREET B&B, *739 W. Main St., (800) 362-6246.* Circa 1843 Greek Revival home in historic district, private baths. $$$

SCHUSSLER HOUSE B&B, *514 Jefferson St., (800) 392-1931.* Circa 1849 Federal/Classic Revival home, antiques, private baths, "sumptuous" breakfasts, afternoon refreshments. $$$

STONEFIELDS DREAM B&B, *411 W. First St., (812) 265-6856.* 1892 home next to Lanier Mansion, antiques, player piano, outdoor deck, '64 Chevelle Convertible. $$$

Where to Eat

KEY WEST SHRIMP HOUSE, *117 Ferry St., (812) 265-2831.* Seafood from Shrimp Panama to Seafood Norfolk to Halibut Oscar to Broiled Walleye. $$

LACY'S, *218 E. Main St., (812) 273-4447.* Sandwiches, quiche, daily specials; bar, evening entertainers. $

NEX-DOOR, *700 Clifty Dr., (812) 273-5151.* American & Italian menu, Black Angus beef the specialty, good salad selection. $ to $$

THE TEAROOM, *Second & West sts.*, *(812) 273-2367*. Soup & Salad Combination, Steak Marsala, Pork Fillets with Mushrooms, Chicken Savinelli, Shrimp & Pasta, Asparagus Pasta; known for salads. $$

THE UPPER CRUST, *209 W. Main St.*, *(812) 265-6727*. "Elegantly simple and simply elegant" European cuisine, proud of sauces. $$

Further Information

Madison Area Convention & Visitors Bureau, *301 E. Main St., Madison, IN 47250 (812) 265-2956/(800) 559-2956.*

Directions

From Louisville (KY), I 65 north to exit 33, IN 256 east to Madison; from Cincinnati (OH), I 71 south to Carrollton (KY), KY 36 west to Milton (KY), cross bridge (US 421) to Madison; from Indianapolis, I 65 south to exit 33, IN 256 east to Madison.

Metamora

Population about 200

Tiny **Metamora's** (first) golden days came in the 1840s and 1850s when the village prospered as a port on the 76-mile-long **Whitewater Canal** (1845). Floods, mismanagement, the coming of the railroad, and other factors ganged up on the canal, and the old waterway fell into disrepair. And so it remained until the 1940s, when the Indiana Department of Natural Resources acquired 14 miles of it and began restoration. Included in the restoration was a covered aqueduct, built in 1843, that carried the canal 16 feet over **Duck Creek**.

Today, the restored canal, aqueduct, and working grist mill make up the **Whitewater Canal State Historic Site**. A horse-drawn canal boat, the *Ben Franklin III*, takes on passengers and travels through the aqueduct, the only operational covered-bridge aqueduct in the United States (hourly departures).

With well over 100 shops, the village has become so popular that it now counts Nashville (which see) as its main rival. Many of the shops are housed in quaint 19th-century houses and other buildings. The goods and wares include dolls, oak and cherry furniture, paintings, oak baskets, candles, home-made horseradish, wooden folk art, Amish cheese, wood signs, nutcrackers, quilts, tinware, and ceramics. Shoppers come from as far away as Cincinnati, Indianapolis, Dayton, and Louisville.

Special Features

In addition to rides on the canal boat, the village offers buggy rides and 1/2-hour steam-engine excursions on the Whitewater Valley Railroad. (Longer rail excursions are available from Connersville, to the north.)

> *Indiana's canal system drove the state into bankruptcy. The experience badly hurt Indiana's reputation and led to legislation that even today prohibits the state from contracting debt.*

Where to Stay

GINGERBREAD HOUSE B&B, *P.O. Box 28, (765) 647-5518.* Early 1870s home with cupola & seven varieties of "gingerbread" rented as unit, period furniture, refreshments. $$

THE GRAPEVINE INN, *P.O. Box 207, (765) 647-3738.* Laura Ashley & "country-decorated" rooms, TV & phones, private baths, balcony with country view. $$

THE METAMORA INN / THE SHEPHERDS HOUSE, *19049 Wynn St., P.O. Box 131, (765) 647-2176.* 1857 home, TV & phones, private baths. $$ to $$$

THE PUBLICK HOUSE B&B, *28 Duck Creek Crossing, (765) 647-6729.* 1830 "canal-town-style" home, TV, private baths, balconies, breakfasts "with a gourmet flair," quiet country atmosphere. $$ to $$$

THORPE HOUSE COUNTRY INN B&B, *P.O. Box 36, (765) 647-5425.* 19th-century Greek Revival home, period furnishings, private baths. $$

Where to Eat

THE CASE HOUSE, *801 Main St. (Brookville), (765) 647-4934.* Roasted Half Chicken with Almond Sauce, Maple-glazed Pork Chops, Channel Catfish, Ribeye; in 1870s bldg. on National Register, century-old recipe ideas. $ to $$

THE HEARTHSTONE RESTAURANT, *US 52, (765) 647-5204.* Skillet-fried Chicken, Country-cured Ham; "Old-fashioned family dining in a warm & casual country setting," since 1930. $

HICKORY LANE AT THE DEPOT, *19063 US 52, (765) 647-4544.* American smorgasbord with especially good variety of salads & pies, since 1970. $

Further Information

Merchants Association of Metamora, *P.O. Box 117, Metamora, IN 47030. Welcome Line: (765) 647-2109.*

Directions

From Indianapolis, US 52 east (via Rushville) to Metamora; from Cincinnati (OH), I 74 west to US 52, US 52 to Metamora.

Nashville

Population 873

Unlike so many other charming villages, **Nashville** didn't arise from the wealth of lumbermen, cotton planters, bankers, or gold miners. Indeed, Nashville and surrounding **Brown County** occupy an area that is relatively poor in natural resources. Nashville's charm originated instead in the backwoods beauty of Brown County, a county with winding country roads, old covered bridges, log cabins, and homey stone buildings.

Standing in contrast with the flatness of so much of the Midwest, the mountainous scenery of Brown County began attracting artists over a hundred years ago. One of the earliest and most prominent of the artists was Theodore C. Steele, the Impressionistic artist of Hoosier Group fame. Steele's home, studio, gardens, and grounds now form the **T. C. Steele State Historic Site**, about eight miles southwest of town. Many of Steele's landscape paintings are on display in the house and studio (1907).

Nashville's center of attraction is the **Brown County Courthouse Historic District** (1873-1937). The district includes a picture-book brick courthouse, the **Historical Society Museum Building**, the **Old Log Jail**, and several other log structures.

Along Nashville's picturesque streets are over 300 art galleries, craft shops, and antique stores. The town is tiny, so park your car and walk. Carriage tours are available for those looking for a little romance.

Special Features

Within the borders of Brown County are **Brown County State Park** (the largest in the state), **Yellowwood State Forest**, and parts of the **Hoosier National Forest**. In and out of the woods are numerous roads and trails, making the county ideal for nature hikes, horseback rides, and bicycle tours.

- *One study has ranked Brown County, along with neighboring Bloomington, among the ten most desirable places in the U.S. in which to retire.*
- *In addition to golf courses, country music establishments, and other attractions, Nashville is home to the charming 60-seat outdoor Melchior Marionette Theatre.*

Where to Stay

5TH GENERATION FARM, *Rt. 4, P.O. Box 90-A, (800) 437-8152.* 1848 farmhouse in country, antique furnishings, private baths, recreation room with pool table. $$ to $$$

THE ALLISON HOUSE INN, *90 S. Jefferson St., P.O. Box 1625, (812) 988-0814.* 1883 home, private baths, full breakfasts, library with fireplace & piano, "Victorian Country Charm." $$$

THE ARTISTS COLONY INN, *P.O. Box 1099, (812) 988-0600.* Locally crafted 19th-century-style furniture, hand-loomed rugs, TV & phones, dining room with paintings & stone fireplace, hot tub on roof deck, craft shop, in heart of town. $$ to $$$

CORNERSTONE INN, *54 E. Franklin St., P.O. Box 275, (888) 383-0300/(812) 988-0300/fax (812) 988-0200.* 1993 Victorian-style B&B hotel, antiques, TV & phones, private baths, whirlpool tubs, full breakfasts, snacks, large balcony overlooking town. $$$

THE STORY INN, *6404 S. IN 135, P.O. Box 64, (812) 988-2273.* Lodgings in cottages & second floor of general store in 19th-century hamlet 12 mi. from Nashville, designer-decorated rooms, private baths, full "country" breakfasts, restaurant. $$ to $$$

Where to Eat

HOBNOB CORNER, *17 W. Main St., P.O. Box 899, (812) 988-4114.* Homemade soups, "exciting" salads, home-baked pastries; in Nashville's oldest commercial bldg., respected. $

NASHVILLE HOUSE, *Main St., (812) 988-4554.* Country-fried Chicken, Baked Hoosier Ham, fried biscuits & homemade baked apple butter. $$

THE ORDINARY, half block S of intersection of Main & Van Buren sts., (812) 988-6166. "Early American Eatery" serving Roast Chicken, Pot Roast, Ham Steak; lounge. $$

THE STORY INN, *(see above).* Dining among memorabilia or on screened porch overlooking gardens & brook, fresh local foods, dinner by reservation, variable hours. $$

Further Information

Nashville/Brown County Convention & Visitors Bureau, *P.O. Box 840, Nashville, IN 47448 (800) 753-3255.*

Directions

From Indianapolis, I 65 south to exit 68, west on IN 46 to Nashville.

New Harmony
Population 846

New Harmony was laid out and settled by Harmonists – Lutheran Separatists – in 1814. Ten years later the town was taken over by a second communal society, this one lasting only a couple of years. Both communities faded, and their utopian ideals were never realized, but each stressed intellectual and cultural achievement, and that legacy lives on. For today the quaint little town of New Harmony is alive with musical performances, workshops and conferences, summer theater productions, craft demonstrations, and art exhibitions. In addition, many of the tour sites (see below) offer permanent exhibits of art, history, and science.

The bridge between New Harmony's past and present is a unique one. Beginning in 1937 various preservation and restoration efforts were undertaken. In the late 1950s construction began on the first of several contemporary structures. In the years since, the town has been zoned and its infrastructure upgraded and modernized. New buildings, including a visitors' center, medical clinic, and townhouses, have gone up. Their architecture has often united modern elements with traditional ones, especially those of the Harmonist tradition. Many of the historic buildings have been restored and converted to museums. The resulting town is a delightful mix of the authentic old with the creative new, of unique shops and good restaurants with history museums and art galleries.

Every visitor should go first to the **Atheneum/Visitors' Center**, a striking contemporary structure designed by Richard Meier. The center offers an orientation film and exhibits, including a scale model of the town in 1824. All tours begin here. The tours range from a 45-minute orientation tour to a three-hour **New Harmony Story Tour**, which includes escorted entry into 11 sites.

There are 15 tour sites in all, as well as several sites open to the public free of charge. Among the tour sites are **Community House #2**, a large dormitory built for single Harmonists and later the site of a Pestalozzian school; **Thrall's Opera House**, originally a Harmonist community house and later remodeled for theatrical performances; and the **Workingmen's Institute**, Indiana's oldest continuously open public library (1838). Another site, the **George Keppler House**, contains exhibits on the life and work of David Dale Owen, Indiana State Geologist and later Chief Geologist for the U.S. Government. The **Maximilian-Bodmer Collection** showcases original artwork from the 1832/1834 expedition of Prince Maximilian and artist Karl Bodmer to the Upper Missouri Territory.

The **Labyrinth**, a restored maze of hedges, is one of the sites open to the public free of charge. Others include the **Roofless Church** (1960), an interdenominational church that won an award for its designer, and **Tillich Park**, the burial place of theologian Paul Johannes Tillich.

Special Features

Nearby **Harmonie State Park** features an Olympic-size pool, 110-ft water slide, and boat launch on the Wabash River. Wildlife, wildflower, and fall foliage viewers have six hiking trails to choose from.

> • *New Harmony was one of the country's most important training and research centers for geology between 1830 and 1860.*
> • *Congressman Robert Dale Owen, a New Harmony resident, sponsored legislation to establish the Smithsonian Institution.*

Where to Stay

THE NEW HARMONY INN, *P.O. Box 581, (800) 782-8605.* Full-service inn, Shaker-style furnishings, fireplaces, balconies, heated pool, tennis courts, health spa. $$

THE OLD ROOMING HOUSE, *916 Church St., (812) 682-4724.* "Lots of reading material, bikes and quiet comfort," quaint. $

RAINTREE INN B&B, *503 West St., P.O. Box 566, (812) 682-5625.* 1899 Classic Revival home, antiques, private baths, balconies, full "gourmet" breakfasts, piano. $$$

Where to Eat

BAYOU GRILL, *504 North St., (812) 682-4431.* Diverse menu ranging from omelets to hearty sandwiches to fried chicken & daily specials. $

NEW HARMONY COFFEE & TEA CO., *Main St., (812) 682-4563.* Pastries, salads, sandwiches, soups, teas, & gourmet coffees; local artwork, gifts. $

RED GERANIUM RESTAURANT, *508 North St., (812) 682-4431.* Prime rib, famed Shaker Lemon Pie; lovely setting, one of Indiana's most popular. $$

YELLOW TAVERN, *521 Church St., (812) 682-3303.* Variety of sandwiches, steaks, & pizzas. $

Further Information

Historic New Harmony, *P.O. Box 579, New Harmony, IN 47631 (812) 682-4488/fax (812) 682-4313.*

Directions

From Evansville, IN 66 west to New Harmony.

Other Charming Indiana Towns

Dana
Fountain City
Spring Mill Village

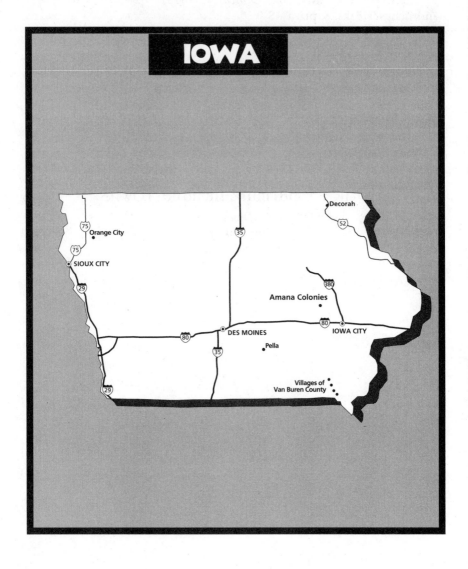

IOWA

The Amana Colonies
Population 1, 700

Iowa's **Amana Colonies** form a little country of their own. The "country" is 26,000 acres large and has seven villages, each at least an hour's ox-cart drive from the next: **Amana**, **Middle Amana**, **East Amana**, **West Amana**, **South Amana**, **High Amana**, and **Homestead**. The villages are laid out in the manner of the "Dorf" of the 19th-century German states, with one long street and several branches, and are distinguished by picturesque gabled sandstone and brick buildings, also from the 19th century. Some buildings are fitted with trellises to support fruit-bearing– and shade-providing–vines. Rich farmlands and wooded hillsides, even a large lily pond (**Lily Lake**), assure that the charm isn't confined to the village limits.

The colonies were begun in 1855 by members of a German/Swiss/French religious group who had come to America seeking a place to worship in peace. The colonists developed a communal lifestyle in which everything–including work and meals–was shared. The villages were built by hand and most of what the colonists needed was made by hand–the formation of bricks and quarrying of stones, weaving of fabrics, construction of grandfather clocks, pressing of grapes for wine, printing and binding of books. In 1932 came "The Great Change," when the free enterprise system was fully adopted and isolation from the outside world ended. Today the Amana Colonies form a National Historic Landmark, one that can boast some 475 sites and structures.

Most of the villages lie along the "Amana Colonies Trail," a loop formed by IA 220 and US 6 and 151 (guide maps and other information are available at several area visitors centers). Amana tends to be the colonies' "capital," and as such has the largest share of shops, restaurants, and other businesses; all villages, however, have their own special attractions.

Five of the seven villages have one or more museums. Amana, for example, has the **Museum of Amana History**, with three buildings of exhibits and an award-winning slide show. In South Amana there is the **Communal Agriculture Museum** and in Middle Amana the **Communal Kitchen and Coopershop**; both provide opportunities to learn more about the Amana Colonies' highly successful communal lifestyle. The **Homestead Church**, a church museum in Homestead, introduces visitors to the colonists' religious practices and beliefs.

It goes without saying that a group of villages respected since the middle of the 19th century for their handcrafted products would possess an exceptional collection of shops. Among the best of the offerings are the hardwood furniture, clocks, woolens, and quilts. The colonies' cheeses, breads, and smoked meats are renowned, as are the wines. Antique lovers should be prepared for a long visit. And even the short-term visitor should experience at least one meal: Some restaurants descend from the original communal kitchens, and their simple but delicious food, often prepared from old Amana recipes, is served family-style.

For visitors seeking a change of pace there are a golf course, a nature trail, and a professional theater troupe (the **Old Creamery Theatre Company**). There is also the bicycle which, depending on time and weather, may offer the very best way to take in this delightful bit of America's heartland.

Special Feature

Kalona, an Amish and Mennonite community, is about 30 miles southeast of the Amana Colonies. Of special interest here is the collection of 19th-century buildings preserved in the **Kalona Historical Village**.

> • *Hearty soups, cucumbers in cream sauce, cooked or pickled red cabbage, fried potatoes, rouladen with dumplings, fried chicken, and rhubarb pie are among the items you can expect to find on local menus.*
> • *The Amana Refrigeration Plant was once part of the Amana Society.*

Where To Stay

BAECKEREI B&B, *507 Q St., P.O. Box 127 (South Amana 52334), (800) 391-8650/(319) 622-3597.* Renovated 1860 communal bakery in quiet setting, antiques, TV, private baths, full breakfasts, cross-stitch works, gift shop. $

CORNER HOUSE B&B, *404 F St. (West Amana 52203), (800) 996-6964/(319) 622-6390.* 1862 sandstone home with antiques, private baths, bridal suite, "unique" full breakfasts. $

DIE HEIMAT COUNTRY INN, *P.O. Box 160 (Homestead 52236), (319) 622-3937.* 1854 stagecoach stop (& later communal kitchen), Amana furniture, quilts, private baths, full breakfasts, some pets. $$

NOE HOUSE INN, *Main St., P.O. Box 127 (Amana 52203), (319) 622-6350.* 1860s colony bldg., hand-stenciled walls, TV, hand-crafted quilts, private baths. $$

ROSE'S PLACE B&B, *1007 26th Ave., P.O. Box 91 (Middle Amana 52307), (319) 622-6097*. Renovated 1870s Sunday School, antiques, private baths, full breakfasts. $ to $$

RAWSON'S B&B, *211 V St., P.O. Box 118 (Homestead 52236), (319) 622-6035*. 1862 communal kitchen home with exposed interior brick walls & original beam structure, antiques, private baths, "full light" breakfasts, 2 whirlpool suites. $$

Where to Eat

THE AMANA BAR RESTAURANT, *4709 220th Trail, P.O. Box 290 (Amana), (319) 622-3214/(800) 325-2045*. Schnitzel, Sauerbraten, Rouladen & Potato Dumplings, Prime Rib, Rib Eye, Hickory-smoked Ham, and other German & American specialties served family-style in rebuilt cattle barn. $$

THE COLONY INN, *741 47th Ave., P.O. Box 130 (Amana), (319) 622-6270*. Amana Bratwurst, Sauerbraten, Chicken Schnitzel (with home-made spaetzle), sandwich platters; dinners served family-style. $$

OX YOKE INN, *Main St., P.O. Box 230 (Amana), (319) 622-3441*. German & American foods served family style in 1870s community-kitchen bldg., Old World-style beers & wines, since 1940, gift shop & museum. $$

THE RONNEBURG, *4408 220th Trail, P.O. Box 224 (Amana), (319) 622-3641*. Sauerbraten with Potato Dumplings, Sliced Amana Ham, Fried Chicken, Hand-breaded Walleye, good selection of sandwiches. $ to $$

Further Information

Amana Colonies Convention & Visitors Bureau, *39 38th Ave., Suite 100, Amana, IA 52203 (800) 245-5465/(319) 622-7622/fax (319) 622-6395*.

Directions

From Des Moines, I 80 east to exits 220 or 225, north to Amana Colonies.

Decorah

Population 8, 063

Decorah is a very pretty Norwegian-American town nestled among the hills, limestone bluffs, and woods of northeastern Iowa. The town is known for its lovely collection of historic homes and its scenic setting on the **Upper Iowa River**. It's also the seat of **Winneshiek County**, rich in history and cultural tradition (see below).

Decorah's most celebrated point of interest is **Vesterheim**, the Norwegian-American Museum. One of the country's top immigrant museums, the Vesterheim covers nearly a city block and consists of a main building, three buildings acquired in the Decorah business district, and nine authentically furnished structures that have been moved to the site. The main museum highlights the Norwegian-American immigrant's experience with carved furnishings, decorative arts, traditional costumes, and a three-story ship gallery. Another building has been converted to the **Gallery of Pioneer Industry**, with exhibits describing the various crafts of the Norwegian settlers. The museum complex also includes an 18th-century Norwegian home and gristmill and two immigrant log houses from the 1850s and 1860s.

The guide for the **Broadway-Phelps Park Historic District** lists over 50 structures. Within the district, entered on the National Register, are houses presenting nearly all major Midwestern architectural styles between the 1850s and 1910. Among those of special note are the 1867 **Ellsworth-Porter House**, now home to the **Winneshiek County Historical Society Museum**; the stucco 1858 **Octagonal House**; the 1862 Gothic Cottage **Grier-Green House**, with elaborate verge board; and the 1867 three-story Gothic Revival **Paine House**.

The natural park-like campus of **Luther College**, a private liberal-arts college (1862), is the result of a 1910 campus landscaping plan. The **Luther College Farm**, acquired by the college in 1929, contains barns, a restored icehouse, and other structures dating from the late 1860s to the turn of the century.

Other structures of note in Decorah include the restored 1888 **Milwaukee Road Passenger Depot**, the 1874 **Methodist Church**, and the 1875 **Steyer Bridge**, one of the very few stone-arch bridges in the state. The 1904 **Winneshiek County Courthouse** is known for its intricate stained-glass dome and its **Soldiers Monument** (1886) honoring county residents who served in the Civil War.

Decorah and Winneshiek County offer a wealth of summer and winter recreational opportunities. There are miles of hiking trails in Decorah's 13 parks, and canoeing and tubing are popular on the Upper Iowa River. The area has three golf courses, groomed snowmobile trails, and miles of stocked trout-fishing streams. The terrain offers good downhill and cross-country skiing.

Special Features

Palisades Parks affords an especially beautiful view of the Decorah area.

Spillville, southwest of Decorah, is the home of **St. Wenceslaus Church** (1860), the Old World-style stone church where composer Antonin Dvorak was once guest organist (1893). The building where Dvorak lived, now the **Bily Clock Museum**, houses a collection of unique clocks hand-carved by Spillville natives Frank and Joseph Bily. Many of the clocks are animated with mechanical figures. A room on the second floor of the museum contains Dvorak memorabilia.

The **Laura Ingalls Wilder Park and Museum**, a National Historical Site, is located in **Burr Oak**, north of Decorah. The pre-1860 hotel was one of the childhood homes of the famous author.

The 140-acre **Heritage Farm**, just a few miles north of town, has as its goals the maintenance and display of endangered food crops. Owned by the Seed Savers Exchange, the farm maintains 8,000 rare vegetables, 600 varieties of old-time apples, and a small herd of extremely rare **White Park Cattle** (visitors welcome).

> *Fort Atkinson, south of Decorah, was the only fort ever built in the U.S. to protect a tribe of Indians (the Winnebagos) from other tribes. The reconstructed 1840 fort is today part of the Iowa State Preserves System.*

Where to Stay

BROADWAY B&B, *303 W. Broadway, (319) 382-2329.* 1890 Queen Anne home in historic district, full or Cont. breakfasts. $ to $$

MONTGOMERY MANSION, *812 Maple Ave., (800) 892-4955.* 1877 home, private baths, full breakfasts, upstairs sitting room with TV. $$

SELVIG HOUSE, *140 Center St. E., P.O. Box 132 (Harmony, MN 55939), (507) 886-2200.* 1910 home of dentist & community leader, original woodwork & beveled leaded glass, full breakfasts, enclosed porch. $$

TAYLOR-MADE B&B, *330 Main St. (Spillville 52168), (319) 562-3958.* Turn-of-century home in village settled by Czechs, antiques, home-made quilts, some private baths, full breakfasts, refreshments, porch & balcony, cabin in back also available, views. $$

Where to Eat

CAFE DELUXE, *421 W. Water St., (319) 382-5589.* "The Area's Greatest Menu Selection." $

MABE'S PIZZA INC., *110 E. Water St., (319) 382-4297. The* pizza place, pasta, broasted chicken; a Decorah tradition. $

RUBY'S RESTAURANT, *120 E. Water St., (319) 382-2558*. Homemade dishes, daily lunch specials, home of the famous "Ronnie Roll." $

STONE HEARTH INN, *Commerce Dr., (319) 382-4614*. Seafood, chicken, steaks, pasta. $

VESTERHEIM DAYTON HOUSE, *520 W. Water St., (319) 382-9681*. Norwegian & American menu, daily specials. $

Further Information

Decorah Area Chamber of Commerce, *111 Winnebago St., Decorah, IA 52101 (319) 382-3990/(800) 463-4692*.

Directions

From Minneapolis/St. Paul, US 52 south to Decorah.

Orange City
Population 4, 940

Some of the shops of this delightful little town out on the prairies of northwestern Iowa stock Delft pottery, wooden shoes, Dutch dolls, and lace and needlework imported from the Netherlands. Other shops sell Dutch pastries, home-cured dried beef, homemade bologna and bratwurst, and imported Dutch cheese. Among the highlights of the three-day **Tulip Festival** on the third weekend in May are a **Volksparade**, **Klompen Dancers**, and a **Straatmarkt**. And colorful tulip beds. **Orange City's** founders were obviously Dutch.

Many of the businesses in downtown Orange City have added facades with architectural elements modeled after 17th- and 18th-century Dutch buildings. Every year the number of Dutch store fronts grows. The city has in fact sent a delegation of its citizens to the Netherlands to study that country's architecture.

There are of course replicas of Dutch **windmills**. Two of them have been built by Orange City businesses: One houses a bank. The other, built by a paint company, is a working mill with authentically furnished living quarters (open to the public).

Although the town was settled by Dutch immigrants (in 1870), the Dutch architecture is relatively new. The town's more historic buildings are solidly American. The most imposing of these is the **Sioux County Courthouse** (1904), built in the Richardsonian Romanesque style and listed on the National Register. This grand building has so much to offer, including a 10-foot bronze statue of "Justice" on top of its tower, that a detailed brochure has been prepared for self-guided tours.

The **Century House** is a restored 1900 home decorated and furnished in the manner of the early 1900s (open for tours). Another restored structure, the **Little White Store** (1870s), was moved to its present location in 1880. Typical of its kind, the building has a false Western front and upstairs apartment (check locally for hours).

Zwemer Hall (1894), on the campus of **Northwestern College**, is listed on the National Register. The sandstone building is open to the public.

Special Feature

Klompen dancers, a Straatmarkt, a Volksparade, and horse-drawn streetcar tours add color to Orange City's annual **Tulip Festival** (third weekend in May). The three-day festival attracts 150,000 visitors.

Loyal to its Dutch heritage, Orange City has two Christmas traditions, Welcoming Sinterklaas and Piet into Holland (the first weekend in December) and the traditional religious holiday of Christmas. The beauty of the lighted religious symbols that decorate the downtown in December is responsible for the town's nickname, "The City of White Lights."

Where to Stay

DUTCH COLONY INN, *IA 10 E., (712) 737-3490.* Full-service motel, Dutch architecture with Hindeloopen painting on shutters & window boxes; "So Clean, So Quiet, So Dutch." $

Where to Eat

THE TOWN HOUSE, *IA 10, (712) 737-3900.* "Homecook'n," menu or all-you-can-eat buffet. $

THE HATCHERY, *121 3rd St. NW, (712) 737-2889.* Quaint eatery housed in small bldg. once used as hatchery, lounge. $

Further Information

Orange City Chamber of Commerce, *P.O. Box 36, Orange City, IA 51041 (712) 737-4510.*

Directions

From Sioux City, US 75 north to IA 10 (just beyond Maurice), IA 10 east to Orange City.

Pella

Population 9, 270

What a delightful contrast! After driving past Iowa cornfields and rolling pastureland, you enter a town whose gardens, streets, even shop windows speak of Holland. Many of the buildings look like those you'd find in Amsterdam, and during the spring and summer months flowers are everywhere. The town is neat, pretty, unusually clean, prosperous. Old World but also very progressive, **Pella** attributes its good fortune to "old-fashioned virtues like hard work, thrift, honesty and integrity."

The **Dutch Fronts** program, an example of "old-fashioned virtues," is responsible for much of the charm of Pella's buildings. The program encourages businesses to incorporate stepped gables and other elements of Low Country architecture in their construction and renovation. As a result, even McDonald's has a delightfully Dutch look.

One of the program's most enchanting accomplishments is the **Klokkenspel** (*Glockenspiels* in German), a musical clock that sets animated figures in motion. On one side the figures tell of Pella's history, on the other side they step out of the Tulip Time festival. A computer-driven 147-bell carillon provides the music. The Klokkenspel is one of only two or three animated clock towers in the United States.

The **Pella Historical Village** encompasses some 20 buildings linked by red-brick walkways and, in season, tulips. Among the most interesting of the sites are the boyhood home of **Wyatt Earp**, the **Sterrenberg Library**, the **Scholte Church**, and the **Miniature Dutch Village**.

The picturesque **Scholte House** (1848), built by Pella's founder, features a fine collection of French and Italian antiques. The National Register house may be toured by appointment. The **Scholte Gardens**, behind the house, display over 25,000 tulips and annuals.

Flowering trees and literally hundreds of thousands of tulips and other flowers contribute to Pella's Old World flavor. (Much of this beauty is the result of a comprehensive planting project, another example of the town's energetic planning.) The tulips and everything associated with them are especially colorful during Pella's annual **Tulip Time**, second weekend in May.

Pella is small enough that its beauty and charm can be absorbed on foot. Park your car and enjoy a little bit of Holland!

Special Features

Lake Red Rock, Iowa's largest lake, is less than four miles from town. The winds make the lake especially popular with sailors, and the over 50,000 acres of diverse habitat attract a variety of nature lovers.

The new **Bos Landen Golf Club** features a 4-star 18-hole championship course. One of Iowa's premier public facilities, Box Landen (Dutch for "Lands of Woods") also boasts an athletic club, 5-acre lake, and 200-year-old hickories and oaks.

> • *Pella shops display Delftware, fine lace, and other imports from the Netherlands.*
> • *Scrubbing the streets before the Tulip Time parade is a Pella tradition.*

Where to Stay

THE CLOVER LEAF B&B, *314 Washington St., (515) 628-9045*. 1892 home, antiques & period decor, full or "Dutch" breakfasts. $$

STRAWTOWN INN, *1111 Washington St., (515) 628-2681*. Mid-1800s buildings on National Register, private baths, "true Dutch" breakfasts, sunroom with hot tub. $$$

Where to Eat

STRAWTOWN INN, *(see above), (515) 628-4043*. Dutch Spiced Beef, Chateaubriand, Stuffed Pork Chop with Apple Dressing & Mushroom Wine Sauce, Dutch apple bread; atmosphere. $ to $$

Further Information

Pella Chamber of Commerce, *518 Franklin St., Pella, IA 50219 (515) 628-2626*.

Directions

From Des Moines, IA 163 southeast to Pella.

The Villages of Van Buren County
Population from about 20 to 1, 020

Here and there in the Midwest and South, usually far from the city, you can still find a little river town where steamboats once stopped, a place that should have died when the boats stopped coming and industry and trains refused to come. Sometimes the town has one or two old brick stores, but not enough to draw many visitors – or merit a listing in a travel book. If **Van Buren County**, tucked away in a remote part of southeastern Iowa, had one town like that, few would care. But Van Buren County has at least *four* such towns, forming a collection that more than merits a visit.

The four riverboat towns of Van Buren County lie along the banks of the winding **Des Moines River**. Each is within biking distance of the next. Each has its own personality.

Bentonsport (1839), a National Historic District and the tiniest of the towns, has a number of buildings dating from the 1840s-1860s. Adding to the charm of the riverside setting are a one-lane iron bridge (1882), open now only to pedestrians and bikes, and a planting of old garden roses within the picturesque ruins of an ancient mill. The town is the only one of the four to boast crafts shops and resident artists. Several of the houses have been renovated by people from Des Moines, Burlington, and elsewhere wishing to make their homes here.

Bonaparte, founded in 1837, is a National Historic Riverfront District and the smallest Main Street Community in the country. Most of the downtown buildings date from the 1850s-1930s, and many have been restored. Separately listed on the National Register are the **Meek Grist Mill** (1878; see restaurant below), the restored **Des Moines River Lock #5** (1852), and the **Aunty Green Museum** (1844), which houses both a museum and the city library.

Keosauqua is the county seat and largest of the towns. The **courthouse**, on the National Register, is the oldest in continuous use in Iowa (tours available). Also on the National Register is the brick and stone **Pearson House** (1847), once part of the Underground Railroad.

Two National Register buildings in **Farmington** are the second oldest church west of the Mississippi (1847), now the **Pioneer Museum**, and a limestone structure (1867) that was once home to a carriage manufacturing company. Farmington is also known for its park on lovely **Indian Lake** and its proximity to **Shimek State Forest** (see below).

Two of the best ways to absorb the charm of Van Buren County are by bike and by river. Country roads in most parts of Iowa are good, open, and often interesting—in other words, ideal for bicycling. In Van Buren County the cyclist has the added advantage of being unencumbered by traffic lights. The towns can also be seen from a canoe, kayak, or tube on the Des Moines River, water conditions permitting.

Special Features

Lacey-Keosauqua State Park, one of the largest parks in Iowa, features trails that wind along the hills and dales of the Des Moines River. One part of the park contains 19 mounds built by an ancient Indian group. Many of the park's structures were built by the Civilian Conservation Corps in the 1930s and are now listed on the National Register.

The trails of the **Shimek State Forest**, the largest continuous stand of forest cover in the state, are ideal for hikers and horseback riders in the warmer months, and cross-country skiers and snowmobilers in the winter.

> *Van Buren County also has eight or so historic towns located away from the river. Several of those in the western part of the county (for example, Cantril and Milton) serve Amish farm communities.*

Where to Stay

Note: Some of the most historic and charming buildings in Van Buren County are those listed below as lodgings and restaurants.

HOTEL MANNING, *100 Van Buren St. (Keosauqua 52565), (800) 728-2718.* "A Steamboat Gothic Gem" & beloved Iowa landmark, spacious lobby with 16-ft ceilings & Vose rosewood grand piano, antique-filled rooms, full breakfasts, lending library. $ to $$

THE MANSION INN, *500 Henry St. (Keosauqua 52565), (800) 646-0166/(319) 293-2511.* Circa 1870 home with carved staircase & stained-glass windows, some private baths, full breakfasts, other meals by reservation. $$

MASON HOUSE INN *(Bentonsport), Rt. 2 (Box 237) (Keosauqua 52565), (800) 592-3133.* Built in 1846 to serve steamboat travelers, antique furnishings, some private baths, full breakfasts served beside 1880 Buck's cook stove, 1882 Estey pump organ. $$ to $$$

Where to Eat

BONAPARTE RETREAT RESTAURANT, *River St. (Bonaparte), (319) 592-3339.* Seafood, Rib Eye Steak, Huge Windsor Chop; in 1878 grist & flour mill on National Register. $ to $$

Further Information

Villages of Van Buren, *P. O. Box 9, Keosauqua, IA 52565 (800) 868-7822.*

Directions

From Des Moines, I 35 south to exit 12, IA 2 east to Van Buren County (in southeast Iowa).

Other Charming Iowa Towns

Bellevue
Walnut
West Branch

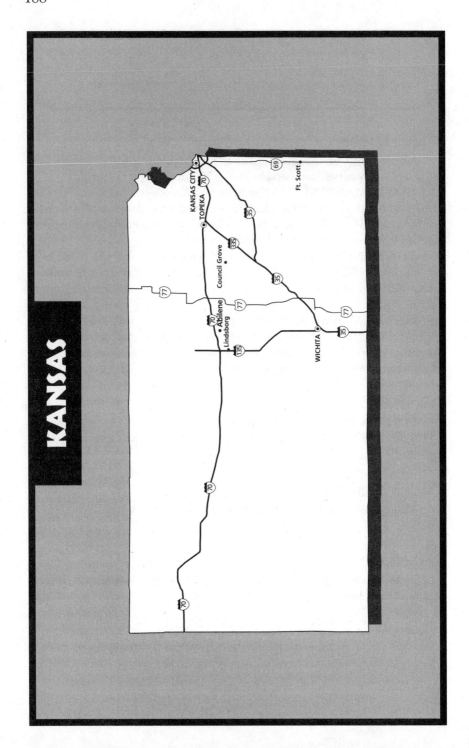

KANSAS

Abilene

Population 6, 742

If American history were to be packaged into its most memorable and romantic eras, one of them would surely be the brawling cow-town era of the Old West; another would be the subsequent turn-of-the-century period with its Victorian wealth and extravagance. **Abilene** was a prominent member of both eras, and important parts of each have been carefully preserved and blended with the accomplishments of more recent periods to create one of the most charming and interesting towns of the American plains.

Abilene began in 1857 as a tiny village and stagecoach stop. A few years later two strangers arrived in town and very quickly made Abilene a legend: One was the railroad which, moving ever westward, made Abilene its terminus for several years. The second was the cowboy, who herded cattle up from Texas along the legendary Chisholm Trail to meet the railroad. Abilene became a booming cow/railroad town, the "wickedest and wildest town in the west," known for its brawling, boozing, betting, and other end-of-trail diversions.

The town's chapter in Western history, at least the hottest part of the chapter, was actually rather short, lasting only five years (1867 to 1872). As the railroad moved farther west, however, Abilene became anything but a ghost town: New businesses flourished and soon handsome mercantile blocks and Victorian mansions lined the streets.

The town's most famous property, the **Eisenhower Center**, commemorates a man with family and childhood roots in Abilene's Victorian era. Occupying 22 acres, the center includes a museum (1954), Eisenhower family home, library (1962), visitors center, and Place of Meditation, the final resting place of Dwight and Mamie Eisenhower and their first-born son. The museum is designed for a self-guided tour through a series of galleries depicting various aspects of Eisenhower's life. Some exhibits are changed periodically to maintain a current relevance.

The best way to enjoy the many mementos of Abilene's Victorian past is with the help of a brochure for a self-guided tour distributed by the Convention and Visitors Bureau (see below). As might be expected, the many beautiful old homes display a variety of Victorian-era architectural styles. The most prominent of the homes are the National Register Italianate **Lebold Vahsholtz Mansion** (1880; guided tours by appointment), the center-towered Second Empire/Italianate **Kirby House** (1885, now a restaurant), and the lovely Neoclassical **Seelye Mansion and Museum** (1905). The latter, on the National Register, displays artifacts from a turn-of-the-century patent medicine company (daily tours).

History is also kept alive at the **Dickinson County Historical Museum**, across from the Eisenhower Center, and the adjacent **Museum of Independent Telephony**, which exhibits antique telephones, switchboards, pay stations, and other memorabilia from an early telephone system. The recently opened **Vintage Fashion Museum** displays women's, children's, and men's clothing in style from 1870 to 1970.

Dedicated to sports history, **The Kansas Sports Hall of Fame** was established "to honor and recognize Kansas athletes, as well as their mentors, who have used their talents to their greatest abilities." The work of Kansans of American Indian descent is featured in the **American Indian Art Center and Gallery**.

Thrillers, comedies, and musicals are presented by the **Great Plains Theater Festival**, a year-round professional theater company. The theater is housed in an 1881 Romanesque church building. Entertainment is also available each evening on the screen of the **Plaza Theatre**, a 1930s Art Deco movie house.

Special Feature

The **Abilene & Smoky Valley Railroad Association** offers a 10-mile round trip between Abilene and Enterprise on a 100-year-old wooden coach/diner.

> • *One of Abilene's most popular family attractions is the hand-carved C. W. Parker Carousel, a working carousel that welcomes riders. The carousel is one of many manufactured by a turn-of-the-century Abilene amusement company.*
>
> • *Nearly 3, 000, 000 cattle were driven from Texas to Abilene during the town's five-year boom period.*

Where to Stay

BALFOURS' HOUSE B&B, *940 1900 Ave., (913) 263-4262*. Contemporary retreat on edge of town with indoor pool & spa, suite with two bedrooms & private entrance, bungalow suite, full breakfasts, some pets. $$

SPRUCE HOUSE, *604 N. Spruce, (913) 263-3900*. 1880s home with bay windows & pocket doors, private baths, full breakfasts, fresh flowers, in heart of town. $$

VICTORIAN REFLECTIONS B&B, *820 NW Third, (913) 263-7774.* Home in turn-of-century residential area, curved stairway, music room, antiques, private baths, full breakfasts, swimming & tennis adjacent. $$

WINDMILL INN, *1787 Rain Rd. (Chapman 67431), (913) 263-8755.* 1917 lavender four-square home on working farm, wrap-around front porch, private baths, full breakfasts, public dining room, hors d'oeuvres. $$

Where to Eat

KIRBY HOUSE, *205 NE 3rd St., P.O. Box 337, (913) 263-7336.* "Serving Traditional Midwestern Fare," Country Fried Steak with mashed potatoes & fresh cream gravy the house specialty, special Sunday lunch menu, Victorian setting. $ to $$

MR. K'S FARMHOUSE RESTAURANT, *407 S. Van Buren, (913) 263-7995.* Seafood, chicken, steaks, barbecued brisket; Abilene landmark, Eisenhower birthday-paddled here. $

WINDMILL INN, *(see above).* Seasoned Shrimp, Filet of Ostrich, 16-oz. T-bone, Seasonal Vegetable Plate; "country with class," by reservation only. $$

Further Information

Abilene Convention & Visitors Bureau, *Union Pacific Depot, P.O. Box 146, Abilene, KS 67410 (800) 569-5915.*

Directions

From Topeka, I 70 west to Abilene; from Wichita, I 135 north to KS 15, north to Abilene.

Council Grove
Population 2228

The prairie town of **Council Grove** straddles the old **Santa Fe Trail** in the middle of the beautiful **Flint Hills** of central Kansas. The site of the town once afforded water, and also wood from groves of hardwood trees, for the use of soldiers, explorers, and merchant caravans moving west along the Santa Fe Trail. The town itself, established in the late 1850s, was for a while the last supply point on the 780-mile trail.

As you walk or drive along **Main Street**, called **Prairie Plaza** today but once part of the Santa Fe Trail, you will see buildings that were among the last traces of civilization seen by thousands of homesick settlers in the

1860s as they faced west. Much of the early town survives today as a National Historic Landmark District.

The name of the oldest commercial building in town, the **Last Chance Store** (1857), obviously tells something about the store's history. Another of the town's oldest buildings, the **Hays House** (1857), is the oldest continuously operating restaurant west of the Mississippi (see listing below). The structure has doubled over the decades as a mail distribution center, court room, tavern, meeting place for Sunday morning church services, and printing room for the first local newspaper.

Another important structure from pioneer times, the lovely stone **Kaw Mission State Historic Site/Museum** (1850-51) was built as a boarding school for Native American boys and later served as a school for the children of settlers.

Although Council Grove is out on the prairie, there is probably no other town in the country that lists more trees among its historic sites. The **Council Oak**, from which the name of the town arose, was the site of an 1825 council, attended by U.S. officials and Osage chiefs, that agreed to a treaty giving Whites free passage along the Santa Fe Trail. (The tree blew down in a 1958 storm, but the site has been marked by a shrine.)

In addition to the Council Oak there was the **Post Office Oak**, a bur oak that is said to have had a cache in its base where people passing along the trail could leave messages. A third tree was the **Custer Elm** under which legend has it George Armstrong Custer camped while patrolling the trail. (Check with the visitors bureau for the locations of the trunks of these two trees.)

Special Feature

KS 177 to the south is one of the state's most scenic routes. Along the way are several little towns that, bypassed by time, are pure Americana. Just outside one of them, Strong City, is the historic **Z-Bar Ranch**, headquarters for the new 10,894-acre **Tallgrass Prairie National Preserve**.

> *Santa Fe Trail ruts can be seen a few miles west of town, just off U.S. 56. They are on private property, so get instructions from the Visitors Bureau on how to visit them.*

Where to Stay

THE COTTAGE HOUSE HOTEL, *25 N. Neosho, (800) 727-7903.* Once an 1870s boarding house and later an elegant Victorian home & hotel, antiques, private baths, Continental breakfasts. $$

FLINT HILLS B&B, *613 W. Main St., (316) 767-6655.* 1913 American Four-Square, antiques, private baths, full breakfasts, boyhood home of former Congressman John Rhodes. $$

Where to Eat

HAYS HOUSE 1857, *112 W. Main St., (316) 767-5911.* Beulah's Ham, Skillet Fried Chicken, Beef Brisket, Chicken Fried Steak; treasures of local history, antiques, original bar, fireplace of native stone, one of finest restaurants in Kansas. $ to $$

ROSIE'S TRAILSIDE DINER, *209 W. Main St., (316) 767-6945.* Mexican food, deli sandwiches, hot beef sandwiches, homemade pies. $

Further Information

Council Grove Convention & Visitors Bureau, *200 W. Main St., Council Grove, KS 66846 (800) 732-9211/(316) 767-5882.*

Directions

From Wichita, I 35 north to exit 92, north on KS 177 to Council Grove.

Fort Scott
Population 8, 362

It seems only fitting that the heartland of America should have one of the country's most beautiful – and beautifully preserved – downtowns. The lawyers, bankers, and socially active women who once moved about **Fort Scott's** streets in their buggies and carriages must certainly have personified Midwestern middle-class respectability. The setting would have it no other way: 30 miles of brick streets lined by tree-shaded, handsome Victorian homes and awning-shaded, colorfully painted Victorian business blocks. The architecture, while varied, has more depth and age to it than can be dismissed simply as "turn of the century"—some of the buildings go as far back as the Civil War.

At one end of **Main Street** is the **Fort Scott National Historic Site**, a restored 1842 frontier military fort. The only one of its kind in the country, the site comprises 20 buildings, including the hospital, powder magazine, bakery, barracks, and officers' row. Within the buildings are 33 historically furnished rooms. During the summer the fort sponsors weapons demonstrations, an Indian encampment, and other events.

Museum exhibits and an audio-visual presentation introduce the visitor to a relatively unknown, but exciting period in America's history.

Other important restorations in the downtown area include the 1873 Gothic-style **Old Congregational Church**, with antique furnishings, and the **Ralph Richards Museum**, an 1893 building displaying turn-of-the-century wedding dresses, railroad memorabilia, antique tools, an old general store, and military artifacts. On the second floor of the museum is a completely furnished Victorian residence with double parlor, library, kitchen, and other rooms.

The downtown area is also the site of two notable memorials, the **Twin Trees Monument** (1965), dedicated to the "Bleeding Kansas" turmoil that occurred before and during the Civil War, and the **20th Century Veterans Memorial** (1990), dedicated to all 20th-century veterans of the U.S. Armed Forces.

Fort Scott's sights may be seen by an hour-long trolley ride (highly recommended). Driving tours, antiquing tours, and walking tours are other options.

Special Feature

A **U.S. National Cemetery**, one of the 12 such cemeteries designated by President Lincoln, lies on the southeast outskirts of Fort Scott. Established in 1862, and older than the Arlington National Cemetery, the cemetery is the final resting place of Indian soldiers, Civil War veterans, and veterans of more recent wars.

> • *A Fort Scott brick business provided 50 million bricks used in the construction of the Panama Canal. Fort Scott brick was also used on the first Indianapolis Speedway.*
>
> • *The traditional pork steak, fried chicken, and "ham and potato bake" often share the small-town Kansas menu with Midwestern-style cheese burritos and other items of Mexican ancestry.*

Where to Stay

THE CHENAULT MANSION, *820 S. National Ave., (316) 223-6800.* 1887 home with ornate woodwork & crystal chandeliers, private baths, full breakfasts. $$ to $$$

COUNTRY QUARTERS, *Rt. 5 (Box 80), (316) 223-2889.* Old farmhouse, hand-carved oak mantle, "great" breakfasts, front porch for Kansas sunsets. $

THE COURTLAND, *121 E. 1st St., (316) 223-0098/(800) 882-4233.* Restored 1906 hotel, family heirlooms, private baths, "sumptuous" breakfasts, sunny Gathering Room. $$ to $$$

THE LYONS' HOUSE, *742 S. National St., (316) 223-0779.* Circa 1876 Italianate mansion, antiques, Tiffany tiles around fireplaces, some private baths, full breakfasts, looms & spinning wheels, murder mysteries. $$ to $$$

Where to Eat

GRANNIE VAIL'S RESTAURANT, *101 State St., (316) 223-0142.* Authentic Midwestern menu with daily & nightly specials, salads, sandwiches, soups; Victorian antiques. $

PAPA DON'S RESTAURANTE, *22 N. Main St., (316) 223-4171.* Specialty pizzas, pasta, deli sandwiches. $

Further Information

Visitor Information Center, *231 E. Wall St., P.O. Box 205, Fort Scott, KS 66701 (800) 245-3678/(316) 223-3566/fax (316) 223-3574.*

Directions

From Kansas City (KS), US 69 south to Fort Scott.

Lindsborg
Population 3076

If you look in one direction, the view is of fields and farms, reminiscent of the Midwest. If you look in another, you see the vast spaces of the West. The countryside is incongruous, and sitting in the middle of it all, and adding to the incongruity, is the delightful little Swedish-American town of **Lindsborg**.

Swedish immigrants settling in the **Smoky Hill River Valley** brought with them a commitment to cooperative farming, but also a love and respect for learning and the arts. The value placed on education led to the founding of **Bethany College**, known today for its liberal arts tradition and beautiful campus.

The love of the arts has manifested itself in many ways, from woodcarving to folk dancing to the establishment of the 400-voice **Bethany College Oratorio Society**. Most obvious to the visitor are the art galleries, two of which are among Lindsborg's top sites: the **Birger Sandzen Memorial Gallery**, on the campus of Bethany College, which displays works by the widely recognized Swedish-American painter and teacher of art, along with works of other artists; and the **Raymer Center for the Arts**, which includes Lester Raymer's studio, home, and collection of artwork and handmade toys.

The best way to soak up Lindsborg's charm is to wander the old brick streets. The tidy compactness of the town makes a map unnecessary, although one is available from the Chamber of Commerce. Craft shops are especially prominent, along with the art galleries and studios. The emphasis in the shops and restaurants is of course on things Scandinavian: imports, folk art and contemporary crafts, Swedish pastries.

The **Bethany Lutheran Church**, near downtown, has a hand-crafted altar and collection of large oil paintings that give the interior an appearance suggestive of churches in rural Sweden.

Several blocks from downtown is the **Old Mill Museum**, which features Indian and pioneer-day artifacts as well as natural history displays. The museum complex comprises several historic structures, including the **Smoky Valley Roller Mill** and the **Swedish pavilion** from the 1904 World's Fair.

Other Lindsborg museums include the **Reo Antique Auto Museum**, located in an annex to a 1930 service station; and the turn-of-the-century **Stenfors Mansion** (shown by appointment).

Special Feature

The panoramic view from **Coronado Heights**, an elevated park and historic site three miles northwest of town, makes it clear that the West is not far away.

• *The Dala Horse, a popular form of domestic art in Sweden, was selected by Lindsborg as the symbol of its Swedish heritage.*
• *The "little" Old Mill Museum displays over 22, 000 items!*

Where to Stay

SMOKY VALLEY B&B, *130 N. Second St., (800) 532-4407/(913) 227-4406*. 1890s Italianate home one block from downtown, family heirlooms, circular staircase, TV, private baths, extensive garden area. $ to $$

SWEDISH COUNTRY INN, *112 W. Lincoln St., (913) 227-2985*. Restored turn-of-century bldg., Swedish pine furniture, TV, homemade quilts, private baths, full Scandinavian buffet breakfast, sauna, bikes, gift shop. $$

Where to Eat

BRUNSWICK HOTEL RESTAURANT, *202 S. Main, (913) 227-2903*. American & Mexican menus, Swedish specialties, luncheon buffet; in hotel bldg. dating to 1887. $

THE CITY BAKERY, *107 N. Main, (913) 227-3908*. Lunches, Swedish pancakes, fresh pastries, ice cream parlor. $

THE HIDEAWAY RESTAURANT & CLUB, *P.O. Box 175, (913) 227-2933*. K.C. Strip, Charbroiled Pork Chops, Malibu Chicken, Shrimp Scampi, Prime Rib (Fridays), burgers; in old barn, recreation membership available for fishing / boating in 2 lakes. $ to $$

SWEDISH CROWN, *121 N. Main, (913) 227-2076*. Swedish & American menus, authentic Swedish meat balls & ham loaf, smorgasbords. $

Further Information

Lindsborg Chamber of Commerce, *P.O. Box 191, Lindsborg, KS 67456 (913) 227-3706*.

Directions

From Wichita, I 135 north to exit 72 (Lindsborg exit).

Other Charming Kansas Towns

Elk Falls
Wilson
Yoder

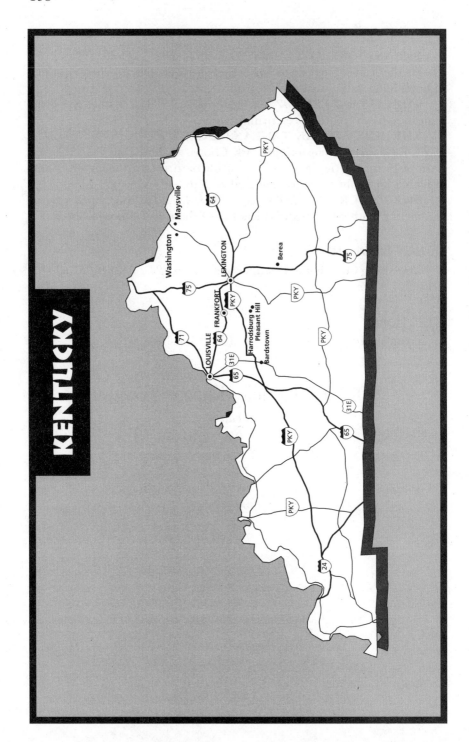

KENTUCKY

Maysville

Washington

LEXINGTON

Berea

FRANKFORT

Harrodsburg
Pleasant Hill

LOUISVILLE

Bardstown

KENTUCKY

Bardstown

Population 6, 801

According to legend, Stephen Collins Foster was inspired by a visit in 1852 to **Federal Hill**, his cousins' home in **Bardstown**, to write *My Old Kentucky Home*, now the Kentucky state anthem and one of the country's most beloved melodies. It isn't clear whether Foster composed the song while in Kentucky or afterward, or whether in fact Foster ever even visited Bardstown. It doesn't really matter, because both Federal Hill and Bardstown look exactly what an "old Kentucky home" ought to look like. Foster couldn't have made a better choice.

Kentucky's second oldest town (1780) and a center of bourbon whiskey production, Bardstown has had its ups and downs (Prohibition was one of its downs). But for reasons relating as much to the townspeople's love of home place as anything, Bardstown has gotten more and more beautiful over the years. The old buildings have been spruced up and restored, the trees have grown bigger and the downtown, although certainly much changed over the decades, looks like it hasn't changed in 150 years. This is a lovely little town that may be closer to the ideal Kentucky home than it was even in Foster's time.

Bardstown has about 200 buildings dating back before 1880. A large number of the older homes were built in the late 1700s and early 1800s. Some are brick, some weatherboarded log, a few frame. Georgian, Federal and, to some extent, Greek Revival styles predominate—the Victorian styles never really caught on. Two of the most famous homes are open to the public. The first, **Wickland** (1813-1830), home of three governors, may be Kentucky's best example of Georgian architecture. The second, the stately Georgian **Federal Hill** (1800-1820), now the centerpiece of **My Old Kentucky Home State Park**, is shown by guides in antebellum costume.

Running a close second behind Federal Hill on the list of historic landmarks is the venerable **Old Talbott Tavern**. Probably built in the late 1700s, the charming brick and stone structure is believed to be the oldest inn in continuous operation west of the Alleghenies. To mention a few who have passed through its doors: King Louis Philippe, George Rogers Clark, Daniel Boone, Queen Marie of Rumania, Henry Clay, General George Patton, Jesse W. James, and John J. Audubon.

St. Joseph Proto-Cathedral, the first Roman Catholic cathedral west of the Alleghenies (1819), is another Bardstown landmark. The restored cathedral has several valuable paintings that were donated by Pope Leo XII and Francis I of the Two Sicilies.

Nearby **Spalding Hall** (1826/rebuilt 1837), once a part of **St. Joseph's College** (for young men), is now home to several businesses and two museums. One of the latter, the **Bardstown Historical Museum**, contains Stephen Foster memorabilia, gifts of Louis Philippe and Charles X of France, Jesse James's hat, and Jenny Lind's velvet cape.

Among the items displayed in the **Oscar Getz Museum of Whiskey History**, also in Spalding Hall, is an 1854 E. G. Booz bottle that gave the world the word "booze," and a copy of the liquor license that Abraham Lincoln and his partners held while running a store in Illinois in 1833.

Other buildings of special note in Bardstown include the **McLean House** (circa 1814), one of Kentucky's finest examples of Georgian-style commercial architecture; the 1827 **Presbyterian Church**; and **Roseland Academy** (1820-1830), noted for its three-flight spiral staircase. The **Old County Jails** (1819/1874) were until 1987 the oldest operating jail complex in Kentucky. Guided tours of the buildings, now a bed and breakfast (see below), are available.

The colorful, costumed cast of the two-hour outdoor musical, *The Stephen Foster Story*, perform more than 50 of Foster's songs.

Special Features

Three local distilleries (**Heaven Hill**, **Jim Beam**, and **Maker's Mark**) offer interesting tours – and good introductions to local history.

To the northwest of Bardstown is the 14,000-acre **Bernheim Forest**. This lovely area contains trails, ornamental gardens, waterfowl ponds, and hundreds of labeled varieties of trees and shrubs.

John Fitch, inventor of the steamboat, died in Bardstown after years of failed efforts to obtain financial and political support for his invention. Ironically, the steamboat and railroad would eventually hurt Bardstown by drawing growth elsewhere.

Where to Stay

ARBOR ROSE B&B, *209 E. Stephen Foster, (502) 349-0014/(888) 828-3330*. 1820 home now in late Victorian style, on National Register, antiques, fireplaces, some TVs, private baths, whirlpools, full breakfasts, refreshments, verandah, gardens, centrally located. $$$

JAILER'S INN, *111 W. Stephen Foster, (502) 348-5551*. Ca 1819 Federal-style jail, on National Register, heirlooms & antiques, TV, private baths, whirlpools, full breakfasts, gardens, one room with resemblance to jail cell. $$ to $$$

KENMORE FARMS B&B, *1050 Bloomfield Rd., (800) 831-6159*. 1860s home on horse farm, antiques & Oriental rugs, private baths, full "country" breakfasts. $$ to $$$

THE MANSION, *1003 N. Third St., (502) 348-2586*. 1851 Greek Revival home on National Register, antiques, hand-crocheted bedspreads, some private baths, "deluxe" Continental breakfasts. $$ to $$$

TALBOTT TAVERN, *Court Square, (502) 348-3494*. Oldest western stagecoach stop in America (1779), antiques, TV, private baths, Cont. breakfasts, dining room, pub, full of character. $$

WM. HEAVENHILL HOUSE, *925 Loretto Rd., (800) 324-5952*. Circa 1820 Federal home, fireplaces, private baths, whirlpools, secluded country setting, home tours. $$$

Where to Eat

BARDSTONIAN RESTAURANT, *521 N. Third St., (502) 349-1404*. Deep Sea Kabob, Chicken Parisienne, Vegetable Kabob, Lobster Tail, Tandoori Scallops, Delmonico, Aged Country Ham; in restored 1846 home. $$

DAGWOOD'S, *204 N. Third St., (502) 348-4029*. New York Strip Marinated in 12-Year-Old Bourbon and Served on White-Oak Barrel Stave with Mushrooms. $ to $$

KURTZ RESTAURANT, *418 E. Stephen Foster, (502) 348-8964*. Southern-style cooking including Skillet-fried Chicken, Fried Cornbread, & home-style vegetables. $

MY OLD KENTUCKY DINNER TRAIN, *602 N. Third St., (502) 348-7300*. Dinner served on fine china in restored 1940s dining cars during 2-hour trip through central Kentucky countryside. $$$

TALBOTT TAVERN, *(see above)*. Federal Hill Catfish, Bill's Chicken Phillippe, George's Aged Country Ham, Judge Rowan's Ribeye Steak, chess pie; in third century of service. $$

XAVIER'S, *112 Xavier Dr., (502) 349-9464*. Sirloin Steak Sauté Arizona, Stuffed Chicken Breast Solanus, Penne Rigate, Grilled Swordfish with Tomato Orange Salsa; highly regarded. $$

Further Information

Bardstown-Nelson County Tourist & Convention Commission, *P.O. Box 867, Bardstown, KY 40004 (800) 638-4877*.

Directions
From Louisville, US 31E/150 south to Bardstown.

Berea
Population 10, 000

Standing in the little park in front of Boone Tavern Hotel in **Berea** is almost guaranteed to bring on feelings of longing and nostalgia. The tulip trees and oaks on the campus across the street have something to do with it. So does the gorgeous white Georgian facade of the hotel, a Kentucky landmark. But it goes beyond that. It is somehow related to what might be called "down home." And Berea has some of the finest of it that our country has to offer.

One of the reasons for this may be that Berea is one of the country's leading centers for the crafting of down-home items. The state in fact has designated Berea the *Folk Arts and Crafts Capital of Kentucky*. It began with the founding in 1855 of the town's centerpiece, **Berea College**, as a place of higher learning for young people, chiefly from Appalachia, who could not afford a college education. Students pay no tuition, and room-and-board costs were – and still are – paid in large part by money earned in the college's labor program. Because ceramics, weaving, woodcraft, broomcraft, and other crafts formed part of the students' work activities, it was inevitable that Berea College and, more generally, Berea would acquire a reputation for quality crafts.

To appreciate the beauty of Berea's crafts, step into the lobby of the **Boone Tavern Hotel** (1909). Although the sheer quality of the work can hide the fact, most of the furniture and furnishings are handmade. The food is also homemade, of course, and let's face it, things like Chicken Flakes in a Bird's Nest, spoon bread, and Southern Pecan Pie can only add to the charm.

Shops offering everything from handmade brooms and patchwork quilts to mountain dulcimers and quality furniture are located in **Old Town** (on N. Broadway) and on campus at The College Square. Some of the work is by local craftspeople, some of it is by students in the college's crafts program. The **Log House Craft Gallery** on Main Street displays student crafts and, on its second floor, the Wallace Nutting collection of early American furniture. In addition to focusing on the history and traditional crafts of Appalachia, the **Berea College Appalachian Museum** sponsors exhibits in which regional artists and craftspeople demonstrate their skills.

Shopping maps and directories are available in the **Welcome Center**, a restored 1917 railroad depot that has been listed on the National Register.

Special Features

A tour of the loomhouse at **Churchill Weavers**, Berea's first non-college industry, provides an opportunity to watch as some of the most beautiful handwoven fabrics anywhere take form on the handmade looms.

While visiting Berea try your skill at skittles, a handcrafted table-top bowling game. Skittles may be played at the Welcome Center on in the lobby of the Boone Tavern Hotel.

Visitors interested in antiques should explore the 400 block of Chestnut Street.

> • *Berea College was the first interracial college south of the Mason-Dixon line.*
> • *The Draper Building on the Berea College campus is a reproduction of Independence Hall in Philadelphia.*

Where to Stay

BOONE TAVERN HOTEL, *Main St., (800) 366-9358.* One of Kentucky's best-known inns (1909), full-service, gift shop with handcrafts from Student Craft Industries. $$

THE DOCTOR'S INN B&B, *617 Chestnut St., (606) 986-3042.* 1948 Greek Revival home, antiques & art, library, private baths, "healthy" breakfast specials or full "country" breakfasts, baby grand piano, fitness area, porch, gardens, mountain views. $$$

HOLIDAY MOTEL, *I 75 & KY 21, P.O. Box 227, (606) 986-9311.* Respected locally owned motel with pool & spacious grounds. $ to $$

THE MORNING GLORY B&B (AND WEAVER'S BOTTOM CRAFT STUDIO). *140 N. Broadway, (606) 986-8661.* Originally grocery store & pharmacy, pressed steel ceiling, furnishings by local artists & craftspeople. $ to $$

SHADY LANE B&B, *123 Mt. Vernon Rd., (606) 986-9851.* Shaded Greek Revival home, works by local artisans, private baths, Cont. or full breakfasts, hors d'oeuvres, croquet & bocci. $ to $$

Where to Eat

BOONE TAVERN HOTEL, *(see above)*. Chicken Flakes in a Bird's Nest, Roast Kentucky Turkey & Dressing, Broiled Haddock, Grilled Kentucky Bourbon Flank Steak, own spoon bread; changing menu, Kentucky cooking at its finest, dress requirements for Sunday noon meal & all evening meals, reservations recommended. $$

Further Information

Berea Tourist & Convention Commission, *201 N. Broadway, P.O. Box 556, Berea, KY 40403 (606) 986-2540/(800) 598-5263.*

Directions

From Lexington, I 75 or US 25 south to Berea (45 minutes).

Harrodsburg/Pleasant Hill
Population 7335

There are no two other towns in the country that in a single day could provide the visitor with a more thorough and delightful introduction to a state than **Harrodsburg** and **Pleasant Hill**. Harrodsburg, the first permanent English settlement west of the Alleghenies (1774), is one of those places where a beautiful setting and collection of historic attractions have blended to produce a town with a truly distinct character—albeit a very Kentucky one. The **Shaker Village of Pleasant Hill**, just seven miles away, provides one of the finest examples of historic restoration in the country. The village is a National Historic Landmark from boundary to boundary.

The **Harrodsburg/Mercer County Tourist Commission** publishes an exceptionally thorough walking/driving tour guide. Among other things, the booklet begins with a glossary that, with no more than a few minutes' study, is guaranteed to turn the reader into someone with a working knowledge of early American architectural history.

St. Philip's Episcopal Church (1860/61), a Gothic Revival gem, has only one truly centered window, the window back of the altar. For as the designer, the Right Rev. Benjamin Bosworth Smith, taught, "Only Providence is perfect, and man should ever be mindful of such." The Greek Revival **Methodist Parsonage** (ca 1840) has housed more than 60 ministers and their families for over a century and a half.

Beaumont Inn (1845), a major local landmark, was for more than seven decades one of the South's leading female colleges. The building has been owned and operated as a country inn by the same family since 1917 (see below). **Morgan Row**, another landmark, is the oldest row house in Kentucky (1807) and the first one constructed west of the Allegheny Mountains.

Old Fort Harrod State Park features an exact replica of the original fort built in 1775. Included on the park grounds are a federal monument dedicated to George Rogers Clark (1934), the oldest pioneer cemetery west of the Alleghenies, and the log cabin in which Abraham Lincoln's parents were married (1806). The Greek Revival **Mansion Museum** (1810 / 1830), also on the grounds, houses exhibits that tell of Kentucky's past, including the Civil War era when state loyalties were divided between North and South. Craft demonstrations are held in the park during the warmer months.

Among the stores downtown is the **Harrodsburg General Store** (circa 1917), built on the site of Daniel Boone's cabin. Visitors may play checkers by a potbellied stove, listen to bluegrass music, and shop for overalls, boot scrapers, oil cloth, and Kentucky jellies.

The Shakers were members of the largest communal society in the country during the 19th century, the *United Society of Believers in Christ's Second Appearing*. Called Shakers because of their ritualistic dance, they were celibate, pacifistic, creative, and hard-working (and obviously had to recruit from the outside).

Pleasant Hill's 33 original buildings and miles of stone fencing are preserved on 2,700 acres of rolling Bluegrass countryside. Among the village's most notable structures are the **Centre Family Dwelling** (1824-1834), which contains a 40-room exhibit of original Shaker crafts and furniture; the **Trustees' Office** (1839), with twin spiral staircases; and the **Meeting House** (1820), where Shaker music is performed.

Special Features

Excursions along the high limestone cliffs of the historic **Kentucky River** can be taken during the warmer months aboard the sternwheeler *Dixie Belle*. The boat departs a short distance from Pleasant Hill, at Shaker Landing.

Evening performances of *The Legend of Daniel Boone* and *Shadows in the Forest*, outdoor drama adventures, are held in Harrodsburg during the summer months in the James Harrod Amphitheater.

> • *Harrodsburg was the site of Kentucky's first law courts, religious service, school, and gristmill.*
> • *The population of Shakers at Pleasant Hill peaked near 500 in the 1830s.*

Where to Stay

BAXTER HOUSE B&B, *1677 Lexington Rd., (606) 734-5700.* Turn-of-century country house among bluegrass horse farms, antique shop. $$

BAUER HAUS B&B, *362 N. College St. (US 127), (606) 734-6289.* 1880s home on National Register, designated Kentucky Landmark, walking distance to Old Fort Harrod. $$

BEAUMONT INN, *638 Beaumont Inn Dr., (800) 352-3992.* Full-service country inn on National Register, antiques, dining room, Kentucky landmark. $$ to $$$

CANAAN LAND FARM B&B, *4355 Lexington Rd., (606) 734-3984.* Ca 1795 home & 1815 log cabin on working sheep farm, National Register, private baths, full "country" breakfasts, pool. $$ to $$$

COLONIAL HILLS FARM & INN, *560 Kirkwood Rd. (Salvisa 40372), (606) 865-2253.* 1850s Greek Revival & Italianate home on farm, private baths, full breakfasts, walking trails. $$ to $$$

SHAKER VILLAGE OF PLEASANT HILL, *3501 Lexington Rd., (606) 734-5411.* Guest rooms throughout village, Shaker reproductions, TV, private baths, restaurant. $$ to $$$

Where to Eat

BEAUMONT INN, *638 Beaumont Inn Dr., (606) 734-3381.* Yellow-legged Fried Chicken, Two-year-old Kentucky Cured Ham, corn pudding; a Kentucky legend. $$

TRUSTEES' OFFICE INN, *3501 Lexington Rd., (606) 734-5411.* Shaker & regional foods served family style in restored Shaker village, home baking, reservations advised. $$

WARD'S LANDING, *4 mi. from Shaker Village on Kentucky River, (606) 734-2875.* Smorgasbord featuring catfish, fried chicken, barbecued ribs, roast beef, bowls of vegetables, "fabulous" biscuits; view of palisades. $ to $$

Further Information

Harrodsburg/Mercer County Tourist Commission, *P.O. Box 283, 103 S. Main St., Harrodsburg, KY 40330 (606) 734-2364/(800) 355-9192.*

Directions

From Lexington, US 68 southwest to Harrodsburg.

Maysville/Washington
Populations 7169 / about 500

Located far from the interstates and in a rather remote part of the state, **Maysville** and neighboring **Washington** are certainly among Kentucky's best kept secrets. Each town reached its heyday during an interesting and romantic time in history, and these times are preserved in the form of two picture-postcard historic districts. Steam-driven riverboats still put into Maysville, an old Ohio River town that once went by the name of *Limestone*, and in Washington, sometimes called *Old Washington*, costumed guides escort visitors along flag-stone walks past buildings that may have known Daniel Boone.

Maysville, or Limestone, was founded in 1784, but didn't reach its golden era until a few decades later. A major tobacco market, the town was a hub of riverboat traffic during the middle years of the 19th century. Maysville remains very much alive, but Kentucky's and adjacent Ohio's major centers of commerce did develop elsewhere, and the town was therefore able to preserve some of its inheritance from the old river days.

Established in 1786 as a pioneer post, Washington developed rapidly into one of the more important towns east of the Alleghenies. Although maybe a little larger now than in the 1790s, Old Washington remains a tiny community that looks in many ways like it did 200 years ago.

One of the loveliest (and most photographed) features of Maysville's historic district is a group of **row houses** (circa 1850) that look like a blend of old New Orleans and antebellum Kentucky. The New Orleans flavor is due to the use of iron grillwork by builders who were familiar with Louisiana because of the riverboat trade.

The **Mason County Museum**, now on the National Register, was built as the public library around 1876. The museum uses changing displays and touch exhibits to introduce the visitor to local history. Included are old photos and detailed river dioramas. A genealogical library and art gallery are also housed in the National Register building. Two other sites of interest in the historic district are the Greek Revival **Mason County Courthouse**, built as a city hall in 1844, and the **National Underground Railroad Museum**, whose exhibits honor the several stations of the Underground Railroad in the Maysville area.

The first stop in Old Washington should be the **Cane Brake**, one of the town's original cabins (1790) and now the visitors' center. In addition to information and historical literature, the center offers an orientation film, guided tours, and a walking-tour map. The historic district lists no fewer than 45 buildings, most built between 1785 and 1812. Four are early buildings that are on tour from the visitors' center: the **Simon Kenton**

Shrine, another of the original cabins; **Paxton Inn** (circa 1810), a station on the Underground Railroad; the **Albert Sidney Johnston House** (circa 1797), birthplace of the famous Confederate general; and **Mefford's Station** (circa 1787), a cabin made in part from planks from a flatboat that brought the Mefford family to nearby Limestone. Two churches are also on tour from the visitors' center, the **Methodist Episcopal Church South** (1848), now known as the Old Church Museum, and the Gothic Revival **Washington Presbyterian Church** (1870).

Several buildings that are not part of the guided tours are nevertheless open to the public. One is **Brodrick's Tavern** (1794), Washington's first tavern; another is the 1845 **Washington Hall**, built as a grand hotel.

Many of the historic homes remain private residences. These include the **George Wood House** (circa 1795), the oldest brick structure in Washington; **Cedar Hill** (1807), which hosted two presidents among other prominent Americans; and **Federal Hill** (1800), built by the brother of John Marshall, Chief Justice of the U.S. Supreme Court.

Another residence, the **Marshall Key House** (circa 1807), was where Harriet Beecher Stowe, a visitor in 1833, witnessed a slave auction that inspired her to write *Uncle Tom's Cabin*. The house is now the **Harriet Beecher Stowe Slavery to Freedom Museum**.

Washington's and Maysville's shops offer a variety of items, including antiques. The out-of-town visitor will be especially interested in the handmade and Kentucky-made crafts.

Special Features

The Maysville area boasts 8 of the 13 **covered bridges** remaining in Kentucky. One, the **Goddard Covered Bridge** (1820), is the oldest covered bridge in the state still open to traffic. A map of the bridges is available from the tourism commission (see below).

Woodworkers, blacksmiths, tinsmiths, and other craftspeople demonstrate their talents in the restored village of **May's Lick** (founded 1780s), 8 miles south of Maysville/Washington. The living village is also home to several antique shops.

On August 19, 1782, almost a year after the surrender of Lord Cornwallis at Yorktown, Kentucky militiamen pursuing British and Indian forces were ambushed near the Licking River. Although the ensuing Battle of Blue Licks lasted only a few minutes, some 60 of the Kentuckians were killed. The battle is commemorated at **Blue Licks Battlefield State Park**, south of Maysville/Washington. In addition to its Pioneer Museum, the park offers camping, swimming, and hiking.

> • *The Simon Kenton Bridge (1931), crossing the Ohio River at Maysville, was a prototype of the Golden Gate Bridge in San Francisco.*
> • *The sternwheelers Delta Queen, American Queen, and Mississippi Queen put into Maysville April through November.*

Where to Stay

THE FRENCH QUARTER INN, *25 E. McDonald Pkwy., (606) 564-8000.* Contemporary full-service inn, whirlpools, restaurant. $$

KLEIER HAUS, *912 US 62 (Maysville 41056), (606) 759-7663.* 1885 home in rolling countryside, porch, TV, some private baths, full "Kentucky" breakfasts, adjacent to golf course. $$

WERNWAG HOUSE B&B, *5079 Main St. (May's Lick), (606) 763-6506.* 1835 home with hand-carved cherry stair rail & parlor mantle, fireplace, private bath. $$

Where to Eat

MOYER WINERY & RESTAURANT, *3859 US 52, P.O. Box 235 (Manchester, OH 45144), (937) 549-2957.* Fettuccine with Shrimp, Poached Scallops, Filet Mignon; surrounded by banks of Ohio River & acres of vineyards. $$

TIPPEDORE'S, *(see The French Quarter Inn above).* Rosemary Chicken, Chef's Quatro Formagi, Chef's "Award Winning" Grilled Ostrich, Mixed Grill, Scrod English Style. $$

Further Information

Maysville-Mason County Tourism Commission, *216 Bridge St., Maysville, KY 41056 (606) 564-9411*; & **Old Washington**, **Inc. Visitor's Center**, *Washington, KY 41096 (606) 759-7411.*

Directions

From Lexington, US 68 north to Maysville/Washington; from Cincinnati, US 52 south along Ohio River to Aberdeen, OH (across river from Maysville).

Other Charming Kentucky Towns

Augusta
Danville
Olive Hill
Shelbyville

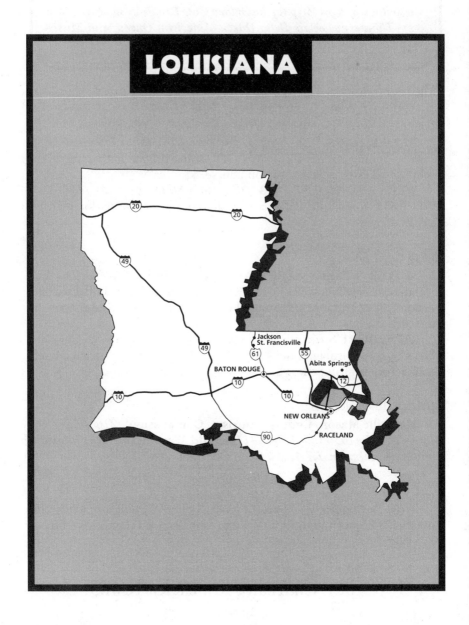

LOUISIANA

Abita Springs
Population about 1, 800

From about 1884 to 1910 New Orleans families used to journey across Lake Ponchartrain to escape the city and the yellow fever epidemics. Resorts in St. Tammany Parish on the north shore of the lake were attractive because of the clean, fresh ozone-rich air emanating from the thick pine forests there. Although the resort towns are still very much around, and continue to attract visitors, most have been altered by the commercial development that follows the automobile. One notable exception is out-of-the-way **Abita Springs**, a village that remains in many ways the delightful little place that it was 100 years ago.

Abita Springs was once an especially popular resort because of its mineral springs. Situated on the banks of the **Abita River**, the **Abita Springs Pavilion** (1888) marks the site of a spring discovered – and enjoyed – by the Choctaw Indians. The town is unique in that its buildings aren't built against one another as in many historic towns. Their wide spacing and location amongst heavy forests give the town a rural, wilderness character.

Many of the buildings are turn-of-the-century "shotgun" houses that once served as second homes for New Orleans's middle classes. There are also "North Shore"-type houses that are variations of the shotguns but that have a projecting section surrounded by galleries on three sides. Adapting to Louisiana's climate, the most dominant features of most of the houses in Abita Springs are the porches.

Abita Springs is for strolling and absorbing. Don't expect much excitement. Here, as elsewhere in the parish, the azaleas, camellias, dogwoods, and other flowers are gorgeous. The **Tammany Trace**, Louisiana's only rail-to-trail conversion – ideal for joggers, cyclists, rollerbladers, and horseback riders – is open from Abita Springs to **Mandeville** (8 1/2 miles).

The best place for shoppers is **Lee Lane** in nearby **Covington**, itself a lovely old town. Here, housed in 19th-century Creole cottages, are unique specialty, antique, and clothing shops.

Special Features

Honey Island Swamp, on the eastern edge of St. Tammany Parish, is one of the most pristine river swamps in the country. Nearly 70,000 acres of the swamp make up a protected wildlife area. Several companies in **Slidell** offer 2- to 4-hour swamp tours, some in environmentally safe craft. The tours provide opportunities to observe alligators, snakes, bald eagles, waterfowl, herons, feral hogs, nutria, otters, mink, and other animals.

Fairview-Riverside State Park south of Abita Springs offers water-skiing, fishing, and crabbing. Under the park's moss-draped oaks is the **Otis House**, built in the 1880s as part of a lumbering camp and renovated in the 1930s to serve as a summer home.

On the grounds of **Fontainebleau State Park**, also south of town, are the ruins of a brick sugar mill built in 1829 by Bernard de Marigny de Mandeville. The park has a swimming pool and a sailboat ramp for launching directly into **Lake Pontchartrain**.

> • *The Lake Pontchartrain Causeway is the longest over-water highway bridge in the world. It is crossed by millions of vehicles each year.*
>
> • *The Abita spring water is a critical ingredient of a beer now produced by a successful local micro-brewery.*
>
> • *The conquest of yellow fever was a major factor in bringing Abita Springs's resort era to an end.*

Where to Stay

THE MAGNOLIA HOUSE B&B, *904 Main St. (Madisonville 70447), (504) 845-4922.* Circa 1850 home with landscaped grounds, antiques, TV, private baths, hot tub, porch swing shaded by magnolias. $$$

RIVERSIDE HILLS FARM B&B, *96 Gardenia Dr. (Covington 70433), (504) 892-1794.* Caretaker's cottage on non-working farm, country kitchen, fishing/boating on Tchefuncte River. $$$

TRAIL'S END B&B, *71648 Maple St., (Abita Springs 70420), (504) 867-9899.* 1890s home adjacent to Tammany Trace, private baths, whirlpools, in center of village. $$$

WINDY PINES B&B, *736 Lafayette St. (Mandeville 70448), (504) 626-9189.* Cypress home on north shore of Lake Ponchartrain, guest lounge, pool, bikes, 5 mins from causeway. $$

Where to Eat

ABITA CAFE, *22132 Level St., (504) 892-5874.* Daily plate specials, po-boys, seafood, salads, omelets. $

BECHAC'S RESTAURANT, *2025 Lakeshore Dr. (Mandeville), (504) 626-8500.* Creole & local specialties; oldest restaurant in St. Tammany, overlooking Lake Pontchartrain. $ to $$

FRIENDS ON THE TCHEFUNCTE, *407 St. Tammany St. in Madisonville, (504) 845-7303.* Seafood, steaks, good assortment of appetizers; inside dining with view of scenic waterway & outside dining with river breezes. $ to $$

LA PROVENCE, *P.O. Box 805 (Lacombe), (504) 626-9598.* French & regional cuisine, outdoor dining, rated one of best in U.S., reservations advised. $$ to $$$

Further Information

St. Tammany Parish Tourist & Convention Commission, *68099 Hwy. 59, Mandeville, LA 70471 (800) 634-9443.*

Directions

From New Orleans, Lake Ponchartrain Causeway north to Covington, LA 36 east to Abita Springs.

Jackson

Population 3, 891

Jackson is a gracious old Southern town nestled in the rolling, forested Louisiana countryside east of the Mississippi River and north of Baton Rouge. Established in 1815, the town has over 100 buildings on the National Register of Historic Places, the second largest number in Louisiana. Included are a number of Louisiana raised cottages as well as several excellent examples of provincial Greek Revival and Victorian architecture.

As in many small rural Southern towns, the most modest and the most pretentious of the buildings often sit side-by-side, or on the same block. Pamphlets are available for self-guided walking and bicycle tours, and guided group tours may be arranged.

Several of the most beautiful of the houses are old plantation homes that today survive in part as bed and breakfasts (listed below). Two homes of historic importance that are not bed and breakfasts are restored **Centenaria** (circa 1840), open for tours by appointment, and **Roseneath** (ca 1832), the town's only full-blown high-style Greek Revival building.

The loveliest buildings from the middle of the 19th century are churches. The **Methodist Church** (1854) and the **Baptist Church** (circa

1860) were both built with brick Gothic Revival basilicas. The **Presbyterian Church** (circa 1852) is of the Colonial style and has finely sculptured windows and the old slave gallery. The **Presbyterian Manse** (circa 1816), now a private residence, was built with wooden pegs rather than nails.

Costumed interpreters conduct walking tours of the **Centenary State Commemorative Area**, the site (1826 to 1908) of the College of Louisiana and, later, Centenary College of Louisiana. Exhibits in an 1837 college dorm and Victorian-era professor's cottage offer a glimpse at student life and education in 19th-century Louisiana.

A good overview of the area's rich and exciting history is provided by the **Jackson Museum and Art Gallery**. The exhibits include antique cars and buggies, Civil War relics, historic ship models, and a diorama of **Port Hudson Battlefield** (Civil War). The adjacent **Old Hickory Village** contains a cotton gin, cane press, general store, and other structures.

Check with the tourism commission (see below) for information on introductory and customized tours of Jackson and the surrounding countryside.

Special Features

Thirteen miles to the east of Jackson on scenic LA 10 lies **Clinton**, another charming old Southern town with strong historical connections. One of the town's most important buildings is the lovely **East Feliciana Parish Courthouse** (1840), the oldest courthouse in continuous use in Louisiana. **Lawyers' Row** (circa 1840 to circa 1860), which in the 19th century housed some of Louisiana's most skilled lawyers, sits just to the north of the courthouse. Both structures are National Historic Landmarks.

One of the best ways to learn about the history of this region is to spend some time examining the tombstones in the **Old Jackson Cemetery** and the **Clinton Confederate Cemetery State Commemorative Area**.

Tastings of muscadine wines and tours are offered by the **Feliciana Cellars Winery** (Jackson) and the **Casa De Sue Winery** (near Clinton).

> • *In 1810 the Jackson area became a part of the Republic of West Florida, a country that lasted only 74 days.*
> • *Jackson was once so well-known for its schools and colleges that it was called the "Athens of Louisiana."*

Where to Stay

ASPHODEL INN, *4626 LA 68 (Jackson), (504) 654-6868*. Townhouses & cabins on grounds of old plantation house (1820), private baths, full breakfasts, restaurant, rocking chairs on verandah, pool, Audubon Society bird sanctuary, gift shop. $$

MILBANK, *102 Bank St. (Jackson), (504) 634-5901*. Circa 1836 Greek Revival mansion with colorful history, on National Register, period antiques, private baths, house tours. $$

OLD CENTENARY INN, *1740 Charter St. (Hwy. 10), P.O. Box 1000, (504) 634-5050*. 1935 inn in historic district, antiques, TV & phones, private baths with whirlpools, Cont. breakfasts, New Orleans courtyard. $$$

Where to Eat

ASPHODEL INN, *(see above), (504) 654-6868*. Plantation dining on verandah or around fireplace. $ to $$

MAJOR'S BEAR CORNERS RESTAURANT, *1674 Charter St. (Hwy. 10), (504) 634-2844*. Trout Almondine Bear Corners, Fresh Water Perch with Crawfish & Hollandaise, Chicken Grand Bayou Stuffed with Spinach & Crawfish, Filet Mignon au Poivre; changing menu, in 1832 bldg. $$

Further Information

East Feliciana Parish Tourism Commission, *P.O. Box 667, Jackson, LA 70748 (504) 634-7155*.

Directions

From Baton Rouge, I 110 north to exit 8B, north on US 61 to LA 68, east on LA 68 to LA 10 (and Jackson).

St. Francisville

Population 1, 700

A great many of the country's millionaires in the antebellum 1850s lived on plantations along the **Mississippi River** between Natchez and New Orleans. Quite a number of them had their homes in **St. Francisville** and West Feliciana Parish. The interesting thing is that despite the Civil War, the boll weevil, natural disasters, and changing times, the situation around St. Francisville hasn't really changed very much: The town and parish are still home to many aristocratic old families, intact working plantations, and some of the country's most elegant plantation houses.

St. Francisville sits proudly on bluffs overlooking the Mississippi in the scenic **Tunica Hills** of eastern Louisiana. The area is known as *English Louisiana* because of the ancestry of its settlers (and to distinguish it from *French Louisiana*). The town is steeped in history and has more than 140 structures on the National Register of Historic Places to prove it. Consistent with both the English and Old Southern roots, tradition is important. The old churches and cemeteries are still in use, and dinner is still served with crystal, china, and silver. Especially enduring is the hospitality.

In and around St. Francisville are at least 10 grand plantation homes that are open to the public. Seven are open for tours year-round and three may be toured by appointment. Many second as bed and breakfasts (see sample listing below). One of the most gorgeous is **Rosedown Plantation** (1835) with its avenue of moss-draped oaks and magnificent restored gardens. Another is the incredibly beautiful **Greenwood Plantation** house (circa 1830), a Greek Revival mansion surrounded by 28 columns. Within are silver door knobs and hinges and a 70-foot baronial hall. Although smaller than its pre-Civil War 12,000 acres, Greenwood is still a working plantation.

The Gothic **Grace Episcopal Church** (1858-1860), the second oldest Episcopal church in Louisiana, has an especially beautiful interior with fine plaster work and carved double-rowed pews.

A visit to the exhibits of the **Museum of the West Feliciana Historical Society** provides a good introduction to the town. A wealth of information is available here, including instructions for a mile-long walking or driving loop tour.

Bicycle tours are becoming a popular way to see the region's plantation houses. Conducted bicycle tours and bike rentals are locally available. Another way to enjoy the area is to take a ferry across the Mississippi.

Special Feature

Audubon State Commemorative Area, to the east of St. Francisville, is the site of **Oakley House**, where John James Audubon completed or began approximately 80 of his bird paintings. The simple but beautiful house was built about 1806 and is listed on the National Register. Oakley's rooms have been restored in late Federal Period style.

In addition to the house, there is a restored formal garden, large detached plantation kitchen, plantation barn, two slave cabins, and other facilities.

• *The builders of Rosedown were among the first Louisiana planters to import camellias.*

• *Although cotton is certainly still grown in the Delta, many of today's working plantations, including those of West Feliciana Parish, produce cattle, hay, and pecans.*

Where to Stay

THE BARROW HOUSE, *P.O. Box 1461, (504) 635-4791*. Circa 1809 house on National Register, period antiques, balconies, beverages. $$$

BUTLER GREENWOOD, *8345 US 61, (504) 635-6312*. Working plantation, 5 dependencies with private baths, swimming pool, guided nature walks, tours of main house. $$$

COTTAGE PLANTATION, *10528 Cottage Lane, (504) 635-3674*. One of few remaining complete ante-bellum plantations, original furnishings, private baths, "plantation" breakfasts, dining room, pool, Andrew Jackson once a guest. $$$

THE MYRTLES PLANTATION B&B, *P.O. Box 1100, (504) 635-6277*. Ca 1796 home with 150 live oaks, Baccarat crystal chandeliers, art treasures, dining room, "America's Most Haunted House!", tours. $$$

ROSEDOWN PLANTATION, *12501 LA 10, (504) 635-3332*. Guesthouse of 1835 mansion, rooms historically decorated, private baths, full breakfasts, pool, tennis courts, access to Rosedown Gardens. $$$

THE ST. FRANCISVILLE INN B&B, *P.O. Drawer 1369, (504) 635-6502/(800) 488-6502*. Ca 1880 Gothic Revival home, full-service inn, full buffet breakfasts, restaurant, New Orleans courtyard, pool, 100-year-old oak trees. $$

Where to Eat

D'JOHN'S RESTAURANT, *US 61 S., (504) 635-6982*. Barbecued ribs the specialty, family atmosphere. $

MATTIE'S HOUSE RESTAURANT, *the Cottage Plantation (see above)*. Variety of seafood, chicken, & steak specialties; homemade bread. $ to $$

MAGNOLIA CAFE, *121 E. Commerce St., (504) 635-6528*. Popular for lunch. $

THE MYRTLES PLANTATION RESTAURANT, *(see above)*. "Upscale bistro cuisine" (reservations requested), afternoon tea by reservation. $$

ST. FRANCISVILLE INN, *(see above)*. Southern Louisiana cuisine, e.g., Fried Catfish Etouffee, Soft Shell Crab Bywater, Chicken St. Francis, Cajun Two Step, Steak Hattie. $ to $$

Further Information

West Feliciana Parish Tourist Commission, *P.O. Box 1548, St. Francisville, LA 70775 (504) 635-6330.*

Directions

From Baton Rouge, I 110 north to US 61, north to St. Francisville.

Other Charming Louisiana Towns

Clinton
Covington
Franklin
Napoleonville
New Roads
St. Martinville

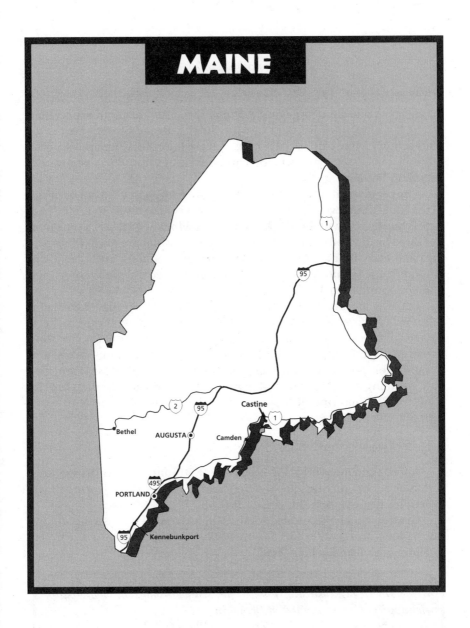

MAINE

MAINE

Bethel
Population 2, 375

Nestled among the scenic **White Mountains** of western Maine, **Bethel** is a village that has appeared on Christmas cards. As you might expect, the village has a National Register historic district, **Broad Street**, lined with 19th-century white clapboard houses that are pure New England (several are now inns – see listings below) and businesses housed in renovated Victorian homes.

The permanent white settlement of Bethel began in 1774 but because of the American Revolution the village grew very little until the 1780s. The oldest house in town, the **Dr. Moses Mason House** (1813), is a museum operated by the **Bethel Historical Society**. On display are period furnishings and early murals; there are also changing exhibits. Another town landmark, the **Gould Academy**, is a highly respected independent school that was founded in 1836.

Bethel's mountainous setting and proximity to **Sunday River** and other major ski resorts make winter the high season here; the area offers some of the best skiing in the East. The sports calendar is four-season, however. The fishing and hiking are superb, the logging roads are designed for mountain biking, and canoeing opportunities vary from lily-pad paddling to whitewater plunging. The renowned **Bethel Inn & Country Club** has one of the top-ranked golf courses in the Northeast (open to the public).

Special Features

About eight miles north of town is the 1870 **Sunday River Bridge**, one of Maine's most picturesque covered bridges. The bridge is sometimes called, for obvious reasons, *Artists' Bridge*.

Grafton Notch State Park, about 14 miles from Bethel, is a mountainous park featuring waterfalls, nature walks, and trail heads for five trails, including the **Appalachian Trail**.

> • *The NTL Institute, known for its workshops on leadership development, was founded in Bethel in 1947.*
> • *The Sunday River Ski Resort offers the only lift-served mountain bike park in the East.*

Where to Stay

BETHEL INN, *on the Village Common, (207) 824-2175.* Full-service inn on 200 acres, outdoor heated pool, golf, skiing, tennis. $$ to $$$ (MAP)

THE CHAPMAN INN, *P.O. Box 206, (207) 824-2657.* Large sunny rooms, full breakfasts, sauna, game room, access to beach. $$

HOLIDAE HOUSE, *Main St., (207) 824-3400.* Late Victorian town house, TV & phones, private baths, "sumptuous" breakfasts with home-baked bread, front porch. $$ to $$$

NORSEMAN INN, *134 Mayville Rd. (US 2 E), (207) 824-2002.* 1790s inn & 1890s barn, some private baths, large fireplaces, breakfasts by the fire. $$

THE SUDBURY INN, *P.O. Box 369, (800) 395-7837.* 1870 three-story inn, private baths, full breakfasts, suites, 2 dining rooms, pub, tavern. $ to $$$

Where to Eat

BETHEL INN, *(see above)*. Candlelight dining, music on the Steinway. $$

THE MATTERHORN, *Rte. 26 & Cross St., (207) 824-6836.* Wood-fired brick-oven pizza, seafood, pasta, "gourmet" salads, "Maine's freshest ice cream cones & sundaes." $

THE MOOSE'S TALE, *P.O. Box 847, (207) 824-3541.* Continental cooking, seafood, steaks, vegetarian dishes. $ to $$

MOTHERS, *Upper Main St., (207) 824-2589.* Popular for lunches & lighter fare, in late 1800s home. $ to $$

SUDBURY INN, *Lower Main St., (207) 824-2174.* Lobster Sudbury, Chicken in Pastry, Sirloin & Shrimp, Vegetable Brochettes; pub for more casual fare, highly regarded. $$

Further Information

Bethel Area Chamber of Commerce, *P.O. Box 439, Bethel, ME 04217 (207) 824-2282/(800) 442-5826 for area lodging reservations.*

Directions

From Portland, I 495 north to exit 11, ME 26 north to Bethel.

Camden

Population 5, 060

Camden is one of those rare places that in real life actually live up to the most romantic of legends. Enticing shops cluster about a picturesque harbor, and time-mellowed New England houses, almost always in white, compete for the prettiest settings along the streets and roads. The grandest or most charming of the houses always seem to have an old sign out front announcing "Antiques" or "Inn." Views of the harbor and bay appear at every turn, and during the warmer months each view includes dozens of white-on-blue sails.

This is sailboat country and to get to know it every visitor should spend at least a couple of hours out on **Penobscot Bay**. Maine needs to be seen from both land and water, weather permitting of course. Camden offers a variety of cruise options on both schooners and motor vessels. Some day trips are as short as an hour, others last all day. For those with more time, overnight, 3-day, and 6-day cruises of the Maine coast are available on classic windjammers. Weekend and week-long courses are offered for visitors wishing to learn how to sail.

Camden's shops, designed as much for the browser as the buyer, tend to shun tee shirts in favor of hand-loomed sweaters and handcrafted jewelry. The restaurants and dining rooms feature some of Maine's most popular products—lobsters, scallops, mussels, clams, haddock, salmon, and swordfish.

Visitors arriving in Camden during the busy summer months might consider leaving their cars in a parking lot on the outskirts of town and taking an air-conditioned bus (the Camden Shuttle) to the downtown area. Free buses run from mid-June to Labor Day.

Special Features

A road ascends to the top of 900-ft **Mount Battie** in **Camden Hills State Park** just north of town. The views of the bay from the summit are spectacular.

Just down the coast from Camden is **Rockport**, another picturesque harbor village popular with artists and writers.

> *In Camden it is possible to take a "cruise" on a working lobster boat.*

Where to Stay

BLACKBERRY INN, *82 Elm St., (800) 833-6674*. Vintage Victorian with parlors, private baths, "scrumptious" full breakfasts, hospitality hour. $$ to $$$

THE BLUE HARBOR HOUSE, *67 Elm St., (800) 248-3196*. 1810 Cape in heart of town, antiques & hand-fashioned quilts, private baths, full breakfasts, suites, dinners by appt. $$$

EDGECOMBE-COLES HOUSE, *64 High St., (207) 236-2336*. Country home in sylvan setting, antiques, fireplaces, private baths, "memorable" breakfasts, ocean views. $$$

HAWTHORN INN, *9 High St., (207) 236-8842*. Victorian mansion & carriage house overlooking harbor, antiques, private baths, whirlpools, full buffet breakfasts. $$ to $$$

NORUMBEGA, *61 High St., (207) 236-4646*. Maine's "Castle by the Sea," hand-carved woodwork, fireplaces, private baths, full breakfasts, suites, bay views, award-winning. $$$

WHITEHALL INN, *P.O. Box 558, (207) 236-3391*. A "landmark for hospitality" since 1901, private baths, dining room, parlors, front-porch rockers, tennis. $$ to $$$

WINDWARD HOUSE, *6 High St., (207) 236-9656*. 1854 Greek Revival home, period antiques, private baths, "gourmet" breakfasts, deck, lighted English gardens, mountain trails. $$ to $$$

Where to Eat

ATLANTICA GRILLE & GALLERY, *3 Sharp's Wharf, (207) 236-6011*. Salmon & Fresh Spinach, Island Style Chicken, Atlantica Seafood Pasta; espresso bar, harbor-side setting. $$

THE BELMONT, *6 Belmont Ave., (800) 238-8053*. Small inn offering "artfully created" New England food, fresh local seafood; good wine list, garden & porch, one of finest in area. $$ to $$$

FROGWATER CAFE, *31 Elm St., (207) 236-8998*. Seafood, pasta, chicken, & beef specialties; homemade breads & desserts. $ to $$

O'NEIL'S, *21 Bayview St., (207) 236-3272*. Lobster, seafood, chicken, pasta, brick-oven pizza. $ to $$

SEA DOG TAVERN & BREWERY, *43 Mechanic St., (207) 236-6863*. "Down East home-style cooking & international specialties," award-winning lagers & ales, brewery tours, overlooking waterfall. $ to $$

WATERFRONT RESTAURANT, *Bayview St., (207) 236-3747*. Fresh grilled fish, lobster, steaks, raw bar; on deck in harbor with view. $$

WHITEHALL INN, *(see above)*. Classical & creative cuisine served in historic country inn, extensive wine list, elegant. $$$

Further Information

Rockport-Camden-Lincolnville Chamber of Commerce, *P.O. Box 919, Camden, ME 04843 (207) 236-4404*.

Directions

From Portland, US 1 north (along coast) to Camden.

Castine

Population 800

Maybe it's because Castine is a harbor village. Or maybe it's because its many lovely historical homes lend a domestic air. Or maybe it's because its location at the end of a small peninsula and off the main tourist routes gives it a sense of cozy remoteness. Whatever the reason, Castine's mood is personal and intimate. And the setting is beautiful.

Castine began as a series of trading posts and forts shadowed by an ever-changing series of flags (French, Dutch, British, and American). Once American sovereignty was established–and given two British occupations, one during the Revolution and the other during the War of 1812, this could never be taken for granted–the village prospered as a port and shipbuilding center. Later, as the day of the sailing vessel waned, the economy found new life with the arrival of the steamboat and its charge of Victorian summer visitors.

Bordering Castine's streets, especially Main and Perkins, are restored 18th- and 19th-century Georgian and Federal homes and a number of beautiful churches, among them the Gothic **Trinity Chapel** (Episcopal, 1897) and the steepled **Trinitarian** and **Unitarian churches** (1829 and 1790, respectively). Adding variety and color are several Victorian and Edwardian summer homes (or "cottages").

The **Wilson Museum** (1921) displays prehistoric, local Indian, and Victorian-era artifacts. Included in the museum complex are a working blacksmith shop and the restored pre-Revolutionary **John Perkins House**, with late 18th-century furnishings (open to public).

Among the locations marking Castine's early history are the archaeological excavation of France's **Fort Pentagoet** (late 1600s), now a National Historical Landmark, and **Fort George State Park**, the site of the Britain's **Fort George** (1779). Another historic site, **Dyces Head Lighthouse** (1828), offers a commanding view of the Penobscot River–as well as a public path to the water.

The **Maine Maritime Academy**, with buildings dating to 1873, offers undergraduate and graduate courses in ocean and marine-oriented programs. The academy's training vessel, the *T. S. Patriot State*, is berthed at the foot of Main Street. Guided tours of the ship are sometimes available.

Clustered near the waterfront are galleries, restaurants, and quaint shops displaying antiques, gifts, books, and other items. Daysailing cruises are available for those who can't get enough of Maine's proverbial coastal beauty.

Special Feature

Blue Hill, another pretty waterside village, is just a few miles north and east of Castine.

> • *One of the country's worst naval defeats ever occurred near Castine in 1779 when 40 some American vessels were lost at the hands of a superior British naval force.*
>
> • *Inhabitants of Castine once included members of the Penobscot Loyalist Society, a group refusing to forswear allegiance to the king. The Castine loyalists were later forced to move to Canada–along with their dismantled houses.*

Where to Stay

THE CASTINE INN, *P.O. Box 41, (207) 326-4365/fax (207) 326-4570.* 1898 Italianate inn with flower-bedecked wrap-around porch, art, private baths, full breakfasts, dining room, pub, suites, English gardens. $$$

THE HOLIDAY HOUSE OCEANFRONT INN, *215 Perkins St., (207) 326-4335.* 1895 mansion on harbor, superb views, private baths, porches overlooking private beach, pets. $$ to $$$

THE MANOR, *Battle Ave., Box 276, (207) 326-4861.* Turn-of-century mansion on 5 acres, on National Register, fireplaces, private baths, candlelight dining, marble oyster bar, pets, cottages, free shuttle from waterfront. $$ to $$$

PENTAGOET INN, *Main St., P.O. Box 4, (207) 326-8616 / (800) 845-1701.* Rambling 1894 inn with turret & gables, front-porch rockers, private baths, full breakfasts, chamber music, library, some pets. $$$

Where to Eat

THE CASTINE INN, *(see above).* Steamed Cod in a Lemongrass Broth with Braised Fennel, Sea Scallops and Spicy Celery Root Puree with Coriander Vinaigrette; reservations suggested, appropriate attire. $$ to $$$

LA CONQUE, *(see The Manor above).* Yellow Fin Tuna Steak, Rotisserie Apricot Ginger Glazed Duckling, Tournedos au Poivre; fireplaced dining rooms, raw bar, award-winning wine list. $$ to $$$

Further Information

Castine Merchants Association, *P.O. Box 329, Castine, ME 04421 (207) 326-4884*; or **Ellsworth Area Chamber of Commerce**, *P.O. Box 267, Ellsworth, ME 04605 (207) 667-5584.*

Directions

From Portland, I 95 to Augusta, ME 3 to Belfast, US 1 to ME 175 (1 mi past Bucksport), south on ME 175 (becoming ME 166) to Castine; from Bangor, ME 15 to Bucksport, then as above.

Kennebunkport
Population 1, 100

The booklet distributed by the **Kennebunk/Kennebunkport** Chamber of Commerce is a virtual album of lovely photographs. The scenes are as remarkable for their diversity as their beauty. Here are the sea, broad beaches, harbors, boat yards, rocky coasts, tree-shaded village streets, Victorian gingerbread, historic churches, quaint shops, sleigh rides, flowers, and frosty ponds. Some of the most beautiful scenes combine the colors of the sea with the red-violet of the wild rugosa roses that grace the coast.

Kennebunkport is in a sense a collection of colorful places, of images. There's something here for about everyone. But maybe especially for someone who loves the sea and wishes a little seclusion mixed with the charms and comforts of a relaxed old New England town.

Along Kennebunkport's beach, sheltered riverfront, and manicured streets stand the magnificent homes of 18th- and 19th-century sea captains, shipbuilders, and well-to-do summer residents. Many of the homes are now bed-and-breakfast inns (see below)—few towns can match Kennebunkport in the number, variety, and quality of its inns. Few, either, can match the experience of the town's innkeepers. Kennebunkport also boasts several restored seaside hotels cut out of another era.

The **Brick Store Museum** (Kennebunk) provides a good introduction to the history of the Kennebunks. The museum's shop features quality reproductions and books on local history and crafts. **The Nott House** (1851-1853), a gracious Greek Revival mansion with original furnishings, also offers a glimpse at the past. The house, open to the public, is maintained by the Kennebunkport Historical Society.

With a collection of over 250 trolleys from around the globe, the **Seashore Trolley Museum** bills itself as the oldest and largest transit museum in the world. Among other attractions, the museum offers its visitors a three-mile ride on an antique electric trolley.

The list of activities open to the visitor is as long and varied as the list of views. Many of the historic buildings on **Dock Square** and elsewhere house galleries and artists' studios, as well as a diversity of interesting little shops. For off-shore excursions there are whale-watching, sightseeing, and sailboat cruises. Deep-sea fishing charters can also be arranged. More active pursuits include scuba diving, canoeing on the ponds and streams, golfing, and cross-country skiing. And, of course, hiking or biking along the coast.

Special Features

Just up the coast from Kennebunkport is the picturesque fishing village of **Cape Porpoise**, home port to a fleet of lobster boats. The coastal scenery here is especially beautiful.

The arrival of Santa Claus by lobster boat and candlelight caroling at the **Franciscan Monastery** are among the events of Kennebunkport's *Christmas Prelude*, celebrated the first and second weekends in December.

Where to Stay

CAPE ARUNDEL INN, *Ocean Ave., (207) 967-2125*. Shingle-style cottage with turret, private baths, "bold" ocean views, restaurant. $$$

THE CAPTAIN JEFFERDS INN, *P. O. Box 691, (207) 967-2311/(800) 839-6844*. Antique-appointed 1804 Federal home, fireplaces, private baths, "bountiful" breakfasts, afternoon teas, carriage house suites, piano, some pets, terrace & gardens. $$$

THE CAPTAIN LORD MANSION, *P.O. Box 800, (207) 967-3141*. 1812 country inn, working fireplaces, private baths, full breakfasts, afternoon refreshments, one of best in country. $$$

THE DOCK SQUARE INN, *P.O. Box 1123, (207) 967-5773*. Classic Victorian decor, TV, canopy beds, private baths, "gourmet" breakfasts. $$$

ENGLISH MEADOWS INN, *141 Port Rd., (207) 967-5766*. 1860 farmhouse & carriage house, hand-sewn quilts, private baths, full breakfasts, sprawling apple trees. $$ to $$$

THE KENNEBUNKPORT INN, *Dock Sq. (P.O. Box 111), (800) 248-2621*. 19th-century mansion & 1930s river house, antiques, TV, private baths, dining room, turn-of-century pub with piano bar, pool. $$ to $$$ (MAP available)

MAINE STAY INN & COTTAGES, *P.O. Box 500A, (800) 950-2117*. 1860 home on National Register, suspended spiral staircase, antiques, TV, private baths, full breakfasts, afternoon tea, garden cottages. $$$

WHITE BARN INN, *P.O. Box 560C, Beach St., (207) 967-2321*. New England period furnishings, private baths, afternoon tea, fresh flowers, suites, restaurant, piano bar, bicycles, one of top inns in country. $$$

THE WILLIAM LORD MANSION, *P.O. Box 1053, 20 Summer St. (Kennebunk 04043), (207) 985-6213*. 1801 home on National Register, family heirlooms, fireplaces, TV, private baths, whirlpools, "gourmet" breakfast buffet, artwork, gardens. $$$

Where to Eat

Note: Kennebunkport is blessed with an unusually large number of fine restaurants. The favorite entree is lobster, of course.

ARUNDEL WHARF RESTAURANT, *43 Ocean Ave., (207) 967-3444.* Baked Stuffed Lobster, Passamaquody Clambake, Broiled Haddock, Shrimp Scampi, Pasta Melange, Chicken Diablo. $$

CAPE ARUNDEL INN, *(see above).* Cape Arundel Seafood Bowl, Roasted Halibut Fillet, Breast of Duckling, Gulf Shrimp with Tuscan Black Beans. $$$

SALT MARSH TAVERN, *Rt. 9, 46 Western Ave. (207) 967-4500.* "Fine Dining in a Wonderfully Restored Old Barn"; for example, A Grilled Breast & Braised Leg of Duckling with a Maine Cider and Dried Cranberry Demi-glace. $$ to $$$

SCHOONERS INN & RESTAURANT, *P.O. Box 709, (207) 967-5333.* Seaside dining, Stuffed Potato with Lobster a delicious specialty. $$

SEASCAPES, *on pier at Cape Porpoise, (207) 967-8500.* "Unique combination of native seafood and best of American cuisine with a Continental flair." $$

WHITE BARN INN, *(see above).* New England seasonal menu, Chargrilled Native Salmon, Oven-roasted Quail; in beautifully restored barn, award-winning. $$$

WINDOWS ON THE WATER, *Chase Hill Rd., (207) 967-3313.* Fresh seafood, "succulent" lobsters, hand-trimmed steaks; wonderful views, entertainment, award-winning. $$

Further Information

Kennebunk Kennebunkport Chamber of Commerce, *P.O. Box 740, Kennebunk, ME 04043 (207) 967-0857.* (ZIP for Kennebunkport is 04046.)

Directions

From Portland, I 95 south to exit 3 (Kennebunk), east to Kennebunkport.

Other Charming Maine Towns

Bar Harbor
Northeast Harbor
Wiscasset

MARYLAND

MARYLAND

Chestertown
Population 4, 000

Heir to the second largest collection of Georgian and Federal homes in Maryland, and only a short drive from some of the largest metropolitan areas on the Eastern seaboard (though sheltered from them by Chesapeake Bay), peaceful little **Chestertown** offers a tempting destination for city dwellers seeking an afternoon or weekend's change of pace. Distinctive shops and topnotch eateries and hostelries can only add to the temptation.

Situated on the banks of the Chester River on Colonial Maryland's Eastern Shore, Chestertown-to-be was chartered as a port of entry by the Maryland Assembly in 1706. The town became the seat of Kent County and, as can be seen from the many mansions of successful merchants, prospered. One of the town's centerpieces, **Washington College**, was founded in 1782 and today ranks as the 10th oldest liberal arts college in the country.

Among the most interesting of the many historic brick homes are the **Geddes-Piper House** (circa 1780), a restored townhouse that is now headquarters to the Historical Society of Kent County (restricted summer hours), and the **Hynson-Ringgold House** (1735-1772), called the "Abbey" in Colonial times. Many of the most historic and architecturally interesting houses open their doors to tours in mid-September and mid-December; several are also open as bed and breakfasts (see below).

The **White Swan Tavern**, now a bed and breakfast (see below), is a town landmark with roots dating to before 1733. Just down the street is **Chestertown Park**, which boasts a fountain (1899) as well as a Saturday Farmers Market.

Two historic churches grace the shaded streets and brick sidewalks of this lovely old town. The first, **Emmanuel Episcopal Church** (1768), is known for its Tiffany window. The second, **Old St. Paul's Church**, is the oldest church in continuous use in Maryland. The church's vestry house, restored, dates to 1766.

Chestertown is designed primarily for two kinds of people: those who seek the spell of another century and those who enjoy exploring quaint little shops–and maybe especially gift, clothing, and antique shops. But the town and its county also cater to other kinds of people: bicycle riders, nature walkers, crabbers, bird watchers, fishermen, sailors. There's a public beach at **Betterton**, and marinas and boat landings lie in virtually every direction.

Special Feature

Catches of clams, oysters, crabs, and fish have made **Rock Hall**, southwest of Chestertown, the "Seafood Capital of Kent County."

> • *One of the sentences for people convicted of minor crimes in Colonial Chestertown was "repairing bridges."*
> • *According to legend, the body of Sir Peter Parker, a British commander mortally wounded in a skirmish near Chestertown during the War of 1812, was returned to England preserved in a barrel of rum.*

Where to Stay

BRAMPTON B&B INN, *25227 Chestertown Rd., (410) 778-1860*. 1860 plantation home on 35 acres, on National Register, 3 1/2-story central staircase, antiques, some fireplaces, private baths, full breakfasts, afternoon tea. $$$

THE IMPERIAL HOTEL, *208 High St., (410) 778-5000/fax (410) 778-9662*. 1903 hotel with full service, winner of restoration award, authentic period furnishings, acclaimed restaurant, Cellar coffee bar & bakery, verandah overlooking sycamore-lined street. $$$

THE INN AT MICHELL HOUSE, *8796 Maryland Pkwy., (410) 778-6500*. 1743 manor house on 10 rolling acres, parlors & fireplaces, private baths, full breakfasts, public dining room weekends. $$$

KITTY KNIGHT HOUSE, *Rte. 213 (Georgetown 21930), (410) 648-5777*. Circa 1755 home overlooking Sassafras River & Georgetown Harbor, original woodwork, some fireplaces, private baths, Kitty Knight Restaurant, Admiral Cockburn Tavern. $$

WHITE SWAN TAVERN, *231 High St., (410) 778-2300/fax (410) 778-4543*. Carefully restored 1733 Georgian home (with service as tavern in early 1800s), private baths, Cont. "plus" breakfasts, afternoon tea, morning paper & fruit basket, museum, garden. $$$

Where to Eat

THE INN AT MICHELL HOUSE, *(see above)*. Butterfly Jumbo Shrimp, Lobster Bisque, Oyster Puffs, & Clam Chowder among appetizers; in 18th-century dining room, fireplace. $$

IRONSTONE CAFE, *Cannon St., (410) 778-0188*. Pan-seared Chicken Breast (with caramelized onion cream & oysters), New York Strip Steak (with mushroom catsup); bistro atmosphere. $$

THE KENNEDYVILLE INN, *P.O. Box 216 (Kennedyville 21645), (410) 348-2400*. Pit barbecue, house-made pasta, seafood specials; microbrewed beers, in renovated home 6 mi N of Chestertown. $$

Further Information

Kent County Chamber of Commerce, Inc., *400 S. Cross St., P.O. Box 146, Chestertown, MD 21620*.

Directions

From Baltimore & Washington DC, US 50/301 across Bay Bridge, US 301 north to MD 213, MD 213 north to Chestertown.

Havre de Grace
Population 12, 000

A walk through **Havre de Grace** offers two pleasures in one: a tour of an historic old Chesapeake Bay town and a 1 1/2-mile stroll along or near the coast. Almost all of the town's top sights are on a more-or-less straight line between the **lockhouse** on the north and the **lighthouse** on the south. Not surprisingly, most of the sights (the lockhouse and the lighthouse for beginners) have a direct connection with the water.

About 800 (!) structures contribute to the **Havre de Grace Historic District**. The most interesting were built in the Canal (1830-1850) and Victorian (1880-1910) periods. It was during the former that the town became an important link in the country's growing network of railroads and canals; it was during the latter that the town enjoyed the economic benefits of the late industrial age.

Two mansions of special architectural interest are the **Spencer-Silver Mansion** (1896) and the **Vandiver Inn** (1886), both now bed and breakfasts (see below). George Washington stopped several times at the **Rodgers House**, the oldest structure in town (1787). The oldest church in town is **St. John's Episcopal Church** (1809), noted for its simple early 19th-century beauty. Another "oldest" is the **Concord Point Lighthouse** (1827), the oldest lighthouse in the country in continuous use when decommissioned in 1975.

The **Susquehanna Museum of Havre de Grace** includes the restored **locktender's house** (1840) and reconstructed pivot bridge adjoining the lock where mule-drawn canal boats once entered the **Susquehanna & Tidewater Canal**. The **Havre de Grace Decoy Museum**, the town's most popular site and home to valuable collections of decoys, celebrates the "historical and cultural legacy of waterfowling and decoy making on the Chesapeake Bay."

The *Martha Lewis* (1955), a two-sail bateau (or "skipjack"), is the only dredge boat still oystering commercially under sail in the country. Rides and charter excursions are available.

Today Havre de Grace is in what might be termed a "tourism, recreation and retirement" era. The waterfront has several marinas, a boardwalk, and a chain of lovely parks. Historians will write of this era's buildings, too. Among the newest are waterfront condos, structures that many locals believe only serve to enhance the town's charm.

Special Feature

The sites of a once-working Harford County farm are preserved at the **Steppingstone Museum** in **Susquehanna State Park**, northeast of town. The sites include a farmhouse furnished in turn-of-century style and shops that "preserve and demonstrate the rural arts and crafts of the 1880-1920 period."

> • *The annual Duck Fair, held on the grounds of the decoy museum, features a head-whittling contest, punt-gun demonstration, and duck-&-goose calling contest.*
> • *A $2,000 no-questions-asked reward still awaits the person who returns the original lighthouse lens, missing since 1975 and presumed stolen.*

Where to Stay

THE CURRIER HOUSE, *800 S. Market St., (800) 827-2889/(410) 939-7886.* Early 1800s home overlooking juncture of river & bay, family heirlooms, private baths, full "watermen's" breakfasts, occupied by same family since 1861. $$$

LA CLE d'OR GUESTHOUSE, *226 N. Union Ave., (888) 554-8378/ (410) 939-6562/fax (410) 939-1525.* 1868 home with historic associations, French antiques, Strauss crystal chandeliers, one private bath, full breakfasts, outdoor spa. $$$

SPENCER-SILVER MANSION, *200 S. Union Ave., (800) 780-1485.* 1896 High Victorian stone mansion, antiques, some private baths, "gourmet" breakfasts, carriage-house suite, city tours. $$ to $$$

VANDIVER INN, *301 S. Union Ave., (800) 245-1655.* Large Queen Anne cottage with five multi-flued chimneys, private baths, full breakfasts, "gourmet" dinners weekends. $$ to $$$

Where to Eat

CRAZY SWEDE, *400 N. Union Ave., (410) 939-5440*. Seafood & prime rib, friendly atmosphere accented by brass & natural wood, a fun place. $$ to $$$

ICE DREAMS, *209 N. Washington St., (410) 939-1525*. Prize-winning crab cakes, old-fashioned ice cream parlor, waterview dining. $

MACGREGOR'S RESTAURANT & TAVERN, *331 St. John St., (410) 939-3003*. Seafood, steaks, chops, pasta; all-glass dining room with deck & outside bar. $$ to $$$

PRICE'S SEAFOOD, *654 Water St., (410) 939-2782*. Old-fashioned crab house with homemade crab cakes, crab soup, steamed crabs & shrimp, clams, oysters, soft shell crabs. $$

TIDEWATER GRILLE, *300 Franklin St., (410) 939-3313*. Linguini Pescatore, Crab Cakes, Fresh Flounder Orange, Filet Mignon; on water's edge with great views, outdoor dining, popular. $$ to $$$

Further Information

Havre de Grace Chamber of Commerce, *224 N. Washington St., Havre de Grace, MD 21078 (800) 851-7756*.

Directions

From Baltimore, I 95 north to exit 89, MD 155 east to Havre de Grace.

St. Mary's City
(not incorporated)

St. Mary's County, not far south of Washington, D.C., is an agricultural and forested part of Maryland that remains – at least for the present – relatively free of commercial development. Situated on a peninsula bounded by the **Potomac River** on one side and **Chesapeake Bay** on the other, the county is served by highways that go nowhere but the sea. Denied the flocks of tourists that migrate along interstates, the county's restaurants offer seafood at what may be the lowest prices on the Eastern Seaboard north of the Carolinas.

St. Mary's City, in the southern part of the county, was the location of Maryland's first capital (1634-1695) and site of the fourth permanent English settlement in the New World. Although the original town eventually disappeared following the removal of the capital to Annapolis, some of it has been re-created as **Historic St. Mary's City**, a grand 800-acre outdoor history museum.

The museum's Visitors Center complex features an archaeology exhibit hall, orientation materials, and museum shop. Self-guided walking tours begin here. The various exhibit areas are connected by a walking trail system. Scripts highlighting events in the town's history are acted out by costumed interpreters. Included in the re-creation is a 66-acre natural history area that preserves woodland, marsh areas, and bluffs along the **St. Mary's River** in much the same state that the settlers found them.

The meticulously reconstructed 1676 brick **State House** is one of the museum's centerpieces. Actual 17th-century court cases, concerning everything from pig stealing to treason, are re-enacted in the first-floor **Assembly Room**.

The re-created **Godiah Spray Tobacco Plantation** is a living history farm. Complete with livestock and crops, the farm portrays the lives of a middle-class planter family in the 1660s. Farm structures include the one-room main **Dwelling House** (even the middle classes had little privacy in Colonial Maryland), tobacco sheds, and animals pens.

The square-rigged *Maryland Dove*, equipped with 17th-century instruments, is a replica of one of the two ships that carried Leonard Calvert, his settlers, and colony supplies from England. The tiny size of the ship – which was probably used to carry supplies – nicely underscores the extent of the risks the settlers had to face.

Farthing's Ordinary is a reconstructed 17th-century inn. "Dyett and Drink" are served to modern visitors by **Farthing's Kitchen**, to the rear of the building.

Trinity Episcopal Church, adjacent to Historic St. Mary's City, was constructed in 1829 of bricks from the original State House (1676). The **Leonard Calvert Monument** (1890) stands on the church grounds.

Special Features

Point Lookout State Park is located to the south of St. Mary's City at the confluence of Chesapeake Bay and the Potomac River. In the park is the site of Fort Lincoln, a fort built by Confederate prisoners of war. Two memorials honor the 3,364 Confederate prisoners who died here. A Civil War museum is in the Visitor's Center. Cruises to sparsely populated **Smith Island** depart from the park during the summer.

St. Ignatius Church (1785), in St. Inigoes near St. Mary's City, is a Roman Catholic church with magnificent stained-glass windows and altar. The church has one of the oldest cemeteries in the country. The floor of **St. George's Episcopal** ("**Poplar Hill**") **Church** (1740), in nearby **Valley Lee**, contains ancient gravestones of four early rectors. Both churches are on the National Register of Historic Places.

> *The Margaret Brent Memorial honors the first woman in America to request the right to vote in a legislative assembly (1648). The request was denied.*

Where to Stay

BARD'S FIELD B&B, *15671 Pratt Rd. (Ridge 20680), (301) 872-5989.* Small manor house built ca 1798, on creek overlooking Potomac, "large country" breakfasts, original porch. $$

OLD KIRK HOUSE, *P.O. Box 83 (Scotland 20687), (301) 872-4093.* Circa 1800 home overlooking creek, full breakfasts, balcony. $$

ST. MICHAEL'S MANOR, *Rt. 5 (Box 17-A) (Scotland 20687), (301) 872-4025.* 1805 home overlooking creek, antiques & Oriental rugs, full breakfasts, boating/biking. $$

Where to Eat

SCHEIBLE'S CRABPOT RESTAURANT, *23 Wynne Rd. (Ridge), (301) 872-5185.* Crabcakes, seafood, daily specials; nautical atmosphere, overlooking Smith Creek. $

SPINNAKER'S AT POINT LOOKOUT MARINA, *Wynne Rd. (Ridge), (301) 872-5145.* Fresh seafood, steaks, daily specials. $

Further Information

Tourist Information Center, *St. Mary's County Chamber of Commerce, 28290 Three Notch Rd., Mechanicsville, MD 20659 (301) 884-5555.*

Directions

From Washington (DC), MD 5 south to St. Marys City.

St. Michaels

Population 1, 301

There are ideal retirement communities and there are communities ideal for raising families. Although maybe qualifying for either or both of these, the little harbor town of **St. Michaels** clearly sets the standard for yet a third kind of ideal community: the post-family, pre-retirement community, the perfect place for people who, having raised a family and achieved some degree of professional or business success, wish to change careers and pursue second lives.

St. Michaels is in fact home to many people living "second lives," and it's not hard to understand why. With its narrow streets, pastel-tinted houses, and tidy little gardens, the town is certainly picturesque. It is also gently lapped by a sailboat-trimmed harbor, historic to the tune of 350 years, and remote from, but not too much so (maybe two hours), several East Coast metropolises. The natives welcome newcomers, and the shops, restaurants, and inns range from the solid to the downright upscale. Biking is a favorite travel mode.

The **Chesapeake Bay Maritime Museum**, one of the finest in the country, features an outdoor portion with skipjacks, log canoes, and a restored 1879 lighthouse. The indoor portion has an aquarium of bay life and exhibits that detail, among other things, the history of steamboating on the bay and the impact of migratory birds on the bay's economy, sport, and art.

On the green around which the town was built is **St. Mary's Square Museum** (main building circa 1800), with displays of local memorabilia. The **Cannonball House** (circa 1805), on the square, is a Georgian house whose roof was penetrated by a cannon ball during the War of 1812. St. Michaels's other historic sites include the red brick **Old Inn** (circa 1816) and the restored **Freedom's Friend Lodge** (1883).

Special Features

Sightseeing cruises on **Chesapeake Bay** and the **Miles River** range from the part-day to the overnight, from the narrated historic to the nature-loving.

The incredibly beautiful waterside village of **Oxford**, not far to the southeast, is a smaller but quieter and more sedate relative of St. Michaels.

> • *British cannon balls generally overshot the town in the War of 1812 because the forewarned citizens hoisted lanterns to masts of ships and tops of trees.*
> • *Many visitors to St. Michaels arrive by boat and rent bikes to get around town.*

Where to Stay

BARRETT'S B&B INN, *P.O. Box 279, (410) 745-3322.* Late 1860s Colonial-style house, Oriental rugs, quilts, double whirlpools, private baths, full breakfasts with home-baked breads. $$$

HAMBLETON INN, *202 Cherry St., P.O. Box 1007, (410) 745-3350.* Circa 1860 home on harbor, private baths, "delicious" breakfasts, upstairs porch, water views. $$$

INN AT PERRY CABIN, *308 Watkins Ln., (800) 722-2949.* Full-service Ashley Inn in 1812 Colonial mansion on Miles River, English & American antiques, indoor pool, health facility, restaurant, sports & recreations, very highly rated. $$$

KEMP HOUSE INN, *P.O. Box 638, (410) 745-2243.* 1807 Georgian house, period furnishings, working fireplaces, private baths, pets, Gen. Robert E. Lee once a guest. $$$

THE THOMAS HARRISON HOUSE, *201 Green St., P.O. Box 852, (410) 745-2417.* Oldest 2-story dwelling in St. Michaels (ca 1790), period & reproduction furniture, private baths, library, water views, brick patio, bicycles. $$$

VICTORIANA INN, *P.O Box 449, (410) 745-3368.* 1883 doctor's home on harbor, period furniture, some private baths, "hearty country" breakfasts, porches, gardens. $$$

WADES POINT INN ON THE BAY, *P.O. Box 7, (410) 745-2500.* On circa 1819 120-acre farm, rooms with bay views, balconies & screened porches, jogging/nature trail. $$$

Where to Eat

208 TALBOT, *208 N. Talbot St., (410) 745-3838.* How about Baked Oysters with Prosciutto Ham, Pistachio Nuts & Champagne Cream for beginners?; 4 small dining rooms in 1870 bldg., one of best in region, reservations recommended. $$ to $$$

MICHAEL RORK'S TOWN DOCK RESTAURANT, *125 Mulberry St., (410) 745-5577.* "Creative" American cuisine, seafood specialties prepared by owner/chef; beautiful waterfront location. $$ to $$$

MORSELS, *205 N. Talbot St., (410) 745-2911.* Seasonal eclectic menu: Cioppino, Morsels Crab Cakes, Smoked Turkey Quesadilla, Filet au Poivre; cozy upstairs bar. $$

ST. MICHAELS CRAB HOUSE, *305 Mulberry St., (410) 745-3737.* "All-U-Can-Eat" steamed crabs served in oldest bldg. on harbor, extensive seafood menu $$

WINDOWS, *101 N. Harbor Rd., (410) 745-5102.* "Creative" Eastern Shore & American cuisine, seafood specialties; lovely view of St. Michaels harbor. $$ to $$$

Further Information

Talbot County Chamber of Commerce, *P.O. Box 1366, Easton, MD 21601 (410) 822-4606. (ZIP for St. Michaels is 21663.)*

Directions

From Washington (DC), US 50 east (via Chesapeake Bay Toll Bridge) to Easton, MD 33 west to St. Michaels.

Other Charming Maryland Towns

Easton
New Market
Oxford
Snow Hill
Solomons

MASSACHUSETTS

MASSACHUSETTS

Chatham

Population 6, 800

Thrust farther out to sea than any other part of Cape Cod–and with the possible exception of the eastern fringe of Nantucket Island, any other part of southern New England– **Chatham** likes to call itself the "First Stop of the East Wind." The sea–and more specifically, fishing and shellfishing– has been important to Chatham pretty much since the arrival of the Pilgrims in 1656. And as can be seen from the catches being unloaded down at the **Chatham Fish Pier**, it still is.

In more recent times the sea has also brought tourists, enough in fact to nearly quadruple the town's population in the summer. Location on Cape Cod would be more than enough to attract visitors, but Chatham itself offers about everything a vacationer might want in a New England town (except, of course, skiing): for the swimmer or beachcomber, town beaches as well as the famous sands and dunes of **Cape Cod National Seashore**; for the harried or overworked, a solid selection of quiet old inns; for the sports-minded, superb salt-water and fresh-water fishing; for the art collector, galleries with works of Cape Cod artists; for the bicyclist, the **Chatham Bike Route** and **Cape Cod Rail Trail**; for the naturalist, nature trails and some of the best birdwatching in New England.

The **Old Atwood House** (1752), owned by the Chatham Historical Society, offers an excellent introduction to the cultural and natural history of the town and Cape. On display are collections of shells, Sandwich glass, antiques, paintings, and other art objects. Changing exhibits use relics and old photographs to recall Chatham's past.

The Railroad Museum, one of New England's best, features a 1910 caboose, exceptional collection of model trains, and wide range of railroad memorabilia. Of special interest to miniaturists is a diorama of the Chatham railroad yards as they looked in 1915. The museum is housed in the depot that served Chatham from 1887 to 1937.

Visitors interested in learning more of Chatham's past will enjoy a tour of the restored **Mayo House**, an 1820 Cape Cod home with period furnishings (check locally for hours). **Chatham's Old Grist Mill** (1797), which once used wind power to grind corn, is another of Chatham's preserved historic treasures (occasionally open to public).

The Chatham Fish Pier has a visitors' balcony so that the return of the fleet (shortly after noon, depending on tidal conditions) and unloading of the haddock, cod, flounder, lobster, and other catches can be viewed, photographed, and maybe even sketched or painted. Also at the pier is *The Provider* (1992), a monument erected to honor the Chatham fishing industry. The monument's design was selected from some 100 entries in an international competition.

It is only to be expected that a New England town with a long history of tourism should evolve one or two special tourist traditions. And Chatham has done just that. First, visitors love to drive "Down to the Light" and park for an especially grand view of the Atlantic. (*The Chatham Light*, or simply *The Light*, refers to the town's 1877 **lighthouse**.) A second tradition is heading for Kate Gould Park on Friday evenings during the summer months for a concert by the celebrated **Chatham Band**. The concerts include community singing as well as dance numbers for both children and adults.

Special Feature

Guided tours are available of the **Monomoy National Wildlife Refuge** on Monomoy Island. The refuge, one of a chain for migratory waterfowl along the Atlantic Flyway, provides nesting, feeding, and resting grounds for at least 285 species. Boat liveries are also available.

> *Chatham's summers tend to be cool and prone to morning fogs; the Chamber of Commerce describes the fog as "just another conversation piece." Many believe that the most beautiful season here is Indian summer.*

Where to Stay

THE CAPTAIN'S HOUSE INN OF CHATHAM, *369-377 Old Harbor Rd., (508) 945-0127/(800) 315-0728/fax (508) 945-0866.* 1839 inn on 2 acres, antiques, fireplaces, TV & phones, private baths, whirlpools, "extensive gourmet" breakfasts, afternoon tea, English gardens, bikes. $$$

CHATHAM WAYSIDE INN, *512 Main St., (800) 391-5734/(508) 945-5550.* Full-service renovated & expanded 1860s inn in heart of town, fireplaces, balconies, restaurant, heated pool. $$$

CYRUS KENT HOUSE INN, *63 Cross St., (800) 338-5368/(508) 945-9104.* 1877 sea captain's home & carriage house, English antiques, original art, fireplaces, TV & phones, private baths, full breakfasts, award-winning restoration. $$$

MOSES NICKERSON HOUSE INN, *364 Old Harbor Rd., (800) 628-6972/(508) 945-5859.* 1839 sea captain's house, antiques, fireplaces, private baths, full breakfasts, gardens. $$$

THE OLD HARBOR INN, *22 Old Harbor Rd., (800) 942-4434/(508) 945-4434/fax (508) 945-7665.* 1930s inn featuring English country decor, wicker sunroom, antiques, fireplaces, private baths, Cont. "plus" breakfasts, gardens, highly rated. $$$

Where to Eat

THE BISTRO, *595 Main St. (upstairs), (508) 945-5033.* Grilled Garlic Marinated Chicken & Angel Hair, Pan Roasted Cape Sea Scallops, Baked Pumpkin & Sage Raviolis, Grilled Angus Rib Eye Steak; open-wood grill. $$

CAPTAIN LINNELL HOUSE, *137 Skaket Beach Rd. (Orleans), (508) 255-3400.* Atlantic Salmon (poached, with plum tomato, fresh herbs & creme fraiche), Chicken & Shrimp (sauteed, with raisins & a marmalade demi-glace). $$

IMPUDENT OYSTER, *15 Chatham Bars Ave., (508) 945-3545.* Steak Barnard, Pasta Primavera, Chicken Bella, The Impudent Oyster's Bouillabaisse, Pesca Fra Diablo, Oyster Stew. $$ to $$$

L'ALLOUETTE, *787 Main St. (Harwich Port), (508) 430-0405.* Steamed Norwegian Salmon in Court Bouillon, Atlantic Halibut Sauteed with Pistachio Crust, Casserole of Cassoulet, Chateaubriand Bouquetiere. $$

Further Information

Chatham Chamber of Commerce, *2377 Main St., P.O. Box 793, Chatham, MA 02633-0793 (800) 715-5567/(508) 945-5199.*

Directions

From Boston, I 93 south to MA 3 (Exit 7), south to Sagamore Bridge over Cape Cod Canal, US 6 east to MA 137 (Exit 11), south to MA 28, east to Chatham center.

Edgartown
Population 1, 138

Located seven miles off the Massachusetts coast, **Martha's Vineyard** is in some ways its own little country. Made self-sufficient and independent by their separation from the mainland, the islanders refer to the rest of the world as *off island*. Even the climate is different here: Bathed by the

Gulf Stream, the island enjoys cooler summers and milder winters than the rest of New England. When islanders wish a summer home, they buy or build it on another part of the island. Why travel to the mainland when your own little "country" offers six very different towns and a landscape that varies from beaches and wetlands to hills and forests?

Over 350 years old, **Edgartown** is Martha's Vineyard's county seat and oldest town. It is best known for its harbor, filled with sailboats and yachts, and its beautiful old Federal-style whaling captains' homes. Many of the homes can be seen by touring **North** and **South Water Streets**. Some now serve as inns and restaurants (see listings below).

The 12 rooms of the **Thomas Cooke House** (1765) feature antiques, ship models, costumes, and artifacts of the whaling and early farming industries (tours available). The house is just one of several historic exhibits maintained by the **Vineyard Museum**.

The painstakingly restored **Vincent House** (1672), owned by the **Martha's Vineyard Historical Preservation Society**, is the oldest known house on the island (open to the public). Also owned by the Historical Preservation Society, the six-columned Greek Revival **Old Whaling Church** (1843) has been transformed into a performing arts center.

Few places in our country have as many good restaurants and charming inns per capita as Edgartown. There are no fast-food restaurants nor discount department stores.

Special Feature

Each of the towns on Martha's Vineyard has its own character, and no one can agree on which is most charming. In addition to Edgartown, the towns are **Chilmark**, **Gay Head**, **Oak Bluffs**, **Vineyard Haven**, and **West Tisbury**.

> • *The spreading pagoda tree on South Water Street was brought to Edgartown as a seedling from China in the early 19th century.*
> • *Old box pews that are entered through little doors still occupy the Federated Church (1828).*
> • *Early 19th-century camp meetings of the Edgartown Methodists helped pave the way for the development of a summer resort industry.*

Where to Stay

THE DAGGETT HOUSE, *59 N. Water St., (800) 946-3400.* Inn comprising several bldgs., "finest" breakfasts in ca 1660 dining room, restaurant, harbor & garden views. $$$

THE EDGARTOWN INN, *56 N. Water St., Box 1211, (508) 627-4794.* 1798 captain's home, antiques, some private baths, patio garden, Daniel Webster & Nathaniel Hawthorne once guests. $$ to $$$

HOB KNOB INN, *128 Main St., P.O. Box 239, (800) 696-2723/(508) 627-9510/fax (508) 627-4560.* 19th-century Gothic Revival home, antiques, TV & phones, down comforters, private baths, full breakfasts, afternoon tea, fresh flowers, library, verandah, gardens, classic bicycles, charter fishing boat, JFK once a guest. $$$

THE SHIRETOWN INN, *21 N. Water St., (800) 541-0090.* Collection of historic homes including 18th-century captains' houses, on National Register, full-service inn, Cont. breakfasts, restaurant, pub, lovely gardens. $$ to $$$

THE SHIVERICK INN, *Pent Ln., (508) 627-3797.* Pillared 1840 mansion, antiques & Oriental appointments, fireplaces, private baths, guests "beamed home" by chandelier in cupola. $$$

THE TUSCANY INN, *22 N. Water St., Box 2428, (508) 627-5999.* Captain's home, "elegant" furnishings & fabrics, private baths, full breakfasts, cappuccino & homemade biscotti. $$$

THE VICTORIAN INN, *24 S. Water St., (508) 627-4784.* Circa 1820 captain's home on National Register, antiques, private baths, full "gourmet" breakfasts, refreshments, balconies with scenic views, gardens. $$$

Where to Eat

L'ETOILE, *27 S. Summer St. (at The Charlotte Inn), (508) 627-5187.* For example, Grilled Wild Striped Bass Fillet with a Tropical Vegetable, Frisse & Mango Slaw with Preserved Lemon, Lime, Honey & Curry Vinaigrette; reservations, proper dress. $$$ (prix fixe)

THE NEWES FROM AMERICA, *23 Kelly St., (508) 627-4397.* Colonial pub serving New England Clam Chowder, Caesar Salad, Smokin' Musket Turkey, Wicked Bean Burrito, Eggplant Piago, Fish & Chips; 10 micro-brewed draft beers. $

STARBUCK'S, *131 N. Water St., (800) 225-6005.* "The Seafood House" serving Continental & traditional New England dishes, in famed Harbor View Hotel. $$$

THE WHARF PUB, *Lower Main St., (508) 627-9966.* "Affordable Pub Grub at its best," fresh seafood, live entertainment, popular with islanders. $ to $$

Further Information

Martha's Vineyard Chamber of Commerce, *Beach Rd., P.O. Box 1698, Vineyard Haven, MA 02568 (508) 693-0085. (Zip for Edgartown is 02539.)*

Directions

Year-round ferries from **Woods Hole** (MA) carry passengers and cars (car reservations recommended). Seasonal passenger ferries sail from **New Bedford, Falmouth**, and **Hyannis**, MA; and from **Montauk**, NY. The island is also connected via regularly scheduled plane service to **Boston, Hyannis, Nantucket**, and **New Bedford**.

Lenox

Population 5, 600

When a village nestled in a **Berkshires** valley has a summer performing arts schedule rivaling that of many large cities, it should be obvious why by November its inns are nearly booked solid for the following summer. Many of the towns listed in this guide can boast of art galleries, summer stock productions, concerts, and other celebrations of the arts. None, however, possesses the cultural splendor of **Lenox's** billings:

There is first of all the **Tanglewood Music Center**, an estate comprising a mansion, music halls, and elegant gardens. And, of course, the **Shed**, the internationally famous summer home of the **Boston Symphony Orchestra**, with a lawn offering unlimited seating under the stars.

There is also the 1,200-seat concert hall of the **Berkshire Performing Arts Theatre** of the **National Music Center**, where top artists perform every genre of American music. A major music library, a hands-on museum, and a home for retired performers are among the projects planned for the center.

Then there is **The Mount**, Edith Wharton's 1902 summer estate (now the **Edith Wharton Restoration**). The Mount is home to *Shakespeare & Company*, a festival with performances of Edith Wharton, Henry James, and Shakespeare in two indoor and two outdoor theaters.

Lenox also has its off-stage attractions. In addition to one of the finest and most romantic collections of inns in the nation, there are eight or nine art galleries and some of the best shopping in western Massachusetts. Tucked among the woods and hills about Lenox are estates built as summer houses by late 19th- and early 20th-century East Coast millionaires. Most of the houses remain private and their magnificence must therefore be admired from the distance. Some have been converted to inns (see below).

The development of cross-country ski areas and the proximity to great downhill skiing are adding winter to the list of Lenox's most popular seasons.

But irrespective of season, and beyond the on stage and off stage, Lenox is a place of quiet beauty and refinement. It's a place to relax amongst reminders of a more gracious time. One senses that Wharton and James and others of their era still choose to linger here.

Special Features

The grounds and miles of trails of the 1,112-acre **Pleasant Valley Wildlife Sanctuary** north of Lenox provide a beautiful all-season retreat for people as well.

Among the attractions at the **Berkshire Scenic Railway Museum** are model railroads and a 10-minute train ride.

> *Tea is served between performances staged in the drawing room at The Mount.*

Where to Stay

Note: In addition to an excellent selection of B&Bs and small inns (see sample below), Lenox boasts a number of larger inns, many of them full-service. These were often built in the 19th century as elegant country houses, or "Berkshire Cottages." They include the **Apple Tree Inn**, **Blantyre**, **Cornell Inn**, **Gables Inn**, **Rockwood Inn**, **Village Inn**, and **Wheatleigh**.

AMADEUS HOUSE, *15 Cliffwood St., (413) 637-4770/(800) 205-4770*. Victorian home on quiet street, antiques, private baths, full breakfasts, afternoon tea, suite, verandah, classical music. $$$

BIRCHWOOD INN, *7 Hubbard St., P.O. Box 2020, (800) 524-1646*. 1767 home on National Register, antiques, fireplaces, multi-course breakfasts, 18th-century library & parlor, adjacent to Kennedy Park. $$ to $$$

BROOK FARM INN, *15 Hawthorne St., (413) 637-3013*. 1890s home, private baths, full breakfasts, English tea, firelit library, pool, garden hammock. $$ to $$$

CLIFFWOOD INN, *25 Cliffwood St., (413) 637-3330*. "Belle Époque" spaciousness, fireplaces, private baths, evening wine/hors d'oeuvres, verandah. $$ to $$$

SUMMER HILL FARM, *950 East St., (413) 442-2057/(800) 442-2059*. Late 18th-century farmhouse in rural setting, antiques, fireplaces, private baths, full breakfasts, cottage. $$

WALKER HOUSE, *64 Walker St., (413) 637-1271*. 1804 Federal home with antique furnishings & artwork, private baths, full breakfasts, afternoon tea, library video theatre, 3 acres of wooded grounds. $$ to $$$

WHISTLER'S INN, *5 Greenwood St., (413) 637-0975*. 1820 English Tudor mansion, antiques, private baths, buffet breakfasts, sherry/port, music room with Steinway piano & Louis XVI palace furniture, gardens & woodlands. $$$

Where to Eat

CAFE LUCIA, *90 Church St., (413) 637-2640.* Linguine alla Marinara, Crispy Pancetta & Thyme Roasted Free-Range Hen, Ravioli Bandiera al Forno, Bistecca ala Fiorentina. $$

CHURCH STREET CAFE, *65 Church St., (413) 637-2745.* For example, Seared New England Cod with a Bouillabaisse of Shrimp, Mussels, Potatoes, Tomato & Lobster Broth. $$

CANDLELIGHT INN, *35 Walker St., (413) 637-1555.* Fettuccine with Summer Vegetables, Cold Poached Salmon with Chive Remoulade, Grilled Quails with Wild Rice Stuffing; cozy tavern. $$ to $$$

SEMOLINA, *80 Main St., (413) 637-4455.* Shrimp Farfalle, Seared Fresh Cod Fish Bacalao, Linguine all Norma, Seared Filet Mignon au Poivre. $$

SEVEN HILLS INN, *100 Plunkett St., (413) 637-0060.* Grilled Sea Bass with a Delicate Citrus and Chervil Glaze accompanied by Lobster Ravioli; good presentation. $$$

ZAMPANO'S, *579 Pittsfield-Lenox Rd., (413) 448-8600.* Seafood, chicken, beef, pasta, vegetarian entrees, daily & weekly specials, sandwich board. $ to $$

Further Information

Lenox Chamber of Commerce, *P.O. Box 646, Lenox, MA 01240 (413) 637-3646.*

Directions

From Springfield (MA), I 90 (Massachusetts Turnpike) west to Interchange 2, US 20 north to MA 183, MA 183 into the village.

Nantucket Island

Population approximately 7, 000 (year-round)

Now and then history and nature collaborate to produce an ambiance so distinctive and compelling that it has to have a name. The usual practice is to select the name of the town most closely associated with the ambiance. **Nantucket** is a good example. For many Americans "Nantucket" refers to more than a town or island: It refers to fishing boats and wharves and surf, to old shingled houses with potted flowers, to candlelit dinners in 18th-century dining rooms, to harbors and lighthouses and models of old ships.

Nantucket is all of this, and more. The town is also a leading art colony, a major yachting and recreational fishing center, a living museum (the entire island is an historic district). And the beaches are some of the best in the country, if not the world.

The importance of whaling to Nantucket's history is highlighted by the engaging exhibits of the **Whaling Museum** (1847), one of Nantucket's top sites. The restored Greek Revival **Hadwen House** (1845), built by a whale-oil merchant, and the elegant decor and furnishings within offer another glimpse of whaling's importance to Nantucket (open to public).

The **Oldest House** (1686) provides a good example of the late 17th-century house plan of the Massachusetts Bay Colony (tours). Built a few decades later, the **Macy-Christian House** (1723) combines the Colonial style of its inhabitants with the late 19th-century revival of its most recent owners (tours).

For a magnificent view of Nantucket Town and Island, climb the tower of the **First Congregational Church** (open to public). Another church, the **Unitarian Universalist Church** (also open), houses the town clock and 1810 bell in its gold-domed tower. The church's interior is decorated with trompe l-oeil painting.

Special Feature

The **Nantucket Life Saving Museum** is a re-creation of the original station built by the U. S. Life Saving Serving in 1874. Picnickers are attracted by the scenic location (open to the public).

> • *The Old Mill (1746) still grinds corn during favorable weather. The mill is the sole survivor of four that once served the island.*
> • *The two-story Old Gaol (1805), made of logs fastened with iron bolts, may have been the first jail in the U.S. to allow prisoners to go home at night.*
> • *Nantucket Memorial Airport is the second busiest commercial airport in Massachusetts (after Boston's Logan International).*

Where to Stay

ACCOMMODATIONS ET AL, *11 India St., (508) 228-0600/(800) 588-0074.* Group of restored 18th-century inns & cottages; most with canopy beds, fireplaces, antiques, private baths, harbor views. $ to $$$

ANCHOR INN, *66 Centre St., (508) 228-0072.* 1806 home with unspoiled interior, antique paneling, private baths, once owned by famed Gilbreth family. $$ to $$$

CARLISLE HOUSE INN, *26 N. Water St., (508) 228-0720.* Restored 18th-century inn, antiques & Oriental rugs, fireplaces, some TVs, canopy beds, private baths, Cont. "plus" breakfasts, refreshments, local art, gardens. $$ to $$$

THE CARRIAGE HOUSE, *5 Ray's Ct., (508) 228-0326.* Circa 1865 carriage house in center of historic district, private baths, home-baked breakfasts, guest living room with TV. $$ to $$$

THE CENTURY HOUSE B&B, *10 Cliff Rd., (508) 228-0530.* Gray-shingled home with wrap-around porch in historic district, private baths, "bountiful" buffet breakfasts, refreshments. $$$

CLIFF LODGE, *9 Cliff Rd., (508) 228-9480.* 1771 whaling captain's home, TV & phones, private baths, "magical" views from widow's walk, garden patio. $$ to $$$

GREAT HARBOR INN, *31 India St., (800) 377-6609.* 18th-century sea captain's home, American antiques, handmade quilts, TV, private baths. $$$

SEVEN SEA STREET INN, *7 Sea St., (508) 228-3577.* New post-and-beam country inn, private baths, whirlpool, widow's walk for sunset views. $$$

THE WOODBOX INN, *29 Fair St., (508) 228-0587.* Nantucket's oldest inn (1709), fireplaces, private baths, "gourmet" breakfasts, dining room with candlelight dinners. $$$

Where to Eat

THE ATLANTIC CAFE, *15 S. Water St., (508) 228-0570.* Famous Quahog Chowder, "Super Sandwiches," specialty salads, South of Border entrees; casual, a local favorite. $ to $$

LE LANGUEDOC, *24 Broad St., (508) 228-2552.* American & Continental cuisine served in intimate dining rooms, cafe wine bar. $$ to $$$

THE SEAGRILLE, *45 Sparks Ave., (508) 325-5700.* Local fish & shellfish, lobster, steaks, pasta; open year-round. $ to $$

THE WOODBOX, *(see above).* Native seafood, Beef Wellington, hot popovers; "Nantucket's oldest dining rooms." $ to $$$

Further Information

Nantucket Island Chamber of Commerce, *48 Main St., Nantucket Island, MA 02554 (508) 228-1700.* Contact the Chamber of Commerce for a copy of their very colorful and comprehensive annual guide.

Directions

Comfortable ferries, some operating year-round, serve Nantucket from **Hyannis** (MA). Cars require reservations, but passengers and bicycles do not. Visitors are discouraged from bringing cars to the tiny island. Several major as well as local airlines have regularly scheduled flights from a variety of East Coast locations.

Rockport
Population 7, 432

Rockport's harbor is one of the most picturesque on the Eastern seaboard. Anyone who enjoys paintings and watercolors of American fishing villages and harbor scenes has seen the harbor in a gallery somewhere. Indeed, an old red shack on Bradley Wharf has been so popular with art students that it has been nicknamed *Motif No. 1*. Many of the famous names in American art, including Winslow Homer and Edward Hopper, placed their easels at or near Rockport Harbor at some stage in their lives.

Rockport is designed for walking. The main and back streets of the town are bordered by many fine homes built between 1692 and 1864, most in the 1700s. Many are adorned with shutters, fan lights, and old-fashioned gardens. Also along the streets is a goodly collection of studios and galleries. Of special note (and popularity) are the diverse exhibits in the galleries of the **Rockport Art Association**.

The harbor, **Headlands**, and beaches, including a couple right in town, are ideal for hiking and strolling (the Chamber of Commerce publishes a guide that describes three short in-town walks originating from Dock Square). Wildflowers abound in the area's waysides, salt marshes, and ponds. Birdwatchers spot not only the upland birds of New England, but also a wide selection of shore and sea birds. Island cruises and informative lobstering trips are available for those looking to the water.

> • *Rockport became the American landfall of the trans-Atlantic cable in 1884.*
> • *Rockport granite was used in the construction of New York's Woolworth Building, New Orleans's Federal Reserve Bank, Philadelphia's Kensington National Bank, and dozens of other structures in the U.S. and elsewhere.*

Special Features

Halibut Point State Park affords splendid views of Ipswich Bay and, on a clear day, points in New Hampshire and Maine. Closer at hand in the park are tidal pools and a beautiful water-filled granite quarry.

A house constructed of approximately 100,000 copies of Boston newspapers may be visited at nearby **Pigeon Cove**. The house and its furniture, also made of newspapers, required some 20 years to "build."

Where to Stay

ADDISON CHOATE INN, *49 Broadway, (508) 546-7543/(800) 245-7543*. Mid 19th-century Greek Revival home with ocean view, private baths, Cont. "plus" breakfasts, awning-shaded porch, pool. $$$

THE CAPTAIN'S HOUSE, *109 Marmion Way, (508) 546-3825*. 1910 ocean-front home, private baths, enclosed sunporch, attractive yard & patios. $$ to $$$

LINDEN TREE INN, *26 King St., (508) 546-2429*. 1840 home, private baths, afternoon treats, gardens, leisurely stroll to beaches. $$ to $$$

SEACREST MANOR, *131 Marmion Way, (508) 546-2211*. "Intentionally quiet" with magnificent views, private baths, "famous" full breakfasts, afternoon teas, gardens, one of finest. $$$

Where to Eat

Note: Rockport has been "dry" since 1856, when some 200 women hatcheted the kegs and poured the contents into the streets. Bring your own paper bag.

BRACKETT'S OCEANVIEW RESTAURANT, *29 Main St., (508) 546-2797*. Hot Boiled Lobster, Shrimp Scampi, London Broil, Baked Crab Casserole, fried seafood plates, New England-style Chowder; seaside dining. $ to $$

ELLEN'S HARBORSIDE, *1 T-Wharf, (508) 546-2512*. Three generations of experience specializing in fresh seafood. $ to $$

THE GREENERY CAFE/RESTAURANT, *Dock Sq., (508) 546-9593*. Fresh seafood, ethnic cuisine, pastas; bakery, overlooking harbor. $ to $$

MY PLACE BY-THE-SEA RESTAURANT, *68 South Rd., (978) 546-9667*. Steamed Lobster with Corn on the Cob & Red Bliss Potatoes; My Place Swordfish with a Tangy Bernaise Sauce, Pecan Butter & Parslied New Potatoes; spectacular outdoor oceanfront setting, award-wining. $$

PEG LEG RESTAURANT, *18 Beach St., (508) 546-3038*. Fresh seafood, "Yankee favorites;" on edge of the sea, highly regarded. $ to $$

Further Information

Rockport Chamber of Commerce, *P.O. Box 67, Rockport, MA 01966 (508) 546-6575*.

Directions

From Boston, US 1 north to MA 128, MA 128 east to exit 9, MA 127 north to Rockport.

Stockbridge
Population 2, 311

The oldest village improvement society in the United States, the Laurel Hill Association, was formed in **Stockbridge** in 1853. The goal of the association, the oldest preservation society in the U.S., was and remains to "glorify God's grandeur by gracefully combining Art and Nature." Stockbridge is also home to the oldest private land trust in the country, The Trustees of Reservations, founded in 1891. The townspeople of Stockbridge were clearly among the first in the nation to draw attention to the beauty of the past, and to the need to protect it.

Given the village's cultural heritage and beauty, the interest in preservation isn't really surprising. For instance, the buildings and architectural styles along Main Street combine to create one of the most picturesque village scenes in the country. The street is the kind of main street that small American towns are supposed to have – which is probably why Norman Rockwell chose to portray it in his famous painting, *Stockbridge Mainstreet at Christmas*.

Among the structures along the street are the famed **Red Lion Inn** (1773, rebuilt 1897; on the far right of Rockwell's painting), the **Cat and Dog Fountain** (1862), the Greek-Revival **Stockbridge Town Hall**, and the **Stockbridge Library**, one of the oldest libraries in western Massachusetts (original part built in 1864). On the lower level of the library is a history museum and research center, known as the Historical Room.

Then there are the *Cottages*, summer homes built during the closing years of the 19th and beginning of the 20th centuries by the barons of America's post-Civil War industrialization. Although many of the mansions have since disappeared, enough remain to add color and an Old World sense of aristocracy to Main Street and the other byways in and round the village (see also Lenox). Most are private, but several of the most important – along with a few earlier, Colonial houses – are open to the public.

The oldest house of these is **Mission House** (1739), the home of John Sergeant, first missionary to the Stockbridge Indians. The restored house has period furnishings and a warm Colonial garden. Other historic – and beautiful – homes include:

Naumkeag (1885) is one of the village's best-known Cottages. The 26-room gabled mansion, built by an ambassador to England, boasts a collection of Chinese porcelain, elegant furnishings, and especially lovely gardens. Although built much earlier (1820s), the Federal-style **Merwin House** displays late 19th- and early 20th-century furnishings. The house and its peaceful grounds also go by the name of *Tranquility*.

Chesterwood is the name of the studio (1898) and Colonial Revival summer home (1901) of sculptor Daniel Chester French. One of the country's foremost artists, it was French who created the *Minute Man* (1875) in Concord, Massachusetts, and the seated *Abraham Lincoln* (1922) in the Lincoln Memorial in Washington, D.C. Chesterwood is home to nearly 500 pieces of sculpture, as well as to gardens and rolling woodlands.

The **Norman Rockwell Museum**, dedicated to a man unrivaled as a perceiver and illustrator of American charm, contains Rockwell's studio and the world's largest collection of original Rockwell art. Architect Robert A.M. Stern has skillfully fashioned Colonial elements to create a new museum building that is itself a masterpiece of American charm. The museum's 36 acres of scenic grounds are available for picnicking and relaxation.

Stockbridge's shops display American and European items ranging from paintings and antiques to gourmet foods, contemporary glass, candles, and hand-knit sweaters. During the summer months the renowned **Berkshire Theatre Festival** presents classic, contemporary, and children's theater.

Special Features

For a healthy hike leading up to three-state mountain views, ask for directions to the nearby historic Ice Glen area.

The 15-acre **Berkshire Botanical Garden**, northwest of town, features plantings of primroses and conifers, herb garden, rose garden, ponds, woodland walks, and in general, quiet beauty.

West Stockbridge, less frequented than Stockbridge and Lenox, is another charming Berkshires village.

Where to Stay

ARBOR ROSE B&B, *8 Yale Hill, (413) 298-4744.* New England millhouse with pond, antiques & watercolors, home-baked breakfasts, gardens, mountain view. $$ to $$$

BROAD MEADOWS, *P.O. Box 485, (413) 298-4972.* 1902 summer estate on spacious grounds, antiques, private baths, full breakfasts, library/music room with Steinway. $$$

CONROY'S B&B, *P.O. Box 191, (413) 298-4990.* 1830 brick Federal-style farmhouse with spacious lawns, antiques, fireplaces, some private baths, breakfast buffet, gardens, scenic views. $$ to $$$

THE INN AT STOCKBRIDGE B&B, *P.O. Box 618, (413) 298-3337.* Georgian Colonial inn on 12 secluded acres, antiques, private baths, full breakfasts, wine/cheese, baby grand. $$$

ROEDER HOUSE B&B, *P.O. Box 525, (413) 298-4015.* 1856 home with flower gardens, country antiques, Audubons, private baths, full breakfasts, pool. $$$

THE WILLIAMSVILLE INN, *MA 41 (W. Stockbridge 01266), (413) 274-6118.* 1797 white clapboard Federal farmhouse on 10 acres, antiques, private baths, full breakfasts. $$$

Where to Eat

CACTUS CAFE, *54 Main St. (Lee), (413) 243-4300.* Mexican cantina serving Vegetable Quesadillas, Enchiladas, Chimichangas, Caldo Quintanaroo, Chicken Mole, Pescado del Dia (served grilled with a mango salsa). $$

FEDERAL HOUSE INN, *Main St. (S. Lee), (413) 243-1824.* Highly acclaimed cuisine in restored 1824 country home. $$$

THE MORGAN HOUSE INN, *33 Main St. (Lee), (413) 243-0181.* Innovative & traditional New England cuisine served in historic stage-coach inn, lighter fare in tavern, chef-owned. $$

THE RED LION INN, *Main St., (413) 298-5545.* Famed landmark, elegant antique-filled dining room, flower-laden courtyard, reservations. $$$

Further Information

Stockbridge Chamber of Commerce, *P.O. Box 224, Stockbridge, MA 01262 (413) 298-5200.*

Directions

From Springfield, I 90 west to Interchange 2, MA 102 west to Stockbridge.

Other Charming Massachusetts Towns

Concord
Great Barrington
Hyannis
Sheffield
Williamstown

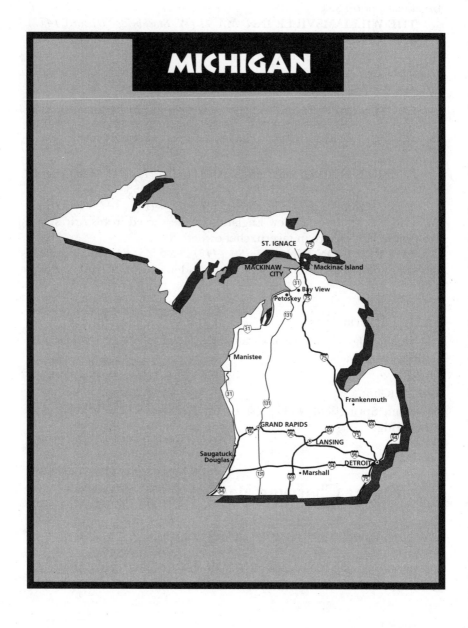

MICHIGAN

ST. IGNACE
MACKINAW CITY
Mackinac Island
Bay View
Petoskey
Manistee
Frankenmuth
GRAND RAPIDS
LANSING
Saugatuck Douglas
DETROIT
Marshall

MICHIGAN

Frankenmuth

Population 4, 408

Frankenmuth, Michigan's *Little Bavaria* is one of the more unusual of our country's towns. Gabled and towered Bavarian buildings dot the landscape, giving the town a romantic European appearance. At the same time, landscaped parkland and the American love of detached construction put distance among the buildings, giving the town a spacious American appearance. The colorful Bavarian-inspired architecture of many of the structures, including the glockenspiel tower and covered bridge, is delightful. At the same time, many of the visitor attractions along the two-mile business stretch could exist only on this side of the Atlantic. A tug of war exists between the authentic and the copied, with charm the sometimes victor.

In 1927 a Frankenmuth restaurant began serving chicken dinners family-style. Word got around and by the 1940s "Frankenmuth-style" chicken was attracting people from as far away as Detroit. The use of Bavarian-style architecture made its appearance around 1948. Today, two restaurants (see below) serve over 2,000,000 dinners, mostly chicken, annually. And the architecture is more popular than ever.

Unlike many towns with more natural sources of charm, Frankenmuth has plenty to keep all members of the family busy. Tours of woolen mills, woodcarving shops, a restored grist mill, and a brewery inform and entertain at the same time. Among the many interesting shops is one specializing in pewter, another that boasts the world's largest outdoor cuckoo clock, and yet another that displays thousands of dollhouse miniatures in over 100 room settings.

Bronner's Christmas Wonderland, the world's largest Christmas store, offers 500 different styles of Nativity scenes, 260 decorated trees, 200 styles of nutcrackers, and over 50,000 unique trims and gifts.

For those tiring of the commercial, there are guided tours of Gothic **St. Lorenz Lutheran Church** (1880). The church has a 167-foot steeple, vivid stained-glass windows, and a carved baptismal font that is a replica of the font in the original St. Lorenz Church in Bavaria.

• *"Franken" refers to the province in Bavaria from which the town's settlers came, and "Muth" means "courage" in German.*
• *Three million people visit Frankenmuth each year.*

Where to Stay

BIRCH RUN'S CHURCH STREET MANOR, *12274 Church St. (Birch Run 48415)*, *(517) 624-4920*. 19th-century home offering full breakfasts. $$

FRANKLIN HAUS B&B, *216 S. Franklin St., (517) 652-3939*. 1911 home with antiques, private baths, full breakfasts. $$

Where to Eat

BAVARIAN INN RESTAURANT, *713 S. Main St., (517) 652-9941*. Famous Frankenmuth-style chicken dinners, Bavarian entrees including Sauerbraten & Kasseler Rippchen. $$

ZEHNDERS, *730 S. Main St., (517) 652-9925*. Famous family-style chicken & other American dinners served in 9 dining rooms. $$

Further Information

Frankenmuth Convention & Visitors Bureau, *635 S. Main St., Frankenmuth, MI 48734 (517) 652-6106/(800) 386-8696*.

Directions

From Detroit, I 75 north to exit 136, MI 83 east and north to Frankenmuth.

Mackinac Island

Population about 550 year-round

The stately **Grand Hotel**, white with yellow awnings. The magnificent Victorian "cottages" lining the **West** and **East Bluffs**. The red geraniums against the white clapboards and fence pickets. The purples, lavenders, and whites of the lilac trees in the spring. The sound of horses and carriages. The neatness, cleanliness, and civility. Above all, the blue waters of **Lake Huron**, everywhere. **Mackinac** (MACK in awe) Island offers spectacular views and a glorious diversity of images.

Strategically located between **Lakes Huron**, **Michigan**, and **Superior**, Mackinac Island has been a special place for centuries. The Indians, the French, the English, and finally the Americans all passed through. The island slipped from beneath one flag to another, but always without bloodshed. The history, the beauty, and the pollen-free environment began to attract steamships in the latter half of the 19th century, and Mackinac Island became a resort. Most visitors came to spend a few days. A few, the wealthy, built cottages so that they might spend the summer.

More than 80 percent of the island is now a state park. The island is closed to motor vehicles (except for snowmobiles in the winter, and even these are restricted). All travel is by foot, bicycle, or horse. Horse-and-carriage taxi service is available, as are tours and "drive yourself" hourly rentals. There are also private liveries and an abundance of bicycle liveries.

The most important of the historic sites is **Fort Mackinac** (1780), a **Mackinac State Historic Park** and National Historic Landmark. Given by the U.S. Government to the State of Michigan in 1895, the fort is manned by "soldiers" who portray the military life of the very Victorian 1880s. The fort comprises 14 restored buildings, including the **Soldiers' Barracks**, **Post Hospital**, the **Guardhouse**, and the **Officers' Stone Quarters**. The latter was built with 4-foot-thick walls and is one of Michigan's oldest buildings. Each building tells its own special story using exhibits, multimedia programs, costumed reenactments, and period craft demonstrations. There are also concerts.

The 1817 **Robert Stuart House**, the home of an Astor Fur Company manager, is now a museum displaying local artifacts, including records of the American Fur Trading Company, and period rooms. The displays of the **Beaumont Memorial** describe the famous 1820s experiments of Dr. William Beaumont, who furthered knowledge of the human digestive system by examining the stomach of a man with a gunshot wound in the abdomen. Other historic buildings include the 1830 **Mission Church**, the three-story **Indian Dormitory** (now a museum with period furnishings), and the **McGulpin House**, a restored Canadian log residence.

Even visitors staying elsewhere should spend some time at the majestic **Grand Hotel**. Non-registered guests may stroll the 700-foot verandah, examine the photos in the lower lobby, and after obtaining a special guest pass, explore the Grand Hotel gardens. Luncheon may be taken at any of six restaurants. High tea is served mid-afternoon, and music and demitasse follow dinner in the Parlor. The bar atop the hotel has one of the finest views on the island. An orchestra plays in the evening: There are few experiences so romantic as going by carriage up to the ballroom of the Grand Hotel for an evening of dancing (dress code after 6:00 p.m.).

If you like pure white snow, clear blue skies, tranquillity and stillness, consider visiting Mackinac Island in the winter. A number of businesses remain open to serve cross-country skiers, snowmobilers, and sleigh riders. Ferry boats continue until after the holidays (this is a wonderful place to spend Christmas) and airplane service from **St. Ignace** is available after the straits freeze. Check with the Chamber of Commerce for information on transportation, lodging, and snow conditions.

Special Features

A bicycle or carriage tour around the island on MI 185 (8.1 miles) includes such sights as Arch Rock, a natural limestone arch that stands nearly 150 feet above the water; Lover's Leap, a 145-foot limestone pillar; and Devil's Kitchen, a cave with a spectacular view of the Lower Peninsula and **Mackinac Bridge**.

> • *It should come as no surprise to learn that Mackinac Island's MI 185 is the only state road in Michigan that has never had an automobile accident.*
> • *Mackinac Island's beautiful lilacs were introduced in the 1600s by French missionaries.*
> • *More than 800, 000 people visit Mackinac Island each year.*

Where to Stay

Note: Mackinac Island is blessed with some of the country's loveliest classic resort hotels. Among these are the **CHIPPEWA, GRAND, IROQUOIS, ISLAND HOUSE, & LAKE VIEW**.

BAY VIEW AT MACKINAC, *P.O. Box 448, (906) 847-3295.* 1891 home on water's edge, private baths, own coffee blend, verandah, spectacular seascapes. $$$

CLOGHAUN B&B, *P.O. Box 203, (906) 847-3885.* 1884 home on spacious grounds, private baths, Cont. "plus" breakfasts, refreshments, antique melodeon, verandah, private balconies. $$ to $$$

HAAN'S 1830 INN B&B, *P.O. Box 123, (906) 847-6244.* Greek Revival home with period antiques, some private baths, Cont. "plus" breakfasts, porches. $$$

MADAME LA FRAMBOISE HARBOUR VIEW INN, *P.O. Box 1207, (906) 847-0101.* Remodeled 1820 manor, fireplaces, private baths, whirlpools, porches, harbor views. $$$

METIVIER INN, *P.O. Box 285, (906) 847-6234.* 1877 home with "Country French flavor," private baths, deluxe Cont. breakfasts, large porch with wicker. $$$

Where to Eat

Note: Mackinac Island is best known for its Great Lakes whitefish and trout. For between meals, try one of the town's famous fudge shops.

THE CARRIAGE HOUSE, *Hotel Iroquois, (906) 847-3321.* Broiled Lake Superior Whitefish, Seafood Linguine, Iroquois Filet Mignon; dining with a sweeping view. $$$

THE PUB OYSTER BAR, *Main St., (906) 847-3454*. Oysters, spiced shrimp, chowders, seafood, pasta, steaks. $ to $$

VILLAGE INN, *Hoban St., (906) 847-3542*. VIP Planked Whitefish, lake perch, chicken, steaks, specialty soups, Special Steakburger. $$

THE WOODS, *in forest near Grand Hotel, (906) 847-3699*. Mackinac Whitefish Baked in Parchment, Rotisserie Chicken/Jarlsberg Sauce, Rib Eye Steak; casual, Bavarian charm. $$

THE YANKEE REBEL TAVERN, *3 Astor St., (906) 847-6249*. Balsamic Chicken Pasta, Yankee Pot Roast, Great Lakes Walleye, Bleumoon Caesar Salad, deep-dish homemade pies; early 1800s decor, wooden beams. $$

Further Information

Mackinac Island Chamber of Commerce, *P.O. Box 451, Mackinac Island, MI 49757 (906) 847-6418 or 3783.*

Directions

Commercial air service is available to the island, but most people prefer to go by ferry, departing from either **Mackinaw City** or **St. Ignace**. The ferry ride is itself an experience. Among the many spectacular views is that of the 5-mile-long **Mackinac Bridge** that connects Michigan's Lower and Upper Peninsulas.

Manistee

Population 6734

The Victorian Port City of Manistee can be reached by air, land or, if you prefer, by freighter or sailboat or canoe. The shores of Lake Michigan border the town's west side, to the east is **Manistee Lake** (and the Manistee National Forest), and through the heart of town flows the **Manistee River**.

Manistee's heyday came in the years after the Civil War when, thanks to the vast pine forests, the town became one of Michigan's most important lumbering centers. Seeing no virtue in frugality, the lumber barons built elegant Victorian mansions and a downtown business district that, today, displays what is probably the finest collection of Victorian commercial buildings in Michigan.

The Romanesque **First Congregational Church** (1892), listed on the National Register, was designed by noted Chicago architect William LeBaron Jenney. Two of the 36 stained-glass windows are Tiffany and two others were displayed at the 1893 Columbian Exposition (tours by reservation). Another National Register church, **Our Saviour's Church** (1868/69), is the oldest Danish-American Evangelical Lutheran Church in America. It has a hand-carved pulpit and Viking ship and is topped by an octagonal spire with finial weathervane (tours by reservation).

The Italianate **Ramsdell Theatre** (1903), on the National Register, is acoustically one of the best in the U.S. Among other things, the theater boasts its original thunder machine and an act curtain by Walter Burridge, who designed the sets of the original stage production of *The Wizard of Oz* (tours available).

An especially popular place, in part because visitors are always welcome, is Manistee's Romanesque Revival **Fire Hall** (1889). Now a State Historic Site, the structure hasn't undergone usage or design alterations since it was built and is reputed to be one of the oldest continuously operating firehouses in the state (open for tours).

The 1882 **Babcock House** features period furniture, Oriental rugs, unusual automatic musical instruments, and the original gas light system (guided tours).

There are several ways to explore the Victoriana. Probably the most leisurely and rewarding is a stroll down **River Street**, the main street, followed by a stroll back along the lovely **Manistee Riverwalk**. Both parallel the river, and each other, and do what some of the most charming byways in the world do, twist and turn. A tour aboard a 1900s-replica trolley (hourly) is another option.

Wednesday evening concerts on the river's edge are held in the beautiful new Victorian **Gazebo Bandshell** (1991) during the summer months. A variety of performances by the **Manistee Civic Players** delight audiences at the Ramsdell Theatre.

Special Features

But a few blocks from downtown, the white sand beaches of **Lake Michigan** provide a beautiful backdrop for swimming, picnicking, enjoying nature, or just plain lazing.

Chartering and other marine services are available for those seeking coho and chinook salmon, lake trout, steelhead, brown trout, and large, yellow lake perch.

> • *Boat watching is a favorite Manistee pastime. Freighters often pass through the center of town on the Manistee River.*
> • *The North Pier Catwalk (1880), on the National Register, is one of five remaining pier catwalks on the entire coast of Lake Michigan.*
> • *James Earl Jones began his career at the Ramsdell Theatre.*

Where to Stay

E. E. DOUVILLE HOUSE B&B, *111 Pine St., (616) 723-8654.* 1879 home, ornate hand-carved woodwork, soaring staircase, antiques, walking distance to Lake Michigan. $ to $$

LAKE SHORE B&B, *3440 Lakeshore Rd., (616) 723-7644.* Home on Lake Michigan with private sandy beach, TV, Cont. "plus" breakfasts, private decks with lake views. $ to $$

MANISTEE COUNTRY HOUSE, *1130 Lakeshore Rd, (616) 723-2367 / fax (616) 723-9914.* 1901 brick home with pressed tin ceilings, antiques, some private baths, pedestal sinks, full breakfasts, refreshments, potpourri pots on radiators, verandah, gardens. $ to $$

MANISTEE INN & MARINA, *378 River St., (800) 968-6277.* New full-service inn on waterfront, Cont. breakfasts, kitchenettes, hot tubs, boat docks, fishing charters, yogurt shop. $ to $$

OLD CAMP TOSEBO INN B&B, *7228 Miller Rd., (616) 889-4242.* Restored 1912 lodge at former camp in woods on Portage Lake, some private baths, coffee & scones. $ to $$

Where to Eat

FOUR FORTY WEST, *440 River St., (616) 723-7209.* Perch, cod, white fish, prime rib; varied menu, overlooking river. $ to $$

Further Information

Manistee Area Chamber of Commerce, *11 Cypress St., Manistee, MI 49660 (616) 723-2575 / (800) 288-2286.*

Directions

From Grand Rapids, I 96 west to US 31, US 31 north to Manistee.

Marshall

Population 6891

Fountain Circle in **Marshall** is without qualification one of our country's grandest circles. Anchored in the center by a Greek Revival Fountain and surrounded by a set of handsome buildings, the circle looks like the product of a marriage between a lovely Continental city and a prosperous Midwestern town. The adjacent streets continue the flavor, except that a little of New England seems to get into the mixture as well.

It was once assumed that Marshall would become the capital of Michigan – moving the capital from Detroit to Marshall was in fact written into the original state constitution. However, when in 1847 the state legislature voted on the matter, Marshall lost by just one vote and Lansing was chosen.

As a kind of consolation prize, and a considerable one at that, the battle's loser went on to become one of Michigan's most beautiful towns. Today, with 867 designated buildings, Marshall is the largest National Landmark District in the country in the "Small Urban" category.

The Chamber of Commerce's self-guided tour brochure includes no fewer than 130 buildings and 46 historic markers! Several of the houses and sites are open to the public during the **Annual Historic Home Tour** on the first weekend after Labor Day.

The **Honolulu House Museum**, on Fountain Circle, was built by a Chief Justice of the Michigan Supreme Court to resemble the mansion he had occupied in Honolulu as U. S. Consul to the Sandwich (Hawaiian) Islands. A blend of Italianate, Gothic Revival, and Polynesian influences, the house has received a number of awards for the recent restoration of the paint-on-plaster wall and ceiling decorations.

Also on Fountain Circle are the lovely stone **Town Hall** (1857), built as a stage coach stop and livery stable, and the **National House Inn** (1835), the first brick building in the county and the oldest operating inn in Michigan (see below).

Throughout the historic district, but especially along the streets to the east and north of Fountain Circle, is a virtual museum of 19th- and early-20th-century American residential architecture. Most of the homes have been restored. The shade trees for which Michigan's towns are well-known make touring the streets especially pleasurable.

Special Feature

Marshall's **Michigan Avenue** ranks as one of the finest (and healthiest) main streets in the country. A shopping guide is available from the Chamber of Commerce. Abundant parking is available behind the shops.

> • *The 1839 Greek Revival Governor's Mansion was built on the hopeful assumption that Marshall would become Michigan's capital.*
> • *In the 1840s members of Marshall's leading families were sued and heavily fined for their efforts to prevent slave hunters from returning an escaped slave to his former owner in Kentucky.*

Where to Stay

McCARTHY'S BEAR CREEK INN, *15230 C Drive North, (616) 781-8383*. In restored home & converted barn overlooking creek, private baths, Cont. "plus" breakfasts. $$$

NATIONAL HOUSE INN, *102 South Parkview (on Fountain Circle), (616) 781-7374*. Restored 1835 stagecoach stop on National Register, massive open-hearth fireplace, private baths, afternoon tea, sitting garden, mystery weekends. $$$

Where to Eat

CORNWELL'S TURKEY HOUSE, *18935 15 1/2 Mile Rd., (616) 781-4293*. Turkey served in Michigan's only professional dinner theater. $

MALIA ITALIAN BISTRO, *130 W. Michigan Ave., (616) 781-2171*. Italian dining on historic main street. $$

MOONRAKER, *11401 17 Mile Rd., (616) 789-0058*. Seafood, prime rib, Mexican entrees, sandwiches. $

SCHULER'S RESTAURANT, *115 S. Eagle St., (616) 781-0600*. Northern Michigan Rainbow Trout, Schuler's Saucy Chicken Scaloppini, Schuler's Classic Roast Prime Rib of Beef; bakery, a Michigan tradition. $$

Further Information

Marshall Area Chamber of Commerce, *109 East Michigan Ave., Marshall, MI 49068 (616) 781-5163*.

Directions

From Detroit, I 94 west to exit 110 (Marshall exit).

Petoskey/Bay View
Population 6, 056

Back in the days before the three-car family and air-conditioned house, residents of large Midwestern cities could escape the summer's heat and humidity–and pollen–by boarding a train or steamboat and traveling up to the clear waters and rolling forests of northern Michigan. Two favorite destinations were **Petoskey** and **Bay View**, adjacent resort communities on Lake Michigan's beautiful **Little Traverse Bay**.

Chartered in 1879, Petoskey started as both a lumbering center and a resort. The town's first passenger train arrived in 1873 and the first brick hotel (still in operation–see Stafford's Perry Hotel below) opened in 1899. Next door, tiny Bay View was founded as a summer retreat in 1875 by the Methodist Church. The village was (and remains) noted for its programs of lectures, concerts, and Sunday evening vespers; it is now a National Historic Landmark with more than 440 cottages, most dating to before 1890.

The many **Victorian buildings** make leisurely walking tours of Petoskey and Bay View appropriate–and very enjoyable. (Check with the Convention & Visitors Bureau–see below–for walking-tour brochures.) One of downtown Petoskey's most important structures is the **Little Traverse History Museum**, once the passenger depot (1892) for the Chicago & West Michigan Railroad. Exhibits in the Richardsonian Romanesque structure include memorabilia associated with author Ernest Hemingway and historian and journalist Bruce Catton. The Italianate **Symons General Store** (1879), also downtown, was Petoskey's first brick building. The oldest building in Petoskey is the timbered **St. Francis Solanus Indian Mission** (1859; closed).

Boyne Country (which includes Petoskey and Bay View) offer a near-limitless range of recreational pursuits. Petoskey's **Gaslight Shopping District** is respected throughout the upper Midwest, and beyond. Bay View has a substantial summer calendar of musical and theatrical performances. More than 25 public courses beckon the golfer, and a lovely slice of Lake Michigan shoreline plus several good-sized inland lakes invite swimmers, boaters of all kinds, and water enthusiasts in general. Public fishing sites provide access to trout, bass, walleye, salmon, and steelhead. Those seeking more unique pursuits might enjoy hunting for morel mushrooms, or maybe *Petoskey Stones* (fossilized coral).

Sometimes billed as the "Midwest's favorite winter destination," Boyne Country has more than 90 downhill ski runs and several hundred kilometers of groomed cross-country trails. There are also sledding hills and excellent facilities for skating, snowmobiling, and ice fishing. The apres-ski scene is reputed to be the best between New England and the Rockies.

Special Features

Boyne Country has a wealth of scenic–and quiet–**back roads**. Many are ideal for bike tours.

Varying from the bright reds and oranges of the maples and oaks to the yellows of the birches and basswoods, northern Michigan's **autumn foliage** is among the country's most spectacular. Five fall tours ranging in length from 45 minutes to 2 1/2 hours are described in a special brochure distributed by the Convention and Visitors Bureau.

The Petoskey area provided lumber for the rebuilding of Chicago after the Great Fire of 1871.

Where to Stay

THE GINGERBREAD HOUSE, *205 Bluff, P.O. Box 1273, (616) 347-3538*. 1881 Bay View cottage, porch with rocking chairs, private baths, Cont. "plus" breakfasts, views of Little Traverse Bay. $$$

MONTGOMERY PLACE, *618 E. Lake St., (616) 347-1338/fax (616) 348-8311*. Originally 1879 hotel, on National Register, hand-carved 8-ft front door, private baths, full breakfasts, wines & snacks, 80-ft verandah overlooking Little Traverse Bay. $$$

SERENITY, *504 Rush St., (616) 347-6171*. Turn-of-century home on hill overlooking Little Traverse Bay, antiques, private baths, Cont. "plus" breakfasts, afternoon tea, glass-enclosed porches. $$$

STAFFORD'S BAY VIEW INN, *613 Woodland Ave., P.O. Box 3, (616) 347-2771/(800) 258-1886*. Full-service 1886 inn on Little Traverse Bay, Michigan Historic Site, antiques, public dining room, wicker & chintz sunroom, bayside gardens. $$$

STAFFORD'S PERRY HOTEL, *Bay & Lewis sts., (800) 456-1917/(616) 347-4000*. Full-service 1899 hotel in Gaslight District, balconies, multinational menus with "lots of American comfort foods," al fresco dining in summer, live music in Noggin Room Pub. $$ to $$$ (golf packages available)

TERRACE INN, *216 Fairview, P.O. Box 266, (800) 530-9898/(616) 347-2410*. Full-service 1911 inn with wood paneling, period furniture, front porch, Cont. breakfasts, dining room (see below), private beach. $$ (packages available)

Where to Eat

THE NEW YORK, *101 State St. (Harbor Springs 49740), (616) 526-1904*. Salads & cold plates, sandwiches, Great Lakes Whitefish, Chicken Tuscany, "Bill's Burger"; est. 1904. $

CITY PARK GRILL, *432 E. Lake St., (616) 347-0101*. "A Victorian cafe" serving "tastes from Italy, the Southwest, the Orient"; cherry back bar in Pub. $$

ROAST & TOAST CAFE, *309 E. Lake St., (616) 347-7767*. Grilled Vegetable Lasagna, Bourbon Teriyaki Chicken, New Orleans Chicken Bienville, soups & salads, lunch specials; coffeehouse, bakery. $

TERRACE INN, *(see above)*. Planked Whitefish the specialty, Chicken Hemingway, Fettuccine Alfredo. $$

Further Information

Petoskey-Harbor Springs-Boyne Country Visitors Bureau, *401 E. Mitchell St., Petoskey, MI 49770, (800) 845-2828/(616) 348-2755.*

Directions

From Grand Rapids, US 131 north to Petoskey.

Saugatuck/Douglas
Population 954/1, 040

With a combined population of less than 2,000, the snug Lake Michigan harbor villages of **Saugatuck** and **Douglas** boast 35 bed and breakfasts, 30 art galleries, 3 golf courses (including Michigan's second oldest), a **Chamber Music Festival,** and a summer stock theater. They are also home to **Oxbow**, the summer camp of the internationally respected Chicago Institute of Art.

Saugatuck and Douglas are the kinds of places where bed and breakfasts place illustrated histories of Great Lakes steamers on coffee tables. Appropriately, the *SS Keewatin*, a 1907 Canadian Pacific Railway passenger liner, is moored here as a museum. Guided tours allow a glimpse of the comfort once enjoyed by steamship travelers on the Great Lakes.

The two villages share one of the 10 best harbors in the U.S., and that means some world-class Great Lakes sailing. The villages also share beautiful unspoiled beaches and, not far away, towering dunes. In the waters outside the harbor, sports fishermen pull in salmon, trout, walleye, and perch.

Touring options are unusually broad: bicycle, dune buggy, paddlewheeler, cruise boat, ice skates, horse and buggy, hot-air balloon (etc.). The villages' campground is especially attractive and is located directly on the water.

Special Feature

The dunes of **Saugatuck Dunes State Park**, just north of the villages, provide beauty and challenge for hikers and cross-country skiers.

> • *The old hand-cranked ferry that connected Saugatuck and Douglas before construction of the bridge is still in operation.*
> • *The Goose Festival (third weekend in October) in nearby Fennville celebrates the return of 300, 000 Canada Geese.*
> • *The townspeople are openly proud of the fact that nearly all—if not in fact all—of their businesses are locally owned.*

Where to Stay

BEECHWOOD MANOR, *736 Pleasant St. (Saugatuck), (616) 857-1587.* 1874 Victorian diplomat's home, on National Register, full breakfasts, verandah with rockers, croquet. $$$

THE BELVEDERE INN, *3656 63rd St. (Saugatuck), (616) 857-5501/ fax (616) 857-1813.* Restored 1913 mansion on 5 acres of landscaped grounds, private baths, full "gourmet" breakfasts, afternoon tea, dining room. $$$

FAIRCHILD HOUSE, *606 Butler St. (Saugatuck), (616) 857-5985.* Circa 1919 Craftsman home, sparkling crystal, antiques, European feather beds, private baths, whirlpool, champagne breakfasts, gardens. $$$

LAKE SHORE RESORT, *2885 Lake Shore Dr. (Saugatuck), (616) 857-7121.* Motel-resort with private beach, TV & phones, private baths, Cont. breakfasts, pool, wooded nature trails, overlooking Lake Michigan. $$ to $$$

THE PARK HOUSE, *888 Holland St. (Saugatuck), (800) 321-4535.* Saugatuck's oldest residence (1857), on National Register, private baths, suites, cottages, Susan B. Anthony once a resident. $$$

ROSEMONT INN, *83 Lakeshore Dr. (Douglas), (616) 857-2637.* 1886 Victorian inn across from Douglas Beach, fireplaces, TV & phones, private baths, full buffet breakfasts, whirlpool, sauna, heated pool, English garden, bicycles, highly rated. $$$

WICKWOOD INN, *510 Butler St. (Saugatuck), (616) 857-1465.* English-style inn, arts & antiques, private baths, breakfast & cocktail-hour buffets, English library-bar, garden room, gazebo. $$$

Where to Eat

CHEQUERS OF SAUGATUCK, *220 Culver St. (Saugatuck), (616) 857-1868.* English pub offering Shepherd's Pie, Toad in the Hole, Bangers & Mash, Beef Tips Sherwood, Mixed Grill, Tahini Shrimp, Chicken Stilton, sandwiches with homemade English chips; English antiques. $$

CLEARBROOK GOLF CLUB & RESTAURANT, *6494 Clearbrook Dr. (Saugatuck), (616) 857-2000.* Skewered Carolina Style Pork, Vegetarian Pasta Sauté, Fresh Canadian Walleye, Lobster Risotto "Clearbrook Style," 8 oz. Filet Mignon; also lighter fare, overlooking gardens & golf course. $$

RESTAURANT TOULOUSE, *248 Culver St. (Saugatuck), (616) 857-1561.* Country French fare, including bouillabaisse, cassoulet, & wild game. $$

Further Information

Saugatuck/Douglas Convention and Visitor's Bureau, *P.O. Box 28, Saugatuck, MI 49453 (616) 857-1701. (ZIP for Douglas is 49406.)*

Directions

From Chicago, I 94 east to I 196 (near Benton Harbor, MI), I 196 north to exit 36 (Saugatuck/Douglas exit).

Other Charming Michigan Towns

Allegan
Calumet
Gaylord
Grand Haven
Lexington
Romeo
St. Clair
South Haven

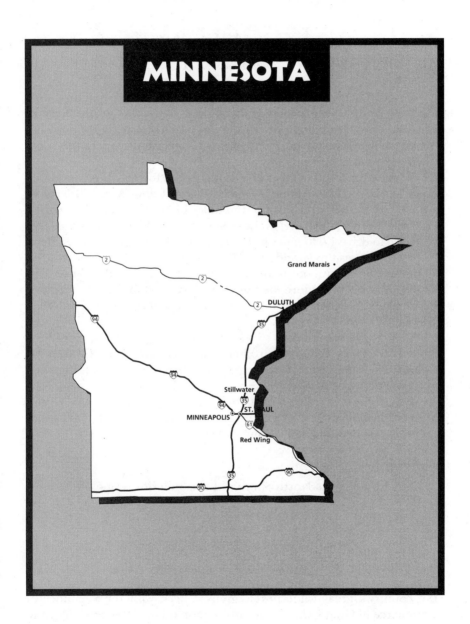

MINNESOTA

Grand Marais

Population 1, 171

Grand Marais is a picturesque little harbor town situated on one of the most beautiful shorelines in the United States, the **North Shore of Lake Superior**. Walk along Grand Marais's beach or scan the harbor from the deck of a boat offshore and you can't help but respect the sheer vastness of the northlands.

Beyond the town lie miles of mountains and forests, largely undeveloped, and beyond these is the **Boundary Waters Canoe Area Wilderness**, a natural area that stretches for 150 miles in Minnesota and along the Canadian border. Then there is **Lake Superior**, an inland sea so great that you have to drive 1,026 miles just to get around it! It is uncrowded here.

Start your visit to Grand Marais with a tour of the shops. Then stroll along the harbor and out to the lighthouse. Finally, by all means take a couple of hours to explore the tiny peninsula most aptly named **Artists' Point**. The views from here of Lake Superior and its renowned shoreline are magnificent.

If you have several days to spend in this beautiful area, consider a guided canoe trip, or maybe enrollment in a class at the **Grand Marais Art Colony**. The latter offers week-long classes in watercolor, oils and acrylics, pottery, and other media

One of the best places to turn for indoor entertainment is the **Grand Marais Playhouse**. The playhouse presents plays, concerts, and other events and shows during its summer season.

Special Features

MN 61 along the North Shore of Lake Superior is one of the most scenic routes in the country. From Duluth to the Canadian border, and beyond, rugged cliffs and thick forests vie for attention with grand expanses of blue water.

The **Gunflint Trail** connects Grand Marais with the eastern entrance to the Boundary Waters Wilderness. The black-topped highway winds for 58 miles through and around the wooded hills and glacial lakes of one of the country's great wilderness regions. Check with the Chamber of Commerce in Grand Marais for information on outfitters, lodging, and resorts.

Motor vessels make daily passenger runs between Grand Portage (farther up the coast) and **Isle Royale National Park**.

> • *Northeastern Minnesota's shape has earned it the nickname,* *"Tip of the Arrowhead."*
> • *Grand Marais is the ideal place to come for a second spring after the spring flowers of more southern climes have begun to fade.*

Where to Stay

DREAMCATCHER B&B, 2614 CR 7, (800) 682-3119. New North Woods-style home overlooking Lake Superior, art & antiques, private baths, full breakfasts, refreshments, porch, gardens. $$$

THE NANIBOUJOU LODGE, *20 Naniboujou Trail, HC I (Box 505), (218) 387-2688.* Exclusive 1920s private club converted to full-service inn, on National Register, largest native rock fireplace in state, pine-walled guest rooms, "North Woods" breakfasts, afternoon tea, restaurant, views, hiking to waterfall. $$ to $$$

PINCUSHION MOUNTAIN B&B, *220 Gunflint Trail,* (800) 542-1226. Overlooking Lake Superior 1,000 feet below, private baths, full breakfasts, Finnish sauna. $$$

THE SHORELINE, *20 S. Broadway, P.O. Box 667,* (800) 247-6020. Motel owned by same family for more than 40 years, lakeview rooms, guest library with coffee & fresh donuts from "world's best donut" bakery, sun deck & beach on Lake Superior. $ to $$

THE SUPERIOR OVERLOOK B&B, *P.O. Box 963,* (800) 858-7622. New home 200 feet from Lake Superior, Danish "aebleskivers" sometimes on breakfast menu. $$$

Where to Eat

ANGRY TROUT CAFE, *"on the harbor," Box 973,* (218) 387-1265. Grilled Lake Superior Fish of the Day, Deep-fried Alaska Cod, Maple Grilled Chicken Breast, Grilled Shiitake Mushrooms & Vegetables; seating on the water, seasonal. $$

BIRCH TERRACE, *P.O. Box 217,* (218) 387-2215. Fresh Lake Superior fish, steaks, famous ribs; in 1898 log mansion overlooking harbor. $ to $$

EAST BAY HOTEL FAMILY DINING ROOM, *P.O. Box 246,* (218) 387-2800. Fresh fish, homemade Swedish rye bread; overlooking Lake Superior. $ to $$

THE NANIBOUJOU LODGE, *(see above).* Lake Superior Trout with Fresh Lemon Sauce, Walleye Sauteed with Seasoned Almonds, Cranberry Pork Tenderloin, Apricot Roast Chicken. $$

Further Information

Grand Marais Chamber of Commerce, *P.O. Box 1048, Grand Marais, MN 55604 (888) 922-5000 / (218) 387-2524.*

Directions

From Duluth, MN 61 northeast (along Lake Superior) to Grand Marais.

Red Wing

Population 15, 134

You'd think that having an historic town tucked amongst the scenic bluffs and forests of the upper Mississippi would be enough. Not for the people of **Red Wing**. Apparently believing that everyone wins when nature and humankind work to complement each other, the people of Red Wing have added some 26 parks and hung 220 flowering baskets from the downtown lampposts. The result is a stunning union between an already handsome downtown and one of the most beautifully landscaped riverfronts in the U.S.

It doesn't hurt either that the historic preservation board has the authority to say "no" to about any downtown construction that doesn't remain true to the middle of the 19th century (1858 to be exact). The results of the board's efforts can be enjoyed either by a summer trolley ride or by one of three walking tours—brochures are obtainable at the Chamber of Commerce or front desk of the St. James Hotel (listed below). Twenty-six of the sites along the way are on the National Register of Historic Places.

One of the most visited of the sites is the restored **T. B. Sheldon Auditorium Theatre** (1904), the first municipal theater in the country. The Renaissance Revival theater presents a varied slate of attractions year round. Probably most important to the visitor is a public tour and multimedia program on Red Wing's history.

Boathouse Village is one of Red Wing's most famous attractions. Located on the Mississippi in **Bay Point Park**, the "village" consists of boat storage houses that ride up and down on poles, adjusting to the water's level. The poles are called *gin poles*, because gin bottles were tied to them and hidden in the water during Prohibition. The place is very popular with photographers and artists.

What with the stores downtown, 52 factory outlet and other shops in the **Pottery Place Outlet Center** (itself a National Historic Building), and the **St. James Hotel Shopping Court**, Red Wing offers fabulous shopping.

Red Wing has a number of scenic views of the **Mississippi**, and the visitor has an array of sightseeing options. By all means the most time-honored is the 600-foot climb to the top of dramatic **Barn Bluff**. Henry David Thoreau made this climb in 1861 and wrote glowingly of the views. Today there are marked paths and stairways to make the climb easier. Another beautiful view, this time of Red Wing as well as the river, can be reached by driving up to **Sorin's Bluff**. In addition to the views, there are hiking trails and caves to explore.

In 1890, 98 people perished on the excursion boat "Sea Wing" in a storm on Lake Pepin, downriver. The tragedy is marked by a memorial in Levee Park.

Where to Stay

THE CANDLE LIGHT INN, *818 W. Third St., (612) 388-8034*. 1877 home, private baths, full breakfasts, library with fireplace, inviting front porch. $$ to $$$

GOLDEN LANTERN INN, *721 East Ave., (612) 388-3315*. Tudor Revival home of three presidents of Red Wing Shoe Company, private baths, whirlpools, full breakfasts, afternoon snacks. $$ to $$$

HEARTHWOOD B&B, *17650-200th St. E. (Hastings 55033), (612) 437-1133*. Cape Cod log home on 10-acre rural estate, suites, full breakfasts, massive stone fireplace. $$ to $$$

HUNGRY POINT INN, *One Olde Deerfield Rd. (Welch 55089), (612) 437-3660*. New England-style home, 200-year-old antiques, fireplaces, whirlpools, full candlelight breakfasts. $$ to $$$

PRATT TABER INN, *706 W. Fourth St., (612) 388-5945*. 1876 Italianate mansion, original furniture, some private baths, "gourmet" breakfasts, porches, bikes. $$ to $$$

ST. JAMES HOTEL, *406 Main St., (800) 252-1875*. Restored 1875 hotel on National Register, full-service, antiques, champagne, two restaurants, shopping court. $$$

Where to Eat

BRASCHLER'S BAKERY & COFFEE SHOP, *410 W. Third St., (612) 388-1589*. Unique bakery coffee shop serving breakfasts & lunches. $

LIBERTY'S RESTAURANT & LOUNGE, *Third & Plum sts., (612) 388-8877*. American, Italian, & Mexican foods; Red Wing memorabilia, courtesy car from marinas. $

PORT OF RED WING, *(see St. James Hotel above).* Lemon-Pepper Shrimp, Breast of Chicken Rosemary, Filet Mignon, Vegetable Strudel; authentic period restaurant. $$ to $$$

Further Information
Red Wing Area Chamber of Commerce, *420 Levee St., Red Wing, MN 55066 (612) 388-4719.*

Directions
From St. Paul, US 61 south to Red Wing.

Stillwater
Population 15, 350

Stillwater is the kind of town you feel you've seen before. The feeling is a warm one, a very positive case of *deja vu.* It's probably because the town is an amalgam of charming old towns everywhere, towns that many of us visited or passed through as children. There's a beautiful river, and up the hill from the river a turn-of-the-century main street. Yet farther up steeple spires and hints of old houses rise above the trees. Sets of steps link the steeples and the houses with the downtown below.

A first glance suggests that most of the older buildings are turn-of-the-century. Many of them are, but some, especially those on the National Register of Historic Places, go back much further, to the 1840s-1870s. Among the structures of special interest are the predominantly Italianate **Washington County Historic Courthouse** (1867-70), the oldest standing courthouse in the state, and the early Federal-style **Warden's House** (1853), the residence of 11 wardens for the adjacent **Territorial/State Prison** (1851; only remnants remain).

The new (1993) **Stillwater Depot, Logging and Railway Museum** recalls the lumber and rail history of the town. The museum is the home of the 1940s dinner train, the *Minnesota Zephyr,* which offers a three-hour excursion along the bluff-rimmed **St. Croix**. The stern-wheeler, *The Andiamo,* offers river excursions, and the *Stillwater Trolley* offers historical tours. Check with the Chamber of Commerce for narrated walking tours and a self-guided walking/driving tour.

Special Feature
The **St. Croix River**, a National Wild and Scenic River, is designed for boating. Canoeing and kayaking are popular north of town. To the south

sailboats, speedboats, houseboats, and yachts navigate the river to its junction with the Mississippi. Tour boats are available in Stillwater, as are cafes, bars, and shops that cater to boaters. And, of course, fishing is great in this part of the world.

> • *In the mid 19th century, all transportation, mail, and shipping to and from Stillwater depended on the steamboat.*
> • *Believing that a state prison would offer more employment than a state capitol, many Stillwater people back in 1851 sought the prison. And they got it.*
> • *The Stillwater-Houlton (WI) Lift Bridge (1931) is one of two remaining vertical-lift bridges in Minnesota.*

Where to Stay

AFTON HOUSE INN, *P.O. Box 326 (Afton 55001), (612) 436-8883.* Restored 1867 inn on National Register, antiques, TV, private baths, charter boats. $$ to $$$

THE ELEPHANT WALK, *801 W. Pine St., (612) 430-0359.* 1883 Stick-style home with antiquities from around world, private baths, 4-course breakfasts, champagne/wine, porch swing & peacock chairs. $$$

JAMES A. MULVEY RESIDENCE INN, *622 W. Churchill St., (612) 430-8008.* 1860s Italianate home with black walnut trees, English faux marble fireplaces, private baths, clawfoot & whirlpool tubs, 4-course breakfasts, porch & gardens, bikes. $$$

THE LAUREL STREET INN, *210 E. Laurel St., (612) 351-0031.* 1859 Greek Revival/Italianate home, fireplaces, private baths with whirlpools, full breakfasts, 1 1/2 acres of lawn & gardens overlooking St. Croix River, bicycles. $$$

LOWELL INN, *102 N. Second St., (612) 439-1100.* Full-service inn nicknamed "The Mount Vernon of the West," one of best in Midwest. $$$ (American & European plans)

OUTING LODGE AT PINE POINT, *11661 Myeron Rd. N., (612) 439-9747.* 1858 "poor farm" renovated as inn on 350-acre wooded park, Louis XV reproduction furniture, private baths, whirlpools, wine, culinary outings. $$$

THE RIVERTOWN INN, *306 W. Olive St., (800) 562-3632.* 1882 lumberman's mansion, fireplaces, private baths, whirlpools, full breakfasts, panoramic views. $$ to $$$

WILLIAM SAUNTRY MANSION, *626 N. Fourth St., (612) 430-2653.* Circa 1890 lumber baron's home, on National Register, original chandeliers, fireplaces, private baths, full "gourmet" breakfasts. $$$

Where to Eat

FREIGHT HOUSE RESTAURANT, *305 Water St., (612) 439-5718.* Seafood, chicken, beef, pork, salads, specialty sandwiches; in 1883 building with deck overlooking river. $$

GASTHAUS BAVARIAN HUNTER, *8390 Lofton Ave., (612) 439-7128.* Old World restaurant in pines serving large variety of Bavarian specialties. $$

THE HARVEST RESTAURANT & INN, *114 Chestnut St., (612) 430-8111.* "Contemporary Cuisine in an Authentic Victorian Atmosphere," acclaimed. $

LOWELL INN, *(see above).* Canadian Walleye Pike, Country Fried Chicken, Brook Trout, Roast Rib Eye au jus, Broiled Breast of Duck, Filet Mignon; Fondue Bourguigonne Dinner with 4-course wine service in Matterhorn Room, award-winning. $$$ (1st & 2nd courses included in table d'hôte pricing)

VITTORIO'S, *402 S. Main St., (612) 439-3588.* Homemade pasta specialties, pizza, good children's menu; guided brewery cave tours, museum. $

Further Information

Stillwater Area Chamber of Commerce, *423 S. Main St., Stillwater, MN 55082 (612) 439-7700.*

Directions

From St. Paul, I 94 east to MN 95, MN 95 north (along river) to Stillwater; also, I 35E north to MN 36, MN 36 east to Stillwater (20 to 30 mins); from Minneapolis, I 35W north to MN 36, MN 36 east to Stillwater.

Other Charming Minnesota Towns

Afton
Grand Rapids
Lanesboro
Mantorville
New Prague
Northfield

MISSISSIPPI

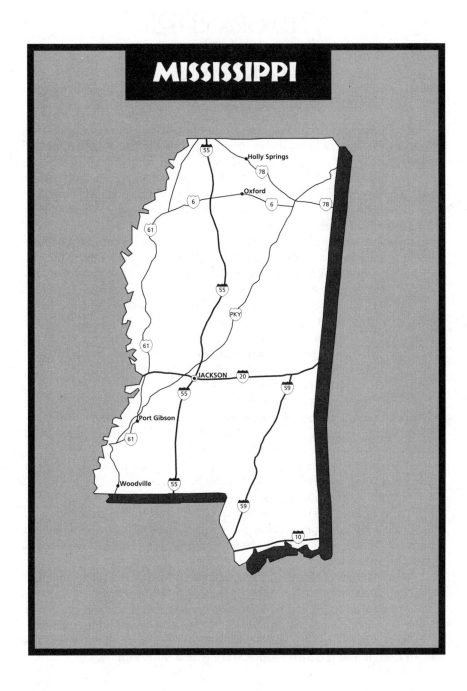

MISSISSIPPI

Holly Springs
Population 7, 261

Holly Springs has an antique square of colorfully painted storefronts and, on the streets just off the square, one of the finest collections of antebellum houses in the South. On seeing the houses, the visitor is going to have three questions, at least. First, where did all the wealth come from? Second, how did so many antebellum mansions get through the Civil War unscathed (especially because Union forces were thick in these parts)? And third, who lives in them?

In answer to the first, much of the wealth arose from land transactions made during the cotton real-estate boom of antebellum days. Many of those who prospered were (surprisingly) lawyers. Also, the town was settled by a number of well-to-do families from Virginia and the Carolinas.

Second, General Ulysses S. Grant was headquartered here for a period during the Civil War. The story goes that when Confederate General Van Dorn occupied the city, Mrs. Grant pleaded with Van Dorn to respect the privacy of her bedroom—and, incidentally, her husband's private papers. The general obliged and, later returning the favor, General Grant ordered that the town not be torched.

Third, the houses are in demand because many people, often young couples, wish the experience of restoring them. It doesn't hurt either that Holly Springs, just 34 miles from Memphis, attracts families who would rather live away from the big city.

The sheer number and variety of 19th-century mansions make Holly Springs a living museum (although most houses are closed to the public, see below). A brief but representative sampling of the homes includes:

Dunvegan (1845), a one-story Greek Revival home furnished with Empire and Regency antiques and decorated in many rooms with painted murals. Dunvegan's style of architecture is sometimes described as "English basement."

Grey Gables (1839-1849), an Italianate house noted for its magnificent spiral stairway and hand-cut Bohemian glass windows.

Montrose (1858), a Greek Revival mansion with a graceful circular stairway, parquetry floors, and beautiful cornices (open by appointment). The arboretum on the grounds, with 50 specimens of native trees, has been designated the **Mississippi Statewide Arboretum.**

Walter Place (1859), a magnificent mansion combining Greek Revival and Gothic Revival elements. It was here that General and Mrs. Grant lived during their stay in Holly Springs.

One of the best ways to take in the houses and their grounds is to get a brochure from the Chamber of Commerce and follow green lines painted on the streets. The *Green Line Tour* may be taken by foot or car. Special group tours of homes, churches, and other buildings may also be arranged through the CoC. Many of the homes are open to visitors during the Annual Pilgrimage, the third weekend in April.

The **Kate Freeman Clark Art Gallery** houses over 1,200 still lifes, portraits, and landscapes by the gifted Holly Springs student of William Merritt Chase. Refusing to sell even one painting, Clark willed all of her work to Holly Springs. Only a few of her paintings are on display at any time (open by appointment).

On display at the imposing **Marshall County Historical Museum** are such diverse items as Chickasaw Indian artifacts, relics from the Civil War and War of 1812, vintage costumes, and antique toys.

Special Feature

An hour or so in the 1837 **Hillcrest Cemetery** can be both an informative and moving experience. Here Victorian cast- and wrought-iron fences enclose old burial plots, and marble and granite obelisks commemorate not only Confederate generals but victims, young and old, of the 1878 yellow-fever epidemic.

> • *Federal troops used the basement of the First Presbyterian Church as a stable for their horses.*
>
> • *Rust College was established in 1866 to educate newly freed slaves. The college's library is named after the Mississippi-born singer Leontyne Price.*

Where to Stay

FORT-DANIEL HALL B&B, *184 S. Memphis St., (601) 252-6807.* Classic 1850 Greek Revival home, antiques, TV, some private baths, full breakfasts, beverages, dinner by arrangement, tour of house. $$

SOMERSET COTTAGES B&B, *135 W. Gholson, (601) 252-4513.* Quaint very private cottages in garden setting adjacent to antebellum home, TV, hot tub, pets. $$

Where to Eat

CROSSROADS FISH SHACK, *Red Banks & Old Hernando rds. (off US 78 about 5 mi west of town), (601) 252-7506*. "All You Can Eat Catfish," fried oysters, slaw, hushpuppies. $

THE GRILLE, KIRKWOOD NATIONAL GOLF CLUB, *785 Hwy. 4 W, (601) 252-4888*. Sandwiches, salads, & buffet served links-side. $

Further Information

Holly Springs Chamber of Commerce, *154 S. Memphis St., Holly Springs, MS 38635 (601) 252-2943.*

Directions

From Memphis (TN), US 78 southeast to Holly Springs.

Oxford

Population 10, 026

Oxford is home to several nationally renowned authors. Endowed by the literary heritage of William Faulkner, served by a major state university, and given character by one of the most colorful (and beautiful) squares in small-town America, Oxford seems designed for the writer.

The courthouse and much of the surrounding square were looted and burned by Federal troops in 1864. Some buildings survived in whole or in part, however, and others were rebuilt. Today the magnificently restored and maintained square is home to the "new" **courthouse** (rebuilt 1873), the **Oxford City Hall** (1885), the oldest continuing department store in the South (1897), and a nationally renowned bookstore, housed in one of the first buildings built after the Civil War. And a host of interesting shops and restaurants.

The walking-tour brochure distributed by the tourism council lists four tours, one focusing on the square area and three on Oxford's other historic areas. One of the latter, the area north of the square, embraces a number of structures dating back to the 1830s. One of the oldest and best known is **Isom Place** (1838-1843), a large planter-style house built of native timber and handcrafted by Indians and slaves (open by appointment).

The area south of the square contains homes from the mid and late 19th century. By all means the most famous is **Rowan Oak** (1848), the home bought and renovated by William Faulkner. Set in a grove of oak and cedar trees, the house was Faulkner's office, home, and quiet refuge from 1930 until his death in 1962. The house, preserved as it was when the Nobel Prize winner died, is open to the public.

The buildings along or near **University Avenue** make up Oxford's fourth historic area. Here are the **University Museums**, a complex of museums boasting excellent collections of 18th- and 19th-century scientific instruments, Southern folk art, Greek and Roman antiquities, and paintings by Oxford folk artist Theora Hamblett. Of special interest on the nearby **University of Mississippi** campus is the restored Classical Revival **Barnard Observatory building** (1848), which houses the **Center for the Study of Southern Culture** (exhibits).

A guide to Oxford's some 15 antique shops is available at the visitor's center.

> • *The building at 520 N. Lamar, built in 1875, was designed by James and Alexander Stewart, designers of three state capitols and the Savoy Hotel in London.*
> • *Don't expect to find lodgings in or near Oxford when Ole Miss has a home football game.*

Where to Stay

BARKSDALE-ISOM B&B, *1003 Jefferson Ave., (601) 236-5600/(800) 236-5696.* Circa 1835 home with Civil War & Faulkner associations, antiques & chandeliers, private baths, "traditional Southern" breakfasts, afternoon wine, library, verandah. $$$

THE OLIVER-BRITT HOUSE INN, *512 Van Buren Ave., (601) 234-8043.* Restored manor house with "charm of Old South," antiques & reproductions, private baths, TV, "Southern" breakfasts weekends. $ to $$

PUDDIN' PLACE, *1008 University Ave., (601) 234-1250.* 1892 "cottage" with screened back porch, antiques; suites with sitting rooms, fireplaces, & private baths; full breakfasts. $$$

Where to Eat

BOTTLETREE BAKERY, *923 Van Buren Ave., (601) 236-5000.* Sandwiches with names like "Van Buren Best Seller," "The Delta," and "The Hummdinger"; baked goods, coffees. $

CITY GROCERY, *152 Courthouse Sq., (601) 232-8080.* Pan-roasted Black Grouper, Grilled Worcestershire-marinated Chicken, Grilled Apple-stuffed Pork Chop; solid lunch menu, good selection of beers. $$

DOWNTOWN GRILL, *110 Courthouse Sq., (601) 234-2659*. Shrimp & Lump Crabmeat Fettuccine, Chicken Sicilian, Filet Paulette, "famous" desserts; in 1888 bldg. on National Register, wrap-around upstairs balcony, piano bar, historic photographs & memorabilia. $$

SMITTY'S RESTAURANT, *208 S. Lamar Blvd., (601) 234-9111*. Catfish Supper, Country Ham Steak Supper, Barbecue Plate Supper (with hot cornbread & "taters"); friendly. $

YOCONA RIVER INN, *MS 334, (601) 234-2464*. "Exquisite" cuisine served in converted country store & house, brown bag. $

Further Information

Oxford Tourism Council, *111 Courthouse Sq., Oxford, MS 38655 (601) 234-4680/(800) 758-9177*.

Directions

From Memphis (TN), I 55 south to exit 243, MS 6 east to Oxford.

Port Gibson

Population 1, 810

According to legend, General Grant proclaimed **Port Gibson** "too beautiful to burn." Whether because of Grant's proclamation or some other reason, the town on **Little Bayou Pierre** was spared. More than a century later it became the first town in Mississippi to be designated a National Historic District. It is one of the South's most beautiful and historic little towns.

Settled around 1788, Port Gibson was chartered as a county seat in 1803. The place was a wide-open frontier town for a spell, but rather quickly succumbed to the advances of civilization. It acquired, for example, the state's first library (1818), second newspaper, and third Masonic Lodge.

Union soldiers crossed the Mississippi River near here in 1863 in what was the largest amphibious landing of troops prior to World War II. The Union victory at the ensuing Battle of Port Gibson, fought a few miles west of town, helped pave the way for the Confederate loss of Vicksburg.

Both within the city and out in the country are a number of lovely historic homes. Several of the most splendid are open for tours, some daily and others seasonally — because these are also open year-round for bed-and-breakfast accommodations, they are described below. Several others open their doors during the annual spring pilgrimage. One of these, the 1817 Federal-style cottage named **Englesing**, boasts the state's oldest formal garden. Another, **Gage House** (1830-1850), has a two-story brick dependency that once contained slave quarters and the house's kitchen.

Also known as the *City of Churches*, Port Gibson's **Church Street** is graced by no fewer than eight churches. The **First Presbyterian Church** (1859) is known for the gilded hand that tops its steeple, and also for its chandeliers, originally on the famous Mississippi River steamboat, the *Robert E. Lee.* **Temple Gemiluth Chessed** (1891) is the state's oldest synagogue, and the only one of its architectural style in Mississippi.

Mississippi Cultural Crossroads operates a (mostly) African-American quilting workshop and the children's **Peanut Butter and Jelly Theater**. Quilts, and art work by both children and adults, are on display and for sale.

Special Features

South of Port Gibson is the **Old Country Store**, an 1875 plantation store that is now home to a mall featuring Mississippi handicrafts.

Southwest of town are the haunting ruins of **Windsor**, the largest antebellum house ever built in Mississippi (1859-1861). Spared by the Yankees, the mansion was destroyed by fire from a cigarette in 1890. Only the 23 columns remain.

Grand Gulf State Park, northwest of town, comprises Confederate forts **Coburn** and **Wade**, several restored buildings, and a museum containing Civil War memorabilia and a collection of horse-drawn vehicles.

Southwest of town near the Mississippi River is the ghost town of **Rodney**. Once a busy river town, Rodney was vacated following a shift in the course of the river. The town's **Presbyterian Church** was built in 1829. Do not attempt a visit before checking locally for instructions.

Where to Stay

CANEMOUNT PLANTATION, *Rt. 2 (Box 45, Lorman 39096), (800) 423-0684.* Individual antebellum cottages adjacent to restored 1855 Italianate home, pool. $$$ (full breakfasts & dinners included in price)

CHINA GROVE PLANTATION, *P.O. Box 426 (Lorman 39096), (601) 437-5189.* Circa 1800 dog trot Greek Revival planters home, "plantation" breakfasts, screened gallery. $$ to $$$

GIBSON'S LANDING, *P.O. Box 195, (601) 437-3432.* Early 1830s home, unusual spiral staircase, faux marble fireplace mantel, private baths, full breakfasts. $$ to $$$

OAK SQUARE PLANTATION, *1207 Church St., (601) 437-4350.*
Circa 1850 Greek Revival home with 30 rooms, on National Register,
private baths, full breakfasts, massive oak trees. $$ to $$$
ROSSWOOD PLANTATION, *(Lorman 39096), (601) 437-4215.* 1857
Greek Revival home on 100-acre estate, on National Register, private
baths, full breakfasts, pool. $$$

Where to Eat
THE OLD DEPOT RESTAURANT & LOUNGE, *S. Market St., (601)*
437-4711. Southern specialties, seafood, catfish, steaks, red beans & rice,
po-boys. $

Further Information
Port Gibson-Claiborne County Chamber of Commerce, *P.O. Box
491, Port Gibson, MS 39150 (601) 437-4351.*

Directions
From Vicksburg, US 61 south to Port Gibson.

Woodville
Population 1, 393

Woodville hasn't changed in 100 years. Not much is happening here
today, and people say that not much will be happening tomorrow, either.
Many like it that way, and that includes the traveler in search of old out-
of-the-way Southern towns that aren't going anywhere.

Woodville is the classic antebellum Southern town. Like most other
small Southern towns, but contrary to common knowledge, the homes of
the black people, who make up well over half the population, share the
streets more or less equitably with the homes of the whites. The old oak
and magnolia trees shade a number of beautiful houses and churches
built during the first decades of the 19th century. The churches are among
the oldest in Mississippi. Several of the antebellum homes bear the
columns of classic Greek Revival.

The homes and churches are best toured with the aid of a brochure
obtainable at the **Wilkinson County Museum**. The **Woodville Baptist
Church** dates from 1809, and the **Woodville Methodist Church** and **St.
Paul's Episcopal Church** go back to the 1820s. (St. Paul's was the church
attended by the family of Jefferson Davis, President of the Confederacy.)
Many of the historic homes are located on **Church Street**. The Wilkinson

County Museum offers small and large group tours of historic sites and/ or nature areas that are not normally open or accessible to the public. The tours include a picnic or lunch/dinner in a home *(for more information, write to the address below or call the museum director at 601-888-3177)*.

Just one mile east of town (on MS 24) is a house that may be visited without joining a tour – **Rosemont Plantation House**, the family home of President Jefferson Davis. Built about 1810 by Davis's parents, this lovely house is centered about a large hall that opens onto front and back galleries. The house was home to five generations of the Davis family and has many of the family's furnishings.

Special Features

About 14 miles west of town on the **Pinckneyville Road** is an old-fashioned general store, called **Pond Store** (1881), that is straight out of the old rural South. The adjacent pond, which gave the store its name, was dug generations ago as a watering hole for animals hauling cotton and other produce to steamboats waiting at **Fort Adams**, just to the west. Tours of the store are available by appointment.

Next to Pond Store is the **Clark Creek Nature Area**, with over 1,200 acres of steep bluff woodlands and winding trails. The state natural area has seven waterfalls, one of them 50 feet high, and is popular with hikers. A park ranger is on duty.

> • *Ft. Adams, an old port city, was a Mississippi River entry point into the United States prior to the Louisiana Purchase (1803).*
> • *Military personnel attached to Ft. Adams built homes in the area of Pond Store following the Revolutionary War. Several of these homes, now over 200 years old, still stand.*
> • *"The Woodville Republican" is Mississippi's oldest newspaper (est. 1824).*

Where to Stay

DESERT PLANTATION, *411 Desert Lane (18 miles from Woodville), (601) 888-6188.* National Register antebellum home on 1,000-acre plantation, period furnishings, private baths, full "country" breakfasts, refreshments on verandah, dinners by appt., pool. $$ to $$$

NEAL'S MAGNOLIA INN, *US 61 S, (601) 888-4826.* Locally owned motel, new. $ to $$

ROSEMONT PLANTATION, *MS 24 E, P.O. Box 814, (601) 888-6809.* Cottage on plantation of President Jefferson Davis's family, full breakfasts, evening cocktails, tour of historic home. $$$

Where to Eat

CORNER GRILL, *corner US 61 & MS 24, (601) 888-4391.* Home cooking, plate lunches, barbecue, sandwiches; lots of local flavor. $

NEAL'S RESTAURANT & LOUNGE, *US 61 S, (601) 888-6180.* Cajun cooking, Mississippi Catfish, Mesquite Prime Rib. $ to $$

SOUTH OF THE BORDER, *US 61 S between Woodville & St. Francisville (LA), (504) 635-3071.* Seafood, steaks, pasta, sandwiches, salads; established 1947, locally popular. $ to $$

Further Information

Wilkinson County Museum, *P. O. Box 1055, Woodville, MS 39669 (601) 888-3998.*

Directions

From Jackson, I 20 west to exit 1b (Vicksburg), US 61 south (via Natchez) to Woodville.

Other Charming Mississippi Towns

Carrollton
Corinth
French Camp
Kosciusko

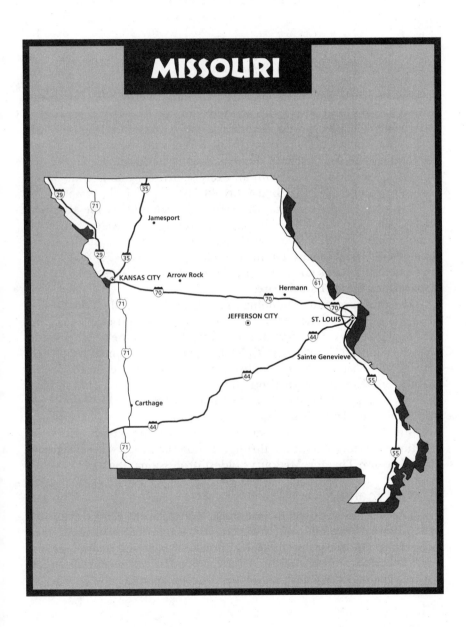

MISSOURI

Arrow Rock
Population 70

Arrow Rock and "weekend" are becoming synonymous for many Kansas Cityans (and others). It's all there, enough for two full but restful days: a quiet and picturesque historic site that can be leisurely toured with or without a guide; a 19th-century Main Street with interesting antique, gift, and specialty shops; craft demonstrations; a top summer repertory theater; good food; a park with an exercise-inviting hiking trail; and a choice of several delightful bed & breakfasts.

It was at Arrow Rock that the **Santa Fe Trail** crossed the **Missouri River**. As such, the village has been catering to travelers since its establishment in 1829. There are a few Victorian houses, but the early date of settlement means that many buildings are of the Federal style, a style uncommon this far west. Many of the older buildings make up the **Arrow Rock State Historic Site**.

The most prominent building in the historic site is the **Old Tavern** (1834), a two-story Federal-style brick building that houses a restaurant (see listing below). The most historic of the houses is the small Federal-style dwelling (1837) of **George Caleb Bingham**, the nationally renowned artist. The house is a National Historic Landmark. Other historic sites include an 1844 **gunsmith shop** and a **newspaper office** with antique presses. Displays at the **state historic interpretive center** highlight these and other town landmarks (open year round).

Musicals, comedies, and a sprinkling of classic dramas are offered in rotating repertory from June through Labor Day at the 420-seat **Arrow Rock Lyceum Theater**, Missouri's oldest professional theater.

Special Feature

The recently restored **Prairie Park**, a 1844 Greek Revival mansion (1845-1849) several miles out in the country, is one of Missouri's premier properties. The house, listed in the National Register, was built by the son of Dr. John Sappington, the physician who popularized the use of quinine for treating malaria. Check locally for tour information.

Where to Stay

BORGMAN'S B&B, *P. O. Box 124, Van Buren St., (660) 837-3350.* 1860s home on National Register, antiques, family-style breakfasts with home baking, porch with swings. $$

DOWNOVER B&B INN & THE OLD LIBRARY BOOK SHOP, *602 Main St., (660) 837-3268.* Rooms with private baths, guest cottage with own kitchen/bath, bicycles, book shop. $$

LA CASITA, *General Delivery, (660) 837-3320.* Small Federal home rented as unit, fireplace, antiques, TV, bath, screened porch, walled patio. $$$

MISS NELLE'S B&B, *606 Main St., (800) 795-2797.* Circa 1853 home, antiques, fireplace, porch swings, close to sights. $$

WESTWARD TRAILS INN B&B, *704 Van Buren, (660) 837-3335.* Suite-size room sleeping five, Ben Franklin stove/fireplace, private bath & entrance, full "country" breakfasts. $

Where to Eat

ARROW ROCK ICE CREAM EMPORIUM, *Main St., (660) 837-3337.* Ice cream parlor, brown-bottled sarsaparilla, sandwiches, soups. $

EVERGREEN RESTAURANT, *MO 41 one block north of Main St., (660) 837-3251.* Continental cuisine served in restored 1840s home, homemade breads, fine wine selection. $$

GRANDMA D'S CAFE, *one block south of Main St., (660) 837-3335.* Homemade soups, breads, & pies; evening entree. $

THE OLD TAVERN, *Main St., (660) 837-3200.* 1834 brick tavern serving catfish, fried chicken, steak, & country ham; spirits, reservations requested. $

SCHOOLHOUSE CAFE, *W. Main St., (660) 837-3331.* Sandwiches & daily specials in homelike setting. $

Further Information

Arrow Rock Area Merchants Association, *P.O. Box 147, Arrow Rock, MO 65320 (660) 837-3305.*

Directions

From Kansas City, I 70 east to exit 89, K Hwy. north to MO 41, MO 41 north to Arrow Rock; from St. Louis, I 70 west to exit 98, MO 41 north to Arrow Rock.

Carthage
Population 10, 747

Enriched by lead and zinc mines, marble quarries, and flour mills, **Carthage** had by the end of the 19th century more millionaires per capita than any other city in the country. Much of the wealth remains, as a drive by the beautifully preserved Victorian homes on **Grand Avenue** and **S. Main Street** will make clear. The town's maple-lined streets are especially lovely in the fall. They're not bad in the spring, either, when the dogwoods are in bloom.

A tour brochure distributed by the Chamber of Commerce provides full architectural histories and color photos for a sample of 20 of the Victorian homes. Dating from the last three decades of the 19th century, the houses represent all major Midwestern Victorian styles. Good examples are the 1870 Italianate **Spencer House**, the magnificent Chateauesque 1887 **Hill House**, and the 1873 **Italian Villa**, known as "Wetzel's Folly."

Two homes, **Kendrick Place** and the **Phelps House**, offer tours. One of the oldest buildings in the Carthage area, Kendrick Place (1849) has been restored to its pre-Civil War appearance. The 1890s Classical Revival Phelps House has 10 fireplaces and a hand-operated elevator that serves all floors between the basement and the third-floor ballroom.

On the square downtown is the magnificent Romanesque Revival **Jasper County Courthouse** (1894/95). Listed on the National Register, the courthouse has several first-floor exhibits of Indian artifacts and mineral specimens from the region's mining days. The building also contains a 1976 mural, *Forged in Fire*, that depicts Carthage's history.

The **Powers Museum** provides a glimpse at local history and the arts; a variety of changing exhibits are featured. As its name indicates, the **Carthage Civil War Museum** tells the story of the role played by Carthage in the Civil War. Included among the exhibits are a diorama and a large mural, both of the Battle of Carthage.

The **Precious Moments Chapel**, southwest of town, was created by artist Samuel J. Butcher. The nondenominational chapel is noted for its murals, carvings, and 15 stained-glass windows, all of the Precious Moments motif. Sharing the beautifully landscaped grounds with the chapel are a gallery, restaurant, gift shop, flower gardens, fountains, and scenic overlooks.

Just outside of town is Lowell Davis's **Red Oak II**, a reconstructed 1930s farming community. Among the restored buildings are a gas station, general store, country school, church, parsonage, art gallery, feed and seed store, cafe, and childhood home of Belle Starr. The village is also home to several "bed and baskets" (breakfast comes in a basket; see below).

Special Feature

About 10 miles south of Carthage is the **Carver National Monument**, the birthplace and childhood home of agronomist George Washington Carver.

> • *The first major land battle of the Civil War occurred in Carthage on July 5, 1861.*
> • *A statue of Carthage's Marlin Perkins, host of TV's "Wild Kingdom" series, is located in Central Park.*

Where to Stay

BREWER'S MAPLE LANE FARM B&B, *Rt. 1 (417) 358-6312*. 20-room home on National Register, original brass light fixtures, Cont. "plus" breakfasts, barnyard of animals, tours. $$

GRAND AVENUE INN B&B, *1615 Grand Ave., (417) 358-7265*. Circa 1890 Queen Anne home with stained-glass windows, antiques, private baths, full breakfasts, wrap-around porch, pool. $$ to $$$

THE LEGGETT HOUSE B&B, *1106 Grand Ave., (417) 358-0683*. 1901 Classical Revival home, lace-curtained guest rooms, some private baths, full breakfasts, mosaic-tiled solarium. $$

RED OAK II BED & BASKETS, *Rt. 1 (NE of city), (417) 358-9018*. Quaint getaways in 1930s village setting, antiques, from rustic decor to "rural Victorian splendor." $$

Where to Eat

CARTHAGE DELI & ICE CREAM, *301 S. Main St., (417) 358-8820*. Homemade soups & thick sandwiches served with 1950s music & decor. $

THE FLOWER BASKET & EATERY, *321 S. Main, (417) 358-0900*. A favorite for lunch; on the square. $

OLD MINERS INN, *208 Main St. (Alba), (417) 525-4332*. Entrecote au Poivre, Poulet Provencale, Filet de Thon Provencale, Chateaubriand (for two), Poitrine de Canard. $$$

TEA & TRUFFLE, *133 E. Third St., (417) 358-9300*. Light lunches served in Victorian atmosphere. $

Further Information

Carthage Chamber of Commerce, *107 E. Third St., Carthage, MO 64836 (417) 358-2373/fax (417) 358-7479.*

Directions

From Springfield, I 44 west to exit 18, US 71 north to Carthage.

Hermann

Population 2, 754

Hermann was founded by the German Settlement Society of Philadelphia in 1836 (settled 1837). It's believed that the founders selected this lovely spot on the **Missouri River** because it reminded them of their native Rhine. The original plans called for a large city that would preserve German culture. The city obviously never materialized, but the townspeople's commitment to preserve their German traditions survived. Picturesque little Hermann remains German, consciously so.

Vineyards, part of Hermann's Rhineland heritage, were planted during the town's earliest years, and grape growing eventually became an important part of the area's economy. Today there are four wineries, each offering daily tours. The oldest, **Stone Hill Winery** (1847), has been declared a National Historic District. At the turn of the century, Stone Hill was the third largest winery in the world. Forced by Prohibition to grow mushrooms (in its vast cellars) rather than grapes, the winery was reopened in 1969; in 1989 it became the first Missouri winery since Prohibition to be awarded an international gold medal. The winery has the largest underground arched cellars in the United States.

Another historic winery, the **Hermannhof Winery** (1852), has a magnificent festhalle. The winery's stone wine cellars and winery building are on the National Register of Historic Places.

The streets of the **Hermann Historic District** (the town has two historic districts) are lined with tidy German-American homes and gardens. Two of the houses are preserved as the **Deutscheim State Historic Site**: the German Neoclassical **Pommer-Gentner House** (1842), with furnishings from the 1840s, and the **Strehly House and Winery** (1844), a German Vernacular house furnished in the 1860s-1880s style.

The **German School Building** (1871) **Museums** provide a comprehensive and fascinating look at Hermann's history. Among the museums' exhibits are a handmade wooden wine press, circa 1835 wood cloth-printing blocks, and boat models and other items depicting the town's river history. One of the museums features dolls and toys from the late 1890s, another displays a hand-made Rococo Revival bedroom set of solid walnut.

The **White House Hotel** (1868) is a three-story brick building, with two-story wing, featuring 15-foot ceilings, arched hallways, and an iron-railed widow's walk. The hotel contains 36 rooms with furnishings and decorations from the late 19th century. The kitchen still has its original cook stove (guided tours).

Hermann abounds with art galleries, antique shops, and quaint craft and gift shops. Crafts include quilts, afghans, handwoven baskets, and handcrafted wood items. Black-powder guns, vintage lighting, and European giftware are among other items displayed in the shops.

Special Feature

The rolling **Missouri River Valley** and the foothills of the **Ozarks** to the south combine to make **MO 19**, which passes through Hermann, an especially scenic highway.

> • *The Gasconade County Courthouse (1896-1898) was the gift of a local merchant.*
> • *Octoberfest, held the first four weekends in October, features a Showboat Theatre, craft demonstrations, German bands and folk dancing, and lots of food, beer, and wine.*

Where to Stay

THE CAPTAIN WOHLT INN, *123 E. Third St., (573) 486-3357.* 1886 home of riverboat captain, antiques & reproductions, private baths, breakfast "an event," suites with private entrances. $$

DREI MADEL HAUS, *108 Schiller St., (573) 486-3552/3558.* Circa 1840 cottage, private baths, German owner's pottery shop on premises. $$

HERMANN HILL VINEYARD & INN, *711 Wein St., P.O. Box 555, (573) 486-4455/fax (573) 486-5373.* Inn on bluff overlooking town, antiques, fireplaces, TV & phones, private baths with whirlpools, private balconies, full or Cont. breakfasts, refreshments, elevator, exercise room. $$$

MARKET STREET B&B, *210 Market St., (573) 486-5597.* Turn-of-century home, antiques, private baths, full breakfasts. $$

MUMBRAUER GASTHAUS, *223 E. Second St., (573) 486-5246.* Circa 1886 home, TV, private baths, full breakfasts, courtesy pickup from Amtrak. $$

Where to Eat

BUCKLER'S DELI & PIZZA, *100 Schiller St., (573) 486-3514.* Unique deli with large menu, homemade soups & desserts; in restored bank building. $

THE LANDING RESTAURANT, *4 Schiller St., (573) 486-2030.* German & American specialties; local antiques, in original high school bldg. $ to $$

VINTAGE 1847 RESTAURANT, *Stone Hill Winery, (573) 486-3479.* German & American specialties, in original winery stable & carriage house, award-winning chef. $ to $$

Further Information

Visitor Information Center, *306 Market St., P.O. Box 104, Hermann, MO 65041 (573) 486-2744/(800) 932-8687.*

Directions

From St. Louis, I 70 west to exit 175, MO 19 south to Hermann.

Jamesport
Population 570

Jamesport is set in the picturesque rolling countryside of northwestern Missouri. The village is surrounded by beautiful old farms, mature woods, and winding rivers. Horses and buggies are common to the roads.

There are really two Jamesports, one complementing the other. The first is the village, a few streets of antique shops and old homes where everyone knows everyone else and no one bothers with street addresses or last names. The second is the surrounding countryside, dotted with Amish farms and country stores.

The village, tiny though it may be, has 16 antique shops and 26 craft and specialty shops. There's an old-fashioned soda fountain, of course. And there are places to sit and relax, quiet places where in the evening only fireflies and whippoorwills disturb.

Although not settling in Jamesport until the early 1950s, the Amish now farm much of the rich land around the village. Amish families also operate several country stores and greenhouses along the highways. The stores sell everything from fabrics and handmade quilts to homemade noodles, jellies, and jams (closed Thursdays and Sundays). Bus tours of the stores and Amish countryside are available.

Special Feature

The little county seat of **Gallatin**, 8 miles west, boasts an 1887 squirrel-cage jail.

- *The Amish maintain seven one-room parochial schools in the Jamesport area.*
- *Visitors need to remember that picture-taking goes against Amish religious beliefs.*

Where to Stay

COUNTRY COLONIAL B&B, *Main & East sts., P.O. Box 46, (816) 684-6711/(800) 579-9248.* Restored 1894 hotel with double verandahs, private baths, study, baby grand piano. $$ to $$$

MARYGOLDS INN, *P.O. Box 224, (816) 684-6122 / fax (816) 359-3573.* New 2-story inn, antiques, theme-decorated rooms, TV, private baths, deck, folk art shop. $$

NANCY'S GUEST COTTAGE B&B, *RR 1 (Box 3), (816) 684-6156.* 2-bedroom house rented as unit, antiques, full "country" breakfasts, dinner menus available, some pets. $$

OAK TREE INN, *Rt. 1, (816) 684-6250.* Three-story Amish-built home in grove of oak trees, "one-of-a-kind" breakfasts, homemade cookies, secluded balconies, barn. $

RICHARDSON HOUSE, *P.O. Box 105, (816) 444-4355.* Turn-of-century farmhouse rented as unit, antiques, "country" breakfasts. $$$

Where to Eat

GINGERICH DUTCH PANTRY & BAKERY, *South and Broadway sts., (816) 684-6212.* Mennonite cooking, homemade pies & baked goods. $

Further Information

Jamesport Community Association, *P.O. Box 215, Jamesport, MO 64648 (816) 684-6146.*

Directions

From Kansas City, I 35 north to exit 61, MO 6 east to Jamesport.

Ste. Genevieve
Population 4, 411

The first thing the visitor approaching **Ste. Genevieve** notices is that the town is nestled in a valley (in an old riverbed in fact) near the **Mississippi River**. The second – if not the first – is that the town is dominated by a tall steeple (of the 1876 **Church of Ste. Genevieve**). The third and fourth are that the church and its steeple share the middle of the town's square with a relatively small old **courthouse** (1821), and that the square is surrounded by 19th-century step-gabled brick storefronts. The most important discovery, however, comes with a stroll down the streets leading off the square. For here lies one of the largest collections of 18th-century houses in the country.

Established between 1725 and 1750 by French settlers, Ste. Genevieve is the oldest town in Missouri. More than 50 of the 18th-century homes built by the settlers survive; many have been restored. Some are private residences and others are house museums (see below). Among them are three of the only four remaining houses in North America of poteaux-en-terre construction (built on poles placed vertically in the ground, with no foundation).

The 19th-century brick buildings on (and off) the square were built by immigrants from southern Germany. These together with the French Colonial buildings form an historic district noted for its craft shops, antique galleries, boutiques, and restaurants.

The two logical starting points for a tour of the district are the Tourist Information Office and the **Ste. Genevieve Museum**. The former provides information for a self-guided walking tour, including take-out cassette tapes. The latter contains collections of local memorabilia. Of note are prehistoric Indian relics, Spanish land grants, and artifacts from the **Saline Creek Salt Works**, Missouri's first industry.

Seven structures, six homes and one inn, are of special architectural and/or historic interest:

The **Guibourd-Valle House** (ca 1784) has elegant furnishings and an attic with hand-hewn oak beams. Outside are a courtyard, rose garden, and old stone well (costumed tour guides).

The **Felix Valle House** (1818), a state historic site, is a Federal-style limestone building with early Empire furnishings and original mantels. Inside is an authentically restocked mercantile store. On the grounds are an attractive garden and original brick and frame outbuildings.

The **Bolduc House** (1770), an authentically restored Creole structure, has original 18th-century furnishings, frontier kitchen, and 18th-century culinary and medicinal herb gardens (open to public).

The **Bolduc-LeMeilleur House** (1820), a frame structure with brick nogging, is furnished with early Federal pieces. The house has early 19th-century herb and scented gardens (open to public).

The **Green Tree Inn** (1789) was the first inn and tobacco shop west of the Mississippi. The inn features original walnut shutters and woodwork and a triangular fireplace that opens into three rooms (under restoration).

The poteaux-en-terre **Amoureaux House** (1770), once the home of a French nobleman, may be the oldest building in Missouri (prearranged group tours only).

The **Bequette-Ribault House** (1778) is another of the four remaining poteaux-en-terre structures in North America (not open to public).

Special Feature

Hawn State Park, southwest of Ste. Genevieve, features pine trees, azaleas, and a 10-mile backpacking trail.

> • *A town square divided into two parts by a street (as in Ste. Genevieve), with one part housing a government building and the other a church, indicates Spanish ancestry. (And indeed, the territory west of the Mississippi was held by Spain from 1762 to 1800.)*
> • *According to legend, the posts used for poteaux-en-terre construction were soaked in arsenic prior to use to repel termites.*

Where to Stay

THE CREOLE HOUSE, *339 St. Marys Rd., (573) 883-7171/(800) 275-6041*. French Creole-style house on 2.5 acres in historic district, fireplaces, TV, private baths with whirlpools, full "gourmet" breakfasts. $$ to $$$

THE FOURTH & JEFFERSON B&B, *406 Jefferson St., (573) 883-5565*. Circa 1887 home in historic district, private baths, full breakfasts. $$

MAIN STREET INN B&B, *221 N. Main St., (573) 883-9199*. Restored late 1870s hotel, private baths, full "gourmet" breakfasts, porch & balcony. $$ to $$$

THE SOUTHERN HOTEL B&B, *146 S. Third St., (573) 883-3493*. Renovated circa 1805 Federal-style building with large front parlors, private baths, full "French" breakfasts, game room. $$ to $$$

STEIGER HAUS, *1021 Market St., (573) 883-5881*. 1882 farmhouse with 1787 guest cottage, private baths, full breakfasts, pool, murder mystery weekends, host an 11th-generation native fluent in French. $$

THE INN ST. GEMME BEAUVAIS, *78 N. Main St., (573) 883-5744*. 1848 country inn in historic district, antiques, private baths, full breakfasts. $$ to $$$

Where to Eat

ANVIL SALOON, *46 S. Third St., (573) 883-7323*. Homemade chili, liver dumplings, German Fries, homemade pies; in oldest bar in continuous operation in Mo. $

CAFE GENEVIEVE *(in Hotel Ste. Genevieve), Main & Market sts., (573) 883-3562*. Seafood, chicken, beef, Kotelett, Country Ham, prime rib the house specialty. $ to $$

OLD BRICK HOUSE, *Third & Market sts., (573) 883-2724*. Fried chicken, liver dumplings; ambiance you'd expect in oldest brick bldg. west of Mississippi River (1785-1805). $

Further Information

Ste. Genevieve Tourist Information Office, *66 S. Main St., Ste. Genevieve, MO 63670 (573) 883-7097.*

Directions

From St. Louis, I 55 south to exit 154, US 61 east to Ste. Genevieve.

Other Charming Missouri Towns

Bethel
Kimmswick
Rock Port
Steelville
Weston

MONTANA

Fort Benton

Population 1, 660

As the head of navigation on the Missouri River and the West's innermost port, **Fort Benton** was destined to encounter some colorful and rowdy days. And the days came: The town was a fur-trading post, the eastern staging post of the **Mullan Trail** (completed in 1859) connecting with Fort Walla Walla in Washington, a steamboat landing for the Gold Rush of the 1860s, and the southern terminus of the **Whoop-Up Trail** (1870/83), along which flowed whiskey and other goods into western Canada. Only with the 1880s did calm and respectability finally come to town.

Today people drive 150 miles across the sweeping wheat fields of central Montana to spend the day in this historic town. Others select *the Birthplace of Montana* to retire to. All it takes to understand why is a stroll along **Front Street**, now peaceful but once infamous for its "bloodiest block in the West." Separating the street from the Missouri is the steamboat levee, site of the **Lewis and Clark State Memorial** (1976). Staked here and there are signs telling about the days when the levee was crowded with boats, freight, and ox and mule teams. Lovely old cotton-woods and various conifers shade the riverbank and **Old Fort Park**, resting place for the remains of **Old Fort Benton** (1847; under restoration).

Bordering the street are historic buildings, some of them brick and most from Fort Benton's Golden Years, the early 1880s. The imposing **Grand Union Hotel** is one of Montana's oldest (1882). Now a National Historic Landmark, the Grand Union was once the most luxurious hostelry between Minneapolis and Seattle. The **Old Firehouse**, on the National Register of Historic Places, dates from 1883. The building housed a steam-powered engine and other firefighting equipment shipped from the East by steamboat.

Built about the same time (1880) but located a few blocks from the river is the recently restored Norman Gothic **St. Paul's Episcopal Church** (visitors welcome). The displays of the **Fort Benton Museum of the Upper Missouri** center on the history of the Fort Benton region from the 1840s until 1887. A second museum, the **Museum of the Northern Great Plains**, depicts the history of the homestead era and the region's farming practices.

Special Features

The *Benton Belle*, a replica of an 1890s riverboat, offers daily excursions on the **Missouri River**.

The scenery and abundant wildlife of some 150 miles of the unspoiled upper Missouri River, designated a Wild and Scenic River, can be seen by canoe (rentals are available) and 3- to 5-day guided boat tours.

> *• People continue to visit the profile monument and marker over the grave of the dog Shep, who spent 5 1/2 years meeting every train at Fort Benton after his master's body was taken away by train in 1936 for burial back East. Although many tried to befriend Shep, the dog faithfully waited for his master's return until killed, ironically, by a train.*
>
> *• Another of the sites on Fort Benton's levee is a replica of the keelboat "Mandan," built for the movie "The Big Sky." Yet another levee site is the hull of the small steamboat, "Baby Rose" (1900).*

Where to Stay

THE SOVEKAMMER B&B, *1109 Third Ave. N. (Great Falls 59401), (406) 453-6620.* Old home close to downtown & C.M. Russell Museum, private baths, full breakfasts made with Danish recipes. $$

Where to Eat

L & R SANDWICH SHOP, *1310 Front St., P.O. Box 1316, (406) 622-5512.* Large selection of sandwiches, specialty sandwiches, L&R Burgers, & basket lunches; bread baked daily, sandwich meats prepared on premises. $

BOB'S RIVERFRONT RESTAURANT, *1414 Front St. (406) 622-3443.* Steak Sandwich, Fettuccini Alfredo, Chicken Terikyaki, Beef-K-Bob, Country Style Pork Ribs, daily specials; view of Missouri River. $

Further Information

Fort Benton Visitors Center, *P.O. Box 988, Fort Benton, MT 59442 (406) 622-5634.*

Directions

From Helena, I 15 north to exit 280 (Great Falls), US 87 northeast to Ft. Benton.

Livingston
Population 7, 500

Robert Redford's selection of Livingston as the setting for his movie, *A River Runs Through It*, was entirely appropriate. The beautiful **Yellowstone River**, the longest free-flowing river in the lower 48, runs right through town. And with no fewer than 436 residential and commercial structures listed on the National Register, and the facades of some 20 buildings on **Main Street** restored to their original designs, much of Livingston should and does look like an early 20th-century Montana town.

One of Livingston's principal landmarks is the grand old **Northern Pacific Railroad depot**. The turn-of-the-century depot was designed by the same firm that designed New York's Grand Central Station. Recently restored at a cost of $800,000, the building is now a museum known as the **Livingston Depot Center**.

Lying among four mountain ranges, some of them snow-capped all year, and astride a world-class river, Livingston has attracted artists, writers, actors, and musicians. Despite the tiny population, the town and its county boast two resident theater companies, the Blue Slipper and the Firehouse 5. The works of local artists are displayed in more than a dozen fine galleries. Some of the art is traditional, centering on Western, wildlife, and angling scenes; much of it, however, is contemporary. Many of the galleries carry pottery, Montana porcelain, basketry, and jewelry.

Special Feature

The Yellowstone River is world-famous for its fishing. The river is also ideal for boating, floating, and kayaking. Both whitewater and scenic trips lasting from a half-day up to a week are available through commercial raft companies.

> • *The fabulous flyfishing scenes in "A River Runs Through It" were filmed on the nearby Gallatin and Yellowstone rivers.*
> • *Livingston is the original and only year-round entry to Yellowstone National Park.*

Where to Stay

THE BLUE-WINGED OLIVE, *5157 US 89, P.O. Box 1551, (800) 995-1366.* An angler's B&B lodge designed for fly fishers, private baths, breakfast buffet, great room, streamside picnic lunches available. $$

DAVIS CREEK B&B, *P.O. Box 2179 (Mill Creek 59047), (406) 333-4768.* In scenic rural setting between Livingston & Yellowstone National Park, cabins, fishing. $$ to $$$

THE GREYSTONE INN B&B, *122 S. Yellowstone St., (406) 222-8319.* Turn-of-century home on National Register, parlor with pocket doors, antiques, TV, private baths, full breakfasts, refreshments, sack lunches available. $$ to $$$

THE ISLAND B&B & GUEST HOUSE, *77 Island Dr., (406) 222-3788.* On island in Yellowstone River, "hearty" breakfasts, afternoon refreshments, hot tub & indoor sauna, privately stocked trout ponds for catch-&-release fly fishing. $ to $$$

PARADISE GATEWAY B&B, *P.O. Box 84, US 89 S., (406) 333-4063/ (800) 541-4113.* Quiet location next to river, private baths, fishing, mountain views. $$ to $$$

Where to Eat

THE CHICO INN, *at Chico Hot Springs Lodge (Pray 59065), (406) 333-4933.* Salmon en Papillote, Curry Chicken, Stuffed Cabbage Leaves, Tenderloin Medallions, prime rib; one of Montana's finest, spectacular setting. $$ to $$$

THE SPORT RESTAURANT, *114 S. Main St., (406) 222-3533.* Steaks, seafood, barbecue, Mexican food, salads, sandwiches; originally 1890s watering hole, featured in movies & books, Hollywood celebrities among guests. $$

UNCLE LOOIE'S, *119 W. Park, (406) 222-7177.* A la carte Italian menu, Chicken Scarpaiello, popular antipasto & Caesar salad, homemade breads. $$

WINCHESTER CAFE, *201 W. Park St., (406) 222-2708.* American cooking, homemade desserts, Western-style breakfasts; extensive wine selection, solid reputation. $ to $$

Further Information

Livingston Area Chamber of Commerce, *208 W. Park St., Livingston, MT 59047 (406) 222-0850/fax (406) 222-0852.*

Directions

From Billings (MT), I 90 west to exits 332 or 333 (Livingston exits); from Yellowstone National Park and Gardiner (MT), US 89 north to Livingston.

Red Lodge
Population 2, 300

Winding through the highest driveable points in both Montana and Wyoming, the 65-mile **Beartooth Scenic Byway** is one of the country's, indeed the world's, most beautiful highways. At one end of the byway is the northeastern gateway to **Yellowstone National Park**. At the other end is **Red Lodge**, an old western town tucked Hollywood-style below spectacular mountains and big blue Montana skies.

Nearly all of Red Lodge's downtown district has been added to the National Register of Historic Places. The district includes many stone and brick buildings, their facades restored, dating from the 1880s to 1915. Especially interesting are the original railroad station house (1889) and a group of buildings, known as *Old Town*, that formed the town's business center from 1886-1893.

Among the displays at the **Carbon County Historical Museum** are rodeo memorabilia, the town's first telephone switchboard, and the homestead cabin of John Johnston, known as "Liver Eatin' Johnson," on whose story the movie *Jeremiah Johnson* was based.

Red Lodge is the site of one of the country's foremost summer festivals, the **Festival of Nations**. The ancestry of the festival can be traced to the 1880s when the discovery of coal attracted hundreds of Finnish, Italian, Scandinavian, and other miners to Red Lodge. Later, about 1949, the Festival of Nations was established to help the various cultural groups learn more about each other.

Each day of the 9-day August festival is assigned to a different culture. There are dances, songs, parades, and other entertainment along with information on cooking, crafts, customs, and languages. On the evening of the day assigned to the Scots, for example, bagpipes, kilts, and dancers fill the streets and bars until the last watering hole closes. It's international learning and party time.

As for outdoor forms of recreation, Red Lodge is a four-season paradise. There's downhill skiing at **Red Lodge Mountain Ski Area**, cross-country skiing at **Red Lodge Nordic Center**, white-water rafting trips, bicycling, horseback riding, golfing, and fantastic trout fishing.

> • *Around 1886 there were four men to every woman in Red Lodge.*
> • *Although just 65 miles long, the Beartooth Scenic Byway will demand at least 2 1/2 to 3 hours of your time—you'll simply not want to speed past the views of the glaciers, snow-capped mountains, and alpine lakes and plateaus.*

Where to Stay

INN ON THE BEARTOOTH, *Hwy. 212 (2 mi S), (406) 446-3555/ (888) 227-7686.* New log B&B with Western flare, fireplace, lodgepole furnishings, down comforters, private baths, full breakfasts, sauna, view of Beartooth Mts. $$ to $$$

PITCHER GUEST HOUSES, *P.O. Box 3450, (406) 446-2859.* Historic 3- and 4-bedroom townhouses with kitchens & woodburning stoves. $$ to $$$

THE POLLARD HOTEL, *2 N. Broadway, (800) 765-5273.* Restored 1893 hotel, full-service, hot tubs, breakfasts, balconies, racquetball, dining room. $ to $$$

WILLOWS INN, *224 S. Platt Ave., (406) 446-3913.* 1909 boarding house with large sundeck, some private baths, Cont. "plus" breakfasts with home-baked pastries, two guest houses, mountain views. $$ to $$$

THE WOLVES DEN B&B, *Rt. 1 (Box 2123) (Roberts 59070), (406) 446-1273.* On banks of Rock Creek, full breakfasts, private entrance & deck, mountain views. $$

Where to Eat

OLD PINEY DELI, *P.O. Box 212, (406) 446-1111.* Seafood, poultry, steaks, & catches of the day served in rustic setting with lovely view; 5 mi out of town. $$ to $$$

THE POLLARD HOTEL, *(see above).* Aubergine Caviar, Smoked Trout Pate, Duck Liver Pate, & Wild Mushrooms among first-course offerings; reservations recommended. $$

Further Information

Red Lodge Area Chamber of Commerce, *601 N. Broadway, P.O. Box 988, Red Lodge, MT 59068 (406) 446-1718.*

Directions

From Billings, I 94 west to exit 434 (Laurel exit), US 212 south to Red Lodge.

Other Charming Montana Towns

Bigfork
Big Timber
Stevensville
Virginia City
Whitefish

308

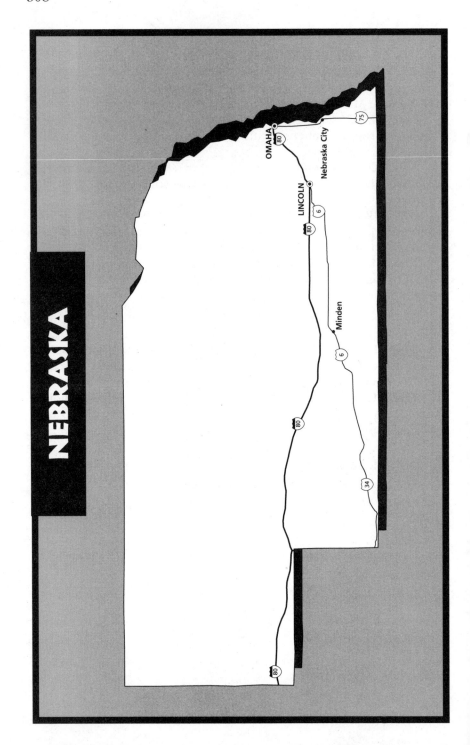

NEBRASKA

Minden
Population 2, 749

The cozy little Nebraska prairie town of **Minden** fits about every romantic notion of what a wholesome American hometown ought to be. In the middle of the town square is an old and imposing courthouse with a magnificent white dome. Around the square are prosperous businesses and, with a nod to the past, no fewer than seven antique shops. Not far from the square is an area of beautiful homes, some with more rooms than really make sense, built by Minden's Victorian-era doctors and lawyers. Finally, there are the farms with their rich irrigated cornfields.

Minden has something else, though, that makes the town just a little different from other prairie towns: A few blocks north of the square is the **Harold Warp Pioneer Village**, one of the top museums of its kind in the country. Within the some 26 buildings of this award-winning museum are exhibits employing 50,000 items to trace the development from 1830 onwards of everything from lighting and bath tubs to motorcycles and musical instruments. Included are the oldest internal combustion engine (1876), the oldest jet airplane (1942), an 1890 combine pulled by 30 horses, and the first "Kelvinator" refrigerator (1925).

Among the museum's buildings are several historic structures situated about a village green. Included are Minden's first church (1884), an original livery stable complete with harness shop, and an authentic replica of a sod house. The museum also presents daily weaving, broom-making, and other craft demonstrations.

Earning Minden the nickname *The Christmas City*, the square and the **Kearney County Courthouse**, especially the dome, are strung every Christmas with 10,000 lights. The lights are turned on as the climax of a Christmas pageant held the last Saturday night in November and the first two Sunday nights in December (the lights are also on every evening from the first production of the pageant until New Year's Day).

Special Features

Fort Kearny State Historical Park northwest of Minden was once an outpost on the **Oregon Trail**. The park features several re-created structures, including a stockade, along with period artifacts.

Fort Kearny State Recreation Area north of town is the site of the sandhill crane spring migration. Nature lovers especially will enjoy the 5-mile hike/bike trail.

Christmas lights were first strung on the courthouse dome in 1915. For many years the bulbs were colored by hand dipping.

Where to Stay

HOME COMFORT B&B INN, *1523 N. Brown, (308) 832-0533/(800) 318-0533*. Colonial-style home on 14 acres, homemade quilts, farm-style breakfasts, antique grand piano, barnyard birds & horses. $ to $$

PRAIRIE VIEW B&B, *1796 L Rd., P.O. Box 137, (308) 832-0123*. Decks overlooking prairie, antiques, full breakfasts, afternoon tea, bicycles & croquet. $ to $$

Where to Eat

CITY CAFE, *413 N. Colorado Ave., (308) 832-2788*. Our Country Fry Steak, chicken, shrimp, hamburger steak, roast beef, ham; solid Midwestern cooking. $

Further Information

Minden Chamber of Commerce, *509 N. Colorado Ave., P.O. Box 375, Minden, NE 68959 (308) 832-1811*.

Directions

From Omaha, I 80 west to exit 279, NE 10 south to Minden.

Nebraska City
Population 6, 547

The old Missouri River town of **Nebraska City** has a downtown that nicely demonstrates how the old and the new can work together. It seems that a factory outlet shop established itself on a downtown Nebraska City street and did so well that other small outlet shops followed, interspersing themselves among the town's regular downtown retail establishments. Perceiving the benefits of the new shops, the community proceeded to plant the area with trees and flowers and to add Victorian park benches and period streetlights and trolleys. The result is a beautiful and healthy old-new downtown street.

Set among apple and cherry orchards and heir to over 300 properties on the National Register of Historic Places, Nebraska City was already special long before the arrival of the factory outlets. A good way to see the town is to park your car (free parking) and hop a trolley. The Chamber of Commerce distributes a map of the "trolley trail" and sights along the way.

Among the historic homes served by the trolley is the 10-room **Wildwood Period House**, a Gothic Revival house of 1860s vintage (open to the public), and the **Taylor-Wessel-Nelson House**, considered the finest example of Greek Revival architecture in Nebraska. The latter is now home to the Nebraska City Historical Society and may be seen by appointment. Other important sights on the tour are the very Victorian 1880s **Farmers Bank**, winner of the President's National Preservation Award, and the **Old Freighter's Museum**, headquarters of an 1859 freight company and now a history museum (open by appointment).

Best times to visit the town's three orchards are during blossom time, usually the first week of May, and at harvest time, beginning around mid-September. The most famous of the orchards is the **J. Sterling Morton Orchard and Tree Farm** (a National Historic Landmark), named in honor of and forming part of the original estate of the founder of Arbor Day. Barns from the early 1900s, apple sorting and packing, and cider making are among the sights open to visitors.

The elegant 52-room Colonial Revival **Morton mansion** is the central feature of adjacent **Arbor Lodge State Historical Park and Arboretum**. A large variety of native trees and shrubs may be seen on the mansion's grounds.

John Brown's Cave and Historical Village features a cabin reputed to be the oldest surviving structure in Nebraska (ca 1852). Beneath the cabin is a cave that was once a station on the **Underground Railroad**. Also on the property are 18 buildings from various periods in Nebraska City's history.

Special Features

The **Meriwether Lewis Steamboat Museum of Missouri River History**, river cruises, and various cultural events add to the charm of **Brownville**, an old steamboat port and one of Nebraska's oldest settlements, downriver from Nebraska City.

> • *Nebraska City is a major antique center.*
> • *Escaping slaves were fed cornbread and water and allowed to spend the night at John Brown's Cave before resuming their trip north.*

Where to Stay

THOMPSON HOUSE B&B, *P.O. Box 162 (Brownville 68321), (402) 825-6551.* 1869 house with period antiques, family-style breakfasts. $$ to $$$

WHISPERING PINES B&B, *21st St. & 6th Ave., RR 2, (402) 873-5850.* Brick Italianate home with wrap-around verandah, antiques, fresh flowers, some TV & phones, some private baths, full breakfasts, refreshments, spa, gardens with ponds & fountains, view of pines. $ to $$

Where to Eat

LIED CONFERENCE CENTER, *2700 Sylvan Rd., (800) 546-5433.* Casual upscale American cooking, overlooking Arbor Day Farm & Arbor Lodge State Park. $$

ULBRICK'S CAFE, *1513 S. 11th St., (402) 873-5458.* Fried chicken, pies homemade with pure lard; converted filling station with plastic-covered tables & family-style service, a local legend. $

Further Information

Chamber of Commerce, *806 1st Ave., Nebraska City, NE 68410 (402) 873-3000.*

Directions

From Omaha, US 75 south to Nebraska City.

Other Charming Nebraska Towns

Arthur
Gothenburg
Valentine
Wayne

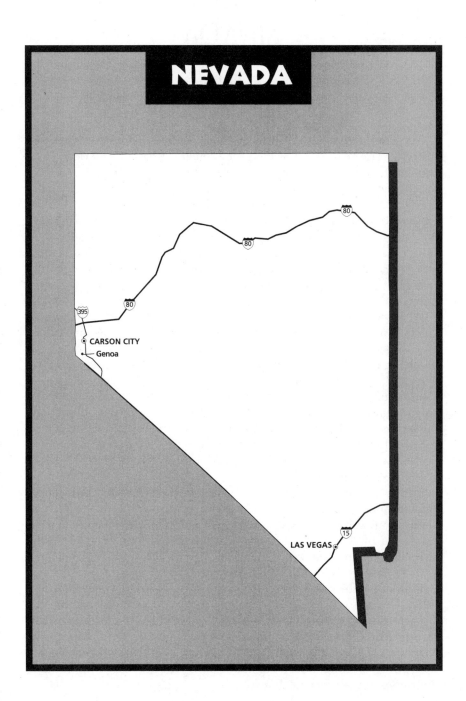

NEVADA

CARSON CITY

Genoa

LAS VEGAS

NEVADA

Eureka
Population 1, 200

A sign welcoming visitors to **Eureka** announces that "You Are Entering The Loneliest Town on the Loneliest Road in America." Even though the townspeople will hasten to note that their home is not truly lonely, they readily admit that it is remote. Situated in the middle of the Nevadan desert, a round-trip automobile excursion to the city (Carson City or Reno in this case) takes about eight hours. And that's counting only driving time. There are few towns in this book where the surrounding "countryside" has changed so little since the first white settlers arrived–Eureka is fortunately in no immediate danger of being engulfed by a sprawling suburbia. The air will hint of sagebrush for many years to come.

Following the discovery of silver in 1864 and the development of smelters a few years later, Eureka boomed into Nevada's second largest city, with a population of over 9,000. There were 100 saloons, dozens of gambling houses, an opera house (see below), and everything else you'd expect in a classic 19th-century mining camp. There was even a Chinatown. On the unromantic side were the soot and pollution from 16 smelters, earning the town the nickname "Pittsburgh of the West." Even though the big boom was over by 1890, mining activity continued to surface on and off over the years, and in fact the town is currently enjoying a boom.

Many of the buildings fronting Eureka's streets were built of brick or volcanic stone in the 1870s and 1880s. Although some are vacant, most continue to house hotels, cafes, bars, shops, and other mercantile establishments. The original pressed-tin ceilings can still be seen in several. A few are private residences. A brochure for a self-guiding tour, published by the Eureka County Chamber of Commerce, provides an excellent way to get to know them.

On display at the **Sentinel Museum** (1879) are the presses and equipment of the *Eureka Sentinel Newspaper*, published between 1870 and 1960. Mementos from other areas of Eureka's past are also exhibited.

The **Eureka County Courthouse** (1879-1880), the town's most important historic structure, once ranked second only to the courthouse in Virginia City as the grandest in the state. The judge's bench in the courtroom (second floor) was made of Spanish cedar. The building continues in use as a courthouse.

The **Eureka Opera House and Theatre** (1880), another enduring landmark, once served as the community auditorium as well as an opera house and theater. Renovated, it is now a convention and cultural arts center. The quaint **St. James Episcopal Church** was built in 1872 to accommodate miners from England.

Special Feature

With the silhouettes of distant mountain ranges acting to dramatize their colors, Eureka's **desert sunsets** are breathtaking.

> *In 1879 six Italian charcoal burners were killed and another ten wounded by a posse in a dispute over the pricing of charcoal. The event, Eureka's most historic, is known as the Charcoal War of 1879.*

Where to Stay

THE JACKSON HOUSE, *Main St., (702) 237-5577*. Restored 1880s hotel with broad second-floor balcony, TV, private baths, saloon, recipient of restoration award. $

THE PARSONAGE HOUSE, P.O. Box 99, (702) 237-5756. 1886 cottage with bedroom, kitchen, living/dining area, 6-ft tub, chandeliers, handcrafted & antique furnishings. $

Where to Eat

LUIGI'S DELI, *(Hwy. 50 S end of town), P.O. Box 27, (702) 237-5477.* The name says it all. $

Further Information

Eureka County Chamber of Commerce & Economic Development Council, *P.O. Box 14, Eureka, NV 89316 (702) 237-5484/fax (702) 237-5175.*

Directions

From Carson City, US 50 east to Eureka.

Genoa

Population 500

A picturesque Old West town tucked in the foothills of the **Sierra Nevada**, **Genoa** is neither the skeleton of a late 19th-century mining town nor a 20th-century resort with glittering casinos. Genoa (accent on second syllable) is very much a 19th-century town, the oldest non-Indian settlement in Nevada in fact, but its careful preservation is very much 20th century, as are its comforts.

Genoa's Old West credentials are impressive. The town was established in 1851 as a trading post, known as **Mormon Station**, that served as a resting place and provisioning station for fur traders and prospectors dreaming of silver or gold. From 1855 until 1916 the town was a county seat, and in 1860 and 1861 it was a stop on the Pony Express.

Today Genoa has nearly 30 buildings listed on the National Register of Historic Places. Construction dates include every decade from the 1850s onward into the early 20th century. The buildings served, and in some cases continue to serve, as guest houses, stores, homes, a dance hall, a Masonic Hall, even a health spa.

By all means the best known and most photographed of the buildings is the charming **Genoa Courthouse** (1865). Now the **Genoa Courthouse Museum**, this lovely brick building served as a courthouse until 1916, then as a school until 1956. The museum has a diversity of exhibits, including the original courtroom, a period schoolroom, a blacksmith shop with hand-forged tools, and antique ranching/farming items, including snowshoes for a horse.

Across the street from the courthouse is a replica of Mormon Station. The replica and historical exhibit inside make up **Mormon Station State Park**. Just down the street is another popular site, the **Genoa Saloon**, allegedly the oldest bar in Nevada (1850s).

The **Carson Valley** can be toured by bicycle, but hot-air ballooning and soaring (world-class) are also exciting ways of getting around.

The townspeople make some 3, 000 pounds of candy in preparation for the annual "Candy Dance, " held the last weekend in September. Now attracting thousands of visitors, the Candy Dance started in 1919.

Where to Stay

THE GENOA HOUSE INN B&B, *P.O. Box 141, (702) 782-7075*. 1872 home on National Register, antiques, private baths, full breakfasts, refreshments, use of Walley's Hot Springs. $$$

WALLEY'S HOT SPRINGS, *2001 Foothill Rd., P.O. Box 26, (702) 782-8155*. Historic cottage accommodations, restaurant, hot mineral springs & spas, pool, tennis, fitness center, President Grant & Mark Twain among guests. $$$

THE WILD ROSE INN B&B, *2332 Main St., P.O. Box 256, (702) 782-5697*. Reproduction Queen Anne home, antiques, private baths, full breakfasts, wine, complimentary visit to Walley's Hot Springs. $$$

Where to Eat

CARSON VALLEY INN-MICHAEL'S, *1627 US 395 N (Minden), (702) 782-9711 (ext. 782) / (800) 321-6983 (ext. 782)*. Sierra Pinon cuisine "with Southwestern flair," good wine list. $$

INN COGNITO, *Genoa Ln., (702) 782-8898*. Continental cuisine, Cajun & wild game specialties. $$

THE PINK HOUSE, *Main St. & Genoa Ln., (702) 782-3939*. Catch of the Day, Chicken Oscar, Long Island Duck; saloon originally a 1904 guest house, fireside dining. $$

Further Information

Carson Valley Chamber of Commerce, *1512 Hwy. 395, Suite 1, Gardnerville, NV 89410 (800) 727-7677. (ZIP for Genoa is 89411.)*

Directions

From Reno, US 395 south (through Carson City) to NV 758 (Genoa Ln.), west to Genoa.

Other Charming Nevada Towns

Lamoille
Unionville
Virginia City

318

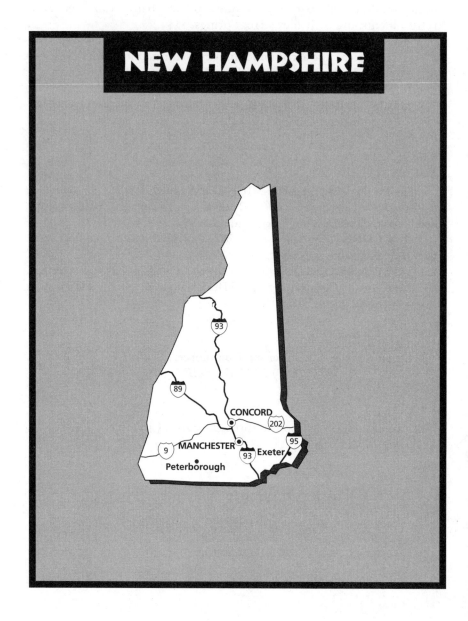

NEW HAMPSHIRE

Exeter

Population 9556

Founded in 1638 and located on a tidal river, railroad line, and major highways, **Exeter** possesses the kind of sophistication that comes with centuries of contact and commerce with peoples from other parts. The town not only has a long, but also a rich history, one distinguished by individualism and Revolutionary rebellion and patriotism.

Exeter's architectural diversity gives tangible expression to its worldly wisdom and long history. Buildings from every era line the town's streets. The best way to explore the architecture is by foot (the Exeter Historical Society publishes a brochure for walking tours). A good starting point is **Front Street**, bordered by an exceptional collection of handsome Federal-style houses. The 1798 **Congregational Church** is also on this street.

The attractive campus of historic **Phillips Exeter Academy** (1781), also on Front Street, has more than 100 buildings. The 1970 library by Louis Kahn and the ornate 1897 Gothic church are of special architectural interest.

Elsewhere is the **Ladd-Gilman House** (1721), a national landmark that is now the **American Independence Museum**. Included in the museum's collections are one of three Purple Hearts awarded by George Washington, handwritten documents of General and President Washington, and one of the 24 surviving copies of the original Declaration of Independence.

The older part of the **Gilman Garrison House** was built in the mid 1600s of hewn logs. Originally a garrison, the structure was remodeled in the 18th century. Period furnishings include Daniel Webster's desk. (open to the public)

Visitors may want to add some of Exeter's specialty shops to their itineraries. Among the offerings are fine old books, unique gifts for children, and imported foods.

> • *The IOKA Theatre (1915) is one of the oldest movie theaters in the country still in operation.*
> • *In 1776 New Hampshire became the first of the colonies to adopt an independent state constitution.*

Where to Stay

THE INN BY THE BANDSTAND, *4 Front St., (603) 772-6352/(800) 665-9335.* 1809 Federal inn, fireplaces, TV, English kettles, down pillows, private baths, homemade pastries. $$$

THE INN OF EXETER, *90 Front St., (800) 782-8444.* Full-service Georgian inn on campus of Phillips Exeter Academy, dining rooms, tennis, swimming, squash, "warmth of a B&B and facilities of a fine hotel." $$$

Where to Eat

THE INN OF EXETER, *(see above).* Creative recipes served in gracious dining rooms, recipient of culinary awards. $ to $$

THE LOAF & LADLE, *9 Water St., (603) 778-8955.* Homemade chowders/soups/stews served cafeteria-style, sandwiches on home-baked bread; riverside dining room & tavern, folk music. $

THE TAVERN AT RIVERS' EDGE, *163 Water St., (603) 772-7393.* Seafood Quesadilla, Chicken in Fillo, Honey Barbecue Pork Chops, Riverside Stuffed French Bread, daily specials. $

Further Information

The Exeter Area Chamber of Commerce, *120 Water St., Exeter, NH 03833 (603) 772-2411.*

Directions

From Manchester, NH 101 east to Rte. 27, Rte. 27 into downtown Exeter.

Peterborough
Population 5, 243

Peterborough is a 19th-century mill town, with old brick buildings that once housed water-powered industries. Unlike many of the New England communities in this guide, which survive largely on tourists and retirees and the past, Peterborough is a working town with business offices, banks, and law firms.

The intriguing **Peterborough Museum**, one of a series of handsome brick buildings facing historic Grove Street, offers an excellent introduction to the town. The museum, showcase of the local historical society, traces the evolution of Peterborough's economy from a farming community through an Industrial Revolution mill town to a present-day center for magazine publishing. Included in the museum is an old-fashioned country store and restored, furnished houses where girls working in the textile mills once lived. Obtain a guide for a walking tour of Grove Street at the Chamber of Commerce.

Long a cultural center, Peterborough is home to one of the best summer theaters in the country, the **Peterborough Players**. The **New England Marionette Theatre**, the country's largest marionette theater devoted primarily to opera, is also here. With the help of skilled puppeteers, the colorful marionettes delight audiences with four performances weekly from May through December.

The galleries of the **Sharon Arts Center**, a few miles south of Peterborough, have shows throughout the year. The center sponsors classes in arts and crafts ranging from painting and weaving to stained glass and printmaking. There is also a shop offering high-quality crafts.

As for the musical arts, the **Monadnock region** offers an impressive series of summer programs. The **MacDowell Colony** is a retreat where composers and other artists can concentrate on their work without outside intrusion. Founded in 1907, the colony evolved from a farm owned by composer Edward MacDowell.

Special Feature

Peterborough is surrounded by tiny villages of the Christmas-card variety. Some of the prettiest are **Hancock**, **Dublin**, **Harrisville**, and **Francestown**.

> • *A stay in Peterborough in the 1930s inspired Thornton Wilder to write "Our Town." Peterborough was the site of the play's world premiere.*
> • *Nearby Mr. Monadnock is the single most climbed mountain in North America.*

Where to Stay

APPLE GATE B&B, *199 Upland Farm Rd. (NH 123 S), (603) 924-6543.* 1832 home in apple orchards, antiques, private baths, full candlelight breakfasts, gardens. $$

PETERBOROUGH MANOR, *50 Summer St., (603) 924-9832.* 1894 mansion on hill, TV, private baths, guest kitchen facilities, travel library. $

Where to Eat

CAROLYN'S BISTRO & DELI, *50 Depot Sq., (603) 924-2002.* "Always Different, Always Fun, Always Homemade." $$

LATACARTA, *6 School St., (603) 924-6878.* "Natural-Creative-International" cooking, in former movie theater. $$

Further Information

The Greater Peterborough Chamber of Commerce, *P.O. Box 401, Peterborough, NH 03458 (603) 924-7234.*

Directions

From Manchester, NH 101 southwest to Peterborough.

Other Charming New Hampshire Towns

Center Harbor
Hancock
Jackson
Jaffrey
Sugar Hill

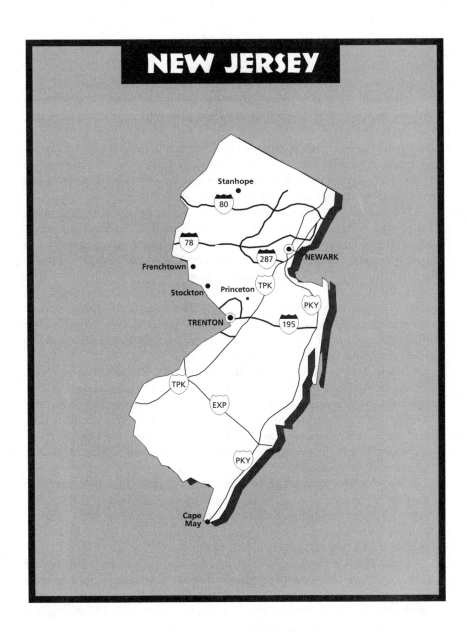

NEW JERSEY

Cape May

Population 4, 668

One of the country's premier Victorian seaside resorts, **Cape May** is among the elite of America's charming towns. If in your mind's eye you can replace the cars with carriages, and the shorts and jeans with bustles and parasols, you can see the town pretty much the way it was. Gorgeous Victorian homes and inns still grace the streets, and visitors still relax on verandahs or stroll the sidewalks and seaside promenade. The views and breezes from the sea are timeless, of course.

No one has yet explained the lure of the sea, but Cape May is surviving proof that, whatever its nature, that lure has been around for many generations. The town was known as a resort when New Jersey was still a British colony. Steamship service between Cape May and Philadelphia began in the early 1800s and was soon followed by regular railroad service. Over the years the resort has entertained a number of presidents and other prominent people – including John Philip Sousa and Congressman Abraham Lincoln. Thanks to the growth of Atlantic City in the early 20th century, Cape May stopped developing and became forever fixed in the colorful closing decades of the 19th century.

Cape May's National Historic Landmark District has over 600 preserved Victorian buildings, a number impressive by any standard. The buildings display an unusually wide variety of architectural styles and ornamentation. A stroll among them is a pleasure any time, including after dark, when the streets are lit by gas lamps. There are maps for self-guided walking tours, and visitors wishing guided tours will be dazzled by the number of options.

The **Emlen Physick Estate** (1881), an 18-room Stick-style mansion designed by Frank Furness, is one of the most important of the historic homes. The house and its Eastlake-style furniture may be seen by tour. Many of the most interesting of the other historic houses are now bed-and-breakfast inns (see expanded listing below).

Cape May's attractions are hardly confined to Victorian homes and inns. The **Cape May Point Lighthouse** (1859) guards the shipping lanes between Delaware Bay and the Atlantic Ocean. Now a museum, the lighthouse features displays on its history as well as a 199-step spiral staircase leading to a spectacular view.

Cold Spring Village, north of town, is a re-created 19th-century South Jersey farm village. Included among the restorations are an old jailhouse, an 18th-century inn, a country store, and a restaurant. There are also craft shops and demonstrations.

Special Features

The **Cape May Bird Observatory** is widely known for its many entertaining programs and bird-watching opportunities.

The **Cape May Whale Watch and Research Center** offers cruises for whale- and dolphin-watchers.

Historic **Lewes, Delaware** is only 70 minutes away on the Cape May-Lewes Ferry. The ferry offers daily service; during July and August twilight and moonlight cruises are also offered. Passengers may walk, bicycle, or drive aboard.

Where to Stay

ANGEL OF THE SEA, *5-7 Trenton Ave., (800) 848-3369*. Elegant Queen Anne home, TV, private baths, full breakfasts, teas, verandahs, opposite ocean/beach, views. $$$

CARROLL VILLA B&B, *19 Jackson St., (609) 884-9619*. 1875 Italianate home in historic district, antiques, private baths, full breakfasts, restaurant, ocean views. $$$

COLVMNS BY THE SEA, *1513 Beach Dr., (609) 884-2228*. Turn-of-century mansion with antiques & 12-ft ceilings, private baths, full gourmet breakfasts, high teas, sherry. $$$

INN AT 22 JACKSON ST., *22 Jackson St., (800) 452-8177*. 1899 Queen Anne home, antiques, suites with sitting rooms & private baths, full buffet breakfasts, afternoon tea, 4 brightly painted verandahs with rockers, bikes. $$$

THE MAINSTAY INN, *635 Columbia Ave., (609) 884-8690*. Victorian inn with fine antiques, fireplaces, private baths, "lucious" breakfasts, afternoon teas, private porches. $$$

THE VIRGINIA HOTEL, *25 Jackson St., (800) 732-4236*. Restored 19th-century hotel with Victorian & contemporary luxuries, dining room, library lounge. $$$

WINDWARD HOUSE, *24 Jackson St., (609) 884-3368*. Antique-filled Edwardian cottage, private baths, full breakfasts, refreshments, beach passes, bicycles, ocean view. $$$

Where to Eat

410 BANK STREET, *410 Bank St., (609) 884-2127*. Louisiana-French cuisine, grilled seafood, steaks; unique ambiance, highly rated. $$ to $$$

ALEXANDER'S, *653 Washington St., (609) 884-2555*. Gourmet dining in elegant Victorian inn; fresh roses, silver, crystal, linen, & lace; tuxedoed waiters. $$ to $$$

THE LOBSTER HOUSE, *Fisherman's Wharf, (609) 884-8296.* Seafood served in quaint seaport setting on working fishing dock. $$

THE MAD BATTER, *(see Carroll Villa), (609) 884-5970.* Eclectic international cuisine, homemade desserts; "Nouvelle Victorian" decor, variety of settings, award-winning. $$ to $$$

THE MERION INN, *106 Decatur St., (609) 884-8363.* Seafood as You Like It, Grilled Swordfish with Lime-Cilantro Butter, Chicken Rovira, Steak as You Like It; intimate Victorian dining rooms, oldest bar in Cape May County! $$ to $$$

WASHINGTON INN, *801 Washington St., (609) 884-5697.* E.g., Oven Roasted Salmon with a maple & mustard glaze laced with a pecan beurre blanc; in 1840 plantation home, largest wine cellar in southern N.J., highly respected, reservations recommended. $$$

THE WATERS EDGE, *On beach at Pittsburgh Ave., (609) 884-1717.* Fresh local seafood, range-fed chicken, steaks, pastas; extensive wine list, ocean views, great reviews. $$ to $$$

Further Information

Chamber of Commerce Of Greater Cape May, *P.O. Box 556, Cape May, NJ 08204 (609) 884-5508.*

Directions

From Philadelphia/Camden, I 76 south to NJ 42, south to Atlantic City Expwy., Atlantic City Expwy. to Garden State Pkwy., south to Rte. 1095, to Cape May.

Frenchtown
Population 1, 528

New Yorkers (and others) seeking a picturesque little river town where the days are relaxed and the nights quiet are discovering **Frenchtown** on the Delaware. It isn't everyday that you can find such a place, especially one just 60 minutes out of New York City.

Frenchtown was on the map, although not necessarily by that name, as far back as the mid-18th century, when a ferry crossed **the Delaware** at this point. During its earlier years the town saw a gristmill, a manufacturer of spokes and wheels, a railroad, even a poultry industry. Around 1875 things began to slow down, however, and the town took a long nap. Then, 20 years or so ago, charm-loving kinds of people began to rediscover the place, and the restorations, art studios, boutiques, and antique shops began to appear.

Although Frenchtown remains quiet, there is more to do than admire the setting, charming though it may be. Sophisticated shoppers will find what they're looking for off the brick sidewalks of the antiqued **Bridge Street**. And sportsmen of all ages can find what they're looking for in or on the waters of the Delaware River. The Delaware is a *play river*, meaning that it's great for canoeing, tubing, fishing, and other river sports.

Special Feature

The bed of the old railroad has been converted to a first-class hiking/biking path.

> *Frenchtown was named after an aristocratic European settler who apparently never bothered to tell the locals that he originated in Switzerland rather than France.*

Where to Stay

HUNTERDON HOUSE, *12 Bridge St., (800) 382-0375/(908) 996-3632*. 1864 Italianate mansion, period pieces, private baths, full breakfasts, sherry, shaded sitting porch. $$$

THE NATIONAL HOTEL, *31 Race St., (908) 996-4871*. Restored 1851 hotel, antique-filled rooms, phones, private baths, suites, Sunday buffet brunch. $$ to $$$

Where to Eat

THE BRIDGE CAFE, *8 Bridge St., (908) 996-6040*. Soups, quiche, home-baked goods, specials; on Delaware River, patio dining. $

THE FRENCHTOWN INN, *7 Bridge St., (908) 996-3300*. Potato Crusted Atlantic Salmon, Rosemary Skewered Gulf Shrimp, Baked Wellington of Pekin Duck; highly respected. $$$

JIM'Z RACE STREET CAFE & GRILL, *2 Race St., (908) 996-3179*. Shrimp Havana, Chicken Savoy, Vegetarian Chili, Tabasco Peppercorn Steak; casual, cozy, quaint & European. $$

LOAFERS AMERICAN BISTRO, *10 Bridge St., (908) 996-0900*. "Unique menu of gourmet-roasted loaves of meat, fish and fowl"; vegetarian loaves a specialty, tantalizing lunch listing, good reviews. $$

Further Information

The Innkeeper, Hunterdon House, *12 Bridge St., Frenchtown, NJ 08825*.

Directions

From Newark, I 78 west to exit 15, County 513 south to Frenchtown (12 miles).

Princeton

Population 12, 016

Stroll down Nassau Street on a warm spring day. Or maybe on an autumn football day when the colors are orange and black. Then cross the street and spend some time exploring the campus. Finally, wander over to the graduate school. You'll find that parts of both **Princeton** and **Princeton University** could have been transplanted from England–Cambridge would be a good bet. You'll also find that the university's campus is indisputably one of the finest in the world. And you'll understand why some might be tempted to vote Princeton the most beautiful town in the United States.

Facing Nassau Street is **Nassau Hall**, in almost every sense Princeton's heart, and one of the country's most hallowed places. The largest academic structure in the Colonies when completed in 1756, the building saw service as the meeting place of New Jersey's first legislature in 1776, as a barracks and a hospital during the Revolutionary War, and as home to the Continental Congress in 1783. To list those who have walked its halls would be to compile an index for a book on American history. Within its walls today are Memorial Hall, honoring the university's war dead, and the faculty room, modeled after Britain's House of Commons.

The university's buildings represent a range of architectural styles and, as might be expected on an Ivy League campus, are often the work of top architects. Structures that may have greatest appeal to the romantic are those of the "Collegiate Gothic" style. One of these, the non-denominational **University Chapel** (1928), is among the largest university chapels in the world; of special interest are the French pulpit and lectern and the American stained-glass windows. The **Graduate School** (1913), with its magnificent tower and lovely quadrangles, provides another splendid example of the Collegiate Gothic style.

Displayed about the campus are the **Putnam Sculptures**, a large collection of modern outdoor works by internationally renowned artists. Other campus sites that merit a visit are the **Art Museum**, the **Natural History Museum**, and the **Woodrow Wilson School of Public and International Affairs**.

Princeton's many lovely and historic homes justify a special tour in their own right. The starting point should be the Georgian **Bainbridge**

House (circa 1766; open), which harbors the Historical Society of Princeton's museum, gift shop, library, photo archives, and administrative offices. The tour of homes should include **Morven** (1755), General Cornwallis's headquarters during the Battle of Princeton and until recently the official residence of New Jersey's governors, and the grand Greek-Revival **Drumthwacket** (1835, enlarged 1890s), official residence of the state's current governors. Both homes are open to the public, although on a restricted schedule or by appointment.

Another home open to the public, the Georgian **Thomas Clarke Farmhouse** (circa 1772), is located in **Princeton Battlefield State Park**, where General Washington defeated the British in 1777. The rooms have period furnishings. Among the many other important Princeton houses are the **Woodrow Wilson House** (1836) and **Westland** (1854), once home to Grover Cleveland (both privately owned).

The Historical Society (Bainbridge House) offers 2-hour guided tours (Sundays) as well as brochures for self-guided walking tours. Check at MacLean House (next to Nassau Hall) for information on campus tours.

Special Feature

In nearby **Rocky Hill** is the homestead (circa 1710) that served as General Washington's headquarters in 1783 and where the general wrote his *Farewell Orders to the Armies*. The dwelling and attendant buildings now form the **Rockingham State Historic Site**. Rooms are furnished in period style.

> *In the days before the Civil War, Princeton University was popular with wealthy Southern as well as Northern families—indeed, students from the South sometimes brought their slaves with them to college. The Civil War subsequently and consequently set close friends and classmates against one another.*

Where to Stay

NASSAU INN, *10 Palmer Square, (609) 921-2853/fax (609) 921-9385*. Full-service Princeton landmark with roots to 1756, 2 restaurants, taproom with Norman Rockwell mural, fitness center, in downtown Princeton across from university. $$$

Where to Eat

ALCHEMIST & BARRISTER, *28 Witherspoon St., (609) 924-5555*. E.g., "Maryland Lump Crab & Maine Smoked Salmon with baby vegetables in puff pastry and a cherried & oyster mushroom creme"; first-class luncheon menu, pub, all-year patio. $$$

PALMER'S RESTAURANT, *(see Nassau Inn above)*. Cuisine in classic tradition, seasonal game & seafood; lovely dining room, respected. $$$

Further Information

Chamber of Commerce of Princeton Area, *216 Rockingham Row, Princeton Forrestal Village, Princeton, NJ 08540 (609) 520-1776/fax (609) 530-9107*; or **Historical Society of Princeton**, *Bainbridge House, 158 Nassau St., Princeton, NJ 08540 (609) 921-6748.*

Directions

From Trenton, US 1 north to Princeton turnoff; from Newark (and New York City), New Jersey Tpk. south to exit 9, follow signs to US 1, south to Princeton turnoff.

Stockton

Population about 600

No more than three miles up the Delaware from Lambertville, **Stockton** consists of a couple of historic inns (see below), a wonderful old railroad station, a couple of craft shops, and maybe one grocery store. There are some interesting old homes on the side of the hill, but you won't see much of them from the main road (NJ 29). A narrow, old-fashioned truss bridge connects the little town with Pennsylvania across the Delaware. Situated as it is alongside the Delaware, the old **Delaware and Raritan (D & R) Canal**, and an old railroad bed turned hiking/biking trail, Stockton is about as likely to be visited today by hikers, bikers, and canoeists as by motorists.

Stockton began as a ferry town in the 18th century. The canal and then the railroad came in the 19th century. Now, with the ferry and railroad gone and the canal (actually a feeder for the main canal) long empty of commercial craft, the town survives on its charm and attractiveness as a home for people commuting to New York City and Philadelphia.

On the northern edge of town is the **Prallsville Mills** section of the **D & R Canal State Park**. Here, clustered on the canal, are an 1877 gristmill (open to the public), a 1794 linseed-oil mill, a sawmill, and several other historic structures. The beginning of the canal is a few miles farther north, at a point now occupied by the **Bull's Island** section of the state park. The park offers excellent canoeing, boating, fishing, hiking, and birdwatching. Approximately 70 feet wide and 8 feet deep, the canal is ideal for canoeing – and safer than the adjoining **Delaware River**.

Special Features

The old railroad-bed trail leads south to **Trenton** and north to **Frenchtown** (see selection). Whether on the trail, canal, or river, Stockton is an excellent place to "put into" for food, supplies, and rest.

Sergeantsville, four miles northeast of Stockton, is the site of **Green Sergeants Bridge**, New Jersey's last covered bridge.

> *The Delaware and Raritan Canal was dug by hand by Irish immigrants between 1830 and 1834.*

Where to Stay

THE STOCKTON INN, *1 Main St., P.O. Box C, (609) 397-1250.* 1710 stone home, reproductions, TV, private baths, restaurant, wishing well. $$ to $$$ (Note: It was about this inn that Richard Rodgers and Lorenz Hart wrote the song about "a small hotel, with a wishing well.")

THE WOOLVERTON INN, *6 Woolverton Rd., (609) 397-0802.* Late 18th-century mansion on magnificent grounds, antiques, private baths, full breakfasts, fresh flowers. $$ to $$$

Where to Eat

ATRIO CAFE, *515 Bridge St., (609) 397-0042.* Pan Seared Atlantic Salmon, Fresh Herb Dusted Breast of Chicken, Grilled New York Sirloin; warm antique setting. $$

THE STOCKTON INN, *(see above).* American & Continental dishes, historic setting, fireplaces, alfresco dining in terraced garden pavilions, bar, entertainment. $$ to $$$

Further Information

Prallsville Mill, *Rte. 29, Stockton, NJ 08559; also,* **Asst. Innkeeper**, *Stockton Inn, 1 Main St., Stockton.*

Directions

From Trenton, NJ 29 north along Delaware River to Stockton.

Waterloo Village

Population: a handful

Situated as it is in a valley alongside a beautiful winding river (the **Musconetcong**) and remains of an old canal, it's hard to believe that picturesque **Waterloo Village** is only minutes from the outer banks of New Jersey's suburbs (it's near the town of **Stanhope**). But it is, even though the setting is rural, in fact as well as appearance.

Deserted as the railroad, iron furnaces, and history in general moved elsewhere, tiny Waterloo Village never emerged from the 18th and 19th centuries. The village was an iron town in the 18th century—the forge in fact provided cannonballs for the Revolutionary effort—and then prospered as a canal town in the 19th century. By the 20th century, however, the place was largely forgotten. Then, after World War II, Waterloo Village was "discovered," restored and opened to the public (1964).

Now a National Historic Site, Waterloo Village embraces over 30 restored structures. A canal museum, working gristmill, blacksmith shop, and sawmill provide excellent glimpses at the commercial and industrial life of another day. Other structures include the 1876 **Wellington House** (now a museum), the **Methodist Church** (1859), and several homes that remain private residences. The village also contains an early farmstead and a 400-year-old **Lenape Indian village**. As a general rule, buildings from the 1700s are of stone and those from the 1800s are frame.

Period-attired guides and craftspeople explain the architecture and demonstrate various crafts. All goods produced by the village's artisans are sold in the original general store.

As part of its new life, Waterloo Village has become a center for the arts. In the summer the **Waterloo Festival Orchestra** is joined by outstanding guest conductors and soloists in the 2,800-seat concert tent. In addition, top artists perform everything from classical music and opera to jazz and rock as part of the special events calendar of the **Waterloo Festival of the Arts**. Also on the calendar are Civil War re-enactments, an arts & crafts festival, an antiques fair, and Irish, Italian, Scandinavian, Inca, and other festivals.

Special Features

Like Waterloo, nearby **Stanhope** was once a forge town, iron-producing center, and port on the **Morris Canal**. The town has many beautiful old houses.

The grounds of Waterloo provide an excellent setting for a family picnic.

Originally named Andover Forge, Waterloo Village received its present name after Napoleon's celebrated defeat in 1815.

Where to Stay

WHISTLING SWAN INN, *110 Main St. (Stanhope), (201) 347-6369.*
1905 Queen Anne home with circular staircase, antiques, rooms furnished in themes, TV & phones, private baths, full buffet breakfasts,
refreshments, gardens, highly respected. $$$

Where to Eat

BARONE'S, *77 US 206, (973) 347-1812.* Fettuccine Mascarpone, Filet
of Sole Veneziana, Chicken Barone, Pork Chops with Vinegar Peppers,
Black Angus Beef, Tortelloni alla Nona. $ to $$

THE BLACK FOREST INN, *249 US 206 (Stanhope), (201) 347-3344.*
Jagerschnitzel in Wine & Mushroom Cream Sauce, Wiener Schnitzel,
Calf's Liver Lyonnaise, Roasted Duck Breast with Apples & Cassis,
seafood, beef; German decor, costumed waitresses, reservations advised.
$$ to $$$

CHEQUERS, *134 NJ 183 (Stanhope), (201) 347-3777.* English pub
food, steak-and-kidney pie, English beers. $

SILVER SPRING FARM, *Flanders & Drakestown Rd. (Flanders), (973)
584-0202.* French Continental menu, e.g., Homard Tourville au Champagne, Cuisses de Grenouille a la Provencale. $$ to $$$

TOWPATH TAVERN, *Waterloo Village.* Hearty luncheon fare, Early
American ambiance. $

Further Information

Waterloo Foundation for the Arts, Inc., *Village of Waterloo, 525
Waterloo Road, Stanhope, NJ 07874 (201) 347-0900.*

Directions

From New York City, I 80 west to exit 25, follow signs to Waterloo.

Other Charming New Jersey Towns

Batsto
Clinton
Flemington
Lambertville
Salem

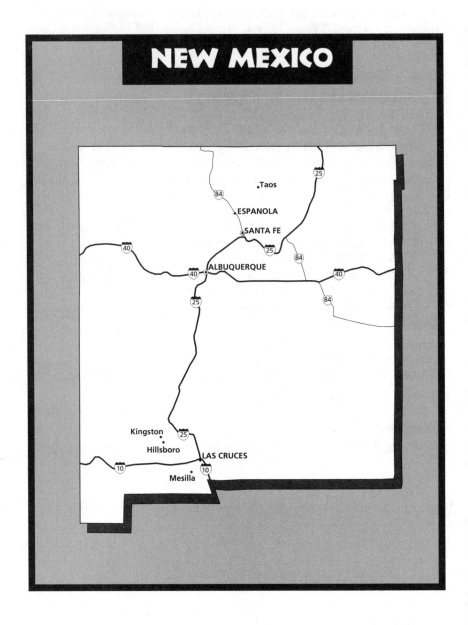

NEW MEXICO

Hillsboro/Kingston
Population 200/30

The old mining towns of **Hillsboro** (gold) and **Kingston** (silver) are two of the major finds of this guide. Few Americans have heard of these tiny spots. Indeed, there are New Mexicans who have never heard of them.

Both villages are tucked away far out on the rolling high desert of southwestern New Mexico. The road that leads to them eventually winds its way through the **Black Range** to the west, but there's nothing in particular on the other side of the mountains—except more spectacular scenery. Overhead the skies are true blue, and the waters coming down from the mountain are sparkling.

Although Hillsboro is on the desert, its **Main Street** passes through a natural grove of old cottonwood trees. Among the trees are several quaint shops, an art gallery, and a bed and breakfast (see below). It's easy to see why movies and commercials have been filmed here. The town also has an old church (1882) that's still in use, the ruins of the old courthouse (the county seat was moved elsewhere in the early 1940s), and on its outskirts, apple orchards, the reason for the town's annual **Apple Festival**. There's also a small museum, the **Black Range Museum**, that displays gold-mining artifacts dating from about 1875 to 1900.

Nothing much remains of tiny Kingston, nine miles down the road, but a few historic buildings and a lovely setting. There's an old brick assay office, the **Victorio Hotel** (now a private residence), and the **Percha Valley Bank Museum**, with its collection of mining artifacts and antiques (open by appointment).

Special Feature

Although virtually in the middle of nowhere themselves, Hillsboro and Kingston are within excursion distance of the beautiful Black Range, the **Gila Cliff Dwellings National Monument**, the **City of Rocks State Park**, and **Elephant Butte Lake State Park**.

> • *Jane Fonda and Ted Turner's Ladder Ranch is located between Hillsboro and Truth or Consequences (to the east).*
> • *Corpses used to be kept in the basement of the Victorio Hotel in Kingston until the spring thaw made burial possible.*

Where to Stay

BLACK RANGE LODGE B&B, *Star Rte. 2 (Box 119), Kingston, (505) 895-5652.* Late 1800s stone lodge, antiques, private baths, game room, balconies, pets, gardens, scenic views. $$

THE ENCHANTED VILLA B&B INN, *Hillsboro, (505) 895-5686.* Historic 2-story adobe home built for British nobleman, full breakfasts, dining room. $$

Where to Eat

ENCHANTED VILLA B&B INN, *(see above).* Home-cooked meals by appointment. $

HILLSBORO GENERAL STORE & COUNTRY CAFE, *Hillsboro.* Some lunch suggestions: Basic Burger, Grilled Chicken & Cucumber, Steak Sandwich, Burrito Supremo, Platos con Dos Enchiladas (smothered in red or green chile & cheese). $

HILLSBORO ORCHARD & SWEETWOOD BAR-B-QUE, *Hillsboro, (505) 895-5642.* "Only brisket in the world smoked over apple wood," chicken, tofu with beans, homemade pies; under-orchard dining. $

Further Information

Black Range Business Association, *P.O. Box 152, Hillsboro, NM 88042 (505) 895-5686.*

Directions

From Albuquerque, I 25 south to exit 63, NM 152 west to Hillsboro/ Kingston.

Mesilla

Population 1, 975

The Mexican-American town of **Mesilla** (*little mesa*) nicely fits the romantic stereotype of the Old Southwest: a plaza, a mission-style church, and of course, old one-story adobe buildings that front directly on the street. Many of the buildings are the same that lined the streets nearly a century and a half ago. Thanks to a zoning ordinance, the original scale of the town and the architectural character of the buildings are carefully preserved.

Also known as *La Mesilla* and *Old Mesilla*, Mesilla has a history that even Hollywood would have difficulty matching: Apache attacks, shootings, the trial of Billy the Kid, cockfights, caravans on the **Chihuahua Trail**, the ratification of the Gadsden Purchase (1854), arrivals and departures of the **Butterfield Overland Mail and Stage Line**. Prospering as a transportation center on a major route to the West Coast, and as a supply center for ranching and mining operations, Mesilla grew from a small settlement in the late 1840s to the largest town between San Antonio and San Diego in the 1880s. Then the inevitable happened: The railroad went to Las Cruces instead of Mesilla. Mesilla was left to wither.

San Albino Church, originally built in 1855 and rebuilt in 1906, overlooks the **plaza**. The church offers masses in Spanish as well as English. Many of the adobe buildings about the plaza now house galleries, boutiques, unique shops, and restaurants (see below). The plaza area is where strolling, shopping, and sightseeing all blend together. The shops offer an excellent selection of Indian and Southwestern handmade jewelry, Kachinas, and Southwestern art and fashions.

About three blocks off the plaza is the **Gadsden Museum**, a house museum shown by guided tour. The museum features possessions, including the famous Gadsden Purchase painting, of the Albert Jennings Fountain family, a family prominent in Mesilla Valley history.

Special Features

During harvest time, chiles, melons, tomatoes, and other produce can be bought at roadside stands along **NM 28** (south) and other highways in the **Rio Grande Valley**.

Nearby **Las Cruces** has two interesting historic districts of its own. The streets of the **Mesquite Street Original Townsite Historic District** are lined with traditional adobe houses tinted with pastels or left in natural shades of beige. Turn-of-the-century houses and other buildings displaying a range of architectural styles, including Spanish-Pueblo Revival and Mission Revival, occupy the **Alameda Depot Historic District**.

> · *The Mesilla Valley is known throughout New Mexico for its chiles. Strings of red chiles, called "ristras," are often hung for decoration.*
> · *The wooden beams that support the roofs of adobe buildings are "vigas." The vigas, exposed on the ceiling, are an important element in New Mexican interior decoration.*

Where to Stay

HILLTOP HACIENDA B&B, *2600 Westmoreland (Las Cruces), (505) 382-3556*. Spanish/Moorish home on 20 acres with panoramic views, antiques & art, phones, private baths, full breakfasts, pets, verandahs & patios, gardens. $$

LUNDEEN'S INN OF THE ARTS, *618 S. Alameda Blvd. (Las Cruces), (505) 526-3327.* 1890 Mexican-Territorial inn adjoining large fine art gallery, vast great room with Jacobean-style furniture, some private baths, full breakfasts, beverages, library, some pets, highly rated. $$ to $$$

MESON DE MESILLA, *P.O. Box 1212, 1803 Avenida de Mesilla, (505) 525-9212/(800) 732-6025/fax (505) 527-4196.* Southwestern adobe inn in peaceful setting, private baths, "gourmet" breakfasts, restaurant, some pets, pool, bicycles. $$ to $$$

Where to Eat

DOUBLE EAGLE RESTAURANT, *on the plaza, (505) 523-6700.* Southwestern & Mexican entrees, dining "amidst the splendor of beautiful antiques." $

EL PATIO RESTAURANTE Y CANTINA, *on the plaza, (505) 524-0982.* "Combining traditional Mexican recipes with innovative New Mexican cuisine," rooms around courtyard once occupied by Mexican customs house. $

LA POSTA RESTAURANT, *just off plaza, (505) 524-3524.* "Serving Mexican food since 1939," in old Butterfield Stage Bldg., a favorite. $

MESON DE MESILLA, *(see above), (505) 525-2380.* "European cooking with a Southwestern flair": Chateaubriand Bouquetiere, Ostrich Black Pepper Steak, Atlantic Salmon Filet, Duck Bigarrade. $$$ (prix fixe)

Further Information

Las Cruces Convention & Visitors Bureau, *211 N. Water St., Las Cruces, NM 88001 (800) 343-7827; also,* **Old Mesilla Association**, *P.O. Box 1005, Mesilla, NM 88046.*

Directions

From El Paso (TX), I 10 north to exit 140 (Las Cruces), NM 28 south to La Mesilla.

Taos

Population 6, 213

Taos is a delightful alternation between ambiance and art. The alternation is almost literal, with attention swinging between strolls along adobe streets and visits to world-class galleries. The ambiance is itself only one step away from art. The walled gardens with their hollyhocks, arched entries, and antique wooden doors have been the subjects of thousands of paintings and watercolors. An old adobe house with blue window frames and sashes and potted pink geraniums can bring out the artist in anyone.

There's more even than the ambiance to induce the artist, however. There are the mountains, always changing in hue and brightness, and mesas, rivers, and forests whose beauty seems only to increase with each change in season. Then there's that New Mexico light, with its special purity. Mix all of this together with the creative traditions of New Mexico's three principal cultures – Native American, Hispanic, and Anglo – and you have one of the world's major art centers.

Taos has 80 plus art galleries! Work varies from traditional to contemporary, and from the pure to the blended and interbred. In one shop you'll find pottery with intricate geometrical decoration from the Acoma pueblo, in the next will be handcrafted contemporary jewelry with shapes and colors defying any description beyond "Southwestern" and "spectacular."

Top exhibits of Taos's art history can be found in the **Millicent Rogers Museum** and the **Harwood Foundation Museum**. The former is distinguished by its collection of Southwestern native American jewelry, textiles, pottery, kachina dolls, painting, and basketry. The latter is operated by the University of New Mexico and features works by Taos artists from 1898 to the present. Two other superb art collections are displayed in the **Fechin Institute**, the historic home of Russian emigre artist Nicolai Fechin, and the **Ernest Blumenschein Home and Museum**, built in the 1700s and furnished as it was when the artist lived there (1919 to 1960).

The new **Van Vechten-Lineberry Taos Art Museum** is a state-of-the-art museum intended to "keep the history of Taos art in Taos" by housing the largest collection of works by Taos Founders in the world. The structure carries the architectural theme of the 1929 studio that forms the main entrance.

The exhibits of the **Kit Carson House and Museum**, a National Historic Landmark, chronicle the history of Taos as well as the life of the legendary Kit Carson. The house was built in 1825 and has exposed ceiling beams (*vigas*) and 30-inch adobe walls. Some of the rooms are furnished in period style.

The massive adobe buttresses of the **San Francisco de Asis Church** (early 1700s) have made the church a popular subject for many artists, including Georgia O'Keeffe. The beautiful interior is famous for its Spanish religious carvings.

Nearby **Taos Ski Valley**, **Red River**, **Sipapu**, and **Angel Fire** offer some of the finest skiing in the U.S.

Special Features

The period rooms of the **Hacienda de Martinez** (circa 1804) open onto two courtyards (*placitas*). As a visit here will show, Spanish Colonial haciendas were self-sufficient villages surrounded by windowless walls to protect against occasional Comanche and Apache raids.

The **Taos Pueblo** is one of Taos's, and indeed the country's, top sites. Composed of multi-story adobe buildings, the pueblo is the finest example of Pueblo architecture anywhere and has inspired the Pueblo Revival style now popular throughout the Southwest. Centuries old and now a World Heritage Site, the pueblo is still inhabited.

> *Contemporary Taos cooking is a creative blend of Mexican, Southwestern Spanish, Continental, and California cuisines.*

Where to Stay

BROOKS STREET INN, *P.O. Box 4954, (800), 758-1489/(505) 758-1489*. Adobe houses with shady walled garden, antiques & art, fireplaces, private baths, full breakfasts with espresso bar, refreshments. $$$

CASA DE LAS CHIMENEAS B&B INN, *P.O. Box 5303, (505) 758-4777*. Adobe home in lush garden setting, fireplaces, TV & phones, private baths, "gourmet" breakfasts, hor d'oeuvres, highly rated. $$$

INN ON LALOMA PLAZA, *P.O. Box 4159, (800) 530-3040*. Walled hacienda on National Register, original art, handcrafted furniture, fireplaces, private baths, "gourmet" breakfasts, patios & fountains. $$$

ORINDA, *P.O. Box 4451, (505) 758-8581*. Old hacienda with mountain views, suites with kiva fireplaces & private entrances, "healthy" breakfasts. $$$

SALSA DEL SALTO, *P.O. Box 1468 (El Prado 87529), (505) 776-2422/ (800) 530-3097*. Convenient to Taos Ski Valley, down comforters, private baths, "gourmet" breakfasts, 2-story stone fireplace, tennis, pool. $$$

Where to Eat

APPLE TREE, *123 Bent St., (505) 758-1900*. Red Curry, Chicken & Chipotle Pasta, Grilled Filet Mignon, Vegetarian Mango Enchiladas; in old adobe house, courtyard, guitarist. $$

DOC MARTIN'S AT THE HISTORIC TAOS INN, *125 Paseo del Pueblo Norte, (505) 758-1977*. Shrimp Burrito, Southwest Lacquered Duck, Sweet Corn Cannelloni; in historic building, courtyard, fireplaces. $$ to $$$

JOSEPH'S TABLE, *4167 S. Santa Fe Rd. (Ranchos de Taos 87557), (505) 751-4512.* Crab & Littleneck Clam Risotto with Tomato & Saffron, Steak au Poivre, Grilled Quail on Polenta with Porcini Mushroom White Wine Sauce; white muslin tablecloths, candles. $$

LAMBERT'S OF TAOS, *309 Paseo del Pueblo Sur, (505) 758-1009.* Grilled Yellow Fin Tuna, Grilled Breast of Pheasant, Pan Roasted Pork Tenderloin; in historic building in landscaped setting, casually elegant. $$

ROBERTO'S RESTAURANT, *Kit Carson Rd., (505) 758-2434.* "Specializing in New Mexican Food for over 25 years," good recommendations. $

STAKEOUT GRILL & BAR, *4 mi S on NM 68, P.O. Box 453 (Ranchos de Taos), (505) 758-2042.* Stakeout Chicken Roll, Duck Cumberland, Sweetbreads Grenobloise, New York Strip, Salmon Gardini; spectacular views. $$ to $$$

Further Information

Taos County Chamber of Commerce, *P.O. Drawer I, Taos, NM 87571 (800) 732-8267.* **Note**: The new **Taos Visitor Center** on Paseo del Pueblo Sur is open seven days a week.

Directions

From Albuquerque, I 25 north to exit 282 (Santa Fe), US 84 north to Espanola, NM 68 north to Taos.

Other Charming New Mexico Towns

The Acoma Pueblo
Cimarron
Cloudcroft
Las Vegas
Lincoln
Ruidoso
San Felipe Pueblo

342

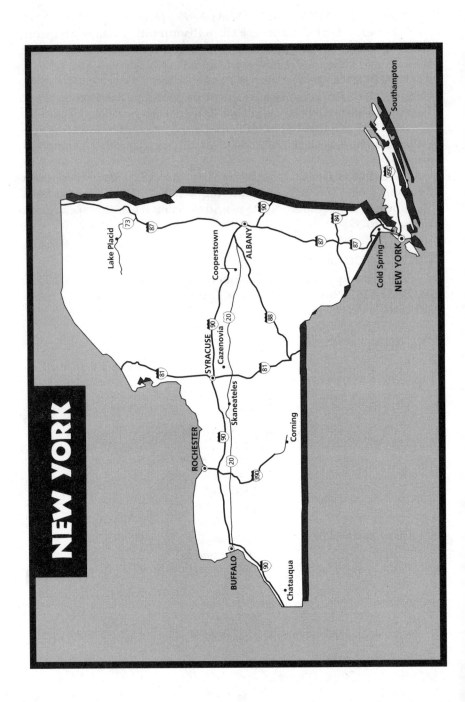

NEW YORK

Cazenovia

Population 3, 007

The similarity of **Cazenovia** to a scenic New England village is something visitors frequently note, especially as they drive down the hill and into town. Dating as far back as the early 1800s, the buildings downtown are of brick or stone with quaint contrasting white or cream door and window surrounds. Listed as a Historic District on the National Register, the downtown area is pure picture-postcard. Of special interest is **Lincklaen House** (ca 1835), one of the most gracious of the country's old inns (see listing below). Inside are high ceilings, carved moldings, Colonial chandeliers, and large fireplaces (visitors are welcome). The rest of the village, primarily residential, consists of stately old homes, tree-lined streets, and lovingly maintained lawns and gardens.

Lorenzo, just south of town, is a stately full front-gabled Adam mansion built in 1807. Preserved as the **Lorenzo State Historic Site**, the house has original furnishings, reproduction wallpapers & fabrics, formal garden, and magnificent views of the lake and surrounding hills.

Cazenovia's rolling setting is also very reminiscent of New England. The village is nestled at the foot of lovely **Cazenovia Lake**, popular with sailboaters. Country inns and cider mills dot the landscape. With winter comes first-class snowboarding and downhill and cross-country skiing (there are numerous groomed trails), and a little later, maple sugaring.

Special Features

At **Chittenango Falls State Park**, just four miles from town, the water plunges 167 feet over ledges and boulders.

One of the best ways to take in the local scenery is to make the 10-mile drive around Cazenovia Lake.

> *Many of Cazenovia's residents work in Syracuse, 25 hilly minutes away.*

Where to Stay

THE APPLE FARM B&B, *3073 E. Pompey Hollow Rd., (315) 655-8466.* 1835 Greek Revival farmhouse in apple orchard, private baths, tennis, trout fishing. $$

THE BRAE LOCH INN, *5 Albany St., (800) 722-0674.* Originally built 1805, Stickley furniture, tartan plaids, private baths, dining room, Scottish gift shop. $$ to $$$

THE BREWSTER INN, *6 Ledyard Ave., (315) 655-9232.* 1890 summer lake home of Standard Oil founder, full-service inn, antiques, 3 dining rooms, library, grounds, dockage. $$$

LINCKLAEN HOUSE, *79 Albany St., (315) 655-3461.* "Hospitality for more than 150 years," full-service inn, individually stenciled rooms, Cont. breakfasts, afternoon tea, President & Mrs. Cleveland among famous guests, dining room & courtyard restaurant, tavern. $$$

NOTLEYMERE COTTAGE, *4641 E. Lake Rd., (315) 655-9419 / (800) 704-4753 / fax (315) 655-8110.* 1888 Victorian Shingle mansion with turrets, arched balconies, & stained-glass windows; antiques, TV & phones, private baths, "hearty or light" breakfasts, lakeside verandah, gardens. $$$

Where to Eat

BREWSTER INN, *(see above).* Farm Raised Salmon Fillet with a Sesame Seed Crust, Tournedos of Beef Tenderloin on Artichoke Hearts; acclaimed. $$

LINCKLAEN HOUSE, *(see above).* Potato-Wrapped Salmon, Grilled Quail, Pan-Seared Filet Mignon; main dining room & flowered courtyard. $$

Further Information

Cazenovia Business Association, *P.O. Box 66, Cazenovia, NY 13035 (315) 655-9243/fax (315) 655-9244.*

Directions

From Syracuse, NY 92 southeast to Cazenovia.

Chautauqua

Population 350 to 10, 000

The **Chautauqua Institution** was founded on the shores of **Chautauqua Lake** in 1874 as a summer school for Sunday-school teachers. A pioneer in adult education, the institution soon expanded to include other summer schools. Along the way lodgings ranging from cottages to grand hotels were built to house students and a wide range of other visitors. Today Chautauqua Institution, a National Historic Landmark, is a self-contained Victorian village. The beautifully restored 1881 **Athenaeum Hotel** (see listing below) is one of the many buildings that in and of themselves would justify a visit here.

During the 9-week session, extending from late June to late August, admission is by gate ticket. In addition to the lodgings, the grounds are sprinkled with restaurants, shops, art galleries, a library, and a broad array of educational and recreational facilities. Many of the activities are designed for children as well as adults. The gate ticket is good for all events and activities except opera and theater performances (for which separate tickets must be purchased). Special 3-, 4-, and 7-night vacation and cultural packages that combine lodgings (American or European plan) and gate tickets are available by reservation.

The arts are represented by a symphony orchestra; opera, dance, and theater companies; chamber music concerts; art exhibits; film festivals; and concerts by popular entertainers. Dozens of 1-day, 1-week, 9-week, and other courses offer instruction in everything from sailing and investment to writing and piano. Also, distinguished speakers deliver lectures on such topics as philosophy, politics, and religion.

> *Admission to the grounds is open when the institution is not in session; many – but not all – of the hotels, restaurants, and other facilities are closed, however.*

Where to Stay

Note: The visitor may choose among a variety of accommodation options on Chautauqua's grounds – for information call (716) 357-6204.

THE ATHENAEUM, *P.O. Box 66, (800) 821-1881*. Restored Victorian hotel facing Chautauqua Lake, full service, tennis, golf. $$$

THE MAPLE SPRINGS LAKE SIDE INN, *4696 Chautauqua Ave. (Maple Springs 14756), (716) 386-2500*. Dutch Colonial mansion fronting on lake, private beach & dock, 11 acres of grounds.

PLUMBUSH B&B, *P.O. Box 864, (716) 789-5309*. Circa 1865 home on 125 acres, private baths, music room with piano & organ, less than mile to Chautauqua. $$$

SPINDLETOP B&B, *Polo Dr. off East Ave. (Greenhurst 14742), (716) 484-2070*. Old home on lake, "comfy" comforters, private baths, dock, heated pool, croquet. $$

STUART MANOR B&B, *4351 W. Lake Rd. (Mayville 14757), (716) 789-9902*. On 3 acres at Prendergast Point, private baths, full "delightful" breakfasts, hot tub. $$

WESTFIELD HOUSE, *E. Main Rd., P.O. Box 505 (Westfield 14787)*, *(716) 326-6262*. 1840 homestead, private baths, full breakfasts with fine china & silver, refreshments. $$ to $$$

THE WILLIAM SEWARD INN, *S. Portage Rd. (Westfield 14787), (716) 326-4151/fax (716) 326-4163*. Circa 1837 Greek Revival mansion with period furnishings, private baths, full breakfasts, dinner by advance reservation, refreshments, library. $$$

Where to Eat

ATHENAEUM HOTEL, *(see above)*. Classic American cuisine, coat & tie, elegant. $$$

HOT ROCK CAFE, *on institution grounds*, *(716) 357-5383*. Meals served on heated rocks. $

(**Tally Ho** and the **Festival Market** are two more of the several restaurants serving Chautauqua's grounds.)

Further Information

Chautauqua Institution, *Chautauqua, NY 14722 (800) 836-2787*; or **Chautauqua County Visitors Bureau**, *4 North Erie St., Mayville, NY 14757*.

Directions

From Buffalo, I 90 south to exit 60, NY 394 east to Chautauqua.

Cold Spring
Population 1, 998

If you take the Hudson Railroad north from New York City along the Hudson River, you'll soon enter a region where the river and the Appalachian Mountains meet. Along an especially beautiful stretch of the river in this region, about 50 miles from Manhattan, the train stops at **Cold Spring**, one of the most picturesque little towns in the **Hudson Valley**.

Main Street is flanked by shade trees and an array of charming 19th-century storefronts. There are more than a dozen shops catering to collectors and lovers of antiques and memorabilia. There are also shops selling books, chocolates, nautical gifts, handcrafted jewelry, hand-knitted Irish sweaters, dried flowers, gourmet foods, and unique clothing. There are also some good pubs. And Cold Spring, neighboring **Garrison**, and the surrounding region are renowned for their excellent restaurants (see sample below).

Cold Spring was a foundry town during the Revolutionary and Civil Wars. A variety of exhibits from those and other days in the town's history are on display in the **Foundry School Museum** – an 1850s schoolhouse and museum of the **Putnam County Historical Society**.

Just south of town and with a sweeping view of the Hudson is **Boscobel** (1804), a fully restored and outstanding example of New York Federal domestic architecture. Inside the house is a superb collection of Federal furniture and decorations (guided tours). On the grounds are an herb garden, orangerie, and rose garden.

Nature enthusiasts are drawn to Cold Spring for several reasons. One of them is the **Constitution Marsh Wildlife Sanctuary**, operated by the National Audubon Society, south of town (canoe tours available). Another is the **Manitoga Nature Preserve**, an 80-acre nature center with beautiful woodlands and waterfalls (self-guided tours). Hikes along country roads and cruises on the **Hudson River** (from **West Point**) are also great ways to enjoy the area's natural attractions.

Special Features

Four miles south of Cold Spring is **Garrison**, another charming Hudson River town – and one also served by the Hudson Railroad. The **Garrison Art Center** houses a gallery and schedules a variety of art classes.

The **United States Military Academy** at West Point is south of town across the river. West Point's Visitors Center offers tours of and information on the academy. The best way to reach West Point is via the Bear Mountain Bridge nine miles south of Cold Spring.

> *Cold Spring's name is believed to have originated with a reference to the local spring by General George Washington.*

Where to Stay

HUDSON HOUSE, *2 Main St., (914) 265-9355*. 163-year-old landmark on banks of Hudson, private baths, public dining room, porches overlooking river. $$ to $$$

ONE MARKET STREET, *1 Market St., (914) 265-3912*. Circa 1830 Federal bldg., private baths, attractive garden, central location. $$$

PIG HILL INN B&B, *73 Main St., (914) 265-9247/fax (914) 265-2155*. 1840s home, fireplaces, wood-burning stoves, some private baths, full breakfasts. $$$

Where to Eat

COLD SPRING DEPOT, *foot of Main St., (914) 265-2305*. Fresh seafood, Chicken Pot Pie, char-broiled steaks, homemade soups; Dixieland Jazz on lawn weekends. $ to $$

HENRY'S ON THE HUDSON, *184 Main St., (914) 265-3000.* Traditional dining in company of 150-year-old cherry bar, murals of Hudson Valley, old tin ceilings, and peanuts on slate floors. $$

HUDSON HOUSE, *(see above).* Fresh fish specials, Maryland-style Crab Cakes, Crispy Roast Long Island Duckling, Char-broiled New York Sirloin Steak. $$ to $$$

PLUMBUSH RESTAURANT & INN, *Rt. 9D, (914) 265-3904.* Continental cuisine, fresh fish, live brook trout, Swiss Apple Fritters a specialty; reservations required. $$$

RIVERVIEW RESTAURANT, *45 Fair St., (914) 265-4778.* Italian cuisine, fresh pasta & seafood, Wood-fired Brick Oven Pizza; outdoor dining with river & mountain views. $ to $$

Further Information

Cold Spring/Garrison Area Chamber of Commerce, *Box 342, Cold Spring-on-Hudson, NY 10516; also,* **The Putnam County News & Recorder**, *86 Main St., Cold Spring, NY (914) 265-2468.* **Note**: Don't confuse with the town of Cold Spring Harbor on Long Island's north shore!

Directions

From New York City, US 9 north to Cold Spring (across from West Point).

Cooperstown
Population 2, 500

At latest count the **Cooperstown** area had about 73 bed-and-breakfast inns, possibly the largest number per capita in the country. Some overlook the shores of beautiful **Otsego Lake**, others grace the geranium-laden streets of the historic district, and yet others are tucked along the winding roads and creeks of the surrounding countryside. They cater to every budget, mood, and personality, and vary from quaint cottages to working farms to Victorian mansions. And they exist for good reason, for even without its lake, rolling hills, forests, and lovely old farms, Cooperstown's arts calendar and world-class sights would make the little town one of the most charming and interesting resorts in the United States.

As with the bed and breakfasts, Cooperstown probably has the largest number of museums per capita in the country. The "Big Three" are the **National Baseball Hall of Fame and Museum**, the **Farmers' Museum**, and the **Fenimore House Museum**.

The **Hall of Fame** was founded in 1939 to honor the game's heroes and to serve as the game's historian by assembling, preserving, and displaying information and memorabilia. More than 6,000 items are on display. A multi-media show is presented continuously in the museum's new 200-seat theater.

The **Fenimore House** (1930s), a grand columned mansion on the shore of Lake Otsego, has three floors of galleries featuring outstanding collections of folk, academic, and decorative arts. There is also a gallery displaying memorabilia associated with novelist and social critic James Fenimore Cooper. A new wing houses the **Eugene and Clare Thaw Collection of American Indian Art**, one of the finest in the country. The Fenimore House is home to the museum and offices of the **New York State Historical Association**.

Life in rural upstate New York between the Revolutionary and Civil Wars is recalled by the buildings, artifacts, and craft demonstrations of the **Farmers' Museum**. Included on the picturesque grounds of the museum complex are the **Main Barn** and the **Village Crossroads**, a collection of buildings comprising a general store, druggist, church, tavern, working farm, and other historic structures.

Cooperstown's other museums include the **American Baseball Experience**, the only baseball wax museum in the country, and the **Fly Creek Cider Mill** (ca 1856), a water-powered mill that uses equipment dating from the late 19th and early 20th centuries.

Everything from jazz to chamber music is performed by top artists during the winter season (ending in December) of the **Cooperstown Concert Series**. In the summer there is the renowned **Glimmerglass Opera**. The visual arts are represented by shows at the **Cooperstown Art Association**, **Gallery 53 Artworks**, and the **Smithy-Pioneer Gallery** (in Cooperstown's oldest building, 1786), as well as by numerous fine craft, antique, and gift shops on Main Street.

Cooperstown's recreational options include bicycle tours, water sports on Lake Otsego, challenging golf, and of course, fun at one of the baseball games or batting ranges. The **Clark Sports Center** includes a complete gymnasium, swimming and diving pools, bowling alleys, racquetball courts, and rock climbing wall.

Because parking in Cooperstown is limited, consider parking in a perimeter parking area (free) and riding the trolley about town.

Special Features

At **Glimmerglass State Park** on the north side of the lake is **Hyde Hall** (1817/1835), a 50-room mansion with two grand public rooms, two libraries, two kitchens, and several dozen other rooms. Although undergoing restoration, the mansion is open weekends and by special tour at other times.

The **Cherry Valley Museum** (1832) in the historic village of **Cherry Valley** northeast of Cooperstown features a unique collection of local memorabilia.

> • *Cooperstown was founded by and named after the father of James Fenimore Cooper.*
> • **Almost 400, 000 visit the National Baseball Hall of Fame each year.**

Where to Stay

ANGELHOLM, *P.O. Box 705, (607) 547-2483.* 1805 Federal home, private baths, full breakfasts, afternoon tea, formal flower gardens, on quiet side street in heart of town. $$$

THE BASSETT HOUSE INN, *32 Fair St., (607) 547-7001.* 1816 brick Federal home, antiques, TV, private baths, American clock collection, 1895 billiard table, across street from Baseball Hall of Fame. $$$

GREEN APPLE INN, *81 Lake St., (607) 547-1080.* Colonial Revival home, private baths, full "gourmet" breakfasts, guest living room, gardens. $$$

THE INN AT COOPERSTOWN, *16 Chestnut St.-CB, (607) 547-5756.* 1874 hotel in heart of historic district, private baths, Cont. breakfasts, recipient of preservation awards. $$$

THE J.P. SILL HOUSE, *63 Chestnut St., (607) 547-2633.* 1864 Italianate house in historic district, marble fireplaces, original antiques, down comforters, full breakfasts, on spacious grounds. $$$

NINETEEN CHURCH STREET B&B, *19 Church St., (607) 547-8384.* Circa 1820 home in central location, private baths, full breakfasts, painted murals. $$$

THISTLEBROOK B&B, *RD 1 (Box 26), (800) 596-9305.* Converted 1866 barn overlooking valley, American & European antiques, private baths, full breakfasts. $$$

TOAD HALL, THE B&B, *RD 1 (Box 120) (Fly Creek 13337), (607) 547-5774.* 1820s stone farmhouse on 80 acres, antiques & art, private baths, "hearty" breakfasts. $$$

Where to Eat

THE 1819 HOUSE, *South of town on County 11, (607) 547-1819.* Gulf Shrimp Stuffed with Atlantic Blue Crab, Three Grain Risotto with Smoked Duck Breast, 1819 Surf and Turf. $$

BLUE MINGO GRILL, *P. O. Box 190, (607) 547-2543*. Blackboard menu featuring grilled fresh fish, beef; on Adirondack porch overlooking Lake Otsego, recommended. $$

COOPERSTOWN DINER, *136 1/2 Main St., (607) 547-9201*. Huge hamburgers, onion chips, breakfast all day. $

THE HAWKEYE BAR & GRILL *(in Otesaga Hotel), P.O. Box 311, (607) 547-9931*. American entrees from grill served in English pub atmosphere, respected. $$

ROSE & KETTLE RESTAURANT, *4 Lancaster St. (Cherry Valley), (607) 264-3078*. Seafood, poultry, meat; everything prepared on premises in circa 1810 family home, roses, chef-owned, reservations recommended. $ to $$

Further Information

Cooperstown Chamber of Commerce, *31 Chestnut St., Cooperstown, NY 13326 (607) 547-9983/fax (607) 547-6006*.

Directions

From Albany, US 20 west to NY 80, NY 80 south to Cooperstown.

Corning
Population 11, 938

Corning receives high points on the ideal-American-hometown dimension. First, nestled on the banks of the **Chemung River** and surrounded by the rolling woodland of southwestern New York, the town has a scenic setting. Second, home to the headquarters of two Fortune 500 companies, it also has a sound economic base. And third, Corning has an active downtown/historic district and a town plan that encourages walking. The car is often left home, and sidewalk visiting and old-fashioned friendliness are the beneficiaries.

The **Market Street Historic District** is a four-block area of fine old commercial buildings that have been restored to a late 19th-century appearance. The district's brick sidewalks are lined with shade trees and a colorful collection of specialty shops, restaurants, antique stores, and – in case the visitor forgets this is Corning – glass-blowing shops. There's also a restored 1880 ice cream parlor and the beautiful new **Riverfront Park** (a gift of Corning, Incorporated).

One of Corning's (and New York's) top attractions is the **Corning Glass Center**. The center depicts all aspects of glass, including its history, uses, manufacture, and service as an art form. The center comprises the incomparable **Corning Museum of Glass**, the **Hall of Science and Industry**, the **Steuben Glass Factory**, and several retail shops. (tours)

The **Rockwell Museum**, another top attraction, is housed in an historic Romanesque Revival building. The museum has superb collections of American Western art, Carder Steuben glass, and antique toys. Films and changing exhibitions are also featured.

Centering more on local and regional history, the **Benjamin Patterson Inn Museum Complex** boasts an impressive collection of restored structures. Foremost among them is the furnished 1796 **Benjamin Patterson Inn**, a former stagecoach stop. Others include the log **DeMonstoy Cabin** (1784), the authentically furnished one-room **Browntown School** (1878), and a replica of the 1868 **Starr Barn**.

In the summer months daily performances of the **Mark Twain Musical Drama** are held just a few minutes away. The spectacular production's music and dancing celebrate the life and writings of the much-loved author. (Twain wrote *Adventures of Huckleberry Finn* and several other works while residing at a nearby farm.)

Special Feature

The **National Soaring Museum**, located between Corning and Elmira, focuses on aviation history. Featured are the country's largest glider and sailplane collection, a cockpit mockup, and films on soaring. A glider field and scenic overlook are adjacent.

> • *The Corning area is one of the best in the country for soaring.*
> • *Much of today's Corning is the result of a major reconstruction effort undertaken after the devastating flood of 1972.*

Where to Stay

"1865" WHITE BIRCH B&B, *69 E. First St., (607) 962-6355*. 1865 home, antiques, some private baths, full breakfasts, common room with TV & games, short walk to Market Street. $$

ADDISON ROSE B&B, *37 Maple St. (Addison 14801), (607) 359-4650*. Queen Anne home, period furnishings, full breakfasts, afternoon tea on verandah. $$

DELEVAN HOUSE, *188 Delevan Ave., (607) 962-2347*. Southern Colonial home in quiet surroundings, full breakfasts, cold summer drinks, airport pick-up. $$ to $$$

ROSEWOOD INN, *134 E. First St., (607) 962-3253.* 1855 home, fine antiques, private baths, "gourmet" breakfasts served in Victorian wood-paneled dining room. $$$

Where to Eat

BLOSSOM'S, *at Lodge-on-the-Green, US 15 & NY 417 (Painted Post), (607) 962-2456.* American cuisine served in beautiful setting. $$

BOOMERS' BISTRO, *58 W. Market St., (607) 936-1408.* Broad family menu with seafood, chicken, beef, pasta, pizza, Oriental, & Mexican offerings; English pub atmosphere. $

LONDON UNDERGROUND CAFE, *69 E. Market St., (607) 962-2345.* European & American menu, fresh seafood, "desserts to die for"; unique three-level seating, London Underground art. $$

MARKET STREET BREWING CO. & RESTAURANT, *63-65 W. Market St., (607) 936-2337.* Pasta Melange, Baked Rainbow Trout, Baron Steuben Steak, Seared Duck Breast, good selection of sandwiches & salads; 6 fresh brews, rooftop seating, biergarten. $$

PELHAM'S UPSTATE TUNA CO. RESTAURANT, *73 E. Market St., (607) 936-8862.* Grilled seafood, poultry, & meat; pasta dishes; over 100 beers/wines, kids' menu, in historic bldg. $$

Further Information

Corning Chamber of Commerce, *42 E. Market St., Corning, NY 14830 (607) 936-4686.*

Directions

From Rochester, I 390 south to NY 17, NY 17 east to Corning.

Lake Placid
Population 2, 485

Host to the Olympic Winter Games of 1932 and 1980, and situated among the hills and lakes of the lovely **Adirondacks**, **Lake Placid** is a place of scenery and spectacular sports facilities. **Main Street's** sophisticated shops and restaurants add a cosmopolitan air. Yet the charm of Lake Placid only begins with the setting. For arising from the sports complexes, and echoed by the hillsides, is the nostalgic kind of charm that comes with grand memories, memories of gold-medal achievements and cheers and national anthems.

Lake Placid is as complex as its charm. There are many Lake Placids, and all have to be sampled if the town is to be known. Each sports facility is its own village. Even the lake is too complex to be grasped by a glance. Unless you have time to spare, take some kind of organized tour. The bus tours are good, the 1-hour narrated boat cruise wins raves from visitors, and the **Lake Placid Olympic Site Tour** (sponsored by Eastman Kodak Company) offers a convenient, comprehensive self-guided motor tour of the sports complexes. For a geographical overview, scan the region from a scenic flight.

One of the most active of the sports complexes is the **U.S. Olympic Training Center**, where visitors are free to watch as athletes from all over the country train. The **Olympic Center**, another complex open to visitors, is the largest indoor ice facility in the world. Figure skaters, hockey players, and speed skaters train on the center's rinks. At the **Olympic Jumping Complex** even watching can be breathtaking as athletes train on the 70- and 90-meter ski jumps . Training takes place all year, with plastic matting replacing snow in the warmer months.

The **Lake Placid Sinfonietta** concerts, held weekly during the summer, are among the most popular of Lake Placid's many cultural events.

Special Feature

On a clear day the summit of **Whiteface Mountain** offers one of the most spectacular panoramic views in the country. Drive the 5-mile **Whiteface Mountain Veterans Memorial Highway** (in **Wilmington**) to the parking area near the summit, then complete the climb by a short hike or by a unique elevator ride through the heart of the mountain.

> *The internationally famous figure skater Sonya Henie won a gold medal in 1932 for her performance in the Olympic Center.*

Where to Stay

ADIRONDAK LOJ, *Adirondak Loj Rd., P.O. Box 867, (518) 523-3441.* Lodge in wilderness setting at trail head (since 1890), family-style dinners available, back country information & lectures, packages. $

BLACKBERRY INN, *59 Sentinel Rd., (518) 523-3419.* Comfortable old home, flannel sheets, private baths, full breakfasts, common room with piano, car plug-ins. $$

HIGHLAND HOUSE HIDEAWAY, *3 Highland Pl., (518) 523-2377.* Centrally located 1-bedroom cottage rented as unit. $$ to $$$

INTERLAKEN INN, *15 Interlaken Ave., (518) 523-3180/(800) 428-4369*. Victorian-style country inn, private baths, full "country" breakfasts, afternoon tea, restaurant. $$ to $$$

MOUNTAIN HEARTH INN, *338 Old Military Rd., (518) 523-1114*. 19th-century farmhouse, full breakfasts, mountain views. $$ to $$$

STAGECOACH INN, *370 Old Military Rd., (518) 523-9474*. "Guests welcomed since 1833," antiques & Indian art, some private baths, full breakfasts, birch-trimmed fireplaces, highly rated. $$ to $$$

WILLKOMMEN HOF, *NY 86 (Wilmington 12997), (800) 541-9119*. European-style guesthouse, German cooking, sitting room with fireplace & piano. $ to $$

Where to Eat

ALPINE CELLAR, *E on NY 86, (518) 523-2180*. Authentic Swiss & German dishes, imported beers. $$

CASCADE INN, *Cascade Rd., NY 73, (518) 523-2130*. Chicken Francese, Mixed English Grill, 20 oz Boneless Jumbo Steak, Linguine Marinara, good seafood selection. $ to $$

INTERLAKEN INN, *(see above)*. Regional Continental cuisine, changing prix fixe menu, highly recommended, reservations required. $$$

JIMMY'S 21, *Main St., (518) 523-2353*. Italian-American menu, fresh seafood, "scrumptious" desserts. $$

LAKE PLACID LODGE, *Whiteface Inn Rd., (518) 523-2573*. Grilled Rainbow Trout, Chicken Parmentiere, Entrecote Bordelaise; views, reservations advised. $$ to $$$

Further Information

Lake Placid Convention & Visitors Bureau, *Olympic Center, Lake Placid, NY 12946 (800) 447-5224*.

Directions

From Albany, I 87 north to exit 30, NY 73 northwest to Lake Placid.

Skaneateles

Population 2, 724

Skaneateles (pronounced scan ee AT las) lies at the top of a gorgeous lake by the same name. The village and the lake complement each another, the one enhancing the already remarkable beauty of the other.

Skaneateles's **downtown** is an historic district containing numerous brick buildings constructed in 1835 to replace wooden structures destroyed in a fire. Brick-lined sidewalks and cast-iron lampposts complete the scene to produce something out of an old photo album. Trees, hanging floral arrangements, and hand-painted storefronts give the photo color. Proud of the beauty and vitality of the downtown, the village has been successful so far in keeping shopping malls at bay.

In the surrounding neighborhoods are faithfully restored and landscaped homes dating from the early 1800s onward. Here as well as downtown, the streets are notable for the attention given to maintenance, cleanliness, and historic authenticity.

Skaneateles Lake is one of the most beautiful and popular of New York's **Finger Lakes**. The 16 x 1 1/2-mile lake has crystal-clear water, with a through-the-water visibility of 25 feet (the lake has New York's highest water-quality rating). The lake is ideal for virtually all water sports, including scuba diving. The village has two waterfront parks, one for swimming and one for enjoying the scenery.

Special Feature

Sightseeing, lunch, Sunday brunch, and dinner **cruises** (see below) offer one way to tour the lake. Driving tours around the lake offer another—check with the Chamber of Commerce for itinerary suggestions.

Woven among the Finger Lakes of central New York is some of the most beautiful countryside in the nation. Whenever possible, got off the main highways and explore it.

Friday-evening gazebo concerts and Sunday-afternoon polo matches form part of Skaneateles's entertainment calendar.

Where to Stay

EVERGREEN MANOR B&B, *98 W. Genesee St., (315) 685-6829.* 1815 Early Classical Revival home, once safe house on Underground Railroad, private baths available, full "gourmet" breakfasts, near shops & lake. $$

THE GRAY HOUSE B&B, *47 Jordan St., (315) 685-0131.* 1909 home, antiques, private baths, large parlors, walking distance to shops & lake. $$

LADY OF THE LAKE, *2 W. Lake St., (315) 685-7997/(888) 685-7997.* Turn-of-century Queen Anne home, antiques & Oriental rugs, comforters, private baths, full breakfasts weekends/Cont. breakfasts weekdays. $$$

MILLARD'S AT THE SUMMIT RESTAURANT & B&B, *1715 E. Lake Rd., (315) 673-2254.* Old home with panoramic view of lake, full breakfasts, restaurant/tavern downstairs. $$

SHERWOOD INN, *26 W. Genesee St., (315) 685-3405.* 1860s stage-coach stop, full-service, antiques, opposite beach, two restaurants. $$ to $$$

Where to Eat

DOUG'S FISH FRY, *8 Jordan St., (315) 685-3288.* Casual dining on indoor & outdoor picnic tables, very popular. $

KREBS, *53 W. Genesee St., (315) 685-5714.* "All-you-can-eat" served family style, no printed menus, regionally renowned. $$$

MID-LAKES NAVIGATION CO., LTD., *11 Jordan St., P.O. Box 61, (315) 685-8500/(800) 545-4318.* Champagne dinner, Sunday brunch, & luncheon cruises on Skaneateles Lake aboard double-decked & classic wooden cruisers. $$$ (including cruise)

SHERWOOD INN, *(see above).* American menu offering seafood, chicken, steaks, prime rib, pastas; tavern dining available. $ to $$

Further Information

Skaneateles Chamber of Commerce, *P.O. Box 199, Skaneateles, NY 13152 (315) 685-0552.*

Directions

From Syracuse, I 81 south to exit 15, US 20 west to Skaneateles.

Southampton
Population 4, 023 (village)

Esteemed for decades as a resort of the celebrated and very wealthy, **Southampton** is renowned for its grand estates and beautiful beaches. Although once thought of as a summer beach colony, the village has become a "community for all seasons," offering a wide range of recreational activities, shops, restaurants, and cultural outlets. The year-round population has increased as various professional people have been drawn by the area's successful marriage of cultural sophistication and natural beauty. Reminding that this is still resort territory, however, the population swells during the summer months when thousands flock to enjoy the trendy, affluent, and artsy mood that represents the summer "Hamptons."

The **Southampton Historical Museum** comprises a number of sites, including **Captain Rogers' Homestead**, a grand two-story whaling captain's house (1843). The house's exhibits include a sea captain's living room and bedroom, a Colonial bedroom, Indian relics, and antique toys, costumes, china, etc. Among the displays on the grounds are a furnished one-room schoolhouse, a carriage shop, a post office and country store housed in a pre-Revolutionary barn, and a village street from a century ago.

The restored **Old Halsey Homestead** (1648), another of the museum's possessions, is Southampton's oldest surviving house, and indeed the oldest English frame house in New York State. The house contains authentic 17th- and 18th-century furnishings. Outside is a Colonial herb garden and border gardens.

Yet another structure belonging to the historical museum is the restored **Elias Pelletreau Silversmith Shop** (circa 1750). Pieces of Pelletreau silver, very rare, are highly valued by collectors of early American silver.

The **Parrish Art Museum** (1898), housed in a handsome Italianate structure, features 19th- and 20th-century American art, collections by William Merritt Chase and Fairfield Porter (two renowned artists/residents of Southampton), Renaissance pieces, and other works. The permanent collection includes more than 2,000 pieces.

The shingled **St. Andrew's Dune Church** was originally a Life Saving Station built by the U.S. Government (in 1851). A church since 1879, the building's walls and windows have beautifully inscribed Biblical passages. On the grounds are remnants of old shipwrecks.

Southampton boasts many sophisticated boutiques, art and craft galleries, and gourmet food shops. It is also home to the country's oldest department store, **Hildreth's** (established 1842). The Southampton region (and the southern coast of Long Island in general) is blessed with miles of beautiful beaches and dunes. Beach access can be a problem, however, so check in advance with an innkeeper or the Chamber of Commerce.

The Southampton area harbors attractive farms that abound with vegetables and fruits. Eastern Long Island is rapidly becoming an influential wine region and Southampton has several vineyards that offer tours, tastings, and sales. The region is ideal for hiking, biking, and rollerblading (bike and Rollerblade rentals are available).

Lodging reservations are a must during the summer months and restaurant reservations are recommended (although some restaurants do not accept reservations during the summer months).

Special Features

Westhampton Beach, **Sag Harbor**, **East Hampton**, and other picturesque coastal towns are just a few miles away. Each presents its own unique view of the Hamptons.

The **Southampton Cultural Center** offers art education programs, children's activities, chamber-music concerts, and art exhibitions. Another cultural center, the **Bay Street Theatre** in Sag Harbor, stages literary readings, musical events, and plays throughout the year.

Several oceanside state parks are located at the eastern tip of Long Island, among them **Montauk Point State Park**, site of the 1795 **Montauk Lighthouse**.

> • *A locally published tour of antique shops and sources lists no fewer than 82 establishments!*
> • *Suffolk County is dotted with 18th- and 19th-century windmills. All are of English design.*

Where to Stay

CALDWELL'S CARRIAGE HOUSE, *519 Hill St., (516) 287-4720.* Carriage-house suite with private entrance, TV, 2 baths, kitchenette, garden with outdoor eating & grill facilities, near village & beach. $$$

MAINSTAY, *579 Hill St., (516) 283-4375.* 1870s guest house (once a country store), antique iron & brass beds, some private baths, pool, walking distance to village & beach. $$$

Where to Eat

75 MAIN, *75 Main St., (516) 283-7575.* American recipes with Asian, French, Southwestern, & Italian influences: Peppercorn Grilled Atlantic Salmon, Homemade Whole Wheat Angle Hair, Flourless Chocolate & Macadamia Nut Cake with Raspberry Coulis. $$$

BARRISTER'S, *36 Main St., (516) 283-6206.* Mesquite Grilled Chicken, Asparagus & Roma Tomato Ricotta Pie, Sliced Turkey with Spinach Leaves, Penne Pasta Pompadour, & Baked Flounder among daily lunch specials. $$

THE DRIVER'S SEAT, *62 Job's Ln., (516) 283-6606.* "Southampton's Meeting Place" serving Shrimp Scampi, Chicken Piccata, Prime Rib of Beef, Sliced Steak Sandwich, Barbecued Spare Ribs; tempting lunch menu. $$

FELLINGHAM'S RESTAURANT, *17 Cameron St., (516) 283-9417.* Sports bar featuring 17 kinds of burgers. $

JOHN DUCK JR., *N. Main St., (516) 283-0311.* Long-established eatery known for Long Island Duckling & German dishes; Our Famous Steak Sandwich, Sauteed L.I. Duck Livers, & Sauerbraten with Potato Pancakes among luncheon offerings. $$

LOBSTER INN, *162 Inlet Rd., (516) 283-9828*. Splat (lobster, snow crab, clams, steamers, mussels, & shrimp steamed together & served for two) a house specialty; casual waterfront setting. $$ to $$$

POST HOUSE RESTAURANT, *136 Main St., (516) 283-9696*. Continental cuisine, famed Sunday brunch, patio dining; in National Register bldg. dating to 1684. $$ to $$$

SOUTHAMPTON PUBLICK HOUSE, *52 North Sea Rd., (516) 283-2800*. Microbrewery restaurant listing Pan-seared Lemon Peppered Chicken Breasts, 18 oz. Boneless New York Sirloin, & Amber Battered Fried Shrimp among entrees. $$

Further Information

Southampton Chamber of Commerce, *76 Main St., Southampton, NY 11968 (516) 283-0402*.

Directions

From New York City, I 495 (Long Island Expwy.) east to Exit 70, south on Manorville/County Road 111 to NY 27, east past Southampton College to Southampton/North Sea Rd. exit, south to Main Street.

Other Charming New York Towns

Annandale-on-Hudson
East Hampton
Hammondsport
Rhinebeck
Wyoming

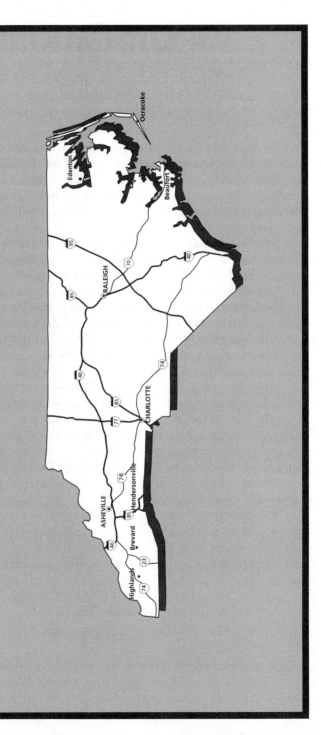

NORTH CAROLINA

Beaufort
Population 3808

Sometimes the sights are themselves active, and then sightseers need only linger passively by to enjoy them. And so it is along the old waterfront of the picturesque port and county seat of **Beaufort**. Sailboats bob at anchor or dock, dinghies and harbor cruise boats come and go, sailors talk of shrimping, restaurants smell of fresh seafood, and street musicians entertain.

Settled around 1710, and once the target of attack by pirates, Beaufort is North Carolina's third oldest town. Proud of their history, the people of the town have done much to preserve and restore their architectural heritage. As with the waterfront, much of the town's history can be enjoyed with little effort—the harbor area from the deck of a cruise boat, the streets from the seat of an English double-decker bus.

The **Beaufort Historic Site** comprises several restorations. One of the most prominent, the **Joseph Bell House** (circa 1767), provides an excellent example of early Beaufort architecture. The house has 18th-century furnishings. The **Josiah Bell House** (circa 1825), another restoration, has a beautiful side garden maintained by the Garden Club.

The oldest surviving public building in the county, the **Carteret County Courthouse** (1796), has authentic furnishings and boasts among its possessions an original thirteen-star American flag. Other restored structures include the circa 1829 **Carteret County Jail** and a circa 1859 **apothecary shop**. The **Safrit Historical Center** welcomes and orients visitors to the historic site.

The **North Carolina Maritime Museum**, one of Beaufort's top sites, displays boats and boat models, outstanding shell collections, and other exhibits concerned with the maritime and natural history of the North Carolina coastal region. The museum also offers field trips, lectures, and other programs.

Among the graves of the **Old Burying Grounds**, which date to 1731, are those of victims of the Indian Wars.

Special Feature

Wild herds of ponies, with ancestors dating back to Colonial times, are Beaufort's most novel attraction. **Carrot Island** and **Bird Shoals**, which form part of a nature reserve system and are visible from Beaufort's waterfront, are home to many species of birds, some endangered, as well as to the ponies. Check locally for information on ferry service to the sites.

> • *Ann and Queen Streets were named for Queen Anne, who ruled at the time the town was surveyed in 1713.*
> • *Hurricanes in the late 19th century eventually drove as many as 600 people from nearby Shackleford Banks, now part of the Cape Lookout National Seashore.*

Where to Stay

BEAUFORT INN, *101 Ann Street, (800) 726-0321.* Full-service contemporary inn (1986) on waterfront, "famous" breakfasts, bicycle & boat slip rentals. $$ to $$$

CAPTAINS' QUARTERS, *315 Ann St., (919) 728-7711/(800) 659-7111.* Turn-of-century home in quiet location, family heirlooms, private baths, full breakfasts, refreshments, verandah, 1 block from waterfront. $$ to $$$

THE CEDARS INN, *305 Front St., (800) 732-7036.* Circa 1768 home on harbor, antiques, private baths, full breakfasts, dining room, suites, rocking-chair porches. $$ to $$$

DELAMAR INN B&B, *217 Turner St., (919) 728-4300.* 1866 home, antiques, private baths, "delightful" breakfasts, upper porch, on historic homes tour. $$ to $$$

INLET INN B&B, *601 Front at Queen streets, (919) 728-3600.* Full-service contemporary inn on harbor, private porches, ceiling fans, views of Cape Lookout & Beaufort harbor. $$ to $$$

THE LANGDON HOUSE, *135 Craven St., (919) 728-5499.* Home dating to 1732, Colonial/Federal furnishings, private baths, Cont. or full breakfasts, original glass in windows, host an historian/guide/maitre d'. $$$

PECAN TREE INN, *116 Queen St., (919) 728-6733.* Mid 19th-century home with Victorian additions, antiques on pine floors, private baths, Cont. "plus" breakfasts, large English flower & herb garden. $$ to $$$

Where to Eat

BEAUFORT GROCERY CO., *117 Queen St., (919) 728-3899.* French cafe atmosphere with flowered tablecloths & "Beaufort Green" decor, own baking. $$

THE FRONT STREET GRILL, *419 Front St., (919) 728-3118.* New American bistro known for pasta & fresh seafood, paintings & sculpture by NC artists. $ to $$

HARPOON WILLIE'S, *500 Front St., (919) 728-5247*. Savory Shrimp, Crab Cakes Supreme, Soft Shell Crabs, Zoup of the Willy a must-try dish; overlooking waterfront. $$

LOUGHRY'S LANDING, *502 Front St., (919) 728-7541*. Fresh local seafood, prime rib, original salads, varied pastas. $ to $$

THE SPOUTER INN, *218 Front St., (919) 728-5190*. Rustic Grilled New York, Fried Chicken & Penne, Seafood Reunion, Lusty Crab Cakes; seasonal selections, good lunch menu, overlooking creek. $$

Further Information

Carteret County Tourism Development Bureau, *P.O. Box 1406, Morehead City, NC 28557 (800) 786-6962. (ZIP for Beaufort is 28516.)*

Directions

From Raleigh, US 70 southeast to Beaufort.

Brevard

Population 5, 388

Brevard (accent on second syllable) is the seat of **Transylvania County**, a place of thick forests and some of the highest mountains in the **Appalachians**. The mountains and forests give rise to trout-filled streams, and the streams tumble over waterfalls with names like **Looking Glass**, **Slippery Witch**, **Turtleback**, and **Horsepasture**. One of them, **Whitewater Falls**, is the tallest east of the Mississippi. The county is home to more than 250 waterfalls!

A major cultural center, Brevard adds its own kinds of beauty. The **Brevard Music Center** attracts talented musicians from around the world to its stage. Spotlighting the center's summer season are operas, operettas, musicals, pops concerts, chamber music, and performances by renowned soloists.

On Thursday evenings the sounds of bluegrass and original mountain music can be heard at **Silvermont**, an historic mansion. Contributing to the cultural calendar during the winter, spring, and fall are the **Brevard Little Theatre** and the **Brevard Chamber Orchestra**. Brevard is also home to **Brevard College**, which, as might be expected, has a respected music department.

In or near downtown are the 1851 brick courthouse (site of a summer art show) and a number of 19th-century homes, some of which offer lodging (see below). **Main Street** is known for its thriving specialty, antique, and craft shops. All sorts of crafts are practiced in the Brevard area, including weaving and quilt making. The handcrafted furniture is especially sought after.

Not far from town are more than 500 miles of hiking and biking trails that wind through mountains and along rivers and streams. The **French Broad River** is popular with canoers and kayakers. In the winter the **Blue Ridge Parkway** offers good cross-county skiing, and glorious scenery.

Special Feature

One of the county's most popular waterfalls, Sliding Rock, is a 150-foot natural water slide. About 11,000 gallons of cold water flow down the slide every minute.

Situated in the **Pisgah National Forest** is the **Cradle of Forestry**, the country's first forestry school. The restored turn-of-the-century campus is now a hands-on museum.

US 276 north of Brevard has been designated a Scenic Byway.

> • *Pisgah Forest, once owned by George Vanderbilt, was the country's first managed woodland.*
> • *Rare white squirrels may be seen scampering about in Brevard's city parks.*

Where to Stay

INN AT BREVARD, *410 E. Main St., (704) 884-2105.* Turn-of-century inn on National Register, antiques, private baths, full breakfasts, dining room. $$ to $$$

KEY FALLS INN, *Everett Rd. (2.5 miles from town), (704) 884-7559.* 1860s farmhouse, private baths, "sumptuous" breakfasts, porches, tennis, waterfall, mountain views. $$ to $$$

THE PINES COUNTRY INN, *719 Hart Rd. (Pisgah Forest 28768), (704) 877-3131.* Inn & four cabins/cottages on 12 acres of pine woods, private baths, full "country" breakfasts, optional dinners, open fireplace, verandah. $$

THE RED HOUSE INN, *412 W. Probart St., (704) 884-9349.* 1851 home with rich history, antiques, some private baths, full breakfasts, walking distance to downtown. $ to $$

RED LION INN, *US 178 (10 mi S of town), Star Rte. (Box 200, Rosman 28772), (704) 884-6868.* Verandah by mountain stream, large open fireplace, restaurant, hiking, fishing. $$ to $$$

SASSY GOOSE, *US 276 (12 miles from town)*, *(704) 966-9493*. On 50 wooded acres, private baths, 6-acre lake, swimming, croquet. $$ to $$$

WOMBLE INN, *301 Main St., P.O. Box 1441, (704) 884-4770*. New Orleans-style home with 18th- & 19th-century antiques, private baths, large & comfortable parlor, restaurant, verandah. $$

Where to Eat

CHIANTI'S, *NC 280 and US 276 and US 64, (704) 862-5683*. Italian cuisine, one of most popular in North Carolina. $ to $$

OCTOBER'S END, *115 US 64 W. (Lake Toxaway), (704) 966-9226*. Trout Romano, Fettuccine di Pomadora, Chicken Valentino, Eggplant Parmigiana with Pasta. $$

OH SUSANNA'S, *230 W. Main St., (704) 883-3289*. Soups, salads, sandwiches, daily dinner specials; local flavor. $ to $$

RAINTREE, *US 276 S., (704) 862-5832*. Smoked Trout, Lemon Chicken, New York Strip & Prime Rib the house specialties, pasta, catch of the day. $$

Further Information

Brevard Chamber of Commerce, *35 W. Main St., Brevard, NC 28712* *(800) 648-4523*.

Directions

From Asheville, I 26 south to exit 9, NC 280 southwest to Brevard.

Edenton

Population 5, 000

Retirees searching for the perfect place to live often end up with a North Carolina address. Many who do so settle in Brevard, Hendersonville, Highlands (see selections), or other mountain communities in the western part of the state. Those preferring to be near the water and, at the same time, longing for the charm of a bygone era are more likely to look to Beaufort (see selection) or **Edenton**, an historic and architectural gem sometimes called "the South's prettiest town."

Lying on little Edenton Bay on the northern shore of **Albemarle Sound**, Edenton is very much near the water. And the town is certainly in a position to evoke the charm of bygone eras: The second largest port in the Colonies in the early 1700s and capital of North Carolina Colony until 1743, Edenton (incorporated 1722) had a collection of fine homes and other buildings long before North Carolinians even thought of breaking with the king. An eventual decline in commercial importance combined with a relatively remote location–and local commitment to preserving traditional ways–ensured that this charming bit of the past would survive.

Today Edenton has a lovely tree-lined historic district of handsome 18th-, 19th-, and early 20th-century buildings. Bordering the district at its southern end are waterfront parks with picture-postcard views of the bay and sound. People who have retired here talk with pride about the area's friendliness, safety, and absence of traffic congestion.

Edenton's business district offers the shopper a variety of boutiques and collections of antiques and–remembering North Carolina's tradition of fine cabinet-making–reproductions. The sports-minded will find marina services and two golf courses.

Special Features

Some of the finest beaches in the world are in North Carolina's famous **Cape Hatteras National Seashore**, an hour or so to the east of town.

Two plantations with beautifully restored houses are a short driving distance from Edenton. One, **Hope Plantation** (circa 1803), features the frame Federal-style home of North Carolina statesman David Stone. The second, **Somerset Place**, is a complex consisting of a fine verandahed house (circa 1830), outbuildings, and grounds; it was once one of the largest plantations in North Carolina. Both plantation houses are open to the public and are furnished in period style.

> *After the Great Lakes, Albemarle Sound is the largest body of fresh water in the country.*

Where to Stay

ALBEMARLE HOUSE B&B, *204 W. Queen St., (919) 482-8204.* 1904 home with antiques & stenciling, private baths, "gourmet" full breakfasts, refreshments, 2-room suite, sailing lessons & cruises available. $$

GOVERNOR EDEN INN B&B, *304 N. Broad St., P.O. Box 1145, (919) 482-2072.* Neoclassical home with beveled glass entrance, wrap-around porch, TV, private baths, full breakfasts. $$

GRANVILLE QUEEN THEMED INN, *108 S. Granville St., (919) 482-5296/fax (919) 482-4319.* Elegant circa 1907 home, European & Asian furnishings, TV & phones, private baths, balconies, 5-course breakfasts, wine-tasting gatherings. $$$

THE LORDS PROPRIETORS' INN, *300 N. Broad St., (919) 482-3641.* 4 bldgs. (1801 to 1975) in historic district, spacious parlors, TV & phones, private baths, full breakfasts. $$$ (4-course dinner)

TRESTLE HOUSE INN B&B, *632 Soundside Rd., Rt. 4 (Box 370), (800) 645-8466/(919) 482-2282.* 1972 private estate with massive redwood beams, private baths, full breakfasts, exercise room, billiard table & shuffleboard, private lake on wildlife refuge. $$

Where to Eat

WATERMAN'S GRILL, *427 S. Broad St., (919) 482-7733.* Broiled Crabcakes, Cajun Grilled Tuna, Gingerbread Cake from "The Lovin' Oven"; 2-story restaurant with nautical memorabilia & original watercolors. $$

Further Information

Chowan County Tourism Development Authority, *116 E. King St., P.O. Box 245, Edenton, NC 27932-0245 (919) 482-3400 / (800) 775-0111 / fax (919) 482-4925.*

Directions

From Raleigh, US 64 east to US 17, north to Edenton; from Portsmouth (VA), US 17 south to Edenton.

Hendersonville
Population 9, 668

With its mild and healthful climate and glorious mountain scenery, **Hendersonville** is a retreat, and it has been for close to 200 years. Maybe longer, because the Cherokees are believed to have come here to seek solitude long before the arrival of any Europeans.

Rice and indigo plantation owners from Charleston and other lowland towns once built summer homes in the Flat Rock area just south of here so that their families could escape the heat, humidity, and malaria of the coastal region (see also Pendleton, SC). The plantation families were followed by Georgians and Floridians seeking to escape the yellow fever epidemics. Later, victims of tuberculosis and other chest ailments were attracted by the region's altitude. Maintaining the tradition, retirees from the East and Midwest wishing to escape the cities and cold winters began settling here in the 1940s and 1950s.

Hendersonville is today as popular as ever as a place to escape to. The air and water are pure, crime is low, and the pace of life easy. The town is one our grandparents or great grandparents could have lived in. The country is rural, a place where people watch birds or go on wildflower walks.

There are two historic districts, one in **Flat Rock**, three miles south, and the other in Hendersonville. The Flat Rock historic district is older, dating back to the summer days of antebellum planters. Hendersonville grew as businesses developed to serve those retreating to the area, and so its district dates to a later stage of the 19th century.

Many of the summer homes built by privileged Charlestonians and others from the coastal region remain in private hands as estates and can only be seen from the distance, if at all. There is one most notable exception to this rule, however: **Connemara** (circa 1838), the farm where Carl Sandburg and his family lived for 22 years. Now the **Carl Sandburg Home National Historic Site**, the home and grounds of the beloved American poet are open to the public. The house is kept very much like it was when Sandburg lived there, and numerous hiking trails lead to the goat farm and to panoramic views of lakes, rolling hills, and in the distance, the **Blue Ridge Mountains**.

Another structure from the days of the Southern aristocracy open to the public is the Episcopal **Church of St. John in the Wilderness**, in Flat Rock. The church was built in 1833 as a chapel for the estate of an English-born family. Later, it was turned over to the Episcopal Diocese and, in 1852, doubled in length. The church has been entered in the National Register.

The historic **Hendersonville Depot** (1879) is now home to the 420-square-foot **Apple Valley HO Scale Model Railroad**. The model has over 500 feet of track, 95 switches, and a variety of scenic, rural, and industrial landscape features. Celebrating another mode of transportation, the **Western North Carolina Air Museum** exhibits restored and replica antique airplanes. Included in the collection are a 1931 Piper E-2 and a 1943 Stinson Reliant.

Ten blocks long, Hendersonville's **Main Street** has 194 businesses. The late 19th-century buildings, many with restored storefronts, house antique shops, upscale clothing shops, bakeries, and coffee shops. An alternative form of shopping is offered at the **Henderson County Farmer's Curb Market**, in operation for more than 60 years. Here there are garden-fresh vegetables, baked goods, afghans, and aprons, all home-grown or homemade.

Hendersonville's recreation scene is consistent with that of a community that has no fewer than seven banks on Main Street. There are several well-known golf courses, each unique, and others are being built (many are open to the public). Comedy, classic, musical, whodunit, and other kinds of hits from the Broadway and London stages are presented each summer at the **Flat Rock Playhouse**, one of the ten best summer stock theaters in the country. Other productions are offered by the **Hendersonville Little Theater**, the **Belfry Players**, and the **Absolute Theatre**. Inquire at the visitors center for information on these and other events, including performances of mountain music.

Special Feature

Chimney Rock Park, 20 minutes east of Hendersonville, offers an eye-dazzling 75-mile view of the rugged western North Carolina landscape. Within the park is a 400-foot waterfall, rock formations, and nature trails.

> *The Hendersonville area ranks as the seventh largest apple producer in the country. And, yes, there's an annual apple festival (September).*

Where to Stay

APPLE INN, *1005 White Pine Dr., (704) 693-0107*. Home dating to circa 1900, private baths, home-cooked breakfasts, hammocks & rocking chairs on grounds, badminton, croquet. $$ to $$$

CLADDAGH INN, *755 N. Main St., (800) 225-4700/(704) 697-7778/fax (704) 697-8664*. Turn-of-century inn on National Register, TV & phones, private baths, full breakfasts, refreshments, wrap-around porch. $$ to $$$

ECHO MOUNTAIN INN, *2849 Laurel Park Hwy., (704) 692-4008*. Massive 1896 stone-and-frame structure, antiques & reproductions, fireplaces, TV & phones, suites, pool, mountain views. $ to $$$

FLAT ROCK INN, *2810 Greenville Hwy. (Flat Rock 28731), (800) 266-3996*. 1888 summer retreat on National Register, private baths, family-style breakfasts, refreshments, croquet, horseshoes. $$ to $$$

HIGHLAND LAKE INN, *P.O. Box 1026 (Flat Rock 28731), (704) 693-6812 / (800) 762-1376*. 180-acre retreat with wide choice of accommodations, full-service, dining room, canoeing, fishing, tennis, hiking trails, ropes course. $$$

THE WAVERLY INN, *783 N. Main St., (800) 537-8195*. 1898 inn on National Register, phones, private baths, full breakfasts, refreshments, rocking chairs on verandah. $$$

WOODFIELD INN, *US 25 2 miles S, P.O. Box 98 (Flat Rock 28731), (800) 533-6016*. Originally the Farmer Hotel (1850), antiques, antebellum atmosphere, restaurant, Civil War reenactments. $$ to $$$

Where to Eat

EXPRESSIONS, *114 N. Main St., (704) 693-8516.* "Creative" American & Continental cuisine, seasonal specialties, changing menu; in historic Main Street bldg., highly recommended. $$ to $$$

HIGHLAND LAKE INN, *(see above).* Continental cuisine, e.g., Broiled Salmon with Horseradish Crust; French countryside setting, oak-beamed rooms, one of best in region. $$ to $$$

HUBERT'S, *Laurel Park Village, US 64 W., (704) 693-0856.* International menu, good presentation, chef-owned & operated. $$

THE PARK DELI CAFE, *437 N. Main St., (704) 696-3663.* 15 pasta dinners, barbecued ribs, full-meal salads, celebrated desserts; unique park setting. $

QUARTER HOUSE, *1508 US 25, (704) 692-1429.* Trout Almondine, Chicken Schnitzel, Prime Rib, main-course salads, known for red meats; candlelight dining. $$

SINBAD MEDITERRANEAN RESTAURANT, *133 4th Ave. E, (704) 696-2039.* Eastern Mediterranean & Indian menu, Middle Eastern ambiance, locally respected. $$

Further Information

Visitors Information Center, *201 S. Main St., Hendersonville, NC 28792 (800) 828-4244.*

Directions

From Asheville, I 26 south to exit 18A (Hendersonville exit).

Highlands

Population 948 (village only)

Tucked in the middle of a national forest in western North Carolina's Blue Ridge Mountains, **Highlands** is a place of mountain streams, dogwood and rhododendron, autumn brilliance, snow-capped mountains, waterfalls and craft shows. There are no theme parks, chain restaurants, factory outlets, or video arcades. Highlands is a place for lovers of nature.

Established in the 1870s, Highlands was known by the 1880s as a health resort and refuge from the heat of Southern summers. (Several of the inns of those days have been renovated and once again greet visitors – see below.) With a cool average altitude of 4,118 feet, the little town became a summer hideaway for the affluent from the South, especially

Atlanta. For Atlanta's privileged, Highlands became synonymous with "summer mountain retreat." Many built second homes here, expensive second homes. They still do.

The wealth of Highlands's summer residents is reflected in the merchandise in the shops, the restaurant menus, and the many fine country clubs. It's indeed possible that Highlands has the largest number of excellent restaurants per capita in the United States. The town boasts a multitude of boutiques and quaint shops. Some offer art, others antiques, and yet others hand-made items of wood, iron, fabric, etc. Shop windows display music boxes, custom-designed jewelry, porcelain, Oriental rugs, bird and even bat (!) houses.

The cultural scene is similarly rich. The **Highlands Playhouse** stages professional productions in its hilltop theater, and each year music lovers make their way here to attend the highly respected month-long **Highlands Chamber Music Festival**. Local artists display their works in the **Bascom-Louise Gallery**, located in the Hudson Library, as well as in private galleries.

It is nature, however, that dominates Highlands. The **Highlands Nature Center** features indoor wildlife exhibits, botanical gardens, and seminars and lectures. The area around Highlands is known for its mountain trails, challenging golf courses, and trout-fishing streams. There are excellent campgrounds and scenic highways. Of very special note are the waterfalls (see also **Brevard**). At least seven sizable falls are located within a few miles of town. (Visitors are cautioned to view the falls from a distance and not to climb them.)

Special Features

Franklin, 16 or so miles northwest of town, is famous for its gem mining. Visitors are invited to mine for rubies, sapphires, and other stones. The drive to Franklin (**US 64**) is one of the most scenic in North Carolina.

Where to Stay

HIGHLANDS INN, *P.O. Box 1030, (704) 526-5036.* Renovated 1880 inn on National Register, antique furnishings & Colonial stenciling, private baths, Cont. "plus" breakfasts. $$ to $$$

LAKESIDE INN B&B, *Rt. 1 (Box 189A), (704) 526-4498.* 1930s hunting lodge on Lake Sequoyah, private baths, "gourmet" breakfasts, patio & landscaped grounds, canoe. $$

MORNING STAR INN, *480 Flat Mountain Estates Rd., (704) 526-1009.* Quiet 2-acre setting, antiques, down-filled duvets, private baths, "Southern gourmet" breakfasts, hospitality hour, wicker-filled porch. $$$

THE OLD EDWARDS INN, *P.O. Box 1030, (704) 526-5036*. Restored 1878 Inn on National Register, antiques & Colonial wallcoverings, private baths, Cont. "plus" breakfasts, restaurant. $$ to $$$

PHELPS HOUSE B&B INN, *270 Main St., (704) 526-2590*. 1885 inn, antiques, private baths, "hearty" breakfasts, evening coffee/tea, lunches & dinners available, porch. $$

Where to Eat

THE CENTRAL HOUSE, *(see The Old Edwards Inn above)*. Cajun Shrimp, Maryland Crab Cakes, Central House Chicken, steaks; antiques, Colonial atmosphere. $$

NICK'S, *NC 28 S, (704) 526-2706*. Seafood, local salmon trout, prime rib, steaks; casual, family owned & operated for 20 years. $ to $$

ON THE VERANDAH, *US 64/NC 28 W, (704) 526-2338*. Applewood Smoked Salmon, Grilled North Carolina Quail, Creme Brulee a favorite dessert; wine bar, rustic contemporary setting overlooking Lake Sequoyah. $$ to $$$

PAOLETTI'S RESTAURANT, *E. Main St., (704) 526-4906*. Classic northern Italian cuisine. $ to $$

Further Information

Highlands Chamber of Commerce, *P.O. Box 404, Highlands, NC 28741 (704) 526-2112*.

Directions

From Asheville, I 26 south to exit 9, NC 280 southwest to US 64 (near Brevard), US 64 west to Highlands.

Ocracoke
Population 700

A quiet and relaxed way of life continues among the picturesque **Outer Banks** houses and live-oak trees that cluster about the pretty little harbor. Unless there's a rush on to catch the next ferry, there's no reason to hurry. The bicycle is the best way to get around town. This is one of the Atlantic Coast's true treasures!

Located on **Ocracoke Island** in the middle of **Cape Hatteras National Seashore**, **Ocracoke Village** relaxes next to 17 miles of unobstructed oceanfront. Because buildings may not be built near the ocean, the shops and restaurants stick close to the village. Just down the beach is the photogenic **Ocracoke Lighthouse** (1823), the oldest lighthouse still in operation in North Carolina.

One of the most popular ways to tour Ocracoke Island's beaches is by horseback.

Special Feature

Day trips are available to **Portsmouth**, an abandoned village on nearby Portsmouth Island. Some of the village has been restored under the supervision of the National Park Service.

> • *The waters and coves hereabouts were once the haunt of Edward Teach, otherwise known as Blackbeard, and other pirates.*
> • *Four Royal Navy sailors killed near here in 1942 are buried in the village's British Cemetery.*

Where to Stay

THE BERKLEY CENTER COUNTRY INN, *P.O. Box 220, (919) 928-5911.* Estate on harbor, private baths, character & atmosphere. $$ to $$$

CREWS INN, *P.O. Box 460, (919) 928-7011.* 1908 home with wrap-around porch, antiques, private baths, breakfasts on porch, gardens, secluded location in center of village. $$

EUGENIA'S B&B, *P.O. Box 611, (919) 928-1411.* 1907/08 home brimming with antiques, full breakfasts. $$

THE ISLAND INN, *P.O. Box 9, (919) 928-4351.* Full-service turn-of-century inn "with a flavor of yesterday," antiques, restaurant, heated pool, open year-round. $ to $$$

SILVER LAKE INN & MOTEL, *P.O. Box 303, (919) 928-5721.* New structure of salt-treated lumber & hand-split cedar shakes, full-service, hot tubs, Victorian suites, deep-water docking, harbor views. $$ to $$$

Where to Eat

THE BACK PORCH RESTAURANT, *Ocracoke, (919) 928-6401.* Broad range of seafood specialties, homemade breads & desserts; own cookbook. $ to $$

CAFE ATLANTIC, *P.O. Box 123, (919) 928-4861.* Fish fresh from Ocracoke nets, Seafood Kabobs, Cafe Atlantic Crab Cakes, Sauteed Scallops; popular. $ to $$

CAPTAIN BEN'S, *Ocracoke, (919) 928-4741.* Clam chowder, prime rib; old high school gym converted to restaurant. $ to $$

COCKLE CREEK, *Hwy. 12, (919) 928-6891.* Fresh Tuna, Shrimp Scampi, Scallops, Seafood Platter, Ribeye, Fettuccine Alfredo. $$

HOWARD'S PUB & RAW BAR, *NC 12, (919) 928-4441.* Ocracoke's oldest imbibery & raw bar serving subs, burgers, pizza; darts & games, wide-screen TV, open year-round. $

Further Information

Outer Banks Chamber of Commerce, *P.O. Box 1757, Kill Devil Hills, NC 27948 (919) 441-8144. (ZIP for Ocracoke is 27960.)*

Directions

Toll ferries connect Ocracoke with the mainland at **Cedar Island** (crossing time approximately 2 1/4 hours) and **Swan Quarter** (approximately 2 1/2 hours). Reservations for the toll ferries are strongly recommended. The ferry to **Hatteras Inlet** (approximately 40 minutes) is free. *Call (919) 928-3841 for reservation and schedule information.*

Other Charming North Carolina Towns

Bath
Cashiers
Dillsboro
Manteo
Saluda

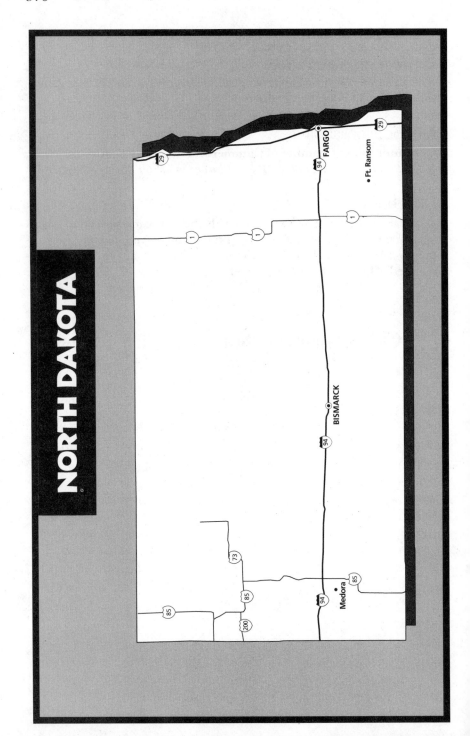

NORTH DAKOTA

NORTH DAKOTA

Fort Ransom
Population 111

Fort Ransom is a quaint little Norwegian-American village nestled in the scenic **Sheyenne River Valley** of southeastern North Dakota. Along its recently paved main street are buildings with rosemaling, inside as well as out, and on the wooded slopes of the valley above the main street, houses climb apparently without pattern. This is the kind of place that yearns to be painted and photographed. It is the site of a major arts and crafts festival.

Of special interest in the village is the **Ransom County Historical Museum**, which houses exhibits and artifacts from Fort Ransom's pioneer years. Nearby are the restored one-room **Bear Creek Schoolhouse** and the **T.J. Walker Historical Site** (1882), consisting of a mill, barn, and residence.

Fort Ransom is remote from the interstates and beaten tourist route – it may be the only community in this guide that isn't served by at least one state highway. Yet the village is almost literally surrounded by scenic and recreational attractions: One mile south, at the **Fort Ransom Historic Site**, are the archaeological remains of a log fort that was used from 1867 to 1872 to guard a settlement trail and the **Northern Pacific Railroad**, then under construction.

One mile north is **Fort Ransom Ski Area**, popular with downhill skiers. Two miles north is beautiful **Fort Ransom State Park** (see below). Three miles southeast is the 509-acre **Sheyenne State Forest**, great for canoeing and snowshoeing. And traversing the village is the 46-mile-long **Sheyenne Valley Snowmobile Trail**.

As if all of this weren't enough, the area is rich with old farmsteads, reminders of the Norwegian farm families who settled here in the 1870s and 1880s.

Special Feature

Fort Ransom State Park features camping, picnicking, horseback riding, cross-country ski trails, canoe rentals, and a canoe campsite. There is also a scenic overlook that provides spectacular views of the Sheyenne River Valley.

The park is best known, however, for its **Fort Ransom Sodbusters Days**, a July get-together that attracts thousands with turn-of-the-century

378 AMERICA'S MOST CHARMING TOWNS & VILLAGES

plowing and threshing demonstrations, displays of antique farm equipment, quilting, ice-cream making, farm-style cooking, and other early
farming and household re-creations.

> • *The original buildings of two early homesteads (1879 and 1884)*
> *have been incorporated as part of Fort Ransom State Park.*
> • *The Sheyenne Valley Snowmobile Trail is maintained with funds*
> *from snowmobile registrations, required in North Dakota.*

Where to Stay

THE PRESIDENTS HOUSE, *Valley City State University (Valley City
58072), (800) 532-8641*. Former home (1901) of VCSU presidents &
families, private baths, breakfasts if requested, close to downtown, scenic
drive to Fort Ransom. $$

VIKING VIEW RESORT, *Ft. Ransom, (701) 973-2101*. One- & two-
bedroom log cabins. $ to $$

WAGON WHEEL INN, *455 Winter Show Rd. (Valley City 58072), (701)
845-5333/(800) 319-5333*. Full-service motel with cozy lobby & fireplace,
suites, Cont. breakfasts, indoor pool & whirlpool. $

Where to Eat

FORT CAFE, *107 E. Main St., (701) 973-2301*. Daily dinner specials
served in grocery store, steaks, Sodbuster Burger the house specialty. $

J. S. CORRAL BAR & GRILL, *Main St., (701) 973-9161*. Established
1884, rustic atmosphere with Western window murals & unique wall
displays. $

Further Information

Fort Ransom State Park, *5981 Walt Hjelle Pkwy., Fort Ransom, ND
58033 (701) 973-4331*.

Directions

From Fargo, I 29 south to exit 48, ND 46 west to Ransom County 58,
Ransom County 58 south – look for the signs.

Medora

Population about 101

There are few better ways to recapture the spell of a small 1800s cattle town than to stroll **Medora's** boardwalks. Along the way are restored buildings like the **Rough Riders Hotel** (1884; see below) and **St. Mary's Catholic Church** (1884). The spell isn't hurt by the awesome beauty of one of the country's finest Western settings – the **North Dakota Badlands**. Nor the knowledge that Theodore Roosevelt once rode these parts. In the evening the gas street lights are turned on and the quiet stirred by the sounds of a vaudeville show (the *4M Review* in the old town hall).

Medora was named for the wife of the Marquis de Mores, a French aristocrat who in 1883 founded the town. De Mores came to Dakota Territory to seek his fortune in the cattle and meat-packing industry. The fortune was never made and the family was seldom seen here after 1886, but during his stay the marquis built a town and a legacy.

De Mores is best remembered today through his 26-room frame summer home, or *chateau*, which overlooks Medora. The house, along with the stables and several other outbuildings, is now the **Chateau de Mores State Historic Site**. Most of the furnishings are European and American antiques, some of them summer-cottage rustic, original to the family.

The **Medora Musical** is a grand spectacle of music, dancing, comedy, and variety acts that pay patriotic tribute to Theodore Roosevelt's "Bully Spirit." The show, performed by professional entertainers, is presented in a 2,750-seat amphitheater reached by a large outdoor escalator. The amphitheater is positioned to offer a breathtaking view of the Badlands. While here, inquire about tickets to one of North Dakota's major eating events, the **Pitchfork Steak Fondue**.

Special Features

Medora is the entrance to the **South Unit** of the **Theodore Roosevelt National Park**, a park known for its Badlands scenery and wildlife, including buffalo, wild horses, and elk. A visitors center, museum, and Roosevelt's **Maltese Cross Ranch cabin** are near the entrance.

Several miles north in the park is the **Peaceful Valley Ranch**, an old dude ranch and now a park concession that offers a variety of horse-back trail rides. The rides vary in length from 1 hour to overnight. Several, lasting from 4 to 5 1/2 hours, journey to the park's **Petrified Forest** and **Painted Canyon**. A trail ride is a must for those who have the time.

• In addition to Theodore Roosevelt and the Marquis de Mores, Medora has attracted such notables as silent-screen star Tom Mix and Marie, Queen of the Rumanians.
• General George Armstrong Custer camped just a few miles south of Medora's site in 1876 on his way to Little Big Horn.

Where to Stay

ROUGH RIDERS HOTEL, *Downtown Medora, (701) 623-4422.* Restored 1880s hotel, full-service, operated as B&B October 1 to May 1, restaurant. $$

Where to Eat

ROUGH RIDERS HOTEL, *(see above).* Steaks & buffalo burgers served in rustic dining room of historic hotel, good wine selection. $$

Further Information

Site Supervisor, *Chateau de Mores State Historic Site, Medora, ND 58645 (701) 623-4355.*

Directions

From Bismarck, I 94 west to exit 24 (Medora exit).

Other Charming North Dakota Towns

Devils Lake
Kenmare
Walhalla

381

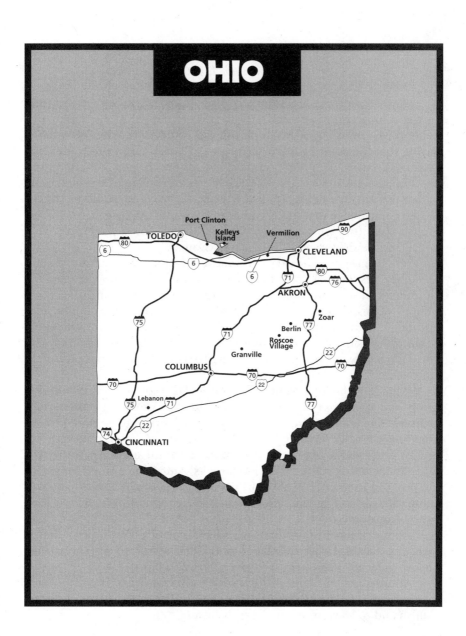

OHIO

Berlin

Population 1, 000

Maybe about half of all Amish people in the world have their farms in the rolling countryside around **Berlin** (accent on first syllable) and other towns and villages in this part of east central Ohio. It goes without saying that the countryside is picturesque: Amish farms are traditional American farms, with big barns and proper farmhouses. Shunning the modern, the Amish drive buggies rather than cars and use kerosene lamps rather than electric lights. They love the handmade and the home-baked. It's no coincidence that several other towns in this guide lie in or close to Amish areas (the villages of Van Buren County, Iowa; Jamesport, Missouri; and Lewisburg and Lititz, Pennsylvania).

People have been heard to say that "Lancaster County, Pennsylvania is like the Disneyworld of Amish; Berlin is the real thing." The some 70 businesses in and around the town are locally owned, and the area's volume of business is too small to pose much danger to the countryside. Although "country" malls, "country" markets, "country" stores, and other "country" businesses that capitalize on country charm occasionally dot the main highways, visitors find Berlin's back-road landscapes pleasantly untouched.

A guided tour of **Behalt**, a 10-foot by 265-foot cyclorama, offers a good and very enjoyable introduction to the Amish and Mennonite peoples. The enormous painting traces the history of these people from their beginning in 1525, in Zurich, Switzerland, to the present.

Another way to learn about the Amish is to visit an Amish farm that's open to the public. One choice is **Schrocks' Amish Farm and Home** east of town (on Rte. 39). Here visitors may tour two Amish homes, pet farm animals, have a buggy ride, and otherwise take a somewhat romantic look at the Amish lifestyle.

A large number of Berlin stores sell locally crafted furniture, often of oak. The town is also a good place to shop for fine quilts. Food shops offer delicious locally made cheeses, ice creams, and pastries.

Another way to shop for local foods and crafts is to travel the back roads. Many Amish farms have shops. This is also a good way to meet the Amish and to learn more about their farms.

Special Feature

Farmerstown, **Charm**, **Mount Hope**, and **Kidron** are among the most charming and unspoiled of the area's towns and villages.

> • *Remember that the Amish regard the photograph as a sign of vanity, something forbidden by the Bible.*
> • *Founded in 1816, Berlin had a population of 75 by the time of the 1830 census.*

Where to Stay

CARRIAGE HOUSE INN, *P.O. Box 422, 5453 East St., (330) 893-2226.* Home with view of woods & field, TV, locally made furniture, private baths, sunroom, walking distance to shops/restaurants. $ to $$$

CHARM COUNTRYVIEW INN B&B, *OH 557 (nr. Charm 44617), (330) 893-3003.* Home with porch overlooking Amish countryside, private baths, full "country" breakfasts, evening snacks. $$$

DONNA'S B&B & COTTAGES, *East St., (800) 320-3338/(330) 893-3068.* Home with country decor, TV, private baths, full breakfasts, freshly baked evening snacks; honeymoon cottages with fireplaces, TV, kitchenettes, & whirlpools. $$

GILEAD'S BALM MANOR, *8690 CR 201 (Fredericksburg 44627), (330) 695-3881.* New inn on 5 acres of landscaped grounds overlooking lake, 12-ft ceilings, fireplaces, TV, private baths, whirlpools, kitchenettes, indoor heated pool. $$$

THE MILLER HAUS, *P.O. Box 126 (Charm 44617), (330) 893-3602.* Amish-style home on 23 acres, antiques, quilts, private baths, full breakfasts, refreshments, porches with hickory rockers, small dogs by special request. $$$

POMERENE HOUSE ACCOMMODATIONS, *P.O. Box 185, (330) 893-2842.* 1879 Italianate home on National Register, 10-ft ceilings, 2-room Victorian suites rented as units, candy shop. $$

Where to Eat

BOYD & WURTHMANN RESTAURANT, *P.O. Box 140, (330) 893-3287.* Home-style cooking, homemade desserts; a local favorite. $

CHALET IN THE VALLEY, *OH 557, (330) 893-2550.* Swiss-Austrian-Amish cooking including schnitzels, bratwurst, steaks, fondues, German potato salad; pleasant setting, gift shop & cheese house. $ to $$

HOMESTEAD RESTAURANT, *4450 Rte. 557 (Charm), (330) 893-2717*. Pan Fried Chicken, Sauerkraut 'n Pork, Homemade Pot Roast, Roast Beef; "down country" charm in especially charming country village. $

Further Information
Amish Country Visitors Bureau, *P.O. Box 177, Berlin, OH 44610 (330) 893-3467.*

Directions
From Akron, I 77 south to exit 83, OH 39 west to Berlin.

Granville
Population 4, 353

Granville's settlers came from Massachusetts and Connecticut in the opening years of the 19th century. They brought with them their New England ways, including some of their architecture. Even today their heritage can be seen – and felt – in Granville. But there are also strong Midwestern elements here, and the fusion of the New England with the Midwestern has produced a lovely town.

Granville is a place to relax, to stroll, to think or read. It's also the place for the Midwesterner seeking a meal in a gorgeous old inn. The restored facades and beautiful landscaping along **Broadway**, Granville's main street, maintain a New England flavor, with maybe a little Continental color thrown in. As is true of central Ohio in general, Granville's trees and shrubs seem especially lush.

The **Robbins Hunter Museum**, housed in an 1842 Greek Revival mansion, displays 18th- and 19th-century American, European, and Oriental antiques in 11 furnished rooms. The grounds are maintained by the Granville Garden Club. Collections of hand tools, costumes, and other artifacts from settlement days are on exhibit at a second museum, the stone **Granville Historical Society Museum**. The museum is the oldest (1816) of more than 100 buildings on the National Register of Historic Places. A third museum, the brick Italianate **Granville Life Style Museum and H.P. Robinson House**, features a state-of-the-art 1949 kitchen as well as Victorian furnishings and a collection of 19th-century photographs.

The chapel and 11 other campus buildings of **Denison University**, a private liberal arts and sciences college, are listed on the National Register. The lovely campus should be part of every tour of Granville.

Special Feature

Licking County has paved old railroad routes to construct trails for walkers, bikers, skaters, and skateboarders.

Where to Stay

THE BUXTON INN, *313 E. Broadway, (614) 587-0001*. Restored 1812 stagecoach tavern on National Register, full-service inn, period antiques, dining rooms, fountains & formal gardens. $$ to $$$

FOLLET-WRIGHT HOUSE B&B, *403 E. Broadway, (614) 587-0941*. 1860 village home, private baths, homemade Danish rolls a breakfast specialty. $$

THE GEORGE T. JONES HOUSE B&B, *221 E. Elm St., (614) 587-1122*. 1861 home on National Register, period furnishings, private baths. $$

THE GRANVILLE INN, *314 E. Broadway, (614) 587-3333*. Full-service inn "in tradition of an English country house," plump comforters, dining room. $$

GRANVILLE MANOR B&B, *4058 Columbus Rd., (614) 587-4677*. 1850s home on three rolling acres, private baths, hot tub, 3 mins to Granville. $$

THE PORCH HOUSE B&B, *241 E. Maple St., (614) 587-1995/(800) 587-1995*. Circa 1903 home with antiques, quilts, private baths, full "country" breakfasts, pets by arrangement. $$

Where to Eat

ALADDIN RESTAURANT, *122 E. Broadway, (614) 587-0253*. Home-cooked food, local favorite. $

BREWS CAFE, *128 E. Broadway, (614) 587-0249*. "Best burgers & over-stuffed sandwiches anywhere!", wood-fired pizza oven, 250 bottled beers, 8 kegs on tap. $

THE BUXTON INN, *(see above)*. Coquille of Seafood, Chicken Victoria, Baked Double-Cut Pork Chop, Choucroute Garnie, Buxton Pot Roast. $$

THE GRANVILLE INN, *(see above)*. Fresh seafood, Chicken Oscar, prime rib, famous raisin bread, elegant Sunday buffet. $$

VICTORIA'S OLDE TYME DELI & ICE CREAMS, *134 E. Broadway, (614) 587-0322*. Light dining in one of Ohio's favorite places. $

Further Information

Granville Business & Professional Association, *P.O. Box 135, Granville, OH 43023 (614) 587-4490*.

Directions

From Columbus, OH 16 or 161 east to Granville.

Kelleys Island

Population 200

For many years, even before the Civil War, excursion steamers plied the waters of the Great Lakes. One of the ports of call was the **Village of Kelleys Island** on the shores of the largest American island in **Lake Erie**. Today the boats are smaller, but Kelleys Island is still a port of call, and an especially pleasant one at that.

Following a common scenario, the charm of Kelleys Island is due in part to "undevelopment." At the turn of the century the island was home to numerous wineries, limestone quarries, orchards, and logging and fishing industries. The population was four times what it is today. Then the industry began to disappear, and the 2,800-acre island became relatively undeveloped (one third of it now belongs to the state). Rich in flora and fauna as well as reminders of another day, the island is today known for its quiet and relaxed atmosphere and is listed in its entirety on the National Register of Historic Places.

The island has two unique state memorials. The first, the **Glacial Grooves**, discovered back when there was blasting in the quarries, has been described as the most spectacular example of glacial carvings in the country. The second, **Inscription Rock**, contains pictographs inscribed by Erie Indians hundreds of years ago.

Cars are permitted here, but many visitors rent bikes or golf carts and tour the island at a pace more befitting the setting. Hiking is also popular, and the island has nature trails that boast fossils (very popular these days) and abandoned quarries as well as a diversity of bird species. Other activities include summer swimming, winter ice fishing, and year-round wine tasting.

Special Feature

The 352-foot **Perry's Victory and International Peace Memorial**, commemorating Commodore Perry's victory over the British fleet in the War of 1812, is located in nearby **Put-in-Bay**. There is daily summer boat service to Put-in-Bay from Kelleys Island.

• Datus and Irad Kelley purchased the island for $1.50 an acre in the 1830s.

Where to Stay

CRICKET LODGE B&B, *P.O. Box 323, (419) 746-2263*. 1905 lakefront home on National Register, "leisurely" full breakfasts served on screened porch, old-fashioned porch glider. $$$

EAGLES NEST, *P.O. Box 762, (419) 746-2708*. Home surrounded by lawn & trees, private baths, studio & efficiency suites available. $$$

FLY INN, *P.O. Box 471, (419) 746-2525*. Modern home with private baths, whirlpool, pool table, pool. $$$

SWEET VALLEY INN, *Division St., P.O. Box 733, (419) 746-2750*. Victorian home on National Register, antique-filled rooms, full breakfasts, spa, gardens, lake views. $$$

WATER'S EDGE RETREAT, *827 E. Lakeshore Dr., (419) 746-2455*. Victorian lakefront home, private baths, whirlpools in suites, sailing packages. $$$

Where to Eat

FRESCH'S ISLAND HOUSE, *131 Division St., (419) 746-2304*. Victorian home serving Italian & Continental cuisine. $$

KELLEY'S ISLAND WINE CO., *Woodford Rd., (419) 746-2537*. Wine-tasting room & gourmet deli in 19th-century vineyard. $

VILLAGE PUMP, *W. Lakeshore Dr., (419) 746-2281*. Local hangout known for fresh Lake Erie perch, home-prepared food, Brandy Alexanders. $ to $$

WEST BAY INN, *W. Lakeshore Dr., (419) 746-2597*. Old winery now serving sandwiches, soups, & salads; bar. $

Further Information

Kelleys Island Chamber of Commerce, *P.O. Box 783, Kelleys Island, OH 43438 (419) 746-2360*.

Directions

You can get to Kelleys Island by island-hopping cruisers out of **Sandusky**, by ferries and cruisers from **Marblehead** (another charming village), and by air from Sandusky and **Port Clinton** (see selection). And, of course, by private boat.

Check with the Chamber of Commerce for schedules. No matter how you get there, do allow at least four or five hours, preferably several days.

Lebanon

Population 11, 646

Lebanon is the kind of town that an expatriate from the Midwest could easily long for. Quiet streets and mature trees. Porch swings and overhanging eaves. A nicely preserved downtown with brick sidewalks, linden trees, and a handsome slice of the 19th century. Lots of history (settled 1796). A major antique center.

The Golden Lamb, an imposing brick landmark that began as a two-story inn and coach stop in 1803, is Ohio's oldest hotel and restaurant (see below). Its halls have echoed the voices of 10 presidents and such other dignitaries as Mark Twain, Henry Clay, and Charles Dickens. Also a museum, the hotel has antique-furnished rooms and an outstanding collection of Shaker pieces and Currier and Ives prints (open to diners and guests).

Glendower State Memorial, a mansion built between 1836 and 1840, displays one of Ohio's finest examples of Greek Revival architecture. The interior is furnished with Empire and Victorian pieces.

One of the best county museums in the country, the **Warren County Historical Society Museum** houses collections ranging from the paleontological and archaeological to the Victorian, folk art, and horse-drawn (including a magnificent sleigh). On the third floor is the Robert and Virginia Jones Shaker Gallery, an outstanding collection of Shaker furniture, spinning wheels, and other memorabilia.

The **Turtle Creek Valley Railway** offers passengers a 14-mile, approximately 1-hour trip through the Ohio countryside. The tracks follows an old stage coach route and 1880 railroad bed. Complete with a 1950s diesel/electric locomotive, 1930 passenger coaches, and gondola car with open-air seating, the train offers Sunday and mystery dinner tours as well as shorter rides.

Over 30 antique and specialty shops dot Lebanon's downtown streets. What with several good eateries and an old-fashioned soda fountain serving as additional incentives, it's understandable why shoppers from nearby cities love to head this direction for a day of browsing.

Not least among Lebanon's attractions is a location that makes the town ideal as a vacation center. To the south is Cincinnati, one of the country's truly unique cities. Only a few miles from Lebanon, on the northern fringes of Cincinnati, are two of the nation's top recreation parks, **Paramount's Kings Island**, with world-class roller coasters, and **The Beach**, a premier water park. A scenic river popular with rafters and canoers (see below) and a series of lakes and state parks offering boating, swimming, hiking, and camping lie to the east. Also to the east are the rolling woods and pastureland of pretty southern Ohio, a rural landscape designed for a little relaxed motoring.

Special Features

Boasting more than 35 antique shops of its own, **Waynesville**, a charming little town just up the highway, is sometimes called the *Antiques Capital of the Midwest.*

Just east of Lebanon is the **Little Miami Scenic State Park & Bike Trail**, a 50-mile linear park on the east bank of the **Little Miami River**. Canoe and raft liveries are located at several points along the river.

Overlooking the Little Miami Valley, **Fort Ancient State Memorial** is the site of a very large hilltop enclosure built by prehistoric Indians. A museum focuses on the earthwork as well as on Ohio's Indian heritage.

Nearby Waynesville was the birthplace of branch banking (1877) and home of the originator of the Stetson hat.

Where to Stay

THE ARTIST'S COTTAGE, *458 E. Warren St., (513) 932-5938.* 1860 carriage house with sleeping loft & full kitchen rented as unit, fireplace, full breakfasts, access to heated pool & hot tub. $$$

BURL MANOR, *230 S. Mechanic St., (513) 932-2910.* Circa 1844 Greek Revival home, private baths, formerly home to state senators & other prominent citizens. $$

HARDY'S HAVEN, *208 Wright Ave., (513) 932-2951.* Furnished apartment in Victorian residential area, next to golf course/tennis courts. $$

THE HATFIELD INN, *2563 Hatfield Rd., (513) 932-3193.* Home on historical farm, period furnishings, custom tin chandeliers, private baths, combination Cont./buffet breakfasts, circular porch, herb garden, ponds. $$

WHITE TOR, *1620 Oregonia Rd., (513) 932-5892.* 1862 Ohio farmhouse offering 2-room suite with private bath, fireplace, TV; full "English" breakfasts, porch for watching sun set over Little Miami Valley, gardens. $$

Where to Eat

THE BEST CAFE, *17 E. Mulberry St., (513) 932-4400.* Chicken Stroganoff, Sauerbraten, Cabbage Strudel, Portobello Pizza; English pub feel with English beers on tap, since 1949. $$

THE GOLDEN LAMB, *27 S. Broadway, (513) 932-5065.* Traditional Midwestern favorites served in 4 dining rooms of historic inn; antiques, extensive wine list, servers in period attire, Black Horse Tavern. $$

THE GOURMET ON BROADWAY, *20 N. Broadway, (513) 933-8377.* Soups & salads made from scratch, Chocolate Marble Cheesecake one of homemade desserts; espresso, cappuccino, & gourmet coffees. $

THE SYCAMORE TREE, *3 S. Sycamore St., (513) 932-4567.* "Upscale" sandwiches & salad plates, Biscuit Pudding among "desserts to die for," variety of coffees. $

Further Information

Lebanon Area Chamber of Commerce, *120 E. South St., Lebanon, OH 45036 (513) 932-1100.*

Directions

From Cincinnati, I 71 north to South Lebanon exit (Exit 28), north on OH 48 to Lebanon.

Port Clinton
Population 7, 106

Port Clinton is an old fishing town with a colorful waterfront, beautiful trees, and lovingly maintained buildings from the last decades of the 19th and early decades of the 20th centuries. The houses sport a variety of hues. The town is also a summer resort and gateway town, a place on the way to **Catawba Island**, to **South Bass Island** way out in Lake Erie, and to anywhere else in or on Lake Erie where boats can go. Port Clinton is where fishing and sightseeing trips begin. It is one of those towns whose appeal is based in part on anticipation.

Nicknamed the *Walleye Capital of the World*, the port was once a center for commercial fishing, boat building, and various industries related to the water. Although commercial fishing remains, many of the water-based industries have given way to water-based recreations. Thanks to civic pride and the efforts of the regional planning commission, the town has become a delightful little lakeside resort with a touch of class and an unmistakable, though unpretentious, upscale ambiance.

Sailors and other visitors will find Port Clinton's attractive downtown amply stocked with shops and restaurants. There are several structures of historic interest here as well. One is the venerable **Island House Hotel**, now restored (listed below). Another is the magnificent sandstone

Romanesque Revival **courthouse**, listed on the National Register of Historic Places. Of special interest are the murals on the upper floors depicting **Ottawa County's** history.

Bounded by beaches on one side and a series of lovely homes on the other, **East Perry Street** offers one of the few places on the southern shore of Lake Erie where the beauty of the lake can be enjoyed from the seat of a car.

Foremost among Port Clinton's recreations are fishing and boating. Charters are available for the pursuit of smallmouth bass, walleye, perch, and other lake fish. There are also marinas and outfitters for private boaters. For sightseers in general, there are excursion boats serving the resort and "party" village of **Put-in-Bay** on South Bass Island.

> • *The Portage River Lift Bridge, linking downtown to western Ottawa County, was designed by a female engineer in the late 1920s. It seems that the program printed for the bridge's dedication listed the engineer only by first initial and last name, whereas all men involved with the project were listed by their first as well as last names. The bridge, carefully preserved, still operates to allow boats to pass out to Lake Erie.*
>
> • *The National Rifle and Pistol Matches have been held each July and August at Camp Perry, west of Port Clinton, since the turn of the century.*
>
> • *Movie stars used to stay at the Island House Hotel while outfitting their classic wooden Matthews yachts, built in Port Clinton.*

Where to Stay

THE ISLAND HOUSE, *102 Madison St., (800) 233-7307*. "Lake Erie's Centennial Hotel," full-service, restaurant, established 1886 & restored 1986. $$ to $$$

Where to Eat

THE GARDEN AT THE LIGHTHOUSE, *226 E. Perry, (419) 732-2151*. Fresh local fish served in old home of lighthouse keeper, Fish Market Salad popular. $$

ISLAND HOUSE, *(see above)*. American cuisine with fresh Lake Erie perch & walleye among specialties. $$

MAYHEW'S RESTAURANT, *128 W. Perry, (419) 732-3259*. The place for breakfast. $

Further Information

Ottawa County Visitors Bureau, *109 Madison St., Port Clinton, OH 43452 (800) 441-1271.*

Directions

From Toledo, OH 2 east to Port Clinton.

Roscoe Village
Population about 500

Roscoe Village is a little canal community cut from the 1830s. The village is an authentic restoration, not a reconstruction; a living community, not a museum. The sidewalks are brick and the lampposts and signs antique. Guides wear 1830s clothing. Period crafts are demonstrated and the products sold in quaint shops. There's an inn (which happens to have one of the finest dining rooms in Ohio - see below) and lovely perennial gardens. Some of the restorations are private homes. The population is almost exactly what it was in the 1830s.

Adding to the realism is a 1 1/2-mile restored section of the old **Ohio and Erie Canal**. Tours of the canal aboard a horse-drawn replica of an 1800s canal boat are one of the village's most popular attractions (45 minutes).

Founded in 1816, Roscoe Village was from the 1830s to the 1860s a busy canal port. The railroad and, terminally, a disastrous flood in 1913, drove the little village into oblivion. Following a scenario almost exactly that of Waterloo Village in New Jersey (see selection), the town was rediscovered in 1968 and restoration of its buildings begun. Roscoe Village was to become Ohio's – and one of the country's – premier restored villages.

The **Visitor Center & Exhibit Hall** features miniature dioramas and a wide-screen high-tech theater presentation on early transportation. Within the village are several living history buildings, including a working 19th-century print shop, a blacksmith shop, an 1825 working man's home, the kitchen and rooms of a doctor's home, and the **Toll House**, whose exhibits demonstrate 19th-century building techniques as well as modern restoration techniques. The separately administered **Johnson-Humrickhouse Museum** is noted for its collections of Native-American, Eskimo, and Asian artifacts.

The **Living History Tour** gives the visitor a glimpse of what life was like in an 1800s community.

Special Features

Coshocton, just across the Muskingum River, has a beautifully restored downtown area.

South of Roscoe Village in Muskingum County is **The Wilds**, the largest private land preserve in the world. Built on 9,154 acres of reclaimed land, the preserve is designed to protect rare wildlife. The land may be toured by car or tram.

Food baskets may be purchased at nearby **Rainbow Hills Vineyards** and enjoyed with a glass or bottle of wine by the pond or on an outdoor deck in the woods behind the winery.

> • *Roscoe Village's Whitewoman Street got its name from a white captive, Mary Harris, who was married to an Indian and lived in the area in 1750.*
> • *The Muskingum River is the only river that both begins and ends within Ohio.*

Where to Stay

APPLE BUTTER INN B&B, *455 Hill St. (Coshocton 43812), (614) 622-1329*. 1840s Greek-Revival home overlooking village, private baths, "lazy-day" rockers. $$ to $$$

BUTLER MILL HAUS, *17845 OH 60 S. (Dresden 43821), (614) 327-7965*. Restored feed mill with 18-ft ceilings, private baths, life-sized folk art. $$

MARY HARRIS HOUSE B&B, *42768 US 36 (Warsaw 43844), (614) 824-4141*. Ancient shade trees & stone garden on 4 acres, private baths, full breakfasts, porch swing, highly recommended. $$

ROSCOE VILLAGE INN, *200 N. Whitewoman St., (800) 237-7397/ (614) 622-2222/fax (614) 623-6568*. Full-service inn within village, Shaker-style furnishings, two restaurants. $$ to $$$

VALLEY VIEW INN, *32327 OH 643 (Fresno 43824), (216) 897-3232/ (800) 331-8439*. Porch overlooking woods & Amish farms, locally made furniture, private baths, family-style breakfasts, player piano. $$ to $$$

Where to Eat

KING CHARLEY'S TAVERN *(see Roscoe Village Inn above)*. Rustic tavern serving light meals. $

THE OLD WAREHOUSE RESTAURANT, *400 N. Whitewoman St., (614) 622-4001*. Family-style dining in restored 1838 canal warehouse, char-grilled entrees. $ to $$

ROBSON'S, *442 Main St. (Coshocton)*, *(614) 622-8262*. Crab Legs, Farmhouse Chicken, Prime Rib, Spaghetti "Our Way"; known for sandwiches, salads, exceptional desserts. $$

ROSCOE VILLAGE INN CENTENNIAL ROOM, *(see Roscoe Village Inn above)*. Traditional American & international repertoire prepared by award-winning chef, fireside dining. $$

THOMAS STEAK HOUSE, *131 N. 3rd (Coshocton)*, *(614) 622-7112*. Seafood, chicken, pasta, char-broiled steaks & chops, roast prime rib of beef the house specialty. $$

Further Information

Roscoe Village Foundation Marketing & Public Relations Dept., *381 Hill St., Coshocton, OH 43812 (800) 877-1830/(614) 622-9310.*

Directions

From Cleveland, I 77 south to exit 65, US 36 west to Coshocton (and Roscoe Village); from Columbus, OH 16 east to Coshocton.

Vermilion
Population 11, 127

Vermilion is sometimes described as a "New England seaside community" and a home of steamship captains. The reference to New England is given in quotes because Vermilion isn't of course in New England, but no qualification is needed for the reference to the steamship captains: More than 50 Great Lakes captains made their homes here in the latter part of the 19th century.

An active Lake Erie port as far back as the early 1800s, many of Vermilion's people, and their homes, had New England roots. The roots can still be seen in a downtown waterfront area that has been restored as **Harbour Town 1837**. Here are gracious captains' homes, the old **Town Hall**, the old **Opera House**, and numerous specialty shops and unique restaurants. You can also see the town's roots in the lovely white Cape Cod homes nestled on the lagoons of the **Vermilion River**.

The two floors of the **Inland Seas Maritime Museum** tell the fascinating story of the Great Lakes using paintings, photographs, models, and artifacts. The museum features a simulated ship's bridge and a replica of the **Vermilion Lighthouse**.

Reflecting its popularity with fishing and recreational craft, Vermilion has an excellent small-boat harbor. The town also has several fine beaches. Sail and power boat rentals, fishing charters, and bicycle rentals provide good ways to enjoy this charming "New England" port city and summer resort.

Where to Stay

CAPT. GILCHRIST GUESTHOUSE, *5662 Huron St., (216) 967-1237*. 1885 home on National Register, antiques, private baths, majestic buckeye trees. $$ to $$$

Where to Eat

ALIZE AT ELBERTA, *4320 Liberty Ave., (216) 967-2200*. Seafood, steak, prime rib, pasta, garlic soup; small, quaint. $ to $$

CHEZ FRANCOIS, *555 Main St., (216) 967-0630*. Filet de Sole Douvre/Veronique, Coquillage a la Provencale, Supreme de Vollaile/Noisettes et Homard, Filet de Boeuf Wellington a la Perigourdine, daily seasonal specials; also prixe fixe 4-course menu & special 5-course wine dinners; in 1840 bldg. with brick floors/walls & dark wood beams, outdoor cafe. $$$

McGARVEY'S, *5150 Liberty Ave., (216) 967-8000*. Riverfront restaurant serving fresh seafood & Lake Erie fish, dockside service. $ to $$

OLD PRAGUE RESTAURANT, *5586 Liberty Ave., (216) 967-7182*. Czechoslovakian cuisine: Roast Pork with Sauerkraut & Dumplings, Chicken Paprikash, Bohemian Goulash; Lake Erie Yellow Perch; old-world ambiance. $ to $$

Further Information

Vermilion Chamber of Commerce, *5495 Liberty Ave., Vermilion, OH 44089 (216) 967-4477*.

Directions

From Cleveland, OH 2 or Ohio Turnpike west to OH 60, north to Vermilion. Avoid US 6 east, a once-scenic route that is succumbing to "development." US 6 west of Vermilion still retains some of its original beauty.

Zoar Village
Population 177

The streets of the picturesque little village of **Zoar** are entering the 21st century looking in good measure like they did in the first half of the

19th century. Just how this happened is a little piece of classic American history.

Persecuted for their religious beliefs in Germany, a group known as German Separatists immigrated to the United States and founded the town of Zoar – named for Lot's Biblical town of refuge – in 1817. Finding themselves unable to provide for themselves and to pay for their new land, the Zoarites chose to pool their individual properties and operate as a commune. The commune prospered, and by the middle of the century the *Society of Separatists of Zoar* had acquired assets valued at more than $1 million. Among their holdings at one point were four boats on the Ohio & Erie Canal (see Roscoe Village selection).

Economic and social factors were eventually to plague the group, however, and in 1898 the Society disbanded. During the years following, members of the younger generations left to seek brighter futures elsewhere, and outsiders bought and restored the buildings as members of the older generations died. Ten of the buildings have been restored by the Ohio Historical Society. Prominent among the other restorers have been families from Canton, just a few miles to the north.

Five of the historic buildings are log cabins; the rest are two-floor structures, some brick and some frame (but filled with brick masonry, or nogging). The solid old-world construction of the buildings has added to their value and encouraged restoration efforts.

Visitors should first stop by the **Zoar Store** (1833) to purchase tour tickets and to see an introductory video. Reproductions of 19th-century wares are also sold here. (Note – tours are only offered during warmer months.)

The historic district comprises 12 blocks. The most imposing of the buildings maintained by the **Ohio Historical Society**, and therefore open to the public, is the **Number One House** (1835-1845), a Georgian-style house that was the home of Zoar Society leader Joseph Baumeler and several other families. Among the historical society's other properties are the bakery (1845), tin shop (1825), blacksmith shop (1834), wagon shop (1840), and garden and greenhouse (1835).

Zoar may be best known for the beauty of the formal **community garden**. The garden occupies an entire village square and is arranged with geometric precision according to a Biblically-inspired pattern.

The old **Town Hall**, now a museum maintained by the **Zoar Community Association**, displays old photos, tinware, furniture, and other Zoar memorabilia (by appointment). The majority of buildings are private residences, shops, restaurants, and bed and breakfasts (see below). The 1868 **schoolhouse** (usually closed) and 1853 **Meeting House** (now United Church of Christ) are among the village's most handsome buildings.

> • *Because there is no home delivery, Zoarites treat the post office as a common meeting place.*
> • *Men and women possessed equal political rights in The Society of Separatists of Zoar.*

Where to Stay

THE COBBLER SHOP INN B&B, *2nd & Main sts., (216) 874-2600.* 1828 shop/home, rooms restored & furnished to period, "sumptuous" breakfasts. $$

THE ZOAR TAVERN, *P.O. Box 509, 162 Main St., (216) 874-2170.* 1831 home built by village doctor, full-service inn, hand-hewn beams, antiques, Cont. breakfasts, dining room. $$ to $$$

Where to Eat

INN ON THE RIVER, *S of Zoar off Dover/Zoar Rd., P.O. Box 452, (216) 874-3770.* Seafood, blackened shark, steak, 2-in.-thick pork chops; 1830 canal inn, outdoor gazebo & patio area with grill. $$

THE ZOAR TAVERN, *(see above).* Fresh seafood, fresh-cut steaks, vegetarian selections, sandwiches, salads, "sumptuous" homemade desserts; casual tavern-style atmosphere. $$

Further Information

Zoar Village State Memorial, *P.O. Box 404, Zoar, Ohio 44697 (216) 874-3011/(800) 874-4336.*

Directions

From Cleveland, I 77 south to exit 93 (Bolivar), OH 212 south to Zoar.

Other Charming Ohio Towns

Bath
Bellevue
Milan
Oberlin

398

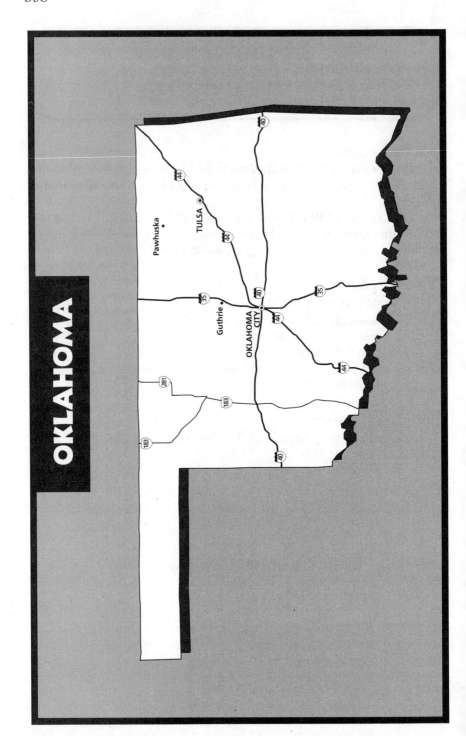

OKLAHOMA

OKLAHOMA

Guthrie

Population 10, 518

At high noon on April 22, 1889 a pistol was shot and thousands dashed across the border into Oklahoma to claim free land in the central part of the state. Some went by train, others by horseback, wagon, or foot. In the morning **Guthrie** consisted of not much more than a train depot; by evening there was a tent and wagon city of some 10,000 *Boomers*. From 1890 until 1907 Guthrie was the territorial capital of Oklahoma, and from 1907 to 1910 the state capital. Then the capital was moved to Oklahoma City, and Victorian Guthrie stood still.

Embracing 400 city blocks and more than 1,300 pre-1910 buildings, Guthrie today has one of the largest urban historic districts in the United States. Virtually every building from the 19th century survives. Much more than a museum, the beautifully restored downtown is alive with shops, restaurants, an original saloon, and turn-of-the-century trolleys. A carriage can frequently be seen conveying newlyweds to the **Harrison House** (see below).

Guthrie is home to several quite unique museums. Site of Oklahoma's first daily newspaper, the **State Capital Publishing Museum** features turn-of-the-century printing equipment. The **Oklahoma Frontier Drug Store Museum**, a turn-of-the-century pharmacy, is furnished with wooden drug-store fixtures and antique wall cabinets with pharmacy memorabilia. Among the displays is a 1910 wooden telephone booth. Yet another museum, the **Oklahoma Territorial Museum**, is a showcase of territorial and early statehood artifacts.

Dominating Guthrie's skyline, the **Scottish Rite Masonic Temple** boasts stained-glass windows, an elegant marble atrium, two theaters, a ballroom, reading salons, and a Gothic library. Many rooms re-create important periods of architecture, including Egyptian, Assyrian, Pompeiian, Italian Renaissance, and Robert Adam. The structure is the largest Scottish Rite temple in the world (open to the public).

A cultural center today as it was in territorial days, Guthrie has the only full-time professional theater in Oklahoma. The **Pollard Resident Theatre Company** performs classic and contemporary plays and musicals in two theaters 11 months each year. As for music, one of the lovely theaters of the Masonic Temple hosts a first-class concert series.

Special Feature

The **National Cowboy Hall of Fame and Western Heritage Center** is about 25 miles south of Guthrie in Oklahoma City. The museum features the Old West with paintings, statuary, portraits of TV and film stars, life-size settings, stagecoaches, and other exhibits.

> • *When the "89ers" reached Guthrie, they found that many of the choicest properties had been claimed by people who had sneaked in before the rush. These, and eventually all Oklahomans, came to be known as "Sooners."*
> • *A Guthrie city directory published several months after the rush listed 39 doctors and surgeons, 40 restaurants, and 46 grocery stores.*

Where to Stay

HARRISON HOUSE, *124 W. Harrison St., (800) 375-1001*. In five restored turn-of-century buildings, antiques, period wallpapers & curtains, private baths, Continental "plus" breakfasts, restaurant, highly rated. $$ to $$$

THE REDSTONE COUNTRY INN B&B, *1016 W. Warner St., (405) 282-0012*. English-style country inn, suites with antiques, private baths, full "gourmet" breakfasts, beverages. $$$

ROSEWOOD MANOR, *401 E. Cleveland, (405) 282-8431*. Oklahoma Territory's first stone-and-brick home (1895), parquetry, full breakfasts. $$ to $$$

SAVANNAH ROSE, *123 S. Capital, (405) 282-7497*. Circa 1904 home, full "gourmet" breakfasts, known for lunches & dinners (by reservation). $$ to $$$

THE SEELY HOUSE B&B & COTTAGE, *701 E. Mansur, (405) 282-8889*. 1893 Classical Revival home, antiques, fireplaces, TV, private baths, whirlpools, full breakfasts, refreshments, verandah. $$ to $$$

THE STONE LION INN, *1016 W. Warner St., (405) 282-0012*. 1907 mansion amongst old pecan trees, private baths, full "gourmet" breakfasts, mystery weekends. $$ to $$$

VICTORIAN ROSE B&B, *415 E. Cleveland St., (800) 767 3015*. Circa 1894 Queen Anne home, antiques, private baths, full "gourmet" breakfasts, coffee/tea, wrap-around porch with wicker swing. $$ to $$$

Where to Eat

THE BLUE BELLE, *224 W. Harrison St., (405) 260-2355*. Sandwiches, steaks, crab legs; Western saloon where Tom Mix bartended (1902-1904). $

GEORGE'S, *202 W. Harrison Ave., (405) 282-7771.* Grilled Swordfish, Roast Duck, Ribeye. $$

GRANNY HAD ONE, *113 W. Harrison St., (405) 282-4482.* Evening buffets featuring chicken, barbecued brisket, beef pot roast, home-made pastries. $

THE STABLES CAFE, *223 N. Division, (405) 282-0893.* Barbecue, hand-cut steaks, chicken-fried steak, spaghetti, Tex-Mex entrees. $ to $$

Further Information

Guthrie Convention & Visitors Bureau, *P.O. Box 995, Guthrie, OK 73044 (800) 299-1889.*

Directions

From Oklahoma City, I 35 north to exit 157 (Guthrie exit).

Pawhuska

Population 3, 825

Up in northern Oklahoma and far from the interstates stretches a region of grassland hills known as the **Osage**. The landscape is reminiscent of the High Plains, although these don't begin for more than another 100 miles to the west. Home to a few ranchers and a sprinkling of little towns, the area hasn't been known to many since the oil-boom days of the 1920s.

Although small, **Pawhuska** is the seat of **Osage County**, capital of the **Osage Indian Nation**, and the largest town for miles. Part of the town's charm is that it doesn't seem to belong. A downtown filled with mostly brick turn-of-the-century and 1920s buildings (89 of them on the National Register) might belong in many places, but not in a valley among the vast expanses of the **Osage Hills**.

The best way to see Pawhuska is to park your car and, as with most charming towns, explore the downtown by foot. Unlike most charming towns, however, the downtown here is still being discovered by outsiders. It's the original. There are a few art galleries and antique and curio shops, but too few (as yet) to impart a touristy flavor. The most historic of the buildings include the **Immaculate Conception Catholic Church** (1887), noted for its beautifully colored stained-glass windows, and the **Constantine Theatre**, opened in 1914 as a grand playhouse after conversion from a hotel built in the mid-1880s. Both structures may be toured by appointment.

The **Osage Tribal Museum**, part of the **Osage Agency Campus**, boasts a collection of over 2,000 rare photographs of early Osage Indians and the town of Pawhuska. The museum, the oldest continually operated tribal museum in the country, is situated on a hill overlooking the town and can be reached by car or by foot using a stairway leading from downtown.

Exhibits of the **Osage County Historical Museum** include a monument to the country's first Boy Scout Troop (established in 1909), two Santa Fe Railroad cars that once served Pawhuska, and a restored one-room schoolhouse.

Just seven miles north of town starts Pawhuska's (and Oklahoma's) most important old-new attraction, the Nature Conservancy's recently established **Tallgrass Prairie Preserve**. The purpose of the preserve is to restore a native American tallgrass prairie ecosystem. The preserve, now totaling over 36,000 acres, may be visited by following a marked drive. Along the way are scenic overlooks where visitors may step out of their cars and take a closer look at the flora and fauna, including perhaps some of the recently reintroduced American bison. Information is available at the Pawhuska Visitors Center (Chamber of Commerce) as well as at the preserve headquarters.

Special Features

Taking a nature walk at **Osage Hills State Park** northeast of Pawhuska offers an especially enjoyable way to become acquainted with the starkly beautiful Osage.

One of the finest Western museums in the country, the **Woolaroc Museum and Wildlife Preserve**, is just a 30-minute drive east of Pawhuska. The museum and preserve are the legacy of a 3,600-acre ranch built by the founder of the Phillips Petroleum Company in the 1920s. The museum is celebrated for its artwork, including paintings by Frederic Remington and Charles Russell, and its outstanding collections of Navajo blankets, Colt Paterson firearms, and other Indian and Western art and artifacts.

Lake Pawhuska, three miles west of town, is a winter trout-fishing lake. Camp sites and other facilities are available.

> • *Until the Allotment Act of 1906 the Osage Indians roamed the prairies as they wished and held the land in common.*
> • *Under President Ulysses S. Grant's "Church Policy," the Quakers were given charge of the country to which the Osage Indians were assigned. However, many of the Indians were (and are) members of the Roman Catholic Church because of an earlier contact with that church.*

Where to Stay

INN AT WOODYARD FARMS, *Rt. 2 (Box 190), (918) 287-2699/fax (918) 287-4616*. 1880s-style farmhouse on 74 rolling acres of working cattle farm, antiques, phones, private baths, full "Oklahoma-style" breakfasts. $$

Where to Eat

BAD BRAD'S BAR-B-Q, *1215 W. Main St., (918) 287-1212*. "Best Bar-B-Q in Oklahoma, Kansas AND Texas!" $
BLUESTEM CAFE, *114 E. Main St., (918) 287-2308*. Home cooking in true main-street cafe. $

Further Information

Pawhuska Chamber of Commerce, *222 W. Main St., Pawhuska, OK 74056 (918) 287-1208.*

Directions

From Tulsa, OK 11 north to OK 99, OK 99 north to US 60, US 60 west to Pawhuska.

Other Charming Oklahoma Towns

Elk City
Freedom
Hominy
Sulphur

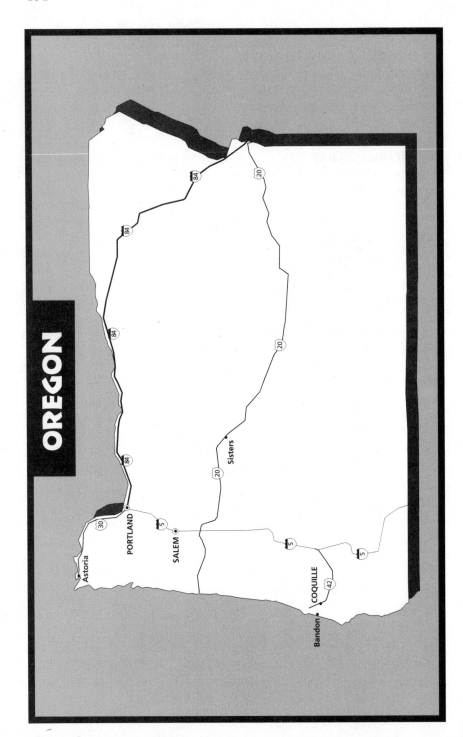

OREGON

Astoria

Population 10, 069

Astoria is in some ways a small American edition of a Scottish port city. In the background are hazy, brooding mountains; closer in are patches of rich green and, in the foreground, the waters of a large estuary, or firth. The city also has a long maritime history, just as do Scottish cities.

The **Astoria Column** up on **Coxcomb Hill** is especially reminiscent of Edinburgh, a Scottish city known for its classical hilltop memorials. The 125-foot column makes an ideal first stop on a visit to Astoria. Dedicated in 1926 and patterned after the Trajan Column in Rome (erected in 114 A.D.), the column bears a pictorial frieze commemorating landmark events in Astoria's history. Inside is a 164-step circular staircase leading to a breathtaking view of the lower **Columbia River** and the **Pacific Ocean**.

Salmon canneries and logging, fishing, and shipbuilding industries turned Astoria into a lively boom town in the late 1800s (the town was apparently also a notorious shanghaiing port), and Astoria's Victorian homes remain a tangible reminder of those times. Many of the homes are now bed & breakfast inns (a few are listed below).

Perhaps the best known of the houses is the 1885 **Capt. George Flavel Mansion**, now a museum of the **Clatsop County Historical Society**. Among the house's many outstanding features are six handcrafted fireplace mantels, each carved from a different hardwood and accented by a different imported tile surround.

The Clatsop County Historical Society also maintains two other museums, the **Uppertown Firefighters** and the **Heritage**. Among the firefighting memorabilia on display at the former are fire engines that range from the hand-pulled to the motorized. The Heritage Museum, housed in Astoria's old Neoclassical city hall (circa 1904), has exhibits tracing the natural and cultural histories of Astoria and the Columbia River.

Astoria is blessed with one of the finest marine museums in the world, the **Columbia River Maritime Museum**. In the Great Hall, designed with a soaring waveform, and in seven exhibit galleries are displays on fishing and whaling, steamboating and sailing, history and adventure. Some of the exhibits are real-life vessels, including the West Coast's last seagoing lighthouse, now a floating National Historic Landmark.

Special Features

Nearby **Fort Stevens Historic Area & Military Museum** offers Civil War re-enactments, historical tours, and scenic views of the Columbia River. Fort Stevens was the only military installation in the continental U.S. to be fired on by the Japanese in World War II (June 21, 1942).

The mouth of the Columbia River provides some of the finest fishing in the world. Boat charters are available.

> • *Known as the "Graveyard of the Pacific, " the region around the mouth of the Columbia River has seen the loss of more than 100 ships and 2, 000 small craft.*
> • *Over four miles long, the Astoria Bridge is the longest continuous truss span bridge in the world.*

Where to Stay

ASTORIA INN B&B, *3391 Irving Ave., (503) 325-8153.* 1890s farmhouse on hillside overlooking river, private baths, full "country" breakfasts, snacks. $$ to $$$

COLUMBIA RIVER INN B&B, *1681 Franklin Ave., (800) 847-2475.* 1870 "Painted Lady," private baths, full breakfasts, river views, quiet & convenient. $$ to $$$

FRANKLIN STREET STATION B&B, *1140 Franklin St., (800) 448-1098.* 1900 home of shipbuilder, antique furnishings, private baths, full breakfasts. $$ to $$$

GRANDVIEW B&B, *1574 Grand Ave., (800) 488-3250.* 3-story Victorian home with river view, some private baths, suites available, close to sights. $ to $$$

ROSEBRIAR HOTEL, *636 14th St., (800) 487-0224/(503) 325-7427/ fax (503) 325-6937.* 1902 Colonial Revival inn, formerly convent, antiques, fireplaces, TV & phones, private baths, spas & whirlpools, full breakfasts, refreshments, verandah, scenic views, winner of preservation award. $$ to $$$

Where to Eat

CAFE UNIONTOWN, *218 W. Marine Dr., (503) 325-8708.* Northwest Cioppino, House-smoked Rock Cornish Game Hen, Filet Mignon, pastas; in 1907 building overlooking river, live music. $$

COLUMBIAN CAFE, *1114 Marine Dr., (503) 325-2233.* Seafood, pastas, crepes, rice dishes, frittatas; unusual & tantalizing menu. $ to $$

PIER 11 FEEDSTORE & DELI, *77 11th St., (503) 325-0279.* Sauteed seafood, chops, steaks; in converted freight depot, unique atmosphere. $ to $$

SHIP INN, *1 2nd St., (503) 325-0033*. A true fish-and-chips house, one of best seafood restaurants in Oregon. $ to $$

SOMEPLACE ELSE, *965 Commercial St., (503) 325-3500*. Spaghettis, linguines, raviolis, Lasagna alla Casserola, Eggplant Parmigiana, Chicken Cacciatori. $

Further Information

Astoria-Warrenton Area Chamber of Commerce & Visitor Center, *P.O. Box 176, Astoria, OR 97103 (503) 325-6311.*

Directions

From Portland, either US 30 or US 26 northwest to Astoria.

Bandon

Population 2, 770

Within the city limits of **Bandon** (or **Bandon-by-the-Sea**) is one of the most beautiful beaches on the West Coast. Rock-studded and with smooth white sand, it may be the most beautiful between Alaska and Acapulco. At least the locals think so. Off shore are spectacular rocks, or *seastacks*, home to seals and other animals. Bandon also has a river, the **Coquille**, and two national wildlife refuges within its limits.

Bandon's **Old Town** embraces a colorful collection of art galleries and craft shops. Not only do visitors admire and/or shop for arts and crafts, they watch the works take shape as quilters, silversmiths, leathersmiths, and others display their skills. Some of the shops are in historic buildings that were fortunate enough to escape devastating fires in 1914 and 1936. Cranberry products are among the items unique to Bandon's shops – one shop offers free samples of cranberry candy.

Even considering its marine location, Bandon offers the visitor an unusually wide variety of activities. Seal watching and, in season, whale watching are popular. (Don't disturb seal pups resting on the shore—their mothers may reject them.) Birdwatching is also popular—puffins, for example, can be seen in the spring on **Elephant** and **Table Rocks**. Fishing, both dockside and deep-water, is excellent. So are clamming and crabbing. Crab rings as well as fishing gear can be rented.

Among the many other beach activities are kite-flying, horseback riding, and tidepooling. Beachcombing is rewarded with finds of driftwood, petrified wood, agate, and jasper. Windsurfing is popular on the river and local lakes; there's a windsurfing school south of town.

Special Features

Several tempting tour sites for the beach- and shopping-weary: a seafood processing plant, a cheese factory, a cranberry bog (seasonal), the **Bandon Historical Society Museum**. Check with the Chamber of Commerce for details.

Hundreds of free-roaming birds and animals may be met, petted, filmed, and talked to at **West Coast Game Park** south of town.

The restored Coquille River Lighthouse (1896) is probably Bandon's most photographed landmark and one of the few American lighthouses ever to be rammed by a ship (in 1903).

Where to Stay

BAILEY'S CEDAR HOUSE B&B, *2226 Seven Devils Rd., (541) 347-3356.* In wooded country setting near secluded beaches, suite with private entrance & bath, TV, full breakfasts, hot tub. $$

BANDON BEACH HOUSE, *2866 Beach Loop Dr., (541) 347-1196.* Ocean-front inn, river-rock fireplaces, private baths, full breakfasts, ocean views, easy beach access. $$$

FLORAS LAKE HOUSE B&B, *92870 Boice Cope Rd., (541) 348-2573.* New home over sand dune from ocean/beach, private baths, Cont. "plus" breakfasts, common room with open-beamed ceiling & wood stove, decks. $$$

LIGHTHOUSE B&B, *650 Jetty Rd., P.O. Box 24, (541) 374-9316.* On beach, fireplaces, private baths, whirlpools, full breakfasts, wine, panoramic views. $$$

PACIFIC HOUSE, *2165 Beach Loop Dr., (541) 347-9526.* Home across from "Face Rock," original art, TV, private baths, Cont. "plus" breakfasts, some pets, outdoor spa, ocean view, access to miles of beach. $$ to $$$

SEA STAR GUESTHOUSE, *370 First St., (541) 347-9632.* In heart of Old Town, open-beam ceilings, TV, private baths, optional full breakfasts, lofts, suites, decks, harbor & beachland views. $ to $$

Where to Eat

BANDON BOATWORKS, *S. Jetty Rd., (541) 347-2111.* Fresh seafood, clam chowder, poultry, steaks, prime rib; ocean-view dining. $ to $$

CHRISTOPHE AT FACE ROCK, *3225 Beach Loop Dr., (541) 347-3261/(800) 638-3092.* Fresh Salmon, Duck Breast & Fresh Oyster Chardonnay, Jambalaya, Pasta Nicoise; European-style inn. $$ to $$$

HARP'S, *480 First St. SW, (541) 347-9057.* Garter Filet (filet mignon marinated in garlic & teriyaki), Scampi Montezuma, Halibut (charbroiled with a hot pistachio sauce); on bay & river, view of lighthouse & marsh, popular. $$

LORD BENNETT'S, *1695 Beach Loop Dr., (541) 347-3663*. Seafood entrees, broiled steaks, house specialties; panoramic views of coastline. $$

Further Information

Bandon Chamber of Commerce, *300 Second St. SE, P.O. Box 1515, Bandon, OR 97411 (541) 347-9616/fax (541) 347-7006.*

Directions

From Portland, I 5 south to exit 120, OR 42 west either to Coquille (and 42S to Bandon) or to US 101 (and south to Bandon).

Sisters

Population 820

Sisters is a tribute to what can happen when a spectacular setting is complemented with human planning and imagination. Overlooked by the snow-capped peaks – including those of the **Three Sisters** – of central Oregon's **Cascade Range**, and bordered by forests of towering ponderosa pines, Sisters's setting would itself guarantee the town high marks.

But what makes the little town so special is its Old West flavor. Originally because of special incentives, and more recently a building code, buildings in the downtown area conform to an 1880s' architectural style. The building code also restricts elevations to 30 feet or less, thereby preserving the panoramic views of the Cascades. The result is a business district with charm and character—the kind of place where people linger even when they've got nothing particular to buy.

The range of goods in the shops is impressive for a small town (although Sisters serves an area of several thousand). Bordering the Western streets are galleries, boutiques, and an especially interesting and diverse array of gift and specialty shops.

Sisters opens onto an outdoor paradise. There are no fewer than nine public and private golf courses within 25 miles of town. The region's many unspoiled rivers, lakes, and streams provide opportunities for sailing, boating, swimming, rafting, and fishing. The mountains and forests beckon horseback riders, hikers, and climbers. For the winter months there are two major downhill ski areas and hundreds of trails for cross-country skiing, snowshoeing, and snowmobiling. The snowmobile trails rank among the best in the country.

410 AMERICA'S MOST CHARMING TOWNS & VILLAGES

The Sisters area is dotted with resorts and campgrounds. Several outfitters cater to those planning trips into the wilderness.

Special Features

The approximately 100-mile loop of a National Scenic Byway begins just west of town. One part of it, **McKenzie Highway (OR 242)**, is closed in the winter. Check locally for routing and road conditions.

The crystal-clear **Metolius River** emerges from the ground at the base of **Black Butte** in **Camp Sherman**, a community northwest of Sisters. The 42-degree water forms one of the largest spring-fed rivers in the country.

> *Many of the peaks in the nearby Cascades are potentially active volcanoes, especially South Sister and Mt. Bachelor.*

Where to Stay

CASCADE COUNTRY INN, *15870 Barclay Dr., P.O. Box 834, (503) 549-4666/(800) 316-0089.* New home with custom wall murals, antiques, handmade quilts, private baths, full breakfasts, refreshments, mountain bikes. $$$

CONKLIN'S GUEST HOUSE, *69013 Camp Polk Rd., (503) 549-0123.* 1910 ranch house with panoramic views of mountains & forests, private baths, full "country" breakfasts, refreshments, heated pool, gardens, trout ponds. $$ to $$$

LAKE CREEK LODGE *(in Camp Sherman), Star Route (Sisters), (503) 595-6331.* Rustic cabins, since 1935. $$$ (MAP, summers)

SQUAW CREEK B&B INN, *68733 Junipine Ln., P.O. Box 1993, (503) 549-4312/(800) 930-0055.* Home in 8.5 acres of ponderosa pine & aspen groves, TV, private baths, full breakfasts, hot tub. $$$

Where to Eat

THE GALLERY RESTAURANT, *230 W. Cascade St., (503) 549-2631.* "Old-Fashioned Family Restaurant." $ to $$

HOTEL SISTERS RESTAURANT, *105 W. Cascade St., (503) 549-7427.* Western saloon & restaurant in renovated 1914 hotel. $$

KOKANEE CAFE, *25545 SW FS Rd. 1419 (Camp Sherman), (541) 595-6420.* Kokanee Trout, East Coast Bay Clams, Fresh Fish of the Day, Chicken Metolius, New York Steak, Grilled Tofu & Noodle Stir Fry; lodging upstairs, seasonal. $$

Further Information

Sisters Area Chamber of Commerce, *P.O. Box 430, Sisters, OR 97759 (503) 549-0251.*

Directions

From Portland, I 5 south to exit 233 (Corvallis), US 20 east to Sisters.

Other Charming Oregon Towns

Cannon Beach
Hood River
Jacksonville
Newberg
Yachats

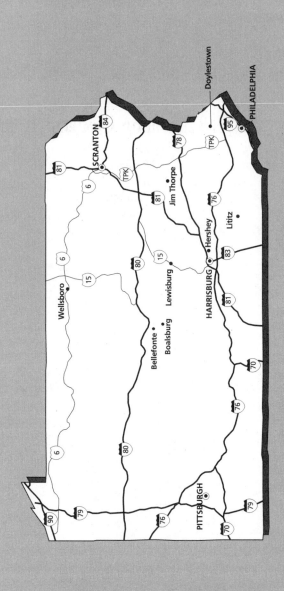

PENNSYLVANIA

Bellefonte

Population 6, 358

Visitors sometime arrive expecting the **Big Spring** in **Bellefonte** to be another Old Faithful. They shouldn't. The Big Spring doesn't gush, or do anything else very dramatic, although it does produce 11,500,000 gallons a day, enough for Bellefonte's water supply. The Big Spring is a looking pond, a peaceful place to be. Adjacent is **Talleyrand Park**, with gazebo and foot bridges, where people stroll on Sundays and listen to concerts by local musicians. A nice place to relax awhile.

Bellefonte is a relaxed kind of town in general. Maybe it's because the town's growth leveled off around the turn of the century and a little of the way of life of another century still lingers. The old residential streets as well as downtown share in the attitude.

The walking-tour brochure distributed by the Chamber of Commerce is in fact an 1874 city map with 45 little numbers superimposed to show the more important sites. The map's message is clear: A lot of what was Bellefonte in 1874 is still around.

Throughout the town are fine old buildings, with the accent on fine as much as old. Especially noteworthy are the early **Georgian buildings**. A beautiful example is the gray-stone, white-shuttered 1815 **Potter Home**. This lovely building now houses an interesting historical museum. Other notable structures include the handsome Gothic Revival **Brockerhoff Hotel** (1864/1865), the largely classical **Hastings Mansion** (1840s), and the flamboyant but picturesque **Crider Exchange Building** (1872).

Visitors who enjoy strolling shaded streets flanked by 19th-century mansions should include Linn, Curtin, and North Allegheny streets in their tour. For the evening, the **Garman Opera House**, a restored 1890s vaudeville house, stands ready to entertain with live theater, concerts, and other presentations.

Special Feature

At the old brick **Train Station** the **Bellefonte Historical Railroad** offers seasonal excursions aboard its two rail diesel cars. The excursion to **Curtin Village**, a 19th-century ironworks village with restored furnace and 1831 ironmaster's mansion, is particularly recommended.

> • *Bellefonte ("beautiful fountain") started out as Big Spring, but was renamed after "Big Spring" was visited by the French statesman, Talleyrand, in exile in America from 1794 to 1796.*
> • *Bellefonte was one of the first towns in the world to have electricity (1884).*

Where to Stay

THE ANNIE NATT HOUSE B&B, *127 W. Curtin St., (814) 353-1456.* 1882 Italianate vernacular home, Oriental carpets, fireplaces, private baths, choice of full or Cont. breakfasts weekends. $$ to $$$

EARLYSTOWN MANOR, *RR #1 (Box 181A; Centre Hall 16828), (800) 644-4842/(814) 466-6118.* Home that "reproduces exquisite splendor of early 1900s," private baths, full breakfasts, panoramic views of central Penn. countryside. $$$

REYNOLDS MANSION B&B, *101 W. Linn St., (814) 353-8407/(800) 899-3929.* 1885 red sandstone home with blend of late 19th-century styles, marble vestibule, inlaid parquet floors, fireplaces, private baths, whirlpools, full "gourmet" breakfasts, billiard room. $$$

Where to Eat

THE GAMBLE MILL TAVERN & RESTAURANT, *160 Dunlap St., (814) 355-7764.* Maryland Crabcakes, Seafood Strudel, Kirshwasser Pork, Butternut Ravioli; in restored grist mill with origins in 1786, bar. $ to $$

Further Information

Bellefonte Intervalley Area Chamber of Commerce, *320 W. High St. (Train Station), Bellefonte, PA 16823 (814) 355-2917/fax (814) 355-2761.*

Directions

From Scranton/Wilkes-Barre, I 81 south to I 80, west to exit 23, PA 150 south to Bellefonte.

Boalsburg

Population 2, 206

Quiet, shady sidewalks nudging friendly old two-story houses. Black shutters against white on some houses, lots of gingerbread on others.

Picket fences and potted flowers. People chatting on broad, cool porches. Shops and other businesses just a stroll down the tree-canopied street. A romanticized image of the 19th-century small American town, true, but maybe one that's not far off the mark. **Boalsburg** is living proof of that.

Settled by families of Scots-Irish background in 1808, Boalsburg came of age during the 19th century. Major action–including the establishment of Penn State's ancestor at nearby State College–tended to bypass the town, however, and Boalsburg was able to retain much of its 19th-century townscape and flavor.

The furnishings of nine generations of the Boal family, the town's founders, may be seen in the family home (1789), now the **Boal Mansion Museum**. On the mansion's grounds are several interesting 18th- and 19th-century structures, but of very special note is the **Columbus Chapel**, which contains religious and secular heirlooms, some dating as far back as the 1400s, that belonged to Christopher Columbus and his family. Described as "the strongest link with Columbus in the USA," the chapel was inherited by a member of the Boal family and moved to the family estate from Spain in 1909.

Another first-class attraction, the **Pennsylvania Military Museum & 28th Division Shrine**, honors the "citizen soldiers" of Pennsylvania from Benjamin Franklin's first military unit in the Revolutionary War through the troops of Operation Desert Storm. Displays in the 65-acre park are both inside and outside and include military equipment, weaponry, monuments, and memorials. Of particular interest is a walk-through exhibit designed to give the visitor a chilling look at World War I trench warfare.

Every tour of Boalsburg must begin, end, or resume with a walk down picturesque Main Street. Here is the **Boalsburg Heritage Museum**, housed in an 1825 home, featuring pieces from old homes in the area as well as a gallery. Here also is **Duffy's Tavern**, a handsome stone stage-coach tavern (1819; see below). And here also are little establishments that will delight shoppers, window as well as serious, with their selections of antiques, gifts, quilts, gourmet items, cookware, and seasonal crafts.

Special Feature

State College, home of the **Pennsylvania State University** (1855), is only three miles from Boalsburg. Points of interest on the attractive campus include the administration building, **Old Main** (rebuilt 1929), and its land-grant frescoes by Henry Varnum Poor; the **creamery**, renowned for its ice creams; and several important museums, including the **Palmer Museum of Art**.

Where to Stay

THE CHATELAINE AT SPLIT FINE FARMHOUSE, *P.O. Box 326 (Pine Grove Mills 16868), (814) 238-2028/(800) 251-2028.* Federal-style farmhouse, some private baths, full breakfasts, tea on Belleek ware. $$$

THE HOUSE ON TOP OF THE HILL B&B, *1800 Earlystown Rd., (814) 466-2070 .* Home on 11 hilltop acres with panoramic view, TV, private baths, full breakfasts. $$$

NITTANY MEADOW FARM, *P.O. Box 311, Rt. 322, (814) 466-7550.* Converted wagon shed with rural views, hand-stenciled walls, designer linens, private baths, adjacent to golf course & ski resort. $$$

SPRINGFIELD HOUSE B&B, *126 E. Main St., P.O. Box 240, (814) 466-6290/(888) 782-9672.* 1847 Federal/Victorian home with wrap-around porch, central location, private baths, full breakfasts, afternoon tea, cottage with apartment. $$$

Where to Eat

DUFFY'S TAVERN, *113 E. Main St., (814) 466-6241.* Seafood, steaks; in historic tavern, antiques. $ to $$

VILLAGE EATINGHOUSE, *109 W. Main St., (814) 466-6865.* Home-style cooking, "delectable" desserts. $ to $$

Further Information

Centre County Convention & Visitors Bureau, *1402 S. Atherton St. (State College 16801), (814) 231-1400/(800) 358-5466/fax (814) 231-8123. (ZIP for Boalsburg is 16827.)*

Directions

From State College, US 322 east to Boalsburg.

Doylestown
Population 8, 575

Doylestown is not a suburb, but neither is it a small rural town. It isn't a tourist spot, but it *is* a spot that many tourists like to visit. Philadelphia isn't far away, but neither is the famed **Bucks County** countryside with its time-mellowed stone farmhouses. Doylestown is a "Main Street" community, with hanging baskets and historic streetlights, but the charm belongs to a real town, a town where families are raised and groceries bought.

Doylestown's 250 years of history, its selection as the county seat of Bucks County, its location and interesting architectural admixture, these and other factors have contributed to an unusually rich cultural heritage and diversity. James A. Michener, Pearl S. Buck, and Oscar Hammerstein II are a few of the creative and accomplished who over the years have chosen to make their homes here.

The town is probably best known for the three unique concrete structures that make up the **Mercer Mile**. The first, **Fonthill Museum** (1908-1910), is the 44-room home built by eccentric millionaire and Renaissance man Henry Chapman Mercer to display his 900 prints and eye-dazzling tile collection. The seven-level building, with no fewer than 32 stairwells and 200 windows of varying size and shape, was inspired by European castles and aided in its design by a good dose of imagination. Fonthill is a National Historic Landmark (guided tour).

The **Mercer Museum** (1913-1916), the second member of the Mercer Mile and also a National Historic Landmark, displays a fabulous collection of more than 50,000 early American tools and other objects. At least 60 Early American trades are represented by the exhibits.

The third building, the **Moravian Pottery and Tile Works** (1912), is a living history museum where decorative tiles and mosaics are produced much as Mercer produced them 90 years ago (self-guided and guided tours).

The **James A. Michener Art Museum of Bucks County**, located in reconstructed buildings of the Bucks County prison, houses a superb collection of 19th- and 20th-century regional American art. The museum is also noted for its outdoor sculpture garden and its permanent exhibition, *James A. Michener: A Living Legacy*, celebrating the famous author's career. The new **Mari Sabusawa Michener Wing** features 12 distinguished Bucks County artists.

Special Features

Just 15 minutes away is **Green Hills Farm**, the 1835 stone farmhouse and 60-acre estate of Nobel and Pulitzer prize-winner Pearl S. Buck (guided tours).

A couple of days can be spent touring lovely **Bucks County**. Among the attractions are storybook farms, wineries, 11 covered bridges, renowned antiquing, historic **New Hope**, and the gardens, shops, and restaurants of **Peddler's Village**.

> • *Concern over the possibility of fire led Henry Mercer to construct the buildings of the Mercer Mile of reinforced concrete.*
> • *The 60-acre Henry Schmieder Arboretum at Delaware Valley College is little-publicized but well worth a visit.*

Where to Stay

DOYLESTOWN INN, 18 *W. State St., (215) 345-6610.* Turn-of-century hotel in heart of town, full-service, designer-decorated rooms, dining room, 2 bars. $$ to $$$

THE INN AT FORDHOOK FARM, *105 New Britain Rd., (215) 345-1766.* 18th-century fieldstone country estate on National Register, family antiques, fireplaces, some private baths, full "farm" breakfasts served on family china, tea/lemonade, highly rated. $$$

MILL CREEK FARM B&B, *P.O. Box 816 (Buckingham 18912), 2348 Quarry Rd., (215) 794-0776/(800) 562-1776.* 1730 manor house on 100 picturesque acres, private baths, full "country" breakfasts, pool/spa, tennis, bass pond, horseback riding. $$$

PEACE VALLEY B&B, *75 Chapman Rd., (215) 230-7711.* 1791 farmhouse on pond, fireplaces, private baths, Cont. "plus" breakfasts, tennis, adjacent Peace Valley Park & Nature Center. $$$

PINE TREE FARM, *2155 Lower State Rd., (215) 348-0632.* 1730 stone farmhouse on 16 pastoral acres, antiques, fireplaces, private baths, full breakfasts, sherry, fresh flowers, pool & pond. $$$

Where to Eat

THE BLACK WALNUT, *80 W. State St., (215) 348-0708.* Vegetable Bouillabaisse, Duet of Fresh Duck, Roasted Breast of Chicken Hunter's Style, Salmon Yin-Yang; in converted town house, high ceilings, great reviews. $$ to $$$

CAFE ARIELLE, *100 S. Main St., (215) 345-5930.* Tilapia St. Peters Fish, Pan Seared Venison Medallions, Wild Mushroom Ravioli; chef-owned French bistro in historical landmark, candlelight ambiance, acclaimed. $$ to $$$

DOYLESTOWN INN, *(see above).* American & Continental menu, local specialties, daily lunch/dinner specials; outdoor dining in season. $$

RUSSELL'S RESTAURANT & BAR, *96 W. State St., (215) 345-8746.* Sauteed Atlantic Salmon, Grilled Ahi Tuna, Sauteed Magret Duck, Grilled Dry Aged Black Angus Sirloin; in restored townhouse, watercolors, courtyard, bistro. $$$

Further Information

· **Bucks County Conference & Visitors Bureau, Inc.,** *152 Swamp Rd., Doylestown, PA 18901 (800) 836-2825.*

Directions

From Philadelphia, PA 611 north to Doylestown. **Note:** Regular train service is available from Center City and other Philadelphia stations.

Hershey
Population 11, 860

Hershey's ancestry is very different from that of other towns in this guide. For one thing, almost all of the town is less than 100 years old. For another, this town is a company town, a *planned* company town. This is where Milton Hershey built the world's largest chocolate manufacturing plant between 1903 and 1905. Hershey built a new community around his factory; deliberately avoiding the usual anonymous company town, however, he chose instead to create a "real home town." And somewhere along the line – 1900 is as good a year as any – Hershey was born.

It's hardly surprising that the major sites of this company town all bear the name Hershey. What is more surprising is that some of the most impressive sites were built during the Depression as part of Milton Hershey's attempt to provide jobs.

A 45-minute trolley tour of Hershey's sites is offered year-round:

At **Hershey's Chocolate World Visitors Center**, cars take passengers on a 12-minute tour that explains the chocolate-making process. A food court, souvenir shops featuring chocolate items, and a cafe ensure that not only the brain gets nourished here.

Hersheypark is an attractive 110-acre theme park that really does have something to please everyone. There are more than 55 rides, some of them state-of-the-art. For those uninterested in mechanical thrills, the park offers shows, strolling performers, theme areas that include nostalgic American and 17th- and 18th-century English and German villages, restaurants, and the 11-acre **ZooAmerica North American Wildlife Park**. The zoo features five environments, including an indoor collection of animals and plants native to the Sonoran Desert.

The **Hershey Museum** (est. 1933) has three major themes: the history of Milton Hershey and the town he founded, an outstanding Pennsylvania German collection, and collections of objects representing several native American cultures. A Victorian house stands in the main gallery.

The lovely 23-acre **Hershey Gardens** (est. 1937) features collections of unusual plants, an All-America Rose Selections display garden, old-fashioned roses, a Japanese garden, and many other plantings. Hershey also has one of the country's grand old cinemas, the **Hershey Theatre** (1933). Clouds appear to move among the stars on the elaborate ceiling.

- *The Hershey Rose Gardens attracted more than 20, 000 visitors on opening day in 1937.*
- *Founders Hall, on the Milton Hershey School campus, is capped by the largest unsupported dome in the Western Hemisphere.*

Where to Stay

THE HOTEL HERSHEY, *Hotel Rd., (717) 533-2171*. Full-service resort listed in Historic Hotels of America Registry, Spanish-influenced Fountain Lobby, lovely grounds. $$$

PINEHURST INN, *50 Northeast Dr., (717) 533-2603*. Large inn once student home of Milton Hershey School, some private baths, full breakfasts, close to attractions. $ to $$

Where to Eat

CIRCULAR DINING ROOM, *in The Hotel Hershey (see above)*. Grilled Swordfish Steak, Rock Cornish Game Hen Provencal, Roast Venison; original stained-glass windows, overlooking formal gardens, legendary. $$$

THE FOUNTAIN CAFE, *in The Hotel Hershey (see above)*. Grilled Salmon Caesar Salad, Poached Chicken Salad/Sweet Peppers, pastas, pizza; informal, hand-painted decor, outdoor dining. $

HERSHEY PANTRY, *801 E. Chocolate Ave., (717) 533-7505*. Grilled Italian Chicken Breasts, Broiled Sea Scallops, New York Strip Steak, Chicken Carbonara Fettuccine Alfredo, Angel Hair Neptune; Victorian atmosphere, popular. $$

Further Information

Hershey Entertainment & Resort Co. (HERCO), *300 Park Blvd., P.O. Box 860, Hershey, PA 17033 (800) 437-7439.*

Directions

From Harrisburg, US 322 east to Hershey.

Jim Thorpe
Population 5, 048

The brick and stone towers, steeples, and gables peering from the mountain valley look almost Old World. The narrow, meandering Victorian streets reinforce the impression. But it isn't clear what part of the Old World the town might belong to, and besides, some of the architecture is certainly American. What is clear is that for people who love charming towns, **Jim Thorpe** is a real find.

With roots deep in anthracite coal, canals, the railroad, county government, and later, tourism, **Mauch Chunk** (pronounced MAWK

CHUNK; now Jim Thorpe) prospered throughout the 19th century, especially in the period between the 1850s and 1890s. Much of the prosperity was converted directly into grand homes and public buildings. The town declined, however, in the early 20th century, in parallel with the decline of the coal industry. In an act of hope and a desire to win publicity and tourists, the town in 1954 offered the widow of the famous 1912 Olympic athlete Jim Thorpe a proper burial and memorial for her husband in exchange for the use of his name.

The visitor's first order of business should be by all means a walking tour of the historic district. A good starting point is the **Jersey Central Railroad Station** (1888), which now houses the **Tourist Welcoming Center**. The station has a unique end tower that helps contribute to the town's quaint appearance.

A more prominent tower highlights the rough-faced sandstone **Carbon County Courthouse** (1893). The building's main courtroom is noted for its oak paneling and stained-glass skylight. Yet another prominent tower belongs to the Gothic Revival **St. Mark's Episcopal Church** (1869). The church's stunning interior, open for tours, is distinguished by Tiffany windows, an ornate baptismal font, and an English Minton tile floor.

Millionaires Row and **Stone Row** are picturesque old residential structures. The former, built between 1860 and 1890, consists of homes of families made wealthy by old Mauch Chunk's industries. The latter (also mid-1800s) contains 16 individualized three-story rowhouses built for employees of the Lehigh Valley Railroad. Renovated or undergoing renovation, many of the homes in both rows now house art galleries and studios, antique and specialty shops, apartments, cafes, and B&Bs.

Overlooking downtown and by all means the most imposing of the 19th-century homes is the 20-room **Asa Packer Mansion** (1860). The rooms of the Italianate mansion, open to the public, are furnished with such items as an ancient Egyptian chair and a solid ebony Steinway grand piano.

Jim Thorpe is known today for its cultural calendar and collection of good studios and galleries. As the Mauch Chunk Historical Society puts it, the town has become a "magnet for people involved with the arts, looking for an economic, emotional, and spiritual haven from the urban experience."

There are several ways to enjoy the surrounding **Pocono Mountains**: hiking or biking the 16-mile old **Switchback Railroad** bed, rafting down the **Lehigh River** (guided tours), and taking a scenic train excursion along the Lehigh River. When the mountains are snow-covered, they can be enjoyed by downhill and cross-country skiing, tobogganing, and snowmobiling.

Special Features

Flagstaff Park offers a panoramic view of Jim Thorpe and the Pocono Mountains.

The 20-ton granite **Jim Thorpe Mausoleum** is just east of town on PA 903.

June is the month for the annual **Laurel Festival of the Arts**, a two-week program of chamber-music concerts. Late September and early October bring the **Art Walk**, a festival of the visual arts that includes the juried Sacred Mountain Art Show.

> • *Also among the furnishings of the Asa Packer Mansion is a chair that belonged to Robert E. Lee and a chandelier that was copied for use in the movie "Gone with the Wind."*

Where to Stay

THE INN AT JIM THORPE, *24 Broadway, (717) 325-2599/(800) 329-2599.* Restored New Orleans-style hotel dating to 1840s, National Register, full-service, fireplaces, some whirlpools, Cont. breakfasts, restaurant, Irish pub, game room, porch. $$ to $$$

JT'S, *PA 209 & Hazard Sq., (717) 325-4563.* Renovated 1830s hotel, antiques, magnificent Victorian barroom. $$

TIFFANY'S GRAND VICTORIA B&B, *218 Center St., (717) 325-8260.* 1846 home with mahogany-beam ceiling, antiques, TV, some private baths, full breakfasts, verandah, pool, grape arbor. $

VICTORIA ANN'S B&B, *68 Broadway, (888) 541-2206.* 1860 townhouse on Millionaire's Row, full or Cont. breakfasts served on crystal & silver, gardens. $$

Where to Eat

BLACK BREAD CAFE, *47 Race St., (717) 325-8957.* Gourmet sandwiches, homemade soups, weekend dinners; first floor of unique Victorian townhouse. $ to $$

THE EMERALD RESTAURANT, *24 Broadway, (717) 325-8995.* Irish foods served with "Irish Hospitality." $$ to $$$

THE LANTERN, *US 209 & PA 93 (Nesquehoning 18240), (717) 669-9433.* Italian dining, Absolute Shrimp & Scallops, Chicken Macaluso, Pork Tenderloin with Raspberry Sauce, nightly features, special salads. $$

Further Information

Carbon County Office, **Pocono Mountain Vacation Bureau**, *P.O. Box 27, Jim Thorpe, PA 18229 (717) 325-3673; also,* **Mauch Chunk Histori-**

cal Society of Carbon County, *14-16 W. Broadway, P.O. Box 273, Jim Thorpe (717) 325-4439.*

Directions

From Philadelphia, I 476 (Pennsylvania Tpk. NE Ext.) north to Interchange 34, US 209 west to Jim Thorpe.

Lewisburg
Population 5, 785

The streets of historic **Lewisburg** are bordered by beautiful old buildings that open directly onto the sidewalks. The buildings are generally brick and display a diversity of Victorian decorations and facades that were added, according to the fashion of the period, subsequent to their construction. Between the sidewalks and the streets are period street lamps. Various little gardens, sometimes planted between buildings and sometimes in windowboxes and elsewhere, add color. Many of the buildings, especially those along **Market Street**, house businesses and, upstairs, apartments. The area is so lively – and at the same time charming – that space is in demand.

An old canal and **Susquehanna River** town, with roots in the 18th century, Lewisburg flourished first in the 1820s and 1830s, then again in the middle of the 19th century, and yet again in the 1920s. A number of Federal-style buildings were constructed during the first period of growth; during the second and even more prosperous period, the architecture was Federal Revival, a style similar to but more spacious than the original. The growth of the 1920s occurred largely in what were then the outskirts of town, and so the older buildings were largely protected. Today, 54 19th-century structures, and groups of structures, of special architectural and/ or historic interest line the streets.

Two of the most important have been converted to history museums. The first, the **Packwood House Museum**, was a late 18th-century log tavern that evolved into a three-story Victorian hotel. The rooms now display a wide variety of early Pennsylvania and American decorations and other artifacts. The second museum is the **Slifer House Museum**, a restored 20-room Italianate mansion (1861) with a wrap-around verandah and gracious lawn (tours).

Bucknell University, a private liberal-arts college, has long been a part of Lewisburg – in fact, the first commencement was held in 1851. One of the buildings on the beautiful hillside campus is the state-of-the-art,

1200-seat **Weis Center for the Performance Arts**. The center presents top artists in the fields of music, theater, and dance.

Lewisburg is a major center in central Pennsylvania for the arts and crafts. Of special interest is an 1883 mill that has been restored and converted to an antique and crafts marketplace. Here over 200 dealers and 35 artisans display their antiques and handcrafted wares.

Special Feature

Rail excursions through Lewisburg and the river and farming country about the town are offered by the **West Shore Railroad**. The trips last 1 1/2 or 2 1/2 hours. Inquire locally for schedules.

Scenic PA 45, west of Lewisburg, wanders through a variety of charming communities. The villages of **Mifflinburg** and **Millheim** are especially attractive.

> • *The original name of Lewisburg was Derrstown, after the town's founder, Ludwig Derr. It's not completely clear why the name was later changed; it probably had something to do with the fact that in English "Ludwig" is "Lewis."*
> • *Lewisburg has one of the lowest crime rates in the country.*

Where to Stay

ANNI'S INN & OUTTINGS, *302 N. Third St., (717) 523-7163*. 1850 yellow brick home, Oriental art, full breakfasts, afternoon tea, refreshments, picnic lunches available, help with arranging self-guided cycling & hiking day trips. $$

THE INN AT OLDE NEW BERLIN, *321 Market St. (New Berlin 17855), (717) 966-0321*. Victorian full-service country inn, antiques, Amish quilts, private baths, full breakfasts, nooks, small-town setting. $$$

PINEAPPLE INN, *439 Market St., (717) 524-6200*. 1857 Federal-style home with Greek Revival trim, antiques, full "country" breakfasts, refreshments, piano. $$

TENERIFF FARM B&B, *PA 45 E., (RR 1, Box 314, Milton 17847), (717) 742-9061*. Working farm, "choice" breakfasts, country atmosphere. $$

Where to Eat

ELIZABETH'S–AN AMERICAN BISTRO, *412 Market St., (717) 523-8088*. Roasted Lemon Bay Chicken, Corn Crusted Salmon, Filet of Beef with Portabella Mushrooms, Linguine with Seared Shrimp; changing menu, in 1860s bldg., reservations suggested. $$

GABRIEL'S, *at The Inn at Olde New Berlin (see above)*. Continental & American cuisine "with a Pennsylvania touch," Chicken & Shrimp St. Michael, Pear & Pork. $$

LEWISBURG INN, *101 Market St., (717) 523-8200*. Nouvelle & classical French cuisine, changing menu; award-winning wine list, in early Victorian home. $$

YODERS FAMILY RESTAURANT, *R.D. 1 (Millmont 17845), (717) 922-4688*. Pennsylvania Dutch cooking, own bakery. $

Further Information

Union County Chamber of Commerce, *219 D. Hafer Rd., Lewisburg, PA 17837 (717) 524-2815*.

Directions

From New York City, I 80 west to exit 30 (just across Susquehanna River), US 15 south to Lewisburg.

Lititz

Population 8, 280

The old Moravian town of **Lititz** nicely illustrates what is turning out to be the next stage in the evolution of many of our country's charming towns – the home away from the city. Blessed with a well-preserved 18th-century historic district (and many fine homes from the next two centuries, too), and located not many country miles from several urban centers, Lititz has become a popular place to live for people who work in Lancaster, Harrisburg, even Philadelphia. As is so often true of adopted towns, newcomers to Lititz like to restore old houses and attend crafts shows and weekend band concerts in the park.

Lititz was founded in 1756 by members of the Moravian Church and remained a closed religious community until the mid-1800s. Then, in the mid-1900s a major preservation effort began as people realized that a priceless 18th-century treasure lay along East Main Street. Now, 50 years later, a stroll down **Main Street** is a stroll into the past, but because the splendidly preserved buildings are still in use, the stroll is into a past that is still very much a part of the present.

Two buildings open to the public are the **Johannes Mueller House** (1792), a living museum of a Moravian home and workplace, and the **Schropp House** (1793) next door, now the **Lititz Museum**. Also on Main Street is the restored house (original from 1871) where General John A.

Sutter, of California Gold Rush fame, spent the last seven years of his life. Sutter was buried in the church cemetery behind **Moravian Church Square**.

Linden Hall, the oldest girls' boarding school in the country, is also in the historic district. The school's Sisters' House and Linden Hall were built in 1758 and 1767, respectively.

Special Features

An entertaining history of American candy-making is on display at the **Wilbur Chocolate Company's Candy Americana Museum**. There is also a candy shop.

The **Heritage Map Museum** displays hundreds of original maps from the 15th to the 19th centuries. The museum was created for "lovers of history, science, geography and art."

Marietta and **Strasburg** are two other very charming Lancaster County towns.

> • *The country's first commercial pretzels were made in the bakery adjoining the Peter Kreider House, known as the "Pretzel House."*
> • *Lititz Springs Park is the site of one of the oldest annual 4th of July celebrations in the country.*

Where to Stay

ALDEN HOUSE B&B, *62 E. Main St., (800) 584-0743*. 1850 brick home in historical district, TV, private baths, full breakfasts, afternoon snacks, three porches. $$

SLEEPY MILL FARM B&B, *470 Snavely Mill Rd., (717) 626-6629*. 1802 stone farmhouse, private baths, full "country" breakfasts, millpond. $$

SWISS WOODS B&B, *500 Blantz Rd., (800) 594-8018*. Swiss chalet with massive sandstone fireplace, goose down comforters, private baths, full breakfasts, Snickerdoodles, gardens. $$$

SPAHR'S CENTURY FARM B&B, *192 Green Acre Rd., (717) 627-2185*. Circa 1855 farmhouse on peaceful 70-acre working dairy farm, country decor. $$

Where to Eat

LOG CABIN, *11 Lehoy Forest Dr. (Leola), (717) 626-1181*. American-style menu; since 1933, 7 dining rooms with 18th- & 19th-century paintings, award-winning. $$ to $$$

THE OLDE GREENFIELD INN, *595 Greenfield Rd. (Lancaster), (717) 393-0668*. Seafood, poultry, beef; in stone farmhouse dating to 1820s, fireplace, piano lounge, brick patio. $$

Further Information

Pennsylvania Dutch Convention & Visitors Bureau, *501 Greenfield Rd., Lancaster, PA 17601 (800) 723-8824/(717) 299-8901. (ZIP for Lititz is 17543.)*

Directions

From Harrisburg, I 76 east to exit 20, PA 72 south to Manheim, PA 772 to Lititz.

Wellsboro

Population 3, 430

The **Allegheny Plateau** of north central Pennsylvania is one of the most rugged and scenic areas of the eastern United States. It is also one of the least populated – and least known. Its most dramatic geographic feature is the spectacular *Grand Canyon of Pennsylvania*, a winding 50-mile-long, 1,000-foot-deep gorge. Its most beautiful little town is **Wellsboro**.

Wellsboro is a community of wide boulevards, gas lights, lovely large homes, and stately old elms and maples. The town is sometimes described as "New England-like". The mood is decidedly relaxed and friendly, the kind of place where a shopping trip becomes a social event.

The townspeople are openly proud of their **Main Street**, a beautifully manicured boulevard lined with nicely preserved Victorian buildings. One of the elms along the way dates back to the 1700s. On the public square, or **The Green**, is another object of pride – a fountain with the delightful bronze statue *Wynken, Blynken and Nod* (1938). Next to the fountain is a plaque bearing Eugene Field's famous poem.

Two of Wellsboro's most handsome buildings are the 1835 **county courthouse**, facing The Green, and the 1894 **First Presbyterian Church**. The **"Lincoln Door House"** has a front door that was an 1858 gift from Abraham Lincoln to the owners; the door came from a building in Springfield, Illinois. The **Wellsboro Cemetery** (1855) has many historic tombs and a beautiful setting.

The **Tioga County Historical Society Museum** is located in the **Robinson House** (circa 1820, with 1840s' additions), listed on the National Register. Originally a tavern, the museum features an 1892 Estey organ and items associated with the life of author George Washington Sears, known by the Indian name of Nessmuk. In the **Museum Annex**, a replica of the Greek Revival 1864 First National Bank, are a 1923 Model T Ford truck and various military, home-making, dressmaking, and millinery exhibits.

The seat of a county with 100 miles of stocked streams, seven lakes, and abundant state forests and parks, Wellsboro is one of Pennsylvania's most popular sporting centers. Summer sports include boating, fishing, golfing, and horseback riding. With the winter come downhill and cross-country skiing, snowmobiling, ice fishing, and skating. The canyon is perfect for white-water rafting and canoeing when the spring waters are up.

Special Features

The streams and lookout points of the **Pennsylvania Grand Canyon** begin just a few miles out of town. Self-guided driving tours through the area are aided by a series of directional arrows of different colors.

> *The statue of "Wynken, Blynken and Nod" was the work of Mabel Landrum Torrey. A marble version of the work may be seen in Denver's Washington Park.*

Where to Stay

CANYON MOTEL, *18 East Ave., (717) 724-1681/(800) 255-2718.* Locally owned motel downtown, pool. $

COACH STOP INN, *US 6, RR 4 (Box 137), (717) 724-5361/(800) 829-4130.* Motel associated with early 19th-century home, on 100 acres 1 mi from Pennsylvania Grand Canyon, restaurant, lounge. $ to $$

COLTON POINT MOTEL, *RR 4 (Box 138), (717) 724-2155/(800) 829-4122.* Motel on 50 acres, 1 mi from Pennsylvania Grand Canyon, "country" breakfasts, stocked pond, rowboat, beach area. $ to $$

THE PENN WELLS HOTEL & LODGE, *Main St., P.O. Box 158, (717) 724-2111 / (800) 545-2446.* Hotel with beginnings in 1869 & modern lodge, both full-service, dining room, pool, health club. $ to $$

Where to Eat

HARLAND'S FAMILY STYLE RESTAURANT, *Pearl St., (717) 724-3311.* Casual family dining with daily specials & homemade soups, breads, & pies. $

THE PENN WELLS HOTEL DINING ROOM, *Main St., (800) 545-2446*. Trout Almondine, Sauteed Chicken Breast, Beef Tenderloin Tips, Broiled Petit Filet, Broiled Scallops, daily specials, Sunday smorgasbord; 19th-century dining room, linens & silver. $$

THE STEAK HOUSE, *Main St., (717) 724-9092*. Seafood, poultry, variety of steaks, daily specials, sandwich platters; reservations encouraged. $ to $$

THE WELLSBORO DINER, *Main St., (717) 724-3992*. Diner in continuous operation since 1939, unique atmosphere, popular. $

Further Information

Wellsboro Area Chamber of Commerce, *P.O. Box 733, Wellsboro, PA 16901 (717) 724-1926*.

Directions

From Rochester (NY), I 390 south to NY 17, NY 17 south to US 15 (near Corning), US 15 south to US 6 (Mansfield), US 6 west to Wellsboro.

Other Charming Pennsylvania Towns

Chadds Ford/Kennett Square
Harmony
Hanover
Marietta
Meadowcroft Village (Avella)
Mechanicsburg
New Hope
Old Economy Village (Ambridge)
Punxsutawney
Shippensburg
Strasburg
Volant

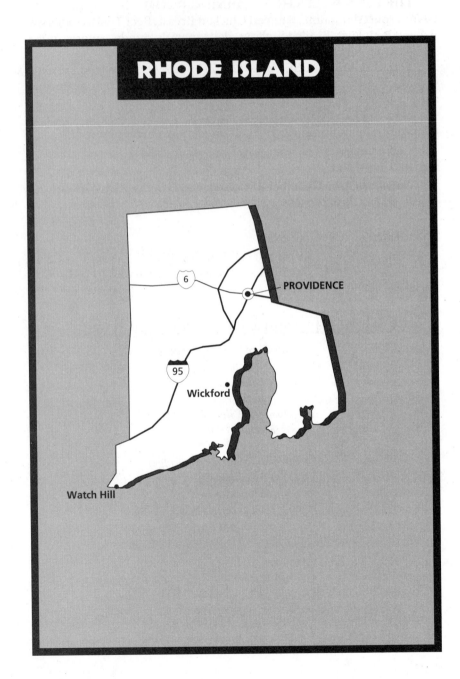

RHODE ISLAND

Rhode Island

Watch Hill

Population 500

Watch Hill, an Historic Landmark Community, is really three villages in one, and there are plenty of breathtaking views of the Atlantic for all of them. The first is a seaside resort, a place where families have been coming for beachside holidays since the 1840s. The second is a charming little harbor village where Westerly people come to shop for a special gift or enjoy a lunch by the sea.

The third is a colony, founded in the late 1800s, of summer homes owned by a tightly-knit group of American aristocrats. The great Victorian homes, or *cottages*, are elegant but sprawl more casually than their cousins in nearby Newport. Although the occupants and the interiors of the mansions are usually inaccessible, the grand exteriors, the winding roads linking them, and the magnificent ocean views are there for everyone to enjoy.

One of Watch Hill's logos is a bronze statue of **Ninigret**, chief of Rhode Island's branch of the **Niantics**, the tribe that once occupied this area. The statue, sculpted in Paris in 1914, overlooks the harbor.

Watch Hill's most unique attraction is the **flying-horse carousel**, the oldest merry-go-round in the country (built prior to 1879). The still-operating steeds, once water-powered but now motor-driven, are suspended by chains from a large turning wheel and "fly" out when in motion. The **Watch Hill Lighthouse**, now a museum, was built in 1858 to replace an earlier structure (special summer hours).

Special Features

The **Napatree Point Conservation Area** occupies a spit of land that extends west from Watch Hill one-half mile into **Little Narragansett Bay**. Although the area is privately owned, beachcombers, bird watchers, and nature lovers in general are welcome. The ruins of a **fort** built during the Spanish-American War may be explored at the end of the point.

Westerly's **Wilcox Park** (1898) is home to a Tree Walk, Colonial Theatre's Shakespeare-in-the-Park, and the 200-member Chorus of Westerly's Summer Pops. The park is named in the National Register of Historic Places.

> • *Every year dozens of people get married in the lovely non-denominational Watch Hill Chapel (1875).*
> • *The nearby Misquamicut Golf Club is one of the oldest in the country (1895; private).*
> • *Summer homes that once dotted Napatree Point were washed to sea in a 1938 hurricane. The area has never been rebuilt.*

Where to Stay

GRANDVIEW B&B, *212 Shore Rd. (Westerly), (401) 596-6384/(800) 447-6384.* Turn-of-century home with wrap-around stone porch, Cont. "plus" breakfasts, ocean view. $$ to $$$

THE INN AT WATCH HILL, *Bay St., (401) 596-0665.* Rooms with ocean views, private baths, balconies. $$$

SHELTER HARBOR INN, *10 Wagner Rd. (Rt. 1, Westerly), (401) 322-8883.* Full-service inn amongst fields with rustic stone walls, originally a farm (ca 1810), full breakfasts, restaurant, own beach, paddle tennis courts, professional croquet course. $$$

THE VILLA, *190 Shore Rd. (Westerly), (401) 596-1054/(800) 722-9240.* Large home on 1.5 landscaped acres, whirlpool & fireplace suites, pool with cabana, private terrace. $$$

WATCH HILL INN, *38 Bay St., (800) 356-9314/(401) 348-8912/fax (401) 596-9410.* Originally built 1845, full-service, Cont. breakfasts, seasonal restaurant, on hill with ocean views & breezes. $$$

WOODY HILL B&B, *149 S. Woody Hill Rd. (Westerly), (401) 322-0452.* On hilltop surrounded by rolling fields, antiques, wide-board floors, handmade quilts, informal gardens. $$ to $$$

Where to Eat

MARIA'S SEASIDE CAFE, *132 Atlantic Ave. (Misquamicut Beach), (401) 596-6886.* Ravioli alla Maria, Pollo Scarpariello, Swordfish Steak, Tournedos Moran, espresso & cappuccino. $$

THE OLYMPIA TEA ROOM, *74 Bay St., (401) 348-8211.* Little Neck Clams & Sausages on Linguini, Fish & Chips, acclaimed lobster salad, World Famous Avondale Swan (cream puff dessert); harborside, Art Deco, since 1916. $ to $$

THE POSITANO RESTAURANT, *(see Watch Hill Inn above).* Italian cuisine in attractive surroundings, overlooking bay. $$ to $$$

Further Information

Greater Westerly-Pawcatuck Area Chamber of Commerce, *74 Post Rd., Westerly, RI 02891 (800) 732-7636. (ZIP for Watch Hill is 02891.)*

Directions

From Connecticut, I 95 north to exit 92 (in Connecticut), CT 2 south to RI 78, RI 78 south (becoming Airport Rd. after crossing US 1) to end, left on Watch Hill Rd.; from Providence, I 95 south to exit 1, RI 3 south to RI 78, proceed as above.

Wickford

Population 2, 750

Located on a harbor stirred by colorful fishing boats, private yachts, and quahog skiffs (the *quahog* is a type of clam), **Wickford Village's** shops would make a perfect setting for a TV commercial showing people loading a station wagon with a just acquired antique or work of art.

Wickford is an unspoiled New England fishing village with tree-lined streets and memories going back to Colonial times. Many of the village's late 18th- and early 19th-century houses survive. A few are bed and breakfasts (see below); some house shops and other businesses. There are also a number of 19th-century summer houses.

One of the most venerated of Wickford's possessions is the Old **Narragansett Church** (1707, moved 1800), the oldest Episcopal church in the northern United States. The church has box pews, a slave gallery, a silver communion set that was a gift from Queen Anne, and the oldest church organ (1680) in North America. A much "younger" church, the Romanesque Revival **St. Paul's**, was built in 1847.

Although not far from Providence, Wickford remains essentially rural, in character as well as setting. The age of the village can be appreciated by noting that several generations of English settlers had lived here before the word "Revolution" was even spoken. There were once even grand plantations in the area that were worked by slaves and indentured servants (although in 1774 Rhode Island became the first colony to outlaw the importation of slaves).

Special Features

Smith's Castle, just north of Wickford, is one of the oldest plantation houses in the country (1678; with 18th- and 19th-century additions). The furnished house and its lovely Colonial, waterfront, and cutting gardens may be seen by guided tour (check locally for hours).

The birthplace of **Gilbert Stuart**, famous for his portraits of George Washington (and many, many others), is five miles south of Wickford. Among the features of the authentically restored house (1751) are corner fireplaces, wooden door latches, and hand-blown window panes. The house is also the site of the country's first snuff mill (still operative; guided tours), a fish ladder, and a partially restored grist mill.

- *The Wickford Art Festival is one of the oldest art shows in the country.*
- *Many visitors choose to visit Wickford by boat.*

Where to Stay

FIFTY SEVEN B&B, *57 Thomas St., (401) 294-7201.* Contemporary Cape cottage in woodland setting, private bath, full English or Cont. breakfasts, pool, near historic district. $$

JOHN UPDIKE HOUSE, *19 Pleasant St., (401) 294-4905.* 1745 Georgian house on waterfront, period decor, fireplaces, suite or apartment, deck & common room. $$ to $$$

MT. MAPLE OF WICKFORD, *730 Annaquatucket Rd., (401) 295-4373.* 1862 home with unique verandah, antiques & period decor, private baths, full breakfasts. $$$

Where to Eat

THE CARRIAGE INN, *Tower Hill Rd., (401) 294-2727/(800) 270-2466.* Jonnycakes, clam cakes; old tavern atmosphere. $$

DUFFY'S TAVERN, *235 Tower Hill Rd., P.O. Box 372, (401) 295-0073.* Seafood fried, grilled, boiled, baked, & steamed; chowder bar, patio dining. $ to $$

THE RED ROOSTER TAVERN, *7385 Post Rd., (401) 295-8804.* Filet of Sole Baked with Almonds, Chicken Wellington, Filet Mignon Italiana; in charming house, award-winning wine cellar, one of Rhode Island's best. $$

Further Information

North Kingstown Chamber of Commerce, *8045 Post Rd., N. Kingstown, RI 02852 (401) 295-5566. (ZIP for Wickford Village is 02852.)*

Directions

From Providence, I 95 south to exit 9, RI 4 to Wickford exit; from NYC and Connecticut, I 95 north to exit 5, RI 102 south and east to Wickford.

Other Charming Rhode Island Towns

Chepachet
Kingston Village
Little Compton
North Scituate

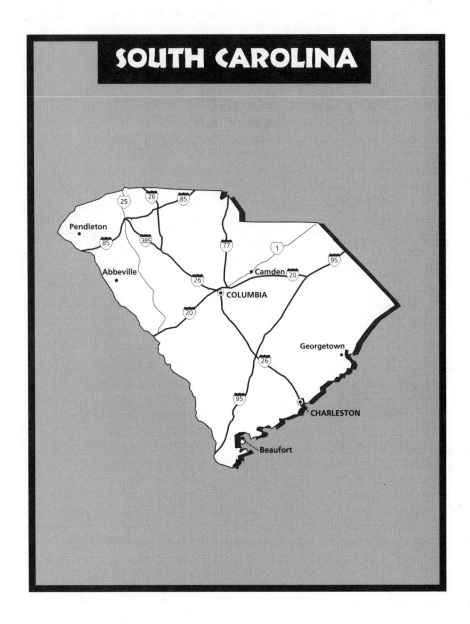

SOUTH CAROLINA

SOUTH CAROLINA

Abbeville

Population 5, 778

Abbeville is a beautiful old Southern town (founded 1758) situated in the rolling countryside of Upcountry South Carolina. The townspeople consciously and successfully cling to a traditional small-town life style. Visiting is in, hurrying is out, and many businesses close on Wednesday afternoons (and Sundays, of course). In recent years Mennonite families from the North have been acquiring area farms. The inevitable result has been an increasingly prosperous and beautiful countryside.

At the center of the **Abbeville Historic District** is a picture-postcard town square. The square is bordered by brick-paved streets and businesses with facades carefully restored to their turn-of-the-century appearance. Traditional hardware and farm-supply stores sit cheek by jowl with antique and chic specialty shops.

Among the buildings on the square is the magnificently restored **Opera House** (1908), pride of the town. Early in the 20th century, when Abbeville was a railroad stopover for road shows, the three-balconied Opera House hosted such vaudeville stars as Fanny Brice, Jimmy Durante, and Groucho Marx. Now in the second chapter of its life, the elegant theater is home to the year-round productions of the professional **Opera House Players**.

A wonderful walking town, Abbeville boasts many gracious 19th-century homes, both antebellum and postbellum, and no fewer than 36 churches. The most historic of the homes is the **Burt-Stark House** (circa 1840), a plantation house where Confederate President Jefferson Davis stayed on his retreat from Richmond at the end of the Civil War (the house may be toured by appointment.) The lovely Gothic Revival **Trinity Episcopal Church** (1860) has hand-carved woodwork and a stained-glass chancel window that was made in England.

Abbeville has two interesting museums. The **Abbeville County Museum**, housed in the three-story county jail (1850s), features artifacts from the town's more than two centuries of history. The **Abbeville County Library** is home to the **Poliakoff Collection of Western Art**, an excellent collection of contemporary Native American ceramics, weavings, and other art objects.

Abbeville may be seen by a self-guided tour or by one of three guided tours—check with the Chamber of Commerce.

Special Features

The nearby town of **Due West** is home to beautiful **Erskine College**, the oldest denominational liberal arts college in South Carolina (1839). Much of this charming little town is on the National Register of Historic Places.

Located on **Richard B. Russell Lake** 13 miles away, **Calhoun Falls State Park** offers water sports and, in the spring, spectacular displays of redbuds and dogwoods.

> • *Site of the first organized meeting to adopt an Ordinance of Secession, and the final meeting place of the Confederate Council of War, Abbeville was "the birthplace and the deathbed of the Confederacy."*
> • *The chancel window of Trinity Episcopal Church made it safely through the Union blockade of Charleston.*

Where to Stay

ABBEWOOD B&B, *509 N. Main St., (864) 459-5822.* Circa 1860 home with wraparound verandah, beautiful hall, some private baths, Cont. "plus" breakfasts. $$

BELMONT INN, *106 Court Sq., (864) 459-9625.* Renovated turn-of-century hotel with elegant lobby, full-service, period furnishings, restaurant. $$ to $$$

SOMEWHERE IN TIME B&B, *P.O. Box 746 (Due West 29639), (864) 379-8671.* 1897 home on National Register, antiques, candlelight breakfasts, wrap-around porch, fish pond. $$

THE VINTAGE INN B&B, *909 N. Main St., (864) 459-4784.* Turn-of-century home with antique furnishings, original clawfoot tubs, suite available, lemonade on wraparound porch. $$

Where to Stay

TIMOTHY'S AT THE BELMONT INN, *(see above).* Grilled Salmon with Raspberry Barbecue Sauce over Creamy Grits, Grilled Chicken Marsala, Rosettes of Beef with Green Peppercorn Sauce, Bourbon Street Pasta. $$

THE VILLAGE GRILL, *114 Trinity St., (864) 459-2500.* Rotisserie chicken, ribs, gourmet sandwiches; "Simple, Fresh and Good." $

Further Information

Greater Abbeville Chamber of Commerce, *107 Court Sq., Abbeville SC 29620, (864) 459-4600.*

Directions

From Columbia, I 26 north to exit 54 (near Clinton), SC 72 south (via Greenwood) to Abbeville.

Beaufort

Population 9, 576

Sometimes described as an "undeveloped Charleston," **Beaufort** (BYUU fert) has become a favorite retirement spot for corporation presidents, prominent writers and artists, and senior military personnel. It's not difficult to understand why. The picturesque coastal town is blessed with one of the most beautiful historic districts in the country, excellent restaurants, seven naturally beautiful golf courses, a variety of cultural opportunities, great fishing, bountiful sunshine, and access to miles of unspoiled beaches.

Early in the 19th century indigo and, later, long staple sea-island cotton, brought wealth to area planters, and magnificent homes to Beaufort's streets. Many of the homes and plantations still survive because Beaufort was occupied by Union forces early in the Civil War and the town and nearby plantations were spared.

Old Point, part of the **Beaufort Historic District**, contains over 150 antebellum homes, many with lovely landscaped gardens. A setting for several films, the enchanting area is made to order for leisurely walking or bicycling. The verandahed white homes, the moss-draped live oaks, and the splashes of color added by the roses, camellias, azaleas, and other flowers produce at times an almost impressionistic effect.

One of Beaufort's historic houses is open to the public: the Federal-style **John Mark Verdier House** (circa 1790), noted for its fine interior details. The Marquis de Lafayette was a guest in the house in 1825. Other beautiful old homes (private) include the Greek Revival **Joseph Johnson House** (1859), the early 19th-century frame **Henry Farmer House**, the double-verandahed **Tidalholm** (circa 1853), and the Greek Revival **George Parsons Elliott House** (1844).

St. Helena's Episcopal Church is one of the oldest churches (1724) still in use in the United States. The building was used as a hospital during the Civil War. The **Beaufort Museum**, once an arsenal, was constructed of brick and tabby in 1798 (rebuilt 1852). The Gothic Revival structure features prehistoric shark teeth, fossils, early Indian pottery, and Civil War and plantation memorabilia.

Both local tradition and retiree interest have fostered a number of cultural organizations. Among them, the **Beaufort Orchestra Guild**, the

Beaufort Little Theatre, the **University of South Carolina at Beaufort's seasonal music program**, and the **Byrne Miller Dance Theatre**.

There are many ways to enjoy the natural beauty of Beaufort's southern coastal setting. Fishing (offshore, surf, or pier) is a favorite pastime; boat rentals and private charters are available. Nearby beaches offer swimming and shelling. The **Beaufort River** can be viewed by a stroll or jog along the sea wall promenade of the **Henry C. Chambers Waterfront Park**. The area boasts many tennis courts and, as noted, beautiful golf courses.

Special Features

The 5,000-acre **Hunting Island State Park**, 16 miles from Beaufort, offers over three miles of unspoiled beaches. Park visitors may survey the scene from an abandoned lighthouse.

Nearby **Port Royal**, one of the state's earliest settlements, has a 1,260-foot boardwalk.

Legend has it that the flat tombstones of St. Helena's Episcopal Church were used as operating tables during the Civil War.

Where to Stay

BAY STREET INN, *601 Bay St., (803) 522-0050.* 1852 planter's mansion overlooking river, antiques & art, fireplaces, private baths, "gourmet" breakfasts, afternoon teas, library, gardens, bikes. $$$

THE BEAUFORT INN, *809 Port Republic St., (803) 521-9000/fax (803) 521-9500.* 1907 home of prominent attorney, full-service inn, guest rooms named after local plantations, fireplaces, "gourmet" breakfasts, high teas, dining room. $$$

OLD POINT INN, *212 New St., (803) 524-3177.* 1898 home in historic district, antiques, private baths, full breakfasts, wine, verandahs, gardens, close to river, scenic views. $$ to $$$

RHETT HOUSE INN, *1009 Craven St., (803) 524-9030.* 1820 home with antique-filled rooms, full-service, full breakfasts, afternoon tea, dining room, bikes. $$$

TWOSUNS INN B&B, *1705 Bay St., (803) 522-1122.* Colonial Revival home in historic district, private baths, full breakfasts, tea/sherry, panoramic bay view. $$$

Where to Eat

11TH STREET DOCKSIDE RESTAURANT, *11th St. W. (Port Royal), (803) 524-7433.* Fresh seafood, steaks, homemade pecan pie; overlooking shrimp boats & Battery Creek. $$

THE ANCHORAGE, *1103 Bay St., (803) 524-9392*. Shrimp Creole, Crawfish Etouffee, Low Country Crab Cakes, Grilled Fresh Salmon with Herb Butter; in 18th-century waterfront mansion with very Southern history. $$

EMILY'S RESTAURANT & TAPAS BAR, *906 Port Republic St., (803) 522-1866*. Tournedos, Fillet Black and White, Steak au Poivre, Fillet of Pork Teriyaki, Canard a l'Orange, large variety of tapas. $$ to $$$

LA SIRENA, *822 Bay St.* Linguini with Grilled Chicken, Salmon Fillet with Salsa Verde, 16 oz. T-Bone Steak, Skillet Seared Tuna, Ligurian Seafood Stew. $ to $$

RIVERWALK RESTAURANT, *19 Marina Village Ln. at Port Royal Landing (Port Royal), (803) 525-6466*. Broiled Founder, Baked Stuffed Shrimp, Catch of the Day, Tender Sea Scallops, New York Strip Steak. $$

WHITEHALL PLANTATION, *Whitehall Dr. (on Lady's Island), (803) 521-1700*. Grilled Swordfish, Poached Salmon, Baked Grouper, Shrimp Beaufort, Gulf Red Snapper; antebellum Low Country setting, gardens, verandah, reservations recommended. $$

Further Information

The Greater Beaufort Chamber of Commerce, *P.O. Box 910, Beaufort SC 29901, (803) 524-3163. (ZIP for Beaufort is 29902.)*

Directions

From Charleston, US 17 west to US 21 (Gardens Corner), US 21 south to Beaufort.

Camden
Population 6, 696

Rare indeed is the old Southern town, especially one in the Deepest part of the South, whose history can be discussed without dwelling on the War Between the States. Created by order of King George II in 1733, **Camden** was a Revolutionary War town. And the town's fame as a horse training and breeding center, although certainly with 19th century roots, belongs more to the 20th century.

The original Camden was a British stronghold during part of the Revolutionary War, fortified with a stockade wall and six small surrounding forts. Although they won the nearby **Battles of Camden** and **Hobkirk Hill**, the British took heavy losses at the latter and evacuated Camden, setting fire to the fortifications as they left. In recent years, excavations at the site have uncovered the remains of the old town, its fortifications, a large powder magazine, and the foundation for the **Kershaw-Cornwallis House**, headquarters for General Cornwallis and other officers during the 1780-81 British occupation.

The excavations provided the basis for **Historic Camden**, a 92-acre partial reconstruction and park. In addition to several reconstructed fort sites, this unique Revolutionary War park features miniature dioramas, a model of the original town, a narrated slide presentation, and nature trails.

The park also has a number of interesting historic buildings that have been moved to the site from other locations. The jewel of the park, however, is the reconstructed Kershaw-Cornwallis House. The exterior of this house is an exact replica of the original 1780 Georgian-style mansion. The inside, with period furniture, is modeled after the interiors of Charleston houses of the same period.

The **Camden Historic District**, not to be confused with Historic Camden, is an oak-shaded area of more than 60 lovely homes and other buildings. Many of the houses are beautifully-maintained, privately-owned mansions that date from the 19th century (Camden came through the Civil War untouched). Of special interest in the district is the Greek Revival **Bethesda Presbyterian Church** (circa 1822), designed by Robert Mills, South Carolina's most prominent architect and designer of the Washington Monument in Washington, D. C.

The Chamber of Commerce has information on walking, driving, taped, and special guided tours of the district.

Special Features

Horses are second only to textiles in importance to Camden's economy. There are two major training centers for horses, one for steeplechase training and the other for flat-race training. There are also two major equestrian events, the **Carolina Cup Steeplechase** and the **Colonial Cup International Steeplechase**. Both take place at the **Springdale Race Course**.

> • *Many of the roads around Camden are dirt rather than paved in deference to the unprotected feet of the horses.*
> • *The horse industry was started during the 1920s in large part by well-to-do Northerners who were attracted by the area's beautiful homes and mild winter climate.*

Where to Stay

ABERDEEN B&B, *1409 Broad St., (803) 432-2524.* Circa 1810 home in historic district, antique furnishings, private baths. $$

A CAMDEN BED & BREAKFAST, *127 Union St., (803) 432-2366.* Federal-style home with morning room, antiques, private baths, full breakfasts, one traveling party accommodated at a time. $$

CANDLELIGHT INN, *1904 Broad St., (803) 424-1057.* On 2 acres of flowers & old oak trees, needlework & antiques, private baths, "expertly prepared" breakfasts. $$

THE CARRIAGE HOUSE B&B, *1413 Lyttleton St., (803) 432-2430.* Circa 1840s cottage, antiques & colorful fabrics, full "country" breakfasts, hostess an interior designer. $$

GREENLEAF INN, *1308/10 N. Broad St., (803) 425-1806/(800) 437-5874.* Circa 1805 & 1890 homes in historic district, full-service inn, "traditional flavor with contemporary convenience," restaurant. $$

Where to Eat

LILFRED'S, *11 Main St., (803) 432-7063.* Fresh North Carolina Rainbow Trout, Succulent Breast of Free Range Chicken, Filet of Beef. $$

LUCY'S, *1043 Broad St., (803) 432-9096.* Pecan Breaded Grouper, Roast Duck with Honey Bourbon Glaze, Grilled Filet with Chevre Herb Crust; lunch/dinner menus changed daily. $$

THE MILL POND RESTAURANT, *84 Boykin Mill Road (Boykin 29128), (803) 424-0261.* Swordfish with Lightly Smoked Blackberry Sauce, Filet Mignon Stuffed with Mushrooms & Peppers; in old mill. $$

THE PADDOCK, *514 Rutledge St., (803) 432-3222.* American, Continental, & Southern specialties. $$

SINCLAIR'S RESTAURANT, *402 Dekalb St., (803)432-9956.* Fried Oysters, Beaufort Crab Cakes, Chicken in Pastry, New York Strip; interesting lunch menu. $

Further Information

Kershaw County Chamber of Commerce, *724 S. Broad St., P.O. Box 605, Camden, SC 29020 (803) 432-2525/(800) 968-4037.*

Directions

From Columbia, I 20 northeast to exit 98, US 521 north to Camden.

Georgetown
Population 9, 912

Whether viewed culturally or geographically, there wasn't just one Old South: There were several, each represented by one or two cities and several towns. One Old South, known as the *Lowcountry*, stretched across the coastal regions of Georgia and South Carolina. It had a long history, reaching back to the earliest years of the 18th century, and was distinguished by its gentility, linkage to the sea, and African and French as well as British heritage. It boasted an American aristocracy, and an economy based on slavery. Its capital cities were Charleston and Savannah. Foremost among its towns was **Georgetown.**

Founded in 1729, Georgetown is South Carolina's third oldest town. Surrounded by large rice and indigo plantations and lying on the banks of the Sampit River with direct access to the open seas, the town became a thriving port with a complement of fine 18th- and 19th-century homes, churches, and public buildings. During the 1800s slaves made up some 85% of the area's population. As with many Southern communities, the town's fortunes have swung up and down since the Civil War; two of its mainstays today are tourists and retirees.

Over 65 Georgetown properties have been listed on the National Register. Georgian, Federal, and Classical and Greek Revival architectural styles predominate, but a sprinkling of New England and other influences add variety. The Greek Revival **Rice Museum** building, the town's lovely centerpiece, is in fact the **Old Market Building** (circa 1842) topped with the town clock and bell tower (circa 1845). Dioramas and other exhibits in the museum focus on the history of the area's rice and indigo production.

Another museum, the **Kaminski House Museum** (circa 1769), displays a number of valuable antiques, including 18th-century pieces made in Charleston. The house enjoys a commanding view of the Sampit River. **Prince George Winyah Episcopal Church** (circa 1747; steeple, 1824) was built of bricks used as ballast in British ships. The earliest inscriptions in the churchyard (circa 1735) go back to 1767.

The **Harborwalk** is a charming boardwalk that meanders along the Sampit River for 1,500 feet. Here and there along its north side are the back entries of shops and restaurants that lie on Georgetown's colorful Front Street.

Georgetown County is dotted with grand plantation houses, resorts, beaches, and other attractions–several are listed below. Reflecting this, Georgetown and its county offer a wide array of organized walking, tram, and boat tours. For those preferring to go it alone, there are maps, brochures, and books about local history (check with the Chamber of Commerce). Opportunities to catch seafood–surf fishing, deep-sea fishing, crabbing, shrimping, clamming–are second only to the many opportunities to eat it (see restaurants below).

Special Features

Rivers in the Georgetown area are lined with dozens of restored **rice plantations**. Some of them are resorts or bed-and-breakfasts; others may be viewed during a spring plantation tour. Two of the most beautiful are open to the public: **Hampton Plantation** (circa 1735), once visited by George Washington, and **Hopesewee Plantation** (circa 1740), built by Thomas Lynch, a signer of the Declaration of Independence.

The grounds of Brookgreen Plantation have evolved into the lovely **Brookgreen Gardens**, where over 500 stunning 19th- and 20th-century American figurative sculptures are displayed among some 2,000 species and subspecies of plants. There is also a 23-acre wildlife park. (open to the public)

> • *Some believe that nearby Pawleys Island/Litchfield is the oldest resort area in the United States.*
> • *Local restaurants serve a melange of Low Country cooking, traditional Southern cooking, and creative American cuisine. Low Country cooking, known for its African as well as European ancestry, features local ingredients, especially fresh seafood.*

Where to Stay

1790 HOUSE B&B INN, *630 Highmarket St., (800) 890-7432/(803) 546-4821*. Circa 1790 West-Indies-style home with original mantles & dentil molding, private baths, full "gourmet" breakfasts, afternoon tea, evening refreshments, cottage with private patio, verandah, gardens, bikes. $$$

ALEXANDRA'S INN, *620 Prince St., (888) 557-0233/(803) 527-0233*. 1880 home with 11-ft ceilings, fireplaces, TV & phones, private baths, full breakfasts, porches, carriage-house suite, pool, gardens & magnolia trees. $$$

DOZIER GUEST HOUSE, *220 Queen St., (803) 527-1350*. Circa 1770 home in historic district, antiques & reproductions, private baths, full "gourmet" breakfasts, once home of prominent politician. $$

DuPREE HOUSE B&B INN, *921 Prince St., (800) 921-3877/(803) 546-0298*. Circa 1740 home in New England style, private baths, full breakfasts, afternoon tea, refreshments, pool; horseshoes, bocce, & hammocks in picnic area. $$

KINGS INN AT GEORGETOWN, *230 Broad St., (803) 527-6937/ (800) 251-8805.* 1825 Federal mansion with original woodwork items, period antiques & reproductions, private baths, "gourmet" breakfasts with china & crystal, afternoon tea & sherry, pool & gardens, croquet, bicycles, highly rated. $$$

THE SHAW HOUSE B&B, *613 Cypress Ct., (803) 546-9663.* Colonial-style home in quiet natural setting, antiques, TV & phones, private baths, full breakfasts, refreshments, birdwatching, bikes, walking distance to historic district. $$

WINYAH BAY B&B, *403 Helena St., (803) 546-9051.* Home overlooking Winyah Bay, TV & phones, private baths, longest private dock in state, small private island. $$ to $$$

Where to Eat

ORANGE BLOSSOM CAFE, *107 Orange St., (803) 527-5060.* Steaks, Grecian dishes, pasta, seafood specialties; good lunch menu. $ to $$

THE PINK MAGNOLIA, *719 Front St., (803) 527-6506.* Chicken Magnolia–grilled chicken breast topped with crab au gratin & served over pasta with salad; soups, salads, sandwiches, traditional Southern dining with cloth napkins & tablecloths. $

RICE PADDY, *819 Front St., (803) 546-2021.* Rice Paddy's Lump Crab Cakes, Bahamian Grouper, Greek Style Baked Shrimp, Port Tenderloin with Green Peppercorn Sauce. $$

Further Information

Georgetown County Convention & Visitors Bureau, *P.O. Box 1776, Georgetown, SC 29442 (800) 777-7705/(803) 546-8436.*

Directions

From Charleston, US 17 north to Georgetown; from Myrtle Beach, US 17 south.

Pendleton

Population 3, 314

The wealthy of the Old South tended to divide their lives between two beautiful worlds: The pillared plantation of novel and screen and the less familiar summer retreat. In South Carolina the former was usually *Low Country*, meaning coastal and often not far from Charleston. The latter was usually *Up Country*, in the higher and cooler elevations of the western part of the state. **Pendleton**, in the foothills of the **Blue Ridge Mountains**, was a favorite Up Country summer retreat (see also Hendersonville, NC).

The town, listed in its entirety on the National Register of Historic Places, is centered about a delightful village green set with period streetlamps and shaded park benches. On the streets about the green stand many lovely homes from the late 18th and early 19th centuries. Some of the finest restaurants in this part of South Carolina are also here.

The first stop for the visitor should be **Hunter's Store** (1850), headquarters for the Pendleton District Historical, Recreational and Tourism Commission. The center offers everything from cassette tape tours in English and French to art exhibits, local crafts, and a book shop.

Fronting on the **village green**, across from Hunter's Store, is the peaceful old **Farmers Society Hall** (1826), town landmark and the oldest continuously used farmers hall in the country. Perhaps the most promi- nent member of the **Pendleton Farmers Society** (in essence an agricul- tural club) was U.S. vice president and statesman John C. Calhoun.

St. Paul's Episcopal Church (1822) has most of its original furnish- ings. Few of the region's early settlers were in fact Episcopalians—but many of the coastal families summering in the town were. The grave- stones in the churchyard read like a South Carolina history book. Many famous South Carolinians are also buried near the **Old Stone Church**, an early Presbyterian church (1802) on the road between Pendleton and Clemson.

In the country just outside town are several old plantation homes; some of them have also served as summer homes. Two, **Ashtabula** (1820s) and four-story **Woodburn** (circa 1830), are now house museums.

Special Feature

Fort Hill plantation house (circa 1806), home of John C. Calhoun, and **Hanover House** (1716), a transplanted Low Country French Hugue- not home, are on the campus of **Clemson University**, just 3 1/2 miles away. Both houses are open to the public.

> • *Several of the streets in Pendleton's historic district bear the names of blacks who have contributed with special distinction to the town and region's heritage.*
> • *The presence of an Episcopal church in non-Episcopal Upcountry is usually a good sign that the area was once a summer refuge for (Episcopal) Low Country planters.*

Where to Stay

LIBERTY HALL INN, *621 S. Mechanic St., (864) 646-7500.* Circa 1840 home with antiques & high ceilings, full-service inn, Cont. "plus" breakfasts, restaurant, wide verandahs. $$

ONE NINETY-FIVE EAST MAIN, *195 E. Main St., (864) 646-5673.* Eclectic home in heart of historic district, antiques & original art, private baths, full breakfasts, fresh fruit, 2-story library, greenhouse. $ to $$

Where to Eat

FARMERS HALL RESTAURANT, *105 Exchange St., (864) 646-7024.* Mixed Grill, Ribeye Steak, Lancashire Hot Pie, daily specials; in historic Farmers Hall, dinner reservations appreciated. $$

LIBERTY HALL INN, *(see above).* Carolina Crab Cakes, Orange Roughy Mediterranean, Tonight's Chicken. $ to $$

PENDLETON HOUSE, *203 E. Main St., (864) 646-7795.* Wide range of traditional entrees; restaurant & pub in 1880 home. $$

Further Information

Pendleton District Historical, Recreational & Tourism Commission, *125 E. Queen St., P.O. Box 565, Pendleton, SC 29670 (864) 646-3782/ (800) 862-1795.*

Directions

From Atlanta, I 85 northeast to exit 14 (in SC), SC 187 north to Pendleton; from Charlotte, I 85 southwest to exit 19 (in SC), US 76/SC 28 north to Pendleton.

Other Charming South Carolina Towns

Cheraw
Edgefield
McClellanville
Walhalla

SOUTH DAKOTA

Deadwood

⊙ PIERRE

90

90

29

81

29

81

90

SIOUX FALLS ⊙

Yankton

SOUTH DAKOTA

Deadwood

Population 1, 830

A heated night life, Old West saloons, and busy gambling parlors have been especially prominent during two periods in **Deadwood's** history. The first, the wild period of the 1870s and 1880s, was triggered by the discovery of gold in the **Black Hills**. Prospectors, claim jumpers, prostitutes, gunfighters, gamblers, hell-raisers, and opportunists breathed fire in **Deadwood Gulch**.

Law and Order amounted to an occasional vigilante court. Those were the days when a Jim McCall could kill a Wild Bill Hickok and get by with it (at least for a while), and a Calamity Jane could boast that she captured the killer when in fact she never did.

The second of the colorful periods began in the 1980s and is in full swing at this moment. In the 1980s Deadwood decided to legalize gambling (maximum wager $5.00) and use 4% of the profits for historic restoration. The town also decided that all restoration, whether funded by gaming or private moneys, would be closely supervised by **Deadwood's Historic Preservation Commission**.

The result is a National Historic Landmark with a cobblestoned **Main Street**, period street lights, trolleys, buried utilities—and more than 80 Old-West-style gaming halls! The best of the first wild period is back, and the worst is buried with Wild Bill Hickok, Calamity Jane, Potato Creek Johnny, and the rest up in **Mount Moriah Cemetery**.

Not that the gambling halls offer the only game in town. Three museums offer good glimpses of Old Deadwood. The exhibits at the **Adams Memorial Museum**, or "Deadwood's attic," include the biggest gold nugget ever found in the Black Hills. The **House of Roses Historic Home**, on the National Register, boasts no fewer than 27 rooms of Victoriana. And the **Ghosts of Deadwood Gulch Wax Museum** displays some 72 life-size figures in 19 haunted settings.

Farther afield, several golf courses and ski resorts offer their own varieties of recreation.

Special Features

Tours of the **Broken Boot Gold Mine** (operated by the Deadwood-Lead Chamber of Commerce) include a guided trip through timbered tunnels and huge underground "rooms" (or stopes) of an historic mine.

Just a few winding miles up the road is mile-high **Lead** (pronounced Leed), another charming town and also on the National Register. Here are a narrow turn-of-the-century Main Street and Victorian houses, modest to mansion, clinging to steep hillsides. One of the top sights is the **Black Hills Mining Museum**, with interesting displays and a walk-through replica of a gold mine.

> • *During its earliest years Deadwood was destroyed three times, twice by fires and once by a flash flood.*
> • *Founded in 1876, the Homestake Gold Mine in Lead is the oldest continuously operated gold mine in the world.*

Where to Stay

BULLOCK HOTEL, *633 Main St., (800) 336-1876.* Restored 1895 city landmark, full-service, elegant gaming parlors & polished staircases, whirlpools, restaurant, gift shop. $$ to $$$

CENTURIA B&B, *784 Main St., (605) 578-2322.* 1890s home, some private baths, walking distance to downtown, quiet surroundings. $$ to $$$

DEER MOUNTAIN B&B, *HC 37 (Box 1214) (Lead 57754), (605) 584-2473.* Unique log home with fireplace, some private baths, full breakfasts, hors d'oeuvres, spa, pool table. $$

HISTORIC FRANKLIN HOTEL, *700 Main St., (800) 688-1876.* 1903 hotel on National Register, full-service, gaming halls, columned porch & sun verandah, restaurant. $$ to $$$

STRAWBERRY BED-N-BREAKFAST, *HCR 73 (Box 264), (800) 423-2149.* On top of Strawberry Hill south of town, private baths, hot tub, communal TV room, deck. $$ to $$$

Where to Eat

THE DEADWOOD SOCIAL CLUB, *657 Main St., (800) 952-9398.* Seafood Fettucini, Honey Bourbon Chicken, Rib Eye, Hawaiian Grilled Chicken Sandwich; casual. $ to $$

THE DEPOT, *155 Sherman St., (605) 578-2699.* "The Best Prime Rib West of the Missouri!", Chicken Cordon Bleu, Beef Oscar, Vegetable Fettuccine, Salmon (baked or grilled), steaks; highly regarded. $$

JAKES RESTAURANT, *677 Main St., (800) 999-6482.* Grilled Walleye, Cajun Seafood Tortellini; one of best in South Dakota. $$$

SILVERADO RESTAURANT, *709 Main St., (800) 584-7005.* Seafood, prime rib, homemade desserts; "Complete gaming and dining experience." $

THE STAMPMILL, *305 W. Main St. (Lead), (605) 584-1984.* Casual fireside dining with shrimp, Black Angus steaks, giant burgers; red brick & polished wood of 1890s. $

Further Information

Deadwood-Lead Chamber of Commerce, *735 Main St., Deadwood, SD 57732 (800) 999-1876/(605) 578-1876; also,* **Deadwood Visitors Bureau,** *3 Siever St., Deadwood (605) 578-1102.*

Directions

From Rapid City, I 90 west to exit 30, US Alt. 14 west to Deadwood.

Yankton
Population 13, 300

Yankton has clean air, no traffic jams, low crime, arts programs, and excellent schools; in other words, it's a model American hometown. Part of the town's appeal lies in its success in blending the old with the new. For while Yankton works to mold a town that will be as proud of its 21st-century heritage as its 19th, this descendant of an old riverboat town and capital of **Dakota Territory** (1861 to 1883) also respects and preserves its historical heritage.

Third Street, Yankton's main street, is protected as part of a National Register Historic District, but the size of the town demands more business space, and so there is also a modern shopping mall. New houses are built, but the town maintains guard over the many lovely homes from the 1870s and 1880s that grace the historic district. New industry is courted, but people point with pride to the oldest continuing industry, the **Gurney Seed and Nursery Co.**, established in 1894.

The same blending of old and new can be seen – and heard – in **Riverside Park.** Here music from a blues or rock concert (for example) in the amphitheater echoes off the walls of a nearby replica of the **Dakota Territorial Capitol.** Here also the traditional and the contemporary mingle at the annual **Yankton Riverboat Days and Summer Arts Festival,** held the third weekend in August.

Yankton's premier tourist attraction, the **Dakota Territorial Museum**, is quite literally jammed with reminders and artifacts of Yankton's territorial days. Included in the museum complex are a rural schoolhouse, **Great Northern Railway Depot** (1892-1893), blacksmith shop, an 1870 parlor, and an office replica of Dakota Territory's first governor.

Special Feature

Just four or so miles down the Missouri is the beautifully developed **Lewis and Clark Recreation Area**. The area is located on the banks of **Lewis and Clark Lake**, a 33,000-acre reservoir that stretches for 30 scenic miles along the Missouri River. The lake and recreation area boast a marina, boat rentals, sandy beaches, excellent camping, biking trails, fishing, everything.

> *French fur traders were in the Yankton area as early as the 1780s and 1790s, several years before Lewis and Clark came through in the early 1800s.*

Where to Stay

THE MULBERRY INN B&B, *512 Mulberry St., (605) 665-7116.* 1873 home on National Register, antiques & walnut paneling, TV, private baths, Cont. or full breakfasts, refreshments, 2 parlors with marble fireplaces, large porch. $ to $$

Where to Eat

HAPPY JACK'S SUPPER CLUB, *E. SD 50, (605) 665-7626.* A Yankton tradition for steaks. $

HARBOR LIGHTS RESTAURANT, *Lewis & Clark Marina/lake area, (605) 665-5650.* Walleye Filet, Chicken Dijonnaise, Pasta Primavera, New York Strip, sandwiches, famous chili. $

JODEAN'S USA, *RR 2 (Box 206), N. US 81, (605) 665-9884.* Daily buffet specials, seafood prepared a variety of ways, chicken, steaks, pork chops, BBQ. $

PANDA INN, *401 Capitol St., (605) 665-0186.* Chinese dining in surroundings of historic Carnegie Library. $ to $$

THE QUARRY STEAK HOUSE & LOUNGE, *RR 1 (Box 286), W. SD 52, (605) 665-4337.* South Dakota Prime Rib the specialty, broad range of seafoods & steaks, sandwiches (incl. Quarry Burger), Quarry Rock Pie; on historic site, "fabulous" views, reservations recommended. $$

Further Information

Yankton Area Chamber of Commerce, *218 W. Fourth St., P.O. Box 588, Yankton, SD 57078 (605) 665-3636.*

Directions

From Sioux Falls, I 29 south to exit 26, SD 50 west to Yankton.

Other Charming South Dakota Towns

Hot Springs
Milbank
Pierre
Spearfish

455

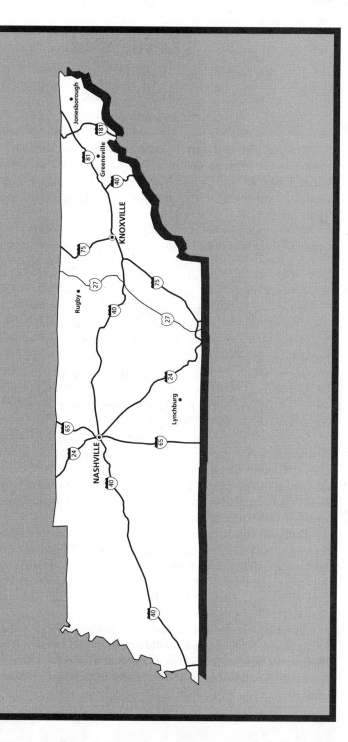

TENNESSEE

Greeneville
Population 14, 400

Greeneville, and east Tennessee in general, has an ambiance that doesn't quite seem to belong to most of the rest of Tennessee, nor to North Carolina just across the border. It is partly mountain, partly Southern, and partly something else, something rooted in pride and self-determination.

Greeneville has always had a mind of its own. The town was once the capital of the **State of Franklin**, a state that because of a complex piece of history existed for a few years in the 1780s but was never recognized by the U.S. Congress. Less than a century later, Greeneville sided with the Union in the Civil War, even though the region is in the South.

Greeneville's downtown historic district has rolling tree-lined streets bordered by lovely antebellum homes and churches of the Federal and Greek Revival styles. The brick sidewalks and absence of power lines (buried) contribute to the beauty. The district embraces more than 35 structures. One of them is an authentic reconstruction of the capitol of the *Lost State of Franklin*. Others include the **Greene County Stone Jail** (1838/1882), the Federal-style **Valentine-Sevier House** (1820), and the **Sevier-Lowry House** (1790s), the oldest structure in Greeneville.

Several of the structures make up the **Andrew Johnson National Historic Site** (Johnson was the 17th president of the United States): the **Visitor Center Complex**, which includes Johnson's tailor shop, a museum, and the president's 1830s house; the **Homestead**, Johnson's home from 1851 until his death in 1875; and the **national cemetery** where Johnson and his family are buried.

Probably the grandest of the homes is the restored **Dickson-Williams Mansion** (1815-1821), known as the *Showplace of East Tennessee*. The circular staircase, which rises three full flights, provides elegant tribute to the craftsmanship of the two Irishmen who designed and built the house. Davy Crockett, Andrew Jackson, the Marquis de Lafayette, and Henry Clay were all guests here.

The historic district includes three churches of special beauty: the 1860s Greek-Revival **Greeneville Cumberland Presbyterian Church**, the 1850 white-frame **St. James Episcopal Church** (which has the oldest organ in Tennessee), and the 1848 Federal-style **First Presbyterian Church**.

Special Features

A $12-million renovation of **Morgan Square**, a late 19th-century railroad hotel district, was completed in early 1996. On the "new" square are the 53-room General Morgan Inn and Conference Center, a reception area, a restaurant, and numerous specialty shops.

The **Andrew Johnson Presidential Library and Birthplace Replica** are on the campus of **Tusculum College**, the oldest college west of the Alleghenies (1794/1818), located just east of Greeneville (check locally for directions). Books printed as far back as the 16th century are housed in the Rare Book Room of the Special Collections Library (access by special permission only). Nine of the college's structures have been established as the **Tusculum College Historic District**. Campus tours are available.

Davy Crockett's Birthplace State Historic Area is east of town on TN 351 (near Limestone).

> *Andrew Johnson was the only senator of a Southern state to reject secession from the Union.*

Where to Stay

BIG SPRING INN, *315 N. Main St., (423) 638-2917*. Circa 1905 home with spacious porches, antiques, private baths, "memorable" breakfasts, homemade treats, dinner by arrangement, guest library, picnic baskets. $$

FLINTLOCK, *790 G'Fellers Rd. (Chuckey 37641), (423) 257-2489*. Rustic 200-yr-old log home, "horseback adventures," antiques, quilts, 3 bedrooms available as suite, porches with swing & rockers, family-style meals available. $$

GENERAL MORGAN INN, *111 N. Main St., (423) 787-1000/(800) 223-2679/fax (423) 787-1001*. "East Tennessee's Premier Historic Hotel" created from 4 late-19th-century railroad hotels, high ceilings & mahogany furnishings, down comforters, 3 dining rooms, bar, golf packages. $$$

HILLTOP HOUSE B&B, *6 Sanford Circle, (423) 639-8202*. 1920s manor house, English antiques, private baths, full breakfasts, dinner by request, mountain views. $$

SNAPP INN B&B, *P.O. Box 102 (Limestone 37681), (423) 257-2482*. 1815 Federal home with antiques, private baths, full breakfasts, country setting. $

Where to Eat

AUGUSTINO'S RESTAURANT & LOUNGE, *3465 E. Andrew Johnson Hwy., (423) 639-1231.* Continental & Italian cuisines, reservations recommended. $$

DEIDRA'S, *140 W. Depot St., (423) 636-8806.* Pan-fried Beef Tenderloin on Smoked Fettucini, Salmon Filet in a Potato Crust, Pork Shoulder Braised in Garlic & Brandy; dark blue ceiling with tiny twinkling stars, 12-ft. trees. $$ to $$$

MILL WHEEL, *435 Afton Rd. (Afton), (423) 638-7111.* American favorites served in old general store, fresh flowers & white linen cloths/napkins. $ to $$

YE OLDE TUSCULUM EATERY, *2281 Tusculum Blvd. (Tusculum), (423) 638-9210.* Shrimp Kabobs, Chicken Green Bean Almondine, Ribeye Steak, Spinach Lasagna; overlooking Tusculum College. $

Further Information

Greene County Partnership, *115 Academy St., Greeneville, TN 37743-5601 (423) 638-4111/fax (423) 638-5345.*

Directions

From Knoxville, I 40 east to I 81, northeast to exit 23, US 11-E east to Greeneville.

Jonesborough
Population 3, 091

Many charming towns can transport the visitor to another era, but they do so with varying degrees of believability and authenticity. **Jonesborough** is among those that do it most believably and authentically. The sidewalks are brick, there are no stoplights downtown, even the power and telephone lines are hidden underground. Here you enter another time, and a beautiful time it is. At night the street lights, which look like gaslights, illuminate with a rare softness. Drive down **Main Street** after dark and you'll know that Jonesborough takes its history seriously.

Jonesborough was founded in 1779 and is Tennessee's oldest town. Its historic district, with over 150 structures, was the first in Tennessee to be listed on the National Register. The town's history is closely linked with the lives of many notable Americans, including three presidents—Andrew Jackson, James Polk, and Andrew Johnson. Records indicate that Andrew Jackson fought several duels here.

The **Jonesborough-Washington County History Museum**, with over 30 professionally designed exhibits, is housed within the Historic Jonesborough Visitor Center. The center offers guided walking tours, brochures for self-guided tours, and information on horse-drawn carriage tours. The **Discover Jonesborough's Times and Tales Tour**, which brings the town to life through stories and anecdotes, has been honored with two prestigious awards (reservations a must).

The place where the presidents stayed, and often conducted official business, was the **Chester Inn** (1797), now restored and painted in authentic (of course) shades of cream and russet. The inn was built on the **Great Stage Road** from Washington, D.C. and is Jonesborough's second oldest building.

The oldest building is the **Hawley House** (1790, with 1818 additions), a log home that today is also a bed and breakfast (see listing below). Among the many other historic homes are the three brick row houses making up **Sisters Row** (circa 1820), built by Samuel Jackson for his three daughters. The brick was handmade on site, and although the houses are very similar, each has a distinctive fanlight and other features.

Jonesborough has several interesting antebellum churches. One of them is the Greek Revival **Presbyterian Church** (1840s), with a slave gallery and original pews and pulpit. Another is the **Baptist Church** (1850), a church with exceptionally rare and beautiful hand-painted etched-glass windows.

This beautiful little town is best seen on foot or by horse-and-surrey tour.

> *• Each October Jonesborough's National Association for the Preservation and Perpetuation of Storytelling sponsors the highly respected National Storytelling Festival.*
> *• The country's first abolitionist paper, "The Emancipator," was published in Jonesborough in 1820. Jonesborough was later a Union stronghold.*

Where to Stay

AIKEN-BROW HOUSE, *104 3rd Ave. S., (423) 753-9440*. 1850s Greek Revival home in historic district, private baths, gazebo, rocking on the porch. $$

HAWLEY HOUSE B&B, *114 E. Woodrow Ave., (423) 753-8869*. 1793 log & frame dwelling, antiques & folk art, private baths. $$

JONESBOROUGH B&B, *P.O. Box 722, (423) 753-9223*. 1848 home in historic district, antiques & period reproductions, fireplaces, TV & phones, full breakfasts, rocking chairs. $$

THE MAY-LEDBETTER HOUSE, *130 W. Main St., (423) 753-7568.* 1904 home with period antiques, full breakfasts, refreshments, restaurant. $$

Where to Eat

Note: Like many communities in this part of the country, Jonesborough is dry. BYOB!

MAIN STREET CAFE, *117 W. Main St., (423) 753-2460.* Homemade soups, sandwiches, salads; a "Fresh Market Cafe" in Old Post Office across from Chester Inn. $

THE PARSON'S TABLE RESTAURANT, *102 Woodrow Ave., (423) 753-8002.* Salmon Cashew, Shrimp Vol au Vent, Filet Mignon, Quail & Petite, Roulade of Pork Tenderloin; Sunday buffet, in 1874 Gothic Revival church. $$$

WINDOWS ON MAIN STREET, *130 W. Main St., (423) 753-7568.* Specialty sandwiches & salads, specials of the day. $ to $$

Further Information

Jonesborough Visitors Center, *117 Boone St., Jonesborough, TN 37659 (423) 753-1010.*

Directions

From Knoxville, I 40 east to I 81, I 81 to exit 23, east on TN 11E.

Lynchburg
Population 4, 721

Nestled among the hills, hollows, and springs of south central Tennessee, **Lynchburg** is virtually synonymous with the **Jack Daniel Distillery**, the oldest registered distillery in the United States (1866). The visitor's itinerary is relatively short, but very pleasant: After making reservations for mid-day dinner at **Miss Mary Bobo's Boarding House** (see below), walk over to the visitors center of the distillery for an especially interesting and informative tour. Regular tours include visits to the **Barrelhouse**, the original 19th-century office, and **Cave Spring** (responsible for a major ingredient of the whiskey). The steps in whiskey-making, including the distillery's famous charcoal-mellowing process, are explained.

After the tour, it's Miss Mary Bobo's for "dinner." The afternoon can be spent napping, browsing through the shops, and relaxing on a bench in the town square. Whittling is still a favorite pastime in the square, and visitors are welcome to take a seat and watch (this may be one of the few places in the country where it's perfectly safe to sit next to a stranger with a knife).

The **Moore County Courthouse** (1884), on the square, was built of bricks made by the people of Lynchburg. On the lawn is a monument (1927) honoring the county's Confederate soldiers.

About the square are little shops that sell white-oak barrels, art, Jack Daniel memorabilia, needlework, antiques. There's even a hardware where locals – and visitors – can pass the time with a game of checkers. One of Lynchburg's most popular products (after the whiskey) is the **Tipsy Cake** (made with the whiskey, of course).

The **Ledford Mill & Tool Museum**, east of town, is home to an old gristmill (1884) and collection of 18th- and 19th-century wood-working tools.

> *The water produced by Cave Spring is pure lime-stone water, always 56 degrees cool and virtually iron-free.*

Where to Stay

GOOSE BRANCH FARM, *Rte. 3 (Box 140), Goose Branch Rd., (615) 759-5919.* Turn-of-century farm nestled in hollow, private entrances & baths, lemonade on old porch. $$

LYNCHBURG B&B, *P.O. Box 34, (615) 759-7158.* Circa 1877 home close to town square, antiques, TV, private baths, shady front porch. $$

MULBERRY HOUSE B&B, *8 Old Lynchburg Hwy. NE (Mulberry 37359), (615) 433-8461.* Circa 1880 home 6 mi from town, antiques, TV, private bath. $$

Where to Eat

MISS MARY BOBO'S BOARDING HOUSE, *just off square, (615) 759-7394.* Mid-day dinner served family-style in lovely old home: 8 or 10 different dishes, home-grown vegetables, homemade pies or cobblers; reservations a must. $

Further Information

Lynchburg & Metro Moore County Chamber of Commerce, *P.O. Box 421, Lynchburg, TN 37352 (615) 759-4111.*

Directions

From Nashville, I 24 south to Manchester, TN 55 southwest to Lynchburg.

Rugby

Population about 75

Although residing in the rough-and-ready wilderness of Tennessee's **Cumberland Mountains, Rugby's** settlers formed literary and theatrical groups, played tennis, and dressed for afternoon tea. Their English village had as many as 70 buildings and a population of around 350 (in 1884). Today only 22 of the gabled buildings survive, but they form what the National Trust calls one of the "most authentically preserved historic villages in America." Nestled among tall trees near a river gorge, it is also one of the prettiest.

It all began in 1880 when English author and social reformer Thomas Hughes established the community as an experiment in cooperative agrarian living. Part of the purpose of the community was to provide a place for the landless younger sons of Britain's landed gentry to learn and practice manual and agricultural trades.

The community wasn't designed to be exclusively English. Some of the settlers were American.

The experiment was not to succeed - drought, harsh winters, a typhoid epidemic, fire, and maybe a little too much tennis and tea drinking all took their toll. Many of the colonists left and in a decade or two the village drifted into a small farming community. Revival of the village began in 1966, when **Historic Rugby** set about preserving, restoring, and exhibiting some of the colony's remaining buildings. The entire village is now listed on the National Register of Historic Places.

Several of the buildings, all painted in their original Victorian colors, may be toured. One of them, the **Schoolhouse Visitors Center**, contains exhibits that chronicle the history of the village. Another, the Gothic Revival **Christ Church Episcopal** (1887), has the original hanging lamps and 1849 rosewood organ. The organ is still used for the church's services every Sunday. The **Thomas Hughes Library**, unchanged since it opened in 1882, has some 7,000 original volumes of Victorian fiction and non-fiction. **Kingstone Lisle** (1884), the delightful rural Gothic Revival cottage built for Rugby's founder, contains original Rugby furnishings.

Most of the surviving homes, now private residences, are normally closed. However, many are open during the **Rugby Pilgrimage**, the first weekend in October.

Rugby has two shops, both truly unique. One carries traditional crafts and British foods, among other items. The other specializes in Victorian gifts and area history books.

Special Features

In the Rugby vicinity are the **Big South Fork National River & Recreation Area, Frozen Head** and **Pickett** state parks, and the **Obed Wild & Scenic River area**. These and other facilities offer hiking, biking, horseback riding, seasonal rafting, remote river canoeing, fishing, and camping.

The popular **Rugby Spring Museum & Crafts Festival** is held every May.

> • *Thomas Hughes, author of "Tom Brown's Schooldays," devoted much of his time to helping the English working classes.*
> • *The trails built by the colonists down to the river are still in use.*

Where to Stay

NEWBURY HOUSE B&B, *Historic Rugby, (423) 628-2441.* 1880 mansard-roofed boarding house, full breakfasts, tea/coffee, verandah. $$

VICTORIAN COTTAGES, *Historic Rugby, (423) 628-2441.* 1879 house (Pioneer Cottage) & reconstructed Gothic Revival cottage (Percy Cottage). $$

Where to Eat

THE HARROW ROAD CAFE, *Historic Rugby, (423) 628-2441.* Cumberland Plateau home cooking & British Isles specialties: Sauteed Catfish, Welsh Rarebit, Shepherd's Pie, Bangers & Mash. $

Further Information

Historic Rugby, Inc., *P.O. Box 8, Rugby, TN 37733 (423) 628-2441/ 2430.*

Directions

From Knoxville, I 75 north to exit 141, TN 63 west to US 27, US 27 south to TN 52 (Elgin), TN 52 west to Rugby.

Other Charming Tennessee Towns

Bell Buckle
Elizabethton
Franklin
LaGrange
Rogersville

464

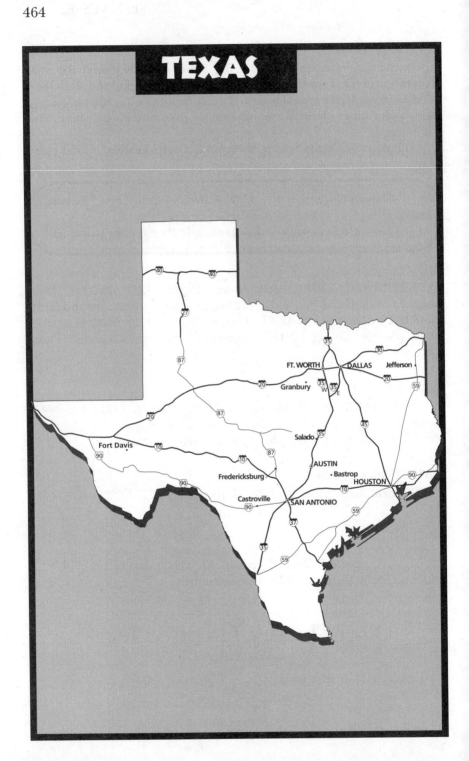

TEXAS

Bastrop

Population 4, 600

Established in 1832, **Bastrop** was here before Texas even became a republic. Built on the banks of the Colorado River and boasting over 130 buildings on the National Register of Historic Places, Bastrop is a peaceful, gracious old town. People who live here report a certain "magical quality" to it. It's the kind of place where a town tour begins with the arrival of a horse-drawn carriage at the bed and breakfast. And yet Bastrop is relatively uncommercialized—unusual for such an historic and attractive (and cosmopolitan) little Texas community, especially one within easy driving distance of Austin and Houston.

The late 19th-century **Main Street**, one of the quaintest and most genuine in Texas, is home to specialty stores, antique shops, restaurants, and other businesses. An especially interesting establishment here is **Lock Drugs**, a 19th-century doctor's office and drug store that still serves sodas and other treats in an old-fashioned ice cream parlor.

Many of Bastrop's historic structures lie in and around the downtown area. They include the **Bastrop Christian Church** (circa 1895), **Old Bastrop County Jail** (circa 1891), and **Courthouse** (circa 1883). The 1889 **Bastrop Opera House** offers year-round dinner-theater productions as well as other special activities.

The streets in and around downtown also contain an imposing collection of antebellum and late 19th-century homes and churches. One, a restored 1850 home, houses the **Bastrop County Historical Society Museum**. The museum's collection includes frontier tools, pictures, furnishings, documents, and other local artifacts.

The Chamber of Commerce maintains information for self-guided driving, walking, bicycling, and Medallion Homes tours. With two lovely city parks on its banks, the **Colorado River** is accessible for fishing, canoeing, and tubing. **Bastrop State Park** (see below) offers fishing, swimming, nature study, and hiking. Bastrop has three fine golf courses.

Special Features

Just east of town, in **Bastrop State Park**, is an especially beautiful stand of loblolly pines. The trees are called the *Lost Pines* because they occur over 100 miles from their normal range in East Texas.

The **Central Texas Museum of Automotive History** is about 12 miles south of town. The museum displays some 85 vintage cars, including Model T's, a Duesenberg, and a 1911 Napier.

The Bastrop area offers a number of beautiful drives, including TX 71 east to Smithville. Inquire locally concerning scenic county roads.

> • The *"Bastrop Advertiser"* is the oldest weekly newspaper in Texas (est. 1853).
> • Bastrop was named after a Dutch nobleman, Felipe Enrique Neri, Baron de Bastrop, an important figure in Texas's settlement days. Unknown to the people of the day, Bastrop was an impostor, wanted in Holland for embezzlement.

Where to Stay

CABINS ON THE COLORADO, *601 Chestnut, (512) 321-7002.* Four small century-old homes with porches/decks, antiques, private baths, swings & rocking chairs, wild flowers, on Colorado River, restaurant, bakery. $$ to $$$

THE COLONY B&B, *703 Main St., (512) 303-1234.* National Register home offering "Southern hospitality," antiques, private baths, full "gourmet" breakfasts, champagne. $$$

HIDE-A-WAY, *Buescher State Park, (512) 303-7378.* Log guest home on acre of pines rented as unit, Cont. breakfast basket, porch swing, stacked wood for fireplace. $$$

THE HISTORIC PFEIFFER HOUSE, *1802 Main St., (512) 321-2100.* 1901 Carpenter Gothic home on National Register, high ceilings, antiques, full breakfasts, collection of old quilts. $$

THE KATY HOUSE, *P.O. Box 803, 201 Ramona (Smithville 78957), (512) 237-4262/fax (512) 237-5000.* Turn-of-century home, American antiques, Battenburg lace, TV & phones, private baths, full "country" breakfasts. $$ to $$$

PECAN STREET INN, *1010 Pecan St., (512) 321-3315.* Eclectic Gothic/Queen Anne home on National Register, 12-ft ceilings, antiques, private baths, Cont. or full "gourmet" breakfasts on china with silver & crystal, guest kitchen, native pecans trees. $$ to $$$

Where to Eat

GIN-U-WINE OYSTER BAR/RESTAURANT, *707 Chestnut St., (512) 321-9864.* Seafood & steaks served in New Orleans-style bistro. $

THE YACHT CLUB, *(see Cabins on the Colorado above).* Grilled Rib-eye Steak, Pork Chop, Chicken Breast, Fish, & Shrimp; Mexican items, sandwiches, soups, salads. $ to $$

Further Information

Bastrop Chamber of Commerce, *P.O. Box 681, Bastrop, TX 78602 (512) 321-2419.*

Directions

From Austin, TX 71 east to Bastrop.

Castroville

Population 2, 159

Settled in 1844 by immigrants from the French-German provinces of Alsace and Lorraine, **Castroville** was by the 1850s a picturesque little Alsatian village. *The Little Alsace of Texas* looks a little more like Texas these days, but the Alsatian flavor is still very much in evidence: Nearly 100 stone buildings from the original Alsatian village remain, Alsatian (a Germanic dialect) is spoken by some of the older townspeople, local kitchens and menus feature Alsatian dishes, and Alsatian folk music is preserved by the **Alsatian Dancers of Texas**.

There was a time when Castroville was one of Texas's largest cities, but in the 1880s the railroad bypassed the town, allowing the picturesque architectural heritage to survive. The historic district, encircled in part by one of those lazy Texas rivers, the **Medina**, contains 97 structures. Most were constructed of limestone and cypress timbers and finished with white plaster. Many go as far back as the 1840s and 1850s. The majority, one-story cottages with the asymmetric rooflines of their Alsatian ancestors, are private residences or homes to businesses, including some of Castroville's dozen or so antique and craft shops. The entire old part of town is a National Historic District.

Among the most imposing of the multi-story buildings are the **Carle House and Store** (1865), the porticoed **Tarde Hotel** (1852; now a private residence), and the unusually beautiful Gothic-style **St. Louis Catholic Church** (1870). The largest structure is the galleried **Moye Center**, now a retreat center but built originally (1873) as a convent and motherhouse.

Castroville's most famous building is the **Landmark Inn**, begun in 1849 and established as an inn in 1854. Now a part of the **Landmark Inn State Historical Park**, the inn still offers overnight accommodations (see below). Other structures in the historical park include a residence, stone grist mill, and arched stone waterway, all dating from the 1850s.

A guide for a walking tour of the historic district is distributed by the Chamber of Commerce. Guided tours are also available, as are tours of homes conducted by the Castroville Garden Club (by appointment).

Special Features

The Olympic-size pool in the **Castroville Regional Park** is the perfect place to conclude a summer's day of sightseeing.

One of the country's most charming cities, **San Antonio**, is 20 miles to the east of Castroville. Top sights in San Antonio: the **Paseo del Rio**, several historic missions, the **Alamo**, and the **Institute of Texan Cultures**.

> • *Castroville is famous for its Alsatian sausage and pastries.*
> • *Only Stephen F. Austin brought more settlers to Texas than the founder of Castroville, Henri Castro.*
> • *Castroville was the first Texas town to be established west of San Antonio.*

Where to Stay

DAS HIESLE GUEST HOUSE, *209 US 90 W, (800) 329-9622.* Late-1800s cottage rented as unit, antiques & vintage fixtures, TV & phone, claw-foot tub, shade trees. $$

THE HABY SETTLEMENT INN B&B, *3980 FM 471 North (Rio Medina 78066), (830) 538-2441.* 1890s farmhouse rented as unit, 11-foot ceilings, antiques, "country" breakfasts, lawn chairs. $$ to $$$

LANDMARK INN, *402 Florence St., (830) 538-2133.* Historic 1860s inn, National Register, antiques, some private baths, gardens, views, old rockers on second-floor gallery. $

THE SWAN AND RAILWAY COUNTRY INN, *P.O. Box 446 (LaCoste 78039), (830) 762-3742.* Small 1912 hotel, antiques, private baths, full breakfasts, long porches, pool. $$

Where to Eat

THE ALSATIAN, *403 Angelo St., (830) 931-3260.* Grilled Shrimp a Quatre Epices, Strasbourg Chicken, Jagerschnitzel; quaint 1800s cottage setting. $ to $$

CHANTILLY TEA ROOM, *309 La Fayette St., (830) 538-9531.* Soups, salads, sandwiches, daily specials; Victorian atmosphere. $

LA NORMANDIE RESTAURANT, *1302 Fiorella St., (830) 538-3070/ (800) 761-1731.* "Traditional French cuisine from Normandy to Alsace": e.g., Gambas aux Amandes, Breast of Capon a l'Estragon, Filet Mignon Sauce Choron; intimate French country home setting, respected. $$

Further Information

Castroville Chamber of Commerce, *802 London St., P.O. Box 572, Castroville, TX 78009 (830) 538-3142.*

Directions

From San Antonio, US 90 west to Castroville.

Fort Davis

Population 1, 200

Fort Davis is truly a town of the Old West, the Old West of history as well as of the movies. Throughout much of the 19th century wagon trains, the Pony Express, and stagecoaches passed through the area on their way west on the old San Antonio-El Paso road. Fort Davis (1854 to 1891) was one of several forts built to guard the road. Almost by Hollywood script, Apaches and Comanches attacked travelers on the road, and troops rode out of the fort to pursue the raiders. Infantrymen from the fort also escorted mail and freight trains and patrolled the region's vast spaces. And all of this took place in the foothills of the Davis Mountains, a made-to-order Western backdrop.

The town of Fort Davis grew up alongside the fort during the latter part of the century. In addition to serving the fort, the town was a center for ranchers and a kind of resort for Texans wishing to escape the heat and humidity of the coastal summers. The elevation, low humidity, and cool climate also attracted people suffering from tuberculosis.

It would be an exaggeration to say that the town's life style hasn't changed in 100 years, but there are those who claim that it hasn't changed much in 50 years. Crime is virtually non-existent, and the water remains clear and the air fresh. Nobody uses street names, and everybody knows everyone else. There are small old adobe houses, a tiny town square, and limestone and adobe buildings, public and commercial, from the late 19th and early 20th centuries. The gift shops and art galleries weren't here 50 years ago, but the old soda fountain was.

Three buildings of special note are churches: the 1904 **First Presbyterian Church**, the 1898 **St. Joseph's Catholic Church**, and the 1884 **Methodist Church**, the oldest Protestant church building between San Antonio and El Paso. The **Union Mercantile**, on the east end of the square, is the town's oldest building (1873).

According to the National Park Service, the old fort, now **Fort Davis National Historic Site**, is "considered the best surviving example of a frontier Indian Wars post in the Southwest." Many of the more than 50 original structures of the fort have been restored; some have been furnished in period and opened as museums. The site includes a visitor center, picnic grove, and nature trail system. During the summer months costumed interpreters present demonstrations and conduct tours of refurnished buildings.

The **Overland Trail Museum** (1883), owned and operated by the **Fort Davis Historical Society**, features a large collection of county photos and a restored frontier kitchen and barber shop (open during the summer on Tuesdays, Fridays, and Saturdays and the rest of the year by appointment). The **Chihuahuan Desert Visitor Center**, just south of town, has gardens and walking trails that introduce the visitor to native flowers, cacti, and trees.

Special Features

The Scenic Loop is a 75-mile road that ascends into the **Davis Mountains**. At one point it reaches the highest elevation in the Texas highway system (6,791 feet). Along the way are the **Davis Mountains State Park**, the **McDonald Observatory** (see below), the **Barrel Springs Stage Stop**, the **Point of Rocks** picnic area, and other scenic and historic points. Most of the land fronting the Scenic Loop is private property, usually working ranches, and travelers are advised not to trespass. Flash floods are possible, as are native animals and cattle on the road.

The **McDonald Observatory**, 17 miles north of town (and on the Scenic Loop), features the second-largest telescope in the world. Check at the visitor center for information on tours of the dome, solar viewing, "star parties," and other public programs.

> *Fort Davis was one of the first posts in the West where black troops, called "Buffalo Soldiers," served (1867 to 1885).*

Where to Stay

HOTEL LIMPIA, *P.O. Box 822 (on the square), (800) 662-5517.* Restored 1912 pink limestone hotel, full-service, 12-ft ceilings with ornamental tin, dining room, bar, glassed-in verandah, rocking chairs (hotel's "trademark"), pets, guest houses, gift shop, nature store. $ to $$$

INDIAN LODGE, *P.O. Box 1458 (Davis Mountains State Park), (915) 426-3254.* Older part a picturesque pueblo-style hotel built in 1930s by C.C.C., full-service, handmade furniture, restaurant, pool. $$ to $$$

NEILL DOLL MUSEUM, *edge of town, (915) 426-3969.* 1898 home, antique furnishings, large doll collection. $$ to $$$

PARADISE MOUNTAIN RANCH, *HCR 74 Box 55, (915) 426-3737/ (800) 738-3320.* Guest houses or roughing it, full "country" breakfasts, trail rides & campouts, horse-riding lessons, roundups. $$ to $$$

THE VERANDA COUNTRY INN B&B, *210 Court Ave., P.O. Box 1238, (915) 426-2233*. 1883 adobe inn, 12-ft ceilings, antique furnishings, private baths, "hearty" breakfasts, gardens & quiet courtyards. $$ to $$$
  WAYSIDE INN B&B, *P.O. Box 2088, (800) 582-7510*. Expanded 1947 residence with scenic views, private baths, "Texas Country" breakfast buffet, antiques & memorabilia. $$ to $$$

Where to Eat
  HOTEL LIMPIA DINING ROOM, *(see above)*. Lasagna Roll-up, Lemon Parmesan Chicken, Burgundy Marinated Roast Beef, Fried Beef Tenderloin, Aaron's Fried Shrimp, Limpia's Vegetarian Fettuccini. $ to $$
  POCO MEXICO CAFE, *TX 17, (915) 426-3939*. Red Enchiladas, Green Enchiladas, Chili Rellenos, Guadalajaras, Flautas, Fajitas, American food. $

Further Information
  Fort Davis Chamber of Commerce, *P.O. Box 572, Fort Davis, TX 79734 (915) 426-3015*.

Directions
  From El Paso, I 10 east to exit 206, TX 17 south to Fort Davis.

Fredericksburg
Population 6, 934

Fredericksburg's considerable charm doesn't fit neatly into any category. The very wide straight streets and their limestone and frame houses, some with Victorian gingerbread trim, don't belong to a German town. Yet the biergartens and the large array of lovely 19th-century stone buildings hardly describe a typical Texas town. Fredericksburg is unique, and belongs on the itinerary of anyone touring Texas.
  By all means the most unique, yet enchanting of Fredericksburg's 80-plus historic sites is the restored **Steamboat Hotel** (1852). Looking very much like an old steamboat getting ready to plough across the Texas Hill Country, the hotel was built and managed by the grandparents of Admiral Nimitz, U.S. five-star admiral and hero of the Pacific in W.W.II. The hotel is today the **Nimitz State Park** and houses a three-floor **Museum of the Pacific War**, with audiovisual exhibits and hands-on displays. The ballroom and four of the hotel's original guest rooms are also on view. Behind

the hotel is the restful **Japanese Garden of Peace**, a gift from the people of Japan.

The **Vereins Kirche Museum** is a replica (1935/36) of an octagonal building (1847) that played a number of roles, including that of school and fort, during the latter half of the 19th century. The landmark building, now owned and operated by the **Gillespie County Historical Society**, houses an excellent local history collection. James Michener is one of several researchers who have used the archives.

A good glimpse of an earlier Fredericksburg is provided by the **Pioneer Museum Complex**. The complex includes the stone **Kammlah House** (1849), which served as a home and store through the 1920s. The building bears a National Historic Trust Site emblem. Eight furnished rooms, a wine cellar, and stone-covered yard (*hof*) are available for viewing. Among other structures in the complex is the limestone Victorian **Fassel House**, a one-room schoolhouse, an authentic Texas Hill Country log cabin, the **Weber Sunday House**, and the **Fredericksburg Volunteer Fire Department Museum**.

Dotting the back streets are smallish houses that were once *Sunday Houses*, weekend houses where farming and ranching families stayed when they were in town to buy supplies, sell produce, dance and party – and attend church. In the era of the horse and buggy, simply getting to and from town took such a large chunk of the day that staying over was often necessary.

The tastes and smells in the town's biergartens are very much like those of the Old Country, but the lovely old limestone walls and the live oaks shielding the tables from the Texas sun are uniquely Fredericksburg. This is Texas German at its delightful best!

Special Features

Fort Martin Scott, two miles east of town, was the first U.S. Army frontier fort in Texas (established 1848). The reconstructed fort, now a state historic site, includes the guardhouse, a civilian log cabin, and two officers' quarters.

This is Texas **peach country**. The Chamber of Commerce/Convention & Visitor Bureau distributes a map of roadside stands and pick-your-own orchards selling homemade peach ice cream, pies, and preserves. The area is also the home of several vineyards and wineries.

More than 3, 000 toys from the 1870-1970 period are on display at the Bauer Toy Museum.

Where to Stay

COUNTRY COTTAGE INN, *249 E. Main, (210) 997-8549*. Consisting of 1850 Kiehne House, 1866 Admiral Chester Nimitz birthplace, & 1995 Courtyard House; fireplaces, TV & phones, private baths, whirlpools, private entrances, in-room full breakfasts, courtyard. $$$

DAS COLLEGE HAUS, *106 W. College, (210) 997-9047/(800) 654-2802*. Monterey-style turn-of-century home, original art, TV, private baths, full breakfasts, suites, wicker furniture on porch/balcony. $$$

DAS GARTEN HAUS, *604 S. Washington St., (210) 990-8408/(800) 416-4287*. Suites overlooking New Orleans-style courtyard, TV, private entrances, full "sumptuous" breakfasts, beverages. $$$

THE DELFORGE PLACE, *710 Ettie, (210) 997-6212*. 1898 home with 12-ft ceilings & antique chandeliers, heirlooms, TV & phones, private baths, "world-class" breakfasts, shaded rock patio, 2 suites also in restored circa 1926 Weber Farmhouse. $$$

MAGNOLIA HOUSE, *101 E. Hackberry, (210) 997-0306/(800) 880-4374*. 1923 home with antiques, fireplaces, TV, private baths, "exquisite" full breakfasts, suites, patio. $$$

SCHMIDT BARN B&B, *231 W. Main, (210) 997-5612*. 1860s limestone barn converted to guest cottage, antiques, phone, sunken tub, "German-style" breakfasts, pets, herb/flower garden. $$

Where to Eat

DER LINDENBAUM, *312 E. Main, (210) 997-9126*. Rhineland-style cooking, schnitzels, sauerbraten, bratwurst, steaks. $ to $$

FRIEDHELM'S BAVARIAN INN, *905 W. Main, (210) 997-6300*. German specialties, seafood, steaks; Boars Nest Lounge, popular. $ to $$

HILL TOP CAFE, *10.5 mi NW of town on US 87, (210) 997-8922*. Shrimp Mytilini, Red Snapper en Pappiote, Cajun-Style Gumbo, Greek salads, Red Raspberry Pie; acclaimed. $$

THE PLATEAU CAFE, *312 W. Main, (210) 997-1853*. Texas/German cooking in "true early Texas environment," biergarten. $

SPANISH CELLAR BISTRO, *201 N. Llano, (210) 997-9076*. Authentic Spanish offerings such as paella & sangria, homemade "greaseless" Mexican food; undiscovered. $$

Further Information

Fredericksburg Convention & Visitor Bureau, *106 N. Adams, Fredericksburg, TX 78624 (210) 997-6523*.

Directions

From San Antonio, I 10 north to US 87, US 87 north to Fredericksburg (approximately 69 miles).

Granbury

Population 5, 001

Granbury is an historic 19th-century town, an antique and art center, a place for Ft. Worthians and Dallasites to go for dinner and a play or musical, a resort nestled along the shores of 30-mile-long **Lake Granbury**.

Granbury's town square was the first in Texas to be listed on the National Register of Historic Places. On the square is the Second Empire-style **Hood County Courthouse** (1891). A Seth Thomas town clock was installed when the courthouse, built of native limestone, was completed. Around the square are beautifully restored late 19th-century and turn-of-the-century commercial structures. One of the handsomest is the 1886 **Granbury Opera House**, a two-story Italianate theater that is still in regular use (see below). Also of note are the limestone **Old Hood County Jail** (1885), which houses the **Jail Museum** (with a hanging tower), and the 1893 **Nutt House**, originally and currently a hotel (see below). The buildings on the square are home to more than 50 antique and specialty shops, art galleries, boutiques, and restaurants.

On the streets off the square is a collection of fine Victorian homes, many of them of the Queen Anne style. Granbury's historic buildings may be seen by guided group tours and by self-guided tours.

Lake Granbury, lined with vacation homes and condominiums, offers a variety of water sports and the setting for some scenic golf. Sightseeing excursions and dinner cruises are available on the *Granbury Queen*, a Mississippi-style riverboat. Lest the visitor forget that this is Texas, Granbury also boasts the world's largest 18-hole miniature golf course.

The **Texas Amphitheater** in nearby **Glen Rose** presents a musical drama, *The Promise*, that portrays the life of Christ. For those preferring old-time entertainment, Granbury also boasts a 1950s **drive-in theater**.

> *Granbury has a rich folklore. Among the legends is that the real John Wilkes Booth, President Lincoln's assassin, was never captured and that he once resided in the town under the name of John St. Helen. Another legend is that Jesse James is buried here rather than in Missouri.*

Special Features

Dinosaur Valley State Park, west of Glen Rose, features the best-preserved dinosaur tracks in the state. The park also has nature trails and a visitor center. Also west of Glen Rose, the **Fossil Rim Wildlife Center** offers a 9-mile drive through a 2,900-acre conservation area containing over 1,000 endangered and exotic animals.

Where to Stay

THE CAPTAIN'S HOUSE, *123 W. Doyle St., (817)-579-6664.* Circa 1875 home overlooking lake, balconies, private baths, shaded park & picnic area, boat parking. $$ to $$$

THE DOYLE HOUSE B&B, *205 W. Doyle, (817) 573-6492.* On the lake, TV, private baths & entrances, full breakfasts on weekends, pool, fishing platform. $$$

THE IRON HORSE INN B&B, *616 N. Thorp Springs Rd., (817) 579-5535.* Craftsman-style home with ornate millwork, private baths, full breakfasts, wine, library. $$$

THE NUTT HOUSE, *on square, (817) 573-5612.* 1893 hotel with air-conditioned guest rooms, dining room, sweet shop. $ to $$

PEARL STREET INN B&B, *319 W. Pearl St., (817) 579-7465.* 1912 Prairie-style home, antiques, individually appointed rooms. $$$

Where to Eat

CUCKOO'S NEST RESTAURANT & CLUB, *south side of square, (817) 573-9722.* Steaks, spirits; live entertainment. $

HENNINGTONS - A TEXAS CAFE, *110 Crockett St., (817) 573-8400.* Eclectic menu ranging from roast duck to country-fried steak, spirits. $$

THE MERRY HEART TEAROOM, *109 N. Houston St., (817) 573-3800.* Quiches, omelets, King Ranch Chicken Crepes, specials, salads, sandwiches; Victorian atmosphere. $

THE NUTT HOUSE, *(see above).* "Country" cooking, homemade light breads & hot-water cornbread. $

RINKY TINK'S SANDWICH & ICE CREAM PARLOR, *west side of square, (817) 573-4323.* Old-fashioned ice cream parlor, live music Saturday evenings. $

Further Information

Granbury Convention & Visitors Bureau, *100 N. Crockett, Granbury, TX 76048 (800) 950-2212.*

Directions

From Ft. Worth, US 377 southwest 35 mi to Granbury, take Business District/Historic District exit across lake to town square.

Jefferson

Population 2, 200

During its early years, **Jefferson** acquired one of the most beautiful collections of mid-19th century homes in Texas. Located on **Big Cypress Bayou**, the town was a major Texas river port, second only to Galveston in tonnage shipped. It was also the "Gateway to Texas" for settlers, a home to wealthy planters, and a Confederate ammunition and food supply center. Then came the *Great Decline*: In 1873, while removing a major log jam on the Red River below Shreveport, Louisiana, U.S. Corps of Engineers dredgers unwittingly lowered the water level on the Big Cypress so much that shipping to Jefferson was no longer feasible.

The **Excelsior House Hotel** (see listing below), one of Jefferson's top sights, has been in continuous operation since the 1850s. Include the hotel and its New Orleans-style courtyard in your tour whether or not you're staying there. Another Jefferson treasure is the *Atalanta*, a private railroad car built in 1888 for railroad tycoon, Jay Gould. There is no better way to apprehend the extravagance of late 19th-century millionaire life than to tour this car.

Jefferson's shady streets can be toured by foot, motorized trolley, horse-drawn carriage, and several other ways. Many of the historic homes may be seen by appointment, several by regularly scheduled tour. Among those in the latter category are the single-story neoclassic **Beard House** (1860), the four-columned Greek Revival **Freeman Plantation** (1850), and the lovely transitional **House of Seasons** (1872), identified by its unique cupola.

Jefferson boasts a number of impressive collections, some public and some private. The **Jefferson Historical Museum** displays many of the public ones: Civil War artifacts, old Bibles, pioneer doctors' instruments, ironstone, old Jefferson bottles, etc. Another public collection, the new **Texas Heritage Archives and Library**, might just as well be called the *Museum of the Republic of Texas*, so extensive and valuable are its holdings from the 1836-1845 period. Private collections of antiques and artifacts may be seen in Jefferson's some 49 arts and crafts and collectibles shops.

> *The final resting place and artifacts from the Jefferson-bound steamboat, the "Mittie Stephens," were finally located in 1993. The boat took the lives of 64 people when it burned and sank on Caddo Lake in 1869.*

Where to Stay

THE CAPTAIN'S CASTLE, *403 E. Walker, (903) 665-2330*. Mid-19th-century Main House plus nearby Carriage House & Cottage, on National Register, antiques, private baths, full breakfasts. $$$

EXCELSIOR HOTEL, *211 W. Austin, (903) 665-2513*. Restored 1850s hotel, antiques throughout, private baths, "plantation" breakfasts, a Texas landmark. $ to $$$

FALLING LEAVES, *304 Jefferson St., (903) 665-8803*. Circa 1855 Greek Revival home on National Register, antiques, private baths, "gourmet" breakfasts, refreshments, huge magnolia & pecan trees. $$$

McKAY HOUSE, *306 Delta St., (903) 665-7322/(800) 468-2627/fax (903) 665-8551*. 1851 home on National Register, antiques, fireplaces, TV & phones, private baths, "Gentleman's Breakfast," refreshments, patio, gardens, Victorian nightgowns & sleepshirts, period hats. $$$

PRIDE HOUSE B&B, *409 E. Broadway, (903) 665-2675*. 1888 home with 12-ft ceilings & ornate woodwork, private baths, "legendary" breakfasts, wrap-around porch. $$$

THE STEAMBOAT INN, *114 N. Marshall, (903) 665-8946*. Greek Revival home on landscaped grounds, antiques, fireplaces, TV & phones, private baths, "gourmet" breakfasts, refreshments, porches, gardens, views. $$$

Where to Eat

AUNTIE SKINNER'S RIVERBOAT CLUB, *107 W. Austin St., (903) 665-7121*. Tex-Mex favorites, Chicken Fried Steak; New Orleans-style eatery in 1866 bldg. $

GALLEY RESTAURANT & LOUNGE, *121 W. Austin St., (903) 665-3641*. Shrimp Scampi, Charbroiled Catfish, Filet Mignon, Ribeye, Creole Bread Pudding; in historic building. $$

THE GROVE, *405 Moseley, (903) 665-2638*. Chef-owned historic home serving seafood, chicken, steaks, pasta; Pecan Praline Cheesecake a winner. $$

STILLWATER INN, *203 E. Broadway, (903) 665-8415*. Shrimp & Pasta, Roasted Cornish Game Hen, New York Strip; in chef-owned 1893 home, period decor, upstairs lodging, gift shop, highly respected. $$

Further Information

Marion County Chamber of Commerce, *118 N. Vale, Jefferson, TX 75657 (903) 665-2672*.

Directions

From Shreveport (LA), I 20 west to US 59, north (16 miles) to Jefferson; from Dallas, I 20 east to US 59, north to Jefferson.

Salado

Population 1, 200

Sitting on the tree-shaded banks of spring-fed **Salado Creek** in central Texas is what may be Texas's most charming little town. Although blessed with a lovely setting and a long and genteel history, **Salado** (sa LAY doh) is so little known that it is sometimes called the "undiscovered jewel of Texas." Many people who regularly travel the nearby interstate have never heard of the village, and there are people living in towns just a few miles away who have never even visited here.

Salado Creek once nourished a stage stop and later a branch of the **Chisholm Trail**. But Salado came into being because of the generosity of plantation owner Colonel Sterling C. Robertson, who in 1859 gave the land for the town. Once born, the town's character was molded by respected **Salado College** (1860 to about 1885), whose students and educators brought to Salado a level of culture and prestige foreign to most other Texas frontier towns.

The railroads bypassed Salado, and the town was destined to become a small, quiet village. The village has undergone a recent revitalization as many of the old homes and other buildings have been restored to house bed and breakfasts (see below), some of the finest restaurants in central Texas (see below), and a very inviting collection of art galleries, potteries, antique and craft shops, boutiques, and book shops. Many of the new homes closely resemble the old; the two mingle comfortably. The setting and character remain strictly rural.

Eighteen of the village's buildings are listed on the National Register. Tapes for a driving tour may be rented at the **Stagecoach Inn** (see below). Several of the houses are open during an historic homes tour held every December.

One of the historic homes is the **Baines home**, a 1866 saltbox built by the great-grandfather of President Lyndon Baines Johnson. Two other interesting homes include the 1868 Greek Revival **Armstrong-Adams House**, once occupied by a series of doctors as well as student boarders, and the old rock **Barton House**, built in 1866 by a Dr. and Mrs. Barton who wished to educate their 10 children at Salado College.

Salado Creek was the first Natural Landmark in Texas. The town is so proud of the creek that a committee has been established to monitor the quality of the water. One of the best places to enjoy the beauty of the crystal-clear waters is at **Pace Park**, once an Indian campground. A bronze statue of **Sirena**, a beautiful Indian maiden who by legend was transformed into a mermaid by a magical fish, graces a bubbling spring of the creek.

Special Feature

In the country south of town stand the 22-room plantation home (1852/1857) and stone slave quarters built by Col. Robertson. The house remains in the hands of the Robertson family. Occasional tours are available – check with the Chamber of Commerce for information.

> • *The ruins of Salado College have been stabilized preliminary to reconstruction efforts.*
> • *Salado hosts the Texas Scottish Games and Gathering of the Clans every November.*
> • *Dr. Barton, builder of Barton House, is believed to have introduced watercress to Salado Creek. The plant flourishes there today.*

Where to Stay

BRAMBLEY HEDGE, *P.O. Box 351, (817) 947-1914/fax (817) 947-9692.* Secluded home on 50 wooded acres, private baths, refreshments, decks, game room, gift shop, fresh flowers, croquet. $$ to $$$

COUNTRY PLACE B&B, *Rt. 1 Box 19VA Holland Rd., (817) 947-9683.* Old Texas-style country house, private baths, full "country" breakfasts, fields of bluebonnets. $$$

GREEN GABLES B&B, *433 Royal St., (817) 947-0520.* Old-fashioned porches, antiques & lace, private baths, "gourmet" breakfasts, old oak tree. $$ to $$$

HALLEY HOUSE B&B, *N. Main St., P.O. Box 125, (817) 947-1000.* 1860 home on National Register, antiques, fireplaces, private baths, "gourmet" buffet breakfasts, garden, oak trees. $$$

INN ON THE CREEK, *P O. Box 858, (817) 947-5554.* Three historic houses & cottage, full "country" breakfasts, porches. $$ to $$$

INN AT SALADO, *P.O. Box 500, (817) 947-8200.* 1872 home on National Register, fireplaces, private baths, tree-covered brick terraces. $$$

THE ROSE MANSION, *P.O. Box 500, (817) 947-8200.* 1870 Greek Revival mansion, grand parlor, fireplaces, acres of landscaped grounds. $$$

Where to Eat

PIETRO'S, *302 N. Main St., (817) 947-0559.* Ravioli, Pasta ala Pietro, Chicken Alfredo, Chicken Marsala, Shrimp Mariana; "Where we feed you like there's no tomorrow." $ to $$

THE RANGE, *101 Main St., (817) 947-3828.* E.g., Grilled Pork Tenderloin with Roasted Vegetables, House Fries and Caramelized Apple Jus. $$

THE SALADO MANSION, *Main St., (817) 947-5157.* Tex-Mex & Southwestern dishes; in 1857 Tyler House, patio dining. $

STAGECOACH INN, *Old Chisholm Trail (Main St.), (800) 732-8994.* Southern Fried Chicken, Chicken Fried Steak, Sugar Baked Ham, Deep Fried Whole Catfish, seafood, steaks; in historic 1861 stage stop. $ to $$

Further Information

Salado Chamber of Commerce, *P.O. Box 81, Salado, TX 76571 (817) 947-5040.*

Directions

From Austin, I 35 north to exit 283 (Salado exit); from Waco, I 35 south to Salado exit, cross under highway to Main Street.

Other Charming Texas Towns

Albany
Alpine
Canyon
Columbus
Comfort
Ft. Stockton
Johnson City
Marathon
Miami
San Augustine
Wimberley

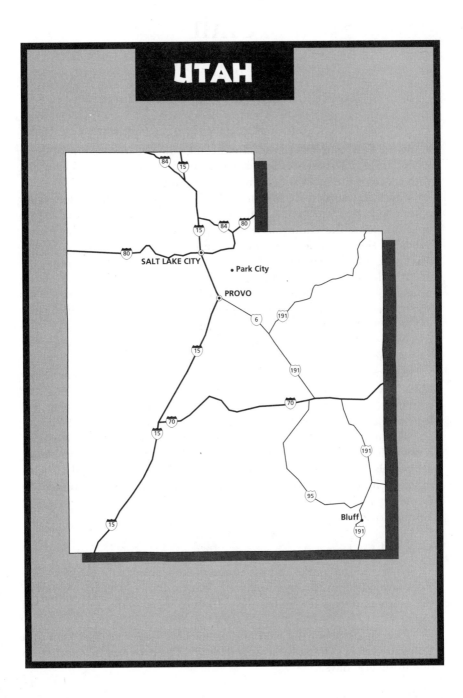

UTAH

Bluff

Population about 290

Guarded by the towering **Navajo Twin Rocks**, **Bluff** lies in a canyon along the **San Juan River** in southeastern Utah. The town is one of those legendary little Western settlements that combine the vestiges of Victoriana with some of the most spectacular scenery in the country.

Bluff was settled by Mormons in 1880. At first the settlers were compelled to group their cabins in a defensive fort, but as the region became safer, the cabins were moved to individual lots. There they provided shelter while larger stone houses were erected. Bluff's growth was to be short-lived, however, for in 1893 the county seat moved to Monticello and the town was progressively abandoned. Many of the houses were eventually torn down, and the remainder lost much of their Victorian ornamentation through negligence or rebuilding. Of the original 30 or so buildings, only about 14 survived. Fortunately, most of the survivors are being preserved, and in many cases restored to their original appearance.

Explore the tiny historic district on foot, and then climb up **Cemetery Hill**. The memorials here remind of a time that was anything but romantic. For example, James Decker, one of the original settlers, and four of his children died of diphtheria in late 1900 and early 1901.

The area around Bluff is rich in prehistoric sites. Within short driving, if not walking, distance are six or seven **Pueblo Anasazi** and **Navajo rock art panels** composed of various representational images and abstract motifs. There are also several **Pueblo Anasazi sites**. One, situated on Cemetery Hill, consists of a Great House, a Great Kiva, and remnants of a prehistoric road.

Special Features

Nine national parks and monuments are within a 2-hour drive. The vast **Navajo Indian Reservation** is adjacent, and the spectacular **Valley of the Gods** is only a few miles away. Inquire locally concerning guided tours.

River trips down the wild and archaeologically rich **San Juan** and **Colorado** rivers can also be arranged locally. The trips vary in length from one to several days.

> • *A unique black-on-red pottery was collected in 1936 at one of the local Pueblo Anasazi village sites. The pottery is now known to Southwest archaeologists as Bluff Black-on-red.*
> • *At one time the Navajos crossed the river by means of a swinging bridge, still in place.*

Where to Stay

BLUFF B&B, *P.O. Box 158, (801) 672-2220.* Frank Lloyd Wright-style home on 17 desert acres, private baths, private canyon. $$

CALABRE B&B, *P.O. Box 85, (801) 672-2252.* In town, full breakfasts. $

PIONEER HOUSE, *P.O. Box 309, (801) 672-2281.* Early 1890s home on National Register available for family get-togethers, field trips, & group outings. $

RECAPTURE LODGE, *P.O. Box 309, (801) 672-2281.* Rustic lodge, private baths, pets, hot tub, pool, slide shows, tour information, nature area. $

Where to Eat

COW CANYON TRADING POST & RESTAURANT, *163 Mission Rd., (801) 672-2208.* Traditional Navajo dishes, TexMex, Italian fare; reservations recommended. $

TURQUOISE RESTAURANT, *Hwy. 191, P.O. Box 306, (801) 672-2279.* Traditional American menu, Navajo Taco a specialty; local artwork. $

Further Information

Bluff Town Board, *P.O. Box 310, Bluff, UT 84512 (801) 672-2281.*

Directions

From Moab (UT) US 191 south to Bluff (100 miles).

Park City
Population 7, 000

Named after its park-like setting, **Park City** is a unique and engaging mixture of the old and the new. The old can be seen in the Victorian buildings and various mementos from the town's mining past. The new is seen in the condos, modern ski resorts, and variety of shops.

But the old and the new don't coexist, they blend. Many of the shops are housed in restored historic buildings, and transportation on **Main Street** is provided by an old-fashioned trolley. The blend is most beautiful in the winter, when people in colorful ski gear stroll through a wonderland of snow-covered Victorian buildings and inviting inns, restaurants, and pubs.

One of the few Utah towns not founded by Mormons, Park City boasted some 27 saloons at one point early in its history. The silver in the surrounding **Wasatch Mountains** helped turn 23 people into millionaires, including George Hearst, father of William Randolph Hearst. By the 1930s, however, it was clear that silver was becoming part of the town's past and the people began to look toward the snow for their future.

And what a future it turned out to be! Park City now has three major ski resorts, three shopping centers (including Main Street), around 15 art galleries, and a free bus system. There are also 90 restaurants, and the apres-ski and night life scenes are among the most highly rated in the country.

Park City has had 64 buildings placed on the National Register of Historic Places. Many are on Main Street. One of special interest to those wishing to know the town is the **Visitor Information Center/Museum**. Once the **City Hall**, the museum tells the story of Park City's mining past and transition to a major resort. In the basement is **Utah's Territorial Jail**, used longer than any other territorial jail in the West (until 1964).

Park City is both a summer and winter resort. The summer tourist will find six distinctive golf courses, hiking and horseback riding trails, and more than 80 miles of mountain-bike trails. A ski lift serves hikers and bikers. In addition to the ski resorts, winter sports fans will find opportunities and facilities for snowmobiling, cross-country skiing, and ice skating. Hot-air balloons color the skies in both summer and winter.

Special Feature

Five Nordic ski jumps, a freestyle jump, a bobsled/luge track, and a snowboard half-pipe have been constructed at **Utah Winter Sports Park**, site of the 2002 Winter Olympic Games. For the summer jumper there is a unique freestyle aerials splash pool, with four aerial ramps, and the 90-meter winter jump is equipped with high-tech materials for use in warm weather. Ski-jump lessons are available.

Among the attractions of the **Park City Silver Mine Adventure** are a 1,500-foot underground elevator and a mine train that travels through 3,200 feet of tunnel.

> • *Park City's ski resorts reported 992, 000 skier days during the 1993-94 season.*
> • *More than 1, 000 miles of tunnels, remnants of the mining area, lace through the surrounding mountains.*

Where to Stay

THE BLUE CHURCH LODGE, *P.O. Box 1720, (800) 626-5467.* Remodeled 1897 church, on National Register, fireplaces, TV & phones, private baths, hot tub. $$$

GOLDENER HIRSCH INN, *P.O. Box 859, (800) 252-3373.* European alpine inn, full-service, Austrian antiques, fireplaces, Cont. breakfasts, hot tub, sauna, restaurant. $$$

IMPERIAL HOTEL B&B INN, *P.O. Box 1628, 221 Main St., (800) 669-8824.* 1904 hotel on National Register, "Western Victorian" decor, antiques, TV & phones, down comforters & pillows, private baths, full breakfasts, refreshments, hot tub. $$ to $$$

THE OLD MINERS' LODGE, *P.O. Box 2639, (800) 648-8068.* 1889 lodge in historic district, antiques, private baths, "hearty country" breakfasts, refreshments. $$ to $$$

OLD TOWN GUEST HOUSE, *P.O. Box 162, (801) 649-2642.* National Register home with suites, "hearty" breakfasts, hot tub. $$ to $$$

THE SNOWED INN, *3770 N. UT 224, (800) 649-5713/(800) 545-7669.* Full-service Victorian inn with art & antiques, suites with down comforters & soaking tubs, restaurant, wrap-around porch, hot tub, scenic views, close to ski resorts. $$$

THE WASHINGTON SCHOOL INN, *P.O. Box 536, (800) 824-1672.* 1889 school refurbished as 4-story inn, on National Register, TV, private baths, full breakfasts, afternoon tea, hot tub, sauna. $$$

Where to Eat

CAFE TERIGO, *424 Main St., (801) 645-9555.* Seafood, fresh pastas, pesto pizza, daily specials; outdoor dining. $$

CHIMAYO, *368 Main St., (801) 649-6222.* Innovative Southwestern cuisine, sweet & spicy chiles; outdoor dining. $$

CISERO'S RISTORANTE & BAR, *306 Main St., P.O. Box 3897, (801) 649-5044.* Cioppino, Eggplant Parmigiana, Stuffed Lumaconi, Lasagna, Joe's Vegetarian Casserole. $ to $$

GRAPPA ITALIAN RESTAURANT, *151 Main St., (801) 645-0636.* Cedar Planked Sea Bass, Open Spit Roasted Game Hen, Baked Gnocchi; fabulous reviews, one of best in Utah. $$$

JUNIPER, *(see Snowed Inn above)*. Poached Tenderloin of Beef, Bronzed Salmon on Roasted Eggplant Cakes, Vegetarian Strudel, Grilled Medallions of Utah Ostrich; extensive wine list. $$ to $$$

THE RIVERHORSE CAFE, *540 Main St., (801) 649-3536*. New American cuisine, fresh seafood, regional specialties. $$

WASATCH BREW PUB, *250 Main St., (801) 649-0900*. Utah Trout, Chicken Milanaise, Grilled Pork Chops, Milwaukee Bratwurst, sandwich board; Wasatch beers. $ to $$

Further Information

Park City Chamber of Commerce/Convention & Visitors Bureau, *P.O. Box 1630, Park City, UT 84060 (800) 453-1360.*

Directions

From Salt Lake City, I 80 east to exit 145, UT 224 south to Park City (30 mi).

Other Charming Utah Towns

Garden City/Laketown
Midway
Springdale
Torrey

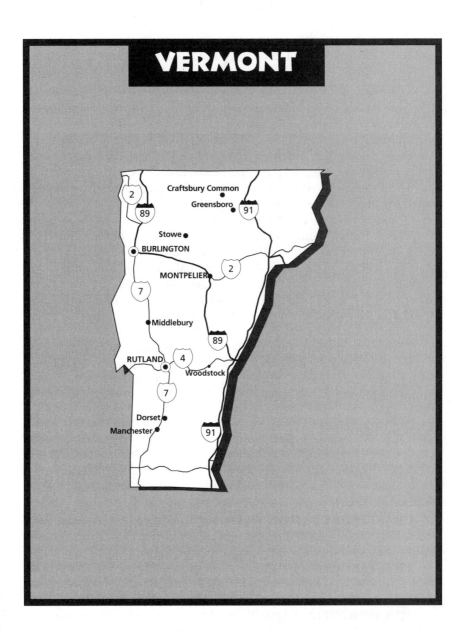

VERMONT

- Craftsbury Common
- 2
- 89
- 91
- Greensboro
- Stowe
- BURLINGTON
- MONTPELIER
- 2
- 7
- Middlebury
- 89
- RUTLAND
- 4
- Woodstock
- 7
- Dorset
- Manchester
- 91

VERMONT

Greensboro/Craftsbury

Population 717/994

Greensboro and **Craftsbury** are up in the Northeast Kingdom of Vermont, a region that looks like what much of our country looked like – or should have looked like – 100 years ago. The setting is strictly rural. The roads, mostly dirt and often tree-lined, wind Currier & Ives style over rivers, through woods, and past farmsteads. Every turn in the road brings a new and delightful view. There is little traffic, leaving the driver free to watch for moose, blue herons, and wildflowers.

Greensboro and Craftsbury do not have many stores or other businesses. Both are little collections of white-painted homes, churches, and a general store or two. Villagers seeking anything more than bread, gasoline, and a few other necessities must make a 30- or 45-minute drive. Craftsbury boasts two libraries and evening concerts on the large **Common** (lovely). There's a charming British woolen shop in **East Craftsbury**. Tucked at the southern end of **Caspian Lake**, Greensboro has an especially well-stocked old general store, **Willey's**.

The gently sloping countryside, the shaded back woods, the deep forests, the lakes and rivers are tailor-made for camping, hiking, biking, fishing, and water sports. There's an extensive trail network for cross-country skiing.

Special Feature

Naturalists and others who prefer their countryside totally undeveloped will find true wilderness not far away in **Essex County**.

Where to Stay

CRAFTSBURY B&B ON WYLIE HILL, *Craftsbury Common (05827)*, *(802) 586-2206*. 1860s hilltop farmhouse, full breakfasts, fresh flowers, birdfeeding windows, scenic views, respected for years. $$

CRAFTSBURY INN, *P.O. Box 36 (Craftsbury 05826), (800) 586-2848*. 1850 Greek Revival home, antiques, some private baths, full breakfasts, dining room, hiking, cross-country skiing. $$ to $$$ (MAP available)

FINCHINGFIELD FARM B&B, *R.R. 1 (Box 1195) (East Craftsbury 05826), (802) 586-7763*. Turn-of-century country house, English antiques, down comforters, some private baths, full breakfasts, library, adjoining farmland perpetually protected. $$ to $$$

HIGHLAND LODGE, *R.R. 1 (Box 1290) (Greensboro 05841), (802)*
533-2647. Small 1860s Greek Revival farmhouse & cottages on lake,
private baths, full breakfasts, children's playhouse, boats, hiking paths,
cross-country skiing, family-oriented. $$$ (MAP)

THE INN ON THE COMMON, *Craftsbury Common (05827), (800)*
521-2233. Colonial buildings with English-style gardens, private baths, full
breakfasts, 5-course "gourmet" dinners, pool, Wellness Barn, clay tennis
court, English croquet, highly regarded. $$$ (MAP)

THE VILLAGE HOUSE INN, *Rte. 14, P.O. Box 228 (Albany 05820),*
(802) 755-6722. 1870s home on 22 acres, antiques, parlor with Vermont
Castings stove, private baths, full country breakfasts, dining room, wrap-
around porch, back deck. $$

Where to Eat

CRAFTSBURY INN, *(see above).* Poached Salmon with a Cucumber
Caper Sauce, Sauteed New York Sirloin with a Red Wine Rosemary Sauce,
homemade desserts; chef-owned. $$

HIGHLAND LODGE, *(see above).* Pepper-crusted Tuna Steak, Grilled
Lemon Pepper Chicken Breast with Thyme Gremolata, Grilled Black
Angus Steak, special desserts. $$

THE VILLAGE HOUSE INN, *(see above).* Shrimp Sterling, Chicken
Pesto, Oriental Saute, Pork Tenderloin Marsala, Sea Scallops Dijonnaise;
also lighter fare. $$

Further Information

Lamoille Valley Chamber of Commerce, *P.O. Box 445, Morrisville, VT*
05661 (802) 888-7607.

Directions

From Springfield (MA), I 91 north to St. Johnsbury exit, US 2 west to
W. Danville, VT 15 north to VT 16, VT 16 to Greensboro Bend, county
road west to Greensboro and Craftsbury.

Manchester/Dorset

Population 3622/550

Manchester and **Dorset** have 19th-century church steeples and
houses, most of them white and *big*, many with green shutters, clustered
about village greens and framed by hills and forests. The predominant
colors are green and white, the particular proportions of each dependent

on the season. Giant shade trees—including of course maples—and winding roads complete the foreground. The scene is perfect for gracious old inns, Colonial dining rooms, and crackling fireplaces.

Manchester Center is a colorful place designed for the shopper. **Manchester Village** and **Dorset**, on the other hand, are places of quiet and incomparable beauty. This is not a place where people typically go to seek work; it is a place to retreat from work. The interesting thing is that this has been true since the middle of the 19th century, at least. In the 1850s, as today, these villages were places of holiday or retirement. Indeed, the history of Manchester is virtually inseparable from the history of its centerpiece, the **Equinox**, Vermont's premier inn (listed below).

While benefiting from the past, Manchester and Dorset do not ignore the present and future: Their buildings are beautifully restored, Manchester's downtown thrives, Dorset's rural charm persists, and development rights for many of the nearby farms are held by land trusts. A lot of work, time, and love have gone to make this true.

Manchester is home to **Hildene** (1905), the 24-room Georgian Revival mansion built by Robert Todd Lincoln, the only son of Abraham and Mary Todd Lincoln to survive to maturity. The house's original furnishings and Lincoln family effects may be seen by daily tours (and candlelight tours during the Christmas season). The formal gardens have been restored. Of the estate's 412 acres, 200 have been set aside as "forever wild."

The **Southern Vermont Art Center** is housed in another Colonial Revival mansion, **Yester House** (1917), in Manchester. Paintings, sculptures, photographs and other works of art are exhibited in 11 of the house's 28 rooms. Classical and chamber music, jazz, and voice and instrumental solos and duets are performed in the adjacent **Louise Ryals Arkell Pavilion**. Also on the grounds are the Sculpture Garden and the lovely **Boswell Botany Trail**, managed by the **Manchester Garden Club**.

The **American Museum of Fly Fishing**, also in Manchester, boasts a collection of more than 1,000 rods and 400 reels. The collection includes fly rods used by Dwight D. Eisenhower, Daniel Webster, Ernest Hemingway, Winslow Homer, Bing Crosby, and other famous Americans.

The **Dorset Playhouse**, noted for good theater, offers a range of performances in both summer and winter. A resident professional group performs in the summer as the **Dorset Theatre Festival**. The **Dorset Players** present periodic shows during the winter.

Manchester is a gateway to several well-known Vermont ski areas. The region also offers groomed as well as ungroomed trails for cross-country skiing. Twenty-one groomed trails are on the grounds of Hildene (see above), along with a warming hut.

Special Feature

From May through October a 5.2-mile winding toll road can be driven to the top of Mt. Equinox. Several states, and even Mount Royal in Montreal, can be seen from the top of the mountain on clear days. Picnicking is available on the grounds of the **Monastery of the Carthusian Order** on the side of the mountain.

> • *Among the summer residents in Manchester during the Civil War year of 1863 were Mary Todd Lincoln and her son Robert Todd.*
> • *Mary Lincoln Beckwith, Abraham Lincoln's great granddaughter, was the last member of the Lincoln family to live at Hildene. Beckwith died in 1975.*

Where to Stay

THE 1811 HOUSE, *Box 39 (Manchester Village), (800) 432-1811.* 1770s Federal-style inn on National Register, antiques, fireplaces, private baths, full breakfasts, Scottish Pub with 49 single-malt whiskies, fine paintings, extensive gardens. $$$

BARROWS HOUSE, *P.O. Box 98 (Dorset), (802) 867-4455/(800) 639-1620.* 1790s Federal home, private baths, full breakfasts, tavern; dining room with Main Crabcakes, Hazelnut Mustard Encrusted Salmon, & Pan Roasted Filet Mignon among menu items ($$). $$$

CORNUCOPIA OF DORSET, *P.O. Box 307 (Dorset), (802) 867-5751/(800) 566-5751.* 1880 country village home on National Register, antiques & art, fireplaces, phones, down comforters, private baths, full "gourmet" breakfasts, dining room, refreshments, cottage suite, marble patio, pool privileges, English gardens, highly rated. $$$

THE DORSET INN, *VT 30 (Dorset), (802) 867-5500.* Oldest continuously operating inn in Vermont (since 1796), private baths, full breakfasts; fresh fish, Baked Eggplant Crepes, Apple Smoked Barbecue Chicken, & Melton Burger on menu. $$$

THE EQUINOX, *P.O. Box 46 (Manchester Village), (800) 362-4747.* 18th-century Vermont landmark on National Register, full-service resort hotel, dining rooms, bar, exercise room, pools, tennis, golf course. $$$

RELUCTANT PANTHER, *Box 678 (Manchester Village), (802) 362-2568.* 1850s landmark & full-service inn, on National Register, antiques, fireplaces, whirlpools, full breakfasts, restaurant, bar, suites, pool, gardens, scenic views. $$$ (MAP)

THE WILBURTON INN, *P.O. Box 468 (Manchester Village), (800) 648-4944.* 1902 Tudor mansion on 20 acres, private baths, "very" full breakfasts, pool, tennis, golf, spectacular views; classical European cuisine & American regional specialties. $$$

Where to Eat

Note: Many of the inns listed above offer superb dining as well as lodging.

THE BLACK SWAN, *VT 7A (Manchester Village), (802) 362-3807.* Continental cuisine "with a California flair," including fresh fish, game, daily specialties; fresh flowers. $$ to $$$

THE CHANTECLEER, *VT 7A (Manchester Center), (802) 362-1616.* Continental cuisine, tableside service, chef-owned, reservations required. $$ to $$$

WILDFLOWERS, *(see Reluctant Panther above).* E.g., Arctic Char Steamed "En Papillotte" with Leeks, Carrots, Herbs and Noilly Pratt Vermouth; New York Strip Steak with a Herbed Mustard Seed Crust & Portwine Demi Glaze. $$$

Further Information

Manchester and the Mountains Chamber of Commerce, *RR 2 (Box 3451), Manchester Center, VT 05255 (802) 362-2100; also,* **Dorset Chamber of Commerce**, *P.O. Box 121, Dorset, VT 05251 (802) 867-2450. (ZIP for Manchester Village is 05254.)*

Directions

From Boston, MA 2 to Williamstown, US 7 north to Manchester and Dorset; from Burlington, US 7 south (via Rutland) to Manchester and Dorset.

Middlebury

Population 8, 034 (excluding students)

With a village green, shuttered Colonial houses, church steeples, museums, beautiful old inns, and a river with a waterfall, **Middlebury** is a resume of New England's charms. The countryside is pastoral. Visible to the east are the **Green Mountains**, to the west the **Adirondacks**. Other New England towns may also have this. What separates Middlebury is that its livelihood depends on a college campus rather than tourist promotion. College towns seem to offer a gentler way of life and a setting more appealing to retirees and others seeking quality in their lives.

Middlebury College is one of the oldest (1800) and most prestigious colleges in the United States. Its beautiful 1,200-acre main campus is dotted with Colonial buildings of gray limestone or white marble. Three of the oldest, **Painter Hall** (1816), **Old Chapel** (1836), and **Starr Hall** (1860) make up nostalgic **Old Stone Row.**

The **Middlebury College Center for the Arts** includes an award-winning concert hall, theater, and library. One of the center's five components, the **Middlebury College Museum of Art**, houses traveling exhibitions as well as a permanent collection. The latter is noted for its Cypriot pottery, 19th-century sculpture, and contemporary prints.

About the village green and along the tree-shaded streets are a number of lovely town landmarks. Of special note are the Federal-style **Painter House** and the much-photographed 1809 **Congregational Church**, with a many-faceted steeple designed to give a little in the wind. The **Community House**, an 1815 home, has hand-carved fireplaces and a spiral staircase. The house is in constant use for art and crafts classes and other community events.

One of the three locations of the **Vermont State Craft Center at Frog Hollow** is in Middlebury. A non-profit visual arts organization, the center displays the works of over 300 Vermont craftspeople in its galleries. The wood, fabric, painting, and other wares are for sale, but visitors are welcome to browse. The Middlebury site also has studios, demonstrations, and classes – and good views of **Otter Creek.**

Vermont arts and crafts may also be seen at the **Vermont Folklife Center**. In addition to displaying folk art, the center uses video tapes to illustrate the state's folk traditions.

The **Sheldon Museum**, the first incorporated village museum in the country, contains one of Vermont's foremost collections of antiques and curios. Housed in an 1829 tavern, later a home, the museum's rooms display furniture, guns, newspapers, and countless other items. In the library are bound copies of everything published in Middlebury since 1801.

The **Historic Marble Works** makes shopping an historic experience. Here on the courtyards of 1890s buildings are restaurants and little shops. A footbridge with a lovely view of the waterfall leads to **Frog Hollow Mill**, an old three-story stone mill housing yet another shop and restaurant.

Middlebury College's **Snow Bowl** offers excellent alpine skiing (open to the public). The Middlebury area also has a good selection of groomed cross-country trails.

Special Features

The **Morgan Horse Farm**, the Home of the Morgans, is located just outside of town. A breeding farm since the 1800s, its mission is to preserve and promote the country's first breed of horses. The farm is operated by the University of Vermont (guided tours).

Round trips between Middlebury and Burlington (and sometimes Rutland) are offered during summer and fall months by Vermont Rail Excursions aboard the air-conditioned vintage cars of the **Sugarbush Vermont Express**.

Peaceful rural landscapes abound in this part of Vermont. Get off of US 7 and roam the valley back roads.

> • *The Pulp Mill Bridge (1806) is Vermont's only two-lane separated covered bridge still open to traffic.*
> • *Otters can often be seen playing in Otter Creek, which flows through town.*

Where to Stay

THE MIDDLEBURY INN, *P.O. Box 798, 14 Court House Square, (800) 842-4666.* 1827 inn now comprising 3 bldgs., on National Register, full-service, Cont. breakfasts, afternoon tea, highly recommended dining rooms, some pets, porch, gardens. $$$ (MAP available)

THE WAYBURY INN, *VT 125 (E. Middlebury, 05740), (800) 348-1810.* Quiet 1810 inn with antiques, private baths, full breakfasts, dining room serving (e.g.) Fresh Atlantic Salmon & Four Seasons Chicken, pub, deck/gardens. $$$

Where to Eat

DOG TEAM TAVERN, *Dog Team Rd., (802) 388-7651.* Broiled Sea Scallops, Dog Teams Famous Prime Rib, sticky buns, Maple Oatmeal Pie; wealth of nostalgic keepsakes. $$

FIRE & ICE RESTAURANT, *26 Seymour St., (802) 388-7166.* Roast Prime Beef—"heavily marbled, aged beef, slow roasted for 7+ hours in our special roasting ovens." $$

MORGAN TAVERN, *(see The Middlebury Inn above).* Salads, sandwiches, New York Strip Steak, Swordfish Steak, Vegetable Strudel, pizza. $ to $$

STORM CAFE, *in Frog Hollow Mill, (802) 388-1063.* Specialty coffee shop serving bagels, croissants, brioche, light lunches. $

Further Information

Addison County Chamber of Commerce, *2 Court St., Middlebury, VT 05753 (802) 388-7951/fax (802) 388-8066.*

Directions

From Burlington, US 7 south to Middlebury; from Rutland, US 7 north to Middlebury.

Stowe

Population 3, 433

Stowe is a white-steepled, picture-book New England village nestled in the **Green Mountains** beneath **Mt. Mansfield**, Vermont's highest peak. One of the first ski resorts in the East, Stowe is second to none in the East in its number – and variety – of fine runs. What is less well known is that Stowe is also second to none in its number – and variety – of bed-and-breakfast inns. Although the village population is only about 450, the number of bed and breakfasts is somewhere between 30 and 40! B&B inns and guest houses vary from private home to stately inn, from rustic to Laura Ashley, from Tyrolean Austrian to Colonial American.

The beauty of Stowe Village is in part due to its age (200 years in 1994) and the charming old buildings, including a covered bridge, that come with age. It's also in part due to a very strict zoning code that governs even the size and shape of signs (neon not allowed). The village is popular as both a summer and winter resort. Because of Stowe's unique climate, flowers do especially well. Indeed, the gardens themselves merit a summer visit.

The **Stowe Recreation Path**, completed in 1989 and already a legend, weaves for 5.3 miles along and over **Mountain Road** (VT 108) and the tumbling **Little River**. Costing $680,000, the award-winning path is one of the country's most beautiful byways for non-motorists.

Stowe is noted for the beautiful crafts and other items displayed in its shops. The **Helen Day Art Center** has changing art exhibits and maintains an active calendar of programs and classes. Among the evening options are summer performances of the **Stowe Theatre Guild** at Town Hall Theatre and beckoning tables in one of the village's cozy pubs.

The Stowe area offers about every outdoor recreation but sponging and deep-sea fishing. Included among the summer offerings are rollerblading, wildlife-watching on Mt. Mansfield, speeding down a 2,300-ft. alpine slide, trout fishing, and sightseeing from an enclosed gondola. In addition to fabulous downhill skiing, winter activities include snowmobiling, ice skating, and thanks to the East's largest groomed-trail network, superb cross-country skiing.

Special Features

The **Stowe Flower Festival** offers sessions on everything from creating ponds and rock gardens to attracting birds and photographing flowers. Both guided and self-guided tours of local gardens are featured.

VT 108 north from Stowe through **Smugglers Notch** offers a particularly scenic drive during the summer months (closed winters). Along the way are waterfalls, hiking trails, and parking areas. Magnificent views can also be enjoyed from an auto toll road that climbs to the top of Mt. Mansfield.

Visitors may watch milking or purchase wool yarns or fresh vegetables at some of the area's **working farms**. Check locally for instructions, and always call the farm in advance.

There are over a dozen **covered bridges** in the Stowe vicinity. Check at the Stowe Visitor Center on Main Street for locations and routing.

> *During Prohibition liquor was smuggled from Canada through the mountain gorge that was named, subsequently and consequently, "Smugglers Notch."*

Where to Stay

BRASS LANTERN INN, *717 Maple St., (800) 729-2980.* Circa 1810 farmhouse, antiques, fireplaces, handmade quilts, private baths, whirlpools, full "country" breakfasts, restaurant, mountain views, packages, award-winning. $$ to $$$

FOXFIRE INN, *1606 Pucker St., (802) 253-4887/fax (802) 253-7016.* Restored country farmhouse, private baths, "hearty" breakfasts, respected Italian dining room, favorite locals' spot. $$ to $$$

THE GABLES INN, *1457 Mountain Rd., (800) 422-5371.* 1850s farmhouse, antiques, fireplaces, TV & phones, private baths, whirlpools, "famous" breakfasts, restaurant, gardens, pool. $$ to $$$

HADLEIGH HOUSE, *Rte. 100, (802) 253-7703.* Early 1800s farmhouse, original post-and-beam rooms, antiques, private baths, old barn & friendly horses. $$

STOWE INN AT LITTLE RIVER, *123 Mountain Rd., (800) 227-1108/ (802) 253-4836/fax (802) 253-7308.* Circa 1825 inn offering full services, antiques & country furnishings, some whirlpools, restaurant, tavern, hot tub & pool, condo suites, pets, gardens, overlooking river & village. $$ to $$$

THE WILKINS HOUSE B&B, *P.O. Box 218, 237 Maple St., (800) 994-5546.* 1842 home in village, original period details, TV, private baths, full breakfasts. $$ to $$$

YE OLDE ENGLAND INNE, *433 Mountain Rd., (802) 253-7558/ (800) 477-3771.* Full-service English-style inn, Laura Ashley decor, whirlpools, dining rooms, pub, suites. $$$

Where to Eat

BLUE MOON CAFE, *35 School St., (802) 253-7006.* Maine Crabmeat Cakes with Tomatillo Sauce & Tequila Lime Mayonnaise, Craftsbury Quail with Cape Gooseberries & Sweet Potato Shoestrings; in restored circa 1850 home, white linen, strongly recommended. $$

GRACIE'S RESTAURANT, *Main St., (802) 253-8741.* Salmon, swordfish, scallops, shrimp, steaks, vegetarian dishes. $ to $$

VILLA TRAGARA, *VT 100, P.O. Box 176 (Waterbury Center 05677), (802) 244-5288.* Involtini di Melanzane, Fettuccine con Gamberi al Limone, Ravioli del Giorno; highly regarded. $$

Further Information

Stowe Area Association, *Main St., P.O. Box 1320, Stowe, VT 05672 (800) 247-8693/fax (802) 253-2159.*

Directions

From Burlington, I 89 east to exit 10, VT 100 north to Stowe.

Woodstock

Population 1, 000 (village), 2, 000 (town)

Back in the middle of the 19th century the American statesman from Vermont, Senator Jacob Collamer, put it very nicely: "The good people of Woodstock have less incentive than others to yearn for heaven." The sentiment could just as well have been expressed at the end of the 20th century. For a long tradition of architectural preservation combined with a century-old commitment to tourism rather than industrial development have kept safe an exceptionally fine collection of vintage New England buildings. When placed along the meandering **Ottauquechee River** in a narrow valley amongst the foothills of the **Green Mountains**, the buildings–along with their village green, of course–become one of Vermont's loveliest and most perfect townscapes.

Woodstock's many beautiful old homes bespeak early wealth. Settled in 1765, the village prospered as a county seat (for Windsor County) and as a center for industries ranging from lumber and woolen milling to animal husbandry and coopering and gin distilling to the manufacture of clocks and musical instruments. Later, as industries moved elsewhere, village leaders turned to tourism and in 1892 opened the famed Woodstock Inn. Tourists have been heading here ever since, and as evidenced by the introduction in 1934 of the country's first ski tow, in all seasons.

Constructed in the early 19th century, the stately homes and churches of the Historic District are generally of the Federal and, less often, Greek-Revival styles. One of the finest of the houses, the Federal **Dana House** (1807), is now maintained as a museum by the historical society (restricted schedule). On display are period furnishings (1740-1900) as well as antique toys and dolls, historic costumes, and local artifacts. The oldest of the several lovely churches are the **Congregational** (1807; remodeled 1880-1890) and the **Unitarian-Universalist** (1835).

There are also two unique bridges: **Middle Bridge**, an authentic covered bridge constructed in 1967-69, and the **Elm Street Bridge**, an iron bridge constructed in 1869-70 and reconstructed in 1979-81 to carry heavier traffic. The historic district is best toured with the aid of a nicely illustrated guidebook prepared by the Woodstock Historical Society (check at the Chamber of Commerce).

The **Billings Farm & Museum** (farm established 1871) includes a working dairy farm, restored 1890s farmhouse, heirloom vegetable garden, and agricultural museum. Housed in several connected barns, the museum employs an impressive range of exhibits to portray life on the farm during the late 19th century. The farm and museum are open to the public.

Twenty-four species of birds of prey, unreleasable because of injury, may be seen in outdoor flight habitats at the **Vermont Raptor Center**. The center, open to the public, also includes a display area with exhibits of snakes and other live animals, nature programs, and self-guided trails (guidebooks are available).

Woodstock's list of things to do and calendar of events rival those of much larger towns. Upscale shops, many located on historic **Central** and **Elm streets**, offer antiques, fine clothing, New England art and handicrafts, maple syrup, and Vermont cheeses. There are also auctions, crafts fairs, and flea markets. Although maybe best known for its golf and skiing, the Woodstock area offers an endless list of recreations–among them, horseback riding, back-road car touring, and sleigh riding. In addition, the Woodstock Inn & Resort (see below) maintains a fitness center with facilities for racquet sports, aerobics, croquet, aquatics, etc. For the evening, a diverse menu of musical and theatrical events is served up, sometimes inside and sometimes under the stars, by the Pentangle Council on Arts.

Special Feature

A parade of horses and carriages, medieval merriment, the singing of the *Messiah*, and other festive events help make **Woodstock's Wassail Celebration**, held the second weekend in December, a warm and colorful time.

Where to Stay

THE 1830 SHIRE TOWN INN, *31 South St., (802) 457-1830.* 1830 home with beamed ceilings on National Register, antiques, quilts, private baths, full breakfasts, one block to village green. $$ to $$$

ARDMORE INN, *23 Pleasant St., (802) 457-3887.* 1850 Greek Revival home in historic district, private baths with Vermont marble, full breakfasts with silver service, afternoon tea. $$$

THE CHARLESTON HOUSE, *21 Pleasant St., (802) 457-3843.* 1835 Greek Revival home on National Register, art & antiques, private baths, "gourmet" candlelight breakfasts. $$$

THE WOODSTOCK INN & RESORT, *On the Green, (802) 457-1100/ (800) 448-7900.* Full-service inn with 18-hole golf course, sports center, downhill & cross-country skiing facilities; restaurants, packages available, a Vermont legend. $$$

THE WOODSTOCKER B&B, *61 River St. (Rte. 4), (802) 457-3896/ (800) 457-3896.* 1830 home, common room with exposed timbers, individual AM/FM/cassette/CD stereo players, private baths, "gourmet" breakfasts, tea, chocolate chip cookies. $$$

Where to Eat

THE PRINCE & THE PAUPER, *24 Elm St., (802) 457-1818.* Poached Norwegian Salmon, Roast Duckling a la Maison, Carre d'Agneau "Royale"; early 19th-century setting, bar, lounge with Windsor chairs. $$$

Further Information

Woodstock Area Chamber of Commerce, *P.O. Box 486, Woodstock, VT 05091, (802) 457-3555.*

Directions

From Boston, I 93 north to I 89 (south of Concord, NH), north to US 4 in Vermont (Exit 1), west to Woodstock.

Other Charming Vermont Towns

Grafton
Newfane
Weston

500

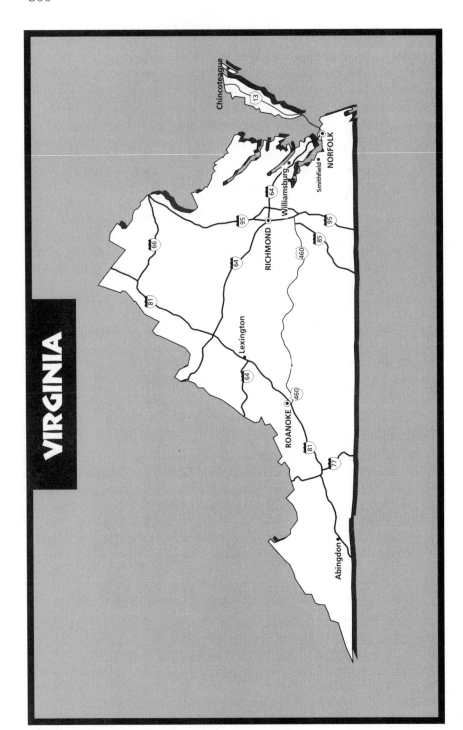

VIRGINIA

Abingdon

Population 7, 003

Abingdon's two "A" words are Ambiance and Arts. Chartered in 1776, Abingdon is the oldest town of British ancestry west of the Blue Ridge Mountains. Bordering the brick sidewalks of the 20-square-block historic district are stately but warm old houses displaying Georgian, Adam, and other traditional architectural styles. Some of the finest now open their doors as bed-and-breakfast inns (see below). Perhaps the most imposing – and renowned – is the **Martha Washington Inn** (1832), originally a private residence but variously a women's college and Civil War hospital since. Now an elegant hotel, the Martha Washington has one of the most respected restaurants in this corner of the world (see below).

As for the arts, Abingdon bills itself as the "cultural center of southwest Virginia." And with excellent reason. For beginners, the town is home to the oldest professional resident theater in the United States, the **Barter Theatre**, State Theatre of Virginia. Earning its name from the Depression-era practice of bartering for tickets with home-grown produce, the theater's three stages present quality performances of classic and contemporary works. Actors appearing at the Barter have included Hume Cronyn, Gregory Peck, Patricia Neal, Ernest Borgnine, and Barry Corbin.

The visual arts are represented by an almost endless array of shops and galleries. The works represent a nice mix of the old and the new and range from contemporary paintings to centuries-old Appalachian crafts. Among the regional crafts are woodcarving, quilting, weaving, dried flowers, and corn shuckery.

Rotating exhibits are held at the **William King Regional Arts Center**, an affiliate of the **Virginia Museum of Fine Arts**. The center houses studios and classrooms as well as galleries. Arts and crafts are also displayed in the **Cave House**, an 1858 Victorian landmark sitting on top of limestone grottos. The building, listed on the National Register, has three-story walnut stair railings and other features that complement the various displays. Yet another setting for the display of art is the **Arts Depot**, a restored 1870 freight station.

In a delightful setting just outside of town is **White's Mill**, the only water-powered commercial mill in southwest Virginia. Across from the mill is an old general store with long counters and a pot-bellied stove. The mill is listed on the National Register of Historic Places (guided tours).

Special Features

The **Virginia Creeper Trail**, a National Recreation Trail, originates just off **Main Street** and travels 34 miles to the foot of **Whitetop Mountain** near the Virginia/North Carolina border. Once a railroad, the pathway is popular with hikers, bikers, horseback riders, and cross-country skiers.

The 115,000-acre **Mount Rogers National Recreation Area** to the east of Abingdon boasts more than 300 miles of trails, including 60 miles of the great **Appalachian Trail**. Some of the trails form circuits. Included in the recreation area are the three highest mountains in Virginia.

One of the country's top tourist events, the **Virginia Highlands Festival**, is held the first two weeks in August.

Abingdonians like to brag that their first visitor was Daniel Boone.

Where to Stay

INN ON TOWN CREEK, *445 E. Valley St., (540) 628-4560.* Home landscaped with brick patios & rock gardens, antiques, private baths. $$$

LITCHFIELD HALL, *247 Valley St., NE, (540) 676-2971.* Historic home with antiques, private baths, full breakfasts, mementos from world travels. $$$

THE LOVE HOUSE, *210 E. Valley St., (540) 623-1281.* Circa 1850 home with original hand-blown glass windows, fireplaces, private baths with whirlpools, breakfasts by professional in culinary field, "gourmet" dinners by arrangement. $$$

SILVERSMITH INN, *102 E. Main St., (540) 676-3924.* 1871 brick home in historic district, private baths, full breakfasts. $$$

SUMMERFIELD INN, *101 W. Valley St., (540) 628-5905.* 1920s brick home in convenient downtown location, private baths, cottage with large honeymoon suite. $$$

VICTORIA & ALBERT INN, *224 Oak Hill St., (540) 676-2797.* Small Victorian inn, fireplaces, private baths, silver-service breakfasts. $$$

Where to Eat

ABINGDON GENERAL STORE & GALLERY, *301 E. Main St., (540) 628-8382.* Two restaurants known for "gourmet flair"; unique store & gallery. $ to $$

THE DINING ROOM, *in Martha Washington Inn, (540) 628-3161.* Pasta with Smoked Salmon, Chicken Preston, Steak Diane; elegant Victorian setting. $$

THE HARDWARE COMPANY, *260 W. Main St., (540) 628-1111.* Seafood, steaks, & pastas served in a renovated 1895 hardware store. $ to $$

THE STARVING ARTIST CAFE, *134 Wall St., (540) 628-8445*. Cafe doubling as a local art gallery. $ to $$
THE TAVERN, *222 E. Main St., (540) 628-1118*. Native American Trout, Carbonara Florentine, Kassler Ripchen; in Abingdon's oldest building (1779). $$

Further Information
Abingdon Convention & Visitors Bureau, *335 Cummings St., Abingdon, VA 24210 (540) 676-2282/(800) 435-3440.*

Directions
From Roanoke, I 81 south to exits 19, 17, or 14 (Abingdon exits).

Chincoteague
Population 3, 572

Part of **Chincoteague's** charm comes from its location on an inviting island off Virginia's **Eastern Shore Peninsula**. Another part comes from its long association with wildlife, especially the abundant waterfowl and the famous Chincoteague ponies.

Chincoteague shares an island 7 miles long and 1 1/2 miles wide with marshes, pastures, and other open spaces. The village's history, going as far back as the 1670s, has largely centered on gathering food from the sea—oysters, clams, and fish. The village/island has developed as a resort in more recent times and offers excellent accommodations, restaurants (see below), shops, and boutiques. The shops are known for their wildfowl carvings and their paintings and photographs of wildlife.

As the name suggests, the **Oyster and Maritime Museum** is designed to tell about the island's oyster and seafood industry. A diorama of the channel area, live exhibits of marine life, and implements used in oyster farming are among the items featured.

Chincoteague is also the gateway to **Chincoteague National Wildlife Refuge** and the **Assateague Island National Seashore**. Located at the southern end of Assateague Island, the wildlife refuge is home to over 316 species of birds and, among other animals, the **Chincoteague ponies**. According to legend (reinforced by Spanish archival evidence), the ponies descend from survivors of a wrecked Spanish galleon. Larger than real ponies but smaller than most horses, the animals won fame in Marguerite Henry's book, *Misty of Chincoteague*. Although allowed to roam wild, they are provided with regular veterinary care and plenty of good food. (Tours of the refuge are available. Pets are not allowed into the refuge, even in a car, so make arrangements with a pet-sitter in advance.)

The Assateague Island National Seashore occupies the only barrier island on Virginia's Eastern Shore that is open to the public. In addition to unspoiled woodlands, marshes, and sand dunes, the seashore offers more than 37 miles of beautiful, open beaches. The 145-foot tower of the **Assateague Lighthouse**, one of the few structures on the island, was built in 1857.

Along with the boating, swimming, fishing, and beachcombing that might be expected around coastal islands, Chincoteague and Assateague Islands offer bird-watching, biking along wilderness trails, crabbing, and shellfishing.

> • *The sale of young ponies from the south (that is, Virginia) portion of the national seashore provides funds for the local firemen – and also the occasion for an annual carnival.*
> • *Unlike the rest of Virginia's Eastern Shore, Chincoteaque Island maintained its association and commerce with the Union during the Civil War.*

Where to Stay

THE GARDEN & THE SEA, *P.O. Box 275 (New Church 23415), (804) 824-0672.* European-style country inn, antiques & Oriental rugs, private baths, afternoon teas, restaurant. $$$

ISLAND MANOR HOUSE B&B, *4160 Main St., (800) 852-1505.* 1848 home of island's first doctor, Federal-style antiques, some private baths, full breakfasts, afternoon teas, brick courtyard with fountain. $$ to $$$

THE MAIN STREET HOUSE B&B, *4356 Main St., (804) 336-6030.* Victorian home of former wildlife refuge manager, wildlife art & carvings. $$ to $$$

MISS MOLLY'S INN B&B, *4141 Main St., (804) 336-6686.* 1886 home on bay, private baths, full breakfasts, afternoon teas, porches for enjoying the breeze. $$$

THE WATSON HOUSE B&B, *4240 Main St., (804) 336-1564.* Victorian home, antiques, private baths with whirlpool baths, full breakfasts, afternoon teas, bicycles, beach chairs & towels, binoculars. $$ to $$$

YEAR OF THE HORSE INN B&B, *3583 Main St., (804) 336-3221/ (800) 680-0090.* Rambling gray & white 1940s home, TV, private baths, sunsets from balconies, 100-ft pier, fishing & crabbing. $$ to $$$

Where to Eat

Note: Chincoteague is understandably blessed with a large number of excellent seafood restaurants.

A. J.'S ON THE CREEK, *6585 Maddox Blvd., (804) 336-5888*. Oysters Rockefeller, Oysters Romanoff, Clams Casino, seafood pastas, fresh grilled fish, steaks, fine wines; "lace & candlelight & mahogany." $$

ISLAND CREAMERY, *6251 Maddox Blvd., (804) 336-6236*. Very popular ice cream parlor.

LANDMARK CRAB HOUSE & WATERFRONT LOUNGE, *Landmark Plaza on N. Main St., (804) 336-5552*. Crab cakes, oysters, shrimp, clams, scallops, soft crabs, Fish of the Evening, Baked Stuffed Flounder, Crab Imperial the house specialty. $$

STEAMERS SEAFOOD RESTAURANT, *6251 Maddox Blvd., (804) 336-5478*. "All the steamed crabs & shrimp you could possibly eat" served on brown-paper-covered tables. $$

THE VILLAGE RESTAURANT & LOUNGE, *6576 Maddox Blvd., (804) 336-5120*. Seafood, chicken, steaks, fresh Chincoteague oysters the specialty; waterfront dining overlooking Eel Creek, reservations suggested. $$

Further Information

Chincoteague Chamber of Commerce, *P.O. Box 258, Chincoteague, VA 23336 (804) 336-6161*.

Directions

From Norfolk, US 13 north (via Chesapeake Bay Bridge/Tunnel) to VA 175, VA 175 east to Chincoteague.

Lexington

Population 7, 568 (including students)

Home to the hallowed halls of **Washington and Lee University** and the **Virginia Military Institute (VMI)**, and once the home of Robert E. Lee and Stonewall Jackson, Lexington is among the South's most historic towns. Nestled in the glorious **Shenandoah Valley**, and boasting a solid collection of restored 19th-century buildings, Lexington is also one of the South's most beautiful towns.

The campuses of Washington and Lee and VMI are both National Historical Landmarks. Washington and Lee, founded in 1749, is a highly respected small (by choice) liberal arts college and law school. The college's most famous president was Robert E. Lee, who took over as head immediately after the Civil War (1865-1870). Probably the most visited building on campus is the **Lee Chapel** (1867), which contains the office (preserved) Lee used when he was the college's president. Also in the chapel are Edward V. Valentine's statue of Lee, Lee's burial place, and Charles W. Peale's famous portrait of George Washington. The 1842 **Lee-Jackson House** was a campus residence of both Stonewall Jackson and General Lee.

Adjacent VMI was the country's first state-supported military college (1839). The college's most famous professor was Stonewall Jackson, its most famous alumnus, George C. Marshall. The **VMI Museum** recalls the history of the college by focusing on the lives of its alums and faculty. Included in the exhibits are the bullet-pierced raincoat that Stonewall Jackson wore at Chancellorsville, 19th-century firearms and daguerreo-types, and uniforms and other items that provide a glimpse of cadet life.

The **George C. Marshall Museum and Library**, also on the VMI campus, features an electric map of World War II, Marshall's Nobel Peace Prize, the Academy Award Oscar won by the producer of the movie *Patton*, and other mementos of the great general's life.

Two sites associated with Stonewall Jackson are the antebellum **Stonewall Jackson Home**, a simple brick townhouse (1801) containing many of Jackson's personal possessions (guided tours available), and the **Stonewall Jackson Memorial Cemetery** (1797), location of Jackson's final resting place and also of Edward V. Valentine's 1891 statue honoring the general. The cemetery also contains the graves of Confederate veterans and two Virginia governors.

Lexington is known for its historic downtown and residential areas. The town is designed for relaxed touring, on foot or maybe on a narrated carriage ride. The visitor center distributes a self-guided walking tour brochure that lists 42 historic sites. The many lovely old Virginia homes date from the last two decades of the 18th century and from virtually every decade of the 19th, especially the 1840s. Among important non-residential structures are a group of offices, known as **Lawyers Row**, built in the 1880s, and the 1845 Greek Revival **Lexington Presbyterian Church**.

The two theaters of the **Lenfest Center for the Performing Arts**, on the Washington and Lee campus, stage a variety of plays, musicals, concerts, and recitals. In the summer, the unique outdoor **Theater at Lime Kiln** presents concerts and original stage productions.

Hikers will enjoy both the 2-mile walking trail through Lexington's beautiful **Woods Creek Park** and the 7-mile **Chessie Nature Trail**, which winds from Lexington to Buena Vista alongside the **Maury River**.

Special Features

Lexington is only minutes away from the **Blue Ridge Parkway**, the **Goshen Pass** (a 3-mile mountain gorge), and the famous **Natural Bridge**, a spectacular 215-foot-high limestone arch.

Horse shows and auctions are among the attractions of the nearby 400-acre **Virginia Horse Center**.

- *VMI's military heritage is colorfully displayed on most Fridays during the school year, when at 4:00 p.m. the cadets present a full military dress parade.*
- *Thomas Jonathan "Stonewall" Jackson taught natural philosophy (physics) and military tactics at VMI for ten years prior to the Civil War.*

Where to Stay

FASSIFERN, *Rt. 5 (Box 87), (540) 463-1013.* Circa 1867 country manor home in park-like setting, private baths, "delicious breakfast choices." $$$

THE HUMMINGBIRD INN, *Wood Lane, P.O. Box 147 (Goshen 24439), (800) 397-3214.* Carpenter Gothic villa (1780-1853) with antiques, private baths, "fantastic" breakfasts, optional dinners, gardens, trout stream, old livery stable. $$ to $$$

THE INN AT UNION RUN, *Rt. 3 (Box 68), (540) 463-9715/(800) 528-6466.* 110-yr-old manor house on creek-fronted mountainside, antiques, private baths, dining room, verandah, pond. $$ to $$$

THE KEEP, *116 Lee Ave., (540) 463-3560.* 1891 home in heart of town, private baths, full "deluxe" breakfasts, tea & sherry, dinners on request. $$

LAVENDER HILL FARM, *Rt. 1 (Box 515), (800) 446-4240.* Circa 1790 farmhouse on 20-acre farm, English country decor, private baths, full "country" breakfasts, creek, fishing & birding, optional dinners. $$

LLEWELLYN LODGE, *603 S. Main St., (800) 882-1145.* Brick home near historic district, private baths, full "gourmet" breakfasts, deck for iced tea. $$ to $$$

The **Historic Country Inns of Lexington**, *11 N. Main St., (540) 463-2044,* include the following properties: **MAPLE HALL**, plantation home (circa 1850) on National Register, antiques, fireplaces, private baths, Cont. "plus" breakfasts, pool, tennis. $$$; **ALEXANDER-WITHROW HOUSE** & **McCAMPBELL INN**, circa 1789 & 1809 homes in historic district, antiques, TV, private baths, Cont. "plus" breakfasts, amenities of Maple Hall available. $$$

OSCEOLA MILL COUNTRY INN, *(Steele's Tavern 24476), (540) 377-6455.* 1843 mill plus miller's home & miller's store, private baths, "hearty" breakfasts, dining room, rocking chairs, pool, bicycles, mill creek & water wheel, museum. $$$

Where to Eat

HARBS', *19 W. Washington St., (540) 464-1900.* Fresh seafood specials, prime rib, pastas, vegetarian dishes, famous nachos, frittatas, salads, homemade baguettes & croissants; outdoor dining. $

IL PALAZZO, *24 N. Main St., (540) 464-5800.* Seafood, pizza, calzone, Italian dinners. $ to $$

MAPLE HALL, *(see above).* Mussels Mediterranean, Chicken Kiev, Saltimbocca, Filet Mignon; seasonal menu, in historic country inn, reservations preferred. $$

VIRGINIA HOUSE, *722 S. Main St., (540) 463-3643.* Southern-style cooking, fried or baked country-cured ham, homemade desserts. $

THE WILLSON-WALKER HOUSE, *30 N. Main St., (540) 463-3020.* "Creative" American cuisine served in circa 1820 Classical Revival home; antique furnishings, outdoor dining, reservations suggested. $ to $$

Further Information

Lexington Visitor Center, *106 E. Washington St., Lexington, VA 24450 (540) 463-3777.*

Directions

From Roanoke, I 81 north to exit 188, west 2 miles to Lexington.

Smithfield

Population 6, 000

Given **Smithfield's** location near the historic **James River** in Virginia's Tidewater, it should come as no surprise to learn that the town and its county (Isle of Wight) lay claim to the oldest Protestant church, the oldest fort, and one of the oldest courthouses in the United States. But Smithfield is in a relatively quiet part of this venerable region–the Jamestown/Williamsburg/Yorktown Triangle, for example, lies by ferry far on the other side of the James–and so the town is perfect for the visitor seeking to mix sightseeing and nostalgia with the slower pace of life of a small Southern town.

Isle of Wight County (or "Shire") was formed in 1634, but the river town of Smithfield wasn't chartered until a relatively "late" 1752. The event that eventually put the little town on the map–and a large map at that–was the establishment of a ham curing business in the late 18th century. Smithfield Hams have been famous ever since and have earned the town the title of "Ham Capital of the World."

Begin your stay in the Smithfield area with a stop at the restored **Old Courthouse of 1750**. The Visitors Center, located here, provides information on a walking tour (guided or self-guided) of the **Historic District** as well as on area attractions. The nicely displayed exhibits of the **Isle of Wight Museum** on Main Street highlight the county's past from prehistoric times to the present.

Just two miles south is Smithfield's most hallowed place, the restored **St. Luke's Church**, the country's oldest existing church of English origin (circa 1632). The brick exterior is distinguished by unique buttresses and stepped gables. On the inside are a rare church organ (circa 1630) and 17th-century furnishings and silver. The structure's original traceried windows are especially lovely.

Fort Boykin, now **Fort Boykin Historic Park**, is the oldest fort on American soil (started 1623). Built in the shape of a seven-pointed star, the fort played a role in the Revolutionary War, the War of 1812, and the Civil War. The tree on the fort's parade ground is believed to the second largest black walnut in Virginia.

Smithfield offers the shopper, especially the antique shopper, a variety of interesting shops and galleries. The area, both town and country, is very bicycle-friendly (rentals available). The Pagan River, which Smithfield borders, and the river's tributaries are also very boat- and canoe-friendly (rentals available).

Special Features

The **Ragged Island Wildlife Management Area**, to the east of Smithfield and overlooking the James River, offers the nature hiker and bird watcher over 1,500 acres of native flora and fauna.

Just a few miles north of Smithfield is **Bacon's Castle** (circa 1665), believed to be the oldest house in Virginia (open to public). Given its age, the house has features that are usually seen only on the other side of the Atlantic.

Many of the region's most prominent settlers came from the Isle of Wight on England's southern coast; hence the name of the county.

Where to Stay

FOUR SQUARE PLANTATION B&B, *13357 Four Square Rd., (757) 365-0749.* 1807 Federal home, antiques, private baths, full breakfasts, "rural serenity." $$

ISLE OF WIGHT INN, *1607 S. Church St., (800) 357-3245/(757) 357-3176.* Attractive contemporary inn offering fireplaces, TV, private baths, some whirlpools, full breakfasts, suites, refreshments. $$ to $$$

MANSION ON MAIN B&B, *36 Main St., (757) 357-0006.* Circa 1890 mansion, antiques, full breakfasts. $$

THE SMITHFIELD INN, *112 Main St., (757) 357-1752.* 1752 home with 240 years of innkeeping experience, suites, some fireplaces, TV, full breakfasts, public dining room, William Rand Tavern, George Washington once a guest. $$$

SMITHFIELD STATION WATERFRONT INN, *415 S. Church St., (757) 357-7700.* New full-service inn on water, restaurant, Boardwalk Raw Bar & Grille, pool, marina, suites available in lighthouse. $$ to $$$

Where to Eat

C.W. COWLING'S, *1278 Smithfield Plaza, (757) 357-0044.* Cajun dishes, pastas, fajitas, steaks, chicken, ribs, seafood, cheddar melts, sandwiches & salads. $ to $$

SMITHFIELD GOURMET BAKERY, *218 Main St., (757) 357-0045.* Sandwiches on variety of homemade breads, daily lunch specials, celebrated desserts. $

THE SMITHFIELD INN, *(see above).* Cioppino, Jumbo Lump Crab Cakes, Stuffed Quail, Tournedos of beef Tenderloin; inviting lunch menu, "casual elegance." $$ to $$$

SMITHFIELD STATION, *(see above).* Wide variety of seafood, Smithfield's "lean generation" pork, good lunch menu, patio/riverview dining. $$ to $$$

Further Information

Isle of Wight Tourism Bureau, *130 Main St., P.O. Box 37, Smithfield, VA 23431 (757) 357-5182/(800) 365-9339.*

Directions

From Richmond/Newport News/Hampton, I 64 to Mercury Blvd. & across James River Bridge, US 258 to Smithfield.

Williamsburg
Population 11, 530

A model of restoration and reconstruction respected round the world, the capital of England's largest colony in America has been – and continues to be - retrieved from the 18th century. To understand and appreciate **Williamsburg**, it must be remembered that for many people the town was never a place of drudgery, of daily routine. Williamsburg was a place of government, of education, of intellectual discussion. It was also a place of balls, gambling, and other amusements for visiting members of Virginia's landed gentry. It was a lovely and pleasurable place, just as it is now.

The main artery of **Colonial Williamsburg** is **Duke of Gloucester Street**. Anchoring the western end of the street is the **College of William and Mary**, at the eastern end is the **Capitol**, and overlooking a mall not far from the street's midpoint is the **Governor's Palace**. On and about Duke of Gloucester Street are over 500 restored or reconstructed public buildings, homes, taverns, and stores. The buildings, scattered across 173 acres, are placed about large gardens and greens, giving the town a wonderful (and deliberate) sense of spaciousness.

Check in first at the visitors center for admission and other information. Additional information is available throughout the restoration from costumed Colonial interpreters. Do not try to do the town and its environs (see below) in a day—allow at least three days. Carriage rides add romance and relax tired feet.

Chartered in 1693, the **College of William and Mary** is the second oldest college in the country. Two of the campus's most interesting attractions are the restored **Wren Building**, the oldest college building in the country, and the **Muscarelle Museum of Art**, known for the quality and variety of its changing exhibitions.

The **Governor's Palace** (1708-1720), restored and one of the town's (and nation's) landmarks, was home to seven British governors and Virginia's first two governors. The gardens are beautiful, especially in the spring. Among the rooms of the reconstructed **Capitol** (1705), another landmark, is the **Chamber of the General Court**, one of the country's most beautiful courtrooms.

Three other well-known structures are the **Bruton Parish Church** (1715), in continuous use since its construction, the restored **Magazine** (1715), and **Raleigh Tavern**, popular in the 18th century as well as today for its billiard room. The restored town contains a number of gracious, architecturally important homes.

Although the restored area is itself a vast living museum, Colonial Williamsburg is also home to two outstanding enclosed museums. The **Abby Aldrich Rockefeller Folk Art Center** features an incomparable collection of American folk art. The **DeWitt Wallace Decorative Arts Gallery** displays English and American silver, glass, paintings, costumes, furniture, textiles, prints, ceramics, rare maps, and other treasures.

Artisans and tradespeople demonstrate 18th-century silversmithing, baking, basket weaving, blacksmithing, furniture making, wig making, bookbinding, gun making, and other skills. The products of their efforts are displayed and offered for sale in quaint restored shops.

The **Virginia Shakespeare Festival** stages productions during the summer months at the College of William and Mary. Visitors to Williamsburg may enjoy golfing, tennis, and swimming.

Special Features

The two other members of the **Historic Triangle**, **Jamestown** and **Yorktown**, are connected to Williamsburg by the Colonial Parkway. Jamestown, the site of the country's English beginnings (1607), is administered by the **Colonial National Historical Park**. Here there are a visitor center, museum, remains of a 1639 church, and several other historical attractions.

Jamestown Settlement is a living history museum depicting life in Jamestown during the early settlement years. Included are the re-created palisaded fort and replicas of three ships that first brought settlers from England.

Yorktown, also administered by the Colonial National Historical Park, is the site of the famous British defeat (self-guided auto tours begin here). The **Yorktown Victory Center**, a battlefield museum, features several excellent indoor exhibits and, outdoors, a re-created Continental Army encampment.

Along the banks of the James River is a series of magnificent plantation homes, many graced by gardens and lovely antiques. Open to the public are **Berkeley**, **Carter's Grove**, **Edgewood**, **Evelynton**, **Sherwood Forest**, and **Shirley** plantations.

Busch Gardens Williamsburg, one of the country's most beautiful theme parks, boasts nine European hamlets, each with its own food, entertainment, etc., and a variety of thrilling rides.

• *The restoration and rebuilding of Williamsburg, spearheaded by Rev. W. A. R. Goodwin and John D. Rockefeller, Jr., began in the late 1920s.*
• *Visitors to the Governor's Palace are often surprised by the communal nature of the royal privy.*

Where to Stay

Note: Colonial Williamsburg's Colonial Houses & Taverns offer lodgings in original 18-century houses and houses reconstructed on their original foundations. The houses accommodate from two to twelve people. Many have private gardens. Reservations may be made by calling (800) 447-8679.

APPLEWOOD COLONIAL B&B, *605 Richmond Rd., (800) 899-2753*. Flemish bond brick with Colonial decor, fireplaces, private baths, full breakfasts, afternoon tea, bikes. $$ to $$$

COLONIAL CAPITAL B&B, *501 Richmond Rd., (800) 776-0570*. Circa 1926 Colonial Revival home, antiques, private baths, full breakfasts, afternoon tea/wine, patio, bikes. $$ to $$$

LIBERTY ROSE, *1022 Jamestown Rd., (800) 545-1825*. Colonial Revival home with antique furnishings, fireplaces, TV & phones, private baths, full breakfasts, refreshments, gardens, on wooded hilltop. $$$

NEWPORT HOUSE B&B, *710 S. Henry St., (757) 229-1775*. Home designed in 1756, period furnishings, private baths, full breakfasts with "historic" recipes, Colonial Country dancing in ballroom Tues. evenings. $$$

WILLIAMSBURG MANOR B&B, *600 Richmond Rd., (800) 422-8011*. Brick Colonial Revival, period furnishings, TV, private baths, "lavish" breakfasts, dinners by appt. $$$

WILLIAMSBURG SAMPLER B&B, *922 Jamestown Rd., (800) 722-1169*. 18th-century plantation-style brick Colonial home, pewter & samplers, private baths, "Skip Lunch" breakfasts, suites/fireplaces, proclaimed "Inn Of The Year" by governor. $$$

Where to Eat

The first four restaurants listed below are housed in restored or reconstructed buildings in the restored area. All offer authentic Colonial dishes and 18th-century furnishings. Colonial balladeers entertain diners in several. *Call (757) 229-2141 or (800) 447-8679 for reservations (recommended) and information.*

CHOWNING'S TAVERN, *100 E. Duke of Gloucester St..* Virginia-style ale house. $$ to $$$

CHRISTIANA CAMPBELL'S TAVERN, *120 Waller St.* Chesapeake Bay seafood. $$ to $$$

KING'S ARMS TAVERN, *409 E. Duke of Gloucester St.* Colonial favorites. $$

SHIELDS TAVERN, *417 E. Duke of Gloucester St., (757) 220-7677.* Scalloped Crab, Roast Pork Chop, Corn Bread-stuffed Quail & Wild Boar Sausage; Syllabub & Sweet Potato Buttermilk Pie among desserts, children's menu. $$ to $$$

THE REGENCY DINING ROOM *(in Williamsburg Inn), Francis St., (757) 229-1000.* Fresh seafood, regional specialties; elegant dining room, award-winning. $$$

THE TRELLIS *(Merchants Square), Duke of Gloucester St., (757) 229-8610.* Fresh seafood, mesquite-grilled dishes; outdoor dining, musicians on weekends, respected, reservations suggested. $$ to $$$

Further Information

The Williamsburg Area Convention & Visitors Bureau, *P.O. Box 3585, Williamsburg, VA 23187 (800) 358-6511.*

Directions

From Richmond, I 64 east to Williamsburg exits.

Other Charming Virginia Towns

Bedford
Middleburg
Monterey
Strasburg
Warm Springs/Hot Springs
Waterford

WASHINGTON

WASHINGTON

La Conner

Population 750

At first glance you might take **La Conner** for a New England fishing village, but one double take later and you'll know that the corner of the country you're in is the northwestern, not northeastern, one. For in the distance lie snow-covered peaks, and dotting the countryside are those tall–magnificently tall–spruces and firs and hemlocks that symbolize the Northwest. The yachtsmen and the browsers in the galleries and shops along First Street are far more likely to be Seattleites than Bostonians.

La Conner, known to old-timers as *Channel Town*, hugs a hillside along the Swinomish Channel at the mouth of the **Skagit River**. Originally a trading post founded after the Civil War, the town became a thriving port for produce from farms on the fertile Skagit Flats. The county courthouse and the railroad eventually ended up elsewhere, however, and these and other developments–or lack thereof–put an end to La Conner's growth. "Progress" stopped and many of the original buildings were spared the wrecking ball. It was only a matter of time–the late 1930s in La Conner's case–before the community was discovered by artists and a new life begun.

Now listed on the National Register, La Conner has an ambiance that remains unmistakably salt-water. The wharves, boat yards, and moorings bustle with activity. A favorite getaway for the city-weary, the village affords a variety of inviting shops (specialty food shops seem particularly popular), restaurants, lodgings, and as might be expected of a town with a long-standing reputation as an art colony, galleries.

Top sights include the colorful **Rainbow Bridge**, which connects the east and west sides of the channel, and two museums, the **Museum of Northwest Art**, with fine examples of the Northwest School of art, and the **Skagit County Historical Museum**, with artifacts from the Skagit Valley's pioneer period. The grounds of the historical museum offer wonderful views of La Conner and the landscape beyond.

Special Features

The **Skagit Valley** is a leading producer of vegetables, vegetable seeds, and **flower bulbs**. Daffodils brighten the landscape during March, and during the first two weeks of April tulips turn the fields into splashes of living color. Irises have their turn in May.

Views of the famed **San Juan Islands** are among the attractions of a 2 1/2-hour cruise through **Deception Pass**.

> • *Two of La Conner's more unusual events are February's La Conner Rotary Club Smelt Derby, when landing a fish takes only a jerk, and September's Orphan Car Show, which celebrates out-of-production makes of cars (e.g., Studebakers and Nashes).*
> • *Grain grown on the Skagit Flats was once shipped to Seattle to feed the horses that pulled that city's streetcars.*

Where to Stay

BENSON FARMSTEAD, *1009 Avon-Allen Rd. (Bow 98232), (360) 757-0579/(800) 685-7239*. 1914 17-room farmhouse 12 mi from town, antiques & old quilts, private baths, full breakfasts, homemade desserts, hot tub, surrounded by gardens. $$

HOTEL PLANTER, 715 First St., *(306) 466-4710/(800) 488-5409*. Restored 1907 inn, TV & phones, private baths, morning coffee, courtyard, garden hot tub, downtown location. $$ to $$$

KATY'S INN, *503 S. Third St., P.O. Box 869, (360) 466-3366/(800) 914-7767*. 1876 home 2 blocks from town, some private baths, full breakfasts, hot tub under gazebo. $$

LA CONNER COUNTRY INN, *107 S. Second St., P.O. Box 573, (360) 466-3101*. Full-service inn, cathedral ceilings & "quaint" furnishings, fireplaces, Cont. breakfasts, dining room, cocktail lounge, library, pets. $$ to $$$

THE PARSONAGE ON PLEASANT RIDGE, *1754 Chilberg Rd. (Mt. Vernon 98273), (360) 466-1754*. Suite in 1894 parsonage, National Register, separate carriage house, private baths, view of tulip fields. $$

Where to Eat

CALICO CUPBOARD, *720 S. First St., (360) 466-4451*. Eclectic & creative breakfast & lunch menus with many "heart-healthy" offerings, "scratch" bakery, antiques, classical music, fresh flowers, award-winning. $

LA CONNER SEAFOOD & PRIME RIB HOUSE, *614 First St., P. O. Box 577, (360) 466-4014*. Fish & Chips, Grandma Lou's Oysters, Steamer Clam Dinner, Pasta Alexander, Prime Rib; extensive lunch menu, waterside dining. $$

PALMERS RESTAURANT & PUB, *205 E. Washington, P.O. Box 599, (360) 466-4261*. Penne Rigatta–smoked salmon, sea scallops, capers, sun-dried tomatoes, wild mushrooms, garlic, white wine, parmesan & cream; turn-of-century reproduction pub. $$ to $$$

518 AMERICA'S MOST CHARMING TOWNS & VILLAGES

Further Information

La Conner Chamber of Commerce, *P.O. Box 1610, La Conner, WA 98257 (360) 466-4778.*

Directions

From Seattle, I 5 north to Conway/La Conner exit (Exit 221), west following directional signs through Conway and across Fir Island to Chilberg Road, west to La Conner.

Leavenworth

Population 1, 692

Lining the streets of **Leavenworth** are colorful Bavarian buildings with signs announcing "Andreas Keller," "Bosch Garten," Bergdorf Gallerie," and dozens of other businesses. The architecture is authentic – some of it in fact was the work of a German designer. The cheerful baskets of flowers hanging from the old (and original) street lamps are distinctly Old World. The dishes in some of the restaurants are genuinely German, in taste as well as name. And although the snow-covered peaks in the background are not the Alps, they are indisputably alpine.

Leavenworth is a true American success story, albeit with a non-American flavor. With its once prosperous lumber and railroad industries gone, Leavenworth needed help. Then, in the 1960s several townspeople began to remodel their businesses using Bavarian styles, styles inspired by the lovely **Cascade Mountain** setting. The idea caught on, although not without controversy, and over the years the town was gradually Bavarianized and revitalized. Today even condominiums, drive-in banks, and motor inns display a Bavarian motif.

Many visitors to the *Bavarian Village of Leavenworth* enjoy the out-doors during the earlier hours of the day and then browse in the shops and relax in the restaurants and pubs during the later hours. The list of outdoor activities seems endless: downhill and cross-country skiing, whitewater or scenery-watching rafting down the **Wenatchee River,** wilderness and scenic canoe trips, guided downhill bicycle trips, rock climbing, fly fishing. For those wishing more passive pursuits there are helicopter tours of the Cascades and dog-sled tours. Neighboring farms and ranches offer old-fashioned sleigh rides, horse-drawn hayrides, horseback rides, and buggy rides.

The list of unique shops also appears endless: There are well over 70 of them. Their offerings describe every conceivable category of arts, crafts, gifts, clothing, foods, and furnishings. Some of the items are American, with emphasis on the Northwest; some are European – for example, Bavarian wax art, Bavarian clothing, and German steins.

Special Features

The **promenade** along the lovely Wenatchee River in **Waterfront Park** offers a cooling break from the shopping, eating, and beer sampling.

East of town, along **US 2**, are some of the world's most important pear and apple orchards. Several of the orchards maintain seasonal fruit stands.

> *The use of authentic Bavarian designs meant that city building codes governing rooflines and other features had to be changed.*

Where to Stay

ABENDBLUME, *12570 Ranger Rd., P.O. Box 9981, (800) 669-7634/ (509) 548-4059.* European-style pension of old-world design, fireplaces, European bedding, private baths, whirlpools, traditional Austrian breakfasts, mountain views. $$ to $$$

ALL SEASONS RIVER INN, *P.O. Box 788, (509) 548-1425.* On the river, rooms with fireplaces, private baths, "gourmet" breakfasts. $$$

ALPEN ROSE INN, *500 Alpine Pl., (800) 582-2474/(509) 548-3000.* Inn combining ambiance of "Old Europe & Pioneer West," fireplaces, private baths, whirlpools, balconies, full breakfasts, large decks, pool & spa. $$ to $$$

CASHMERE COUNTRY INN, *5801 Pioneer Dr. (Cashmere, 98815), (509) 782-4212.* 1907 farmhouse, private baths, "wonderful country" breakfasts, pool & hot tub. $$$

THE HAUS ROHRBACH PENSION, *12882 Ranger Rd. (509) 548-7024.* European country charm, private baths, full breakfasts, pool & hot tub, scenic views. $$$

PINE RIVER RANCH, *19668 WA 207, (509) 763-3959.* Mountain views, fireplaces, private baths, full breakfasts, hot tubs, acres to ski or hike. $$ to $$$

RUN OF THE RIVER, *9308 E. Leavenworth Rd., (800) 288-6491.* Log B&B inn with views, hand-hewn log furniture, private baths, "bountiful" breakfasts; own biking, driving, & hiking brochures; award-winning. $$$

Where to Eat

CAFE MOZART, *829 Front St., (509) 548-0600*. Munchener Sauerbraten, Mailander Piccata, Fresh Catch of the Day, Rindersteak "Maitre d'Hotel"; inviting lunch menu, highly recommended. $$

GUSTAV'S, *617 Front St., (509) 548-4509*. Sandwiches, homemade soups, salads; 20 Northwest draughts on tap. $

LEAVENWORTH BREWERY, *636 Front St. & US 2, (509) 548-4545*. Poached Halibut, Rib Eye, pasta; hand-crafted beers & root beer, pub menu. $

LORRAINE'S EDEL HAUS INN, *320 9th St., (509) 548-4412*. Champagne Vanilla Scallops, Grilled Salmon, Basque Style Chicken; in classic old home, all foods prepared from scratch, outdoor seating. $$

THE PEWTER POT RESTAURANT, *124 1/2 Cottage Ave. (Cashmere), (509) 782-2036*. Traditional dinners, soups, salads, homemade bread & desserts. $$

Further Information

Leavenworth Chamber of Commerce, *P.O. Box 327, Leavenworth, WA 98826 (509) 548-5807*.

Directions

From Seattle, I 405 north to WA 522, WA 522 east to US 2, US 2 east to Leavenworth.

Port Townsend

Population 7, 800

Prosperous from its lumber trade with booming California, **Port Townsend** was just as important in the 1880s as the Port of Seattle, also on **Puget Sound**. Businesses flourished and mansions rose. But the train never came to Port Townsend, and that and several other fateful developments drove Seattle to greatness and froze Port Townsend in time. A hundred years later Port Townsend has the largest collection of Victorian buildings north of San Francisco. It is one of only four towns in the country designated a Victorian Seaport by the National Register of Historic Places.

Sailboats and other craft still move about the harbor of the old port town. The facades of the buildings on **Water Street**, Port Townsend's downtown, are authentically Victorian even if the specialty shops, galleries, and restaurants within are not. Many of the buildings in **Uptown**, on the bluff, are also original, and here too shops, galleries, and restaurants beckon. Elsewhere in the older parts of town are Victorian-era churches, cottages, and mansions. The Chamber of Commerce's historical tour map lists 72 sites. There is clearly much Victoriana to see, and the interested visitor is well-advised to take the self-guided Seagull Tour or one of the van or historical sidewalk tours.

Of special note downtown is the 1889 **Hastings Building**, the first building in town to sport a two-story court with skylight. On the bluff behind is the restored **Old Bell Tower** (1890). The **Jefferson County Courthouse** (1892), one of the two oldest courthouses in the state, is behind the bluff. The building's clock tower is a landmark, offshore as well as in town.

Port Townsend is probably best known for its many fine restored Victorian homes. So many of these are now bed and breakfasts that the town is sometimes nicknamed the *bed and breakfast capital of Washington*. A listing of bed and breakfasts that are also of architectural and/or historic interest is given below.

There are two houses of special historic interest that are open to the public but are not bed and breakfasts. One is the 1868 **Rothschild House**, a state heritage site on the National Register of Historic Places. Most of the house's furnishings, carpets, and wall papers are original. The second house is the **Commanding Officer's Quarters** at **Fort Worden State Park** (see below). This beautiful 1904 home has been carefully and authentically restored and refurnished.

Special Feature

Fort Worden State Park adjoins the town on the north. Turn-of-the-century Fort Worden was built as part of a Puget Sound defense system. On the grounds are restored officers' houses, barracks (now available for conventions and conferences), parade grounds, and artillery bunkers.

The fort is also home to the **Centrum Foundation**, a non-profit organization that promotes the arts. Many varieties of Washington's state flower, the rhododendron, are on display in the **Centennial Rhododendron Garden**, also on the grounds.

> • *Uptown in Port Townsend was established so that Victorian women could shop somewhere other than the rowdy downtown waterfront area.*
> • *The bell in St. Paul's Episcopal Church (1865) was donated by a ship's captain on condition that it be rung in foggy weather to warn vessels.*

Where to Stay

ANN STARRETT MANSION INN B&B, *744 Clay St., (800) 321-0644.* 1889 stick-style home, private baths, full breakfasts, beautiful views. $$ to $$$

F. W. HASTINGS HOUSE/OLD CONSULATE INN, *313 Walker at Washington, (206) 385-6753.* 1889 Queen Anne home, private baths, 7-course breakfasts. $$$

HERITAGE HOUSE B&B INN, *305 Pierce, (206) 385-6800.* 1880 Italianate house, some private baths, breakfast "a delight," water views. $$ to $$$

HOLLY HILL HOUSE, *611 Polk St., (800) 435-1454.* 1872 home in heart of historic district, private baths, full breakfasts. $$ to $$$

JAMES HOUSE B&B, *1238 Washington St., (206) 385-1238.* 1891 home with five chimneys, parquet floors, private baths, full breakfasts, excellent view of harbor. $$ to $$$

ROSE COTTAGE B&B, *1310 Clay St., (206) 386-6944.* Originally an 1868 duplex, private baths, views. $$ to $$$

Where to Eat

BELMONT RESTAURANT & SALOON, *925 Water St., (800) 522-3007.* Fresh seafood, poultry, beef, pasta; casual waterfront dining in Victorian atmosphere. $$

BLACKBERRIES, *Fort Worden State Park, (206) 385-9950.* Contemporary Northwest cuisine — e.g., Halibut-Salmon Braid with Salalberry Beurre Rouge. $$

MANRESA CASTLE, *7th and Sheridan sts., (800) 732-1281.* Fresh local seafood & regional cuisine served in 1892 Victorian inn. $$

SILVERWATER CAFE, *237 Taylor St., (360) 385-6448.* Emperor Oysters, Smoked Salmon Fettucine, Polenta Etienne, Marjoram Chicken. $ to $$

Further Information

Port Townsend Chamber of Commerce, *2437 E. Sims Way, Port Townsend, WA 98368 (206) 385-2722.*

Directions

From Seattle, ferry from downtown to Bainbridge Island (Winslow), WA 305 to WA 3, north on WA 3 to WA 104, west on WA 104 across Hood Canal Bridge to WA 19, north on WA 19 to Port Townsend (approx. 1 3/4 hrs); from Tacoma, WA 16 north to WA 3, continue as from Seattle above.

Nearby **Jefferson County International Airport** is served by Port Townsend Airways flying from Sea-Tac International Airport.

Other Charming Washington Towns

Chelan
Gig Harbor
Ilwaco
Roslyn
Winthrop

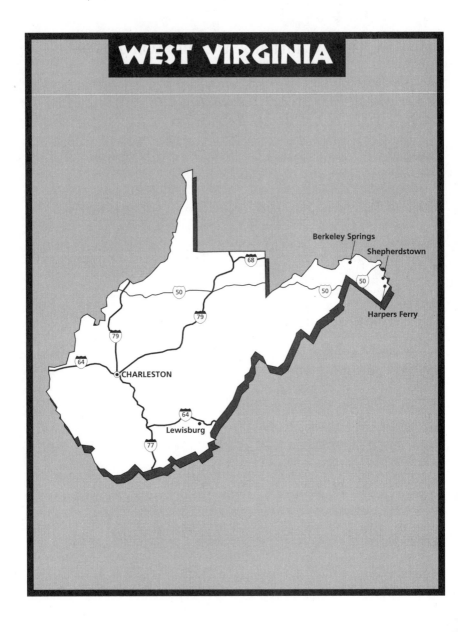

WEST VIRGINIA

WEST VIRGINIA

Berkeley Springs
Population 735

Nestled in the hills of West Virginia, the village of **Berkeley Springs** has the distinction of being the country's first spa. George Washington used to come here to bathe in the warm mineral waters and to promenade and relax with friends. In fact, Washington—along with three signers of the Declaration of Independence, four signers of the Constitution, five Revolutionary generals, etc. – bought lots here when the town was platted in 1776. The place has been a resort ever since.

Today the name "Berkeley Springs" applies to a rather large area: the **springs**, the tiny **state park** that includes them, the tiny town that surrounds the park, the settled area around the town limits, and indeed, the entire eastern side of the mountains in Morgan County. The town is officially known as "Bath," but historically has been postmarked "Berkeley Springs" to avoid confusion with another Bath (in Virginia).

Within the state park, springs discharge about 2,000 gallons of clear, odorless mineral water per minute at a temperature of 74.3 degrees Fahrenheit. The park's two bathhouses allow the visitor a choice among a Roman bath in an individual sunken pool, a soak in a conventional tub, massage treatments, and in the summer, a plunge in a swimming pool. There are also several private spas. The **Roman Bath House** has been in service as a bathhouse since its construction around 1815. A museum on the second floor provides an excellent introduction to the park and its history. A row of unusual shops lines the street facing the park.

The town of Berkeley Springs (or Bath) has a number of quaint late 19th-century structures, some of them now bed and breakfasts (see below). Markers identify the village's first platted lots and their owners. The village and its setting are especially popular with artists.

Special Feature

The overlook at **Prospect Peak**, five miles west of town on **WV 9**, offers a fabulous view. A couple of miles beyond is the quaint river-side hamlet of **Great Cacapon**.

> • *The colors used throughout the state park—yellow, cream, and green—are original colors of the Federal period.*
> • *The large wooden hotels that visitors to the springs used to stay at have all disappeared, often through fire.*

Where to Stay

AARON'S ACRE, *501 Johnson Mill Rd., (304) 258-4079.* Early 1900s home with wrap-around porch, some private baths, full breakfasts. $$$

THE COUNTRY INN, *207 S. Washington St., (800) 822-6630.* Colonial-style full-service inn adjoining village green, dining room, spa, porches & gardens, packages. $$ to $$$

HIGHLAWN INN, *304 Market St., (304) 258-5700.* 1897 bldg. & turn-of-century cottage & town house, TV, private baths, "opulent" breakfasts, verandah overlooking town, flower/herb gardens, silver-service private dinners Sat. evenings. $$$

THE MANOR B&B, *415 Fairfax St., (304) 258-1552.* Victorian home on National Register, private baths, full "country" breakfasts, porch. $$ to $$$

ON THE BANKS GUESTHOUSE, *304 Martinsburg Rd., (304) 258-2134.* 1875 home with mountain view, some private baths, full breakfasts, library & music room. $$ to $$$

Where to Eat

THE COUNTRY INN, *(see above).* West Virginia Rainbow Trout, Old-fashioned Roast Turkey Dinner, Traditional Baked Ham, daily specials; country charm, rustic bar, live entertainment on weekends. $$

TARI'S PREMIERE CAFE & INN, *123 N. Washington St., (304) 258-1196.* Fresh seafood, chicken, pastas, vegetarian dishes, daily specials; lounge, popular. $ to $$

Further Information

Berkeley Springs-Morgan County Chamber of Commerce, *304 Fairfax St., Berkeley Springs, WV 25411 (304) 258-3738/Visitors Center (800) 447-8797.*

Directions

From Washington (DC), I 270 north to Frederick (MD), I 70 (through Hagerstown, MD) to exit 1, US 522 south to Berkeley Springs.

Harpers Ferry
Population about 308

Harpers Ferry is a photogenic little town situated in the **Blue Ridge Mountains** at the confluence of the Potomac and Shenandoah rivers. On a visit here in 1783 Thomas Jefferson described the view from the summit of (now) Jefferson Rock "worth a voyage across the Atlantic." Today a National Historical Park, Harpers Ferry's early to mid 19th-century architecture seems to compliment the scenery. Some of the town's streets look much as they did 140 years ago.

In the 1790s George Washington selected Harpers Ferry as a site for a national armory. Later, during the 1830s, both the **Chesapeake & Ohio Canal** and **Baltimore & Ohio Railroad** came through town. By the middle of the 19th century, Harpers Ferry had become an important arms-producing and transportation center with a population several times what it is today.

Then came John Brown's famous 1859 raid followed in a few months by the Civil War. The armory was burned in 1861 to keep it from falling into Confederate hands. The rest of the town suffered, in spirit as well as structure, during the war years as control swung between the North and the South. A series of floods in the late 1800s pretty much put an end to any remaining hope that Harpers Ferry might revitalize. The little town and its buildings stood still and abandoned.

Many of the buildings have been restored by the National Park Service; others are undergoing, or will undergo, restoration. The best way to see Harpers Ferry is to park at the visitors center and take a shuttle bus to the "Lower Town." The center offers talks by park rangers, conducted tours, and information on self-guided tours.

Many of the town's (and park's) restored buildings have exhibits and media presentations. Of special interest are the **Stagecoach Inn** (1826-1834), which serves as the park's information center/bookstore; the **Master Armorer's House** (1858), now a gun-making museum; and the **Harper House** (1775-1782), the oldest surviving structure in the park. The **Dry Goods Store** (1812) has been restored to look like an 1850s dry goods store. Also of interest is the **Confectionery** (1844-1857), once the home of one of Harper Ferry's most respected citizens. Two of the town's restored buildings house museums that recall the lives and suffering of the townspeople during the Civil War.

On **Camp Hill** are several buildings, constructed in the 1840s and 1850s, that once served as homes for armory officials. Although damaged in the Civil War, they were rebuilt after the war and used to establish **Storer College**, a school for freed blacks. Storer College operated between 1869 and 1955.

The **John Brown Wax Museum**, housed in a historic building, traces the career of the controversial Abolitionist with figures and scenes made life-like with electronic lighting, sound, and animation. Other points of interest in Harpers Ferry include the still-active **St. Peter's Catholic Church** (1830s, remodeled 1890s) and the **Appalachian Trail Confer-**

ence **Visitors Center**, which distributes information and items relating to the country's best-known footpath.

Harpers Ferry and its scenic surroundings support a rich variety of sports and other activities. White-water rafting, canoeing, kayaking, and tubing are popular on the area's rivers and streams. The restored **Chesapeake & Ohio Canal Towpath** offers great hiking and bicycling (bike rentals available). Hikers will find a number of other mapped trails as well, including the Appalachian Trail. Rumor has it that the small-mouth bass fishing doesn't get much better. The same goes for the antique hunting.

The remnants of 19th-century factories and waterways may be explored on **Virginius Island** on the **Shenandoah River**. The National Park Service maintains (and publishes a guide to) an island trail.

Special Features

The National Park Service's **Maryland Heights Trail** leads to Civil War batteries and fort ruins—and a series of magnificent views.

Five minutes to the west is historic **Charles Town**, laid out by George Washington's brother Charles. The tree-lined streets of the town are bordered by many lovely old homes, churches, and other buildings. Not far from Charles Town is delightful little **Middleway**, also historic.

> • *Members of the Lewis and Clark expedition carried arms made by Harper Ferry's armory.*
> • *A popular way to see Harpers Ferry is by an evening "ghost tour."* *Check locally for information.*

Where to Stay

THE COTTONWOOD INN, *Rt. 2 (Box 61-S) (Charles Town 25414), (304) 725-3371.* 200-year-old farmhouse, TV, private baths, full "country" breakfasts. $$ to $$$

THE GILBERT HOUSE B&B, *P.O. Box 1104 (Charles Town 25414), (304) 725-0637.* Circa 1760 Georgian stone house on National Register, antiques, private baths, full breakfasts. $$$

HILLTOP HOUSE, *P.O. Box 930, (800) 338-8319.* Historic stone inn on mountain top, private baths, dining room. $$ to $$$

LEE-STONEWALL INN, *1141 Washington St., (304) 535-2532.* Circa 1795 Georgian-Federal home on National Register, fireplaces, private baths, "hearty country" breakfasts. $$$

RANSON-ARMORY HOUSE B&B, *P.O. Box 280, (304) 535-2142.* 1830 home with Victorian touches, private baths, full "country" breakfasts, refreshments, mountain views. $$

Where to Eat

THE ANVIL RESTAURANT, *1270 Washington St., (304) 535-2582.* Broiled Seafood Saffron, Shrimp & Mussels Cajun, Roulades of Flounder Oscar, Stuffed Lobster Tail. $$

CHARLES WASHINGTON INN, *210 W. Liberty St. (Charles Town), (304) 725-4020.* Original Recipe Crab Cakes, Chicken Pillard, Filet Mignon; in 206-year-old house. $$

CLIFFSIDE INN, *US 340, (800) 782-9437.* Seafood, chicken, steaks, soups, salads, sandwiches, legendary seafood buffet & breakfast buffet weekends. $ to $$

COUNTRY CAFE & GENERAL STORE, *711 Washington St. (Bolivar), (304) 535-2327.* Widely known for sandwiches. $

Further Information

Jefferson County Visitor & Convention Bureau, *P.O. Box A, Harpers Ferry, WV 25425 (800) 848-8687.*

Directions

From Washington (DC), I 270 northwest to Frederick (MD), US 340 west to Harpers Ferry.

Lewisburg
Population 3, 980

It's rare for a town steeped in history and blessed with a scenic setting to show a natural continuity with time, to be more concerned with today's soccer game than with attempts to lure visitors with the contrived. But **Lewisburg** is that kind of town, the way towns used to be, at least according to the romantic. Some say the town is more 1940s than 1990s – the *real* '40s, that is.

Chartered in 1782, Lewisburg's 236-acre historic district has no fewer than 72 sites, including 50 antebellum homes and 11 buildings erected before the War of 1812. The first stop on a town tour should be the four-story **Carnegie Hall** (1902), which houses the visitors center. Funded by Andrew Carnegie and called "the other Carnegie Hall," the hall has 22 classrooms and studios, a 500-seat auditorium, and a 1904 Estey pipe organ.

Two other tour musts are the **Old Stone Presbyterian Church** (1796), the oldest church west of the Alleghenies remaining in continuous use, and the Colonial 1820 **John A. North House**, now home to the museum of the **Greenbrier Historical Society**. (Schedule at least two and a half hours for a full walking tour of the town. Horse-and-carriage tours offer a less energetic option.)

Lewisburg's natural endowment is as rich as its history. Located in the gorgeous **Greenbrier River Valley**, Lewisburg sits amongst mountains and forests just three miles from the beautiful 126-mile unpolluted **Greenbrier River**. Evergreens, maples, rhododendrons, and other flora guarantee four seasons of color.

Special Features

Hikers and bikers will find the 76-mile-long **Greenbrier River Trail** (an old C&O Railroad bed) a custom-made paradise.

Smallmouth-bass fishing is reputed to be better in the Greenbrier River than in any other river in the country. Canoeing is also great.

The Monroe County Historical Society publishes a brochure, *The Springs Trail*, for a driving tour of the many historic springs and resorts of the Greenbrier Valley. Along the way are the 12-columned spring pavilion at **Blue Sulphur Springs**, once a magnificent resort, and the famous Greenbrier Resort at **White Sulphur Springs**. The latter has been a resort since Colonial times.

> *Names scratched by soldiers wounded in the Civil War Battle of Lewisburg can be seen in a section of old plaster in the Greenbrier County Library (1834).*

Where to Stay

THE GENERAL LEWIS, *301 E. Washington St., (304) 645-2600*. Full-service inn, east wing an 1834 house, antiques throughout, suites, dining room, worth a visit in own right. $$ to $$$

LYNN'S INN B&B, *P.O. Box 40, (304) 645-2003*. Shaded front porch with big rockers, antiques & handmade crafts, private baths, "farm-style" breakfasts, country setting. $ to $$

MINNIE MANOR B&B, *403 E. Washington St., (304) 645-4096*. 1830 Methodist parsonage on National Register, private baths, seasonal. $$

SWIFT LEVEL, *Rt. 2 (Box 269A), (304) 645-1155*. Country estate on National Register, ornate trim & mantles throughout, private baths, full breakfasts, equestrian mountain trips. $$$

Where to Eat

CLINGMAN'S MARKET, *102 E. Washington St.* Lunch, country cooking, very large portions, large shared tables. $

DEL SOL CAFE & MARKET, *206 W. Washington St., (304) 645-5515.* New York-style deli, outdoor dining. $ to $$
FOODS & FRIENDS, *213 W. Washington St., (304) 645-4548.* Salads, sandwiches, & pastas with American, Italian, & Southwestern touches. $ to $$
THE GENERAL LEWIS, *(see above).* Mountain Trout, Fried Chicken, Country Ham, Grilled Pork Chops, homemade breads & desserts; reservations suggested. $$
JULIAN'S, *S. Lafayette St., (304) 645-4145.* Classical cuisine in converted Victorian home, everything from scratch. $ to $$

Further Information
Lewisburg Visitor's Center, *105 Church St., Lewisburg, WV 24901 (800) 833-2068.*

Directions
From Charleston, I 64 south to exit 169, south to Lewisburg.

Shepherdstown
Population 1, 287

Shepherdstown is an historic little college time overlooking the **Potomac River**. West Virginia's oldest town (first settled around 1730), Shepherdstown is rich in 18th- and 19th-century commercial and residential buildings. It is also quite cosmopolitan, with sophisticated shops, restaurants, and entertainments. The town is nicely positioned for regional sightseeing – and the region offers much to see, including the **Antietam National Battlefield**, historic Harpers Ferry (which see), and some gorgeous mountain scenery.

The **Historic Shepherdstown Museum**, housed in the **Entler Hotel** (1793/1809), displays items from the town's past. On the grounds is a replica of the world's first working steamboat, built and demonstrated at Shepherdstown by James Runsey in 1787. (Elsewhere in town an impressive monument to James Rumsey, built in 1917, overlooks the Potomac). Other historic structures include the **Public Library** (1800/1845), once a farmers' market, and the **Shepherd Grist Mill** (ca 1738), which boasts the oldest and largest (40 ft in diameter) cast-iron overshot waterwheel in the world (1891).

In June and July **Shepherd College's Contemporary American Theater Festival**, a professional repertory theater, presents new plays.

The festival also offers a late-night improv cabaret. On-screen entertainment is provided at the restored **Old Opera House** (1909); foreign and contemporary American films are featured.

Shepherdstown's shops offer a variety of crafts, antiques, decorative accessories, books, and gifts. One of the bakeries specializes in European breads.

The restored **Chesapeake & Ohio Canal Towpath** is made to order for hikers and bikers (see also Harpers Ferry). Bicycle rentals are locally available.

Special Feature

Antietam National Battlefield and Cemetery is four or so miles northeast of Shepherdstown. On September 17, 1862, more men were killed or wounded here than on any other day of the Civil War.

> • *Shepherdstown, then named Mecklenburg, was the starting point for a contingent of local volunteers who hiked with considerable speed to Boston to join George Washington's Continental Army. The march is remembered as the Bee Line March.*
> • *It was at Shepherdstown Ford where General Lee's army recrossed the Potomac after withdrawing from Antietam.*

Where to Stay

THE BAVARIAN INN & LODGE, *Rt. 1 (Box 30), (304) 876-2551.* Bavarian Alpine chalets with balconies overlooking Potomac, full-service inn, restaurant, pool, tennis court. $$$

MECKLENBURG INN, *128 E. German St., P.O. Box 127, (304) 876-2126.* Circa 1793 home with Federal-style entrance, historic associations, antiques, 1 private bath, sunken garden room, English pub, pets, garden/patio. $$

STONEBRAKE COTTAGE GUEST HOUSE B&B, *P.O. Box 1612, (304) 876-6607.* Victorian cottage with kitchen, rented as unit. $$$

THOMAS SHEPHERD INN, *P.O. Box 1162, (304) 876-3715.* Mid-19th-century Lutheran parsonage in Federal style, private baths, "bountiful" breakfasts, afternoon tea, sherry. $$$

Where to Eat

BAVARIAN INN & LODGE, *(see above).* Variety of German & American specialties, fresh seafood, game dishes; attractive dining rooms. $$

THE OLD PHARMACY CAFE & SODA FOUNTAIN, *131 W. German St., (304) 876-2085.* Gourmet sandwiches & salads, 1911 marble soda fountain. $

UPTOWN CAFE, *129 W. German St., (304) 876-2111.* Catch of the Day, Chef's Choice Chicken, Delmonico Steak, Pasta du Jour, soups, salads, sandwiches; in one of Shepherdstown's oldest bldgs., works by local artists. $

THE YELLOW BRICK BANK RESTAURANT, *Princess & German sts., (304) 876-2208.* Northern Italian & Nouvelle American dishes, large variety of fresh seafoods, fresh pastas, risotto. $ to $$

Further Information

Jefferson County Visitor & Convention Bureau, *P.O. Box A, Harpers Ferry, WV 25425 (800) 848-8687; also, Shepherdstown Visitors Center, P.O. 329, Shepherdstown, WV 25443 (304) 876-2786.*

Directions

From Baltimore, I 70 west to Frederick (MD), US 340 west to Harpers Ferry (WV), WV 230 (two miles past Harpers Ferry) to Shepherdstown; from Washington (DC), I 270 to Frederick (MD), proceed as from Baltimore above.

Other Charming West Virginia Towns

Charles Town
Elkins
Marlinton
Martinsburg
Sistersville
Union

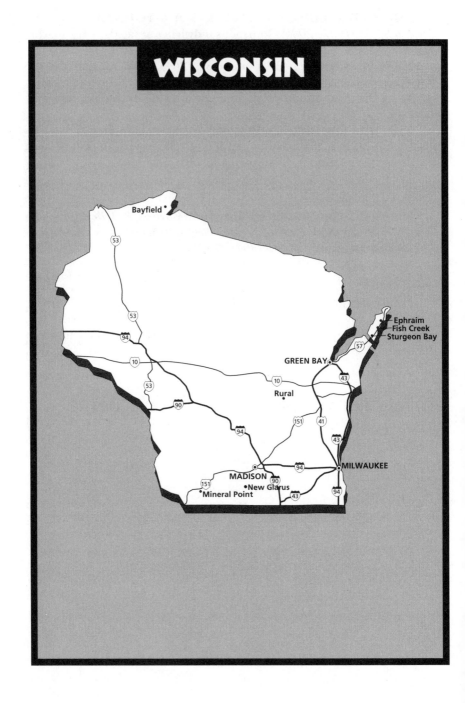

WISCONSIN

Bayfield

Population 686

The tiny fishing village of **Bayfield** lies on a natural harbor on the southern shore of **Lake Superior**. Commercial fishing, lumbering, brownstone quarrying, and tourism helped build the village, especially during the late 19th and very early 20th centuries. In the end tourism proved to be the only really reliable industry, however, and Bayfield stood still as Duluth and other cities took over. Left behind was a village containing, among other things, a delightful collection of Victorian houses.

Bayfield is today a popular summer resort for fishermen and deep-water sailors. Many of the old homes are listed on the National Register; some have been restored and opened as bed and breakfast inns (see below).

One of the town's most interesting indoor stops is the **Booth Cooperage**, where visitors can watch the crafting of barrels. The cooperage is at once a factory and museum. A lush **Nature Trail** winds along a ravine and under the **Old Iron Bridge** (1912; pedestrians only). The trail begins across the street from the **Bayfield Library** (1903). Bayfield's streets can be explored by foot or bicycle. Many of the businesses stay open all winter.

Offshore are the 21 pristine islands of **Apostle Islands National Lakeshore**, guarded by six picturesque **lighthouses**. Information on the lighthouses and other features of the lakeshore can be obtained at the **Apostle Islands National Lakeshore Headquarters**, housed in the brownstone **Old Bayfield County Courthouse** (1894).

The beauty of the Apostle Islands and the lighthouses (all built before 1874) can be experienced by private or excursion boat. A lighthouse tour is one of several excursion options. Check with the Chamber of Commerce for schedules and other tour information.

Bayfield has a kind of "satellite" resort, because a 22nd island, **Madeline**, is big enough to support its own village (**La Pointe**) and other attractions. Access to Madeline Island (population 150) is made interesting by Bayfield's northern latitude. A ferry (20-minute ride) suffices for the warmer months. During the winter, however, the thickness of the ice makes it possible to drive your car to the island. Pine trees are set up on the ice to mark the way. During months when the ice is less thick, people are carried back and forth by a wind sled driven by a large propeller.

Special Features

Madeline Island is home to an historical museum, a state park with nature trails and sailboat charters, and a challenging 18-hole golf course. The historical museum, comprising four historic log buildings, preserves artifacts from the island's Indian, fur-trading, missionary, and later eras. Bus tours of the island are available from late June to early October.

Civil War songs, Broadway favorites, bluegrass, contemporary jazz, Swedish songs, and many other kinds of music fill the tent during the summer months at the **Lake Superior Big Top Chautauqua** three miles south of town.

> • *Swimming does occur in Lake Superior, but because of the temperature most of the swimmers are children.*
> • *The first lighthouse authorized in these waters (1852) was mistakenly constructed on the wrong island.*
> *Scuba divers will find sunken schooners, barges, and ore carriers preserved in the cold waters of Lake Superior. (Divers should register with the National Park Service.)*

Where to Stay

BAY FRONT INN, *City Dock, P.O. Box 406, (715) 779-3880/(888) 243-4191.* Full-service inn on waterfront, private decks, Cont. breakfasts, gift shop, next to restaurant. $$ to $$$

BAYWOOD PLACE, *20 N. 3rd St., (715) 779-3690.* Gabled 1920 home, private baths, full "gourmet" breakfasts, view of Lake Superior. $ to $$

COOPER HILL HOUSE, *P.O. Box 1288, (715) 779-5060.* 1888 home, antiques & family heirlooms, down comforters, private baths, spacious grounds, quiet. $$

GREUNKE'S FIRST STREET INN, *P.O. Box 768, (800) 245-3072.* 1863 & 1880 houses, TV, down comforters, some private baths, full breakfasts, restaurant. $ to $$

OLD RITTENHOUSE INN, *P.O. Box 584, (715) 779-5111.* Three historic homes, antiques, working fireplaces, private baths, whirlpools, full or Cont. breakfasts, dining room, one of Wisconsin's finest. $$$

THE PINEHURST INN AT PIKES CREEK, *Rte. 1 (Box 222), (715) 779-3676.* 1880s country home surrounded by pines, carved stone fireplace, private baths, full breakfasts, refreshments. $$ to $$$

Where to Eat

Note: Bayfield has its own delicacies: fish chowders, blueberry pancakes, fresh fruit pies, homegrown raspberries–and deep-fried white-fish livers! Depending on the age of the fish and skill of the cook, the flavor of the livers can vary from fishy and strong to delicately delicious.

GREUNKE'S RESTAURANT, *(see Greunke's First Street Inn above).* Walnut-breaded Trout, Trout Hemingway, Canadian Walleye Fillets, Roast Loin of Pork, Prime Rib. $$

OLD RITTENHOUSE INN, *(see above).* Regional specialties, no written menu, highly rated, reservations advised. $$$

PIER PLAZA, *City Dock,* *(715) 779-3330.* Fresh fish, award-winning bakery; on waterfront. $ to $$

Further Information

Bayfield Chamber of Commerce, *P.O. Box 138, Bayfield, WI 54814* *(715) 779-3335.*

Directions

From Duluth (MN), US 53 south to WI 13, WI 13 east to Bayfield.

Ephraim/Fish Creek
Population 200/200

Door County and its tiny harbor villages of **Ephraim** and **Fish Creek** are Wisconsin's answer to New England. Both villages have fine old white clapboard houses and inns and attract cyclists and other tourists with their upscale shops and magnificent fall foliage. Both also look out over blue water, shelter yachts in their harbors, and offer sailing cruises.

Maybe departing a little from some New England harbor towns, both back against scenic bluffs. And because they lie on the **Green Bay**, or west, side of the **Door Peninsula**, both depart dramatically from New England by enjoying sunsets over the water rather than sunrises. Indeed, some of the areas along the main road in Ephraim are kept undeveloped just to maintain the open views of the water and the spectacular sunsets.

Separated by five miles, Ephraim and Fish Creek are similar, but they're hardly twins. Ephraim is dry and Fish Creek is wet (this alone gives each a different character), Ephraim stretches along the water and Fish Creek is compact, Ephraim has more historic buildings and Fish Creek has more shops, galleries, and cultural events. Both are engaging.

Ephraim has several historic structures that are open to the public. The best known is the **Anderson Store**, a restored 1858 general store that displays merchandise from the early 20th century. Two other buildings are the 1869 **Pioneer School**, with desks and other artifacts of 1920s vintage, and the **Anderson Barn Museum** (ca 1880), which features historic exhibits and a permanent art collection.

Door County is famous for its strawberries, cherries, and apples – late May is the time to see the blooms. The county is also famous for its windsurfing and other water sports. Bicycle, sailboat, canoe, sea kayak, and cross-country ski rentals are available. So are sailboat and sea kayak lessons.

Special Feature

Peninsula State Park, which lies between the two villages, offers breathtaking views of Green Bay from its limestone bluffs. The park is home to the charming **Eagle Bluff Lighthouse** (1868), also a museum; the **American Folklore Theater**, a professional theater company that does summer musicals; and the beautiful 18-hole **Peninsula Park Course**.

The oldest professional summer stock company in the country, the **Peninsula Players**, performs in the **Theater-in-a-Garden**, an open-to-air theater south of Fish Creek.

> *To do a "Door County Fish Boil," boil new potatoes and baby onions (optional) in a cauldron over an open fire until they're nearly done, add Lake Michigan whitefish or trout, and finally, stoke the fire with kerosene and boil unwanted "fishy" oils off the top. Serve with coleslaw and cherry pie.*

Where to Stay

THE EPHRAIM INN, *P.O. Box 247, 9994 Pioneer Ln., (920) 854-4515.* 1908 home with harbor views, antiques, TV, private baths, full breakfasts, verandah. $$$

FRENCH COUNTRY INN OF EPHRAIM, *P.O. Box 129, (920) 854-4001.* 1912 "summer cottage" in garden setting, French country decor. $$ to $$$

THORP HOUSE INN, *P.O. Box 490 (Fish Creek), (920) 868-2444.* Historic guest house with antique-filled rooms, private baths, cottages, harbor view. $$$

THE WHISTLING SWAN INN, *P.O. Box 193 (Fish Creek), (920) 868-3442.* Circa 1887 inn on National Register, lobby with fireplace & baby grand piano, antiques, TV & phones, private baths, Cont. "plus" breakfasts, refreshments, glass-enclosed verandah, gardens, views, boutique. $$$

THE WHITE GULL INN, *P.O. Box 160 (Fish Creek), (920) 868-3517.* Turn-of-century inn, antique-decorated rooms, private baths, cottages, dining room. $$ to $$$

Where to Eat

AL JOHNSON'S SWEDISH RESTAURANT & BUTIK, *702 Bayshore Dr., P.O. Box 257 (Sister Bay), (920) 854-2626.* "Authentic" Swedish pancakes, sandwiches (on homemade limpa), cheeses, cold plates, dinners; log bldgs. from Scandinavia, goats on roof, gift shop. $ to $$

EDGEWATER DINING ROOM, *10040 WI 42 (Ephraim), (920) 854-4034.* Door County fish boils, cherry muffins & pancakes; on waterfront, reservations advised. $ to $$

HOTEL DU NORD, *P.O. Box 408 (Sister Bay), (920) 854-4221.* Chicken Alexander, Tenderloin a la Oscar, Shrimp du Nord, Fresh Door County Whitefish, Melange of Fresh Vegetable Pasta. $$

INN AT KRISTOFER'S, *734 Bayshore Dr., P.O. Box 619 (Sister Bay), (920) 854-9419.* Spice Rubbed Steak with Fried Leeks, Boudin Blanc, Mandarin Quail with Lingonberry Plum Sauce, Pan Fried Whitefish with Mushroom Cream Sauce; "lighter appetite" menu, across from marina. $$ to $$$

KORTES' ENGLISH INN, *WI 42 between villages, (920) 868-3076.* Seafood, poultry, beef, tableside flambe; Old English atmosphere. $$

TRIO, *4655 County Trunk E (Egg Harbor), (920) 868-2090.* Coq au Cassis, Cassoulet, Whitefish Amandine, Spaghetti with Clams, Beef Roulade; changing menu, country European decor. $$

WHITE GULL INN, *(see above).* Fish boils, Shrimp & Artichoke Romano, Beef Wellington, steaks, home baking. $$

WILSON'S RESTAURANT & ICE CREAM PARLOR, *WI 42 (Ephraim), (920) 854-2041.* Famous ice cream, lighter fare; est. 1906. $

Further Information

Door County Chamber of Commerce, *P.O. Box 406, 1015 Green Bay Rd., Sturgeon Bay, WI 54235 (800) 527-3529/fax (920) 743-7873. (ZIPS for Ephraim & Fish Creek are 54211 & 54212, respectively.)*

Directions

From Milwaukee, I 43 north to exit 185 (Green Bay), WI 57 north to Sturgeon Bay, WI 42 north to Fish Creek and Ephraim.

Mineral Point

Population 2, 428

People from **Mineral Point** traveling in England have been known to remark on the similarity between parts of that country and the rolling, green countryside of their Wisconsin home. The pastoral beauty of southwestern Wisconsin does indeed recall the beauty of rural England, but there is more to the similarity than that.

Families from Cornwall (England) settled in Mineral Point following the discovery of lead early in the 19th century. Bringing with them the skills of the stonemason as well as the miner, the settlers built rock houses similar to those of their native Cornwall. Many of these houses survive, and continue even today to impart a certain English character to Mineral Point.

The hilly, winding streets of Mineral Point carry the similarity to parts of England even further. And so does the state historical society's **Pendarvis Complex**, a group of six restored Cornish miners' cottages built in the 1840s.

The architectural character and variety of many of Mineral Point's other buildings are much more American. The styles range from early log through Federal to Victorian and Italian Renaissance. Of special note are the limestone Italianate **Gundry House** (1867), now a museum owned and operated by the local historical society, and the **Mineral Point Theatre**, a vaudeville and performing arts house with full proscenium and balcony, built in 1914. The latter's magnificent 400-seat auditorium is still used for movie presentations, performances by a local theater group, and other events. A driving-tour brochure focusing on these and other important buildings in Mineral Point is distributed by the visitors bureau.

Mineral Point has been respected as an art center since the 1940s. Over 30 artists and artisans display their work in 11 (at last count) galleries, studios, and shops. The town's woodworkers enjoy an especially wide following. The town also boasts a large number of individual and group antique shops. The various studios and shops are scattered about town. Many are on **High Street** (the English name for a main street).

The **Mineral Point Toy Museum** features antique doll houses, toys, and trains. Old toys are available for purchase in the museum shop.

Special Features

North of Mineral Point is the **House on the Rock**, a contemporary 14-room house built on top of a tower of rock. The house is the original structure of a 200-acre complex featuring such attractions as a gas-lit Main Street, the world's largest carousel, a collection of animated music machines, a miniature circus, and a collection of 250 doll houses. Billed as Wisconsin's number-one tourist attraction, some visitors describe the exhibits as unique and fascinating, others as overwhelming, even dizzying.

North of the House on the Rock, near **Spring Green**, is Frank Lloyd Wright's famous home, **Taliesin East** (open to the public).

> • *Early miners in Mineral Point dug out burrows resembling badger holes in the hillsides for shelter. Hence the Badger State, Wisconsin's nickname.*
> • *A Cornish pasty (PASS tee) usually consists of beef, potatoes, and onions sealed in a flaky crust. The Cornish dessert, Figgy Hobbin, consists of a pastry crust with raisins, nuts, and other sweets served with a caramel sauce. These and other Cornish items are available locally.*

Where to Stay

THE COTHREN HOUSE B&B, *320 Tower St., (608) 987-2612*. 1853 stone family estate on National Register, some private baths, "healthy start" breakfast buffet, guest house & log cabin also available, 3 acres of gardens. $$ to $$$

HOUSE OF THE BRAU-MEISTER, *254 Shake Rag St., (608) 987-2913*. Turn-of-century Queen Anne home, full breakfasts, grand piano, sunny porch in pines. $$

KNUDSON'S GUEST HOUSE, *415 Ridge St., (608) 987-2733*. Antiques, TV, Amish quilts, private baths, full breakfasts. $$

PICK-N-PAW, *359 N. Chestnut St., (608) 987-3985*. 1857 stone-&-brick home, antiques, private baths, dog lovers. $$

THE WM. A. JONES HOUSE B&B, *215 Ridge St., (608) 987-2337*. Turn-of-century mansion, some private baths, full breakfasts. $$

WILSON HOUSE INN, *110 Dodge St., (608) 987-3600*. 1853 home in historic district, antiques, some private baths, full breakfasts. $$

Where to Eat

THE CHESTERFIELD INN, *20 Commerce St., (608) 987-3682*. Daily pasta specials, vegetarian dishes, variety of seafood & steak entrees; in 1850s stone inn, brick-lined patio. $$

GUNDRY & GRAY - PURVEYORS EXTRAORDINAIRE, *215 High St., (608) 987-4444*. In-store delicatessen offering made-to-order sandwiches built on kaiser rolls, also desserts, dinner entrees. $

POINTER CAFE, *US 151 S, (608) 987-3733*. Traditional Midwestern menu. $

RED ROOSTER CAFE, *158 High St., (608) 987-9936.* Homemade Cornish Pasties, Figgyhobbin, Bread Pudding. $
ROYAL INN, *43 High St., (608) 987-3051.* Lunches featuring Cornish Pasties, Mawgan Meatballs, sandwiches, salads, Figgyhobbin, Bread Pudding, Saffron Cake. $

Further Information

Mineral Point Visitors Bureau, *P.O. Box 78, Mineral Point, WI 53565 (608) 987-3201/(888) 764-6894.*

Directions

From Madison, US 151 west (via Dodgeville) to Mineral Point.

New Glarus

Population 1, 900

New Glarus, "America's Little Switzerland," nicely illustrates two reasons why Wisconsin's borders embrace such a large number of charming towns. First, the state is respected among preservationists for its strong commitment to protecting its past, and, sure enough, New Glarus has for decades committed itself to the preservation of its Swiss cultural heritage. Second, Wisconsin is blessed with some of the loveliest countryside in the Middle West, and indeed, New Glarus owes part of its charm to its setting in the rolling woods and pastureland of bucolic south-central Wisconsin.

New Glarus was established in 1845 by immigrants from Glarus, Switzerland. Unlike many towns in this book, the village's ethnic roots didn't gradually go underground and then resurface 100 or more years later; the people have always been conscious–and proud–of their Swiss roots. New Glarus is today a village with Swiss buildings surrounded by festive Swiss flags, canton shields, and gardens. And boxes and wine barrels full of flowers, especially geraniums. The town has been voted the most picturesque (and friendliest!) in Wisconsin in magazine polls.

The Victorian and other styles of most of New Glarus's homes remind that this is after all a wealthy Midwestern town, but many of the commercial and public buildings are of one or another Swiss design, contemporary as well as traditional. A good example is the **Chalet of the Golden Fleece Museum** (1937), built in the Bernese Mountain Chalet style. A recommended stop on any tour of the town, the museum has three floors packed with such unique antiques as a King Louis XVI jeweled watch, Etruscan earrings, a 1661 slate inlaid table, and a circa 1760 Swiss porcelain tile stove. Swiss woodcarvings, painted furniture, and samplers are among the many other items on display.

The **Swiss Village Museum** is a grouping of 13 buildings situated on a beautifully landscaped hilltop. The central building is the **Hall of Harmony**, with exhibits that trace the history of the Swiss immigration to New Glarus. Designed to portray 19th-century Midwestern life, other buildings in the museum include a replica of the town's first log church, a cheese factory, a firehouse, and a Swiss-style bee house. Live demonstrations of various crafts are sometimes offered.

Shops and restaurants offer Swiss food (fondue included), pastries, specialty sausages, cheeses, and European-style beers. Swiss bells, Swiss stoneware, Swiss alphorns, and, of course, Swiss chocolates also reside on shop shelves. Swiss yodelers and accordion players are never far away, neither are speakers of Swiss German. A world-class brewery and a factory that manufactures award-winning cheeses give even the economy a Swiss flavor.

Special Features

The **Swiss Valley Orchard**, just northwest of New Glarus, features dwarf and European varieties of apple trees as well as such treats as apple cider and Swiss & American apple pastries.

One of the best ways to take in southern Wisconsin's delightful countryside is to bike the winding 23-mile **Sugar River State Trail** (bike rentals and shuttle service available). The trail's headquarters and northern entry point are in New Glarus.

New Glarus's many **annual events** (e.g., Polkafest, Heidi Festival, Octoberfest, Volksfest, Wilhelm Tell Festival, New Glarus Winterfest) feature, among countless other entertainments, dancing, dramatic productions, and performances by the Maennerchor, a men's Swiss choral group.

Where to Stay

CAMEO ROSE B&B, *1090 Severson Rd. (Belleville 53508), (608) 424-6340.* 1991 "Victorian" country estate on 120 rolling & wooded acres, antiques, private baths, full breakfasts, whirlpool. $$$

OAK HILL MANOR B&B, *401 E. Main St. (Albany 53502), (608) 862-1400/fax (608) 862-1400.* 1906 American Four Square home, period furnishings & original gasoliers, private baths, 3-course breakfasts, large porch, English country garden. $$

SPRING VALLEY CREEK B&B, *N9098 Old Madison Rd., (608) 527-2314.* 1880s Swiss farmstead, private baths, full breakfasts, suite. $$$

Where to Eat

DEININGER'S, *119 Fifth Ave., P.O. Box 789, (608) 527-2012.* Beef Tenderloin Medallions (with a peppercorn & cognac sauce) a dinner special, Chef Roland's Apple Pancake a lunch specialty, wide variety of wines & beers; in charming Victorian home, family-owned & -operated, strongly recommended. $$

THE DINING ROOM, *209 N. Main St., P.O. Box 262 (Monticello), (608) 938-2200.* Fresh Salmon Filet, Crispy Sauteed Breast of Chicken, Paella, Seared Beef Tenderloin; extensive wine list, fine-art textiles, vintage soft jazz, in 1910 bldg., outstanding reviews. $$

NEW GLARUS BAKERY & TEA ROOM, *534 First St., (608) 527-2916/fax (608) 527-5799.* Breakfast pastries, soups, salads, sandwiches, & desserts served by bakery specializing in European breads & Swiss pastries. $

NEW GLARUS HOTEL-RESTAURANT, *100 6th Ave., (608) 527-5244.* Swiss cuisine served in dining room & balcony overlooking downtown, Swiss decor, polka band weekends. $ to $$

PUEMPEL'S OLDE TAVERN, *18 6th Ave.* Daily soup & sandwich specials; est. 1893, original cherry-wood bar, folk murals painted by traveling artist in 1913, beer garden. $

Further Information

New Glarus Visitor Information, *P.O. Box 713, New Glarus, WI 53574 (608) 527-2095/(800) 527-6838.*

Directions

From Madison, US 18/151 west to Verona, WI 69 south to New Glarus.

Rural

Population about 250

In tiny **Rural** the **Crystal River** twists and turns through back yards, front yards, sometimes both yards. Whenever and wherever you step outside, you're probably going to see this beautiful little river. During the warmer months you can even sit on your porch or in your gazebo and wave at the passing skiffs and canoes. And whenever you walk down the street – and walking is what people do – you're going to cross a bridge.

This idyllic place, now a National Historic District, is the only restored intact village in Wisconsin that was settled by immigrants from the British

Isles. Many of the lovely homes date from the 1850s. Following a not uncommon scenario for charming towns, Rural was bypassed by the railroad and thereby condemned to be frozen in time.

The village measures no more than about two by four blocks. The commercial area is pretty much restricted to one genuinely old-fashioned general store and maybe one or two antique and craft shops. The rest of the village consists of homes, and all but a half dozen date from another era. The homes and intertwining river are exceptionally beautiful when the trees are in their October colors.

To the east of the village is the **Red Mill**, an old mill (1855) that today boasts the largest waterwheel in the state. Close by is a covered bridge authentically constructed in 1970 from original plans. The site also includes a gift shop and a quaint chapel popular for weddings.

Rural is just downstream from Wisconsin's renowned **Chain O'Lakes**, a chain of 22 scenic spring-fed lakes. The lakes can be toured by cruise boats or canoe—of course, if you go very far by canoe, you'll eventually find yourself winding back through Rural.

Special Features

The **Hutchinson House** in nearby **Waupaca** is an 1854 Greek Revival mansion overlooking a lake. The grand old house, now a museum, can be visited by appointment.

Miles of hiking and groomed ski trails can be pursued at **Hartman Creek State Park**, a few miles northwest of town. Among the park's attractions are sandy swimming beaches and facilities for winter camping.

Where to Stay

CRYSTAL RIVER B&B, *1369 Rural Rd. (Waupaca)*, *(715) 258-5333*. 1853 riverside home, fireplaces, private baths, whirlpools, full breakfasts, gazebo, lovely river setting. $$ to $$$

GREEN FOUNTAIN INN, *604 S. Main St. (Waupaca)*, *(715) 258-5171/(800) 603-4600*. Circa 1908 home on spacious grounds, private baths, 1920s decor on main floor, baby grand piano, business library, cottage. $$

THOMAS PIPE INN, *11032 Pipe Rd. (Waupaca)*, *(715) 824-3161*. Restored 1855 stagecoach inn in heart of Amish country, private baths, full breakfasts. $$ to $$$

WHITE HORSE INN, *E. 2341 Crystal Rd. (Waupaca)*, *(715) 258-6162*. Circa 1850 frame farmhouse, private baths, "deluxe" full breakfasts. $$ to $$$

Where to Eat

CARNEGIE'S CLUB ROOM, *321 S. Main St. (Waupaca), (715) 256-1031.* Seafood, pasta, pizza, Mexican dishes, hot/cold sandwiches; in renovated 1914 library, highly praised. $

OAKWOOD, *1040 W. Fulton St. (Waupaca), (715) 258-0181.* Seafood, prime rib, steaks, pastas, Cajun dishes, daily specials, soup & salad specialties. $ to $$

SIMPSON'S INDIAN ROOM, *222 S. Main St. (Waupaca), (715) 258-2330.* Seafood Alfredo, Shrimp a la Romano, Simpson's Special Chicken, New York Strip. $$

Further Information

Gene & Lois Sorenson (Crystal River B&B), *1369 Rural Rd., Waupaca, WI 54981 (715) 258-5333.*

Directions

From Milwaukee, US 41 north to Oshkosh, WI 21 west to Wautoma, WI 22 north to Rural.

Sturgeon Bay
Population 9, 176

Marking the 250-mile shoreline of Wisconsin's scenic **Door Peninsula** are cliffs, rocky coves, harbors, and little villages that are reminiscent of New England (see Ephraim and Fish Creek). In the peninsula's interior are some of Wisconsin's famous cherry and apple orchards. Straddling an isthmus half-way up the peninsula, 40 miles from its tip, **Sturgeon Bay** is ideally situated as a home base for touring this delightful area.

Decades of sawmills, stone quarries, an ice industry, shipbuilding, and most recently, tourism have brought prosperity to Sturgeon Bay and left a legacy of handsome buildings. There are over 100 buildings of historic or special architectural interest in the town; 42 are within two historic districts. Many were built during the last decade of the 19th century and first decade of the 20th. The styles range from those of the Victorian period to Craftsman and American Foursquare. The information center publishes a historic tour map for strollers, bikers, and drivers wishing a self-guided tour.

Sturgeon Bay has two good regional history museums. Among the displays of the **Door County Historical Museum** are a turn-of-the-century fire station with antique fire trucks, a replica of an early Door County home, and exhibits depicting the history of shipbuilding in Door County. The two-story **Maritime Museum** features boats from the early part of the 20th century as well as an actual 1907 Great Lakes pilothouse.

Helping to uphold Door County's traditional stress on the arts, the **Miller Art Center** maintains a permanent collection of 20th-century Wisconsin art and sponsors a series of changing exhibits. The center also maintains a performing arts schedule. Sturgeon Bay is home to a number of art, craft, and antique shops.

Four-hour van tours of Door County depart regularly from Sturgeon Bay. Surrounded as it is by water and beautiful beaches, the Sturgeon Bay area offers a long list of water sports, including snorkeling, scuba diving, and sailing. For those more interested in indoor pursuits, there are guided tours of a microbrewery and a winery.

Special Feature

A magnificent view of **Door County** and **Green Bay** may be enjoyed from the observation platform at **Potawatomi State Park**, just northwest of town.

Laced as it is with interesting country roads, the Door Peninsula is ideal for impulsive, unhurried touring. A few spots, especially along WI 42, are showing signs of strip development, but for the most part the peninsula's pastoral and wooded beauty remains unscarred.

The King of Spain and the late Shah of Iran owned yachts that were built in Sturgeon Bay.

Where to Stay

THE BARBICAN/VICTORIA HOUSE, *132 N. 2nd Ave., (920) 743-4854*. Suites in 2 turn-of-century homes, antiques, fireplaces, TV, private baths, whirlpools. $$$

THE CHANTICLEER GUEST HOUSE, *4072 Cherry Rd., (920) 746-0334*. Suites with antiques, fireplaces, TV, private baths, whirlpools, pool, hiking trails, on 30 acres. $$$

THE GRAY GOOSE B&B, *4258 Bay Shore Dr., (920) 743-9011*. Civil War home in quiet wooded setting, antique-filled rooms, "country" breakfasts, water/sunset views. $$ to $$$

INN AT CEDAR CROSSING, *336 Louisiana St., (920) 743-4200.* Antiques, fireplaces, private baths, whirlpools, refreshments, restaurant, private porches. $$$

SCOFIELD HOUSE B&B, *P.O. Box 761, (920) 743-7727.* Restored 3-story 1902 home, antiques, fireplaces, TV, private baths, whirlpools, full gourmet breakfasts, "sweet treats." $$ to $$$

WHITE LACE INN, *16 N. 5th Ave., (920) 743-1105.* Four Victorian homes (1881-1904), National Register, antiques, fireplaces, TV, down comforters, private baths, whirlpools, full breakfasts, refreshments, verandahs & balconies, garden, highly rated. $$ to $$$

WHITEFISH BAY FARM, *3831 Clark Lake Rd., (920) 743-1560.* 1908 farmhouse on working farm, private baths, full breakfasts, next to state park. $$ to $$$

Where to Eat

DAL SANTO'S RESTAURANT, *341-1/2 N. Third Ave., (920) 743-6100.* Italian & American dishes, pizzas, pastas, salads, sandwiches; in old railroad depot. $ to $$

INN AT CEDAR CROSSING, *112 N. 3rd Ave., (920) 743-4249.* "Creative" fare served in Victorian-era dining rooms, scratch bakery, fine wines/libations, rated one of Wisconsin's best. $$

MILL SUPPER CLUB, *WI 42 & 57, (920) 743-5044.* Fresh perch & whitefish, pasta entrees, family-style chicken, steaks, nightly specials, fish boils. $

Further Information

Sturgeon Bay Area Information Center, *P.O. Box 212, Sturgeon Bay, WI 54235 (920) 743-3924.*

Directions

From Milwaukee, I 43 north to Manitowoc, WI 42 north to Algoma, County S north to Sturgeon Bay.

Other Charming Wisconsin Towns

Alma
Cedarburg
Hudson
Portage

549

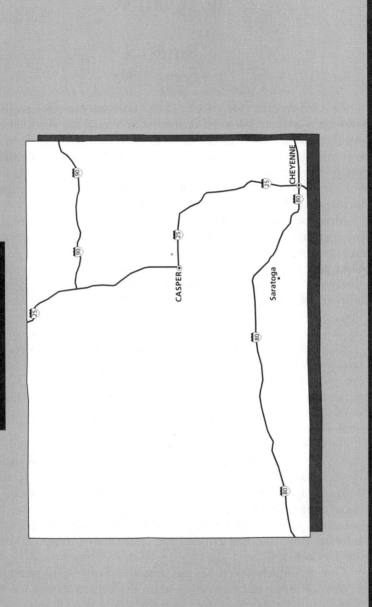

WYOMING

Saratoga
Population 1, 969

Few towns this side of the Hollywood screen can compete with **Saratoga's** *genuine* Western character and majestic Rocky Mountain setting. Away from the interstates and main tourist arteries, the town is large enough to be alive, yet small enough to be more concerned about gossip than crime. Stagecoaches used to stop in front of the old Hotel Wolf (see below). There are still people around who can tell personal stories – truthful ones - about the Old West.

Most people come here for the scenery and the outdoors, but Saratoga has sights of its own. Its natural hot springs (the town was named after its New York cousin and its springs) may be enjoyed in a year-round public pool area. There are also several good art galleries and interesting gift shops. The **Saratoga Museum**, located in the old **Union Pacific Railroad Depot** (1915), exhibits, among other things, railroad memorabilia, a country store, a pioneer home, and a land office. On the museum's grounds are a caboose, restored sheep wagon, and a new pavilion.

One of the town's most popular sights is the **Saratoga National Fish Hatchery** (five miles north). Dating back to 1915, the hatchery raises several kinds of trout, including rainbow and the endangered Greenback cutthroat trout, for stocking. Trout eggs are shipped to other hatcheries. For example, millions of lake trout eggs have been shipped to Great Lakes hatcheries.

Situated on the banks of the **North Platte River**, a blue-ribbon trout fishery, the town's motto reads *Where the Trout Leap in Main Street* (and before the advent of flood control, they did). Fishing is understandably the town's most popular activity, but baited by an especially beautiful golf course (open to public), golfing isn't far behind. Whitewater boating, float trips, cross-country skiing, and kayaking are also popular. The **Medicine Bow National Forest** offers a wealth of trails for hiking and backpacking.

One of the best ways to see this beautiful country is to take advantage of the knowledge and experience of an outfitter. Saratoga has many to choose from. Fishing float trips, horseback fishing trips, tours of historic mining towns, trail rides, and guided snowmobile rides are just a few of the adventures that can be safely undertaken with the aid of an outfitter.

Special Features

The **Grand Encampment Museum** in **Encampment**, 20 or so miles south of Saratoga, uses authentic buildings to recreate a Western community. Included among the buildings and collections are U.S. Forest Service memorabilia, a hat shop, the Palace Bakery, the Lake Creek Stage Station, and a homestead house. A two-story outhouse reminds visitors that the snows in this part of the world can drift well above ground level.

WY 130 between **Saratoga** and **Laramie** has been designated a **National Forest Scenic Byway** (closed winters). There are several spectacular loop tours in and around the Medicine Bow National Forest. Inquire locally for maps and instructions.

> *• Hikers along major creeks in the neighboring mountains will encounter groups of old log cabins known locally as "tie hack camps."* *"Tie hacks" were men who produced ax-hewn railroad ties (during the period between 1868 and 1939).*
> *• Thomas Edison, a member of the Henry Draper Eclipse Expedition, got the idea for the electric light bulb in 1878 at Battle Lake (WY 70, south of Saratoga).*

Where to Stay

BROOKSONG B&B, *Star Rte. Box 9L (Ryan Park), (307) 326-8744.* Home in Snowy Range with panoramic view, antique & country furniture, "hearty" family-style breakfasts, deck & porch swing, trout stream. $$

FAR OUT WEST B&B, *P.O. Box 1230, 304 N. Second St., (307) 326-5869/fax (307) 326-9864.* New B&B with variety of accommodations, full "country" breakfasts, spa, exercise equipment, separate areas for cleaning fish & waxing skis. $$$

THE HOOD HOUSE, *P.O. Box 492, (307) 326-8901.* 1892 Saratoga family home, fishing on owner's ranch by arrangement. $ to $$

HOTEL WOLF, *P.O. Box 1298, (307) 326-5525.* Restored 1893 hotel, on National Register, original dressers & iron beds, private baths, lounge, restaurant. $ to $$

Where to Eat

HOTEL WOLF, *(see above).* Seafood, chicken, many cuts of steak & prime rib, homemade desserts; Victorian setting, old-time saloon. $$

Further Information

Saratoga-Platte Valley Chamber of Commerce, *P.O. Box 1095, Saratoga, WY 82331 (307) 326-8855.*

Directions

From Cheyenne, I 80 west (via Laramie) to exit 235, WY 130 south to Saratoga; alternatively, from Laramie, WY 230 through Snowy Range Scenic Byway.

Other Charming Wyoming Towns

Afton
Alpine
Cody
Jackson
Meeteetse

INDEX

THINGS CHANGE!

Phone numbers, prices, addresses, quality of food, etc, all change. If you come across any new information, we'd appreciate hearing from you. No item is too small! Drop us an e-mail note at Jopenroad@aol.com, or write us at:

America's Most Charming Towns & Villages
Open Road Publishing, P.O. Box 284
Cold Spring Harbor, NY 11724